'The challenge is in the moment;
the time is always now'

James Baldwin

The EY Exhibition

# Picasso 1932

## Love Fame Tragedy

Edited by Achim Borchardt-Hume
and Nancy Ireson

With contributions by
T.J. Clark, Neil Cox, Laurence Madeline,
Alma Mikulinsky and Diana Widmaier Picasso

Tate Publishing

First published 2018 by order of the Tate Trustees by Tate Publishing, a division of Tate Enterprises Ltd, Millbank, London SW1P 4RG
www.tate.org.uk/publishing

on the occasion of the exhibition organised by Tate Modern, London, in collaboration with the Musée national Picasso–Paris

*The EY Exhibition*
*Picasso 1932 – Love Fame Tragedy*
The Eyal Ofer Galleries, Tate Modern, London
8 March – 9 September 2018

Previously shown as
*Picasso 1932. Année érotique*
Musée national Picasso–Paris
10 October 2017 – 11 February 2018

The exhibition at Tate Modern is sponsored by EY

The EY Tate
Arts Partnership

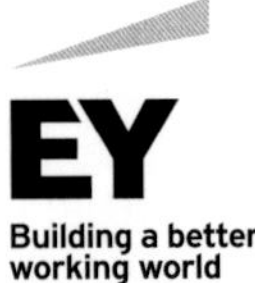


With additional support from the Picasso Exhibition Supporters Circle:
Acquavella Galleries Inc.
Batia and Idan Ofer
Lydia and Manfred Gorvy
Mr Giancarlo Giammetti
The Mead Family Foundation
Thomas Gibson Fine Art Advisory Services
Clore Wyndham
Tate Americas Foundation, Tate International Council, Tate Patrons and Tate Members



A catalogue record for this book is available from the British Library

ISBN 978 1 84976 575 6 (hbk)
ISBN 978 1 84976 576 3 (pbk)

Distributed in the United States and Canada by ABRAMS, New York
Library of Congress Control Number applied for

Project Editor: Judith Severne
Production: Bill Jones
Picture Researcher: Emma O'Neill
Translation from the French of text by Diana Widmaier Picasso and various quotations: Alayne Pullen in association with First Edition Translations Ltd, Cambridge, UK
Designed by Why Not Associates
Printed, bound and colour reproduction by SIZ Industria Grafica, Verona, Italy

Front cover: *The Dream*, *Le Rêve*
24 January 1932

Back cover: *The Mirror*, *Le Miroir*
12 March 1932

Paperback, inside front and back flaps:
The roofs, 23 rue La Boétie; The facade of the chateau at Boisgeloup, lit by a motorcar
Photographs by Brassaï

Hardback, endpapers: marbling by Payhembury Marbled Papers, Cambridge

Back cover quotation: Pablo Picasso, quoted in Françoise Gilot and Carlton Lake, *Vivre avec Picasso*, Paris 1965

Measurements of artworks are given in centimetres, height before width

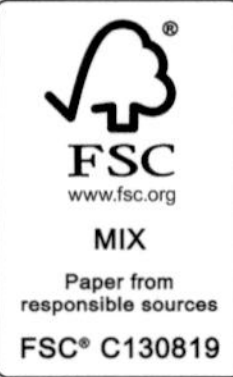

# Contents

# Sponsor's Foreword

EY is delighted to support *The EY Exhibition: Picasso 1932 – Love Fame Tragedy*, a landmark show shedding new light on Pablo Picasso's life and work during the year 1932. One of the most influential artists of the twentieth century, Picasso pioneered a distinct visual language that shook the world of modern art. The artist's legacy continues to captivate people around the globe.

As part of The EY Tate Arts Partnership, we are proud to help make this groundbreaking exhibition possible. Continuing our commitment to strengthening conversations about art and society, we hope these works will offer people a unique perspective on a significant period in Picasso's life and inspire new ways of thinking.

**Michel Driessen**
Sponsoring Partner of
the EY Arts Programme
& Senior Partner TAS, EY

The EY Tate
Arts Partnership

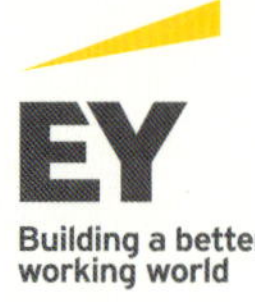

# Foreword

Historians speak of hinge moments as junctures that both separate and connect a clear 'before' and 'after'. The year of 1932 was such a hinge moment: for Pablo Picasso, Europe and the world beyond.

As 1932 dawned, Picasso had just passed the milestone of turning fifty. Given the magnitude of his previous achievements he could well have afforded to be complacent at this stage in his career, which had already spanned thirty years. Invitations for major exhibitions were pouring in from around the world. Despite the Great Depression, his early work broke auction records. A coterie of loyal dealers and collectors encouraged his first retrospective exhibition to be planned for June 1932. Yet the professional challenges Picasso tackled in 1932 remain those that any successful artist must face, with detractors ready to allege that he was no longer 'contemporary'. Consequently, far from simply looking back, Picasso used this moment to reinvent himself. Showing an effort of Herculean proportions, he started to produce paintings that Alfred H. Barr, Jr, the founding Director of The Museum of Modern Art in New York, described as 'unlike anything [Picasso] had done before'. As a result, the works from the first half of the year in particular are among the most esteemed of his entire career. We are delighted to be able to bring together such a stunning group in this, the first ever monographic Picasso exhibition at Tate Modern.

In the second half of 1932, as the political storm clouds began to brew over Europe, the mood of Picasso's work noticeably darkened. For, much as the artist made use of his personal experience to assimilate what was happening in the world, to reduce his work to a claustrophobic entanglement of intimate relationships is overly simplistic. Just as he constantly rethought the traditions and conventions of Western art, he was keenly attuned to the reverberations of the times he was living through, not least the rise of populist nationalism and the anti-individualist rhetoric of fascism.

This is not to say that personal relationships did not play a defining role in the evolution of his work, and rarely more so than in 1932. He continued to juggle the demands of family life: holidays with his wife Olga and son Paulo, entertaining friends, and rites of passage such as Paulo's First Communion. At the same time, and with increasing intensity, he sustained a secretive relationship with the much younger Marie-Thérèse Walter. Though the artist's private life has since become shrouded in myth, with Picasso by turns glorified or vilified, the works he produced over the year suggest a more nuanced dynamic. Loyalties and passions coexisted. The story that emerges through the works and accompanying archival material in this exhibition is not a simple tale of changing affections, but rather one of intertwined lives, of both conflict and personal fulfilment.

Just as Picasso was a true European, so this exhibition is the result of a strong and fruitful collaboration between Tate Modern, London and Musée national Picasso–Paris, also one of the key lenders. The exhibition at Tate Modern is curated by Achim Borchardt-Hume, Director of Exhibitions and Programmes and Nancy Ireson, Curator, International Art following on from the presentation at Musée national Picasso–Paris curated by Laurence Madeline, Curator with Virginie Perdrisot-Cassan, Curator of Sculptures and Ceramics. Together with Juliette Rizzi and Laura Bruni, Assistant Curators they also led and orchestrated the large teams needed for an exhibition of this scope and ambition.

We could not have realised such an ambitious undertaking without the support of our many generous lenders, both institutional and private. We are keenly aware of the trust invested in us and warmly thank all of those who parted with the works in their care to allow us to tell this focused story of one year in the life of Picasso for the benefit of a wide and diverse public. We are especially grateful for the unconditional support we have enjoyed from the Picasso family. It has been a pleasure and a privilege that they joined us so wholeheartedly on our journey.

Picasso's retrospective at Galeries Georges Petit in summer 1932 was organised by four of his dealers. It then travelled to Kunsthaus Zürich, where it became his first-ever museum exhibition. (In 2010 their historic show was the subject of a major exhibition at Kunsthaus Zürich, which we warmly acknowledge.) Today we would call this a public–private partnership. We have been enjoying such a collaboration for the past five years with EY, whose enlightened support through The EY Tate Arts Partnership has benefited a wide array of exhibitions at both Tate Modern and Tate Britain, this being but the latest.

We are also very grateful for the additional support of this exhibition generously provided by the Picasso Exhibition Supporters Circle, which includes Acquavella Galleries Inc., Batia and Idan Ofer, Lydia and Manfred Gorvy, The Mead Family Foundation, Giancarlo Giammetti, Thomas Gibson Fine Art Advisory Services and Clore Wyndham. We would also like to thank Tate Americas Foundation, Tate International Council, Tate Patrons and Tate Members for their support.

We are delighted to collaborate with, and are grateful to, our media partner *The Telegraph*. The Department for Digital, Culture, Media and Sport provides the Government Indemnity Scheme, administered by the Arts Council, without which it would be impossible to organise an exhibition of this level of ambition. Our sincere thanks are due to both.

1932 has also been called Picasso's 'year of wonders'. Eighty-six years later this sense of wonder has not diminished. It is a source of both pride and joy for our two institutions to bring this pivotal moment in Picasso's life and career back to life, and to share it with our audiences at home and abroad.

**Frances Morris**
Director
Tate Modern

**Laurent Le Bon**
President
Musée national
Picasso–Paris

# Curators' Acknowledgements

*The EY Exhibition: Picasso 1932 – Love Fame Tragedy* takes us on a journey across one year of Pablo Picasso's life and work. Both aspects entailed a rich web of networks and conversations involving family and friends; urban Paris and rural Boisgeloup; painting and sculpture; drawing and print-making; explorations of colour and line as much as plunging the depths of love, desire and the subconscious. Eighty-six years later, similar networks and conversations have proved transformational in the making of this exhibition.

We offer our deepest gratitude to all members of the Picasso family: Bernard Ruiz-Picasso and Almine Rech; Maya, Diana and Olivier Widmaier Picasso; Claude Picasso; Paloma Picasso-Thevenet and Dr Eric Thevenet; Catherine Hutin-Blay. Their generous support and advice in numerous matters relating to loans and research have contributed substantially to the success of this project. We also thank the Picasso Administration, especially Christine Pinault, for their essential collaboration and ceaseless efforts on our behalf.

We are deeply indebted to the many private and institutional lenders for entrusting their works into our care: Marie Jager, Archives Painlevé, Paris; Serge Lasvignes, President, Bernard Blistène, Director, Brigitte Léal, Curator and Deputy Director, Collections, and Didier Schulmann, Curator and Chef de Service, Bibliothèque Kandinsky, Centre national d'art et de culture Georges Pompidou, Paris; Bettina and Donald L. Bryant Jr.; Staffan Ahrenberg, Cahiers d'Art, Paris; Grace, Sean and David Carpenter; Luis Lafuente Batanero, General Director, Department of Fine Arts and Cultural Heritage, Ministry of Education, Culture and Sports, Spain; Brigitte Berg, Les Documents Cinématographiques, Paris; Earth Light Foundation, Vaduz; Samuel Keller, Director, and Raphaël Bouvier, Curator, Fondation Beyeler, Riehen/Basel, Basel; Almine and Bernard Ruiz-Picasso, Presidents, François Bellet, Curator and Foundation Secretary, Iro Biehler, Registrar and Thomas Chaineux, Archivist, Fundación Almine y Bernard Ruiz-Picasso para el Arte, Brussels; Giancarlo Giammetti, London; Christoph Becker, Director, Philippe Büttner, Collection Curator, and Thomas Rosemann, Library Director, Kunsthaus Zürich, Zurich; Bruno Ely, Director and Chief Curator, and Florian Rodari, Curator of the Collection Jean et Suzanne Planque, Musée Granet, Aix-en-Provence; Manuel Borja-Villel, Director, The Royal Board of

Trustees, Museo Nacional Centro de Arte Reina Sofía, Madrid; Guillermo Peiró Posadas, General Director and José Lebrero Stals, Artistic Director, Museo Picasso Málaga, Malaga; Glenn D. Lowry, Director, Ann Temkin, The Marie-Josée and Henry Kravis Chief Curator of Painting and Sculpture and Anne Umland, The Blanchette Hooker Rockefeller Curator of Painting and Sculpture, The Museum of Modern Art, New York; Antony William Roland Penrose, Director, and Ami Bouhassane, Curator and Registrar, The Penrose Collection, Chiddingly; Christina Olsen, Director, Joseph Rosa, former Director, and Kathryn Huss, Interim Director, The University of Michigan Museum of Art, Ann Arbor; as well as those who prefer to remain anonymous. We include in our gratitude the many registrars, conservators, assistant curators and researchers – too numerous to mention – who have facilitated the often complex logistics that are a prerequisite for moving these precious works.

For their help in securing crucial loans we thank: William and Nicholas Acquavella and Michael Findlay, Acquavella Galleries, New York; Olivier Camu, Liberté Nuti, and Sandra Carli Karlsson, Christie's; Melanie Clore and Henry Wyndham, Clore Wyndham, London; Cristin Tierney and William Petroni, Cristin Tierney Gallery, New York; David Norman, David Norman Fine Art LLC, New York; Olivia Speer, DWP Editions, Paris; Larry Gagosian, Michael Cary and Millicent Wilner, Gagosian Gallery, New York and London; Harry Smith, Gurr Johns, London; Sandy Heller and Chloé K. Geary, The Heller Group, New York; Helly Nahmad and Georgia Gilbert, Helly Nahmad Gallery, New York and London; Susan Hirschfeld; Libby Howie; Evelyne Ferlay, Krugier & Cie SA, Geneva; Marianna Casimo, Krugier Contemporain SA, Geneva; Nancy Whyte, Nancy Whyte Fine Arts, New York; Arne Glimcher and Tamara Corm, Pace Gallery, New York and London; Sandra Poole; Richard and Paul Gray, and Lilah Aubrey, Richard Gray Gallery, Chicago and New York; Erika Batey, Helena Newman, Florence Sonier and Grace Read, Sotheby's.

An exhibition of this ambition would not have been possible without the aid of individuals outside the museum who helped developing research and broaden our knowledge of Picasso's work. We are deeply indebted to Susan K. Anderson, The Martha Hamilton Morris Archivist, Philadelphia Museum of Art, Philadelphia; Elena Cazzaro, ASAC, Fondazione La Biennale di Venezia, Venice; MaryKate Cleary, Art Historian; Michael C. FitzGerald, Trinity College, Hartford; Simonetta Fraquelli; Carmen Giménez; Christopher Green; Florence Half Wrobel; Silvia Loreti; Marilyn McCully; and Charlie Miller. Conversations with Sir John Patrick Richardson have never been anything but a source of joy and delight. Special thanks are due to Elizabeth Cowling, Professor Emeritus (History of Art), The University of Edinburgh, for acting as the best kind of critical friend.

We salute the contributors to this catalogue and thank them for grappling in such an elucidating manner with Picasso's work: Neil Cox, Professor of Modern Art and Contemporary at ECA, University of Edinburgh; T.J. Clark; Alma Mikulinsky and Diana Widmaier Picasso. The exquisite design of the catalogue owes to the congenial sensibilities of Daniel McGhee and Andy Altmann from Why Not Associates Ltd.

This exhibition is the outcome of a multi-year collaboration between Tate Modern and Musée national Picasso–Paris. It is a daily privilege to work with such a wonderful team of colleagues. In Paris, we are particularly indebted to: Laurent Le Bon, Chief Curator of Heritage and President of the Public Establishment of the Musée national Picasso–Paris, for the many stimulating conversations; Erol Ok, Deputy Director; Emilie Bouvard, Curator of Paintings, Research and Contemporary Art; Claire Garnier, Deputy Director of Collections and Production, Sophie Daynes-Diallo, Head of Exhibitions Management, and Audrey Gonzalez, Exhibitions Registrar, for their tireless attention to every detail concerning the Paris presentation, and François Dareau, Research Assistant, Marie Saussol, Exhibition Intern, and Zoé Prieur, former Exhibition Intern, for their valuable contributions.

At Tate Modern, Maria Balshaw, Director, Tate, and Sir Nicholas Serota, former Director, Tate, have been enthusiastic champions of this ambitious undertaking. We thank Frances Morris, Director, Tate Modern for her unwavering support. Warm collegial thanks go to Helen Sainsbury, Head of Exhibition and Programme Management, and Matthew Gale, Head of Displays, for sharing their expertise with the extended team; to Rachel Kent, Senior Programme Manager, International Collaborations for overseeing the contract and tour logistics with such diligence and to Phil Monk, Design and Production Manager, for his input into the exhibition design.

Laura Bruni and Juliette Rizzi, Assistant Curators, have demonstrated outstanding dedication, diligence and passion throughout the preparation of the exhibition and the catalogue. We are also grateful to Wendy Lothian, Registrar, for steering us through the complex loan logistics with unfailingly good humour. Alyssa Bacon and Stephanie Busson provided invaluable support. Special thanks are due to Judith Severne, Project Editor, and her colleagues at Tate Publishing for their tireless attention to countless details in the making of this book. Jenny Batchelor, Convenor Interpretation, has been an incisive voice in discussions throughout, helping us to articulate often complex ideas with admirable simplicity.

Great institutions as much as great exhibitions are the product of countless hands and minds across many different Departments including Archive and Library, Art Handling, Communications, Conservation, Curatorial, Development, Interpretation, Learning, Legal, Media, Press, Registrars, Special Events and Visitor Experience to name but some. In museums, the work of those operating in the limelight is reliant on the contribution of many colleagues working with equal energy behind the scenes. May each and every one of you feel thanked by us.

Our final salute goes to the artists who nurture our souls by sharing with us their steadfast belief in the power of art to make a difference. Bridging the gulf of time our last and ultimate thanks thus go to Pablo Picasso for giving to the world such a gift of creative abundance.

**Achim Borchardt-Hume**
Director of Exhibitions and Programmes
Tate Modern

**Nancy Ireson**
Curator, International Art
Tate Modern

**Laurence Madeline**
Chief Curator of Heritage

**Virginie Perdrisot-Cassan**
Curator of Sculptures and Ceramics
Musée national Picasso–Paris

# The Painter of Today

Achim Borchardt-Hume

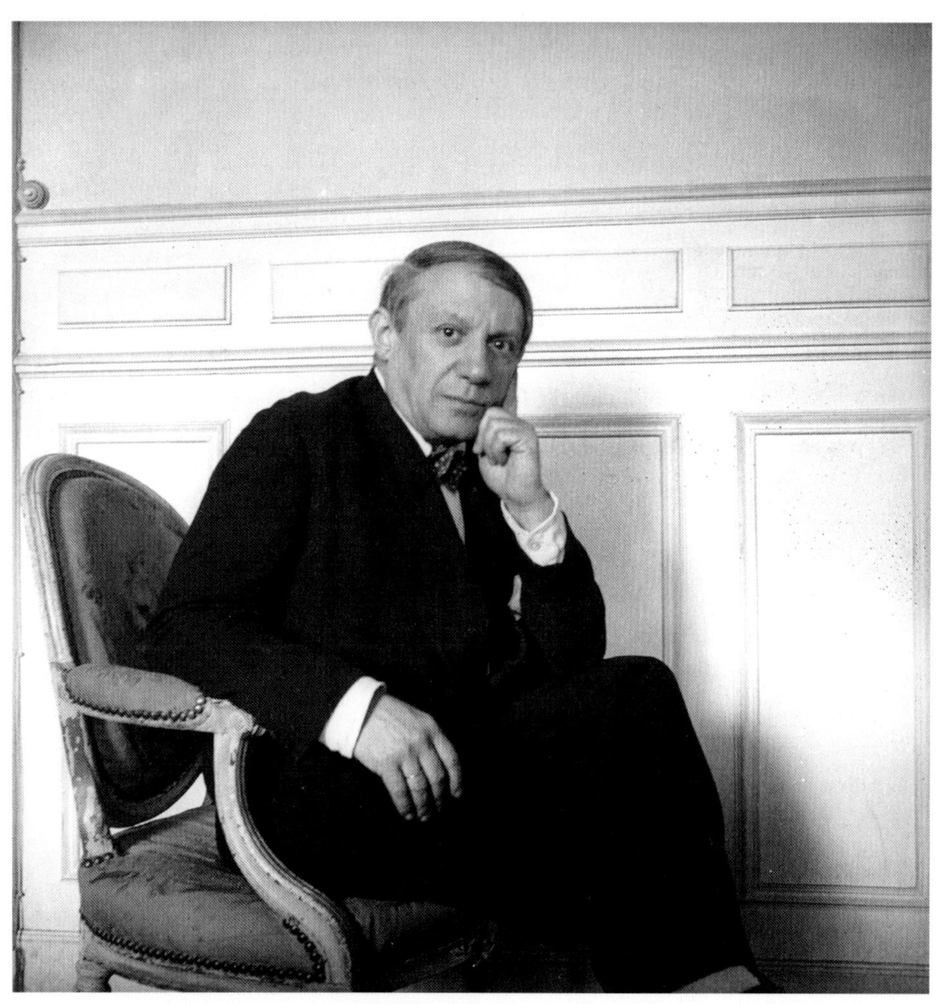

Picasso, rue La Boétie, Paris 1933. Photograph by Cecil Beaton

'The great mass of human beings, absorbed in the toils, cares and activities of life, are only dimly conscious of the pace at which mankind has begun to travel.'

Winston Churchill, *Popular Mechanics*, March 1932

On 25 February 1932 the Brüning government awarded German nationality to Adolf Hitler, paving the way for him to stand in the Reich's March and April presidential elections, both of which he lost. The following day, on 26 February 1932, a painting by Pablo Picasso, *La Coiffure* 1905, sold at the Hôtel Drouot auction house in Paris for an astounding 56,000 francs.[1] Seen as a sign of economic recovery, the sale was widely reported in the international press. Democracy and the market for modern art were both precarious in the wake of the 1929 Wall Street Crash and the Great Depression that followed.

With hindsight, the twelve months of 1932 seem like the proverbial calm before the storm. The most prominent news story of the year was the abduction on 1 March of the twenty-month old son of US aviation legend Charles Lindbergh, which preoccupied the media until the boy was found dead, killed by a massive skull fracture, on 12 May not far from his parents' New Jersey home. In May, 35-year-old Amelia Earhart became the first woman to cross the Atlantic on a solo flight; in July, Frenchman André Leducq won the 26th Tour de France; while at the Summer Olympics, the global recession resulted in fewer than half the nations competing in Los Angeles than had done so four years earlier in Amsterdam (though China, for the first time, sent a single athlete). Also during the summer, a delegation of African-American writers and artists including Langston Hughes travelled to Moscow to participate in the Soviet-sponsored anti-racist film project *Black and White*, soon to be abandoned as a trade-off for recognition of the USSR by the US government. The name 'Yo-yo' was registered as a trademark in Vancouver, Canada, at the height of a North American craze for the toy; Fred Astaire crooned the original version of Cole Porter's perennial jazz hit 'Night and Day'; and at Grauman's Chinese Theater in Los

Angeles, Walt Disney screened *Flower and Trees*, the first of his *Silly Symphonies* animations to be released in full Technicolor, heralding a cinematic revolution. In November, Nadezdha Alliluyeva shot herself after having had publicly to endure one marital insult too many, thereby causing a major public relations challenge for her husband, Josef Stalin. In the same month, fashion designer Coco Chanel launched her first range of precious jewellery; with ironic audacity the collection was called simply *Bijoux de Diamants* (Diamond Jewellery). The pieces were inspired by the beauty of the sky as an encouragement to look upwards during the Great Depression, and certainly helped the ailing diamond trade. In London, the *Times* debuted its custom-designed typeface, Times New Roman, the BBC moved into the recently completed Broadcasting House and undertook its first experiments in television, while on the radio King-Emperor George V inaugurated the now time-honoured tradition of the Royal Christmas Message. The Tate Gallery officially adopted the name of its founding donor, the sugar magnate and philanthropist Sir Henry Tate, and Aldous Huxley published *Brave New World*.

Elsewhere, having made huge gains in the first German federal elections in July 1932, the National Socialists lost thirty-four seats in November. 'Hitler is apparently finished', the composer Richard Strauss wrote in his diary, failing to appreciate the growing collusion between the conservative establishment and the extreme right wing.[2] Rather, these were to be the last free elections in the country for seventeen years. Germany was far from the only nation falling under the spell of Fascist populism: in Italy, Mussolini reached an accord with Pope Pius XI, while in Portugal António de Oliveira Salazar established a dictatorship that was to last for the next thirty-six years. In the autumn, fifteen years after the October Revolution, Stalin's policy of enforced collectivisation led to the first of several mass famines in Soviet Russia. Meanwhile, Picasso's native Spain, a republic since 1931, clung onto its new constitution, though tensions between different political and military factions remained rife – including an unsuccessful coup by General José Sanjurjo in August 1932.

In France, Picasso's adopted home, on 6 May President Paul Doumer was shot by a mentally unstable Russian émigré while visiting a book fair, the first French president to die from a gun wound. Four days later, Albert François Lebrun was elected President of the French Republic, a position he would hold until 1940 when France was overrun by Hitler's armies and Marshal Pétain was made head of the Vichy government (Picasso would be one of the few artists to remain in Nazi-occupied Paris). However, none of these events had a direct bearing on Picasso.

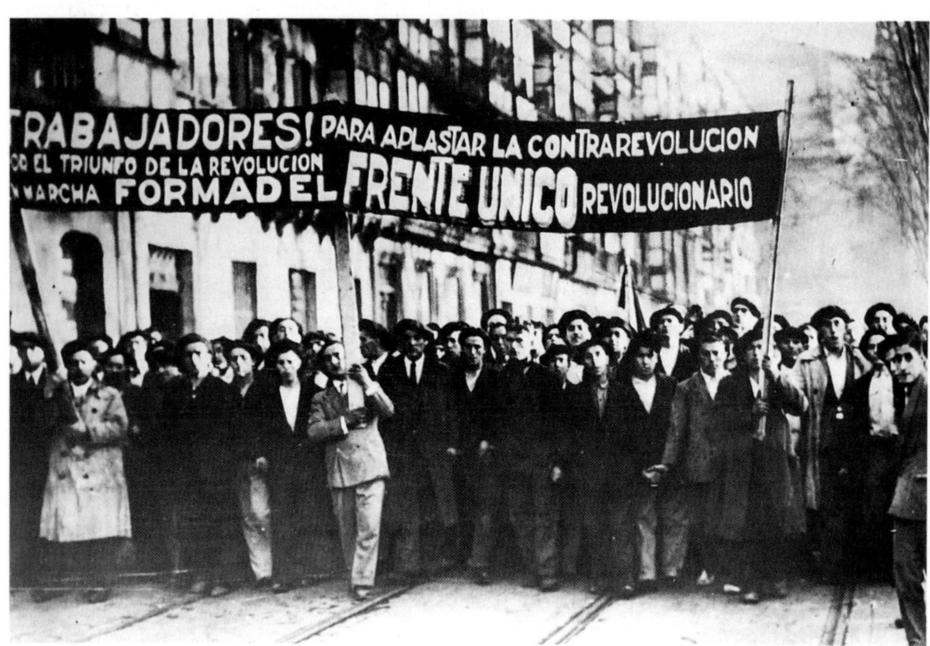


Republican demonstration in Madrid, 1932

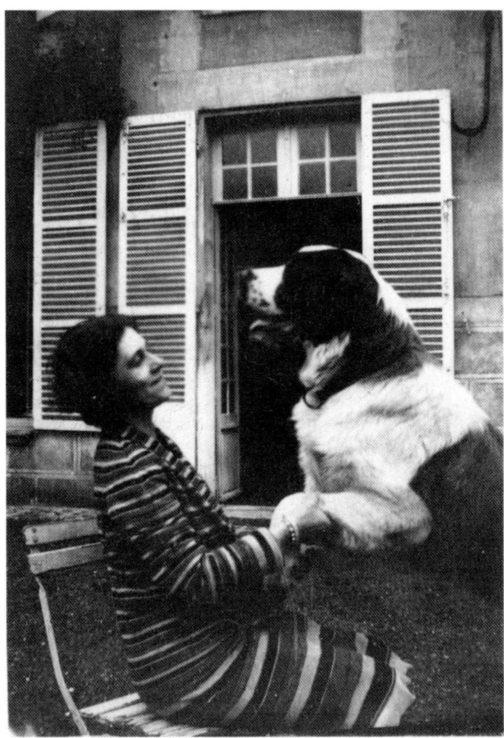

Olga Picasso with Bob, the family's Pyrenean Mountain dog, Boisgeloup, Gisors, early 1930s

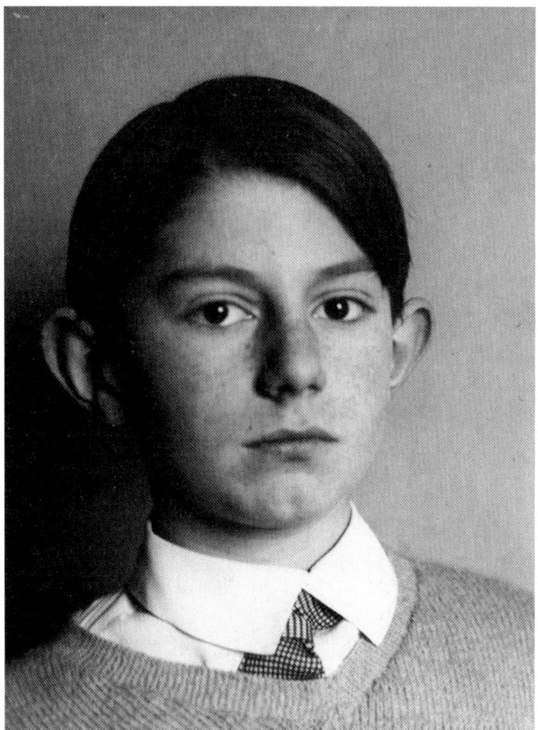

Portrait of Paulo Picasso, rue La Boétie 1932–3
Photograph by Brassaï

Until his epoch-making contribution to the Spanish Pavilion in the Paris International Exhibition of 1937 – a panoramic painting commemorating the bombardment of the Basque town of Guernica – Picasso refrained from mixing art and politics in any overt fashion, and mostly drew on personal experiences in his ceaseless quest for experiment and innovation.

Not that Picasso's private universe was devoid of conflict and tension either – far from it. Between 19 and 25 December 1931, while confined by the imminent Christmas celebrations to the family home he shared with his wife, the former Russian ballerina Olga Khokhlova, and their ten year-old son Paulo, Picasso made a small yet elaborate painting called *Woman with Dagger* (p.41). The image is imbued with the violent subconscious of surrealism. One distorted figure, armed with a slender blade, is shown in the process of killing another female stretched out beneath her. The painting loosely references an icon of classical French art – Jacques-Louis David's 1793 depiction of the murdered Jean-Paul Marat, slumped in the bath he used to soothe his skin condition. In Picasso's version, however, Charlotte Corday assassinates not one of the most radical voices of the French Revolution but her sexual competitor.

On Christmas Day, Picasso rapidly executed another, larger painting (p.43). This shows a singular female figure in a red and black striped armchair. A whirlwind of lines describing various body parts pivots around the figure's sex. Curiously, the sitter's facial features have been wiped out, making her unrecognisable, with a heart drawn into the head's painterly smudge instead. If *Woman with Dagger* is a formally adventurous allegory of jealousy and the darker realm of sexual drives, *Woman in a Red Armchair* is an ode to uncomplicated love and desire – albeit one Picasso clearly had an interest to protect from wider knowledge.

It has become a common trope in the biography-heavy reading of Picasso's work to associate *Woman with Dagger* with the failing state of the artist's thirteen-year marriage to Olga Khokhlova,[3] although it is worth noting that Picasso returned to the subject in the mid-1930s as the political mood across Europe severely darkened.[4] The barely visible tuft of blonde hair in *Woman in a Red Armchair*, on the other hand, leaves little doubt as to the identity of its subject: Marie-Thérèse Walter, then aged twenty-two. This then is Picasso's Christmas in 1931: having translated his sense of domestic entrapment into a disturbing reflection on power, domination, aggression and victimhood, he sought painterly relief in exuberant colour play and free flowing lines by dreaming about his young mistress of four years.

Balancing divergent parts of his professional and private existence remained one of the defining characteristics of Picasso's life throughout 1932: his dutiful roles of husband and father versus his deepening love for a younger woman; the gilded trappings of the successful artist contrasting with his longing for a simpler way of life; a bourgeois apartment in Paris's elegant 8th arrondissement complemented by a chaotic studio and an atmospheric mansion in which to retreat from public life; ambitious paintings made for public display based on sculptures initially known only in photographic reproduction;[5] planning his largest retrospective to date and publishing the first of thirty-three volumes of his catalogue raisonné while forging new paths for the future. Just as in the world at large, so these different facets of Picasso's life and career were soon to come under increased pressure. For the time being, however, their relatively harmonious coexistence created a rich tapestry that made 1932 an exceptionally fertile year – so much so that Picasso's biographer John Richardson has called it an *annus mirabilis*.[6] How then are we to imagine this 'year of wonders'?

On 25 October 1931 Picasso had turned fifty. Since he had first settled in Paris three decades before, his career had been nothing but stratospheric. His early blue and pink paintings had rapidly helped to establish the reputation of the young Spaniard, then barely in his early twenties, as a leading artist of his generation. The invention of cubism, with Georges Braque his closest ally and the German-born dealer Daniel-Henry Kahnweiler their greatest advocate, irrevocably destabilised the foundations of Western painting. After the First World War Picasso moved with ever greater dexterity between a newfound classicism and the most violent distortion of the human figure.

Long gone were the early days of bohemian poverty at the ramshackle Bateau-Lavoir in Montmartre[7] when Picasso, who was always very conscious of the image he projected via his dress, adopted the traditional workman's uniform of baggy patched trousers and jacket, often sporting a cap to complete the look. By now, the Picasso family occupied a grand apartment at 23 rue La Boétie,

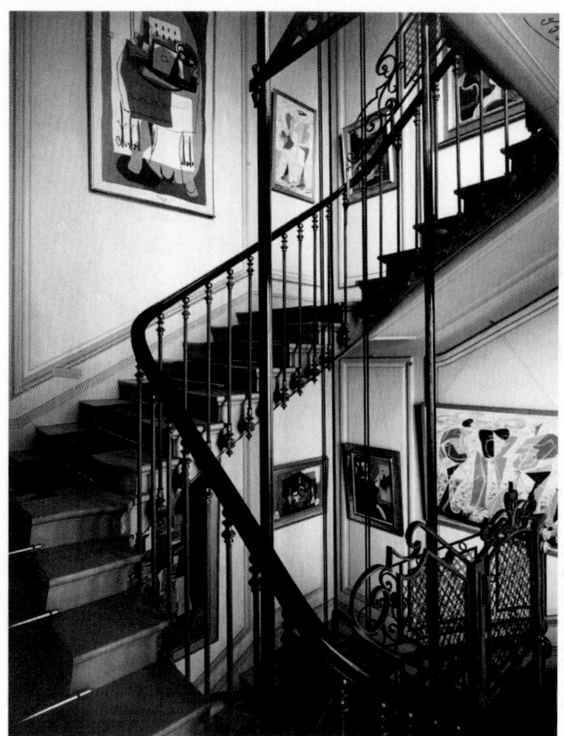

The main staircase of the gallery of Paul Rosenberg on rue La Boétie, with paintings by Picasso and André Masson

not far from the Champs-Élysées. The apartment, which remained Picasso's principal residence until 1940, had been rented for him from 1918 onwards by the dealer Paul Rosenberg, whose gallery and living quarters were next door. Rosenberg enjoyed the privilege of being the first to see and cherry-pick whatever new works Picasso produced. Securing Picasso worldwide representation by working with Georges Wildenstein as a close business associate in the United States, Rosenberg was a formidable force, establishing his ultra-fashionable gallery at 21 rue La Boétie as the epicentre of the 1920s and 1930s Paris art world.[8]

Monsieur and Madame Picasso in turn had become fixtures of an international moneyed jet-set, attending formal dinner and fancy dress parties, theatre and ballet premieres, and joining the trend among the wealthy for holidays in the South of France. The daughter of a Russian colonel, Olga Khokhlova had been a ballerina dancing with Sergei Diaghilev's famous Ballets Russes when Picasso first fell in love with her in 1917. Her strict morals had been as much a part of her appeal as her aspirational life style, which added to Picasso's own sense of success. By now, Olga Picasso dressed in Chanel, the designer of choice for the emancipated modern woman, while her husband liked to wear expensive woollen suits tailor-made on London's Savile Row, and travelled in a chauffeur-driven Hispano-Suiza, the choice of car maker representing a nod to his Spanish roots.[9] At his first meeting with Picasso in Paris, Jim Ede, then a young Assistant Curator at the Tate Gallery fighting the corner of international modern art, offered to pay for a taxi. Noticing Ede's surprise at the sight of the luxury vehicle, Picasso laconically commented in French: 'I am a great master now, you have to have a motor car.'[10] A similar grandeur extended to his living quarters on rue La Boétie. The French-Hungarian artist and photographer Brassaï, visiting in autumn 1932 at Picasso's invitation, described the apartment as 'one of the centres of society life ... No clutter, not a speck of dust. Polished, gleaming wood floors and furniture.'[11] He also observed: 'Olga jealously made sure that Picasso did not impose the powerful imprint of his personality on a realm she considered hers alone.'[12]

While somewhat polemical – after all, the walls were covered in Picasso's works from different periods – Brassaï's comment is indicative of the rising tensions in the Picasso household. Pablo's artist and writer friends of old maintained a well-kept distance from his wealthy lifestyle. Max Jacob, one of his early confidents, mocked Picasso for what he called his 'Duchess period'.[13] Under the strain of his failing marriage, stifled by the conventions of society and family life and eager to reconnect with the world of art and artists he had known as a young man, Picasso created two realms of his own: a studio in the apartment directly above the one he shared with his wife and son, and an eighteenth-century chateau in the hamlet of Boisgeloup near Gisors, 63 kilometres north of Paris, which he had bought in June 1930.

The upstairs apartment at 23 rue La Boétie could not have been more different from the family dwellings below. Brassaï called it 'an apartment turned pigsty',[14] filled with paintings and statues, piles of books, reams of paper, cardboard boxes and the curious objects Picasso was so fond of accumulating. 'No middle-class home had ever been less middle class in its furnishings',[15] Brassaï observed. Crucially, 'Mme Picasso never came up to this apartment. Except for a few friends, Picasso allowed no one in.'[16]

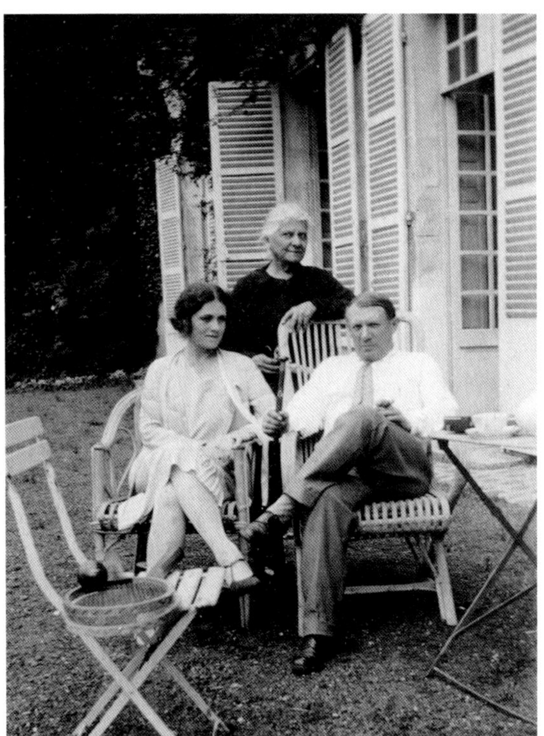

Olga and Picasso with the artist's mother, Doña Maria Picasso y Lopez, in the garden at Boisgeloup, 1930s

Boisgeloup, on the other hand, served a triple purpose: as country retreat for family and friends, as studio for Picasso when on his own, and as a potential bolt hole to spend undisturbed time with Marie-Thérèse Walter. A series of home movies and photographs shows Picasso, Olga and Paulo, along with their Pyrenean Mountain dog Bob, Picasso's mother Doña Maria and others, enjoying their time in the outdoors. The house itself, only one room deep with most of the principal accommodation in the squat stone tower on one corner, was surrounded by an extensive garden. Aside from a row of empty stables, the walled grounds included an impressive dovecote and an ancient chapel which – much to the artist's delight – was still in occasional use. There were few mod cons. The heating was patchy and largely limited to the tower, on whose second floor Picasso also installed his painting studio with views across the village. Plans for a swimming pool, commissioned in summer 1932 soon after his retrospective had opened, were never executed.

Olga Picasso fancied herself as the *châtelaine*, or lady of the manor, visiting frequently and extending the couple's hospitality to an inner circle of friends. Her liking of Boisgeloup was such that the chateau

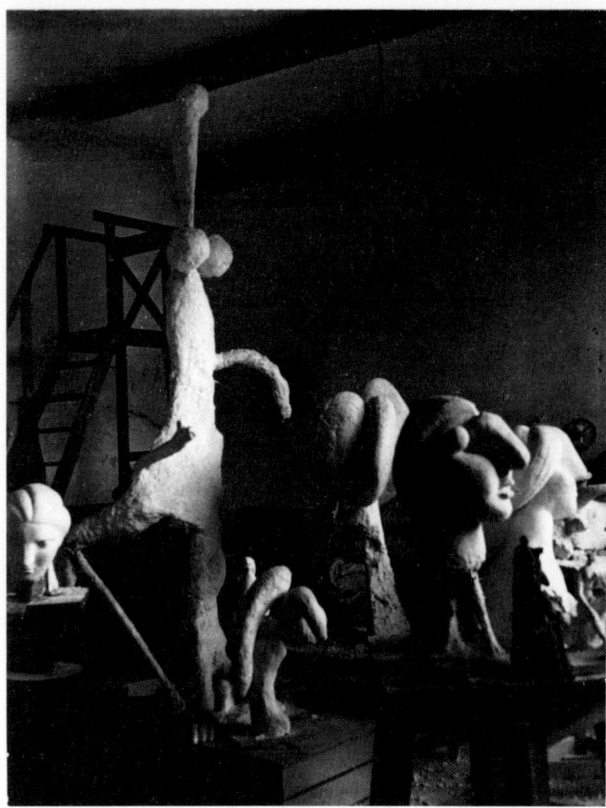

Plaster sculptures in the Boisgeloup studio, December 1932. Photograph by Brassaï

became hers as part of the settlement once she and Picasso formally separated in 1935.[17]

Aside from a welcome refuge from public life, Boisgeloup – and in particular the vacant outbuildings across from the main house – offered Picasso a whole new working environment. He dedicated much of 1931 to the production of a group of extraordinary sculptures: bulbous heads with penile protrusions, neo-classical busts, and large-scale plaster and wood constructions. These were semi-private experiments, revealed to the public for the first time not in an exhibition but in a series of dramatically lit photographs by Brassaï taken in late 1932 and published in the inaugural issue of the surrealist review *Minotaure* in early 1933[18] (pp.184–7). Brassaï vividly recalled the moment when Picasso opened the door to one of the stables and the two men 'were able to see the dazzling whiteness of an entire people of sculptures'.[19] This 'people of sculptures', their differences notwithstanding, orbited around a single source of inspiration: Marie-Thérèse Walter, Picasso's junior by twenty-eight years.

Picasso first met Walter in 1927, outside the Galeries Lafayette department store on Boulevard Haussmann. For the first eight years their relationship remained a well-kept secret, known only to the closest members of her family (and possibly Olga Picasso; as much at least seems suggested by an entry in her address book[20]). This was only to change in 1935 when Marie-Thérèse Walter became pregnant with Picasso's child – María de la Concepción, or Maya for short, named after his sister whose premature death in 1895 from diphtheria, aged seven, haunted Picasso for much of his life. However, it was not until 1958 that the English historian, artist and collector Roland Penrose first mentioned Walter publicly in his biography of Picasso, where he described her (not entirely without gender bias) as always behaving 'according to her own inclination, changing her mind or her manner of living in an inconsequential way as though controlled by the influence of the moon or by some even less calculable force.'[21] Young, athletic, blonde, with a classical profile, Marie-Thérèse Walter was a very different woman from Olga Picasso. Whereas the latter appears refined, melancholic and self-absorbed in Picasso's famous neoclassical portrait (p.129), Walter's strong features sparked both the voluminous Boisgeloup sculptures and the muscular paintings that followed soon after. If the contrast between the downstairs and upstairs apartments at 23 rue La Boétie was symptomatic of the growing rift separating Picasso's public and private personas, so were these two relationships. As Françoise Gilot (herself in a relationship with Picasso from 1943 until 1953 and mother to his son Claude, and daughter Paloma) would observe some thirty years later in her memoirs, Walter 'became the luminous dream of youth, always in the background but always within reach, that nourished his work ... Marie-Thérèse, then, was very important to him as long as he was living with Olga because she was the dream when the reality was someone else.'[22]

The Scylla and Charybdis of reality and dream were the twin monsters that also kept a group of artists and writers in their grip: the surrealists spearheaded by the writer André Breton. While Picasso felt attracted to the surrealist circles, he was also eager to maintain his distance. Hesitant about getting involved in politics (including the surrealists' repeated call for yet another revolution), particularly

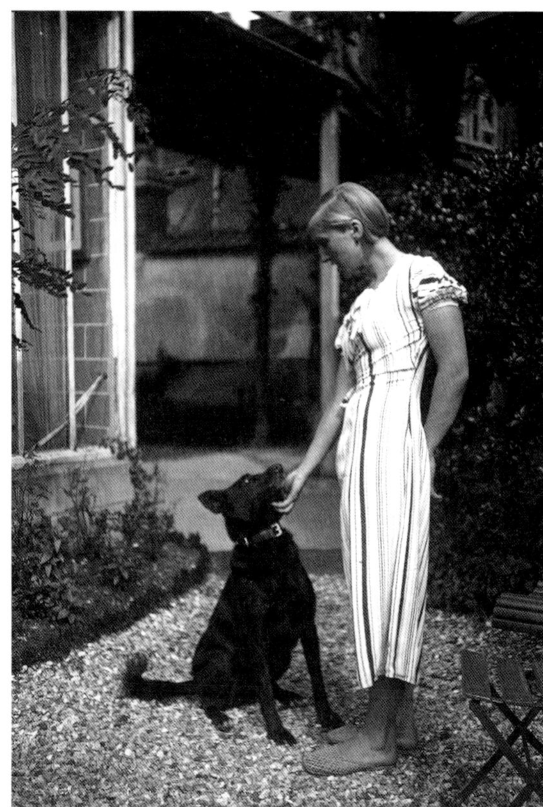

Marie-Thérèse Walter at home in the garden with her dog Dolly, Cité d'Alfort, Maisons-Alfort, c.1930

while living as a foreigner in France with his native Spain edging ever closer to a dictatorship, Picasso was in any case not inclined by temperament to signing up to members' clubs of any kind.[23] He was equally suspicious of manifestos and artist writings which would suggest that art and artist ought to pursue a premeditated programme rather than follow where the work would take them. Surrealism was no different, no matter the very role Picasso had played in its inception when he had asked his poet friend Guillaume Apollinaire in 1916 for a contribution to a programme accompanying a Diaghilev ballet. It was here that Apollinaire had first coined the term 'sur-realism'.[24] Some sixteen years later, Picasso – always more engaged with haptic reality than ethereal dreams – felt ambiguous not just about the movement but the very concept: 'I seek always to observe nature. I cling to resemblance, to a deeper resemblance, more real than the real, attaining the surreal. That is how I understood surrealism, but the word was used in a completely different way.'[25] These lines may as well have referred to the sculptures of 1931 and the paintings that formed the central part of Picasso's production across the first months of 1932. Many of the seated figures, reclining nudes and still-life busts capture and transform Marie-Thérèse Walter's most prominent features: her unmistakable profile, her youthful body and her cropped blonde hair. This metamorphosis provokes yet another gear change in Picasso's work: a new passion for solid volumes and their translation into a particularly flat type of painting, a vigorous dialogue between painting and drawing, a persistent tension between recognisable representation and grotesque distortion. Epitomised by the many depictions of Walter caught asleep or dreaming, it is here that Picasso's *amour fou* or 'mad love', about which so much has been said and written, shares some common ground with the surrealists' conception of the creative drive.[26]

Representation – and the triangulation this entails between physical appearance, the inner experience of this external reality and either's translation into art – remained Picasso's privileged playing field. For him, representation was always also invention: 'Do you think it concerns me that a particular picture of mine represents two people? Though these two people once existed for me, they exist no longer. The "vision" of them gave me a preliminary emotion; then little by little their actual presences became blurred; they developed into a fiction and then disappeared altogether, or rather they were transformed into all kinds of problems. They are no longer two people, you see, but forms and colors: forms and colors that have taken on, meanwhile, the *idea* of two people and preserve the vibration of their life.'[27] This should caution against too literal a reading of one of Picasso's most popular quotes from an interview published in June 1932: 'The work that one does is a way of keeping a diary.'[28] Rarely does biographical circumstance neatly explain the aesthetic choices Picasso made.

To this end, it may be instructive to compare various seated figures from January 1932. These range from the closely affiliated *Reading* and *Young Woman with Mandolin* (pp.48, 49) to the caricature-like *The Yellow Belt* with its erect protuberant nose (p.47), the disturbingly contorted *Rest* (p.54), the tranquil *Sleep* (p.55) and the lyrical *The Dream* (p.57). Two versions from the end of the month dissolve the figure altogether into an assemblage of sculptural volumes reminiscent of prehistoric dolmens and surrealist sculptures such as those of Alberto Giacometti (pp.58–9). These are very different elaborations on a shared theme. The resulting impression then is more complex than is suggested by the frequent focus on *Rest* – its distortion oftentimes equated with Olga Picasso's growing unhappiness – and *The Dream*, generally understood as a portrait of Marie-Thérèse Walter in pre- or post-coital abandon. The January paintings respond at least as much to a set of formal questions as they reflect on the changeability of love and desire, their attractive and their monstrous sides.[29]

Picasso's exploration of the continued possibilities of figurative painting was all the more urgent at a point when the medium was coming under increased pressure from various directions – not least from the rise of abstract art and surrealism with its predilection for automatism, photography, collage, assemblage, curious found objects and their like. This led Picasso to pursue different avenues not just in rapid succession but simultaneously, as is demonstrated by two very different groups of works made during the first two weeks and the final days of March 1932. Between 2 and 14 March, Picasso completed seven extraordinary paintings: two still lifes, three reclining nudes, one fusion of the two genres and one duplicated standing figure. In the first two works, a bust in profile – suggestive of the Boisgeloup sculptures and by extension of Walter – looks across an arrangement of tulips and a bowl of fruit (p.89). In the second version, a palette hung within the bust's sightline creates a quasi-Baroque allegory on the arts of two-dimensional painting and three-dimensional sculpture, the palette's semblance to the bust declaring painterly illusion their meeting ground (p.91). In the majestic canvas of 8 March, the bust no longer gazes at inanimate objects but living beings, a philodendron and a reclining female nude, with the last pieces of fruit pushed to the bottom left corner (p.93). In the subsequent three paintings, the nude takes centre stage, variously draped across a black armchair, turned to reveal her otherwise obscured rear view in a mirror, or asleep burying her head in her arms (pp.95, 97, 99). Finally, on 14 March, the *Girl before a Mirror* gazes at her own reflection in a free-standing looking-glass (p.101). These seven paintings, which Alfred H. Barr, Jr called 'unlike anything [Picasso] had done before in their bold color and great sweeping curves',[30] recall the ancient myth of Pygmalion: sculpture coming to life through the desire of its artist maker. Some forty years after their first encounter, Marie-Thérèse Walter recalled how Picasso made her feel alive by not just looking at her but by truly seeing her for who she was.[31]

Which is not to say that one ought to imagine Walter as an intimate presence in the studio – at least, not the Marie-Thérèse Walter of flesh and blood. Picasso practically never painted from a live model. Furthermore, despite the clear affinity between the sculptures of 1931 and the nudes from early March 1932, the latter were made not in Boisgeloup but at 23 rue La Boétie, a long way away from the sculpture studio with Walter, most likely equally out of reach (though it has been suggested that the diamond wallpaper in two of the paintings references otherwise unidentified lodgings where Picasso and Walter used to meet for their amorous encounters).[32] Longing and desire, both metaphorical and literal, are thus revealed here as the driving forces for Picasso's art. However, aside from Marie-Thérèse Walter, there is a third person in this imaginary room, namely Henri Matisse. The colouristic exuberance of the paintings from early March – painted very much with the coming retrospective exhibition in mind – and their vigorous use of sinuous lines leave little doubt that Picasso was in both dialogue and competition with one of the few fellow artists whose work he never ceased to follow, respect and admire.[33] Around the time that Picasso was at work on the nudes, Matisse – the subject of a large retrospective at Georges Petit one year earlier – conceived his radically simplified monumental canvas mural *The Dance I* for the gallery of the Philadelphia art-enthusiast and collector Albert C. Barnes.[34] Matisse and Picasso, at this moment, were united in their combat for the continued validity of painting rooted in several centuries of representation through a reinvigorated exuberance and sensuality.

Let us compare now the early March paintings with a group of six reclining figures from the end of the month. Picasso – possibly with Olga and Paulo – was spending the Easter weekend in Boisgeloup, following a trip to the seaside near Varengeville and Pourville that had included a visit to the newly built studio of his old friend Georges Braque.[35] Between 25 and 28 March 1932 he produced a series of six mostly small works, with the exception of one large-scale canvas (pp.102–5). Their shared subject

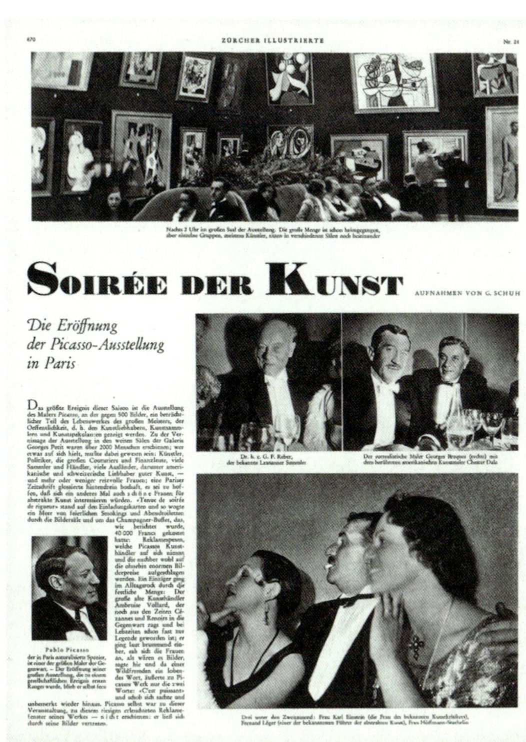

870 ZÜRCHER ILLUSTRIERTE Nr. 28

Nachts 2 Uhr im großen Saal der Ausstellung. Die große Menge ist schon heimgegangen, aber einzelne Gruppen, meistens Künstler, sitzen in verschiedenen Sälen noch beieinander

# SOIRÉE DER KUNST

AUFNAHMEN VON G. SCHUH

*Die Eröffnung der Picasso-Ausstellung in Paris*

Das größte Ereignis dieser Saison ist die Ausstellung des Malers *Picasso*, an der gegen 500 Bilder, ein beträchtlicher Teil des Lebenswerkes des großen Meisters, der Oeffentlichkeit, d. h. den Kunstliebhabern, Kunstsammlern und Kunstspekulanten gezeigt werden. Zu der Vernissage der Ausstellung in den weiten Sälen der Galerie Georges Petit waren über 2000 Menschen erschienen; wer etwas auf sich hielt, mußte dabei gewesen sein: Künstler, Politiker, die großen Couturiers und Finanzleute, viele Sammler und Händler, viele Ausländer, darunter amerikanische und schweizerische Liebhaber guter Kunst, — und mehr oder weniger reizvolle Frauen; eine Pariser Zeitschrift glossierte hintendrein boshaft, es sei zu hoffen, daß sich ein anderes Mal auch s c h ö n e Frauen für abstrakte Kunst interessieren würden. «Tenue de soirée de rigueur» stand auf den Einladungskarten und so wogte ein Meer von feierlichen Smokings und Abendtoiletten durch die Bildersäle und um das Champagner-Buffet, das, wie berichtet wurde, 40 000 Francs gekostet hatte: Reklamespesen, welche Picassos Kunsthändler auf sich nimmt und die nachher wohl auf die ohnehin enormen Bilderpreise aufgeschlagen werden. Ein Einziger ging im Alltagsrock durch die festliche Menge: Der große alte Kunsthändler Ambroise Vollard, der noch aus den Zeiten Cézannes und Renoirs in die Gegenwart ragt und bei Lebzeiten schon fast zur Legende geworden ist; er ging laut brummend einher, sah sich die Frauen an, als wären es Bilder, sagte hie und da einer Wildfremden ein lobendes Wort, äußerte zu Picassos Werk nur die zwei Worte: «C'est puissant» und schob sich sachte und unbemerkt wieder hinaus. Picasso selbst war zu dieser Veranstaltung, zu diesem riesigen erleuchteten Reklamefenster seines Werkes — n i c h t erschienen: er ließ sich durch seine Bilder vertreten.

Pablo Picasso
der in Paris naturalisierte Spanier, ist einer der größten Maler der Gegenwart. – Der Eröffnung seiner großen Ausstellung, die zu einem gesellschaftlichen Ereignis ersten Ranges wurde, blieb er selbst fern

Dr. h. c. G. F. Reber, der bekannte Lausanner Sammler

Der surrealistische Maler Georges Braque (rechts) mit dem berühmten amerikanischen Kunstmaler Chester Dale

Drei unter den Zweitausend: Frau Karl Einstein (die Frau des bekannten Kunstkritikers), Fernand Léger (einer der bekanntesten Führer der abstrakten Kunst), Frau Höffmann-Stachelin

'Art Soiree: The Opening of the Picasso Exhibition in Paris', *Zürcher Illustrierte*, no.28, June 1932, p.870

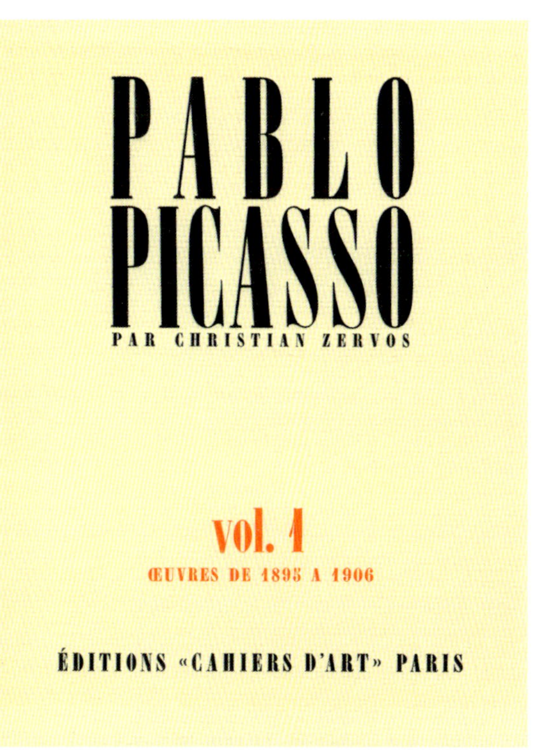


Christian Zervos, *Pablo Picasso. Vol.I: Works from 1895 to 1906*, Cahiers d'Art, Paris (1932)

is a similarly abstracted female nude on the beach, her legs spread ever more extremely to make a provocative display of her bodily orifices, their openings amplified by either the moon or the sun. Various canvases from early 1932 had fused male and female signifiers – the breasts of the *Sleeping Woman by a Mirror* morphing into a pair of male genitals (p.51), the upper half of the sleeping girl's face in *The Dream* resembling an erect penis (p.57) – expressing a desire to overcome sexual separation, whereas the early March nudes were characterised by the smooth uninterrupted surface of their bodies, their sexual organs coyly but hinted at. In sharp contrast, the six reclining figures from later in the month show the body as vulnerable to, and actively inviting, penetration. The works' confrontational subject matter – showing desire as violent rather than placid – finds formal expression in a very different palette, dominated by mixed rather than primary colours, and a network of lines that fuse geometric fragmentation with figurative distortion. As Elizabeth Cowling suggests, if Matisse was Picasso's conversation partner for the early March nudes, Braque and surrealism were his counterparts later in the month (while the paintings' composition responds to Braque's *Bathers* from the same period, the splayed legs and celestial bodies appear to quote from Joan Miró's *Person Throwing a Stone at a Bird* 1926 and Max Ernst's *Men Shall Know Nothing of This* 1923, an icon of surrealism which was at the time in the collection of André Breton where Picasso could easily have seen it).[36] Kahnweiler swooned over the nudes from early March, applauding them as 'perhaps the greatest, most moving things he [Picasso] has produced'.[37] In contrast, Rosenberg refused to show the paintings from the end of the month, telling Picasso in no uncertain terms: 'No, I refuse to have any arseholes in my gallery.'[38] In the June retrospective, the paintings from early March were celebrated as among Picasso's crowning achievements, while those from the end of the month were conspicuously absent, with the small sixth canvas only being reproduced for the first time in a special issue of *Cahiers d'Art* four years later (p.104).[39]

'To me there is no past or future in art. If a work of art cannot live always in the present it must not be considered at all',[40] Picasso had declared in 1923. Now, in early summer 1932, business partners Etienne

Bignou and Gaston and Josse Bernheim-Jeune, with considerable investment from London gallery Alex Reid & Lefevre, used the venerable name and premises of the deceased Georges Petit to organise the largest Picasso exhibition to date, in an attempt to invigorate the flagging art market following the Great Depression. Rosenberg acted as something of a bystander, with one of Picasso's greatest collectors, the German industrialist Gottlieb Friedrich Reber (who was soon to lose both his fortune and collection) among the single biggest lenders. Picasso became closely involved in the planning: many of the paintings from the first half of 1932 were painted specifically with the exhibition in mind.[41] Moreover, he conceived the display to be less *to look back* over his work from the past three decades than *to look at* it from the vantage point of the here and now of June 1932. Rather than on unity, Picasso insisted on multiplicity: he mixed works from different periods, eschewed overly simplistic typologies and refused wall labels with dates. This was the artist throwing down the gauntlet to (art) historians. Not that Picasso was repudiating the idea of history – far from it. At the same time that he was planning his retrospective exhibition, he was also finalising the first volume of his catalogue raisonné, covering the years 1895 to 1906, working with the Greek-French art historian and writer Christian Zervos (who also published the influential magazine *Cahiers d'Art*) as editor. Consequently, not only did he meticulously chronicle his earlier work, he also became more attentive to dating the work he was newly producing.[42]

Aware of doubts as to the continued relevance of his recent work, and weary of being historicised prematurely, Picasso was insistent that his work from the past months would form a key part of any major retrospective effort.[43] Via an intermediary he had communicated as much to Alfred H. Barr, Jr, the director of the newly founded Museum of Modern Art in New York when he expressed reservations about the exhibition Barr was keen to organise for autumn 1932.[44] Picasso's refusal to allow others to parcel his life into neatly defined chapters – blue, pink, analytical cubism, synthetic cubism, and so on – extended to the way his personal relationships manifested themselves in the Georges Petit show. Here, a wall with realist portraits of Olga and Paulo from between 1918 and 1924 was overlooked by a blue self-portrait from 1901, showing his pride in his family, while many of the recent paintings inspired by Marie-Thérèse Walter were peppered throughout the show.[45] Still a secret to most, the repeat appearance of Walter's distinct features was their first inkling as to the existence of this new and mysterious woman in Picasso's life.

The June retrospective marked a watershed: widely reviewed at home and abroad, it cemented Picasso's fame. 'Standing near the door of the great Picasso show at Galeries Georges Petit', the *New York Times* wrote, 'it was impossible not to overhear the voice of the advancing audience, especially as it spoke, for the most part, one's own American tongue. The voice was divided equally between two parts: "Gosh, this is fierce!" followed by rocking laughter; or, "Marvelous, marvelous, what a genius!" in a throat choking with emotion. Perhaps you can imagine with what facial expressions the parties regarded one another.'[46]

As much as it divided public and critical opinion, the June exhibition marked a pivotal turning point in Picasso's work: if a great deal of the first half of 1932 had been taken up with producing 'masterpieces', the second half became a period of energetic experimentation. Soon after the Georges Petit exhibition had opened, Picasso picked up again on the theme of the reclining nude, although from this point on most of the paintings are significantly smaller and more speedily executed. The central figure is circumscribed by fluid lines creating fields that have been coloured in with strong whites, blues and reds, at times overlaid with additional ornamentation. The motif appears to have been something of an anchor point in Picasso's imagination at this juncture, appearing even on the proverbial back of an envelope (p.108). In a painting of 27 July – one of the few larger canvases of the summer – the reclining nude has been rotated by 90 degrees to adopt the position of a seated figure in, as so often before, a red armchair (p.137). Now, however, the sitter is nude, her flesh rendered in luminous pastel shades. The depiction of her face combines a full-frontal portrait with a sideways profile. One is bathed in light, the other veiled in shadow, not unlike in *Girl before a Mirror* (p.101), though the overall mood is softer. Marie-Thérèse Walter here appears as Penrose described her, changeable as if 'controlled by the influence of the moon'.[47] Everything curls and flows in *Nude Woman in a Red Armchair*: the figure, her

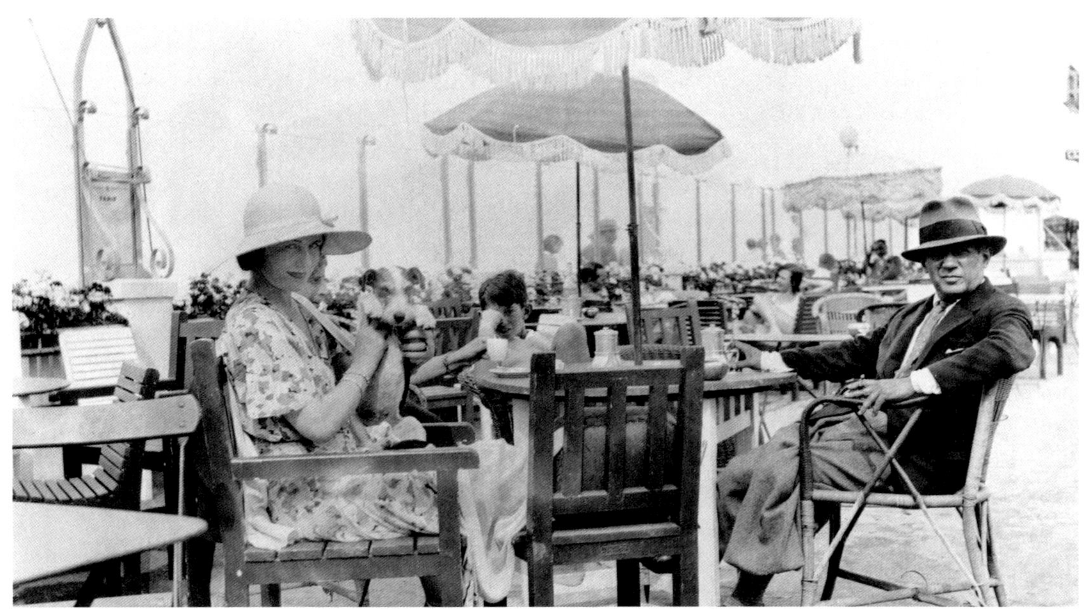

Olga, Paulo and Pablo Picasso on a café terrace, Pourville-sur-Mer, Normandy, August 1932

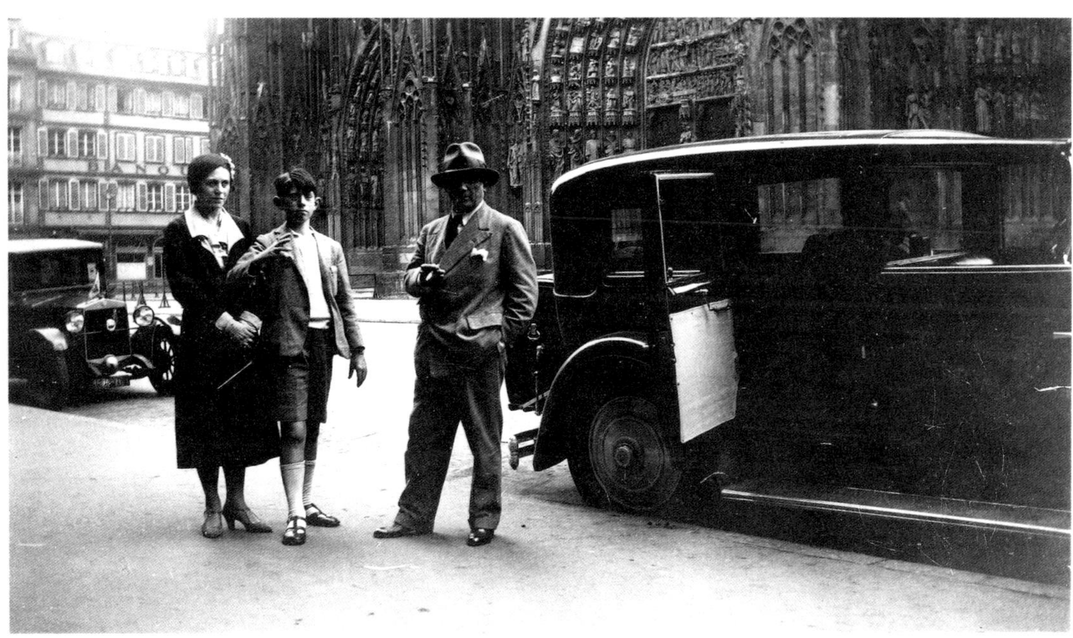

Olga, Paulo and Pablo Picasso standing by their Hispano-Suiza car opposite Strasbourg Cathedral, 7 September 1932

coquettish movement, the lines and even the paint itself. The few straight lines suggesting the corner of a room only serve to heighten the manifold curves. Everything points to this painting having been executed over a short period of time, if not one day.[48] As in the smaller reclining nudes there is a great sense of freedom, as if the opening of the Georges Petit exhibition had lifted a weight off Picasso's shoulders.

The real period of experiment though came with late summer and autumn. Picasso spent much of his time in Boisgeloup, aside from a brief trip to the Normandy coast together with Olga and Paulo. Meanwhile, Marie-Thérèse Walter passed the summer with her sister in the South of France. Holidaymakers frolicking on the beach became a prominent motif in yet another series of small canvases (pp.191–4). In all of these the figures and their movements are extremely stylised, at times to the level of stick figures. On mapping the various constellations of 1932, these intense compositions appear the cousins of the six reclining nudes from late March. The exceptions are two larger canvases from the end of the month, *Seated Woman with Elbow on Knee* and *Bather with Beach Ball* (pp.145, 147), whose painterly ambition aligns more closely with the majestic canvases of the first half of the year. The mauve swimsuits with their triangular patterns are as descriptive of actual bathing costumes as they assert themselves as compositional elements in their own right. The rotundity of the figures is reminiscent of the Boisgeloup sculptures, a small plaster *Bather* from 1931 in particular; and it is hard not to link either to a photograph of Walter taken on a beach holiday (p.146). The disturbingly distorted heads and bodies, however, are a reminder that beauty and terror were rarely far apart for Picasso.

In early September, Picasso, in the company of his wife and son, left for Switzerland where the Georges Petit retrospective had transferred to the Kunsthaus Zürich, making this Picasso's first-ever museum exhibition.[49] The entire permanent collection was removed to make space for a partially revised and enlarged selection that the museum's director Wilhelm Wartmann, together with Sigismund Righini, a Swiss painter who also acted as president of the exhibition commission at the Kunsthaus, installed in a more conventional and less idiosyncratic manner than Picasso had done three months earlier. This

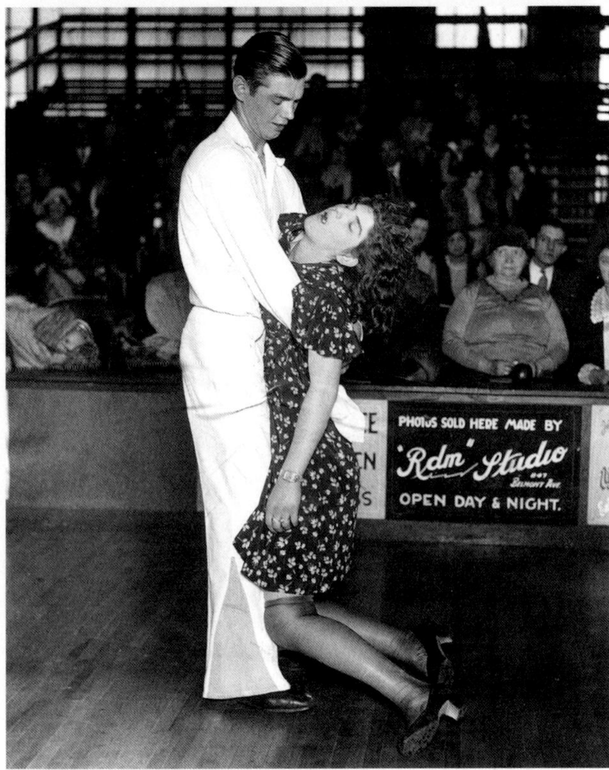


Exhausted contestants during the 3,327th hour of a dance marathon, Chicago, 19 January 1931

did little to appease some of the artist's critics. The psychiatrist Carl Gustav Jung, for one, speculated that Picasso's frequent change of style justified concern about his mental health, suggesting schizophrenia as one possible explanation.[50] Jung's criticism is especially chilling given its echoes of totalitarian regimes' soon-to-come defamation of modern art as degenerate.[51] For now, though, the Picassos were treated as celebrities, their arrival and various engagements making headlines in the local press. Meanwhile, home in France, Picasso even warranted his own entry in the newly published fifth volume of the twentieth-century Larousse encyclopaedia.[52]

Underneath the veneer of successful artist and respectable family man, however, Picasso's sense of unrest and anxiety grew ever more palpable. No sooner had he returned from Zurich via Interlaken and the Alps than he began work on an extraordinary series of black-and-white drawings of the Crucifixion. Picasso had confronted the topic before, most noticeably in a series of drawings from the latter part of the 1920s and a small and densely composed canvas of 1930 (p.180). Over the second half of September and October 1932 he returned to the theme of Christ's agony, the protagonists at times resembling a pile-up of bones, at others the oddly abstracted seated figures of late January. Arcadian scenes of female nudes and flute players provided sporadic relief from the overall darkening mood (pp.196–207).

If the year had begun with genre scenes of seated women, reclining nudes and still lifes, it ended with a return to narrative in the form of animated depictions of women by the seashore – only now the horseplay of the summer turned into scenes of drowning and rescue. There had been some suggestions earlier of water becoming a menace: in a small *Swimmer*, whose subject can barely keep her head above water (p.141), and in some of the autumn beach scenes that share a morphology with the *Crucifixions* (pp.191–3). However, the persistence of the topic in the latter months of 1932 and its formal treatment were entirely new.

Whereas throughout the year most large-scale paintings had been portrait format, now the landscape prevailed; and where female bodies had been curvaceous in the spirit of the Boisgeloup sculptures, now they became increasingly abstracted, with pointy extremities that suggest the thrust of the various figures' actions (pp.223, 231). The palette changed visibly too. Two major works showing women at play are executed entirely in grey tones (pp.224–5); this was a strategy Picasso used repeatedly throughout his career to create works that feed off the tension between story-telling and a heightened autonomy of form, *Guernica* being the most famous example (p.27).[53] Where there is colour, as in two other large compositions, it has come unstuck from the line drawing and operates separately, as it also does in the year's final reclining nude (p.230). This split greatly heightens the restlessness of the scenes. Things here come quite literally apart, especially if compared to the harmony of line and colour in the paintings of the first half of 1932.

While the landscape formats are populated by groups of figures, the portrait formats zoom in on the rescue of a single female figure. One early version, a small-scale canvas, shows a bearded man with classicising features pulling the woman from the water (p.208). Both are naked, their postures reminiscent of the Deposition of Christ as well as of news images of exhausted couples in the dance marathons

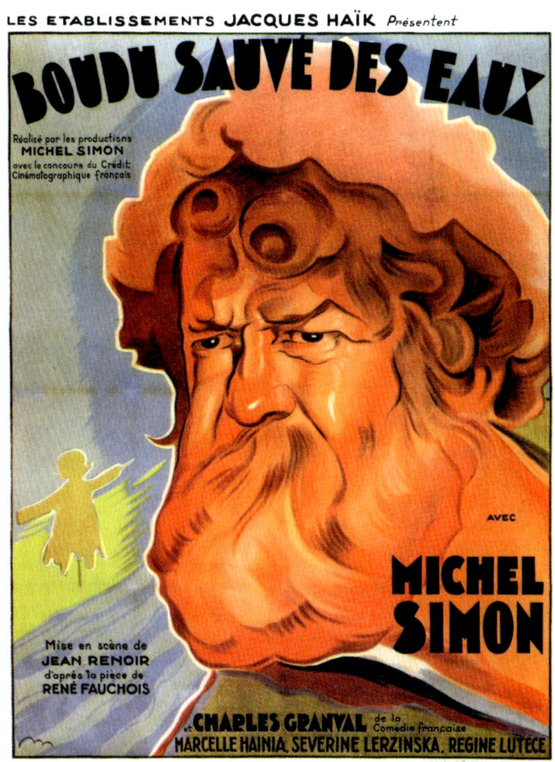


Movie poster for *Boudu Saved from Drowning*, dir. Jean Renoir, 1932

that became a troubling form of entertainment during the Great Depression (p.24). United by the action, psychologically the figures are separated, due to the strong vertical divide in the painting's composition. *The Rescue* of 20 November, by virtue of its scale and format, rich palette and painterly treatment, relates more closely to the paintings from the beginning of the year (p.217). The profile of the rescuer now is recognisably that of one of the monumental Boisgeloup heads as it also appears in the painting of an imposing seated figure of 30 October (p.215). The drowning woman's profile, on the other hand, is not unlike that of the sitter in *Sleep* of 23 January or *Nude in a Black Armchair* of 9 March – but the pose that once suggested peaceful slumber now hints at a lack of consciousness if not death. A third figure – her features similar to those of the other two – emerges from the bottom edge of the canvas, arms outstretched in a gesture that hovers uneasily between coming to the rescue and taking the hapless victim back to the water's bottomless depth. A studio photograph by Brassaï of late 1932 homes in on this character's siren-like quality and the ambiguity of her action by cropping the upper part of the painting (p.216). The kinship of the three women suggests a narrative cycle in which the role of the female protagonist continually flip-flops between that of fatality and rescuer, victim and perpetrator, passive and active. The resulting complexity is markedly different from the way women had been depicted thus far. It is as if the seated figures and reclining nudes from the first half of the year have woken up and risen from their armchairs to turn from passive display to active agency, and from peaceful tranquillity to existential struggle to become if not mistresses of their own destiny certainly active participants.

Scenes of beach play and rescue also feature prominently among the prints Picasso produced alongside the paintings (pp.219, 228–9). Disturbingly, tragic accident turns at rare moments into brutal sexual transgression, when rescue from near death by water morphs into rape (pp.218). Whereas much of the work of 1932 had expressed a hope that sexual separateness could be overcome through love and desire, here it is suggested that conflict and violence were inevitable, that it was impossible for male and female to come to a peaceful balance, be it between people or within the individual sense of self, not least Picasso's own.

If the features of the protagonist in the various versions of *The Rescue* are those of Marie-Thérèse Walter, what does that tell us? For Picasso part of Walter's attraction had been her strong body, highlighted by her prowess as a swimmer. In the reclining nudes of May her physique resembled that of an octopus, a water creature that had been the alluring subject of an early nature documentary by Jean Painlevé, a filmmaker close to the group of surrealists (p.110).[54] Late in 1932, Walter contracted a serious viral infection after swimming in the river Marne. This was akin to her very essence being shaken to the core and certainly did not fail to make a strong impression on Picasso. Life-saving classes were oddly popular in the early 1930s, a fact alluded to in Jean Renoir's humorous parable *Boudu Saved from Drowning*, which was released in early November 1932 (p.25).[55] In it, the homeless Boudu is saved from the waters of the Seine by the bookshop owner Lestingois, only to resist every attempt by his saviour to lead a more respectable existence, exposing the latter's double standards instead by first seducing Lestingois's imperious wife and then his mistress, the maid Anne Marie. Unlike the original play on which Renoir based his script, in the film Boudu does not get reformed by love but forsakes the bourgeois dream of domestic stability in favour of his unconditional freedom. Boudu was played by Michel Simon, a friend of Painlevé with a larger-than-life personality not dissimilar to that of his character. The irreverence of Renoir's film towards marital fidelity (Lestingois is scandalised to find his copy of Balzac's *Physiology of Marriage* covered in spit, whether that of his wife or Boudu remains unclear) is likely to have struck a chord with Picasso, a known cinema enthusiast, especially given his personal circumstances.

Yet, far from the light relief of farce, as the year drew to a close, the mood of Picasso's work grew ever more sombre. As much is suggested by one of the first paintings of 1933, another *Rescue*, in which victim and rescuer have lost their separateness entirely, melding into one (p.233). The scene is reduced to its bare minimum: a strip of water and a mere suggestion of solid land, with most of the backdrop taken up by a brooding sky. Clinched in their desperate embrace, the figures' heads are thrown back in shrieks of agony. Overall, the painting exudes an air of despair.

The year 1932 had seen a force field in which Picasso had managed to construct and control a precarious equilibrium between conflicting demands, different relationships and aesthetic languages; but time was running out. Commercially, his retrospective had been of limited success, with the Kunsthaus Zürich the only institution to buy a cubist still life and doing so at a 50 per cent discount.[56] The Great Depression showed little sign of easing, forcing the dealer Pierre Loeb, for one, to withdraw his loans from the show to seek a quicker sale elsewhere. Meanwhile, the prominence of Marie-Thérèse Walter in the works and exhibitions of 1932 put an even greater strain on Picasso's marriage to Olga. (The birth in 1935 of Maya, Walter's daughter by Picasso, made separation inevitable, leading to what the artist called the worst year of his life.[57]) Storm clouds though were not just brewing in Picasso's personal life. Although Hitler had lost the presidential elections of 1932, on 30 January 1933 Reichspresident von Hindenburg appointed him Chancellor. Europe was hurtling towards an abyss. Within months the first exhibitions of what was now defamed as 'degenerate' art sprang up across Germany with Picasso as one of the anti-modernists' prominent targets. 'I will never fit in with the followers of the prophets of Nietzsche's superman', Picasso presciently acknowledged in 1932.[58] Four years later, the Spanish Republican government invited him to paint a mural for its Pavilion at the Paris International Fair. In a gesture of solidarity with the beleaguered democratically elected government, Picasso, who until now had eschewed any official engagements, especially with his native Spain, accepted the commission in January 1937. For the following months he worked, albeit in a somewhat indecisive manner, on a mural with the perennial theme of the artist in his studio. In one of the sketches the figure of the model, wrapped in slumber, closely resembles the reclining nudes from March and April 1932.

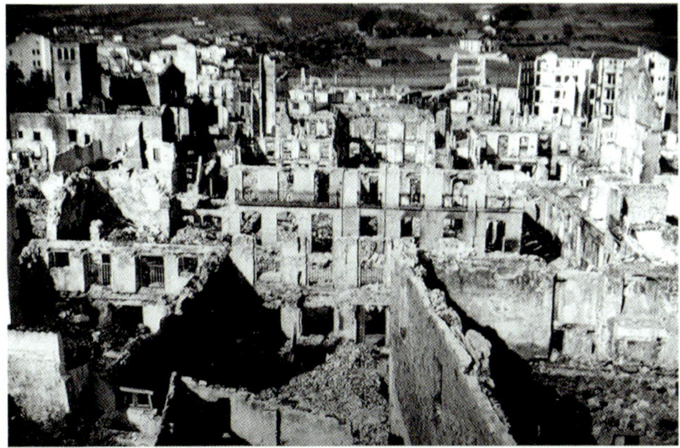

Guernica in ruins after bombing by the German Luftwaffe on 26 April 1937

Then, on 26 April 1937, Nazi German and Italian Fascist planes rained bombs on the Basque city of Guernica, unleashing a hailstorm of machine-gun fire on any civilians trying to escape. As soon as news of the atrocities reached Paris, Picasso changed tack on his project, painting a panorama of terror and destruction instead. To the left of the monumental canvas he prominently depicted a grief-stricken mother holding her dead child, her head thrown back in agony, the child's body slumping in her arm.[59] Their embrace of despair was foreshadowed in *The Rescue* of January 1933. In summer 1932, asked about his imminent retrospective, Picasso had declared: 'When it comes down to it, there is only love. Whatever it may be.'[60] Five years later, with Spain's Civil War opening a period of unprecedented world-wide destruction, his friend the writer and ethnographer Michel Leiris wrote of *Guernica*: 'In a black and white rectangle that looks like an ancient tragedy, Picasso sends us our death notice. Everything we love is about to die, and that is why everything we love must be summed up, with all the high emotion of farewell, in something so beautiful we shall never forget it.'[61]

On the occasion of Picasso's Zurich retrospective, Jung had accused the artist of mental ill health. Perhaps another visitor had been more perceptive. Writing to his wife Lily after his visit to the Kunsthaus, the painter Paul Klee enthused about the exhibition as a whole as much as about the works from 1932. Klee profoundly disagreed with the doubters of Picasso's continued importance and relevance. 'All in all', he wrote, Picasso is 'the painter of today.'[62]

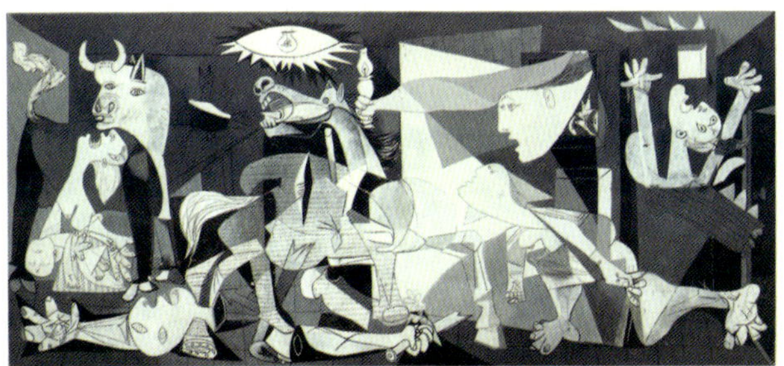

*Guernica* 1 May – 4 June 1937

# Rue La Boétie

In 1918, Picasso moved into a grand apartment at 23 rue La Boétie in the fashionable 8th arrondissement of Paris, close to the Champs-Elysées. The apartment was rented for him by his new dealer and friend, Paul Rosenberg, who lived and worked in the next-door building. Eventually, Rosenberg also rented the apartment on the floor above for Picasso to use as his studio. In late 1932, Picasso invited the Hungarian-French photographer and artist Brassaï to document both apartments. In his 1964 *Conversations with Picasso* Brassaï vividly recalls his visit and the very different atmosphere of what were otherwise identical flats.

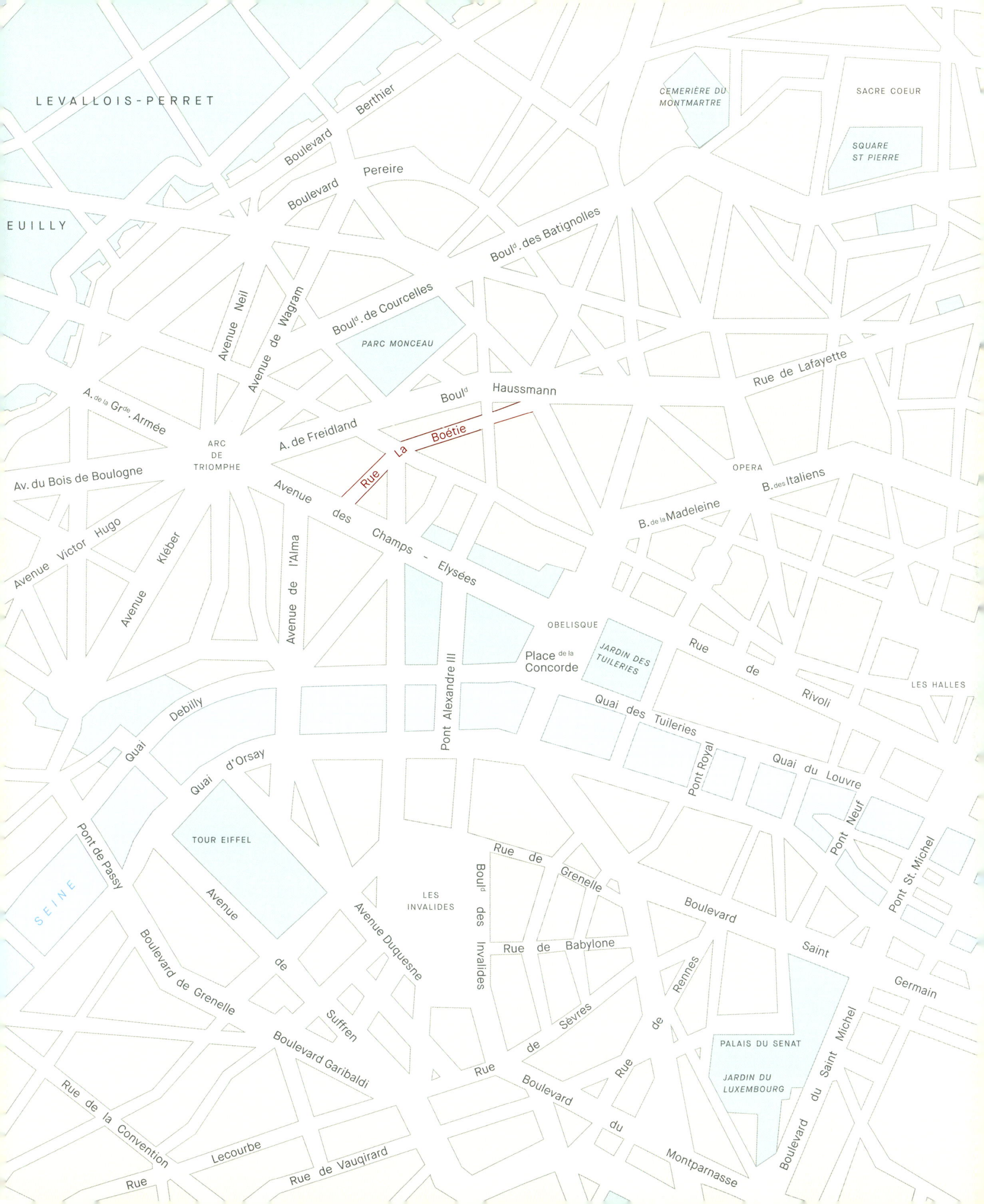

LEVALLOIS-PERRET
EUILLY
Boulevard Berthier
Boulevard Pereire
Bould. des Batignolles
CEMERIÈRE DU MONTMARTRE
SACRE COEUR
SQUARE ST PIERRE
Avenue Neil
Avenue de Wagram
Bould. de Courcelles
PARC MONCEAU
Bould Haussmann
Rue de Lafayette
A. de la Grde. Armée
ARC DE TRIOMPHE
A. de Freidland
Rue La Boétie
Av. du Bois de Boulogne
Avenue des Champs - Elysées
OPERA
B. des Italiens
B. de la Madeleine
Avenue Victor Hugo
Avenue Kléber
Avenue de l'Alma
OBELISQUE
Place de la Concorde
JARDIN DES TUILERIES
Rue de Rivoli
LES HALLES
Quai Debilly
Quai d'Orsay
Pont Alexandre III
Quai des Tuileries
Pont Royal
Quai du Louvre
Pont Neuf
TOUR EIFFEL
Pont de Passy
SEINE
Avenue de Suffren
Avenue Duquesne
LES INVALIDES
Bould des Invalides
Rue de Grenelle
Boulevard Saint Germain
Pont St. Michel
Rue de Babylone
Boulevard de Grenelle
Rue de Sevres
Rue de Rennes
PALAIS DU SENAT
JARDIN DU LUXEMBOURG
Boulevard du Saint Michel
Boulevard Garibaldi
Boulevard du Montparnasse
Rue de la Convention
Lecourbe
Rue de Vaugirard
Rue

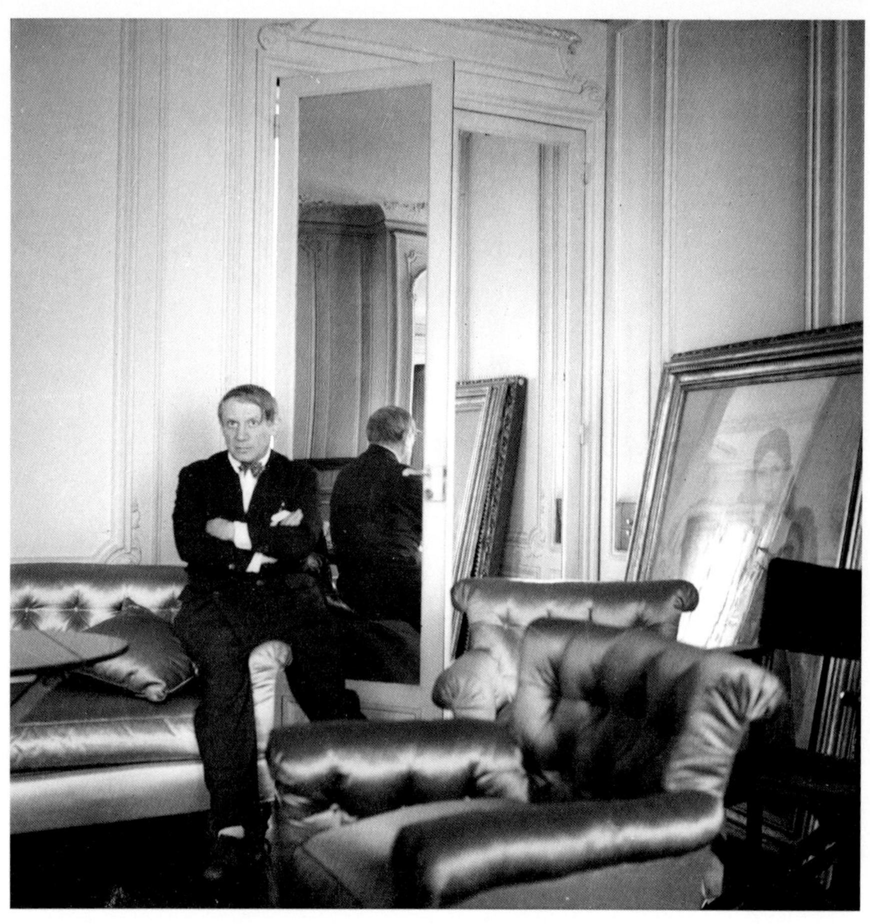

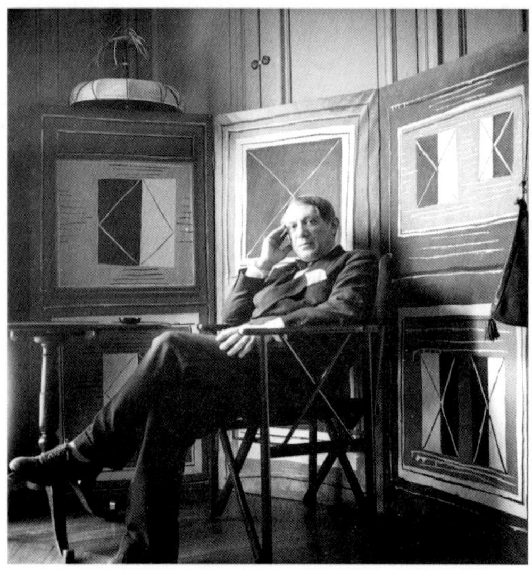

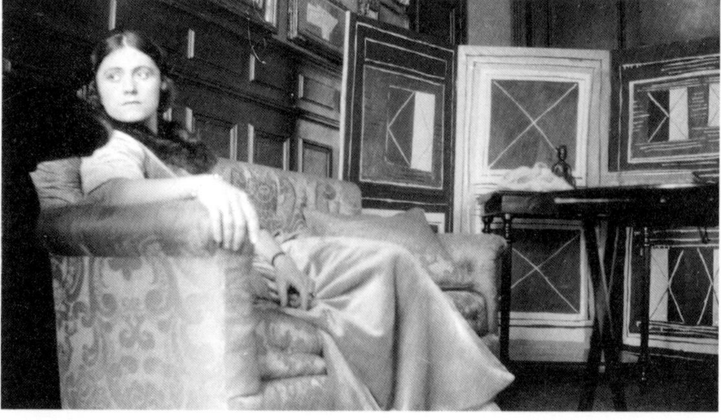

Pablo and Olga Picasso in the downstairs family apartment, rue La Boétie.
Photographs of the artist by Cecil Beaton, 1933

'In 1917, while Picasso was in Spain introducing his young fiancée, Olga Kochlova [sic], to his family ... his Montrouge studio was flooded. He asked Paul Rosenberg, his new art dealer ... to find lodgings for him and to move his things there. Rosenberg rented him an apartment in the building next to his gallery. At his dealer's wish, Picasso was thrust into the new geographic center of the art business. As at the Bateau-Lavoir, he again rented one, then two apartments, identical and on consecutive floors: one to live in, the other to work in. The lower floor became one of the centers of society life, the upper floor his studio. The contrast between them was striking: downstairs, there was a large dining room ... No clutter, not a speck of dust. Polished, gleaming wood floors and furniture ... The extraordinary thing was that, apart from the fireplace mantle, where a bit of his imagination showed through, nothing bore his mark ... This middle-class apartment was completely unlike his usual surroundings. There were none of the extraordinary furnishings he was so crazy about, none of the strange objects he liked to have around him, there were no piles, nothing scattered about, as was his wont. Olga jealously made sure that Picasso did not impose the powerful imprint of his personality on a realm she considered hers alone.'

Brassaï, *Conversations with Picasso*, pp.6–7

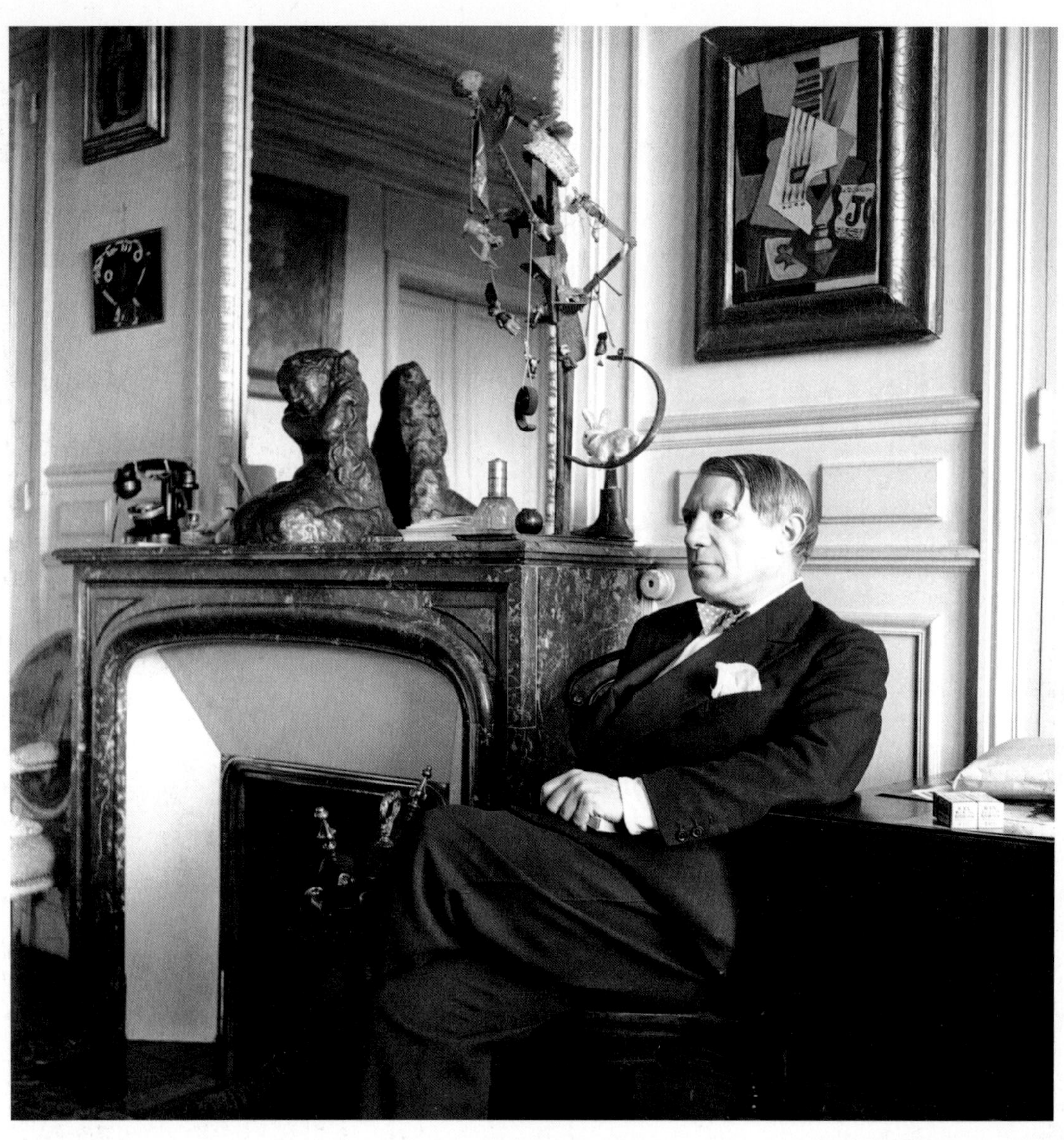

Picasso in the downstairs family apartment, rue La Boétie, 1933
Photographs by Cecil Beaton

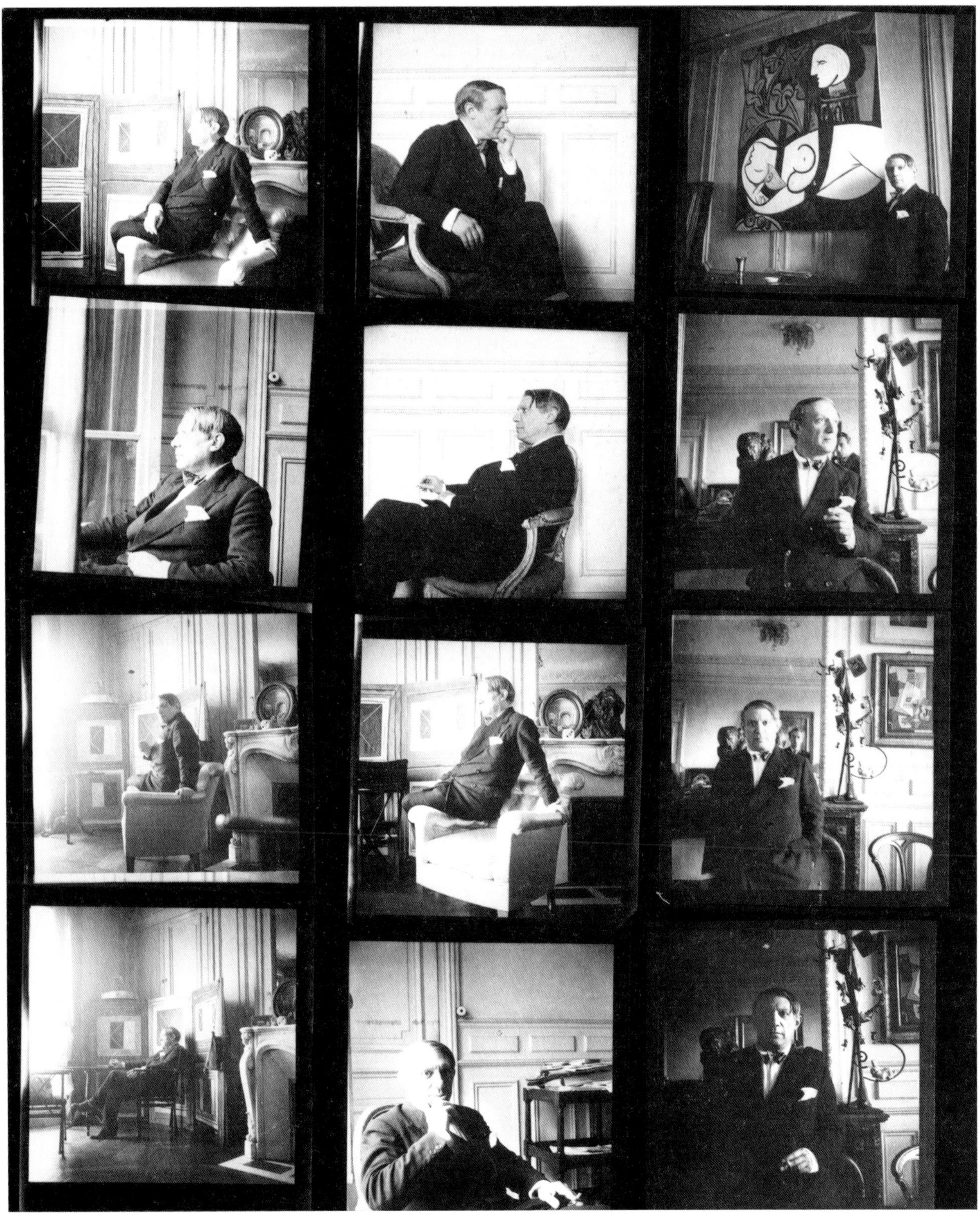

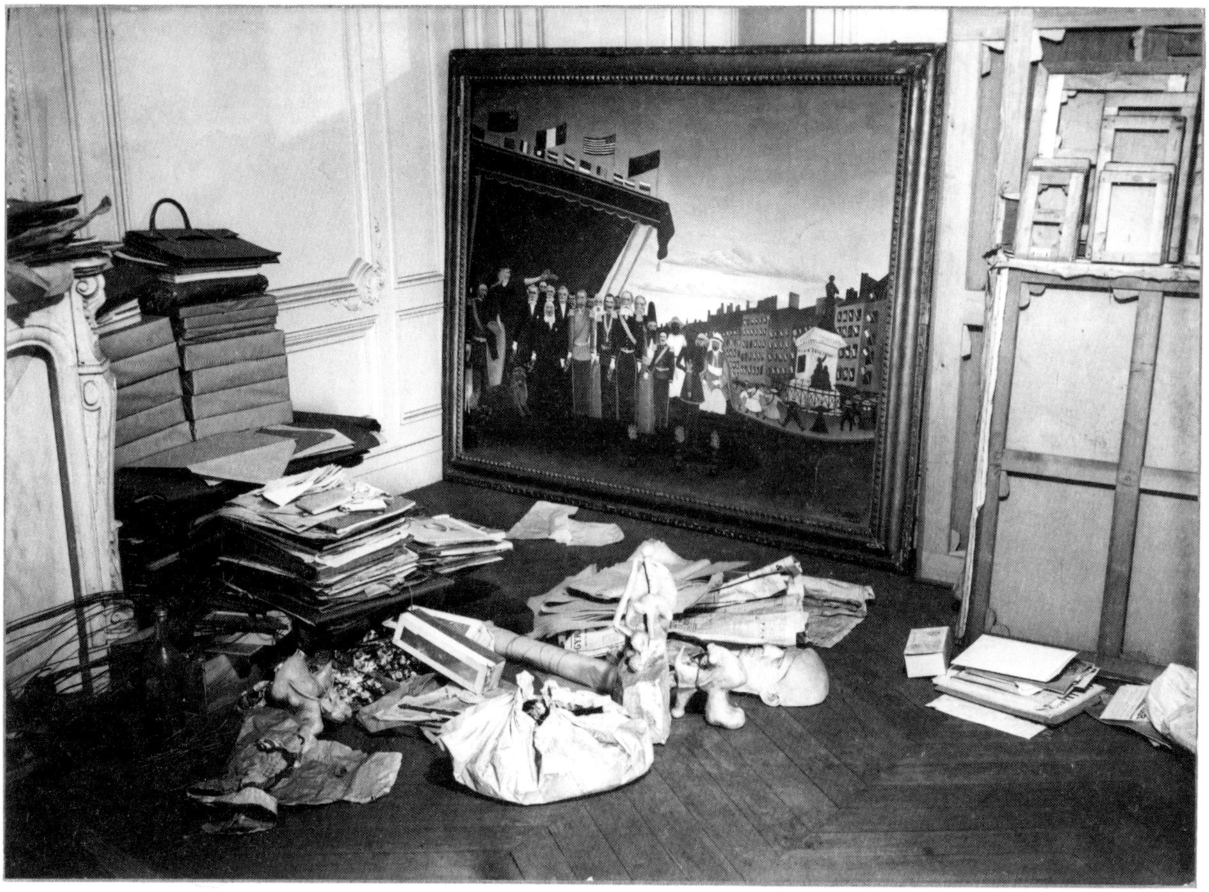

The rue La Boétie upstairs studio in 1932 with Henri Rousseau's painting *The Representatives of Foreign Powers Coming to Greet the Republic as a Sign of Peace* 1907. Photograph by Brassaï

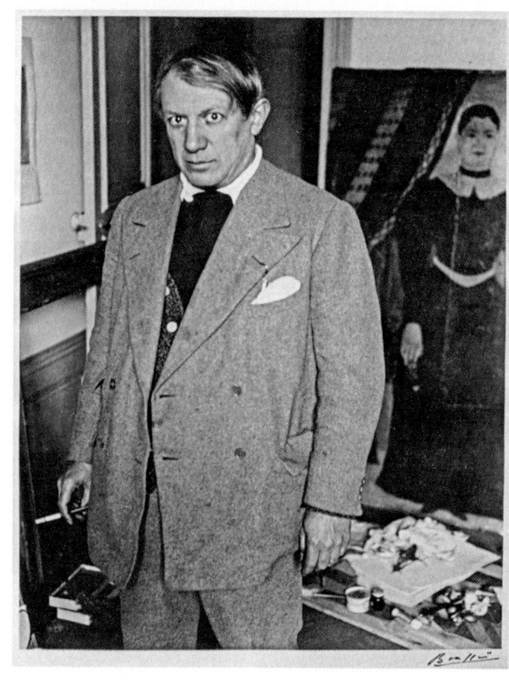

Picasso in the upstairs studio in 1932, in front of Henri Rousseau's *Portrait of a Woman* 1895
Photograph by Brassaï

'I also looked at the strange place: I was expecting an artist's studio, but it was an apartment turned pigsty. No middle-class home had ever been less middle class in its furnishings. Four or five rooms – each with a marble fireplace with a mirror above it – were entirely devoid of all their usual furnishings but filled with piles of paintings, cardboard boxes, parcels, and bundles, most of them containing casts of his statues, heaps of books, reams of paper, odd assortments of objects set every which way against the walls and on the floor, and covered with a thick layer of dust. The doors to the bedrooms were open, perhaps even removed, which turned this large apartment into a single studio fragmented into various nooks for the painter's various activities. You walked on a dull wooden floor, long since stripped of varnish and covered with a carpet of cigarette butts. Picasso had set up his easel in the most spacious, best-lit room – probably the former parlor – the only one that was summarily furnished. The window faced south and offered a fine view of the rooftops of Paris, bristling with a forest of red and black chimneys; in the distance the slender silhouette of the Eiffel Tower could be seen. Mme Picasso never came up to this apartment. Except for a few friends, Picasso allowed no one in. The dust could settle and fall wherever it liked, without fear of some cleaning woman's feather duster.'

Brassaï, *Conversations with Picasso*, pp.4–5

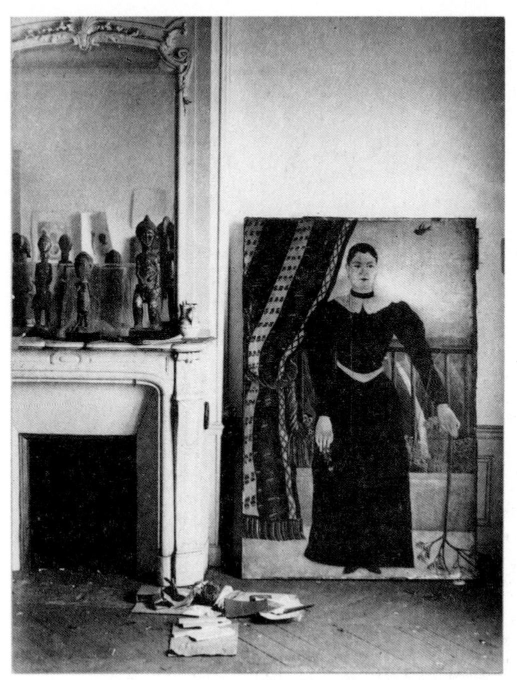

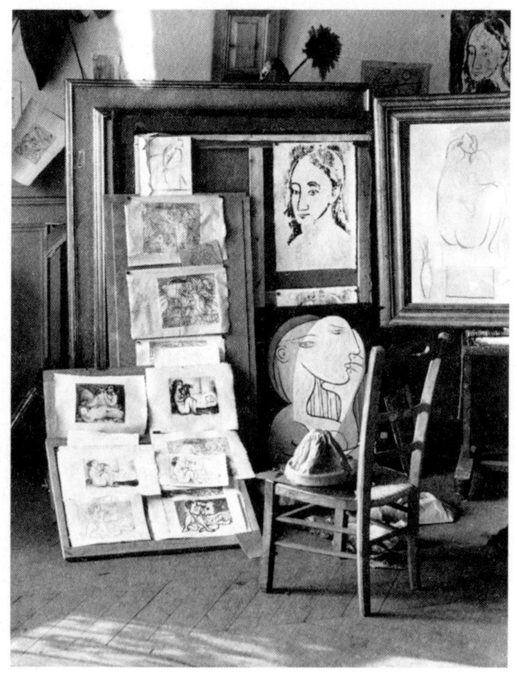

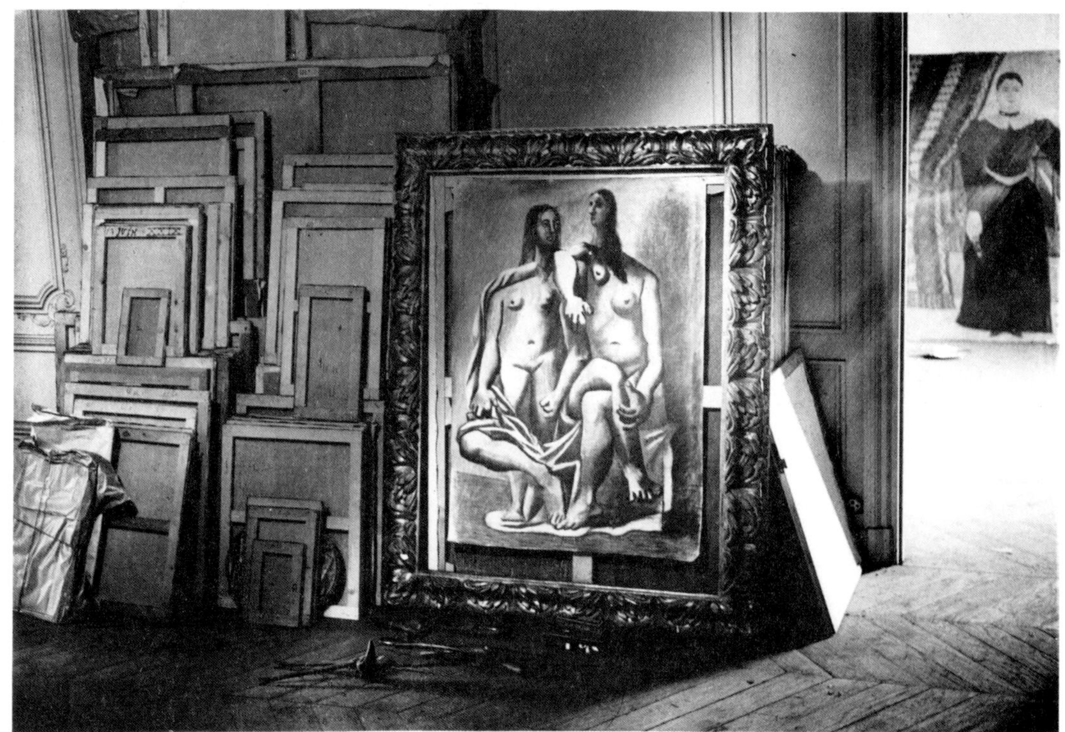

Brassaï

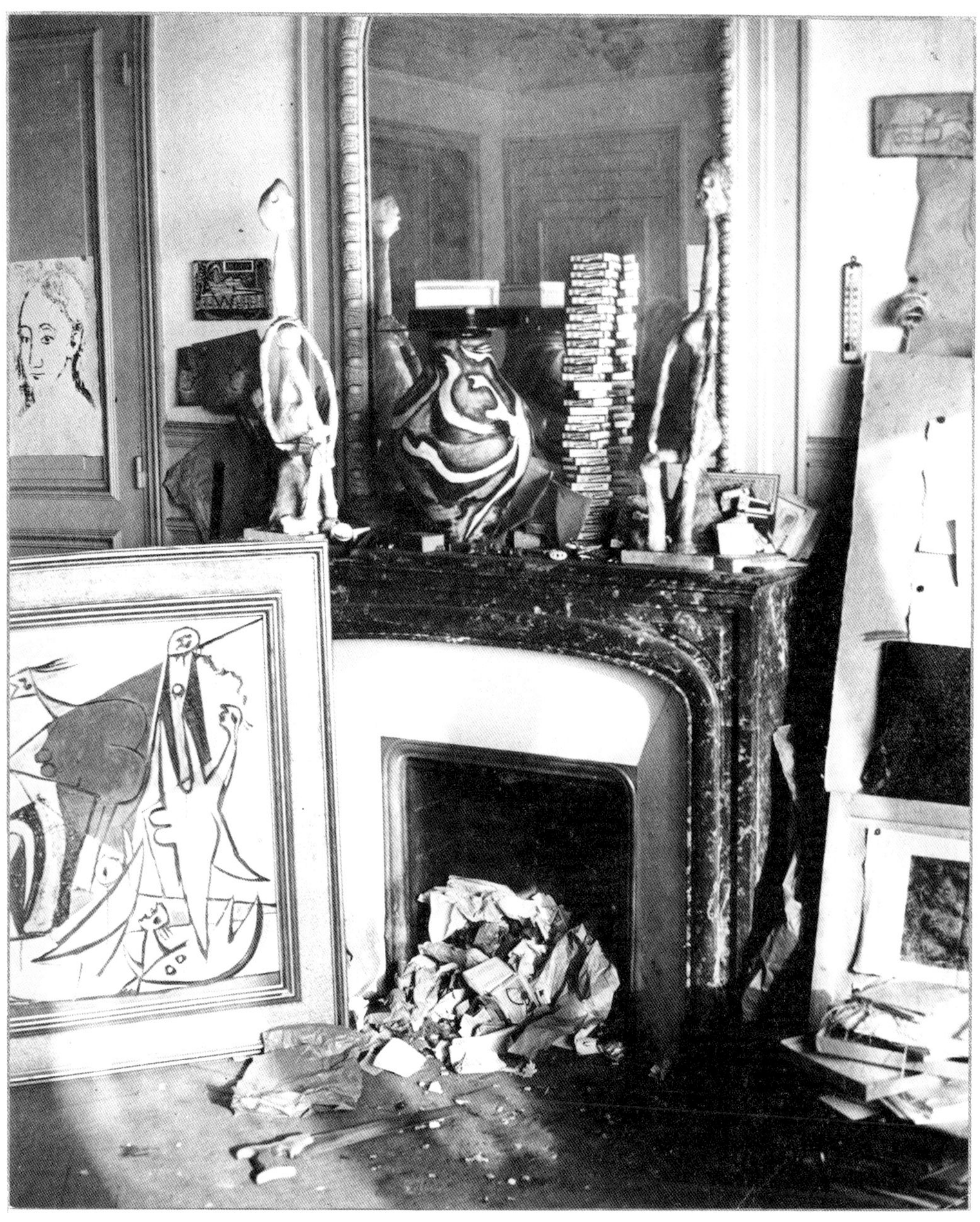

Views of the upstairs studio at rue La Boétie, photographed by Brassaï in 1932
Clockwise from top left:

Carved figures on the mantelpiece and Rousseau's *Portrait of a Woman* (prints reflected in the mirror: *Head with Feather and Tarlatan*, *Tête avec plume et tarlatane* 1932, erwinograph on paper)

A display of engravings and paintings

Fireplace with a stack of cigarette boxes and two sculptures of *Seated Woman* 1929 on the mantelpiece with *The Rescue* 1932 on the floor

*Two Bathers* 1920 and reversed canvases stacked against a wall

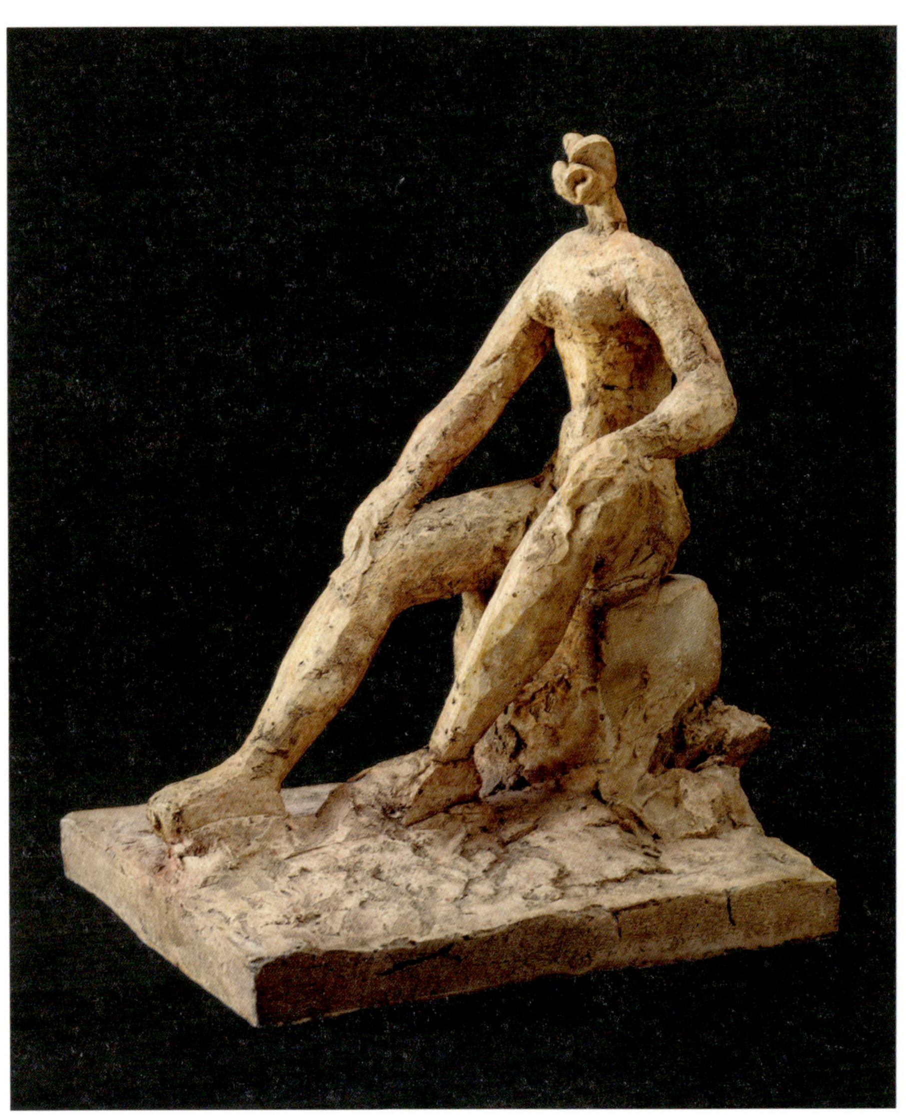



*Seated Woman*, *Femme assise*; Boisgeloup 1931

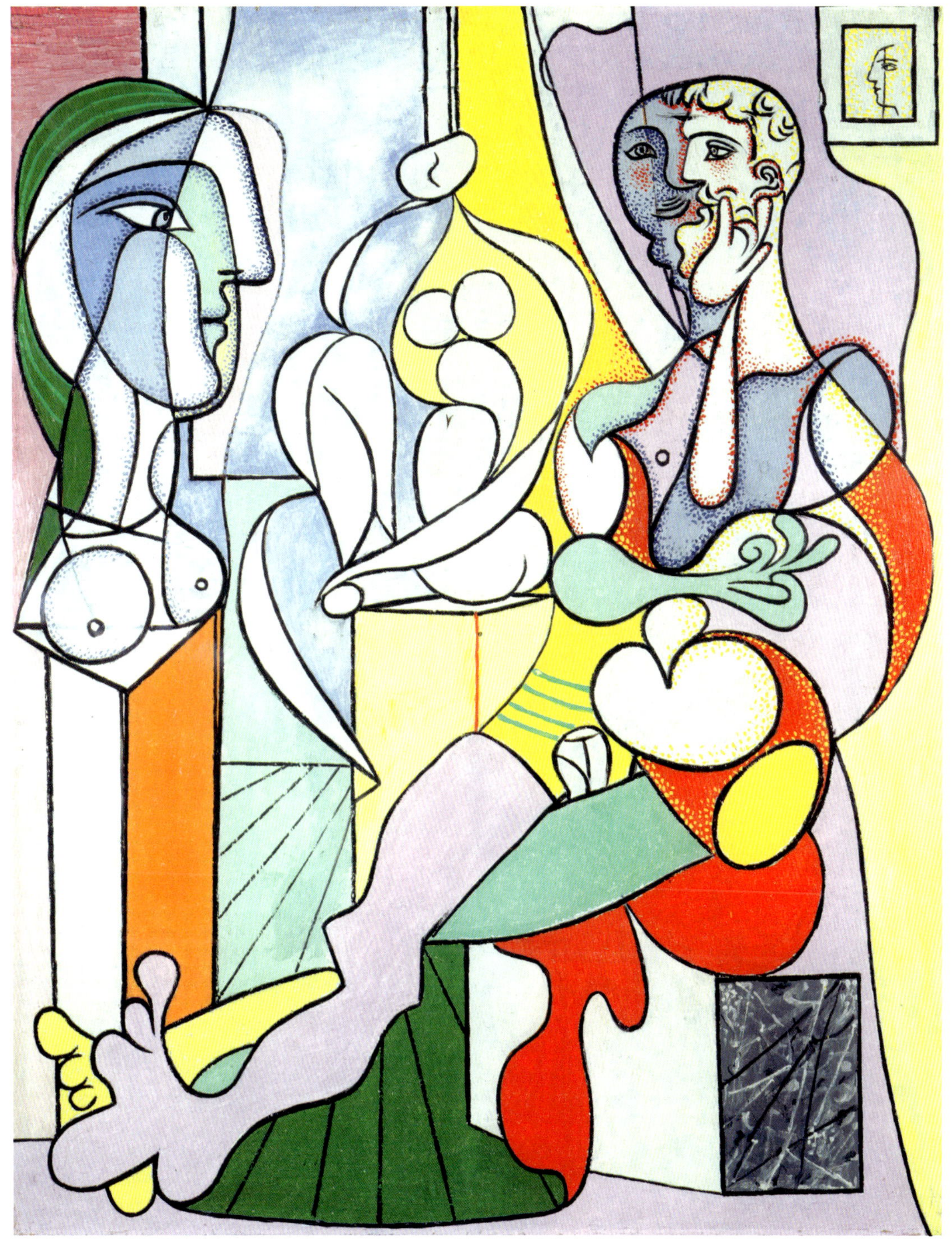

*The Sculptor, Le Sculpteur*

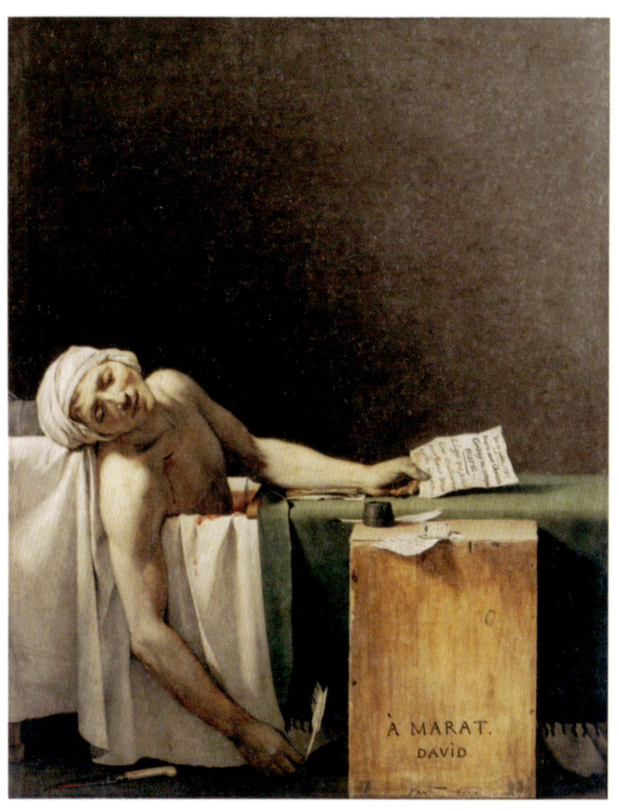




Jacques-Louis David *The Death of Marat* 1793

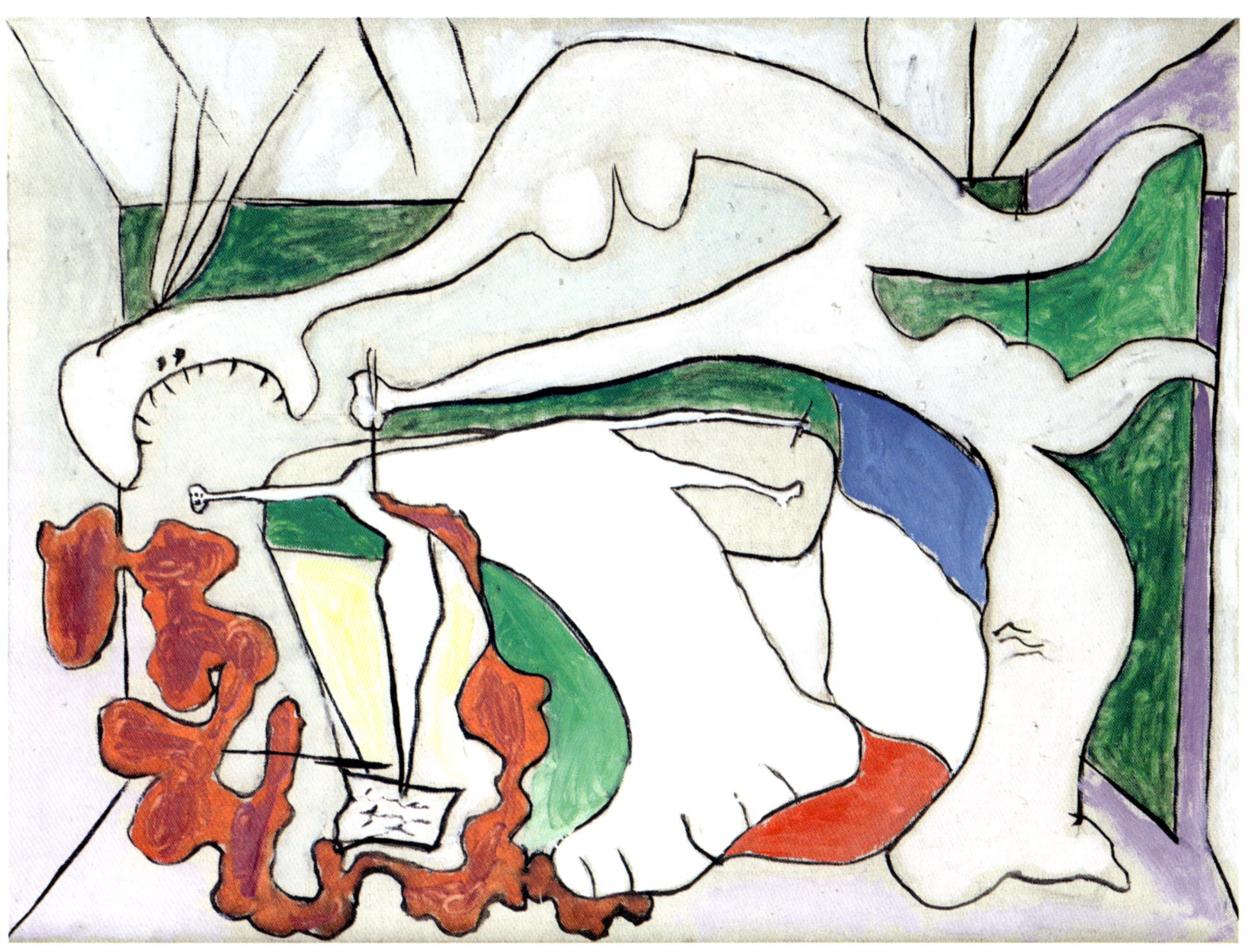

*Woman with Dagger, La Femme au stylet*

'When it comes down to it, there is only love. Whatever it may be.'

Picasso, in Tériade, 'En causant avec Picasso', *L'Intransigeant*, 15 June 1932, p.1

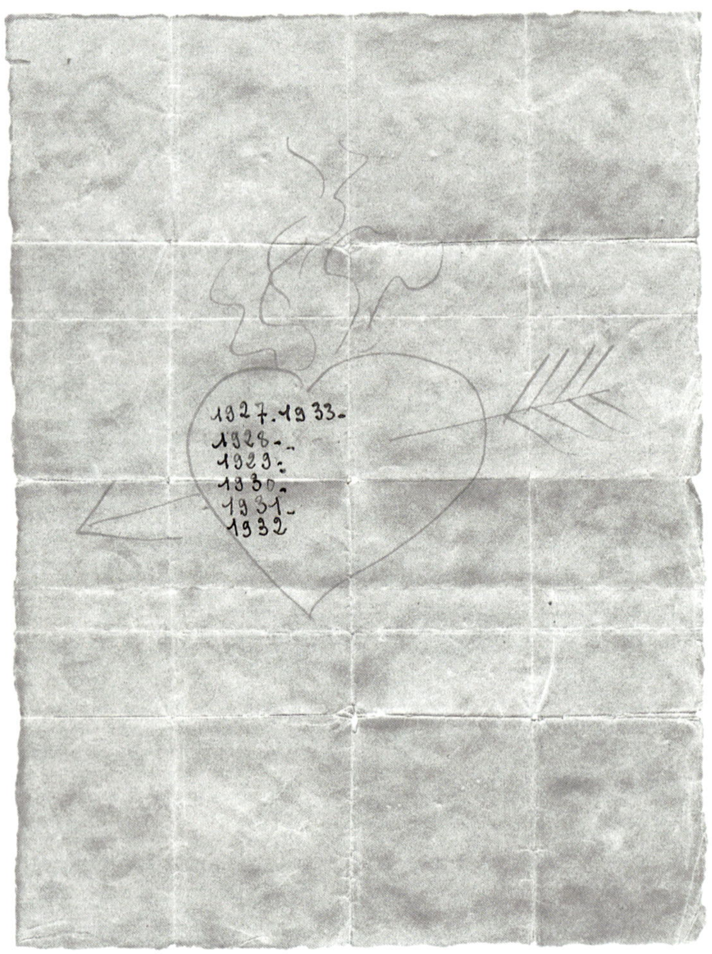


*Flaming Heart, Coeur enflammé* 1933
Picasso has drawn a heart and arrow around the years, written by Marie-Thérèse Walter, marking the duration of their relationship to date

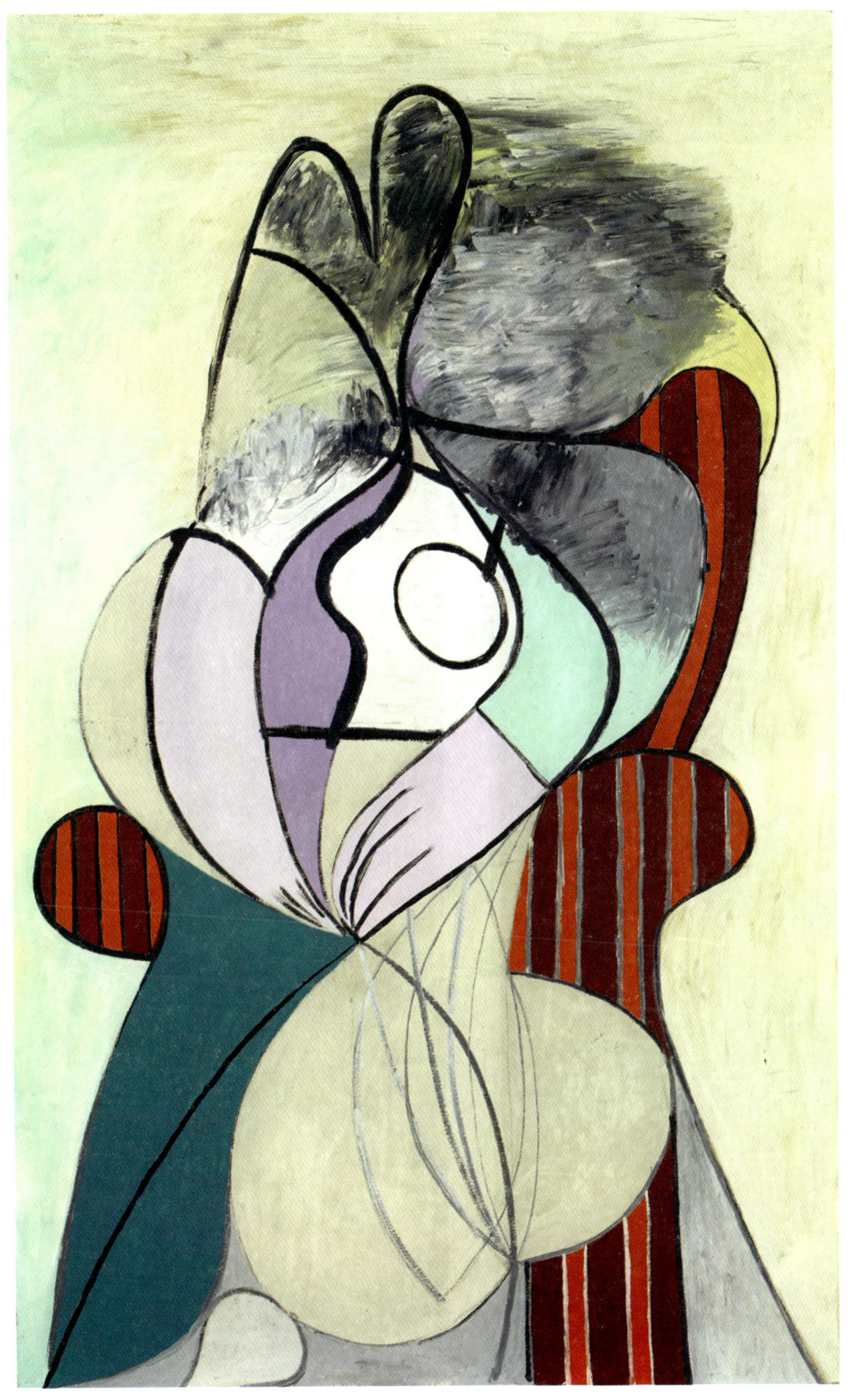

*Woman in a Red Armchair, Femme au fauteuil rouge*

'The work that one does is a way of keeping a diary.'

Picasso, in Tériade, 'En causant avec Picasso', *L'Intransigeant*, 15 June 1932, p.1

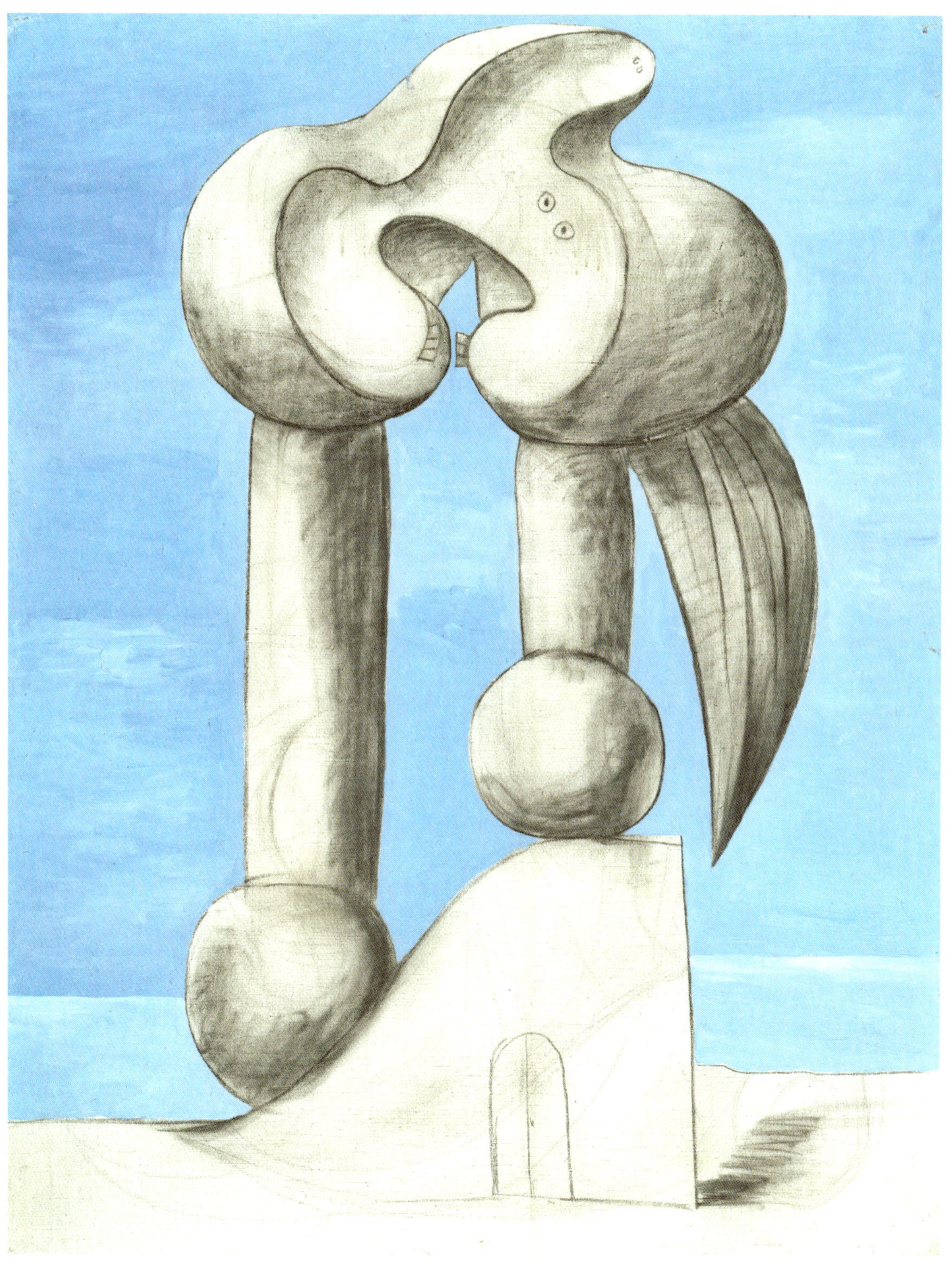

*Figures by the Sea I, Figures au bord de la mer I*

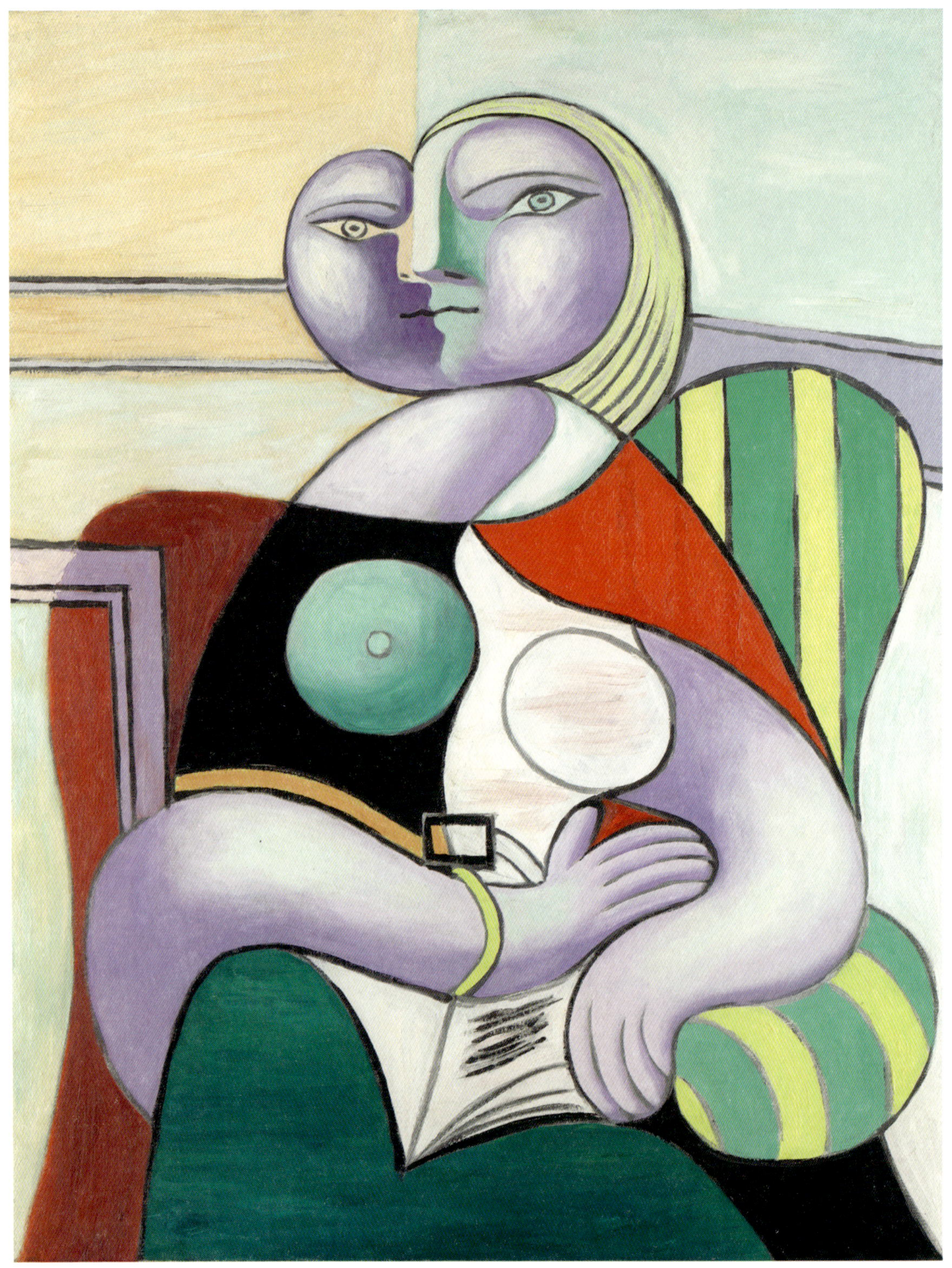

 *Reading, La Lecture*

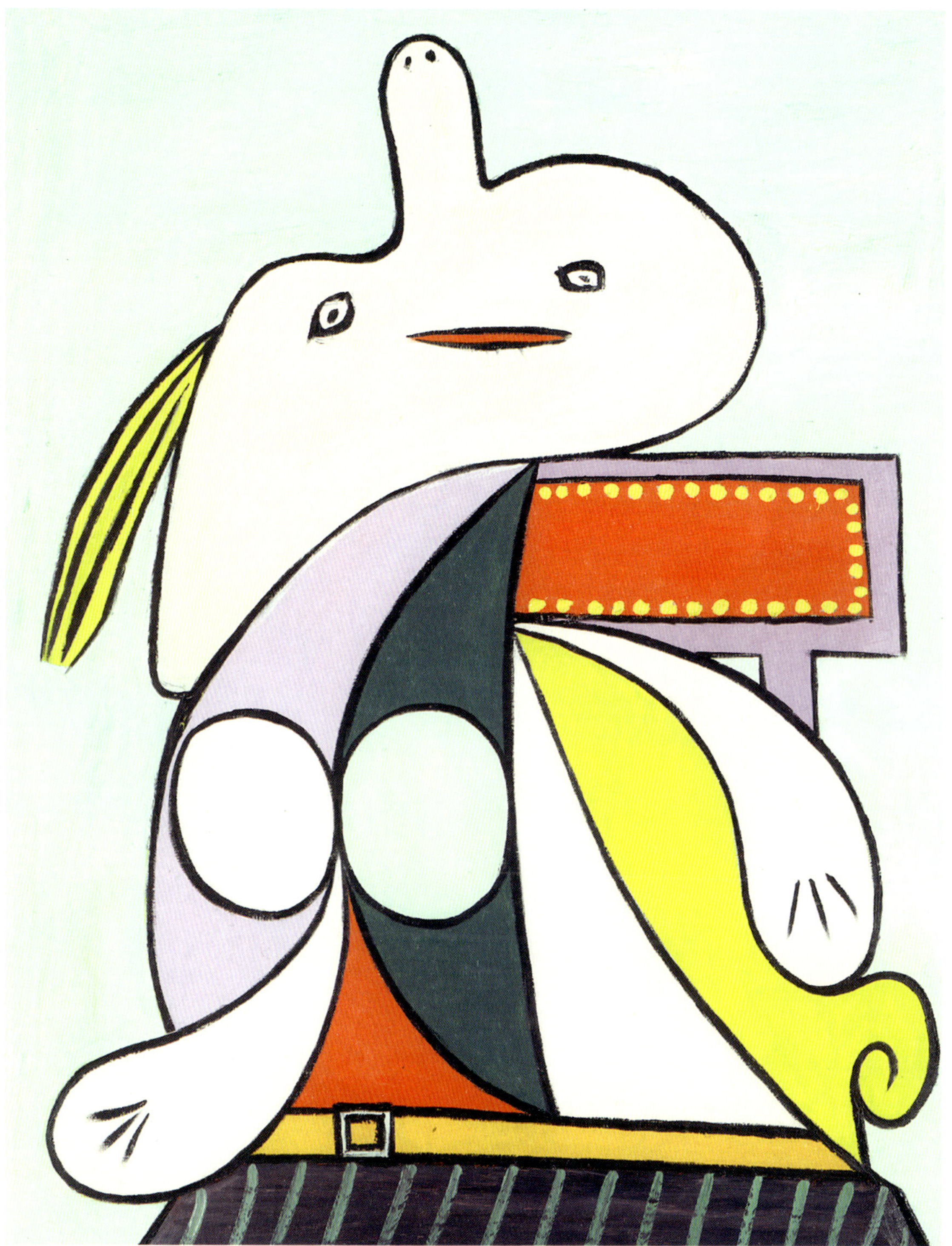

*The Yellow Belt*, *La Ceinture jaune*

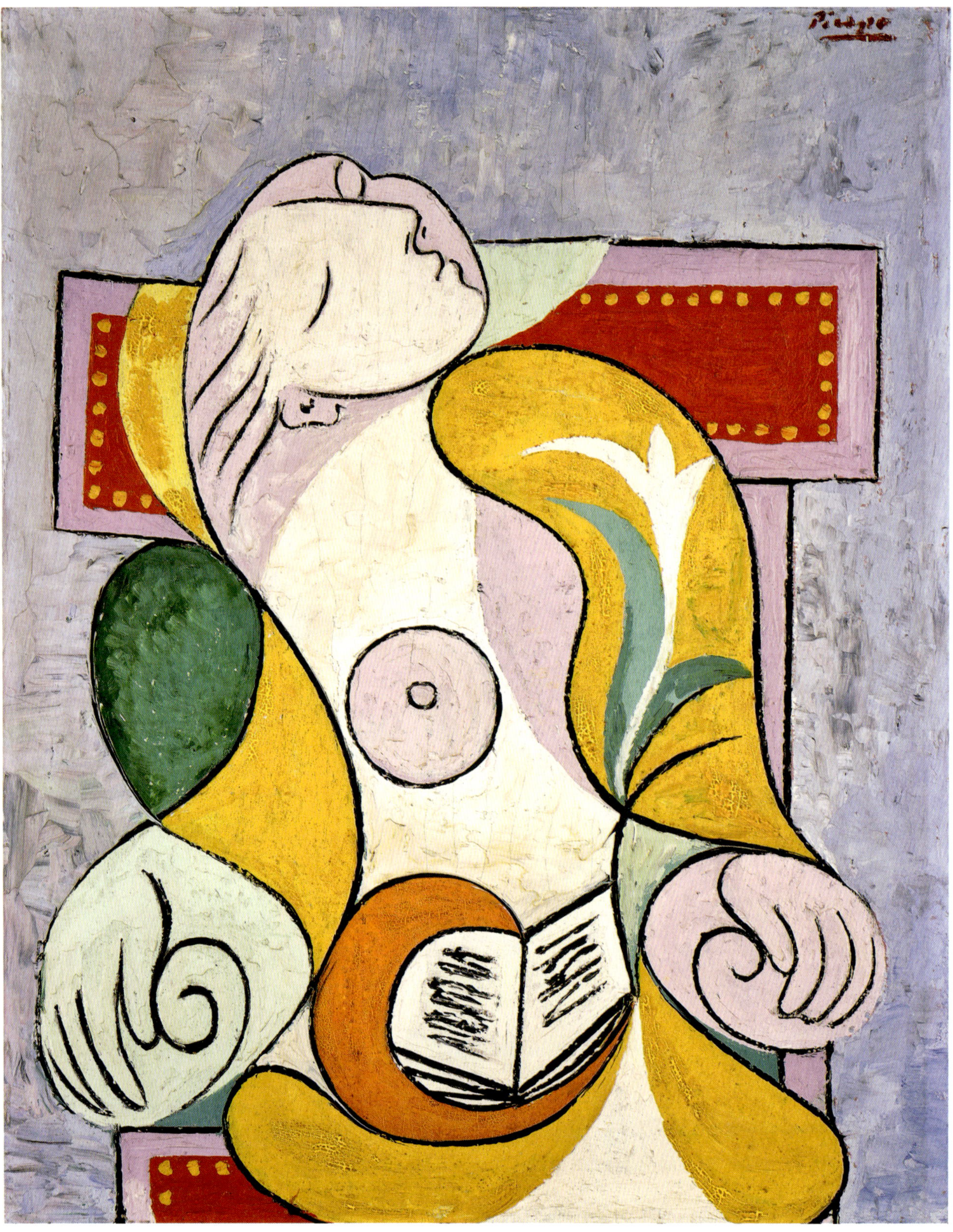

 *Reading, La Lecture*

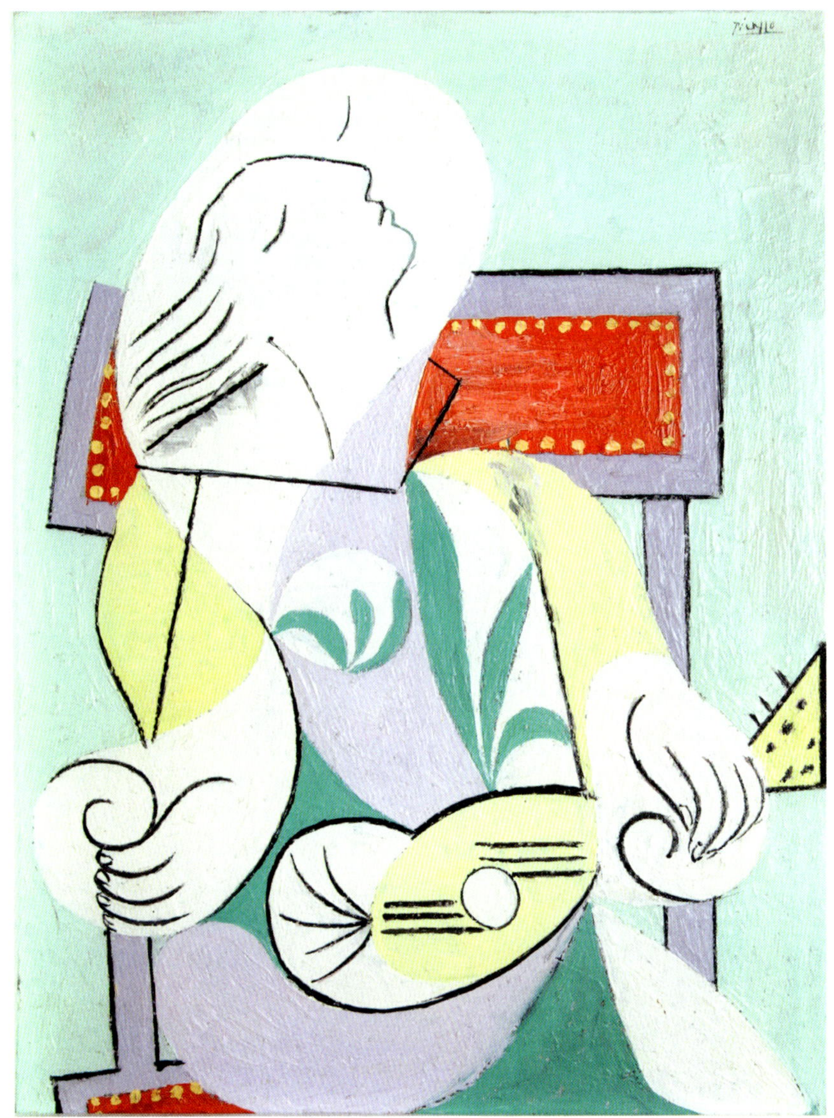

*Young Woman with Mandolin, Jeune Fille à la mandoline*

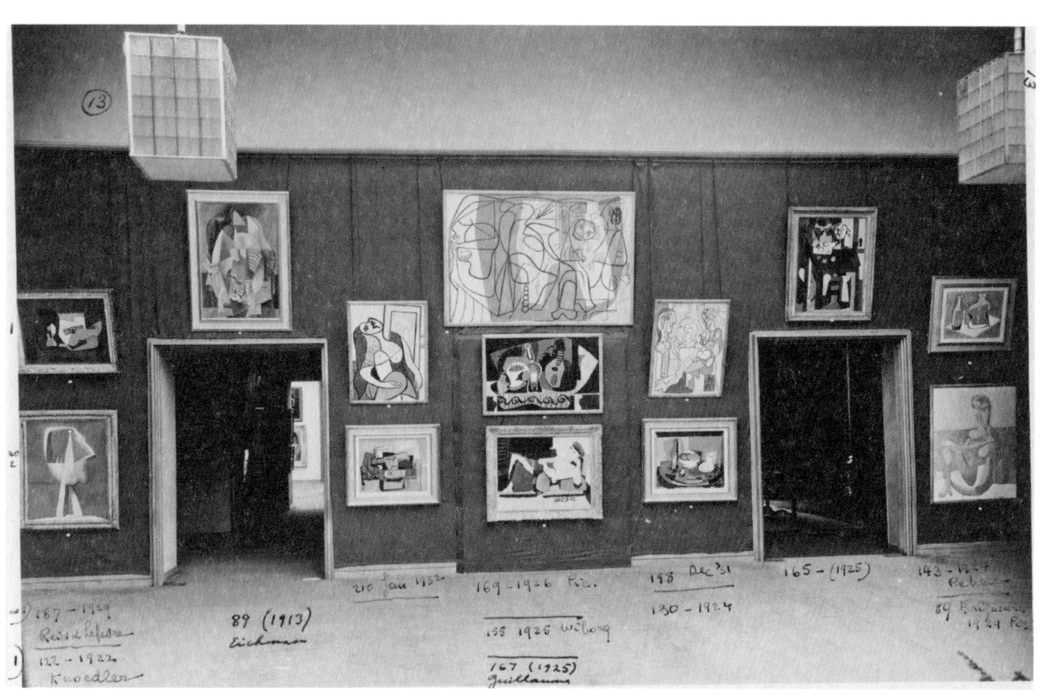


Photograph of the Picasso retrospective at Galeries Georges Petit, Paris, showing *Sleeping Woman by a Mirror* (left of centre). The annotations, by Margaret Scolari Barr, identify the artworks on display by their catalogue entry

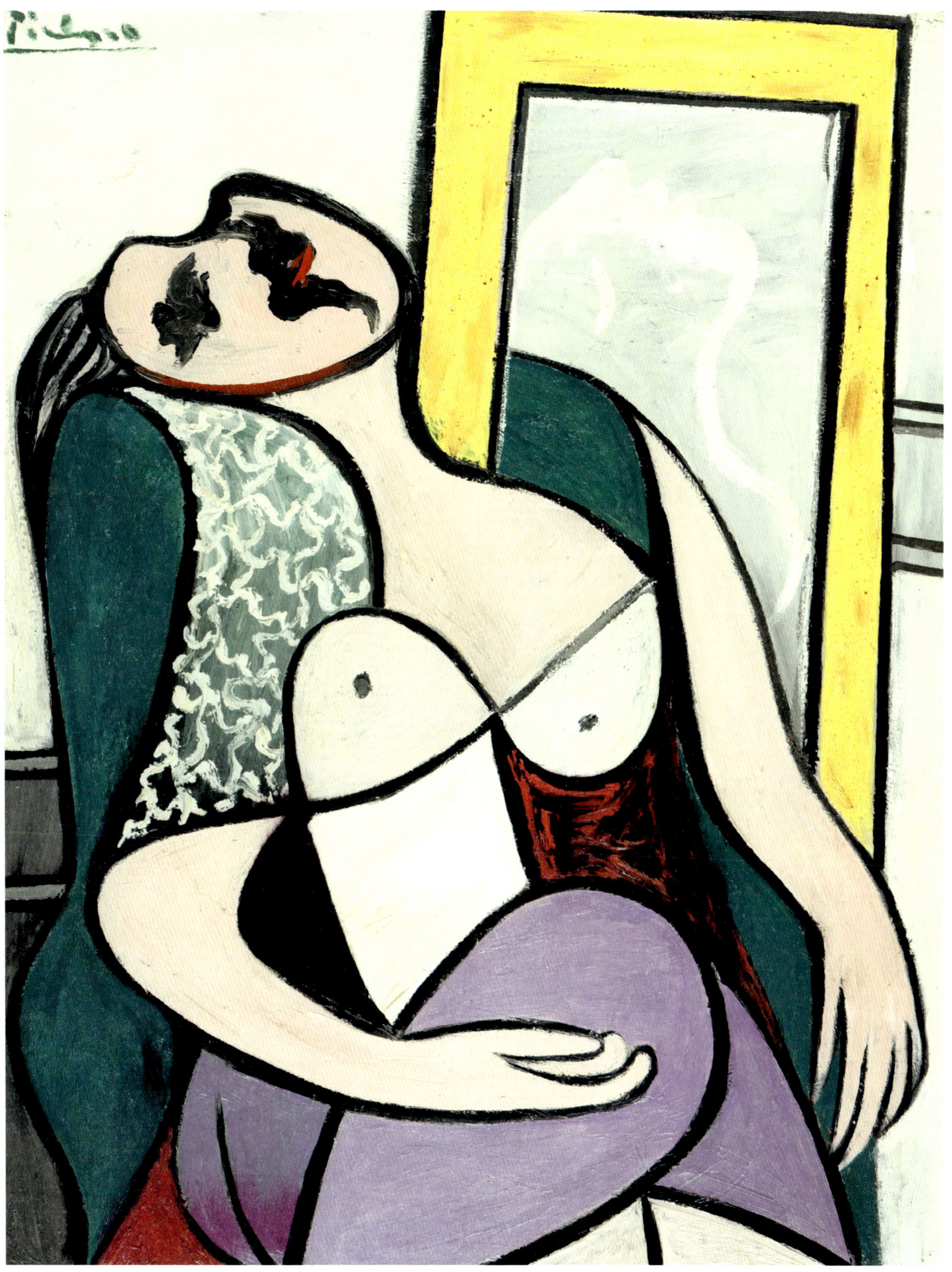


*Sleeping Woman by a Mirror, La Dormeuse au miroir*

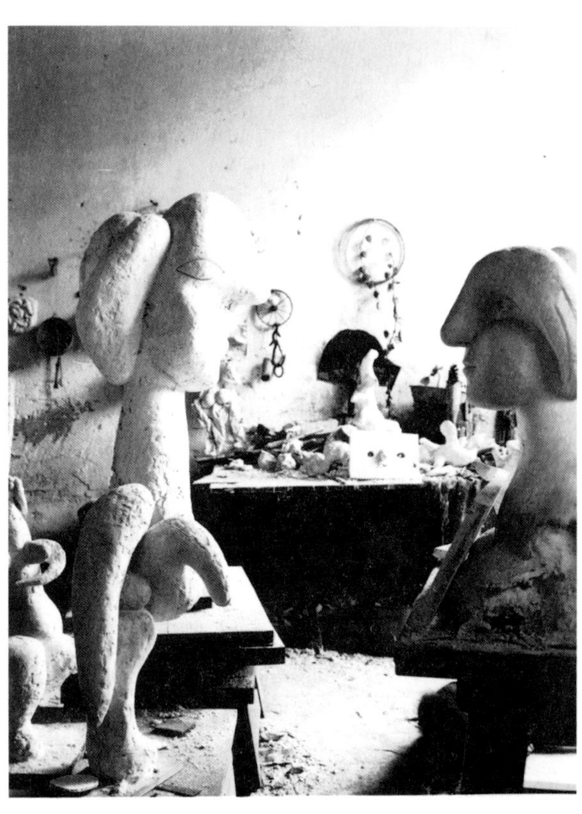

Plaster sculptures in the studio at Boisgeloup, 1933
Photograph by Albert Eugene Gallatin

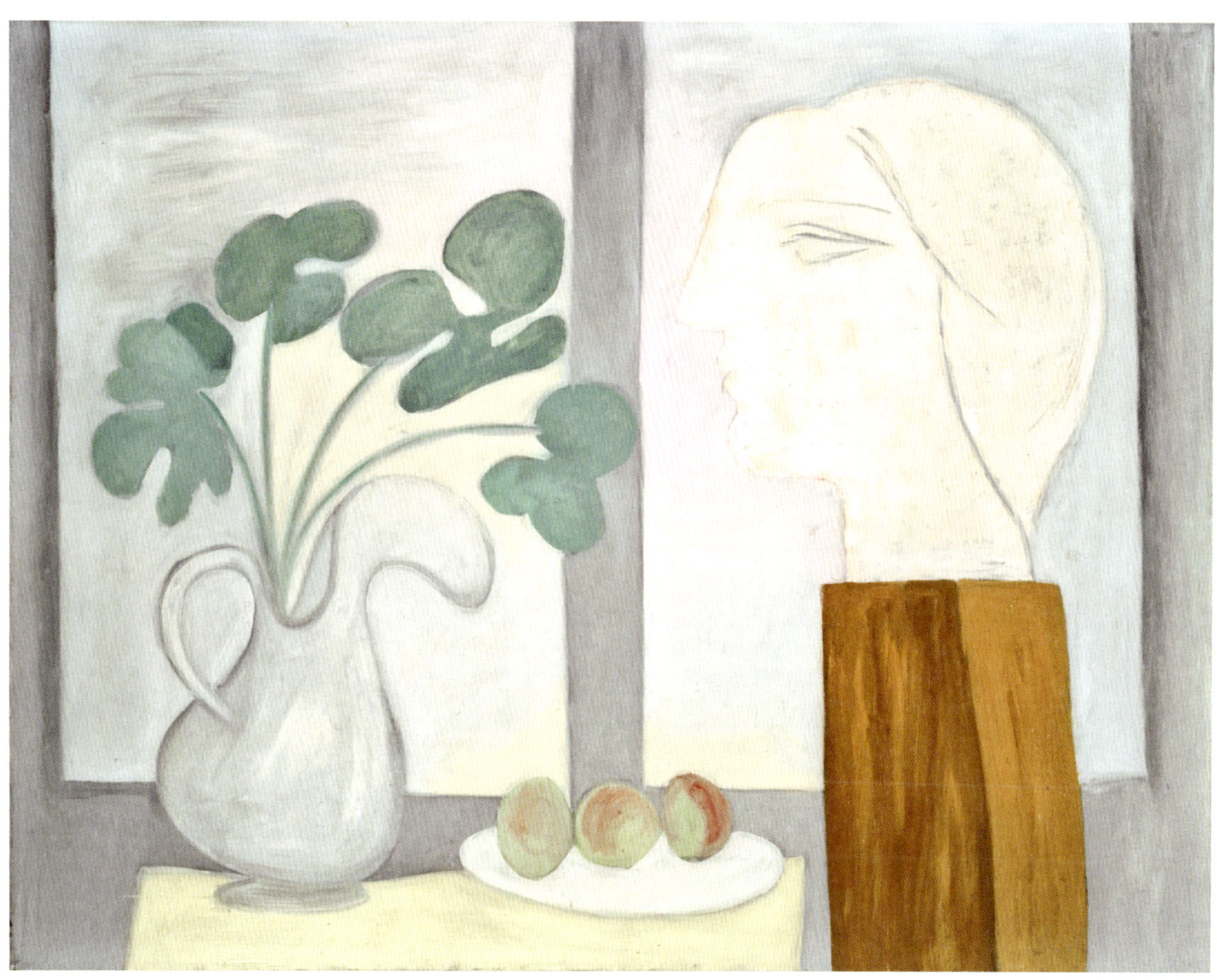

*Still Life at the Window, Nature morte à la fenêtre*

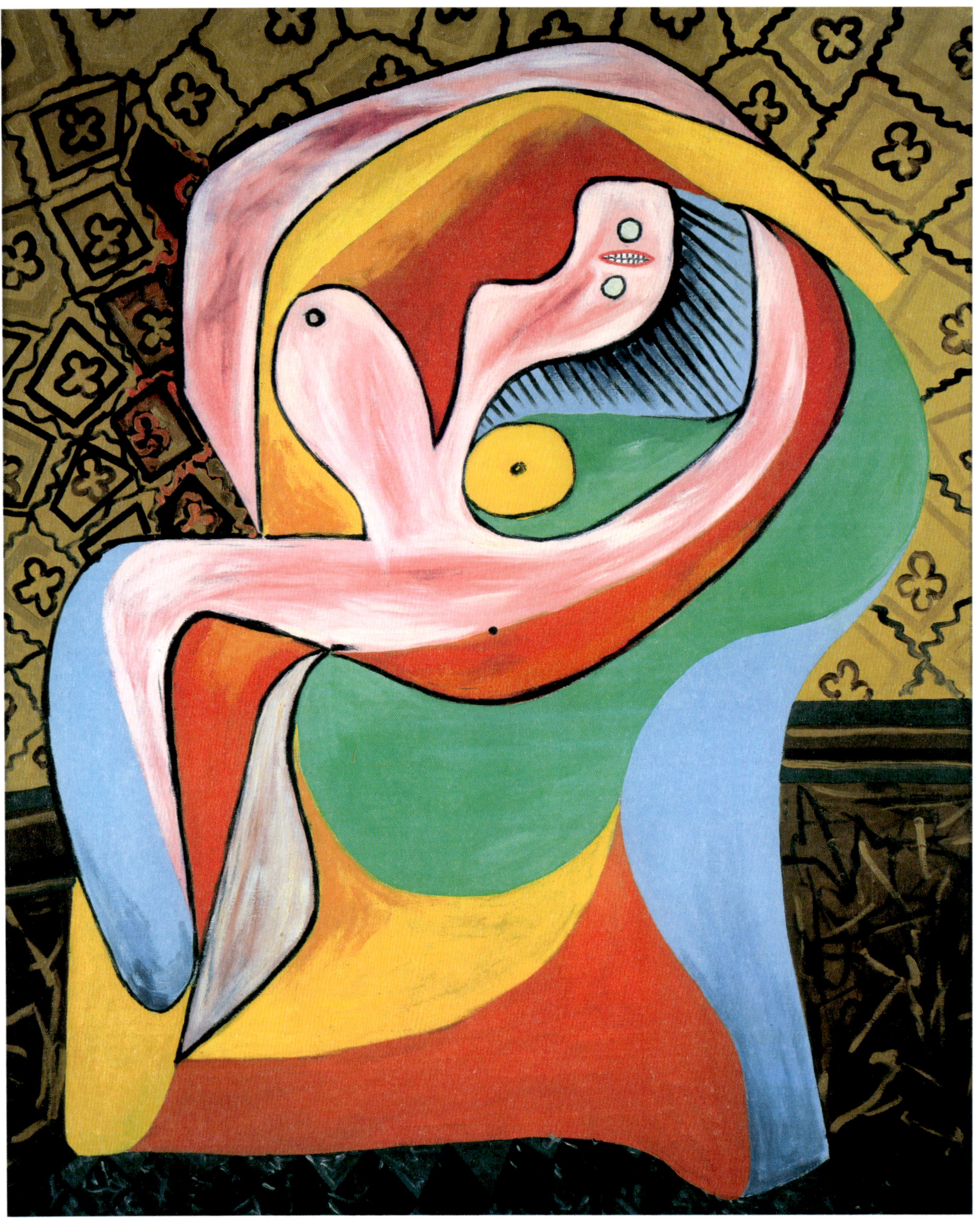

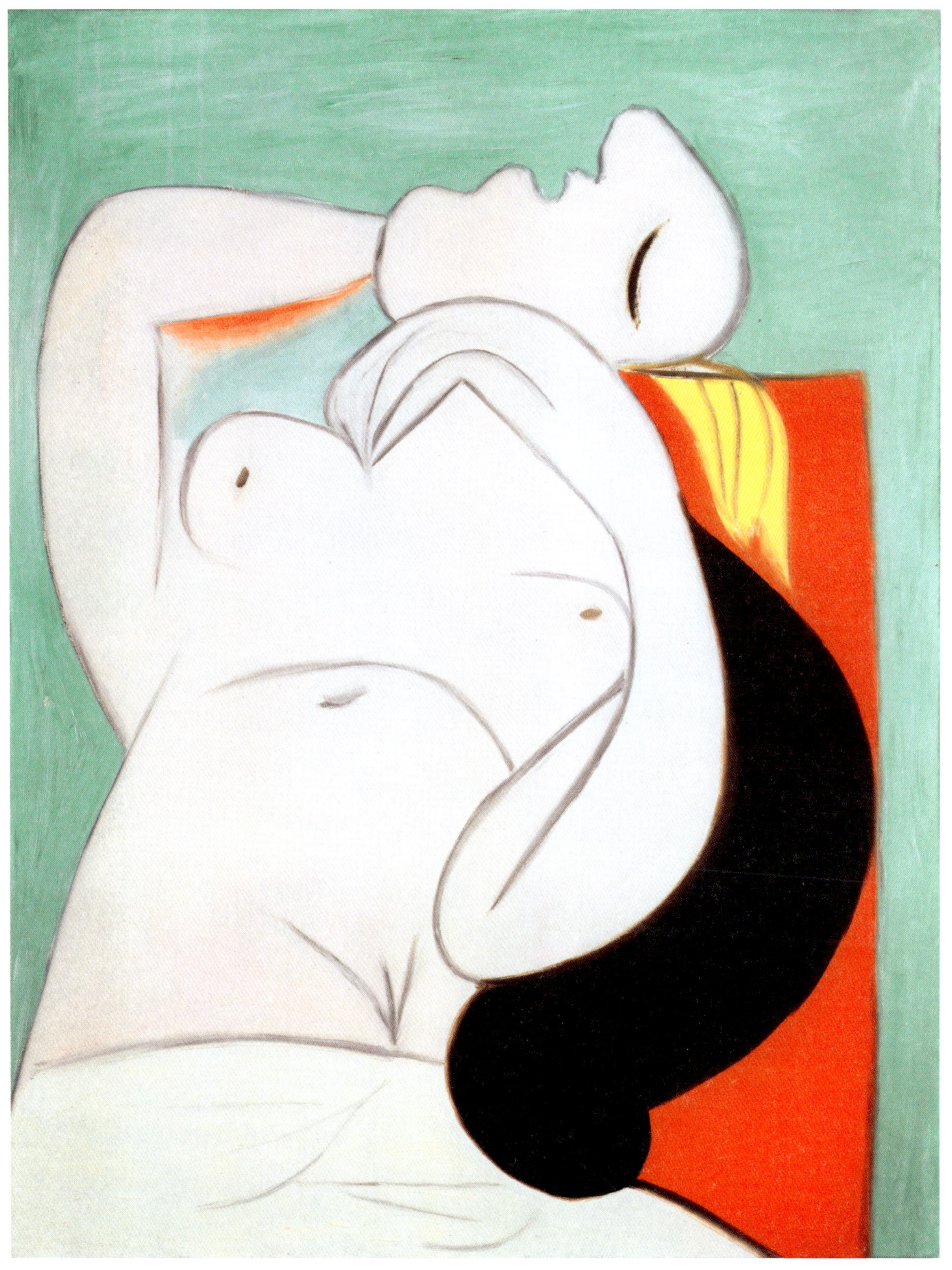

*Sleep, Le Sommeil*

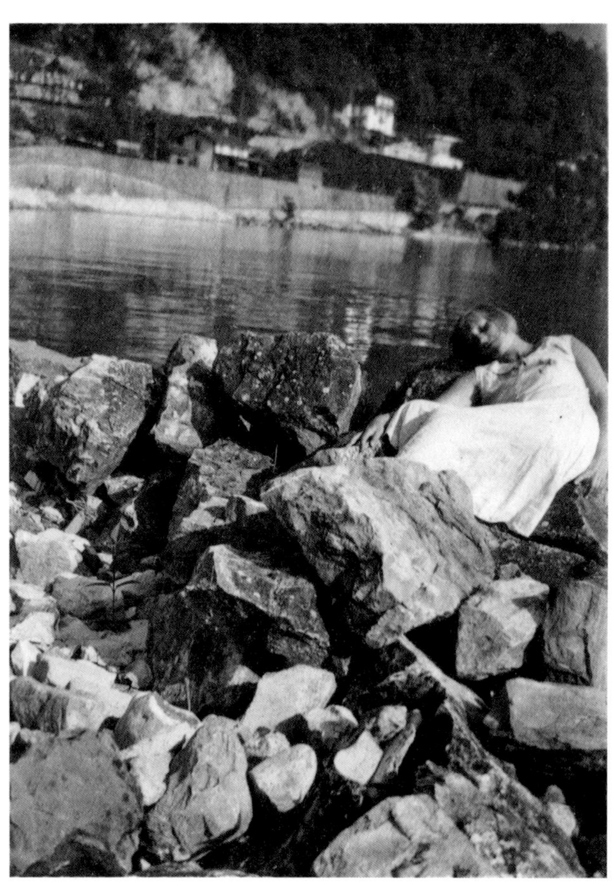



Marie-Thérèse Walter, Leysin, Switzerland, c.1929

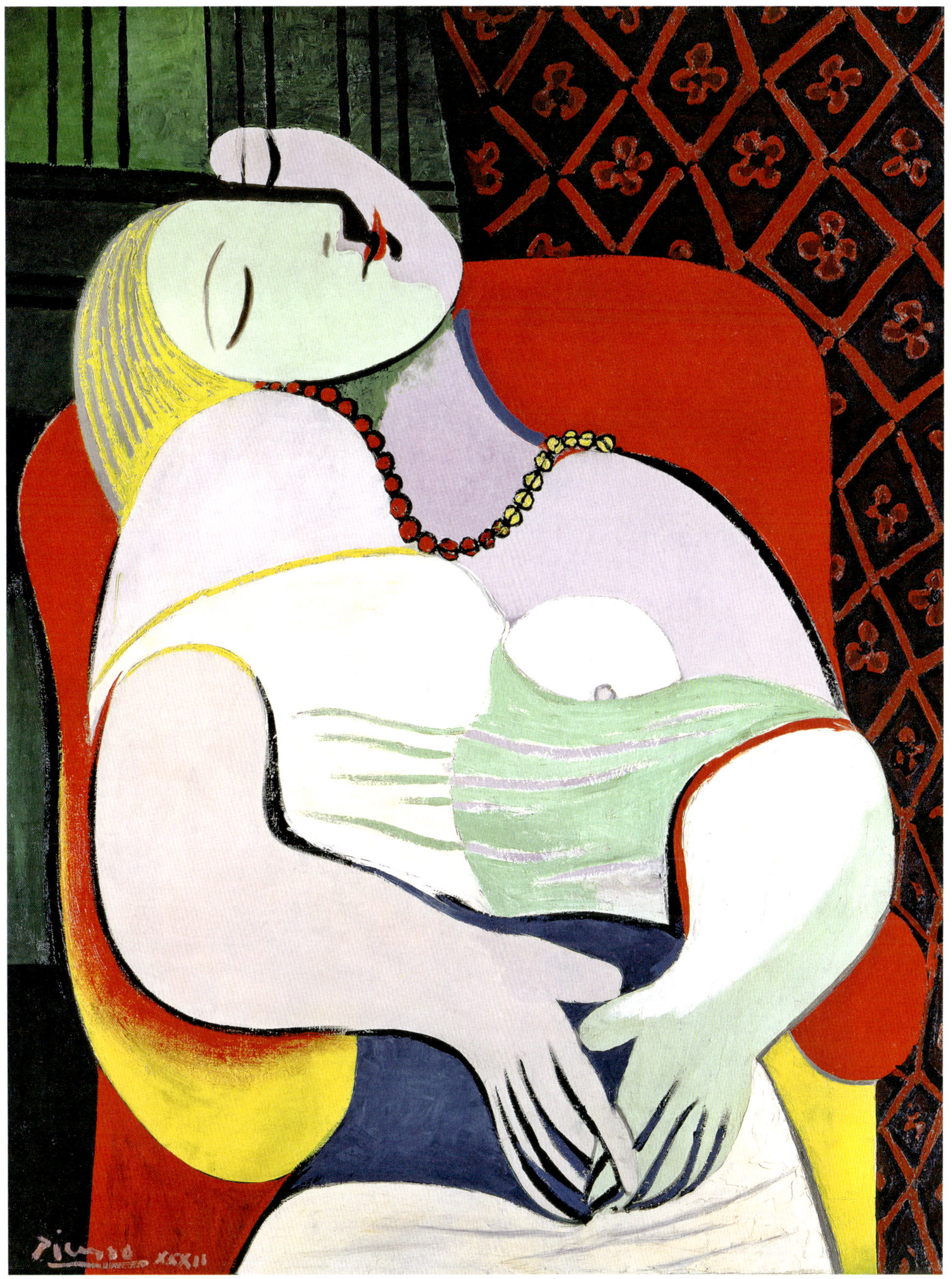

*The Dream, Le Rêve*

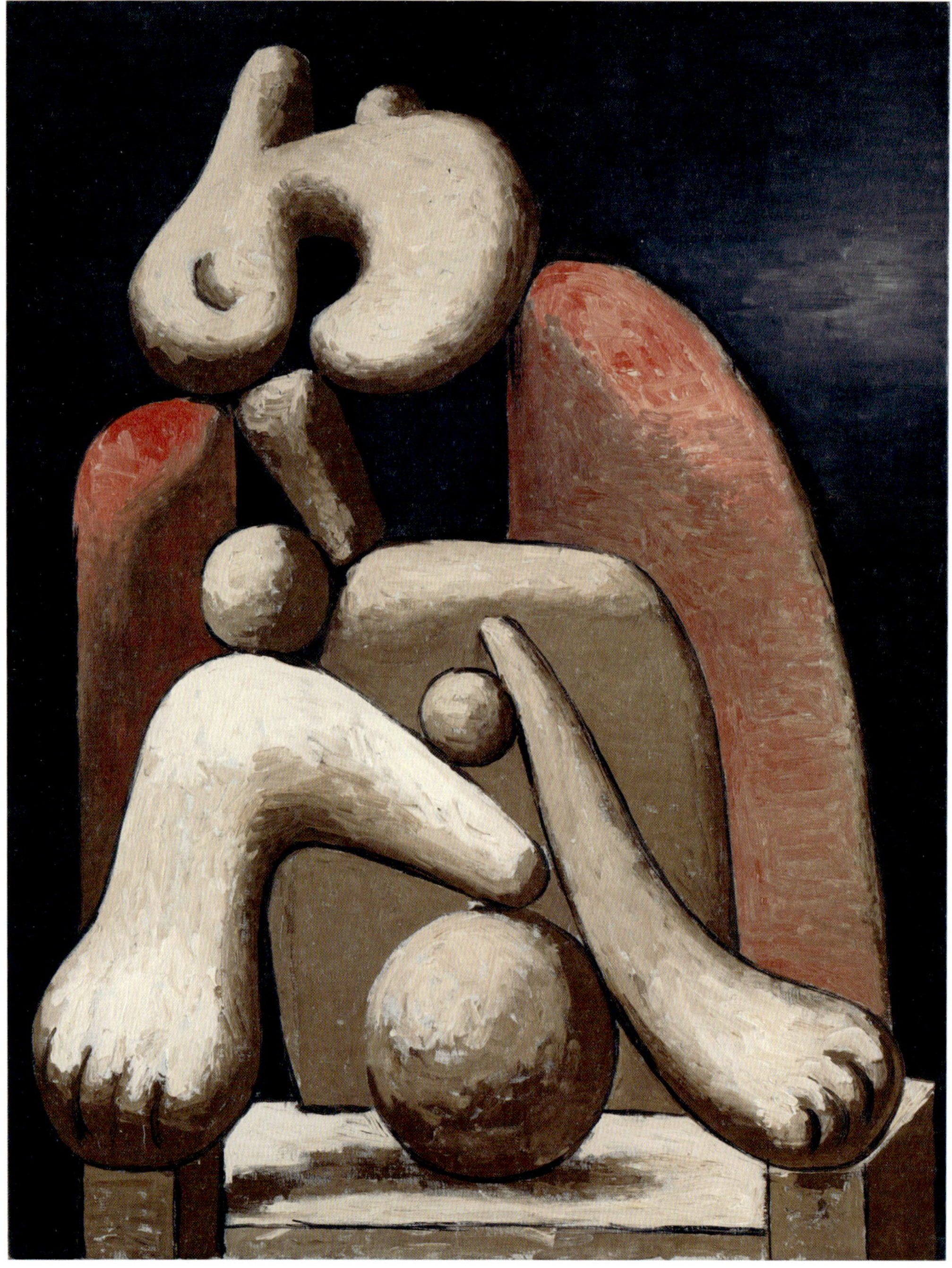



*Woman in a Red Armchair, Femme au fauteuil rouge*

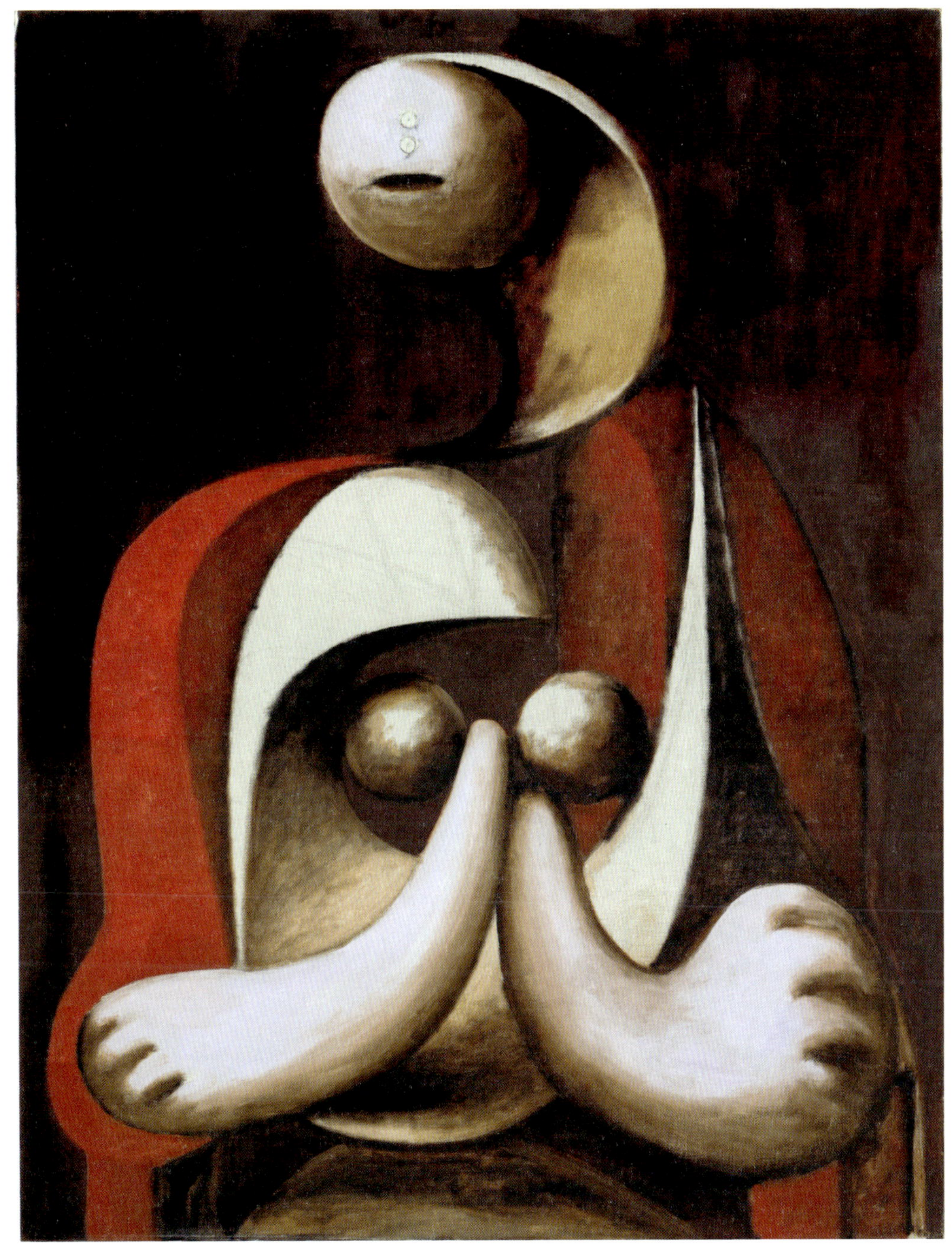

*Seated Woman in a Red Armchair, Femme assise dans un fauteuil rouge*

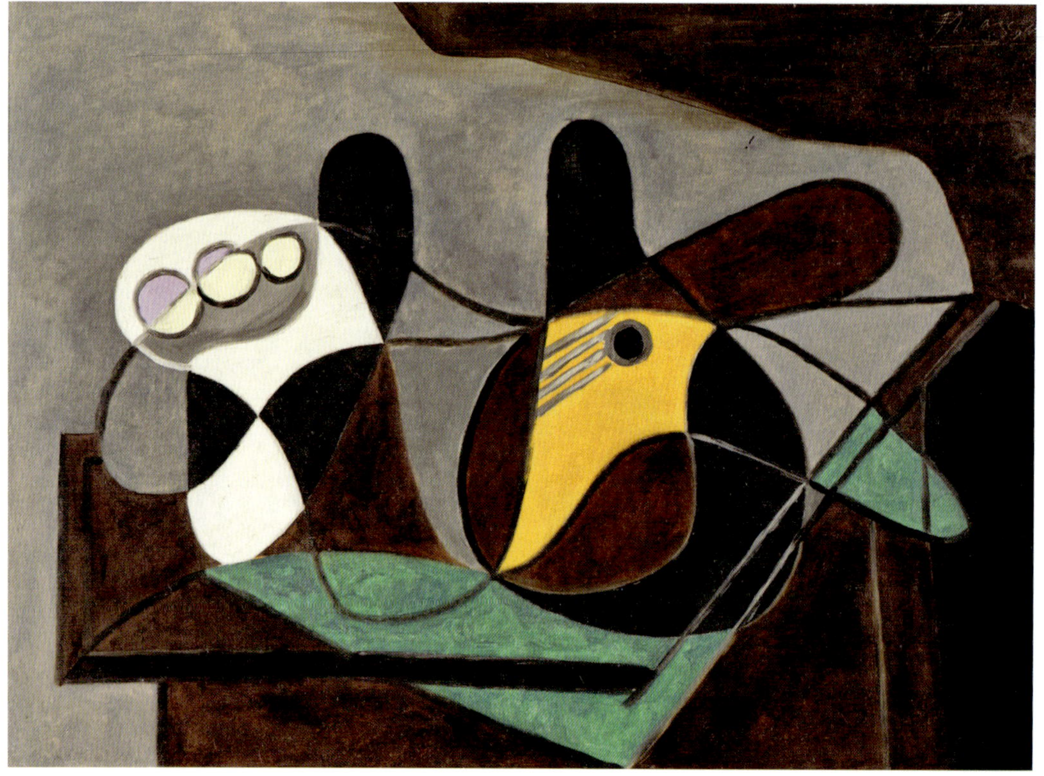

 *Fruit Bowl and Guitar, Compotier et guitare*

'One does not delimit nature, one does not copy it either; one allows imagined objects to take on real appearances.'

Picasso quoted in Brassaï, *Conversations with Picasso*, p.36

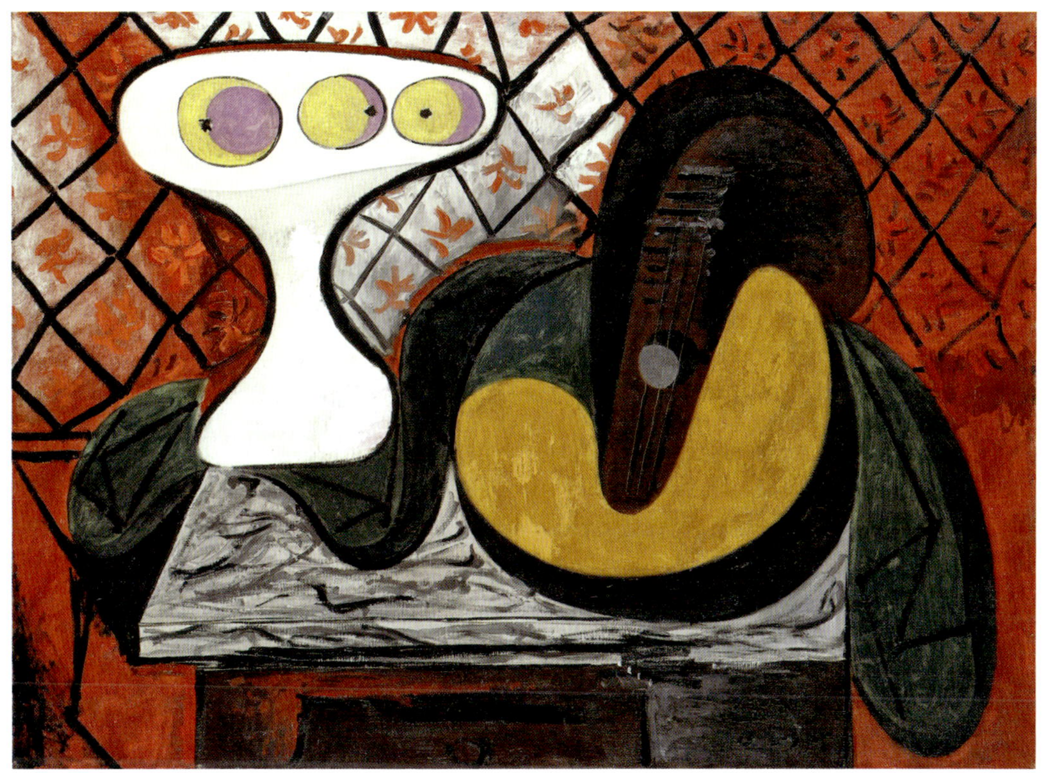

*Still Life with Fruit Bowl and Mandolin, Compotier et mandoline*

# Boisgeloup

In 1930 Picasso bought an eighteenth-century chateau or mansion house called Boisgeloup in the village of Gisors, Normandy, 63 kilometres north of Paris. His purchase freed him from having to load his large Hispano-Suiza luxury car with canvases and paint materials every time he wanted to escape from the city. His new environment led to his work in sculpture, to which he had returned in 1927, dramatically intensifying. Brassaï photographed Boisgeloup in late 1932 and the images were first published in the magazine *Minotaure*. For a long time, this was the first and only way many knew about Picasso's experiments in sculpture.

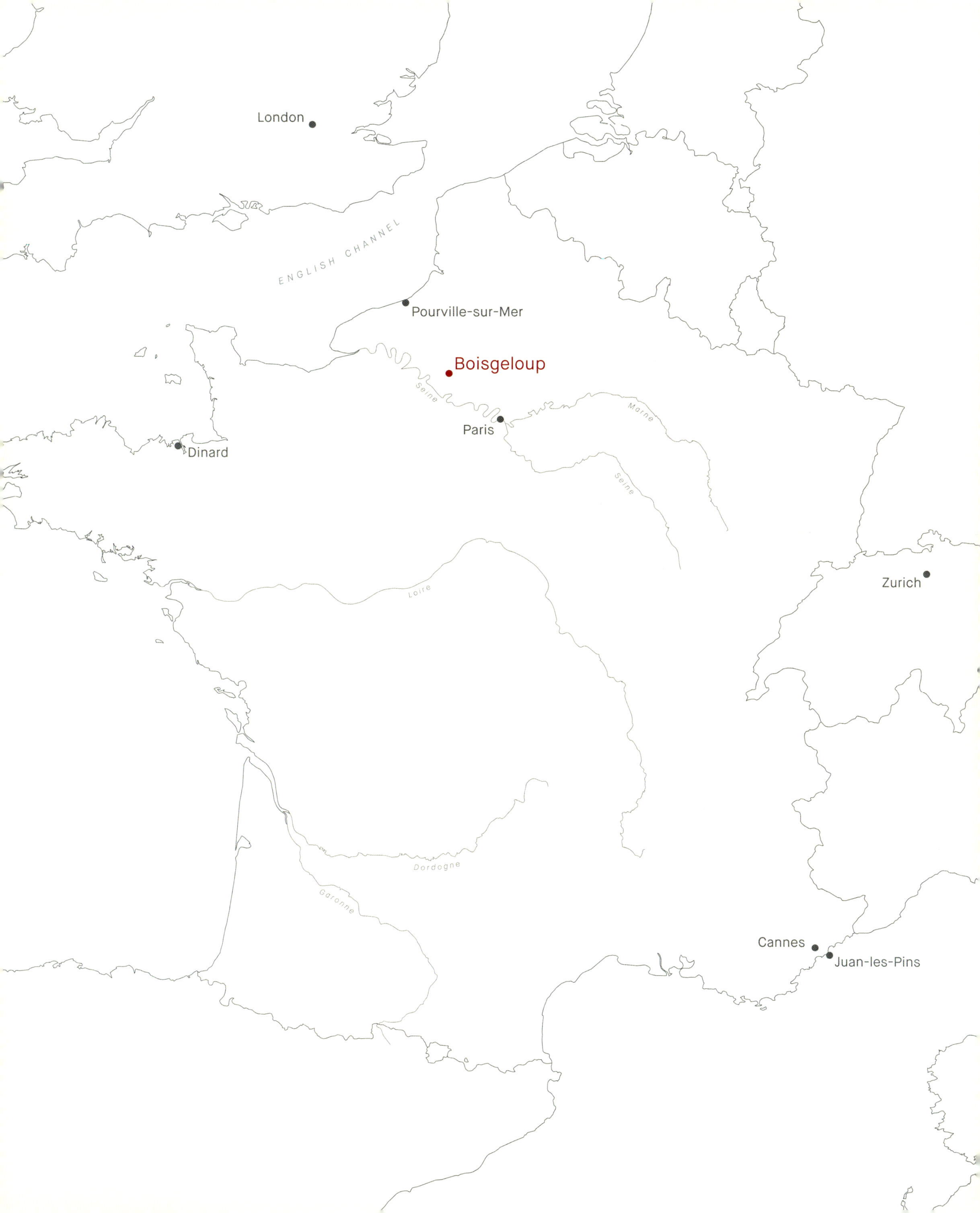
London
ENGLISH CHANNEL
Pourville-sur-Mer
Boisgeloup
Seine
Paris
Marne
Seine
Dinard
Loire
Zurich
Dordogne
Garonne
Cannes
Juan-les-Pins

Picasso and Tériade in front of the sculpture studio at Boisgeloup, December 1932. Photograph by Brassaï

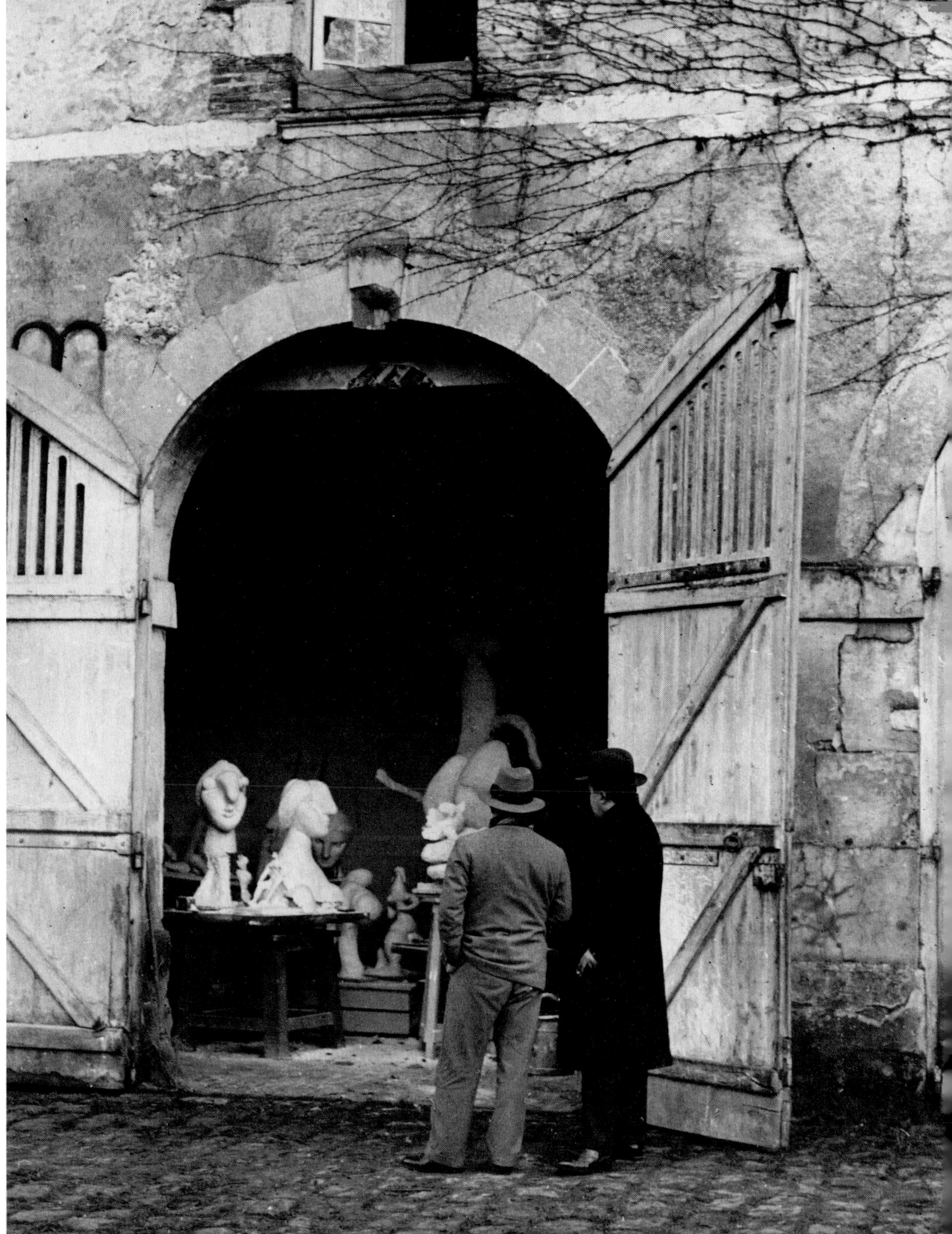

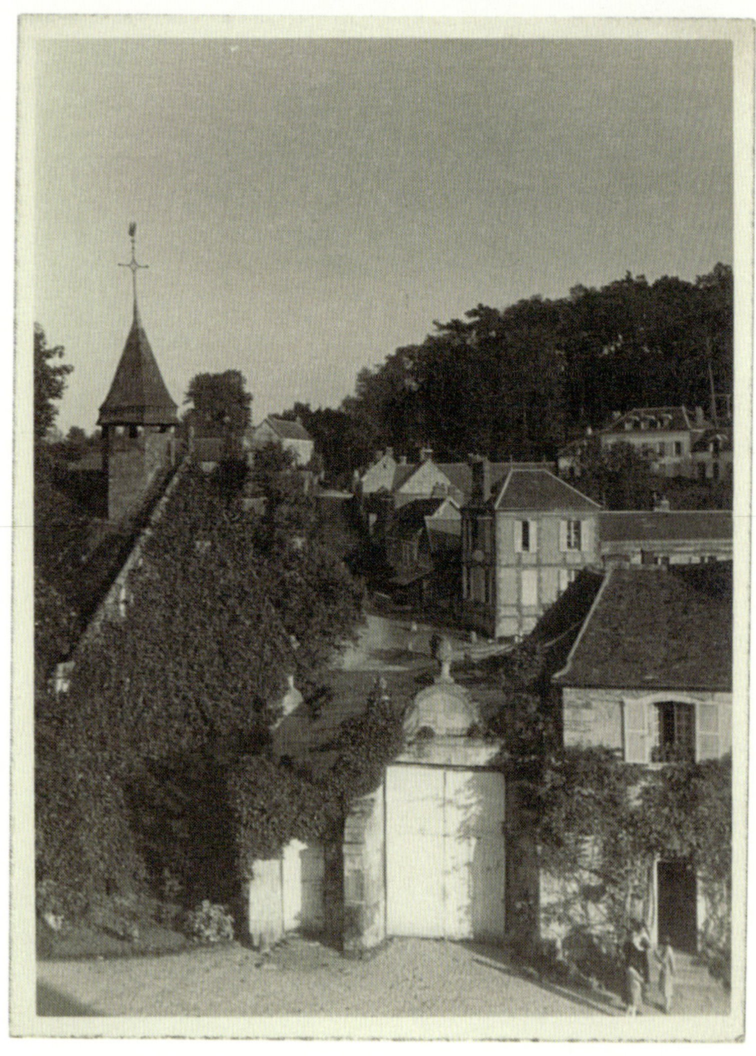

View of Boisgeloup and the village of Gisors, 1930s

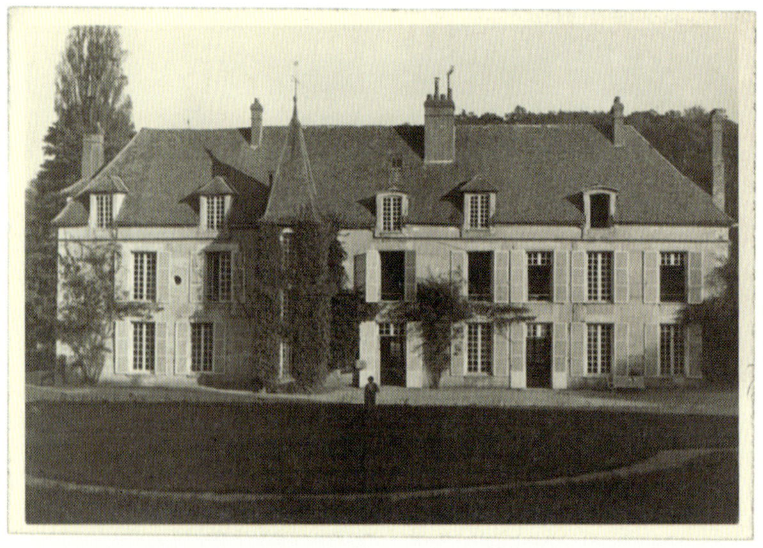

The Boisgeloup chateau with Olga Picasso in the middle of the lawn, early 1930s
Photograph by Brassaï

'The next day round noon, under a dark December sky, I, along with Tériade, Olga, and Paulo, Picasso's eleven-year-old son, climbed into the monumental Hispano-Suiza, which was still brand new, all its brass work still gleaming. The chauffeur, wearing white gloves, closed the door as gawkers looked on. That big black car – roomy, comfortable, elegant – with mirrors and flower vases inside, did not go unnoticed. We left Paris and headed toward Beauvais.

Picasso had bought the property, he confided, because he was a bit tired of bringing the bulky harvest of his summer back to Paris every year from Dinard, Cannes, or Juan-les-Pins, was tired of rewrapping and unwrapping canvases, paints, paint-brushes, sketchbooks, all the gear of his traveling studio. In Boisgeloup he could leave his things there.

Just before reaching Gisors, the Hispano-Suiza veered to the left and onto a small communal road. A signpost indicated: 'Hamlet of Boisgeloup'. A few moments later, I saw the houses of a small village scaling a hill and, at the same time, the portal to a castle attached to an old chapel. We had arrived.'

Brassaï, *Conversations with Picasso*, pp.15–16

'Picasso gave us the owner's tour at a dead run. It was an odd castle: most of the rooms were unfurnished, with simply a few large Picassos here and there on the bare walls. Picasso himself lived with Olga and Paulo in two small rooms in the attic. We also dashed through the small ramshackle chapel, entirely covered with ivy. Picasso explained it was from the thirteenth century and that mass was still sometimes celebrated there. But we were in a hurry. "There are too many sculptures to photograph and it will soon be dark," he said, leading us toward a row of cowsheds, stables, and barns, in the courtyard facing the house. I imagine that, when he visited the property for the first time, it was less the little castle that appealed to him than these vast empty outbuildings to be filled. He could finally satisfy a desire that had long been supressed: to sculpt large statues. He opened the door of one of these large stalls, and we were able to see the dazzling whiteness of an entire people of sculptures.'

Brassaï, *Conversations with Picasso*, p.16

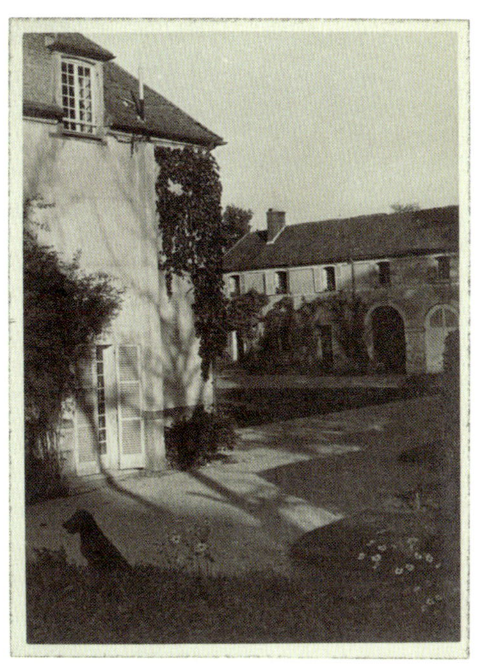

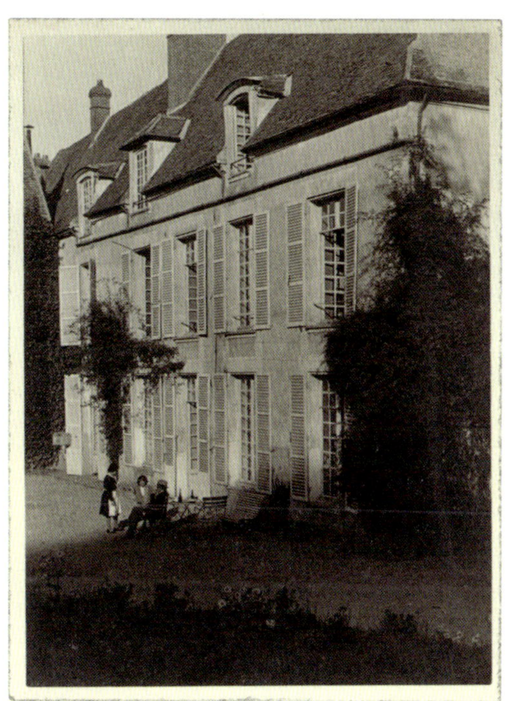

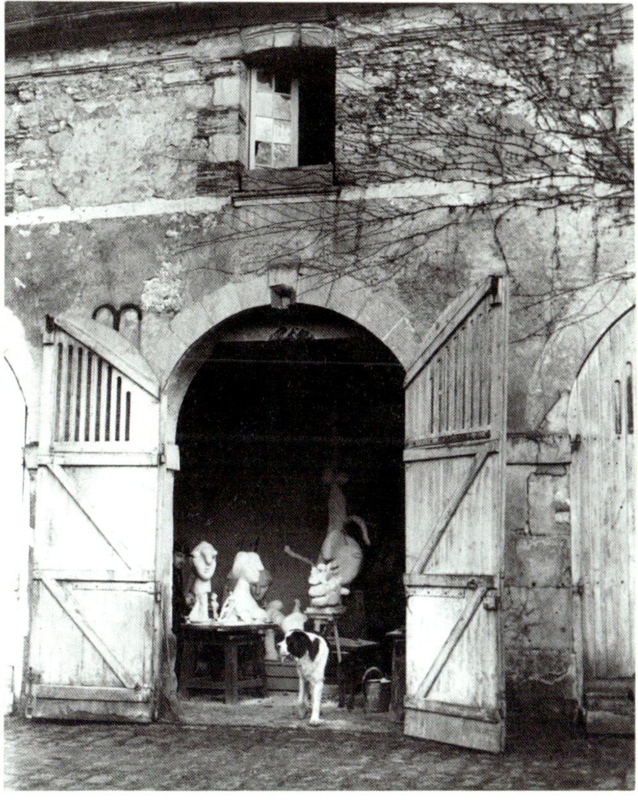

Clockwise from top:

The sculpture studio in the distance, with Elf the dog in the foreground, 1930s

Open door on the sculpture studio with Tériade partly hidden on the left and Bob, the Pyrenean Mountain dog, 1932. Photograph by Brassaï

Partial view of the chateau with Olga and Pablo Picasso and the governess, early 1930s

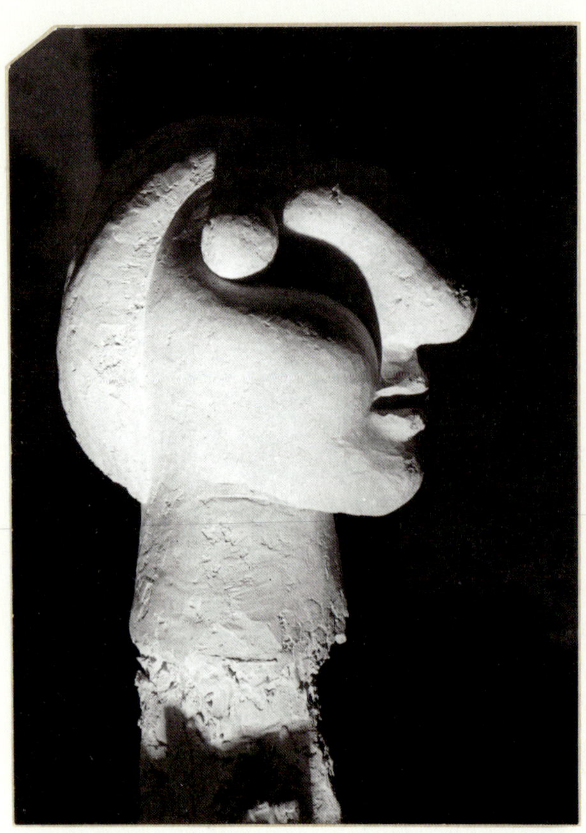

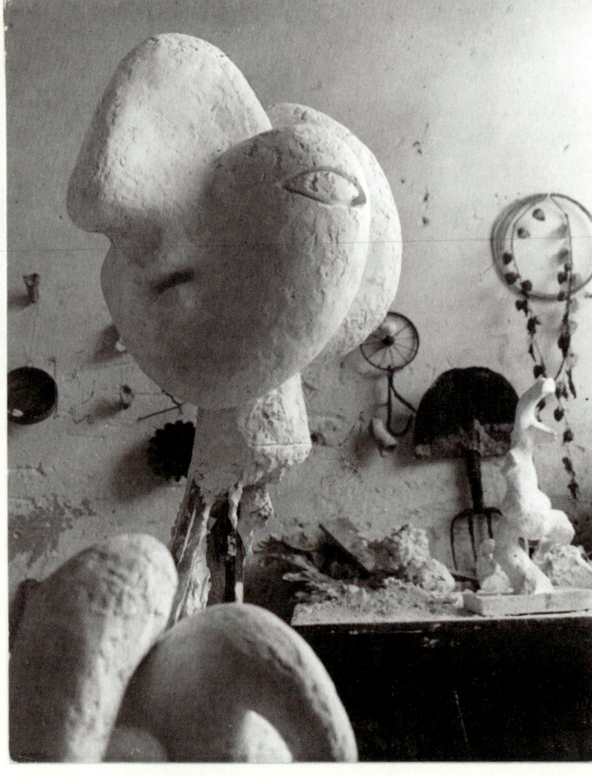

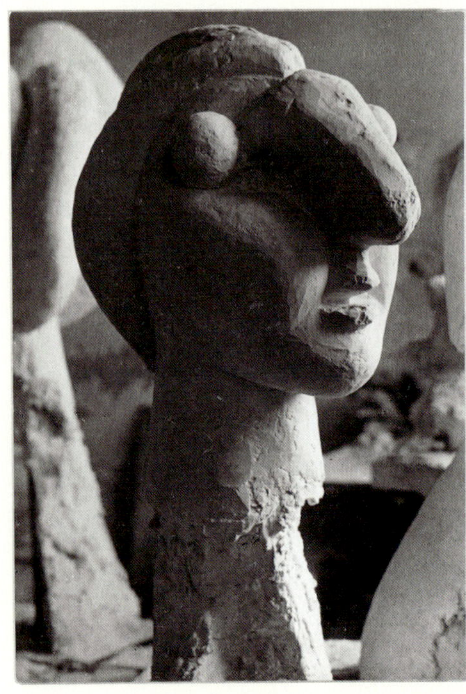

Plaster sculptures in the Boisgeloup studio,
(with Picasso seen from the back)
Photographs on this page by Brassaï, December 1932

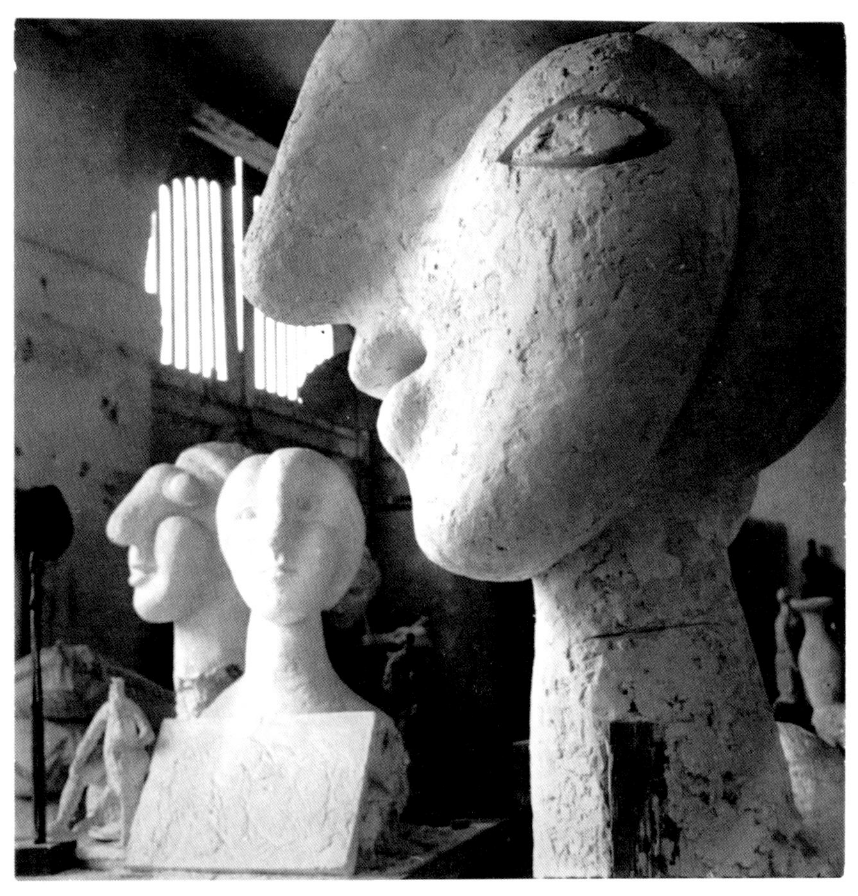

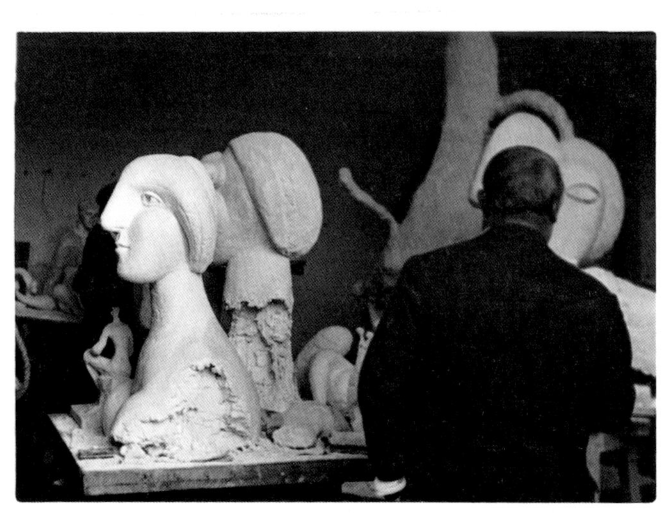

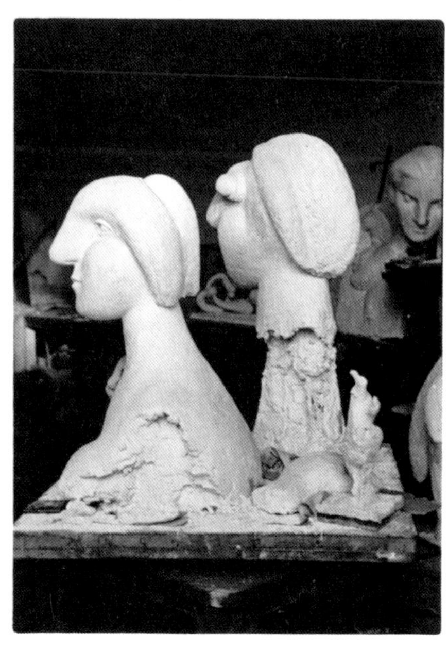

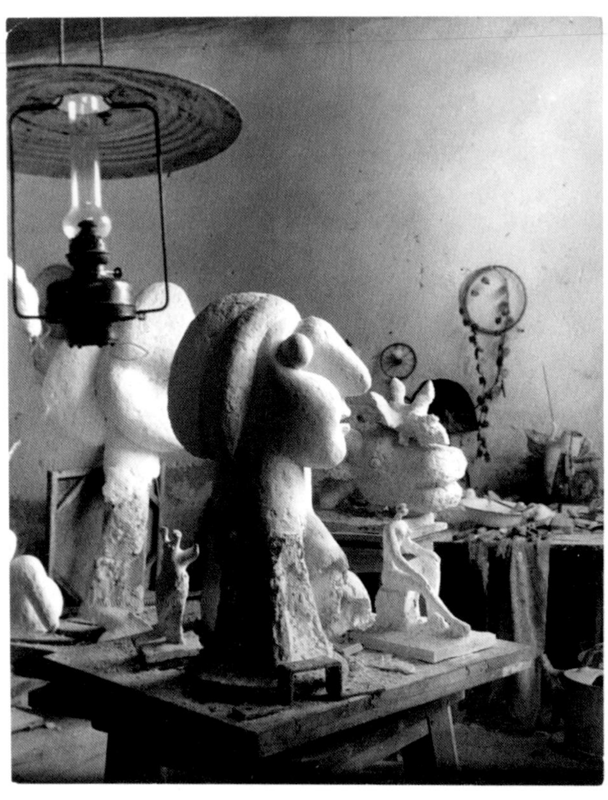

*Head of a Woman* 1931 and other plaster sculptures in the Boisgeloup studio, December 1932. Photograph by Brassaï

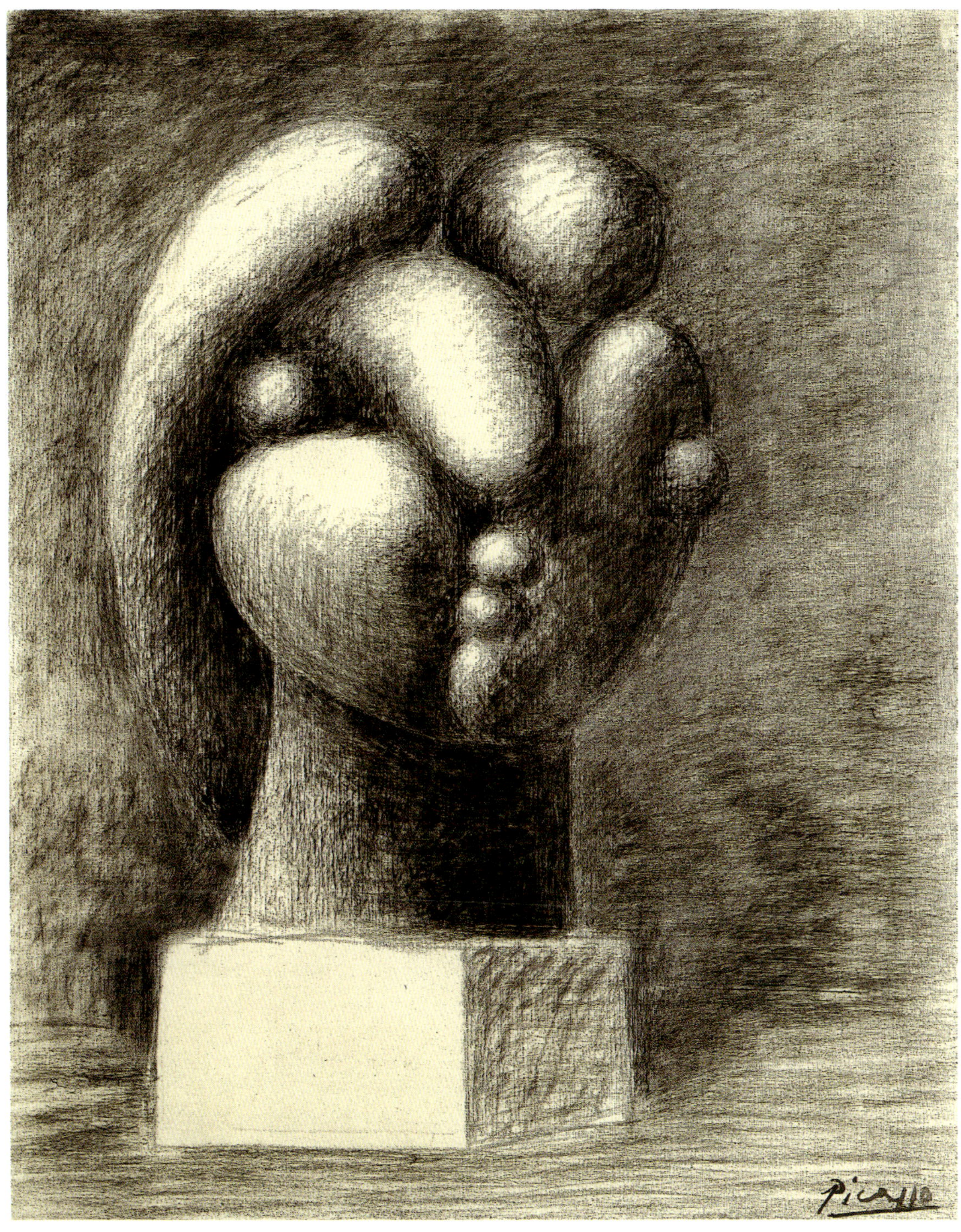


*Sculpture of a Head, Sculpture d'une tête*

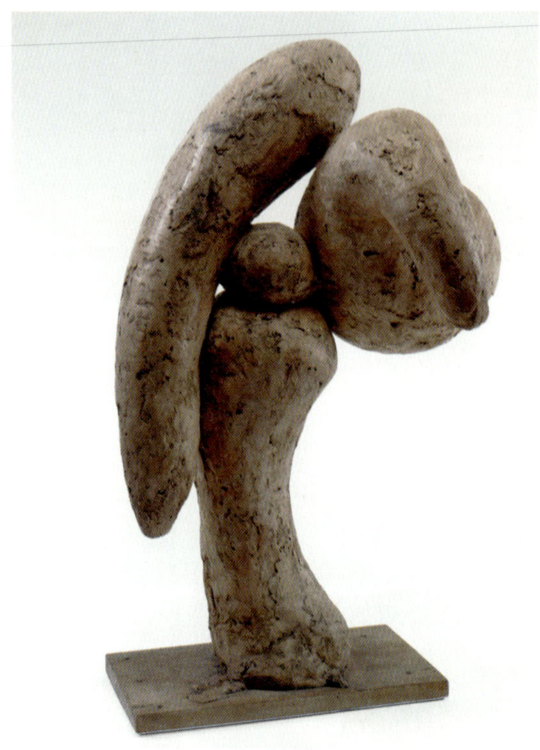

*Head of a Woman, Tête de femme*; Boisgeloup 1931

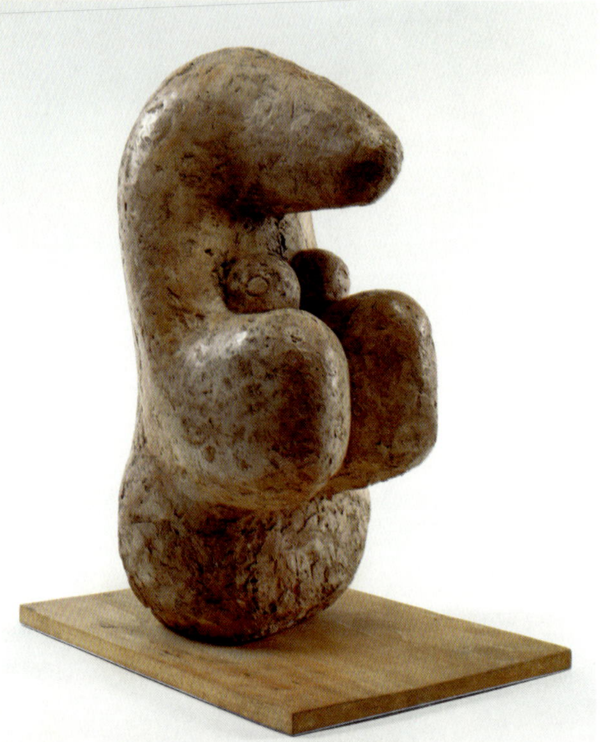

*Bust of a Woman, Buste de femme*; Boisgeloup 1931

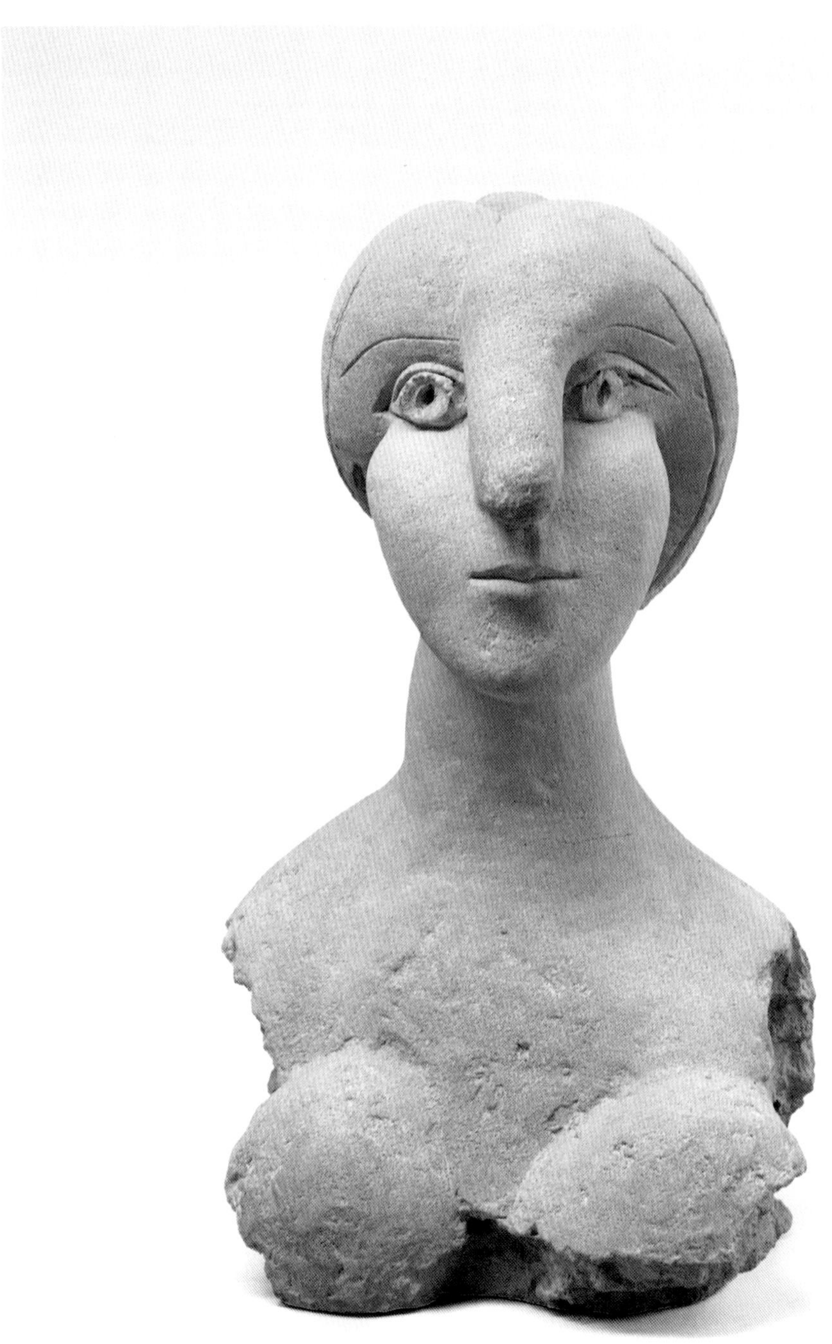

*Bust of a Woman*, *Buste de femme*; Boisgeloup 1931

# ‘I am a woman’: The Spring Nudes

T. J. Clark

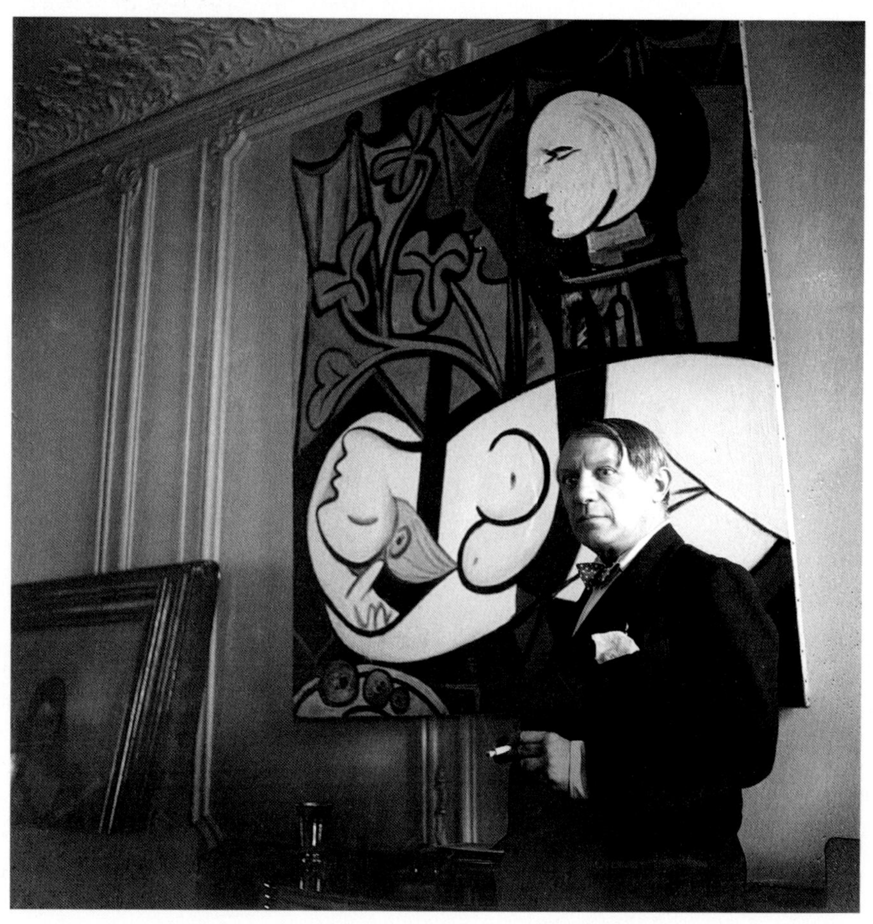

Picasso in the downstairs family apartment, rue La Boétie, 1933. Photograph by Cecil Beaton

One day near the beginning of March 1932 the art dealer Daniel-Henry Kahnweiler wrote to his friend Michel Leiris. The letter to which Kahnweiler was responding has not survived, but what seems to have stuck in his mind from it was the young poet-anthropologist's verdict on the state of painting around 1930. Painting was dead, Leiris had decided, with Picasso the only person capable of breathing life into the corpse.

Leiris had written beautifully about Picasso in the late 1920s – his great essay 'Picasso's Recent Paintings' had appeared in the magazine *Documents* two years before – following the artist further into his new world of monsters and phantoms than any other critic then or since.[1] Kahnweiler, by contrast, had kept his distance for a decade, partly for personal reasons and partly from lack of sympathy with what Picasso had been doing. High cubism remained Kahnweiler's touchstone. He seems to have said nothing, at least in public, about Picasso's turn to classicism after 1918, and certainly nothing about the period of wildness and eroticism inaugurated by *The Three Dancers* of 1925 (p.78).

So what he writes to Leiris in 1932 is astonishing. The prose of his letter is as spontaneous and excitable as Kahnweiler ever could be. Few men were less inclined to gush.

> *Yes, as you say, painting is only being kept alive by Picasso, but how marvellously. Two days ago, at his place, we saw two paintings he had just done.* [The paintings referred to are most probably *Nude in a Black Armchair* and *Nude, Green Leaves and Bust*.] *Two nudes that are*

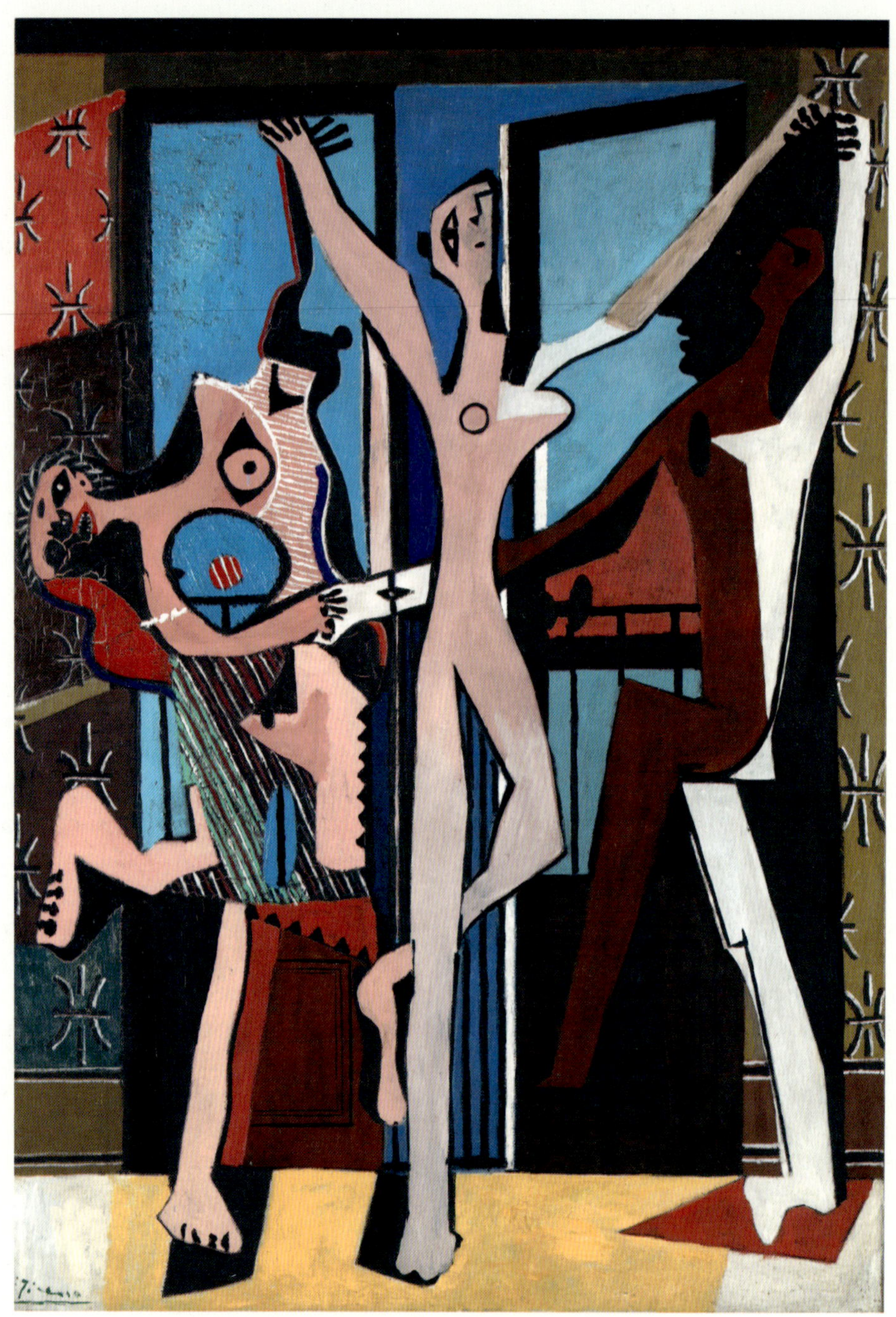

*The Three Dancers*, *Les Trois Danseuses* 1925

*perhaps the greatest, most moving things he has produced. 'It seems as though a satyr who had just killed a woman could have painted this picture,' I said to him about one of the two. It's not Cubist, not naturalistic, it's without any painterly artifice, it's very alive, very erotic, but with the eroticism of a giant. Picasso has done nothing comparable for many years. 'I would love to paint like a blind man,' he'd said a few days before, 'who pictures an arse by the way it feels.' That's it exactly. We came away from there stunned.*[2]

'Stunned' (*écrasé*) may strike us as too much a stock item of Picasso idolatry. And the other fragments Kahnweiler quotes from studio conversation are not likely any longer to impress. Men swap compliments over a nude's dead body. We have been here many times before.

But the tone, to repeat, is entirely out of character for this writer, and the verdict he pronounces – the judgement that the new paintings 'are perhaps the greatest, most moving things' Picasso had ever done – the opposite of routine. No-holds-barred sexuality, it seems – even for as austere a modernist as Kahnweiler – is painting's last hope.

The questions provoked by Kahnweiler's letter concern the character and purpose – the intention, the effect – of Picasso's eroticism; and why painting was thought now to depend on it. But these questions cannot be disentangled from a wider one concerning Picasso's art and 'autobiography': namely, the fact that so much of his art seems, or seems to claim, to be a record of immediate first-person experience.

We happen to know the identity of the woman, Marie-Thérèse Walter, whose 'aliveness' is celebrated in the two 1932 *Nudes*. But who, we might ask, is doing the celebrating? Certainly, empirically, someone called Pablo Picasso. Yet one of Picasso's favourite sayings – it crops up in conversations with Kahnweiler and Romuald Dor de la Souchère, on both occasions thrown out as if it were a well-known formula – was Arthur Rimbaud's '*Je est un autre*' (I is someone [maybe even something] else.' To Dor de la Souchère the painter says: 'I think the work of art is the product of calculations, but calculations often unknown by the artist himself ... So we must suppose, as Rimbaud said, that it is the other that calculates in us.'[3] Picasso's art, in other words, may appear to say 'I', unmistakably; but what in the work does the saying – what force or entity or cloud of unknowing – is precisely Picasso's question. 'Whether he likes it or not,' he explains, 'man is the instrument of nature; it imposes its character, its appearance, on him.'[4] 'You start a painting [this is to Kahnweiler] and it becomes something altogether different. It's strange how little the artist's will matters ... He was completely right, the other, when he said *Je est un autre*'.[5]

So Kahnweiler may be reacting in just the way Picasso would have wanted when he says that the paintings of Marie-Thérèse Walter look as if they had been done by a *non*-Picasso – by some kind of satyr or giant. We could discard the *Après-midi d'un faune* mythology here[6] – the nearest we get to nymphs and satyrs in the 1932 *Nudes* is a bloodless plaster on a plinth – and think about otherness and estrangement in the two paintings more generally, more formally. When Picasso paints a woman, we might ask, is the painting effectively, for the viewer, an act of possession, or does it (whatever Picasso's intention) establish the *woman*'s self-possession? What kind of 'Picasso' – what imaginary place for Picasso as maker and onlooker, and for us in his footsteps – does the picture end up providing? If the atmosphere in both 1932 canvases is ruled by Desire (and I suppose most of us would go along with Kahnweiler at least this far), then what does Desire look like in the two *Nudes*' particular staging? Who desires whom, and what is desire *of*?

I begin with *Nude in a Black Armchair* (p.95). Everything I go on to say about it depends, first, on the canvas's size: it is just over five feet tall and four feet wide, and always seems larger. Kahnweiler's 'giant' responds to this. The photograph Cecil Beaton took at the time of *Nude, Green Leaves and Bust* (whose dimensions are the same), with Picasso smoking proudly in the foreground, dramatises the picture's power over the room (p.76). And size makes the question of the nude's proximity to us – the body's closeness, its excessiveness and openness to our looking – all the more immediate. The nude is pressed close to the picture plane, taking up almost half the painted rectangle: the right-hand edge of the painting cannot contain it, the black armchair projects it forward, the wild vortex of hair invites the touch.

Nearness and availability, then, are part of the painting's story: one understands why Kahnweiler could not escape their spell. But many things in the painting put the first fiction of closeness in doubt. The range of colours Picasso chooses is electric. The tension between the ice blue of the wall and the sunset outside the window could hardly be more intense. No painter since Caravaggio has made a black more lavish and portentous than this one: the clawlike lily in the foreground only emphasises the armchair's enveloping negativity. ('When I paint a woman in an armchair,' Picasso told André Malraux, 'the armchair, it's old age and death, isn't it? Too bad for her. Or maybe it's for her protection.'[7]) Even the green of the rubber plant has a ghastly comic vitality. But does this exacerbation of colour move the nude body *towards* us, imaginatively? Isn't the whole decor – not simply the black and yellow, but the crazy spatiality of armchair, wall, half-open window, escaping pot plant – deeply unreal and estranging? Doesn't it end up making the woman's 'nearness' an abstraction – a form of remoteness as much as proximity? And isn't the seal of that final *un*availability the extraordinary pale mauve Picasso has chosen for the nude's flesh, clamped in its leading of black? Certainly the mauve is 'vital' – in *Nude, Green Leaves and Bust* it is used again, and the difference between it and the white of the bust on the plinth is insisted on – but in 1932 vitality and otherworldliness, or eroticism and de-realisation, seem two faces of the same coin.

Take the blonde-and-brown vortex of hair, for example. Once noticed, it seems the body's pivot. That the configuration is partly an imagining of the model's open vagina is obvious enough: the conjunction of hair and breast is a typical bit of Picasso sex comedy; but this only makes the strangeness of the hair's shape and colour – their fieriness, their twisting, their left-to-right velocity – more striking. The head, we might say, belongs to the hair rather than vice versa: the hair is a life form about to swallow its prey. And what the shape of the hair then does to the nude's neck and shoulders, and even to the lines of her upper breast, and her arm with the flower, and the arc of the armchair, seems to speak to the shape's sheer power – its being a kind of overproductive (maybe malignant) pictorial cell, throwing off approximate versions of itself. The flower claw sets the note.

This returns us to Kahnweiler's letter – to the way he and Leiris seem to agree in the early 1930s that if painting is to be resuscitated, it will be by threading it closer to the excesses and ambivalences of sex. To the power and appeal of eroticism, that is to say, but also to its dangers and uncertainties. Eroticism – this is the hope – will *endanger* painting. It will move painting away from the kinds of ('cubist' or 'classical') orderliness that had been the death of the art form in the 1920s. It will disturb painting's universe.

I turn now to *Nude, Green Leaves and Bust* (p.93). In many ways this painting is more elusive than its companion. *Nude in a Black Armchair* may be ambivalent, but it is not baffling – not a mystery. Its whole handling of form seems directed, single-mindedly, to a central fact of eroticism, and to the ways in which painting, by confronting this fact, might rediscover certain strengths and uncertainties of its own. It aims, in a word, to stage the paradox of 'immediacy' in our relation to others (and therefore ourselves): it turns on the way proximity and openness to possession become, in practice, in the space of Desire, something else – something colder, more abstract, more deeply perplexing. This is a rough characterisation, granted; but at least I feel confident that it is headed in the right direction – its terms correspond to the painting's basic idea. About the intentionality of *Nude, Green Leaves and Bust* I am much less sure.

The latter painting certainly *begins* from the idea of distance and unreality, and (just as much as in *Nude in a Black Armchair*, though very differently) it is this idea that shapes the scene's whole spatiality. Eroticism here is explicitly a kind of theatre, with the naked body framed and confined by a flimsy apparatus of curtains, cushions, strange bands or bonds of black. Notice, for instance, that the cold blue curtain (is it made of blue material, or could it be transparent to the sky?) is pinned to, or hung from, a set of four orange buttons. It is as if the scene takes place inside an improvised alcove or tent. The canvas's initial atmosphere, then, is of elaborate contrivance and enclosure, but what that atmosphere ends up 'saying' about sex – what picture of desire and identification it proposes – seems to me truly hard to decide.

This is, to state the obvious, a darker world than that of *Nude in a Black Armchair*. Darker, and maybe a little more secure. Picasso is an artist – to take up an argument I have made at length elsewhere[8] – whose whole vision of life is premised on nearness and containment. He seems to have taken it for granted that humanity happens within four walls. The room was his model of reality: its walls and windows and few precious possessions were what made life worth living (and painting). That is what makes the abstractness and wafer-thinness of the room in *Nude in a Black Armchair* so chilling: they seem to me Picasso's way of showing true humanness and reciprocity – the space humans have for 'being-in' and 'being-themselves' – under threat. Making an interior in which 'interiority' is on the point of evaporating (following the rubber plant out the window): this, for Picasso, is truly to imagine a world out of joint. The surrounding darkness of 1932 – the Europe of immiseration and dictatorship – seems close.

So the (re)appearance of enclosure and containment in *Nude, Green Leaves and Bust* is intensely charged. The painting seems to be hankering after, and half pretending to provide, the safety and protection of a room. Maybe even the room's erotic warmth – the shared secrecy behind the curtain. But the offer immediately doubles back on itself. The room-space here is transparently an illusion, built – jerry-rigged – out of drapes pinned up inside some further unreadable space. And 'transparently', I have suggested, is a metaphor that the painting brings to life. The extraordinary blue here – three blues, in fact, getting darker from left to right – is not quite diaphanous, not quite airy, but not at all blue-velvety and soft.

The blue of the curtain, further, has been given a face. The face's left-turned profile appears just to the right of the rubber plant, like a set of billowing folds in the curtain itself, wedged between the green leaves of the rubber plant and the grey halo surrounding the sculpture on its plinth. If my experience is typical, the blue face takes time to appear as one looks at the painting: the profiles of the nude and bust are what draw the eye initially, plus the whirligig of the rubber plant; and then, after minutes, the dark face looms. Does the face, at that first moment of materialisation, seem to be male or female? I cannot remember, in my own case; and the longer I look – the harder I try to understand the profile's place in the picture as a whole – the more uncertain the face's gender becomes.

Maybe we could see the face as an emanation – a ghostly double, floating out into three dimensions – of the peculiar wafer-thin bust on the black marble plinth. And that bust does look to be female. It 'is' Marie-Thérèse Walter. A sculpted Marie-Thérèse looks down on a painted one. (The picture would suggest as much even if we did not know, empirically, that Picasso had been making sculpture after sculpture of Walter through the preceding months.) I said that the sculpture 'looks down' on the nude. But equally, if we had only this picture to go on, we might decide that the face of the woman in the sculpture was *not* looking down – that she fixed her cold classical eye on the leaves and drapery, not the inordinate body. But then the blue emanation might help. The blue face does seem to be looking downwards. Gently? Tenderly? Can we put a name to its attentiveness? Or is there something implacable and non-human to it, perhaps deriving from its colour? Nonetheless, isn't the face female? Isn't it some kind of mediating state of Walter herself? It is deeply linked to her. Its double S-curve of lips and nose is closer to the double S-curve of the sleeping woman on the cushions than to the bifurcated profile – nose and forehead stopping the flow of line below – of the plaster head. But then the memory might come back to us of paintings Picasso had done in the late 1920s, where profile heads regularly look on at pictures of (monstrous) women.[9] And those profiles seem to be male – weakly, schematically male, but male all the same. Often in the literature it is taken for granted (maybe too eagerly) that the heads are 'Pablo Picasso'. But looking again at the profile in *Nude, Green Leaves and Bust*, I cannot see it as any more indubitably 'Pablo Picasso' than 'Marie-Thérèse Walter'. It is both. It is neither. It is the face of in-between-ness.

Of course, in a painting by Picasso, 'in-betweenness' is very much more than a matter of shared or distributed features. It is a matter of placement – of the figure's location in space. The blue face looks to be neither outside nor inside the curtain, neither here with us in the space of pleasure – as Picasso so constantly wanted things to be – nor out there in some intangible distance. 'I believe in phantoms,' he said once to Kahnweiler; 'they're not misty vapours, they're something hard. When you want to stick a finger in them, they react.'[10] I do not believe the phantom in this case is within reach of anybody's fingers. And fingers themselves – again, this is a

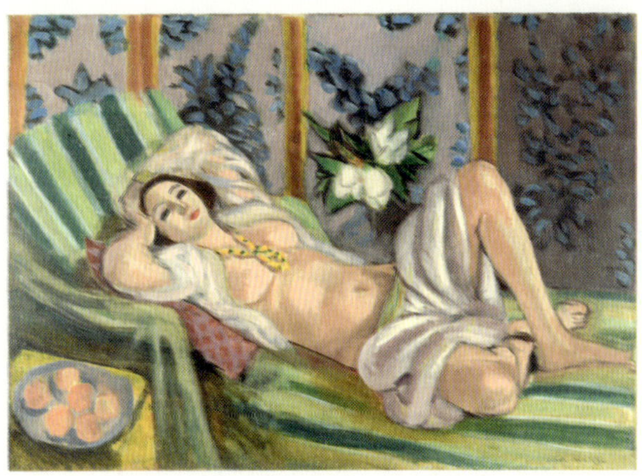

Henri Matisse *Odalisque with Magnolias* 1923–4

charged decision for Picasso, who is a great painter of hands and digits – are reduced in *Nude, Green Leaves and Bust* to a dazzling impalpable double S-curve of pure line. (It is there underneath the nude's thrown-back head.)

Matisse is often on Picasso's mind in the later 1920s and early 1930s.[11] I think he is in *Nude, Green Leaves and Bust*. The picture's pinned-up curtains, and whole atmosphere of elaborate sexual artifice – in contrast to the self-cancelling starkness of *Nude in a Black Armchair* – seem like a direct, maybe half-ironic, homage to the makeshift interiors, part Morocco, part art deco, that Matisse had rigged up inside his Nice apartment after the First World War. *Odalisque with Magnolias* 1923–4 (above) would be a fair comparison. Of course the atmosphere in Picasso is different: wilder, stranger, more secretive, perhaps more ominous. But it is not the case that these latter qualities were simply absent from the paintings Matisse did in Nice. This remains the Matisse paradox: that the absurd Côte d'Azur kasbahs he constructed did repeatedly open onto the unexpected, the unnerving. I would say that most deeply Picasso's *Nude, Green Leaves and Bust* is an answer to the most abrasive of Matisse's interwar paintings, his *Decorative Figure on an Ornamental Background* from the winter of 1925–6 (opposite).

The *Decorative Figure* has always presented Matisse's admirers with difficulties. Alfred H. Barr, Jr, in his great monograph, called it 'a triumph of art over factitious vulgarity'; and then he added: 'Yet because the picture is so clearly an act of will in a field of artifice, the victory seems Pyrrhic.'[12] 'But that's why the painting haunts me,' I imagine Picasso replying. 'It is because the picture so fully admits – makes manifest – the fact that eroticism *is* an act of will in a field of artifice that it remains the painting of Matisse's that I most need to come to terms with, and know I can never quite emulate. The best I can do is replace vulgarity by transparency, and sensual overload by blue gloom.' The cranky leaves and orange pegs in Picasso are a last leftover from Matisse's stifling boudoir.

We return to the question of art and eroticism. The 'unreality' of Matisse's interiors in the 1920s is essential to their worldview: at no point is it punctured by the least hint of irony or even ruefulness. Sex and art *are* 'unreal' for Matisse, and accepted as such: he has made a life inside the twin illusions. He does not mind in the least if the elaborateness of his set-ups strikes the viewer as willful or fussy or even fatuous. 'If you know of a better world, go to it': that seems to me his message.

Of course Picasso agrees, basically, with Matisse's conclusion: he is every bit as dismissive, in his 1932 paintings, of all the surrounding instructions in Paris in the early 1930s that art should engage with 'modern life' or 'the world of the Unconscious', or join forces with the *Association des écrivains et artistes révolutionnaires*. (This association of revolutionary writers and artists was founded in 1932, with several of Picasso's acquaintances involved.) But the tone of Picasso's isolation is different. The cave of eroticism in his work – the pinned-up tent city of art and abandon – is a place of confinement, not simply containment. The black bars of shadow dividing the nude's body in the Picasso only make this explicit. We might say, half-adopting the language of psychoanalysis, that never has a naked body been divided into parts that are *less* 'part-objects' – less the self-sufficient, completely fixated, seemingly natural and necessary whole little totalities conjured up (if we're lucky) by Desire.

The black bands, to dwell on them for a moment, are truly an overdetermined, 'uninterpretable' device. They make me think of William Blake's 'Infant Sorrow' – his 'Bound and weary I thought best/To sulk upon my mother's breast.'[13] And I believe, incidentally, that the bands also emerged from Picasso's continual thinking with and against Matisse. A black that leaks out of its initial home in the picture and moves across the body next to it is a constant

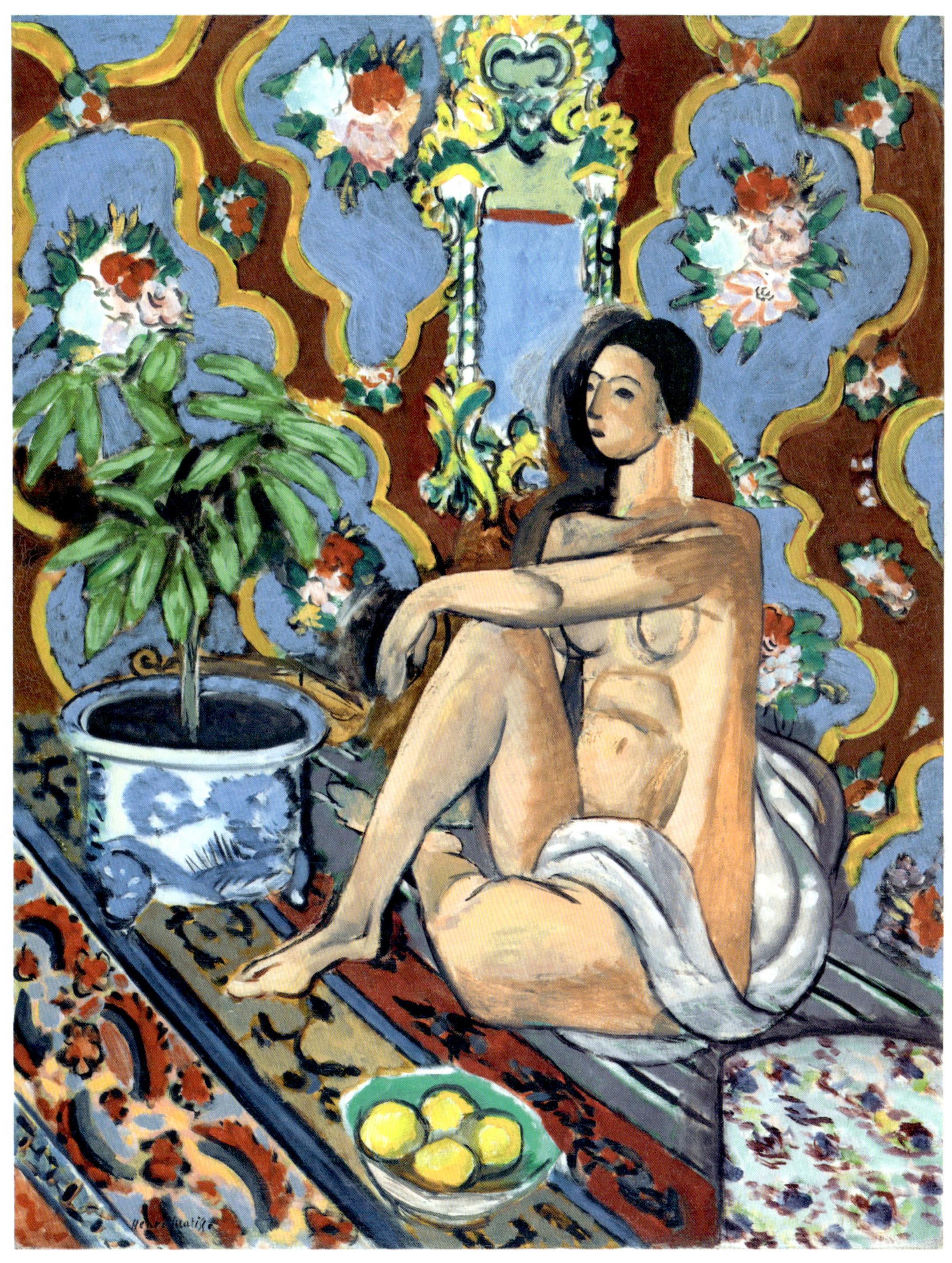

Henri Matisse *Decorative Figure on an Ornamental Background* 1925–6

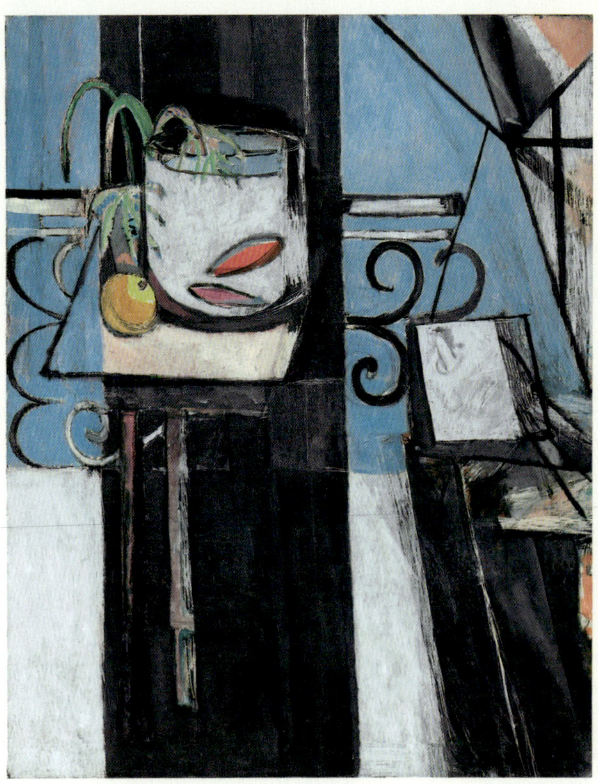

Henri Matisse *Goldfish and Palette* 1914

structuring principle of Matisse's work from 1914 on.[14] *Goldfish and Palette*, done in 1914, is a good example; and it seems to me, pressing the point further, that this very picture was fundamental for Picasso.[15] I think its unplaceable blacks live on in *Nude, Green Leaves and Bust*, and also, come to that, its *blues*... and really its whole weird re-imagining of room and window. I do not think – to come back to the blacks specifically – that Picasso knew why he found Matisse's blacks so transfixing; and I certainly do not think he knew what he was doing when he turned them into the harder, narrower, flimsier black bands of the painting from 1932. Maybe the best we can do, trying to get the measure of the bands, is to see them as representations – enactments – of what 'representation' *is*, in the act of sex: the moment of bounding, dividing, interrupting, which is always the other face of touching, fusing, possessing: the moment at which, perhaps necessarily, body becomes image as we try to steady and incorporate it, and convexity and concavity become abstract 'shape' – form in the eye.

There is a dimension to Picasso's eroticism that I have hardly touched on so far, though with the black bands we are close to it. I imagine that many of the words I have used up to now in this essay to describe the *tone* of Picasso's vision of sex – words like 'ominous' or 'confinement' or 'dangers and uncertainties' – will have struck some readers as euphemisms. The two *Nudes* I have focused on are dated 8 and 9 March 1932 (incidentally, *Nude, Green Leaves and Bust* was the first of the two to be painted). There are other paintings from 1932 just as supercharged and exultant (for example *The Mirror*, p.97); but these are very far from being the year's only notes. Compare the *Nudes* with a canvas done on 10 April, *Woman with a Flower* (p.112). Or go back to 22 January, and put *Nude in a Black Armchair* alongside *Rest* (p.54). It is typical of Picasso that he chose to have himself photographed in front of *Rest*'s shrieking phantasmagoria (opposite), and also typical that two days afterwards he painted a gentle *Dream* as pendant to the nightmare (p.57).[16]

In other words, what I have not properly confronted so far is the thin line in Picasso between beauty and monstrosity; and the fact that for a while, in the late 1920s and 1930s, it is monsters who rule.

What monstrosity came to signify in Picasso's art, and why the threatening or improbable took centre stage for the seven or eight years following 1927, are hard problems.[17] The turn had something to do with the temper of the times. The year 1934 in particular is one of unmitigated horror in Picasso's sketchbooks – rooms fill with lacerated bodies, bomber-swallows swoop down through windows, murderers are on the loose – and looking at the mayhem one inevitably remembers that this is the year of Hitler's Night of the Long Knives. But of course Picasso is (until *Guernica*) essentially a private artist: the century's horrors either appear to him in the very texture of intimate relations – here in the room – or they stay an unpaintable hellish 'background'. For whatever reasons, personal or political (and the biographers' second-hand gossip on this topic seems to me as useless as it is prurient), monstrosity and sex come to be intertwined in Picasso's art. This means that monstrosity, as Picasso understands it, is very much more than a repellent negative. Somewhere at the heart of being human, he believed, lies the moment when bodies present themselves as so many bearers of rotundities and orifices, things to suck or suck with, to bite, to penetrate, to swallow whole. No doubt this is an entirely ordinary, not to

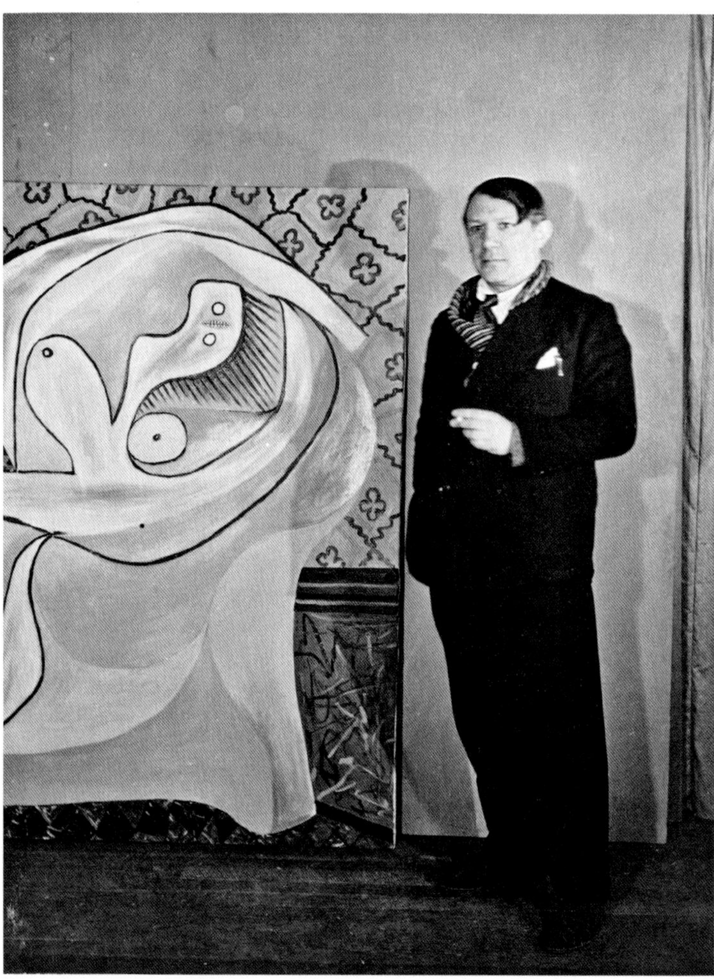

Picasso standing beside *Rest* at his retrospective at Galeries Georges Petit, Paris, June–July 1932

say necessary, dimension to the life of the species; but it has about it something intrinsically frightening – or at least recurrently surprising, unfamiliar. 'Let's play at hurting ourselves,' as a character in a Picasso play has it.[18]

Monstrosity in Picasso, putting things more generally, is the sign of the unknown and dangerous in human dealings. It is an Otherness always lying in wait. This Otherness is there most potently, he insists, in the to-and-fro of sex, but it is clear that Picasso took sex – the psychic and material interpenetration of male and female, preeminently – to be only the strongest and strangest form of the 'human' as a whole. 'When it comes down to it, there is only love', he told an interviewer in 1932.[19] 'Whatever it may be.' Compare *Je est un autre*.

If this seems too abstract, supplement it with a passage from Françoise Gilot's memoir.[20] She tells the story of the writer André Gide paying a call on Picasso in the 1940s, and pronouncing that the two of them had attained the age of serenity. 'There is no serenity for me,' Picasso shot back, 'and, what's more, I don't find any face charming.' The French word for 'face' here is *figure*. A few pages previously in the French edition of the memoir (for some reason the remark does not appear in the earlier American publication), Gilot records Picasso as saying '*Toutes choses nous apparaissent sous forme de figures.*'[21] 'Everything appears to us in the form of figures; and no figure is charming.' 'What is beauty, anyway?' Picasso asks. 'There's no such thing.'[22] Inflect these dicta with the terrible remark, again made to Gilot, about the great paintings he had done of his partner Dora Maar all through the late 1930s: 'Like any artist, I am primarily the painter of woman, and, for me, woman is essentially a machine for suffering ... I want

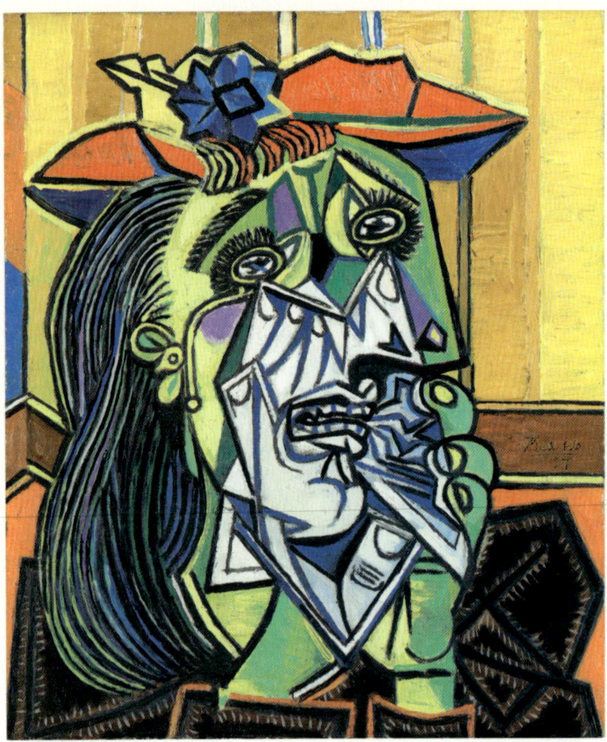

*Weeping Woman, Femme en pleurs* 1937

to underline the anguish of the flesh, which, even in the hour of its triumph, its "beauty", is frightened by the first signs of the alterations of time.'[23]

These seem almost like syllogisms. Sex is at the bottom of things. 'I' is someone else. I am a painter of woman. Woman is essentially a suffering machine. And then finally, in conversation with the poet and filmmaker Geneviève Laporte, Picasso comes up with the concluding aphorism: 'I am a woman.'[24]

'*Je suis une femme*', he says to Laporte. And then he plunges on: 'Any artist is a woman and has to be lesbian. Artists who are pederasts cannot be real artists because they love men. As they are women, they fall back into normalcy.'[25] ('*Tout artiste est une femme et doit être gouine. Les pédérastes artistes ne peuvent pas être de vrais artistes car ils aiment des hommes. Comme ils sont des femmes, ils retombent dans le normal*.')

These are perplexing sentences. However many times I read them, I still get lost in the dance of identities and inversions. And that seems to be the point. Set aside for a moment the ludicrous (period) condescension towards the 'pederast', and stick to the glimpse of Picasso's conception of the structure of desire in representation. Representation, he never tires of reminding us, is Desire's derivative ('When it comes down to it, there is only love'), and therefore dependent on sexual difference; but the driving force of art, he seems to be telling Laporte, is its moment of identification *with* the different, its desire for a woman *as a woman would enact (would feel) the desiring*. As desire for the 'same', in other words – as desire for what a woman already is. But always in the knowledge that this identification-in-representation is a great 'as if' – a breaking of taboo.

Here lies the problem of the homosexual artist, so Picasso imagines. The homosexual artist is drawn to painting men (this seems to be the logic), but from a position – of Woman – that he occupies 'naturally,' continuously, in the everyday life of Desire. Therefore, the act of representation does not disrupt the normal circuit of fantasy – of identification and difference. It confirms it. And this is bad news: it means that the Otherness, the particularity, the unknownness of the object of desire is not jolted into the foreground of perception as the act of representation takes place. It means that the love object does not appear *otherwise* in representation, as seen from somewhere – some other subject-position – that only representation makes possible, and then fleetingly, dangerously. Monstrosity, to repeat, is unknownness.

As an account of fantasy and homosexuality, this smells of Paris in the age of Breton. But as a wild theory of representation and *heterosexuality* – of the one's interference with the other – it is interesting. It has something to tell us about Picasso's life's work.

For good and ill, I mean. The body as it comes to be in a Picasso painting is almost always female, and subject to the force of male fears and wishes. Desire is a will to power. Not without exception, of course; not without there existing a necessary countervailing dream of mutuality, identification, tenderness, care; but these qualities or possibilities are only imaginable as part of – inflections of – a more constant will to manipulate and consume. In such a force field, insofar as the other's body – the other's identity – can be posited at all as self-moving, self-possessed, and in touch with its world, it is in the form of something monstrous, something granted power only grotesquely. The other is conjured up as a *fantastical* threat; and we are always in doubt (and meant to be) whether the monster is just a momentary phantasmagoria, a wish-fulfilment of the male doing the fantasising, or whether it really does register – and try to aestheticise – the moment of dominance that the other, the woman, always actually possesses (and is punished for) in the game of sex.

If this is an explanation for monstrosity, it is not an excuse. And the worst one could say of Picasso's monsters is that they attempt to beautify a world of sexuality whose monstrosity is – the testimonies and statistics go on telling the story – all too real and banal, all too ordinarily acted out.

Nonetheless, I do not think the world would be better without Picasso's two 1932 *Nudes*. Because they, and other nudes like them, are the pictures we have – in some sense *our* pictures, sharing our strange myth of individuality and danger – of bodies belonging fully to a world; pictures of self-possession and self-movement; of elation and abandon and composure. They are images of identity in the making – of the body turning itself to others, without self-loss or abjection or mere ruthless projection of its wishes. In a word, they have life. And I would go further and say – as I tried to initially of *Nude in a Black Armchair* – that in many a painting by Picasso even the 'I am a woman' is realised. Remember that the foiled immediacy of *Nude in a Black Armchair* comes *after* the elaborate, compartmentalised sexual theatre of *Nude, Green Leaves and Bust*. On second thoughts, that is, the Matisse interior is annihilated. 'Unreality' is no more than a moment. The nude in her infinite distance and otherness confronts us.

This puts everyone at risk. The disappearance of room-space in *Nude in a Black Armchair* is as much a threat to the woman's sleeping self-enclosure as it is to our reaching out, imaginatively, to possess her. Desiring her *as she might desire herself* – being suddenly in a space or a circuit of desiring where 'here and there', 'he and she', 'subject and object' are consumed by sheer chilling mauve presence – this is hard to bear. 'Everything is unknown, everything is the enemy,' Picasso said to Malraux.[26] Sex and hostility will never be disentangled. The black armchair is death. The leaves are absurd flaccid penises. Misogyny is part of the picture (with always the hysterical glorification of 'Woman' its other face). No doubt even Picasso's 'Every artist is a woman' could be read as simply another male appropriation *of* the female for the same old purposes.

But I think that this would be ultimately too defensive a reaction – too rejectionist, too despairing. I believe that the viewer of *Nude in a Black Armchair* is truly being invited – maybe even manoeuvred – into a place where the 'normal' to-and-fro and passive-and-active of gender do not quite operate. The body possesses us – *us* just as much as the person it belongs to. Hair and white flower float free of their normal connotations: nobody's fingers will ever quite hold them. Desire is not ours any longer. And that does amount, in a world of subjections, to a glimpse of a better life.

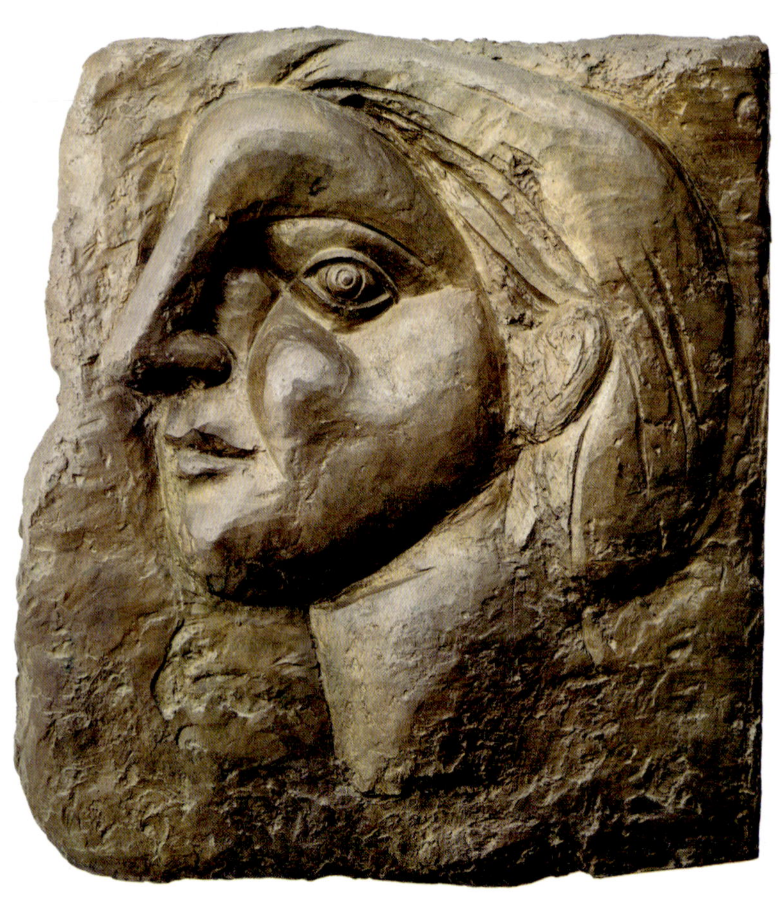



*Head of a Woman, Tête de femme de profil*; Boisgeloup 1931

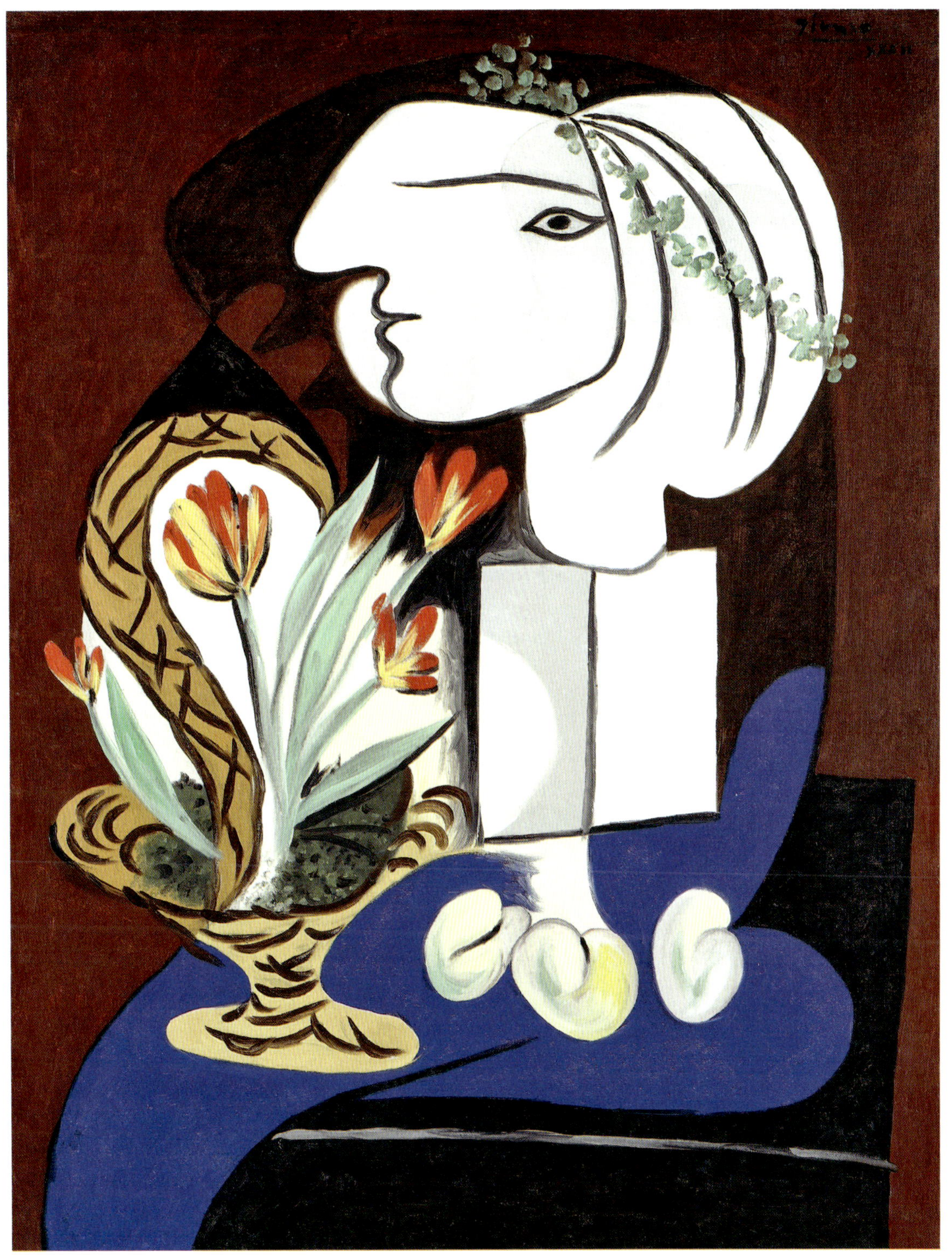

*Still Life with Tulips, Nature morte aux tulipes*

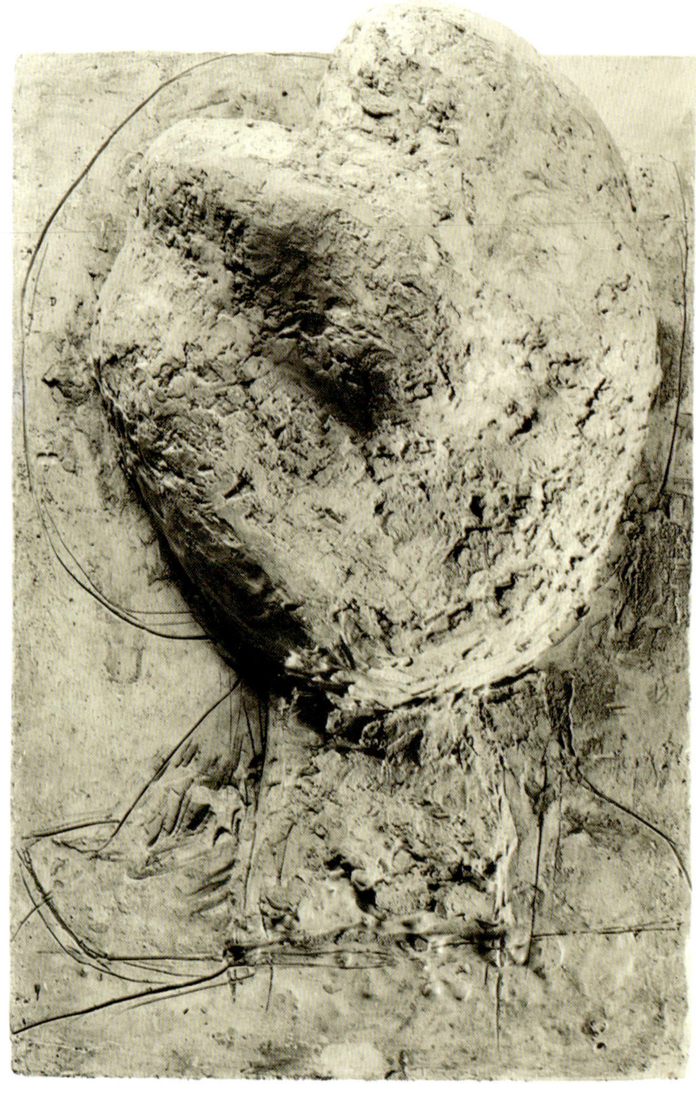



*Head of a Woman, Tête de femme*

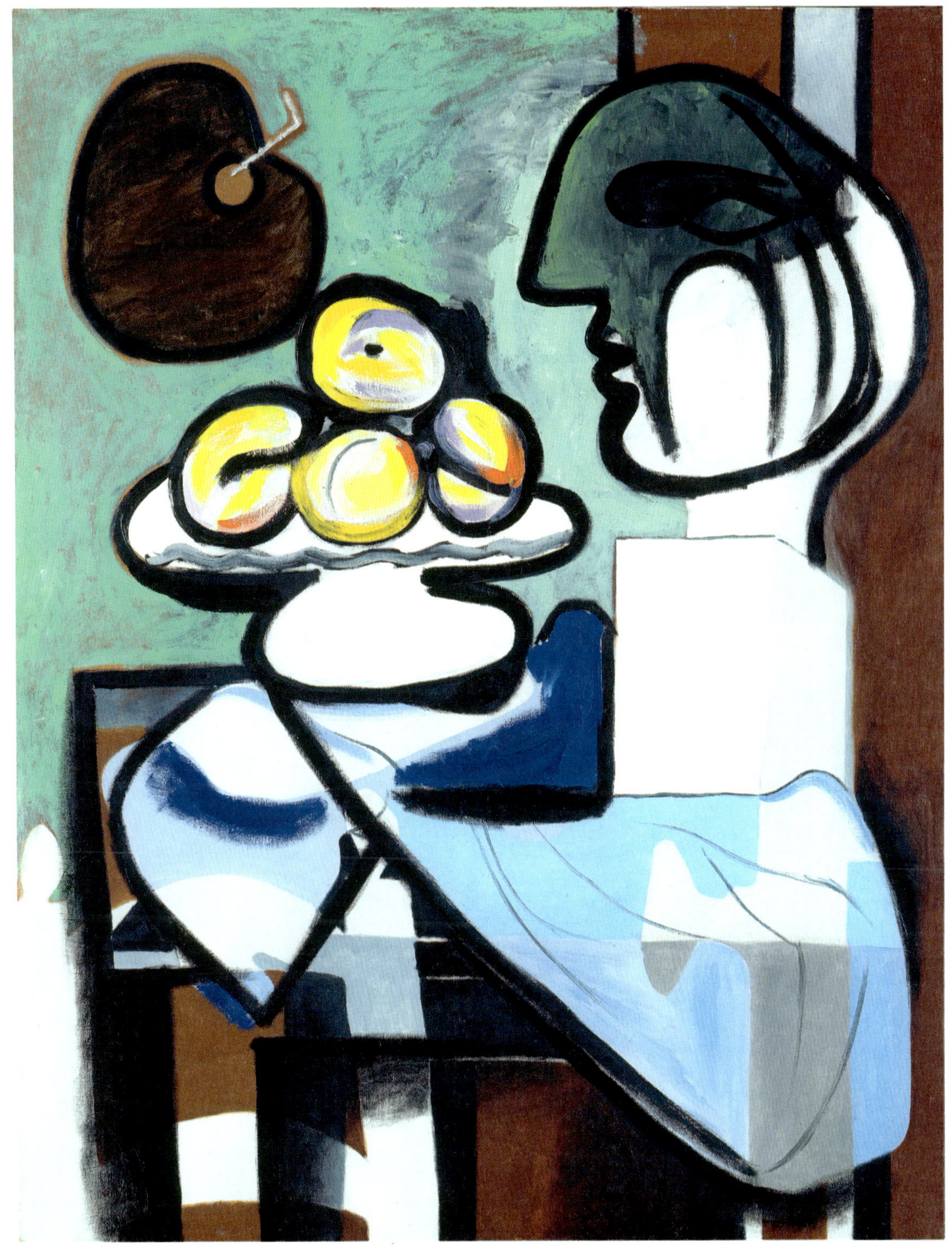

*Still Life: Bust, Cup and Palette, Nature morte: buste, coupe et palette*

'Two days ago, at his place, we saw two paintings he had just done. Two nudes that are perhaps the greatest, most moving things he has produced … We came away from there stunned.'

Daniel-Henry Kahnweiler in a letter to Michel Leiris, 1932

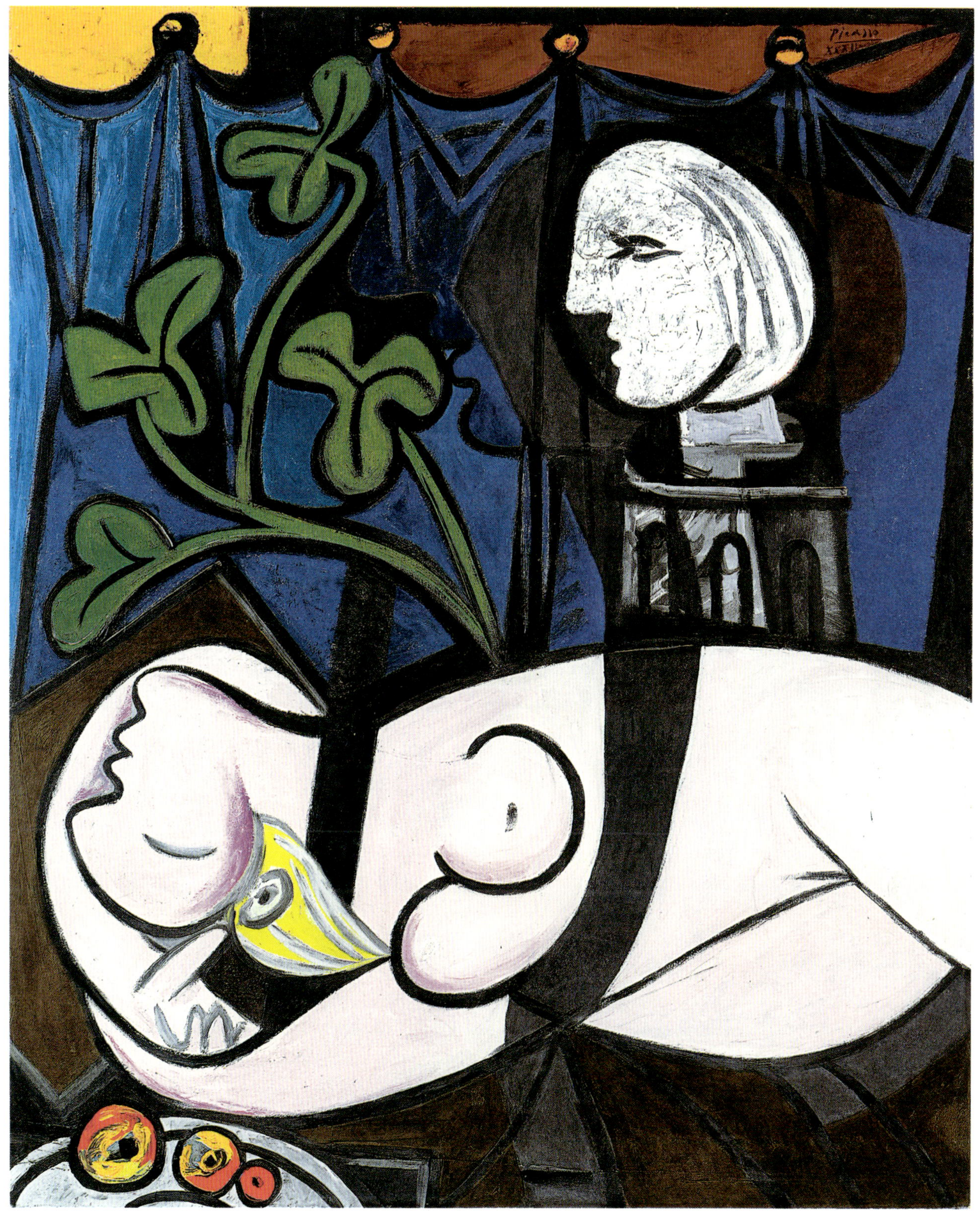

*Nude, Green Leaves and Bust, Femme nue, feuilles et buste*

'It seems as though a satyr who had just killed a woman could have painted this picture.'

Daniel-Henry Kahnweiler in a letter to Michel Leiris, 1932

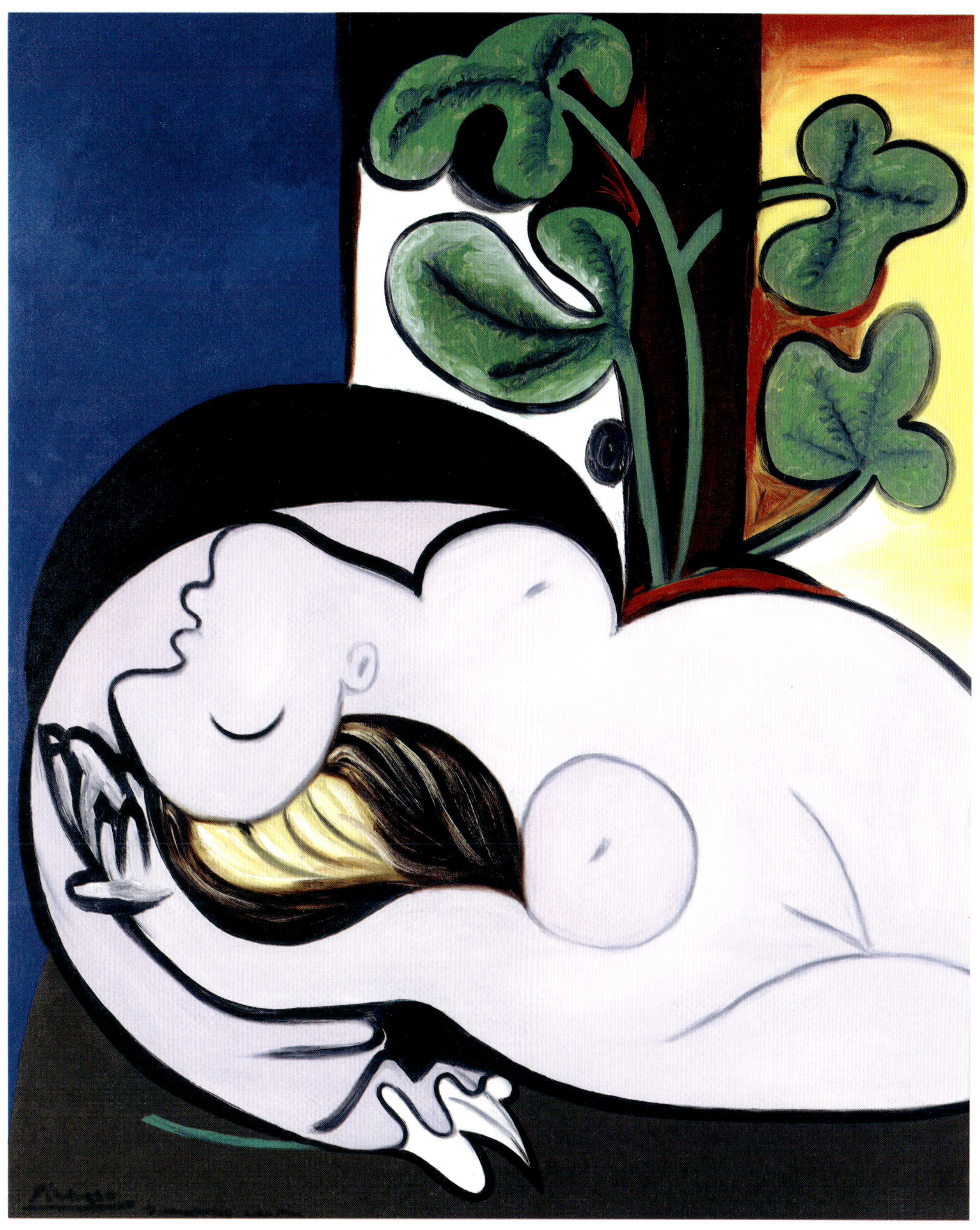

*Nude in a Black Armchair, Nu au fauteuil noir*

'I would love to paint like a blind man who pictures an arse by the way it feels.'

Picasso, reported by Daniel-Henry Kahnweiler in a letter to Michel Leiris, 1932

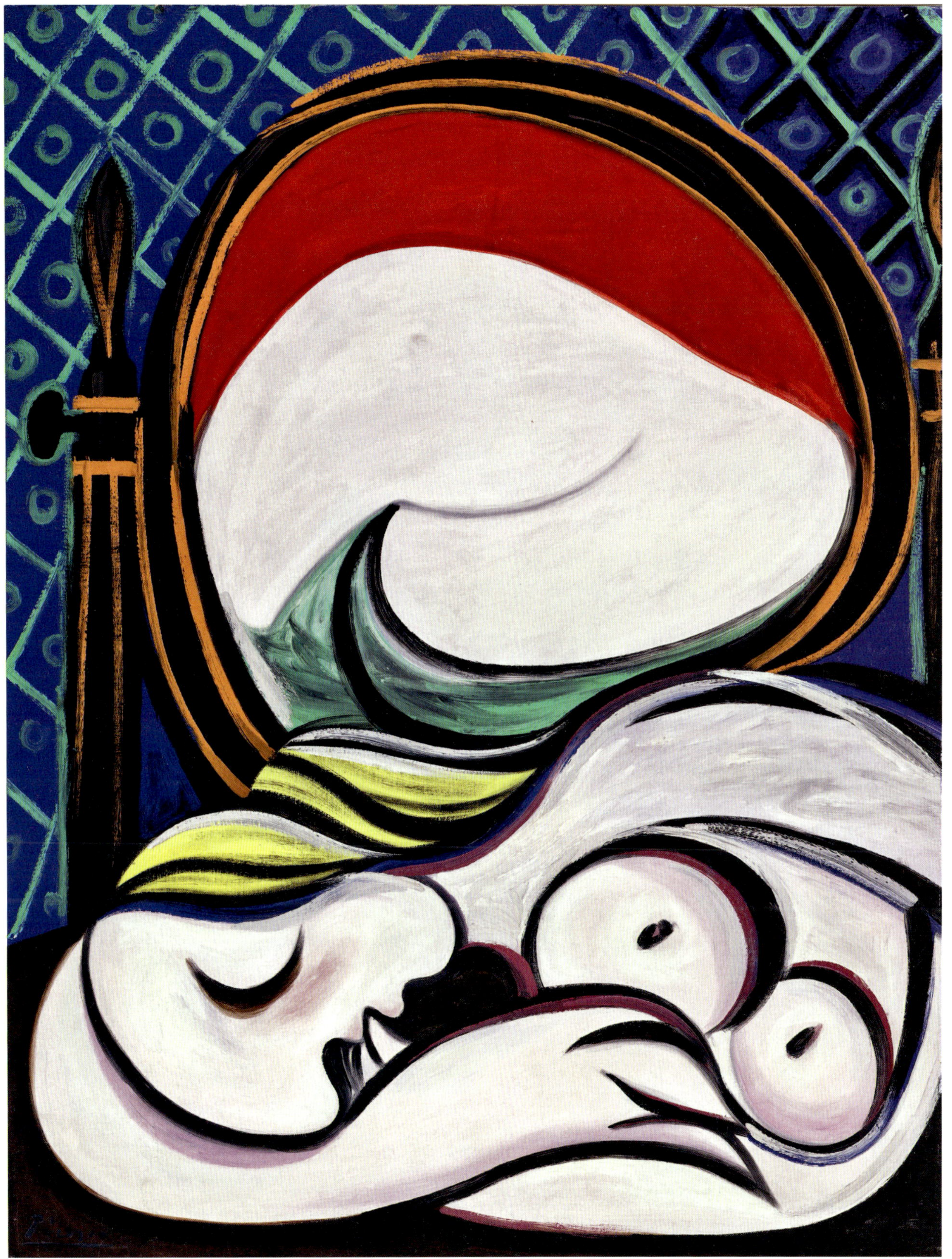

*The Mirror, Le Miroir*

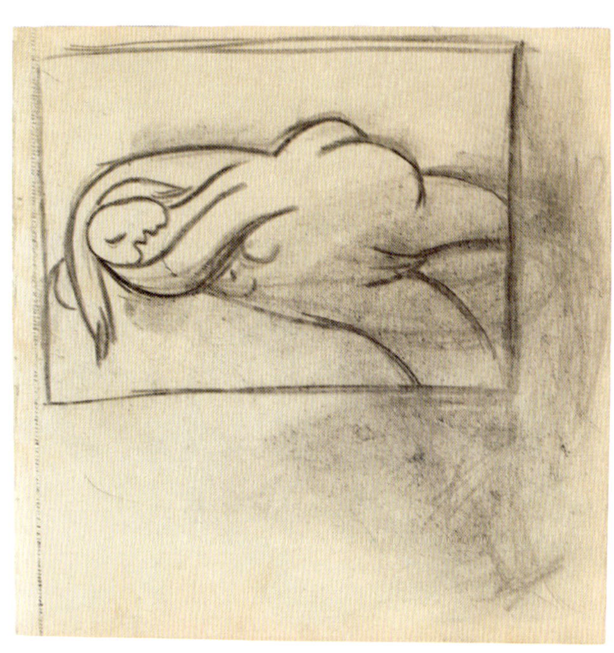

Drawing of *Sleeping Nude* from Sketchbook no.40

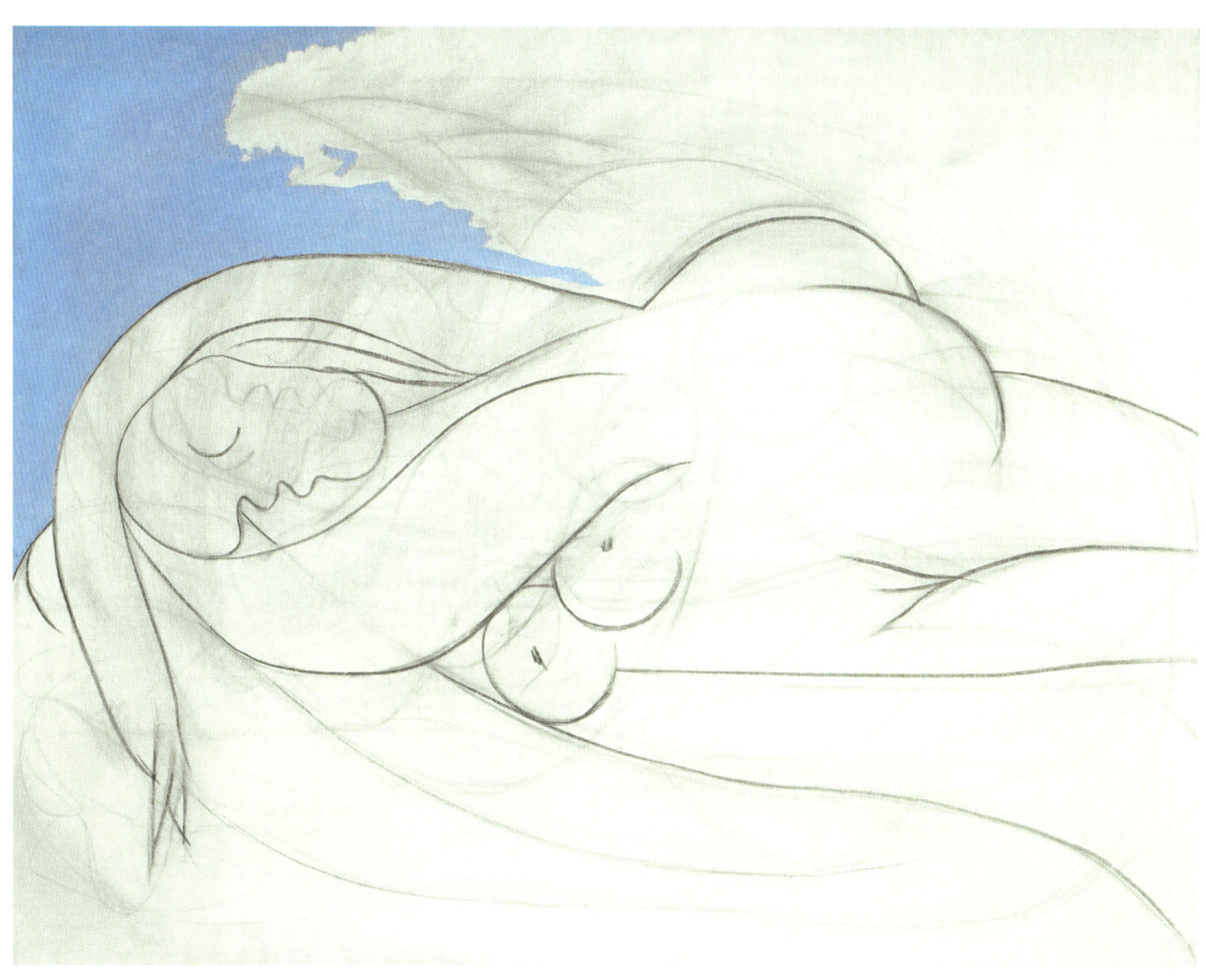

*Sleeping Nude, La Dormeuse (Femme nue couchée)*

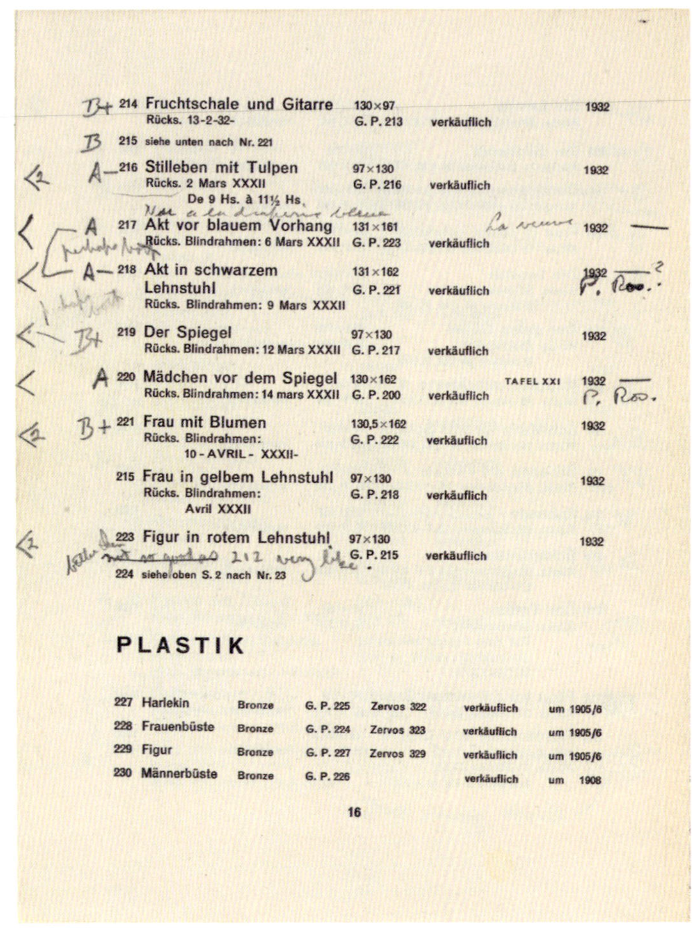

B+ 214 Fruchtschale und Gitarre 130×97 1932
Rücks. 13-2-32- G. P. 213 verkäuflich

B 215 siehe unten nach Nr. 221

A– 216 Stilleben mit Tulpen 97×130 1932
Rücks. 2 Mars XXXII G. P. 216 verkäuflich
De 9 Hs. à 11½ Hs.

A 217 Akt vor blauem Vorhang 131×161 1932
Rücks. Blindrahmen: 6 Mars XXXII G. P. 223 verkäuflich

A– 218 Akt in schwarzem Lehnstuhl 131×162 1932
Rücks. Blindrahmen: 9 Mars XXXII G. P. 221 verkäuflich

B+ 219 Der Spiegel 97×130 1932
Rücks. Blindrahmen: 12 Mars XXXII G. P. 217 verkäuflich

A 220 Mädchen vor dem Spiegel 130×162 TAFEL XXI 1932
Rücks. Blindrahmen: 14 mars XXXII G. P. 200 verkäuflich

B+ 221 Frau mit Blumen 130,5×162 1932
Rücks. Blindrahmen: 10 - AVRIL - XXXII- G. P. 222 verkäuflich

215 Frau in gelbem Lehnstuhl 97×130 1932
Rücks. Blindrahmen: Avril XXXII G. P. 218 verkäuflich

223 Figur in rotem Lehnstuhl 97×130 1932
G. P. 215 verkäuflich

224 siehe oben S. 2 nach Nr. 23

**PLASTIK**

| | | | | | | |
|---|---|---|---|---|---|---|
| 227 | Harlekin | Bronze | G. P. 225 | Zervos 322 | verkäuflich | um 1905/6 |
| 228 | Frauenbüste | Bronze | G. P. 224 | Zervos 323 | verkäuflich | um 1905/6 |
| 229 | Figur | Bronze | G. P. 227 | Zervos 329 | verkäuflich | um 1905/6 |
| 230 | Männerbüste | Bronze | G. P. 226 | | verkäuflich | um 1908 |

16

Page 16 from the catalogue for the Picasso exhibition at Kunsthaus Zürich, with qualitative annotations by Margaret Scolari Barr, 1932

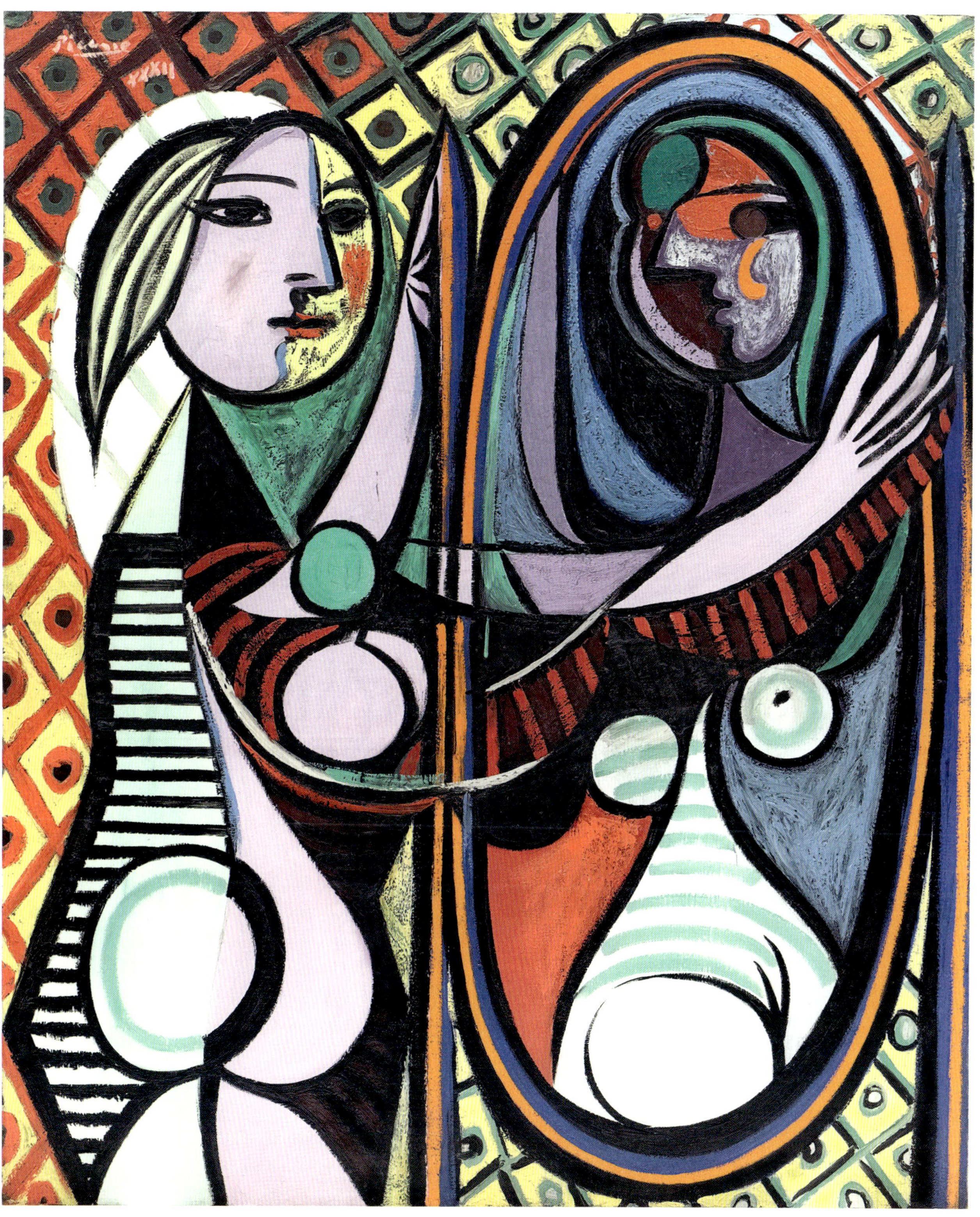

*Girl before a Mirror, Jeune Fille devant un miroir*

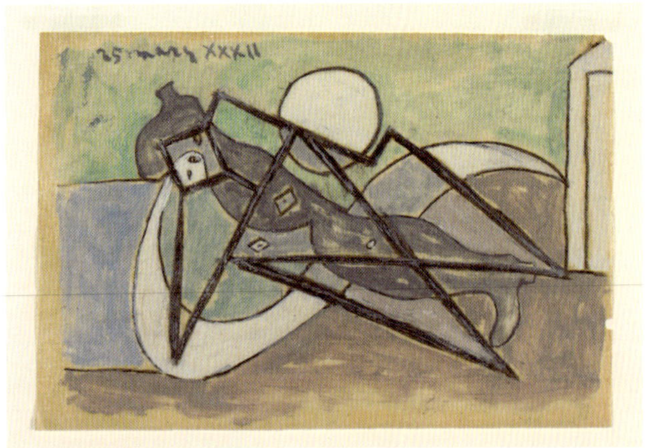


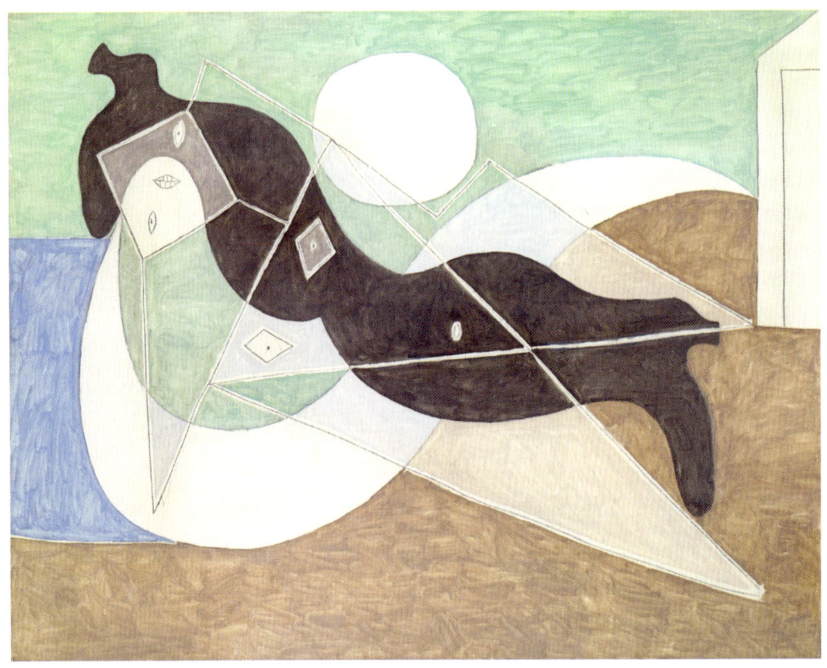

*Reclining Nude Sunbathing on the Beach, Femme étendue au soleil sur la plage*

*Reclining Woman on the Beach, Femme étendue sur la plage*

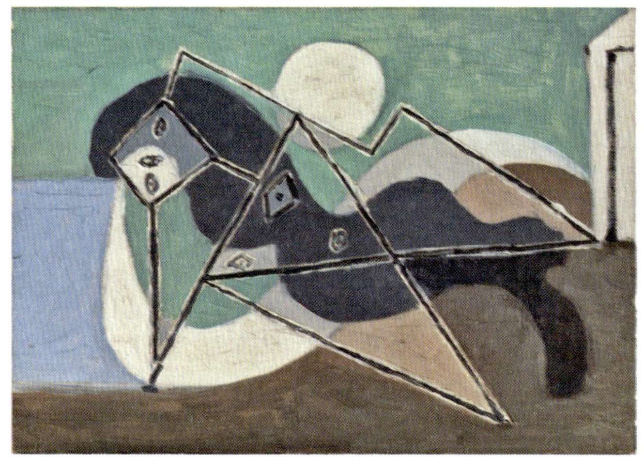

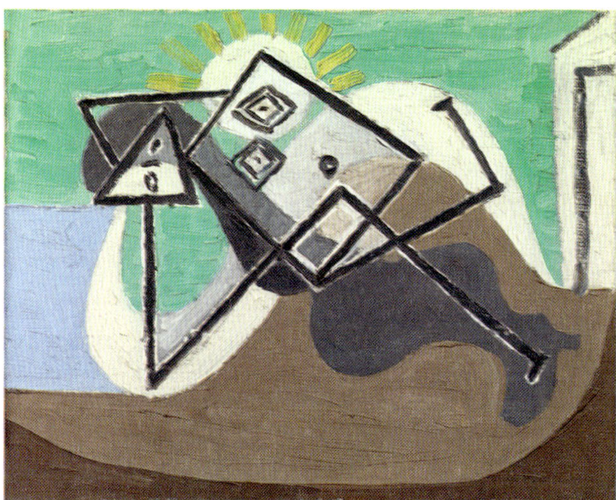

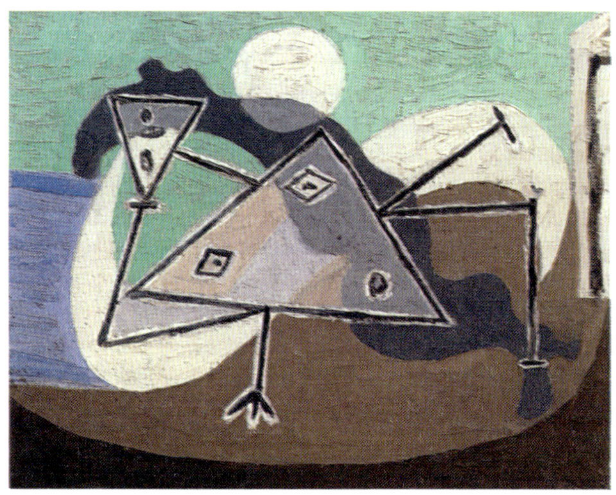

*Reclining Woman on the Beach, Femme nue couchée au soleil sur la plage*
*Reclining Woman on the Beach, Femme étendue sur la plage*
*Reclining Woman on the Beach, Femme étendue sur la plage*

## 'No, I refuse to have any arseholes in my gallery.'

Paul Rosenberg, refusing to exhibit the series of *Reclining Women* in his gallery

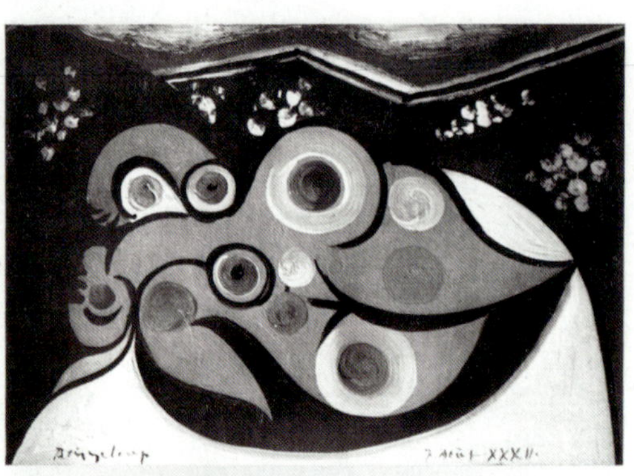

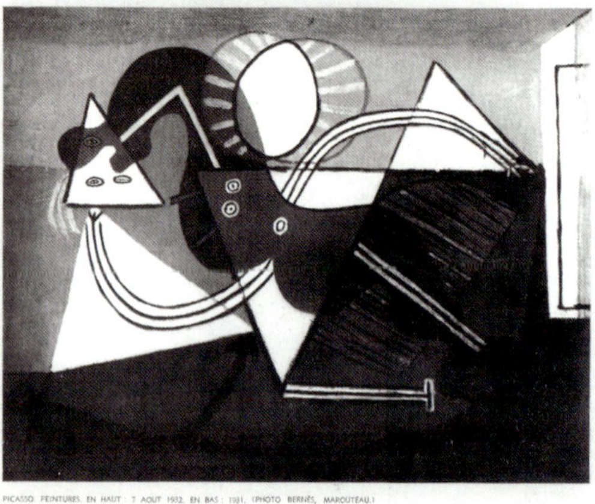

PICASSO. PEINTURES. EN HAUT : 7 AOUT 1932. EN BAS : 1931. (PHOTO BERNÈS, MAROUTEAU.)

*Cahiers d'Art* special issue on Picasso, 1936, p.61, with a reproduction of *Woman on the Beach*

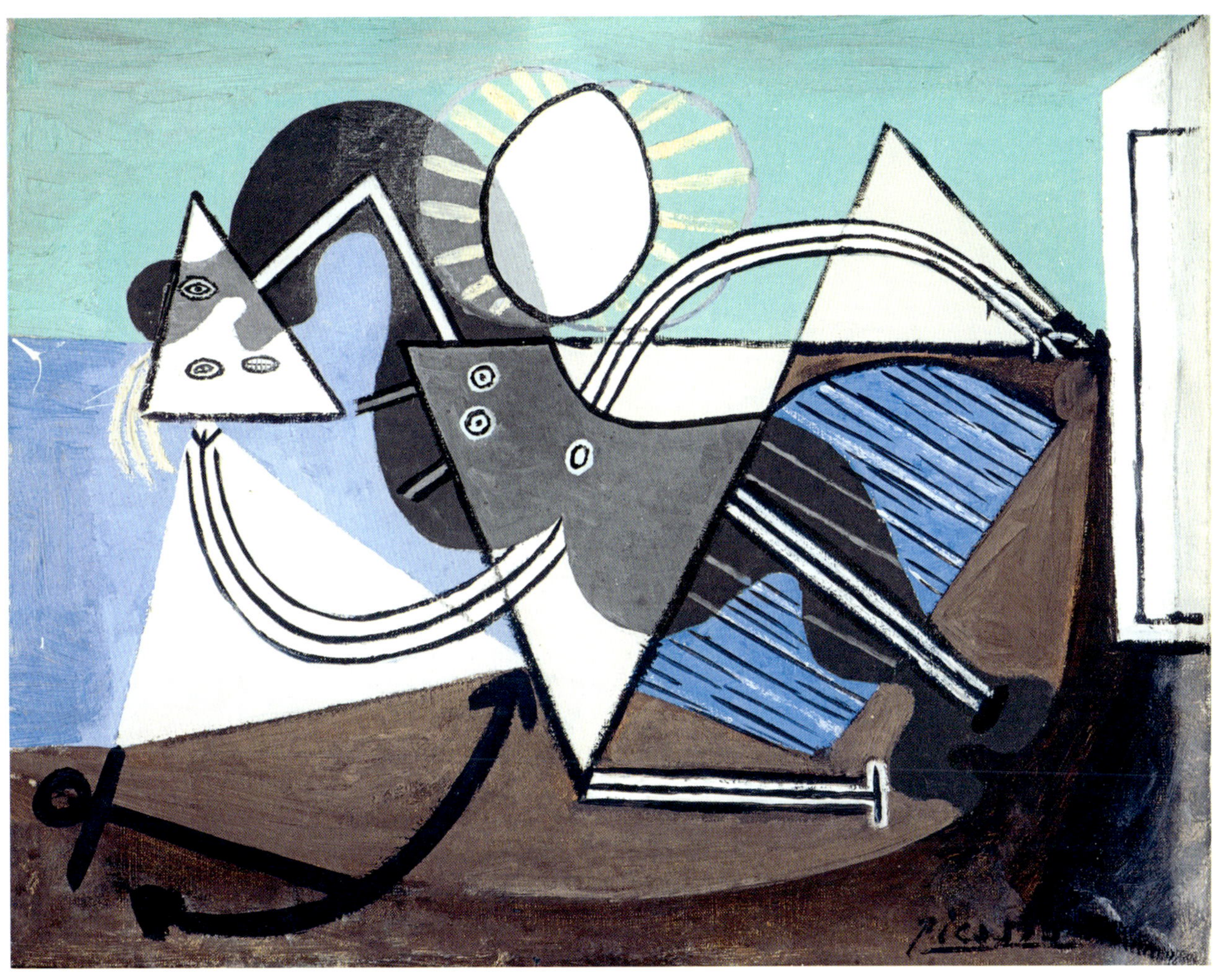

*Woman on the Beach, Nu sur la plage*

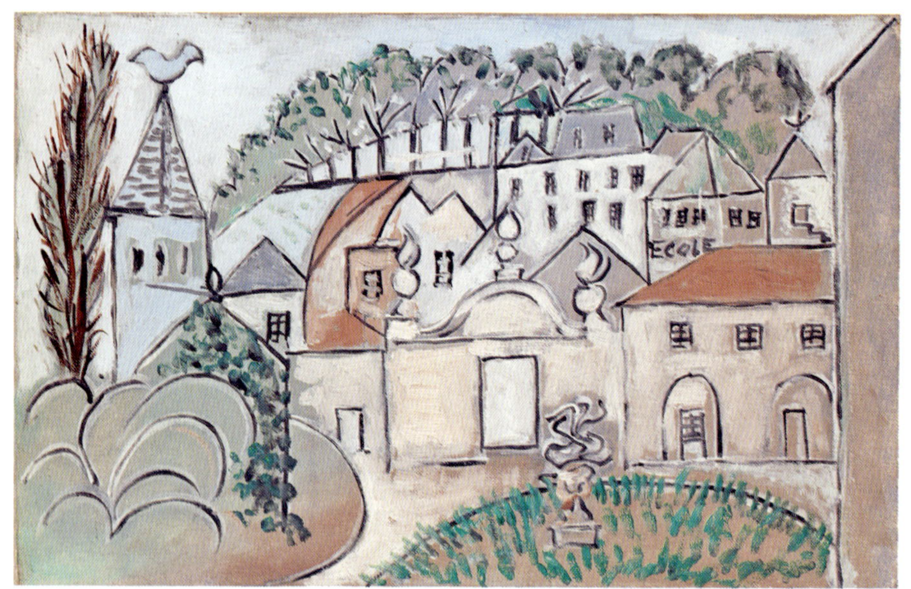


*View of Boisgeloup, Vue de Boisgeloup*

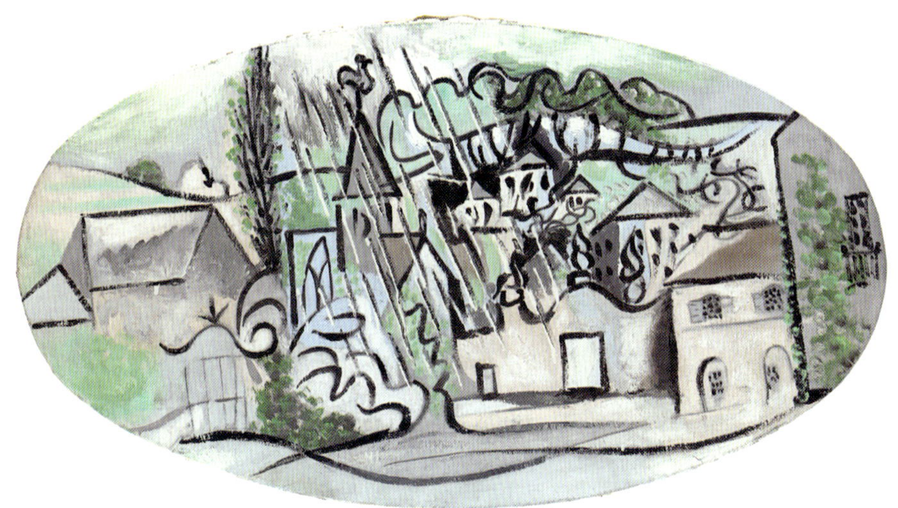

*Boisgeloup in the Rain, Boisgeloup sous la pluie*

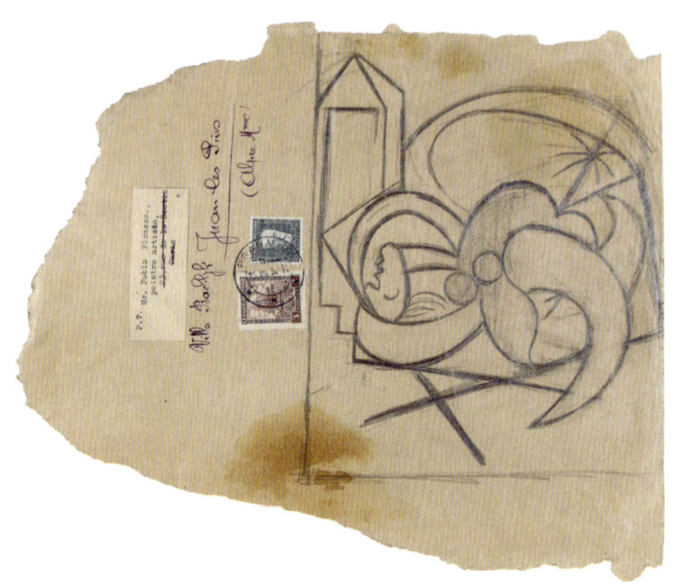



*Bather with Parasol, Baigneuse au parasol* 1932

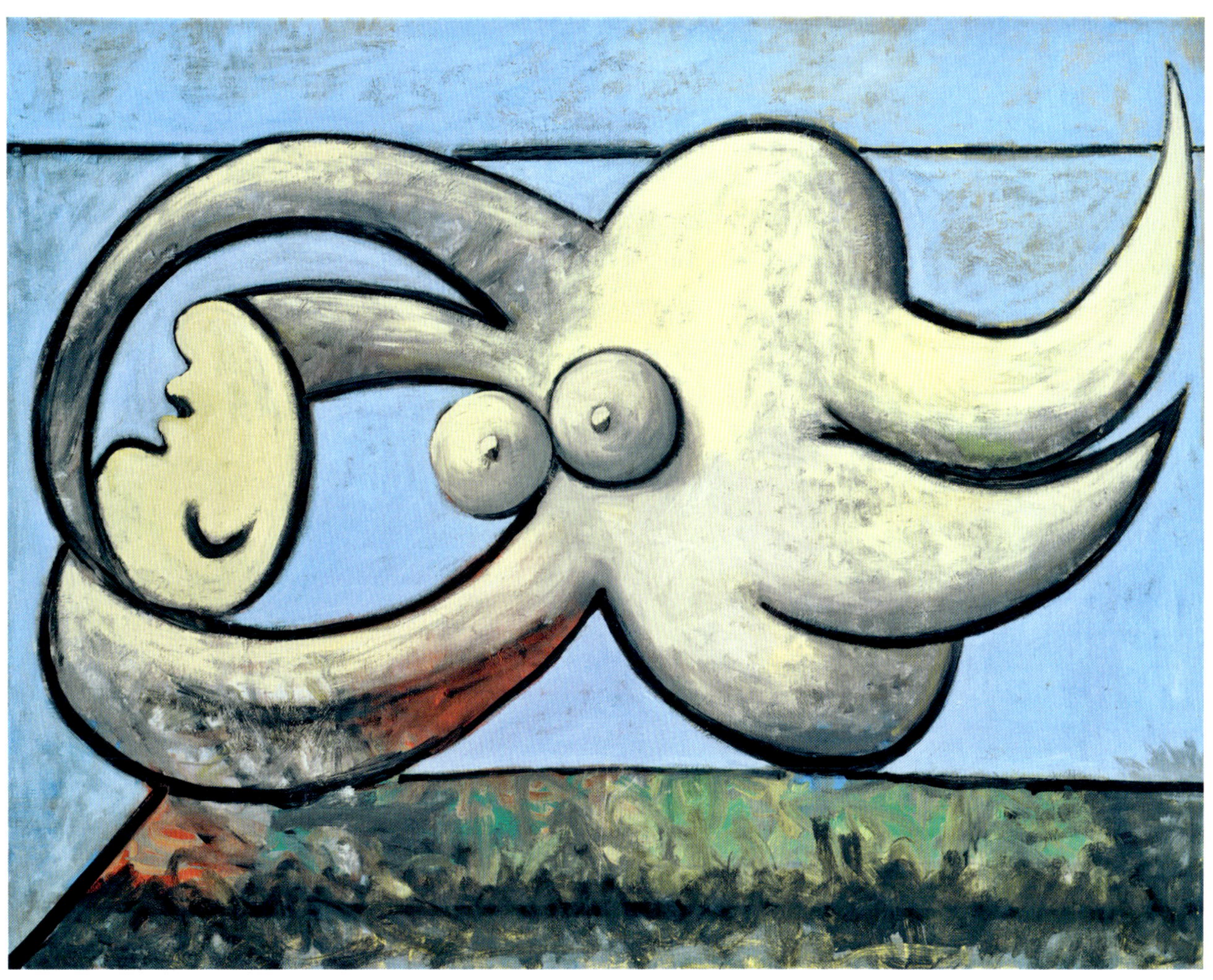

*Reclining Nude, Femme nue couchée*

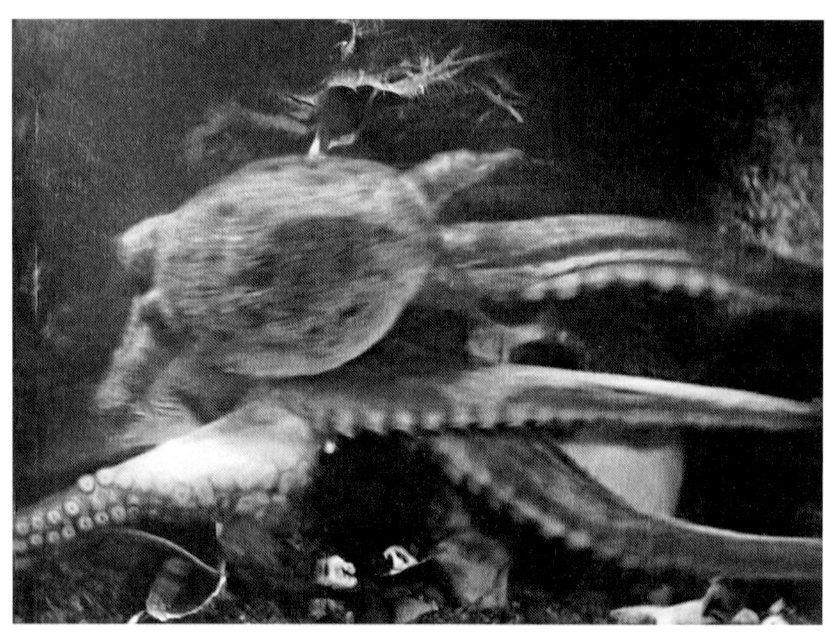



Film still from *The Octopus (La Pieuvre)*, dir. Jean Painlevé 1928

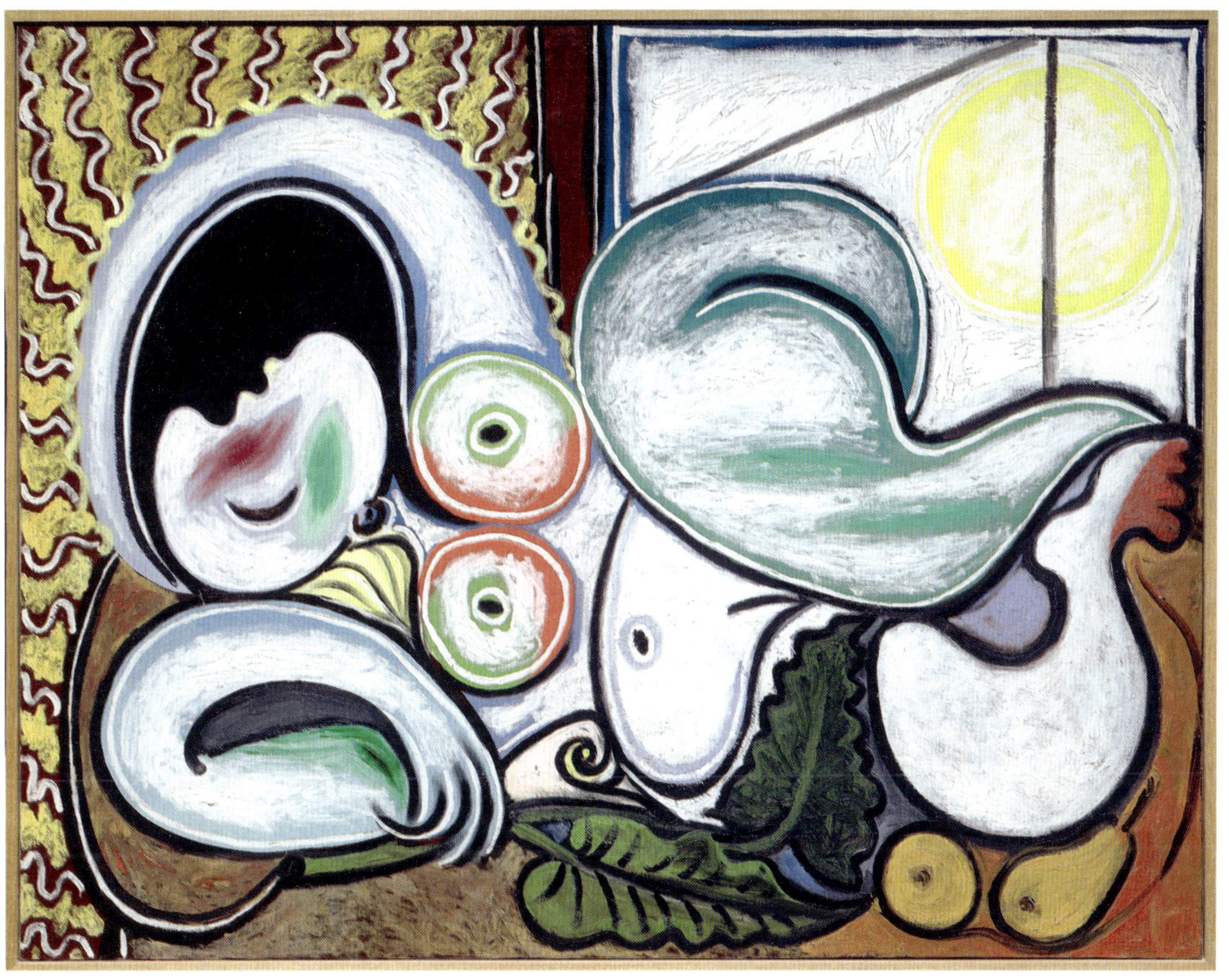

*Reclining Nude, Nu couché*

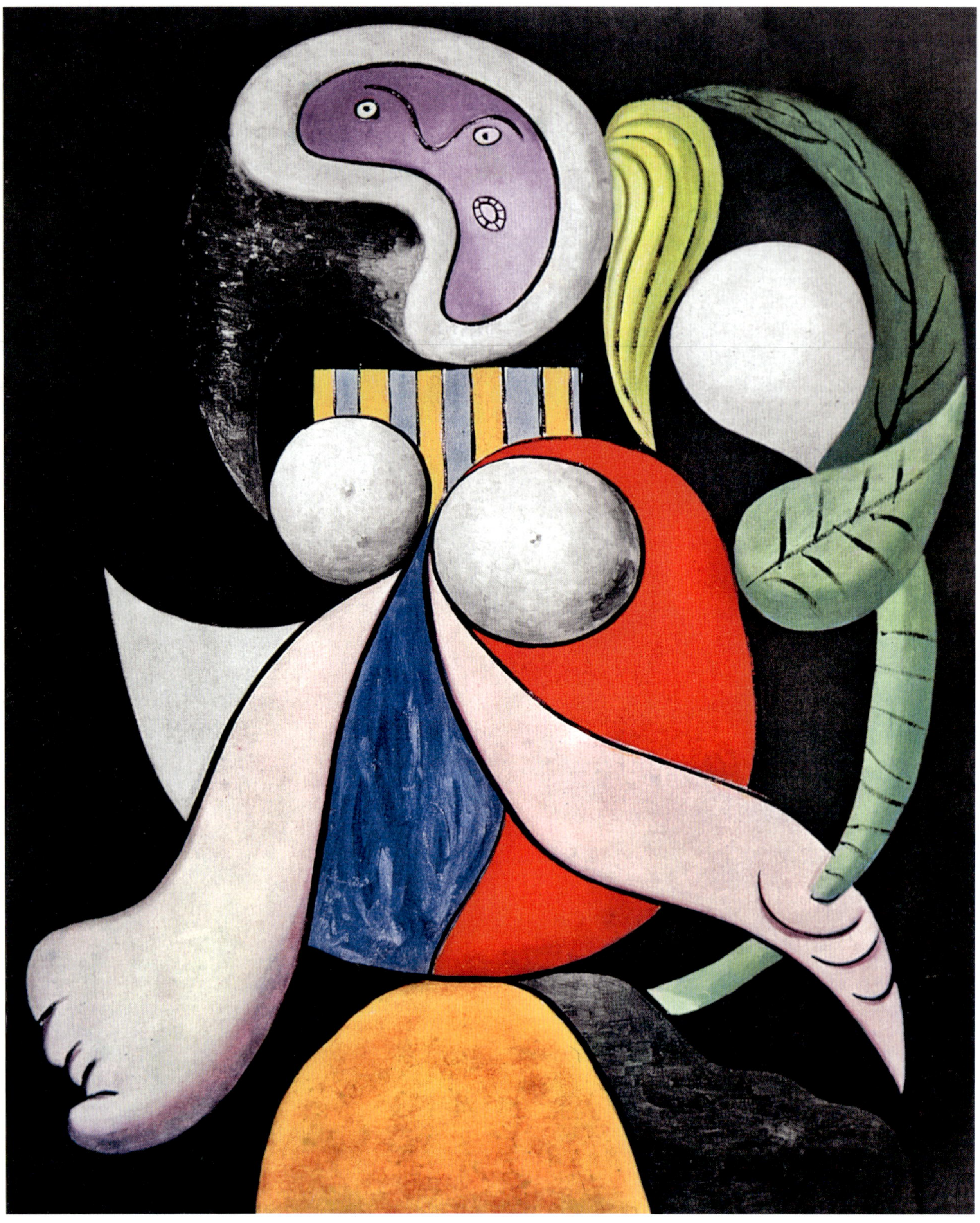

 *Woman with a Flower, Femme à la fleur*

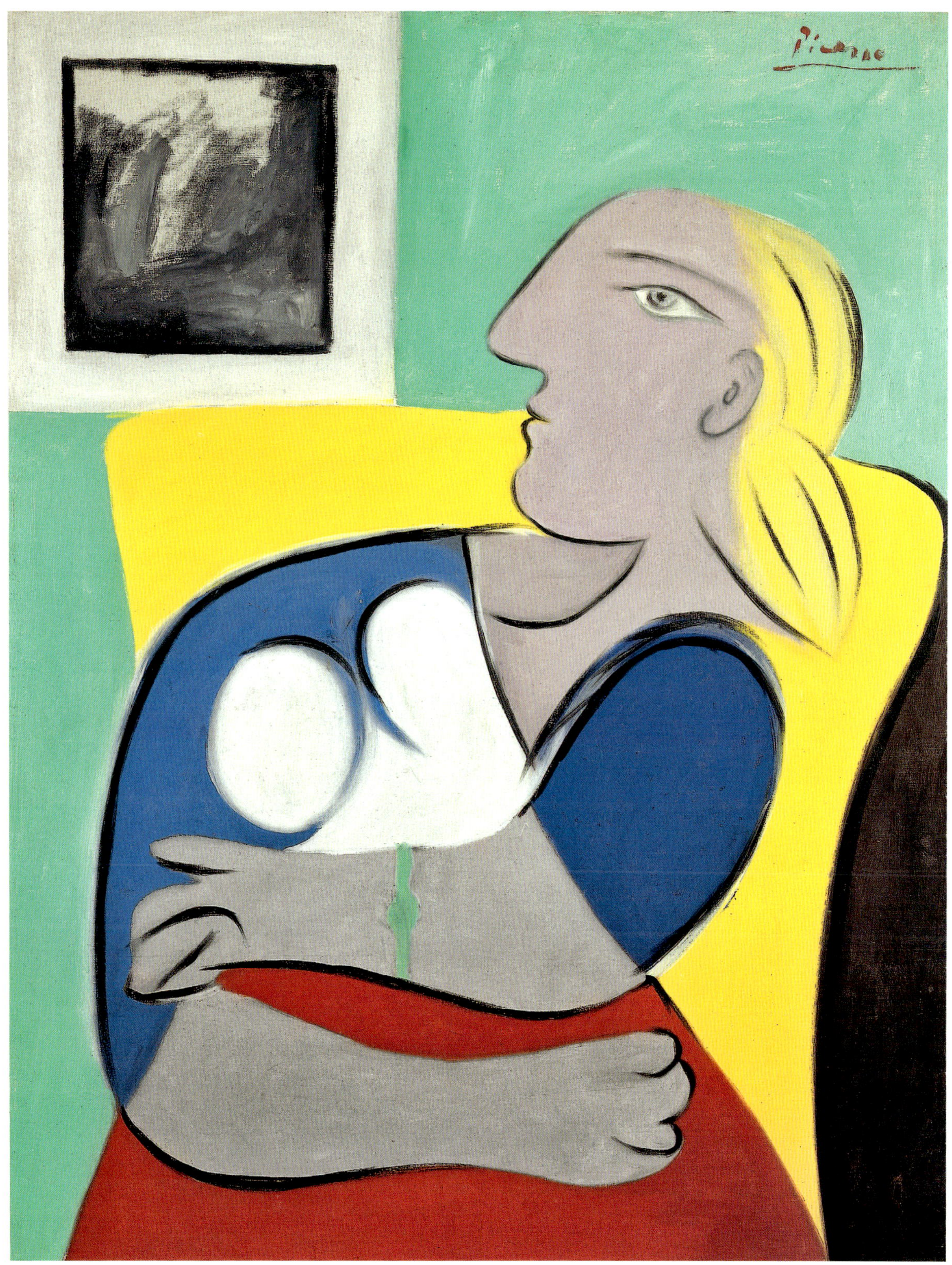

*Woman in a Yellow Armchair, Femme dans un fauteuil jaune*

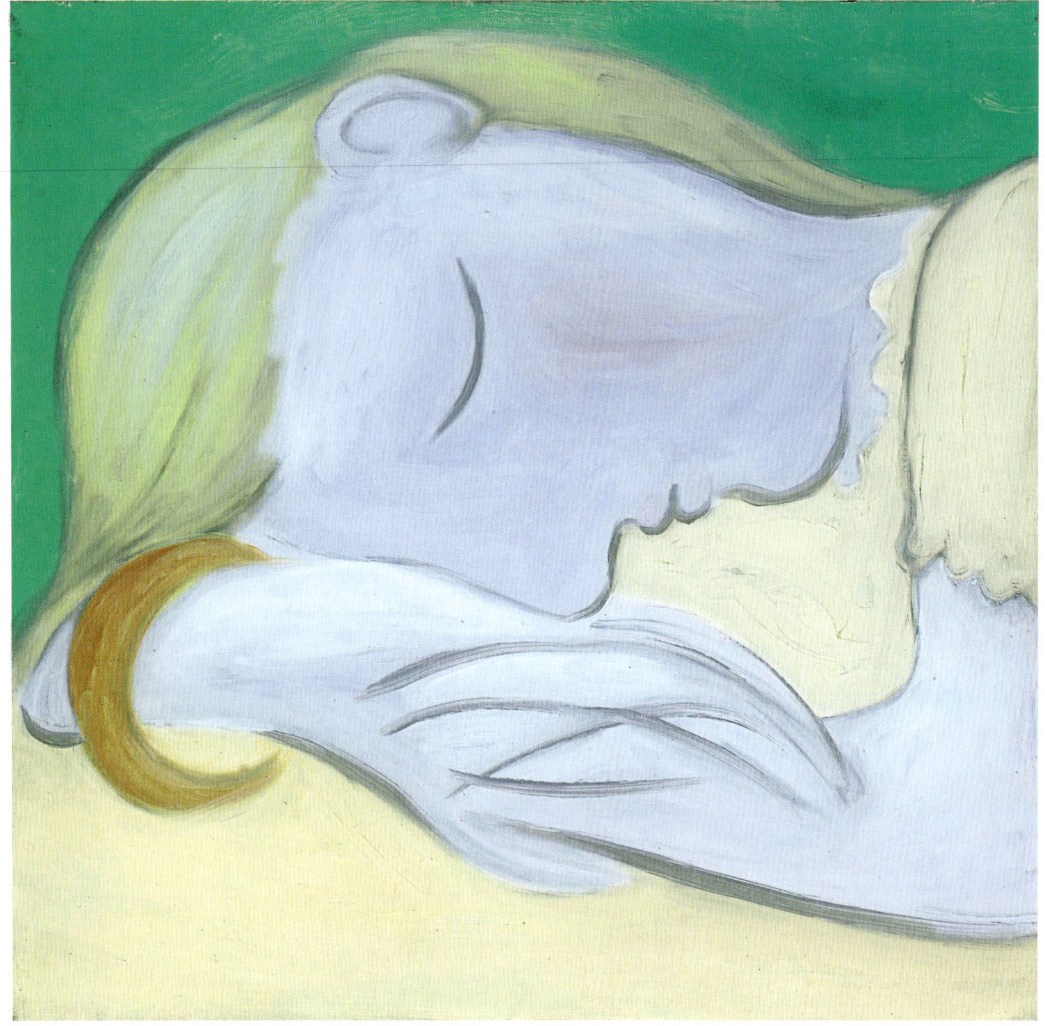



*Woman Sleeping*, *Femme endormie*

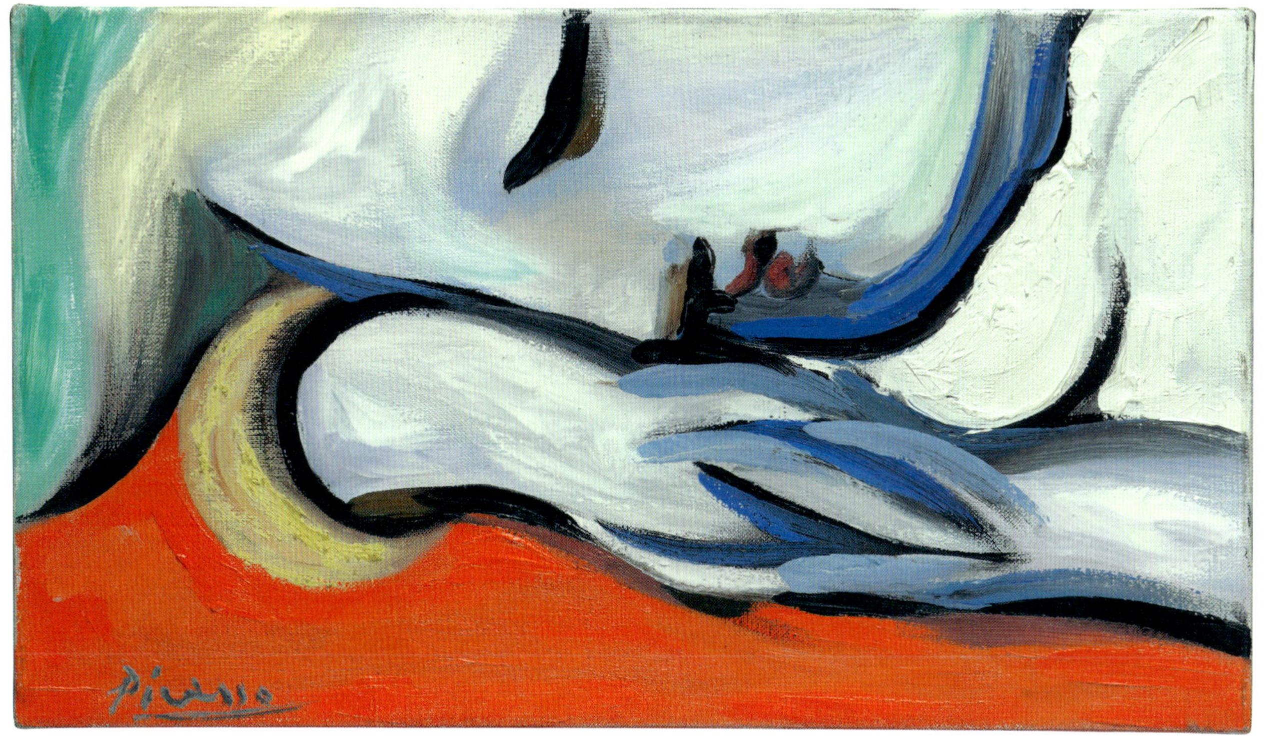


*Rest*, *Le Repos*

# An Art without Past or Future: The Summer Retrospective

Alma Mikulinsky

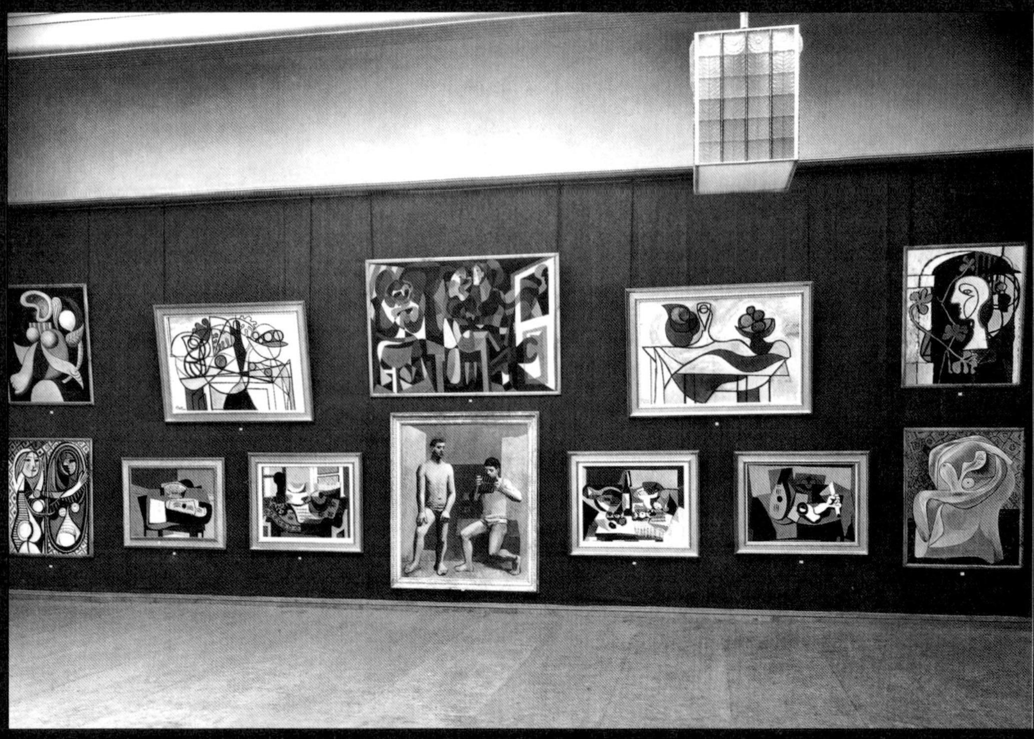

Above and opposite: Views of the Grande Salle, *Picasso* exhibition, Galeries Georges Petit, 16 June to 30 July 1932

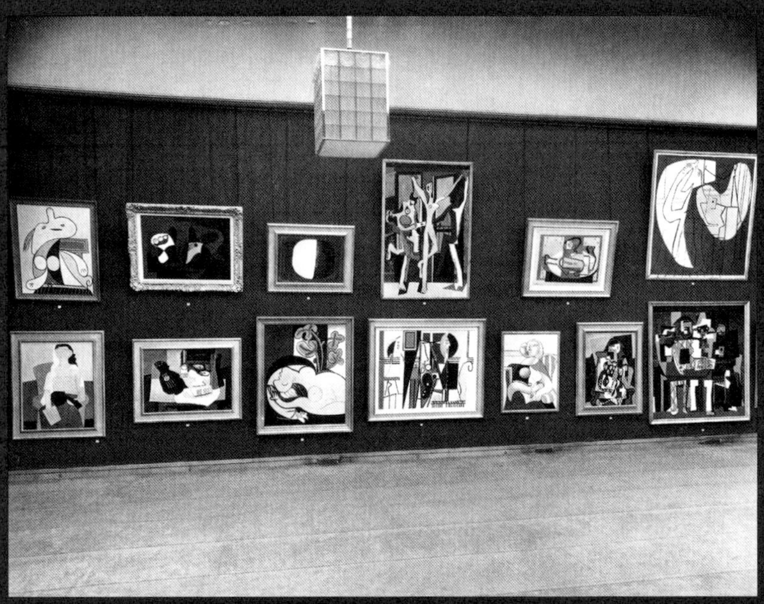

On 16 June 1932 a glitzy private view marked the opening of Pablo Picasso's first large-scale retrospective, an exhibition of 225 paintings, seven sculptures and six illustrated books. These artworks came from all stages of the artist's thirty-year career, and ranged in style from the early neo-impressionist experiments through the blue and rose periods to cubism and neo-classicism, right up to his latest paintings – most noticeably the seated figures and sensual nudes from the earlier months of the year. Margaret Scolari Barr, the art historian, wife and emissary of Alfred H. Barr, Jr, Director of the newly founded Museum of Modern Art in New York, observed that 'the Picasso show at the Galeries Georges Petit … is in part a retrospective but full of recent pictures',[1] unlike the exhibition Barr concurrently hoped to stage in New York, of which more later.

The Paris exhibition took place at the lavish Galeries Georges Petit, a nineteenth-century establishment with new owners, the dealers Etienne Bignou and Gaston and Josse Bernheim-Jeune. Instead of the clean and consistent design expected of modern art spaces, each of the gallery's five rooms was designed differently: one room did indeed have plain light-coloured walls and modish rounded light fixtures, yet another was adorned with floral wallpaper, a dado rail and a marble fireplace with decorated mantelpiece. The largest hall, the Grande Salle, had tall ceilings, modern rectangular light

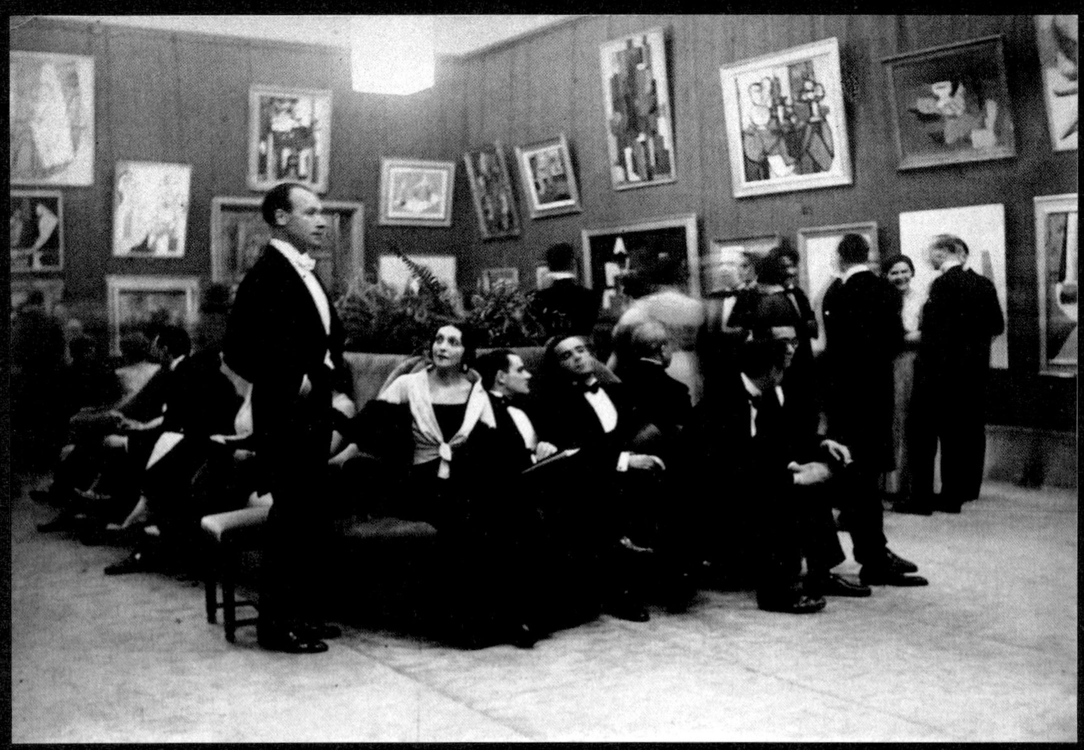

Guests in the Grande Salle on the opening night of the exhibition, 16 June 1932. Photograph by Rogi André

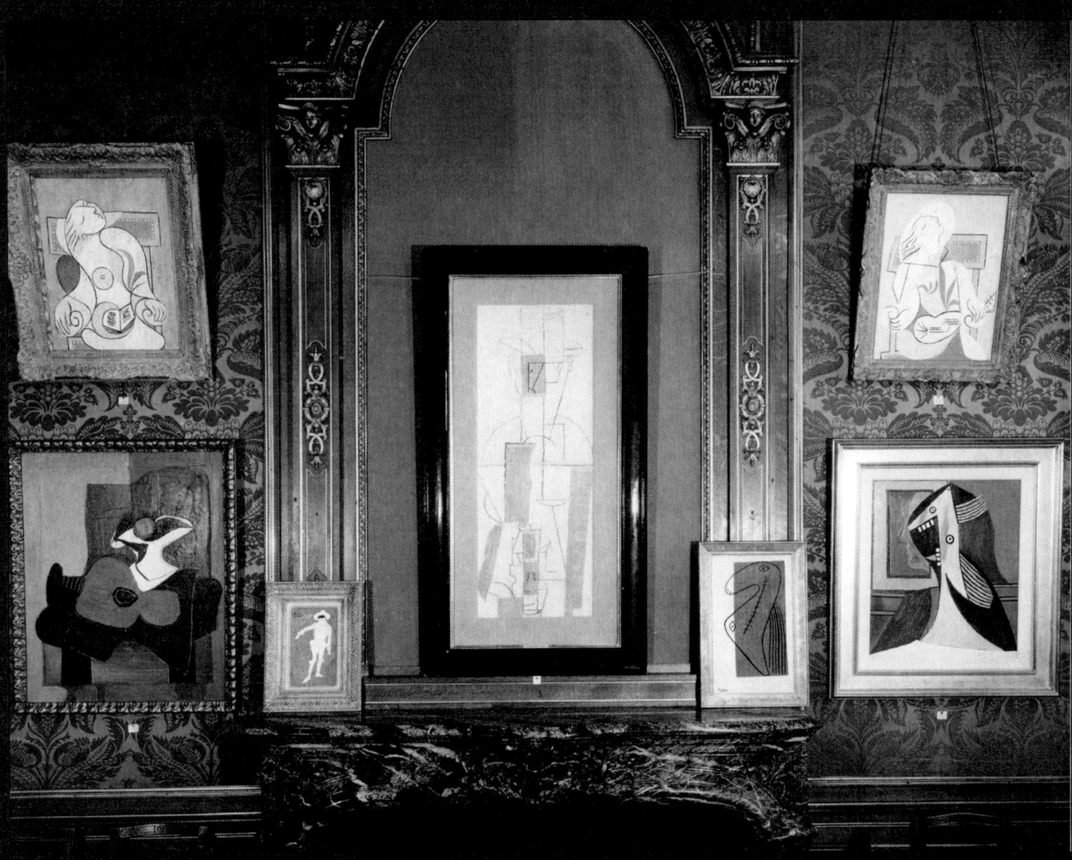

Installation view at Galeries Georges Petit

fixtures and 'royal purple' walls, as well as a spacious seating area with a luxuriant fern at its centre. Despite the eclectic mix of styles, the gallery was considered, at least by some, 'the most beautiful space in Paris.'[2]

Originally the Petit gallery had specialised in impressionist art, but its focus was now contemporary. When it re-opened in the summer of 1931, it did so with a large survey exhibition of the work of Henri Matisse. Picasso's retrospective opened precisely one year later and ran from mid-June to the end of July. Given the competitiveness between the two artists and their towering position within the international discourse around modern art, it is more than likely that one exhibition prompted the other.[3] Other projects – including repeat invitations for a large-scale presentation at the 1932 Venice Biennale, an exhibition at the Prado and plans for a retrospective at the only recently established Museum of Modern Art, New York – all fell by the wayside as Picasso chose to take on spaces that his rival had filled just recently.[4]

Unlike Matisse, who was not involved in the planning of his show, Picasso engaged closely with the project, effectively acting as the exhibition's curator. Picasso selected the artworks (many of which arrived from his own private collection as well as that of one of his strongest collectors at the time, the German industrialist Gottfried Friedrich Reber) and personally arranged them in the space.[5] A desire to outdo Matisse was suggested, not only by the exhibition's size but by its chronological range. Picasso's show was almost twice as large as Matisse's, and was a well-balanced retrospective across his career, as if to counter Matisse's focus on works from the first half of the 1920s (leading some journalists to criticise Matisse's show as insufficiently representative). But the most obvious difference between the two exhibitions was in their layout, with Picasso avoiding the modern convention of art display – equally spaced paintings arranged sequentially – that Matisse's show had followed.

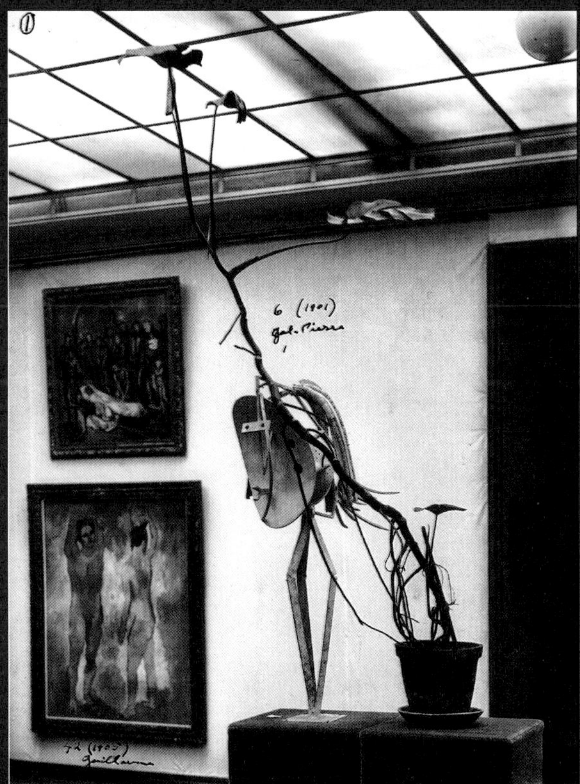


Photograph in the Salle Carrée showing the philodendron, with annotations by Margaret Scolari Barr identifying the paintings on the wall behind according to their catalogue entry

Picasso refused to order his works chronologically. This made it impossible for viewers to discern a linear narrative of changing styles; they were equally unable to distinguish 'periods' of his production. This also went against the format of two book-length publications on Picasso that were published in 1932 by the Greek-French writer, editor and publisher Christian Zervos. Zervos devoted a special issue of the art magazine *Cahiers d'Art* to Picasso's retrospective, in which over 150 artworks in different styles were chronologically reproduced, with the occasional contemporary work inserted into the flow.[6] Simultaneously, he also released the first volume of his ambitious Picasso catalogue raisonné – the first of its kind to be devoted to a living artist.[7] This volume illustrated 384 artworks from 1895 to 1906, spanning the artist's earliest paintings to his proto-cubist era, in a linear arrangement that largely emphasised process through sequencing and chronology.[8] Since this single volume presented more works than the Petit show, writer (and future French culture minister) André Malraux claimed, provocatively, that photo-albums were superior to retrospective exhibitions as they could present an artist's lifework in its completeness. For Malraux the catalogue could potentially change Picasso's reception, claiming that 'the headlong sequence of works is more important than any single one of them, even the best.'[9]

Chronology was soon to become the standard for Picasso's exhibitions, as could be seen both in the unrealised retrospective at the Museum of Modern Art planned by Barr and in the Swiss iteration of the Georges Petit show, which took place in the autumn of 1932 at Zurich's Kunsthaus. This was hung not by Picasso but by Kunsthaus director Wilhelm Wartmann and painter Sigismund Righini, who was also president of the exhibition commission.[10] Despite the difference in displayed works – while the Zurich show exhibited more or less the same paintings as Paris, the planned MoMA show would have relied on borrowing from American collections – both shows shared a similar organising principle: a sequential narrative of Picasso's successive periods and diverse styles.[11]

This could have not been more different to the layout Picasso planned for his exhibition at Georges Petit. Instead of arranging his works according to a chronological timeline, or emphasising a single period in his career, the artist used a mix of strategies to curate 'badly', as he would explain in an interview a day before the show opened.[12] Indeed, being highly personal in character, Picasso's arrangement of his work lacked any logic but his own. On the cusp of becoming the most famous living artist of his time and at a moment of record market prices, Picasso attempted to prevent his practice from ossifying into a canonical narrative. To escape being institutionalised and running the risk of appearing as an artist who had passed his prime, Picasso made public his recent outburst of creativity – with eighteen paintings from the first four months of 1932 making this the most represented period in the show – as well as arranging his art so that past and present would appear intertwined and old and new would resonate with equal intensity. He presented all his paintings as if they were contemporary art – even those he had made thirty years ago. As the artist himself had said in 1923: 'To me there is no past or future in art. If a work of art cannot live always in the present, it must not be considered at all.'[13]

Recalling his visit to the retrospective, the painter and writer Jacques-Émile Blanche described Picasso's curatorial mode of operation. Blanche arrived at the gallery as Picasso was guiding a team of tired installers, who had already been mounting art for a week. When Picasso asked Blanche for his impression, the writer confessed that he was 'exhausted'. Picasso gave Blanche a private tour, as if to offer some guidance, leading him through a series of thematically linked works. They looked at female portraits in diverse styles: the recent *Nude in a Black Armchair* (Georges Petit exhibition catalogue (GP) 221; p.95), a cubist figure, an Ingres-inspired work, and a female torso created from blues and pinks to achieve 'the most luminous white'; yet Blanche was unable to comprehend. He collapsed on a bench, worn out and visually overwhelmed.[14] When reshuffling the art once again for Blanche, Picasso demonstrated the flexibility with which he approached his oeuvre, working through endless interpretations, narratives and possibilities.

The final hang – as seen in the thirty installation photographs that document Picasso's curation[15] – shows how Picasso's display disregarded existing approaches to his oeuvre. While in some spaces he created jarring juxtapositions based on visual alterity, as opposed to relying on stylistic similarities, in others he rhymed paintings from different moments in his career, testifying to his commitment to certain themes and motifs and rejecting ideas of evolution and artistic progress.

In the Grande Salle Picasso hung about seventy works in a dense arrangement, with paintings organised in two and sometimes three rows, reminiscent of the style of the eighteenth- and nineteenth-century French Salon exhibitions. Among these seventy paintings were fourteen works from 1932 including, according to Margaret Scolari Barr, 'an array of the great "bone" pictures ... a recent series of intensely colourful canvases dominated by a semi-abstract blonde head ... monumental stained-glass still lifes [and] the philodendron ... motif.'[16] This double focus on past and present must have left visitors confused: while the recent paintings shared a similar style and themes, Picasso also included earlier masterpieces of opposing idioms, such as the two versions of *The Three Musicians* from 1921 (GP 119, 120), *The Three Dancers* 1925 (GP 168; p.178), 1927's *The Painter and his Model* (GP 177) and the 1928 *Painter and Model* (GP 181), thus avoiding stylistic or periodical coherency.[17] Adding to the visual confusion were the minimal object labels, which only included the works' corresponding number in the exhibition catalogue. Scolari Barr's copy of the exhibition catalogue, is heavily annotated with comments, explanations, and sketches, testifying to her attempt to get to grips with this unclear organisation.[18]

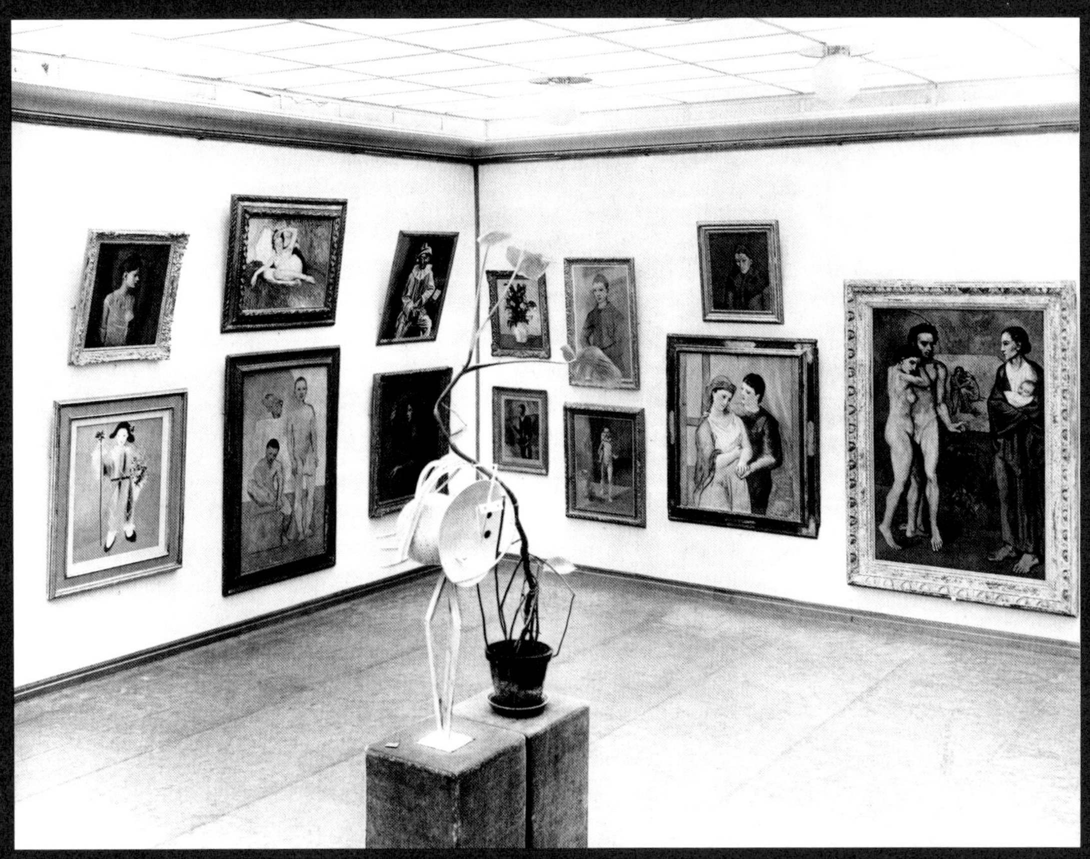

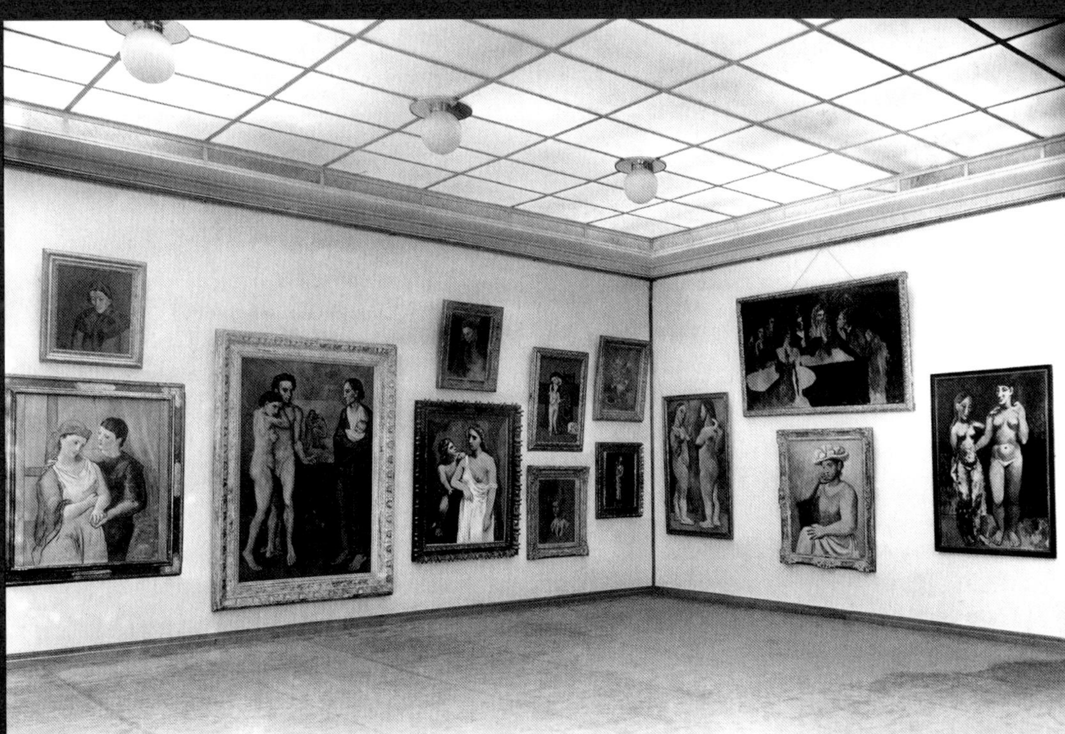

Views of the Salle Carrée

The gallery's inconsistent interior decor added to the erratic impact of Picasso's curation. In the room with the marble fireplace and floral wallpaper, two 1932 paintings were juxtaposed with a cubist composition and four monstrous figures of the late 1920s, forming a series of visual attacks on the human form that contrasted sharply with the surroundings (p.118). Picasso also referred to the Petit decor when he placed his own philodendron houseplant in the exhibition, as if to echo the lush fern that decorated the main room (pp.118, 119). Houseplants were more commonly found in exhibition spaces devoted to decorative arts in France than in commercial fine art galleries, but here it was appropriate given Petit's overall outmoded extravagance.[19] Picasso's plant was not just a decorative element though; at the very centre of Salle Carrée the artist positioned, on two identical pedestals, the 1927 sculpture *Woman's Head* – a construction of diverse iron objects (springs, nails, colander) that were welded to form a female face – and the potted philodendron, which due to its unusual height probably had to be tied to the sculpture to stay erect (p.121).

While writers later commented on this motif in Picasso's paintings and some even noticed the greenery thriving in the artist's studio (Roland Penrose remembered Picasso's delight on returning from a holiday to find the philodendron had taken over the space),[20] only André Breton addressed the odd juxtaposition of sculpture and plant. In 'Picasso in his Element,' published one year after the Petit retrospective, Breton described in a paragraph devoted to the exhibition 'a common plant [which] serves here not only as support but also as *justification* for an iron sculpture that is inseparable from it in the observer's mind.' He claimed that it is the sculpture which was supported by the plant (and not the other way around), in a juxtaposition which further extended the assemblage and explained Picasso's working logic. In Breton's view, the plant transformed into a natural continuation of the sculpture: the philodendron's growth echoed the assemblage's springy curls, and the three top leaves became an extravagant crown. Breton found other examples of juxtapositions of the artistic and the natural in Picasso's work (another plant, bird feathers, a butterfly), suggesting that Picasso's art transcended traditional categories such as the animate and inanimate and therefore became alive.[21] Picasso's admiration for the philodendron's 'overwhelming vitality' in his studio seems to confirm the artist's use of the plant as a metaphor for the unpredictable nature of creativity.[22] The philodendron thus was not only one of the most prominent and recurring motifs in Picasso's recent paintings: by introducing the plant into the exhibition itself an unprecedented link was created between the private world of the studio and the public sphere of the gallery.

Picasso surrounded the plant-sculpture with forty-four paintings dating from 1901 to 1923. His non-linear display was arranged to emphasise themes and compositional connections in such a way that despite the works' stylistic variation there remained a cohesive quality to the hang. The large space, identifiable by the round light fixtures, light walls and glass ceiling, appeared in several installation photographs (p.121). The majority of works on display depicted one or two figures, with a few exceptions such as four multi-figured paintings and one still life. The presence of so many paintings from different moments in time yet with similar composition formed a narrative that highlights homogeneity of themes and ideas, leveraging visual and thematic repetition as a binding element.

This principle of connecting is evident throughout the space, as seen in the two photographs that focus on the three walls with *Life* 1903 (GP 17) at their centre (p.121). *Life*'s composition, for instance, contrasts the embrace of a nearly nude couple with that of an older woman holding a baby. As exhibited, the symmetrically arranged walls mirror the painting's formal division yet do not duplicate the depicted interaction or atmosphere. The painting is the axis around which the room's themes develop – the image's structural relationship and emotional content are taken apart and reworked in nearby paintings. The nude couple's embrace is repeated by the couple in *The Lovers* 1923 (GP 133), but here coyness and awkwardness replace *Life*'s angst. The motif of the woman cradling an infant migrates to other paintings and transforms into a mother softly kissing a child in *Maternity* 1901 (GP 4). It is then refracted in *The Woman with the Crow* 1904 (GP 24) where a woman kisses a crow, in a painting of sharp edges and harsh colours. The opposition between *Life*'s two pairs re-emerges in other images where couples of different sorts and in different configurations present a repertoire of equivalence and difference, a silent theatre of gestures and interpersonal interactions that develops the theme of coupling. This would not have been possible had the displays been strictly linear, and would in turn have limited the understanding of Picasso's past as reverberating in the present.

Despite Picasso's efforts, the show was a critical failure. Most reviewers limited themselves to describe the retrospective in generalising, largely negative terms. Germain Bazin wrote that, regardless of the great achievements of the blue period and the neoclassism of the mid 1920s, 'Picasso belongs to the past' and 'his current downfall is one of the most troubling problems of our time.'[23] Waldemar George criticised Picasso's art for being deeply entrenched in the present so that it lacked any link to the past, suggesting that a connection with tradition is what gives an artwork its ability to live in the future. George also compared Picasso unfavourably with Matisse, stating that while 'Matisse ... transcends his generation, Picasso is a man of his age. The hold he has on his contemporaries springs from the constant "modernity" of his art.'[24] Jacques Guenne did find an art-historical forebear to Picasso, comparing his role and status to that of François Boucher in Madame de Pompadour's court, but the connotations were negative. For Guenne, both were mere entertainers for the French high society, and the establishment and the avant-garde admired Picasso's art because it lacked integrity: 'he created a sort of artistic Esperanto that each can interpret according to his own conscience and taste.'[25]

Roger Lesbats was one of the few reviewers to point to specific elements of Picasso's curation and to analyse its impact on the works' reception. He claimed that the retrospective format – its size and range – as well as the exhibited works, revealed Picasso's art as 'megalomaniac, demonic and desperate'. In his view, the initial effect of seeing the works outside of their chronological order caused 'surprise and temptation ... and one believes in their grandeur'. Yet the impression quickly changed: without the scaffolding of chronological narrative, without the historical context that could have justified the works' stylistic differences, 'they appear to us as unsuccessful trials or successes without future. We overtly perceive the limitation and vanity.'[26] The legacy of Picasso's past achievements appeared as much at stake as his present and future relevance.

There are two possible interpretations of this failure. First, it could be inferred that – despite his attempts to control and shape the narrative through which his art was understood, by both arranging the exhibition and collaborating with the press, dealers, collectors and publishers – Picasso was unable to win over his critics and to foster a more comprehensive understanding of the challenges posed by the multiplicity of his work. Or alternatively it is possible to assume that this was precisely the desired outcome. Instead of being historicised by others, Picasso chose a riskier approach which guaranteed that he would not be classified as an old master.

By staging his art in conflicting and meandering ways and by avoiding clear narratives and straightforward entry points into his body of work, the artist actually used the occasion of a mid-career retrospective to go against the grain. By actively courting controversy and debate, he reasserted himself as non-establishment – and therefore as a continually contemporary artist, and the most famous one at that.

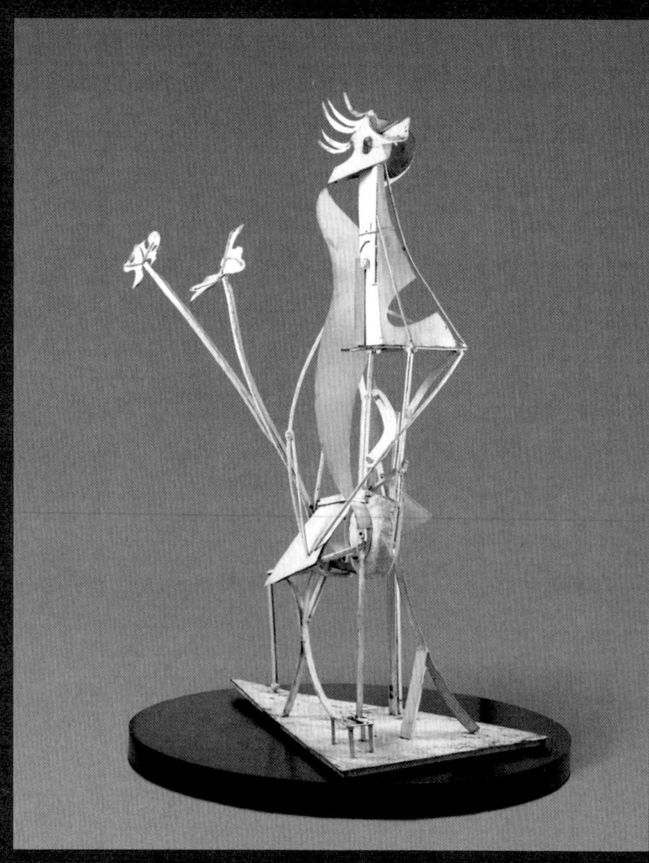

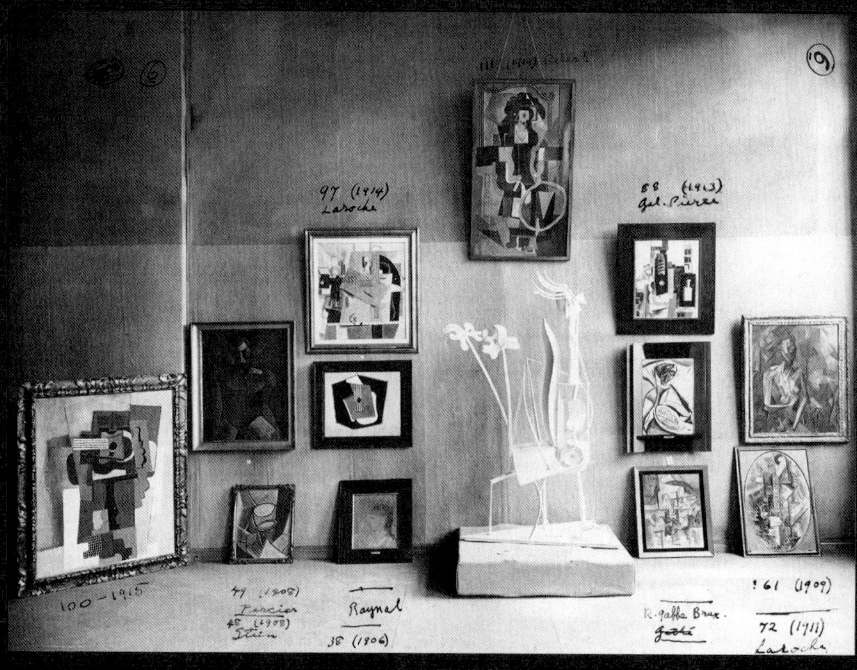


*Woman in the Garden, La Femme au jardin* 1929–30

Photograph taken during installation or deinstallation at Galeries Georges Petit, with annotations by Margaret Scolari Barr identifying the artworks on display according to their catalogue entry

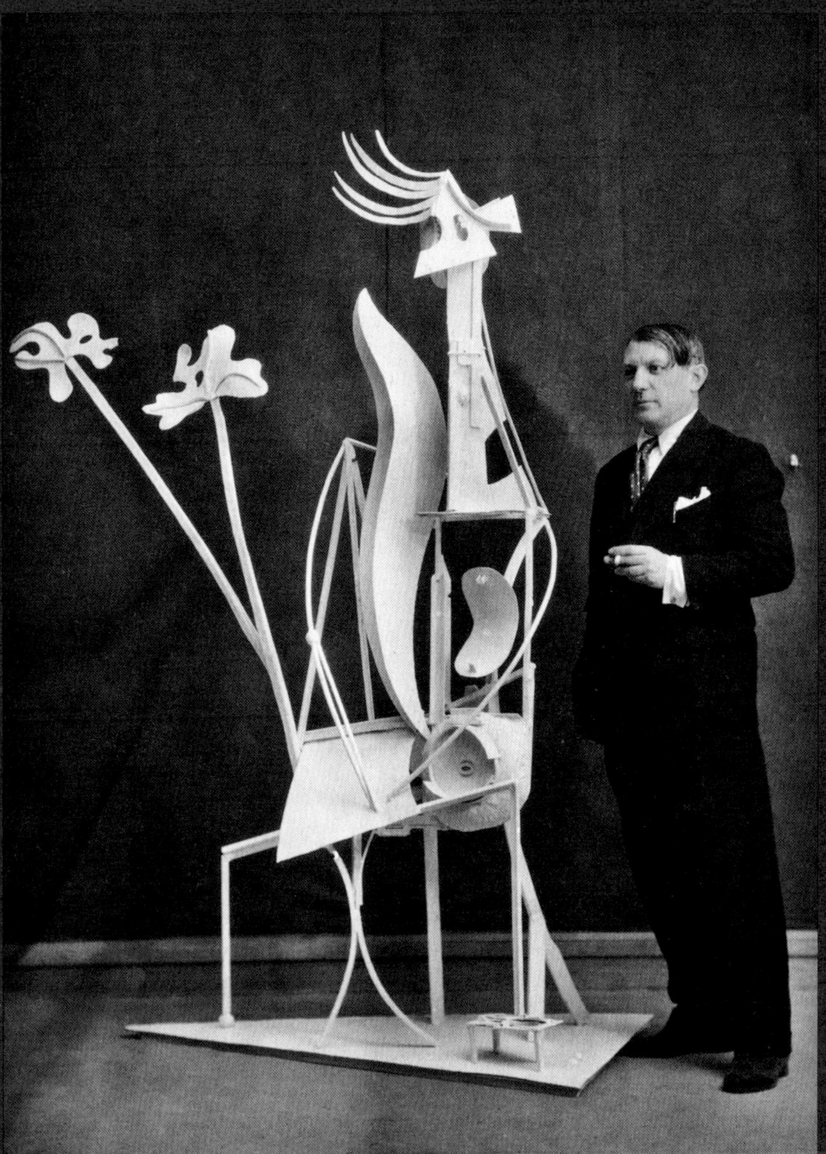

'For a painter who, like me today, when there's an exhibition, sees some of his canvases from a long time ago reappear, it seems that these are prodigal children returning home, but clothed in shirts of gold.'

Picasso, quoted in Tériade, 'En causant avec Picasso', *L'Intransigeant*, 15 June 1932

Picasso with *Woman in the Garden* at Galeries Georges Petit

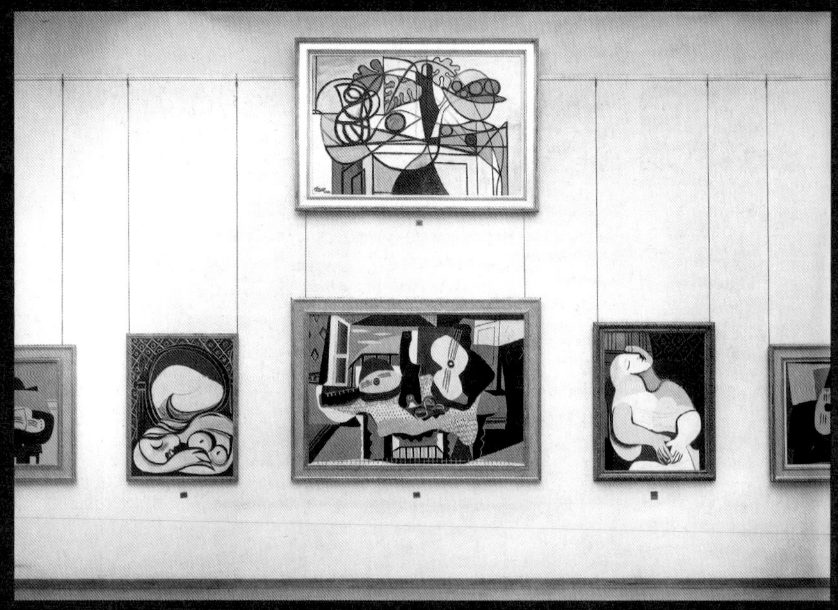

'The Picasso exhibition has won me over once again and the latest very colourful paintings were a true surprise. He has even incorporated some Matisse. Most of the time the formats are larger than one might think. Many of the amusing bather pieces gain a great deal from their tender painting. All in all: the painter of today.'

Postcard from Paul Klee to Lily Klee on seeing the retrospective at Kunsthaus Zürich, 7 October 1932

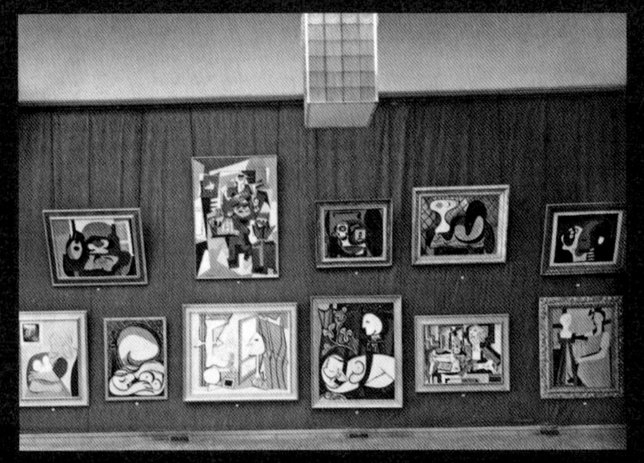

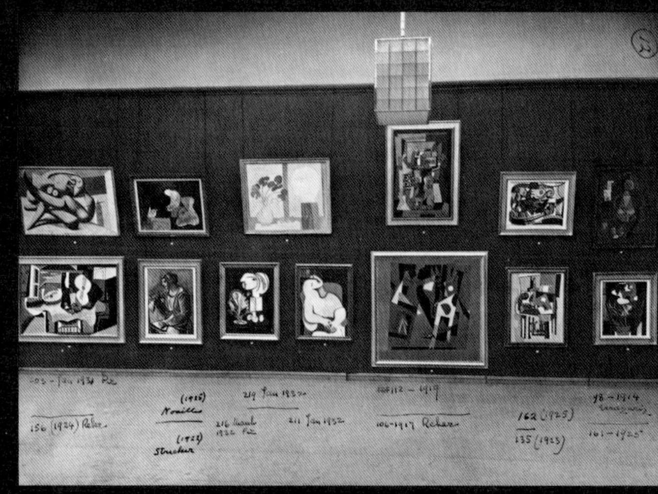

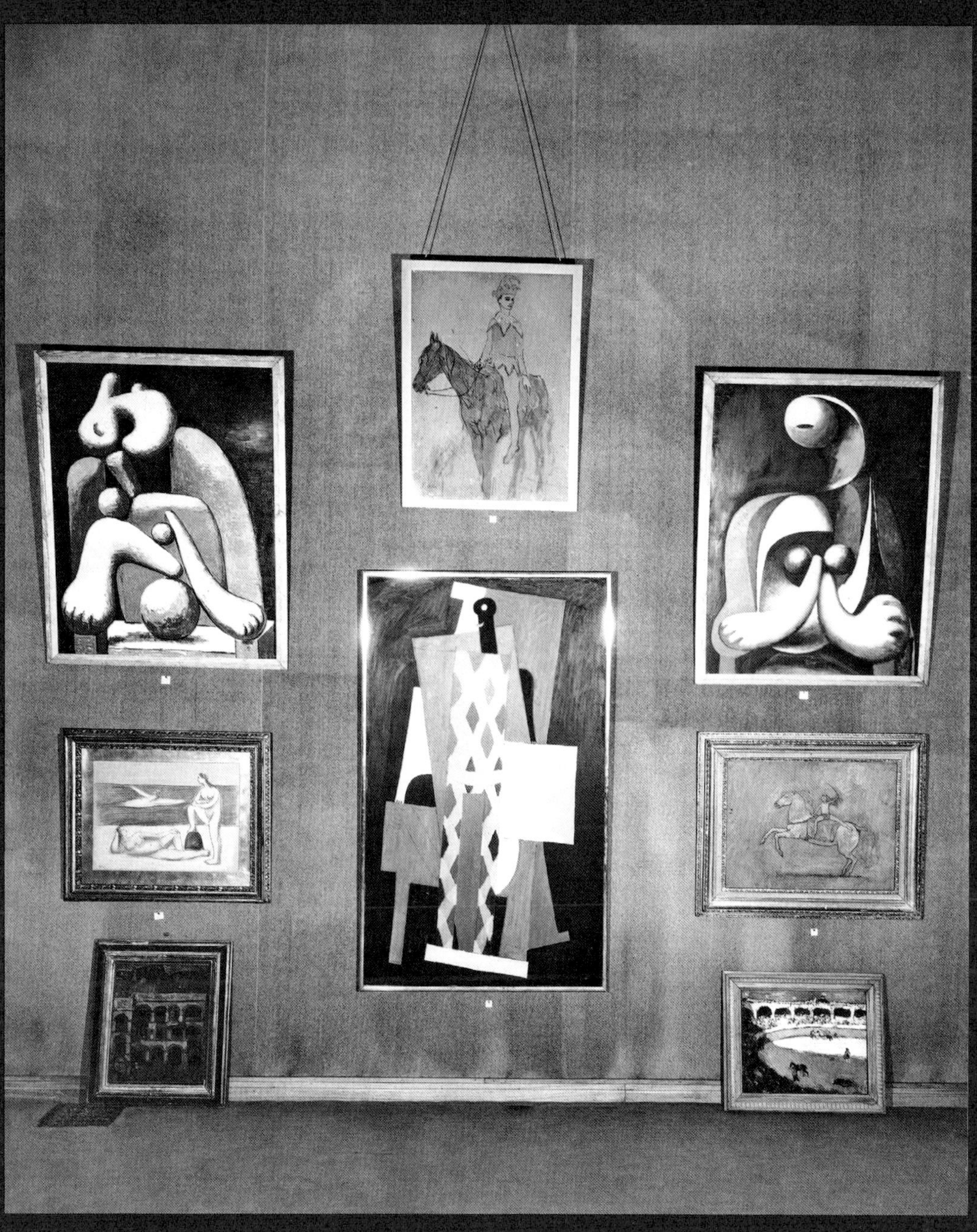

Top left: Installation view of the *Picasso* exhibition at Kunsthaus Zürich,
11 September – 13 November 1932, showing the contrasting style of display there. Photograph by Ernst Linck

Above and left: Installation views at Galeries Georges Petit, Paris. Photograph on the near left annotated by Margaret Scolari Barr to record the works on display according to their catalogue entry

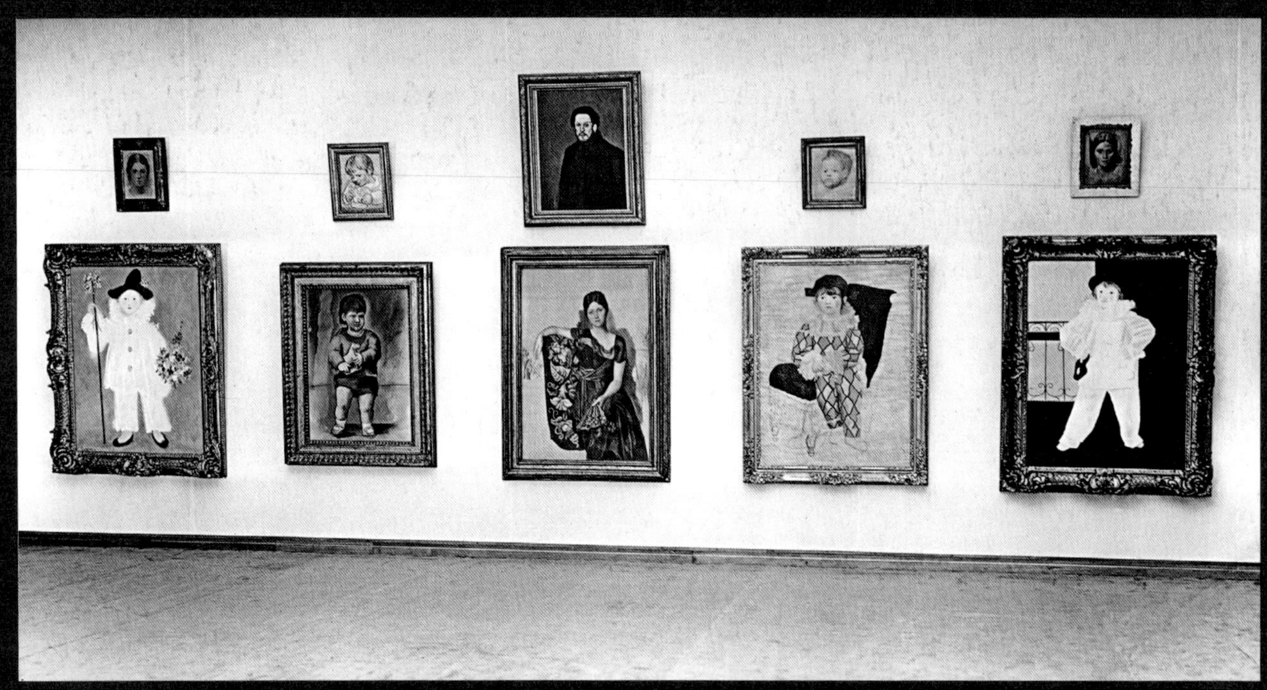

 The so-called 'family wall' at the centre of the retrospective, in the Salle Carrée. Photograph by Thérèse Bonney

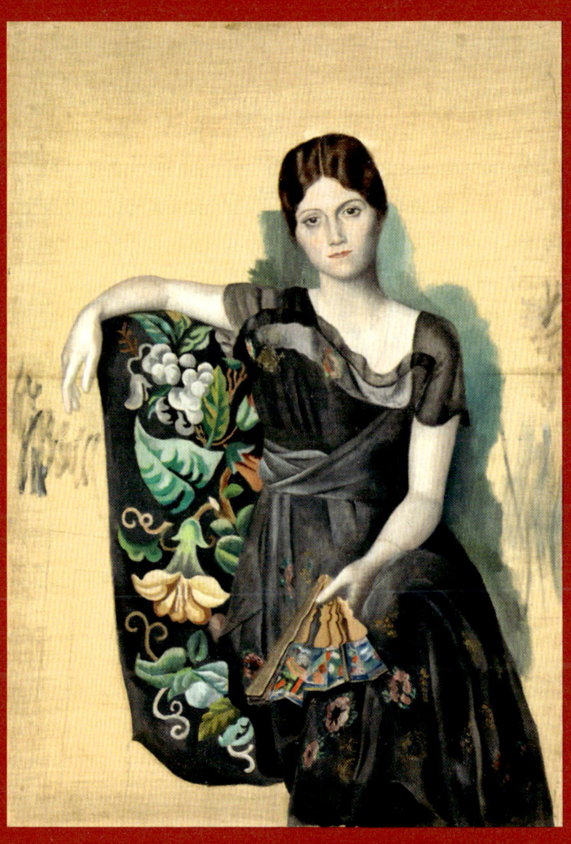

*Portrait of Olga in an Armchair,*
*Portrait d'Olga dans un fauteuil* 1918

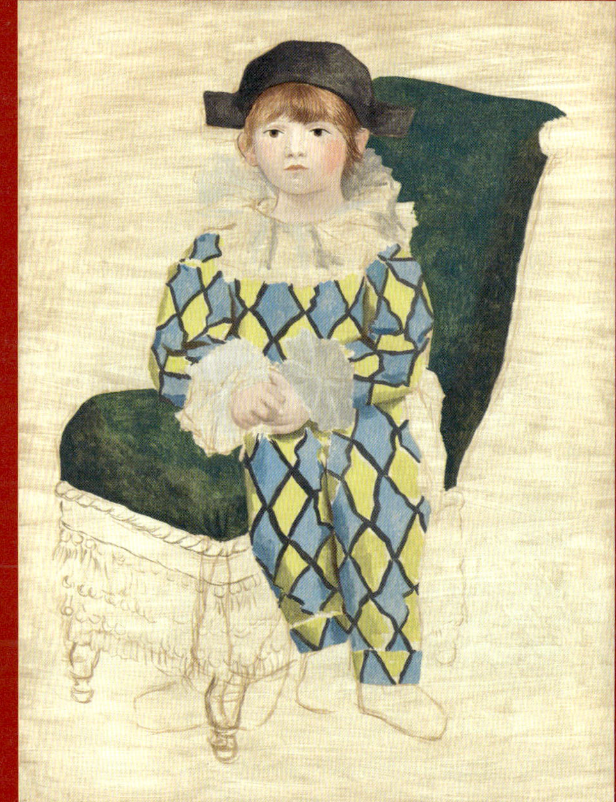

*Paulo as a Harlequin, Paulo en arlequin* 1924

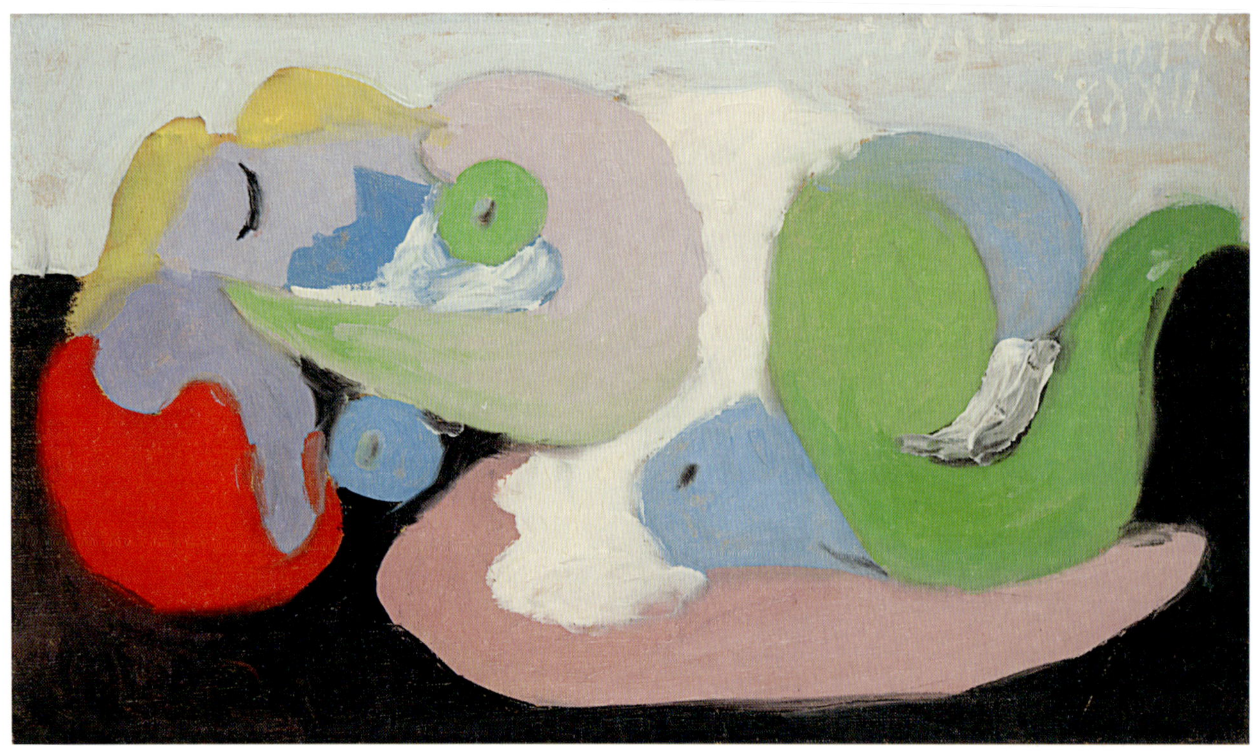

 *Woman Sleeping on a Red Cushion, Dormeuse au coussin rouge*

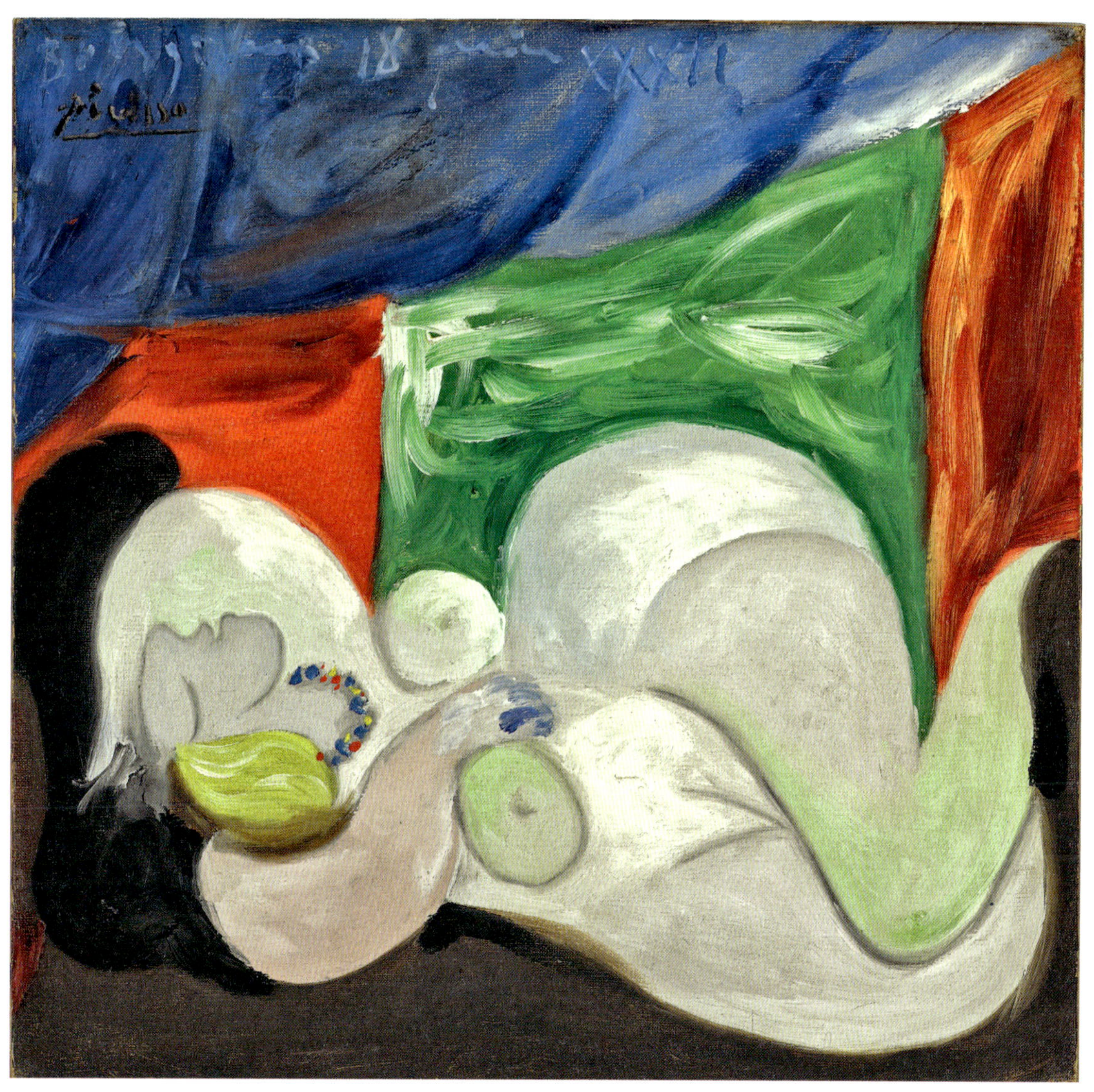

*Reclining Nude with a Necklace, Femme nue couchée au collier*

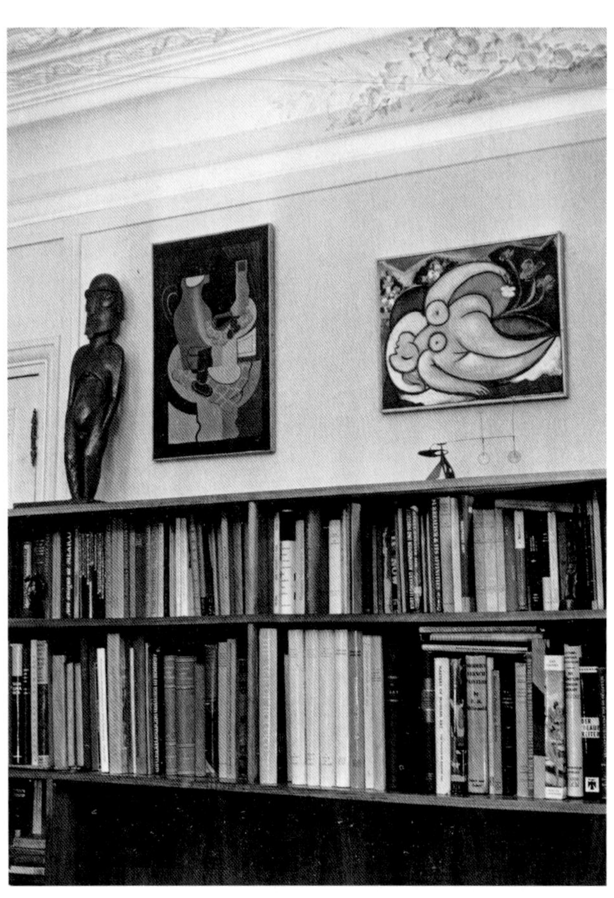

*Reclining Nude* in the home of Daniel-Henry Kahnweiler, Picasso's friend and his dealer during his cubist period. Photograph by Brassaï

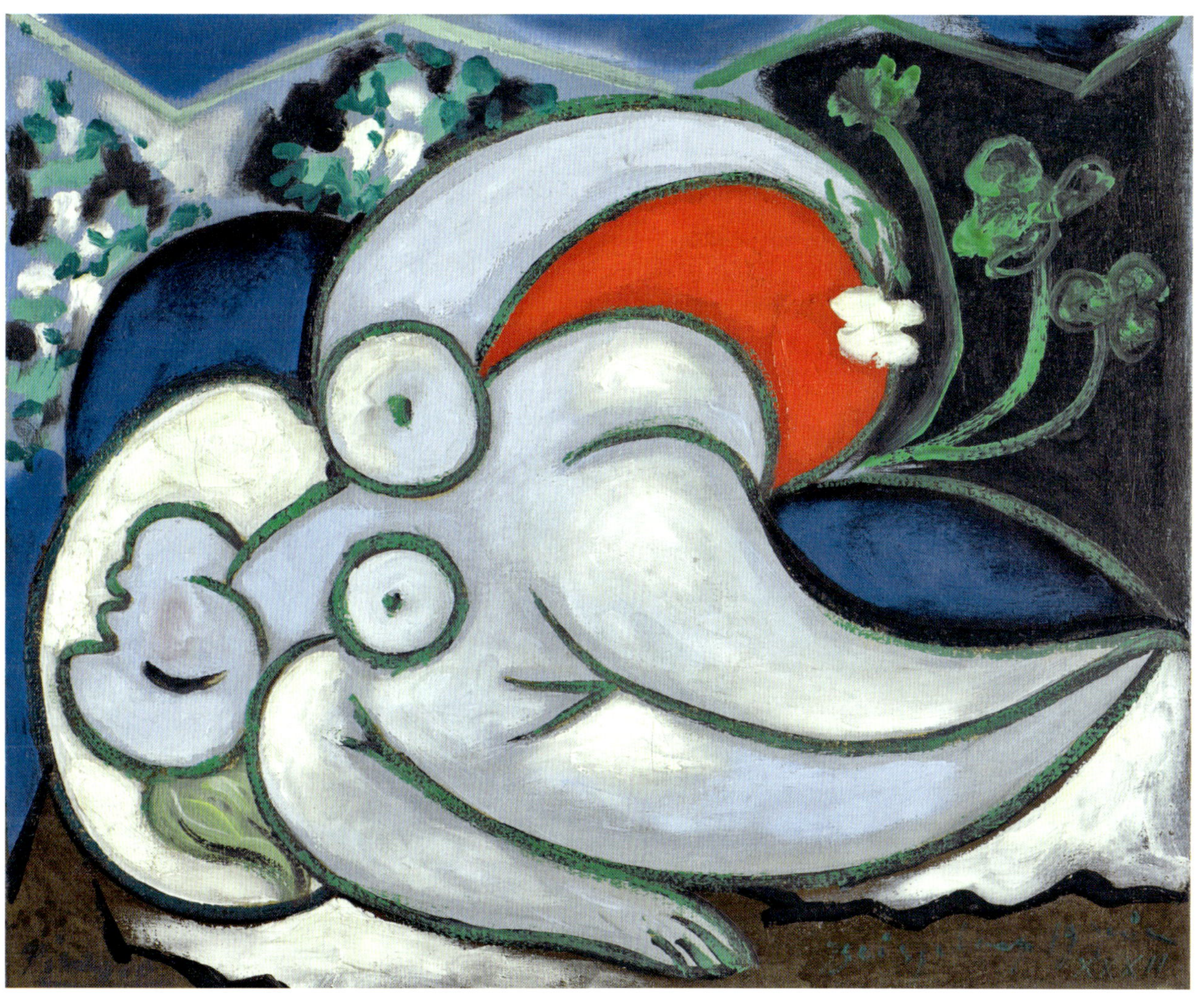

*Reclining Nude, Nu couché*

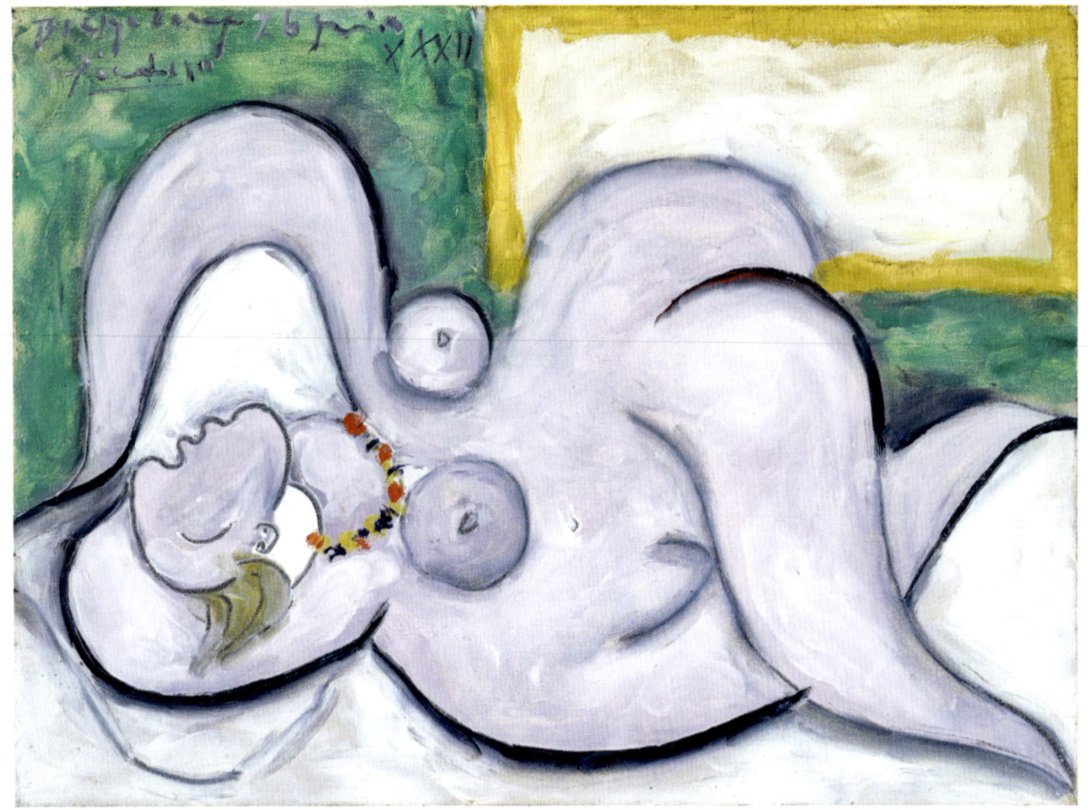

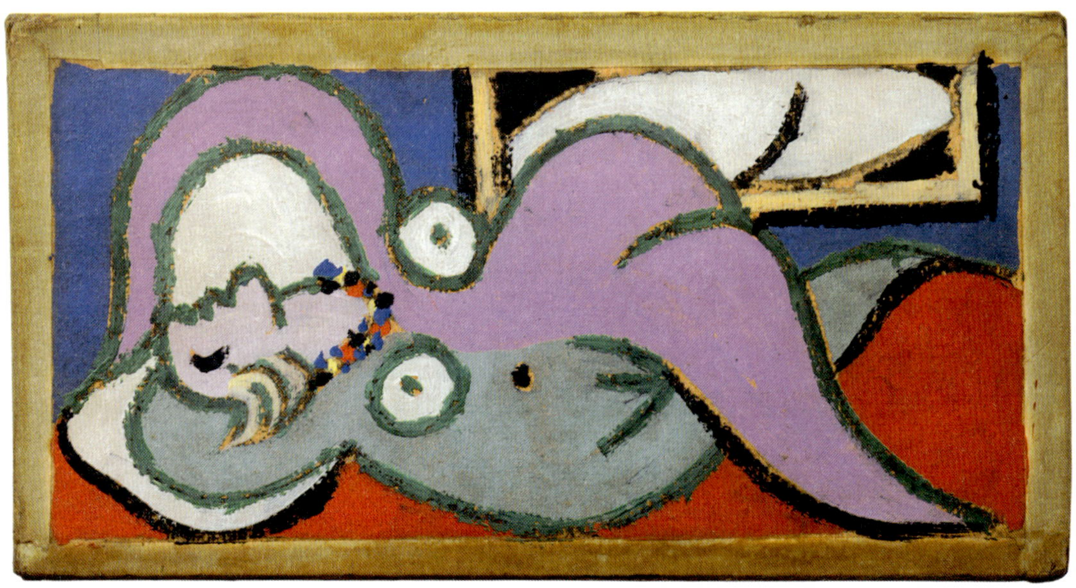

*Nude before a Mirror, Nu devant la glace*

*Reclining Nude, Femme couchée*

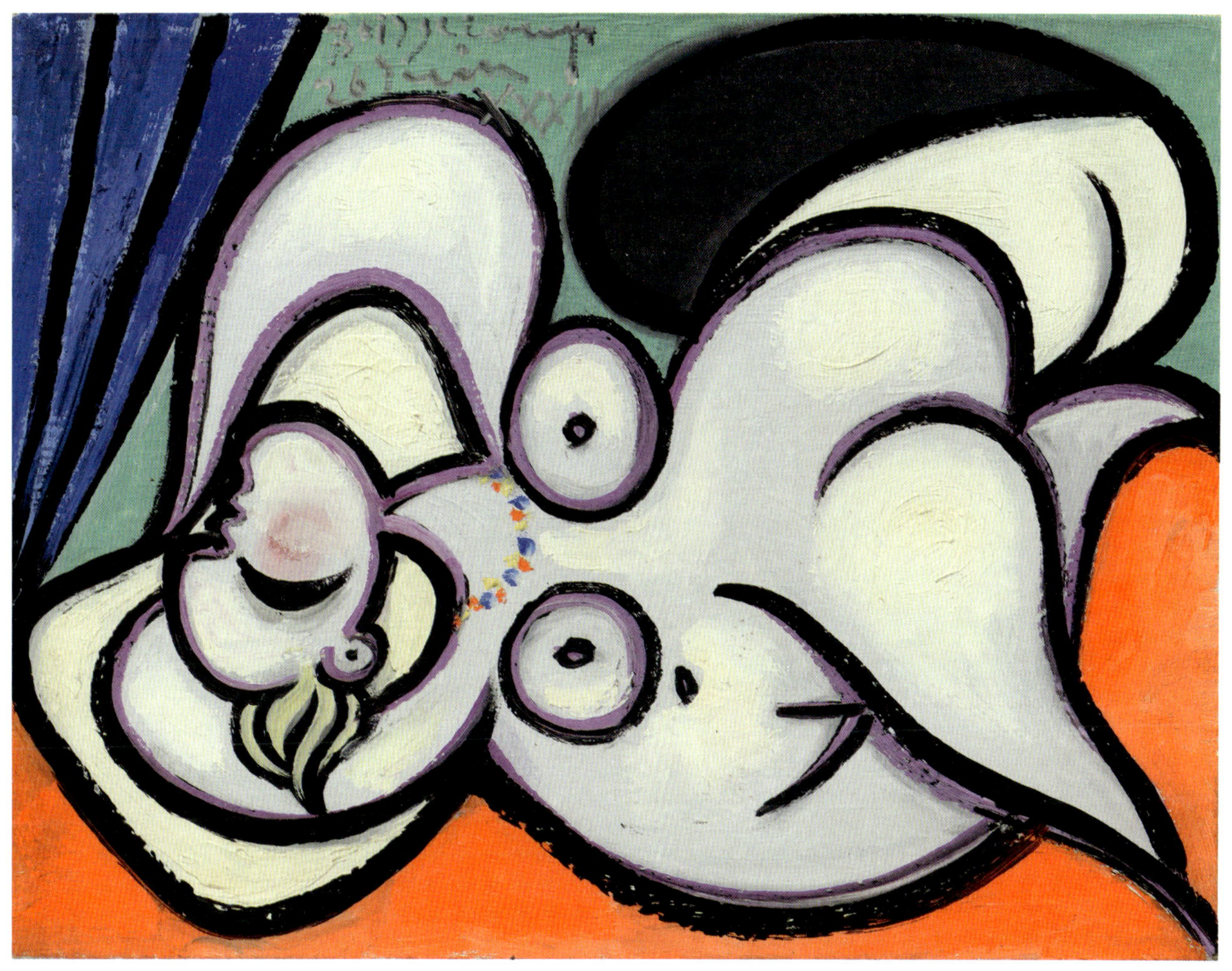

*Nude in Front of a Mirror, Femme entendue les bras sous la nuque sur un lit rouge*

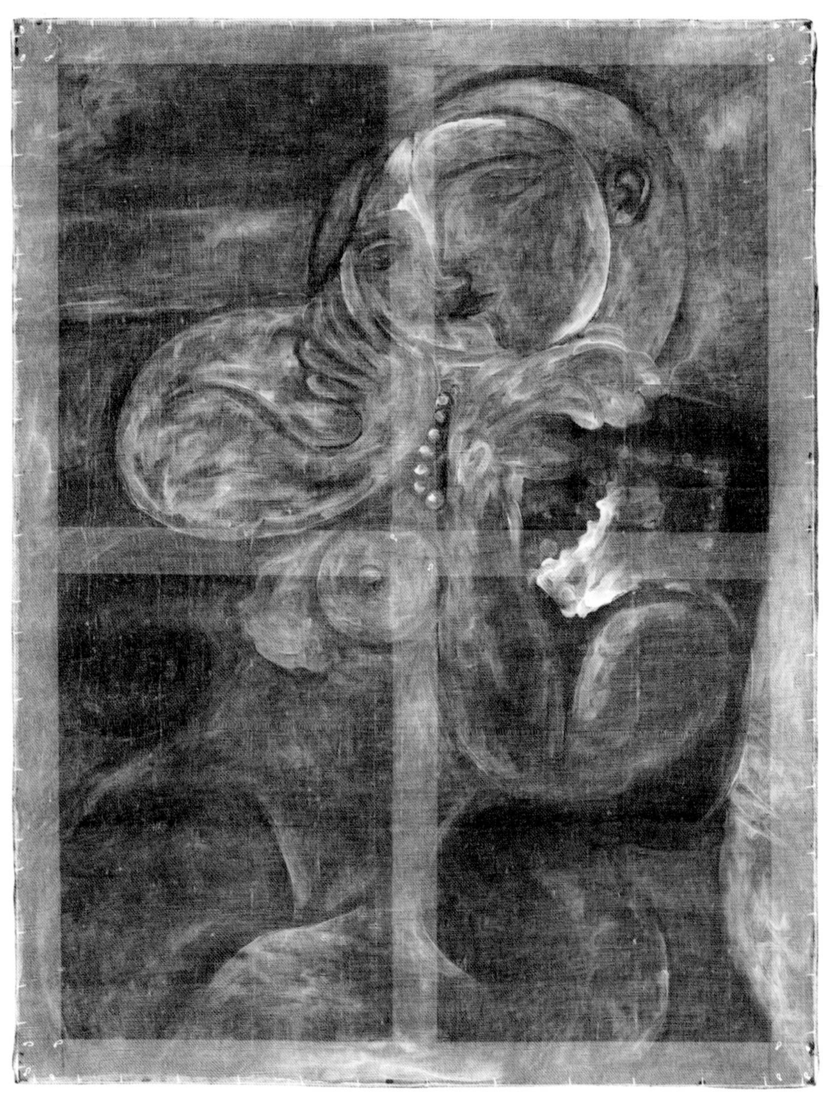

X-radiograph of *Nude Woman in a Red Armchair* confirms that the painting was executed rapidly, with no alterations. It shows a bare minimum of paint, apart from the thicker areas of white in the face, torso and highlights.

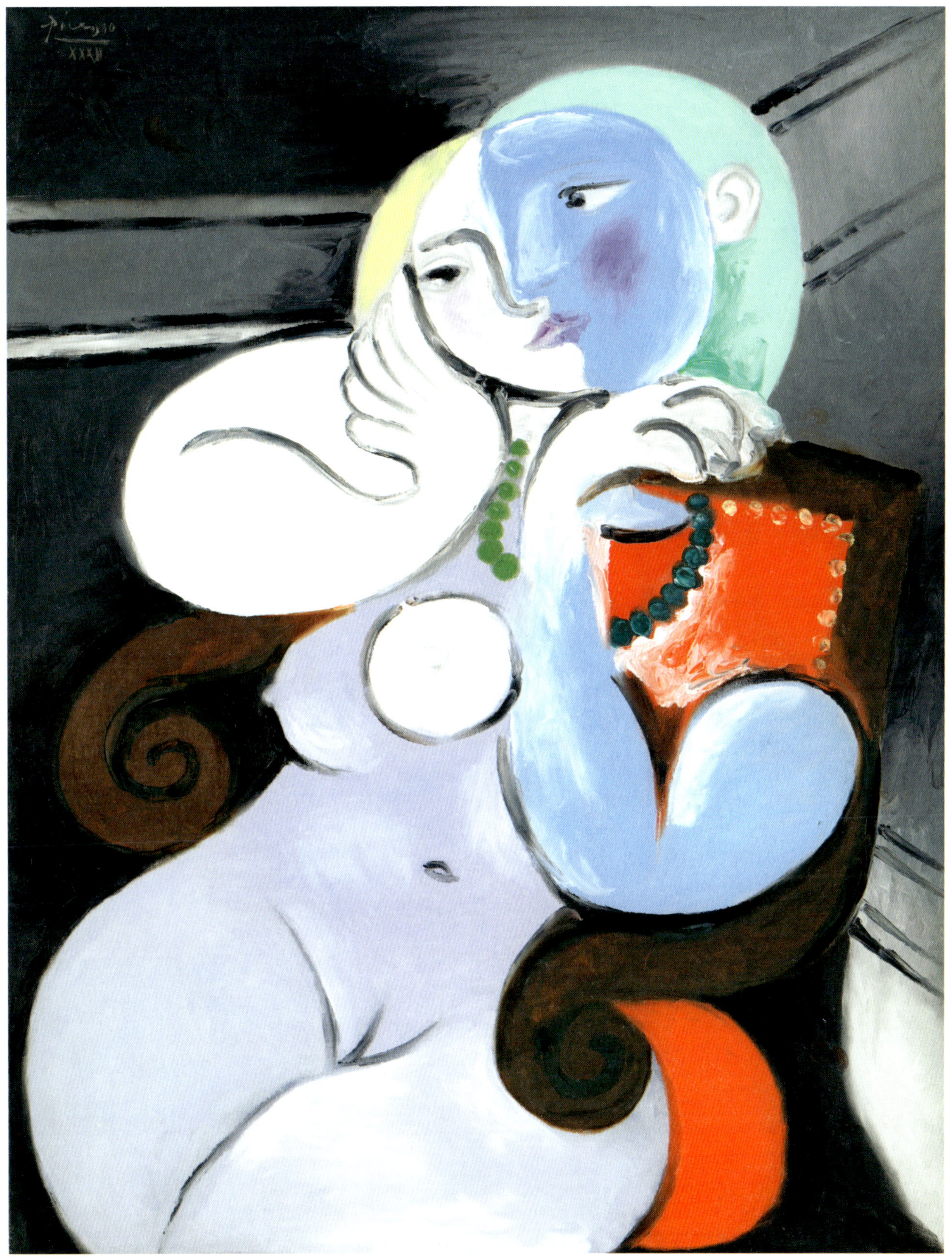

*Nude Woman in a Red Armchair, Femme nue dans un fauteuil rouge*

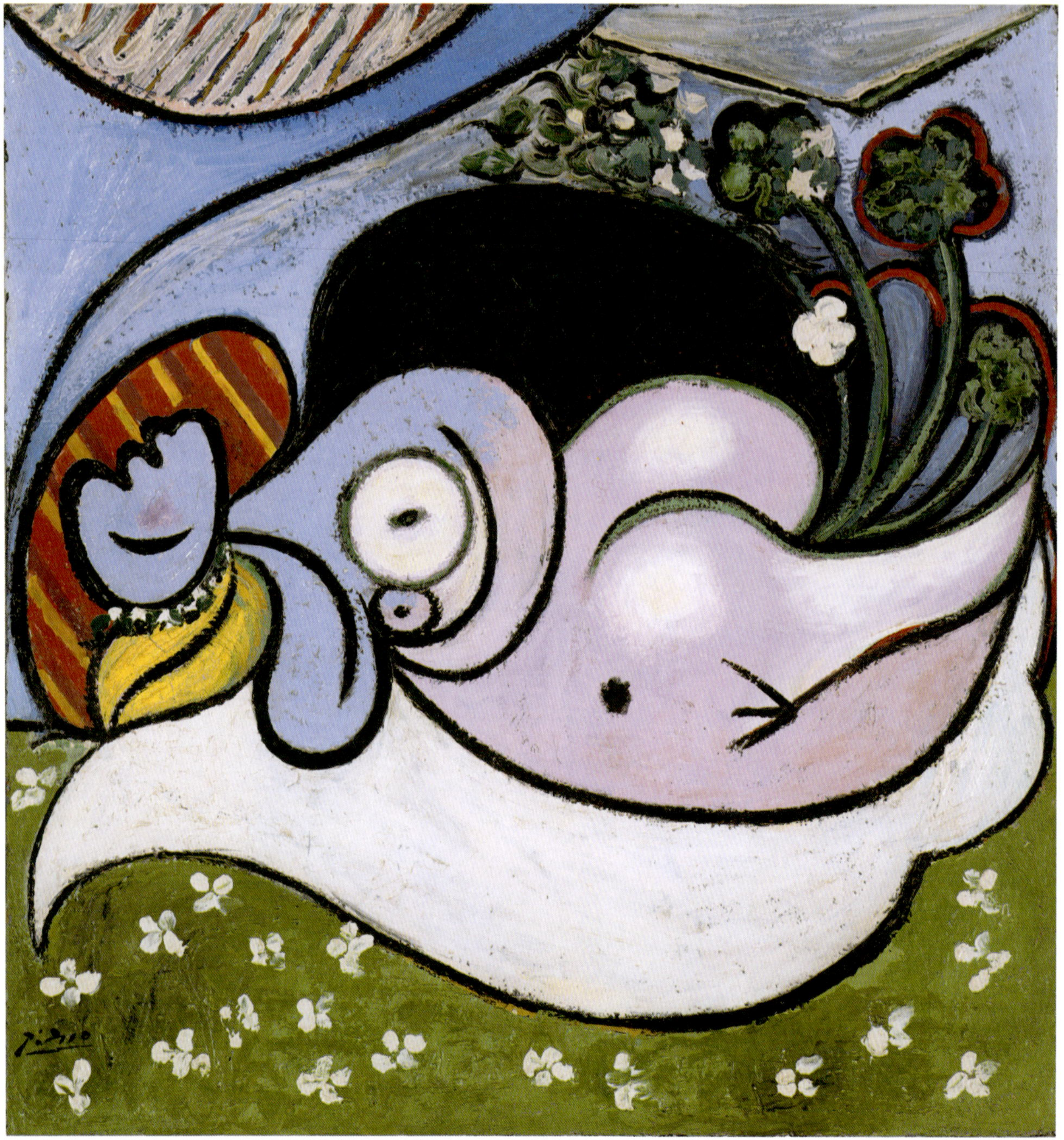

 *The Dreamer, Nu couché aux fleurs*

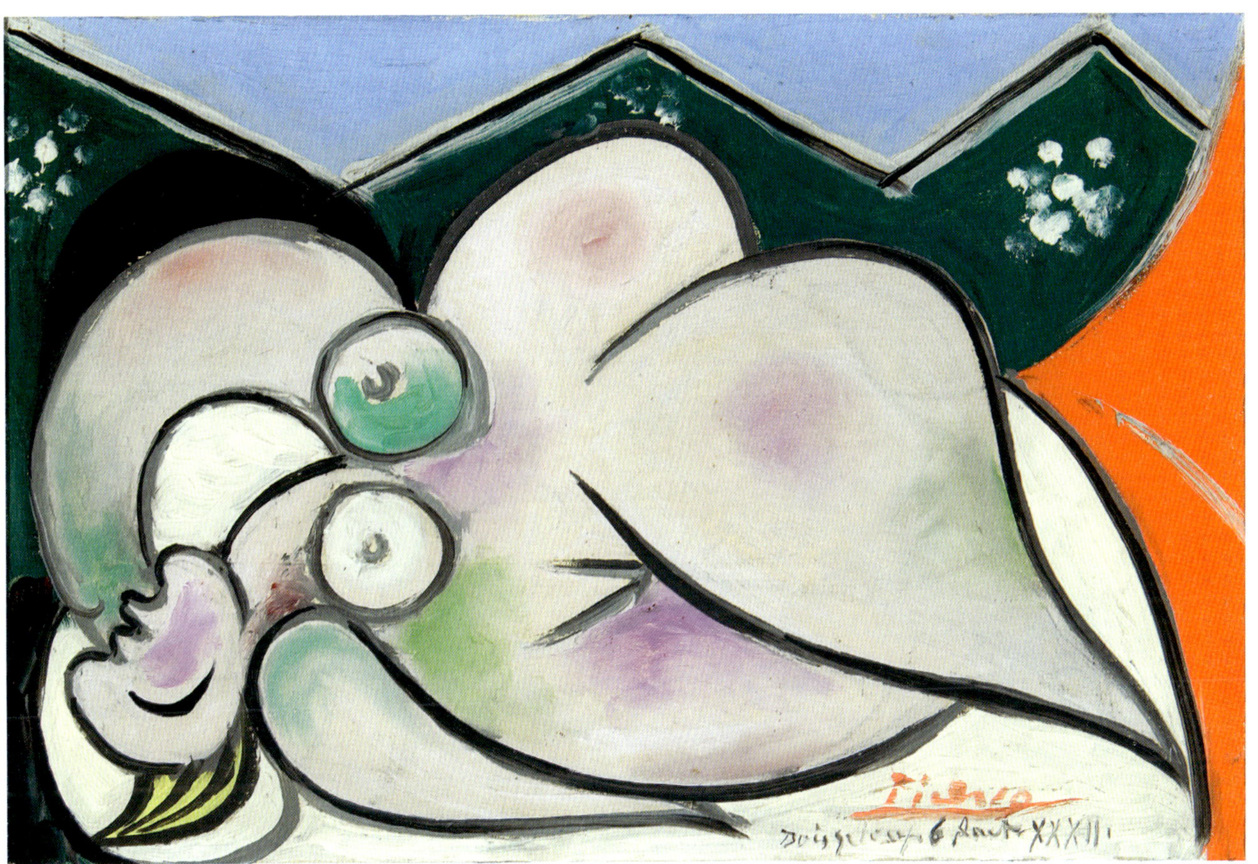

*Reclining Woman, Femme couchée*

'Of course the bull himself is also an image of the sun, but only with his throat slit. The same goes for the cock, whose horrible and particular solar cry always approximates the screams of a slaughter.'

Georges Bataille, 'Rotten Sun', *Documents 2*, no.3, 1930, p.174

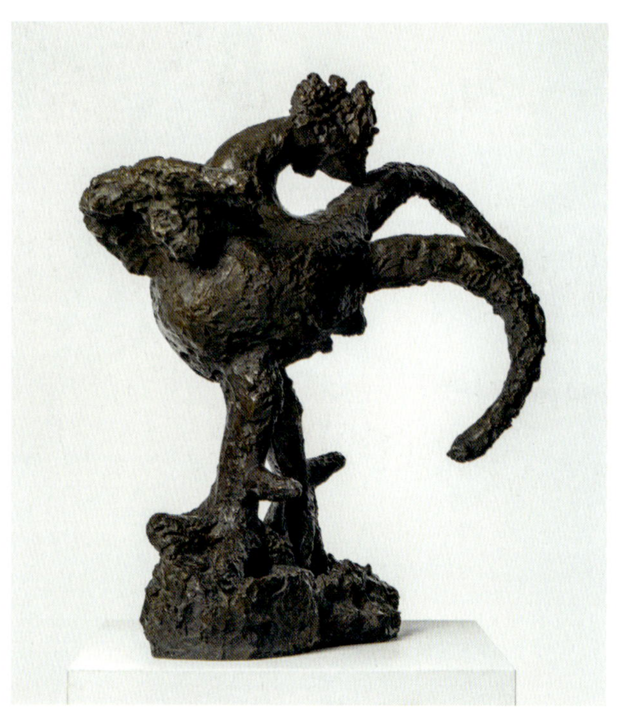

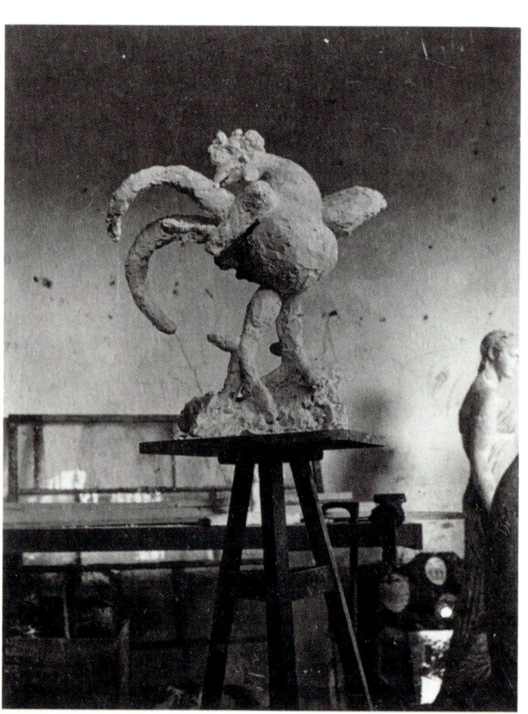

 *Cock, Coq* 1932, cast 1952

*Cock, Coq* 1932. Photograph by Brassaï

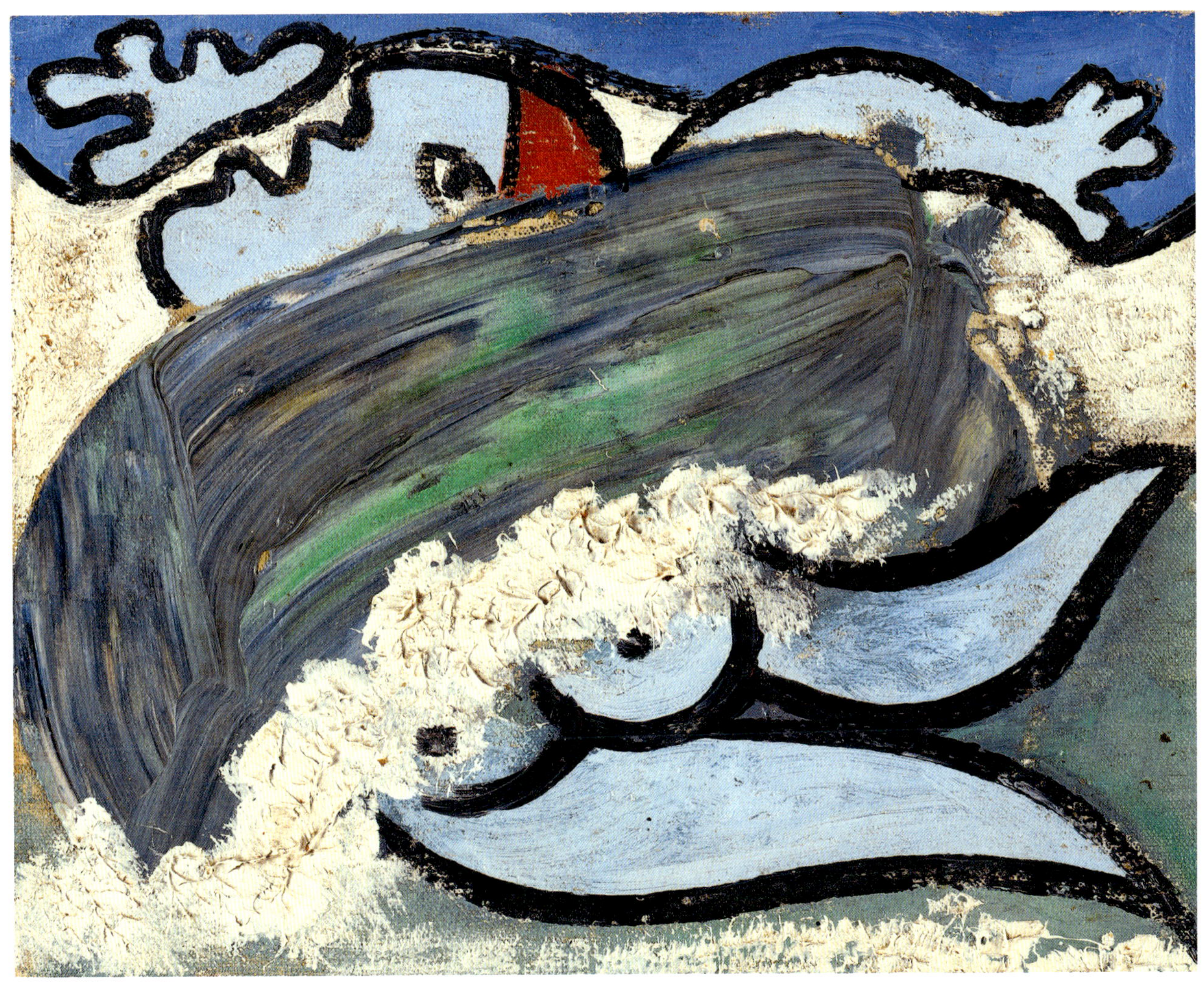

*Swimmer, Nageuse*

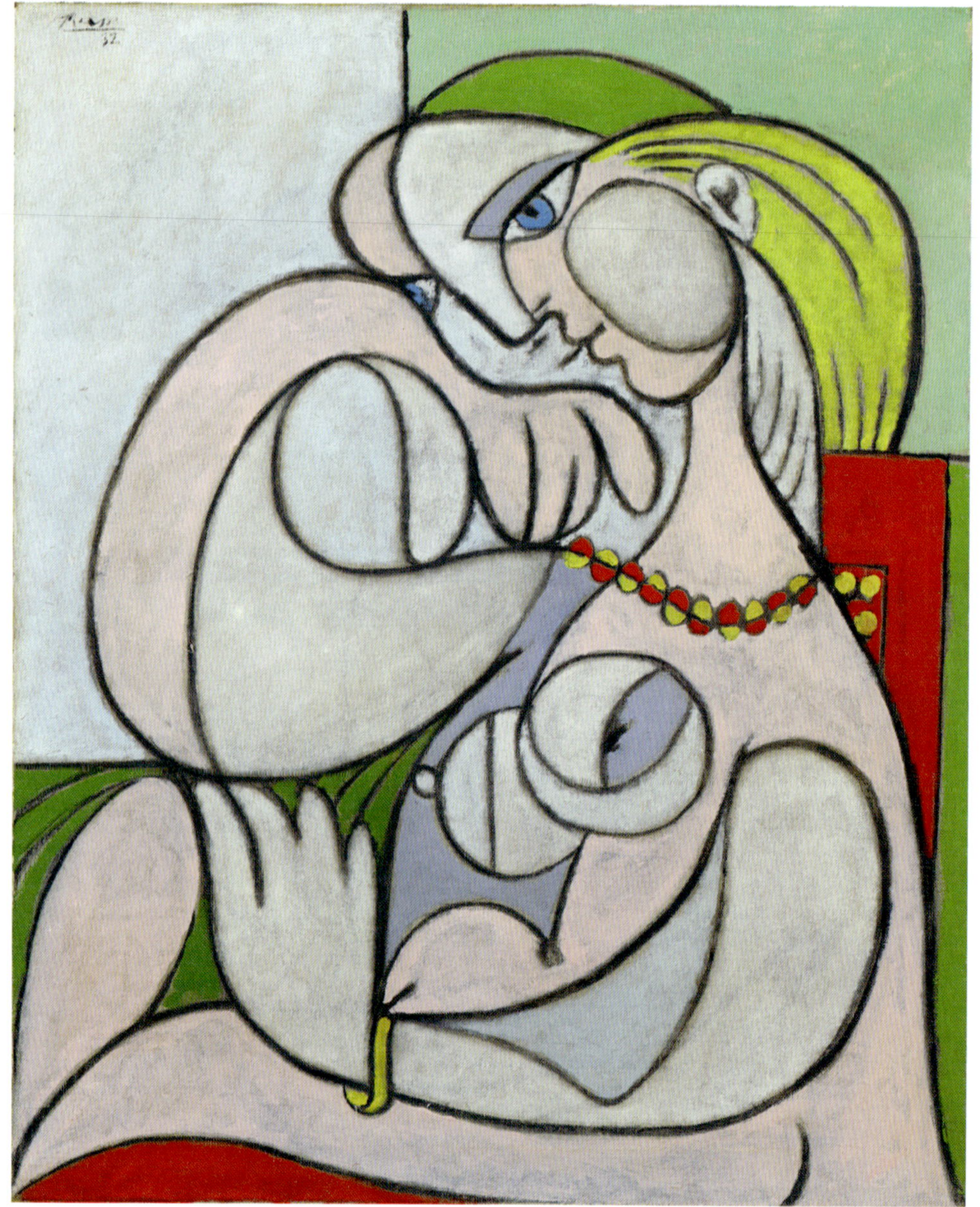

*Nude with Necklace, Nu au collier*

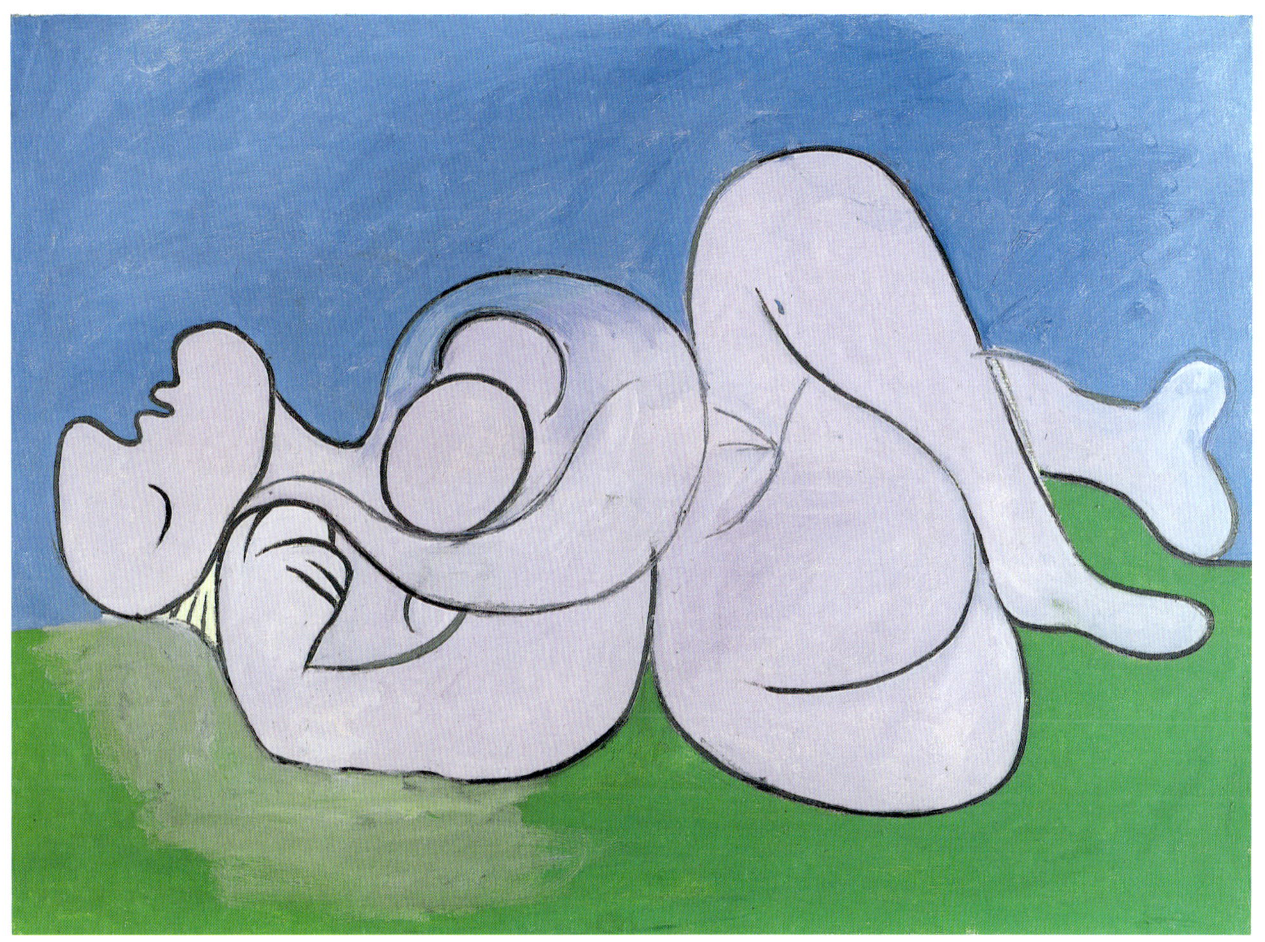

*Sleep, La Sieste*

'I will never fit in with the followers of the prophets of Nietzsche's superman.'

Picasso, quoted in Felipe Cossío del Pomar, *Con los buscadores del camino* (1932)

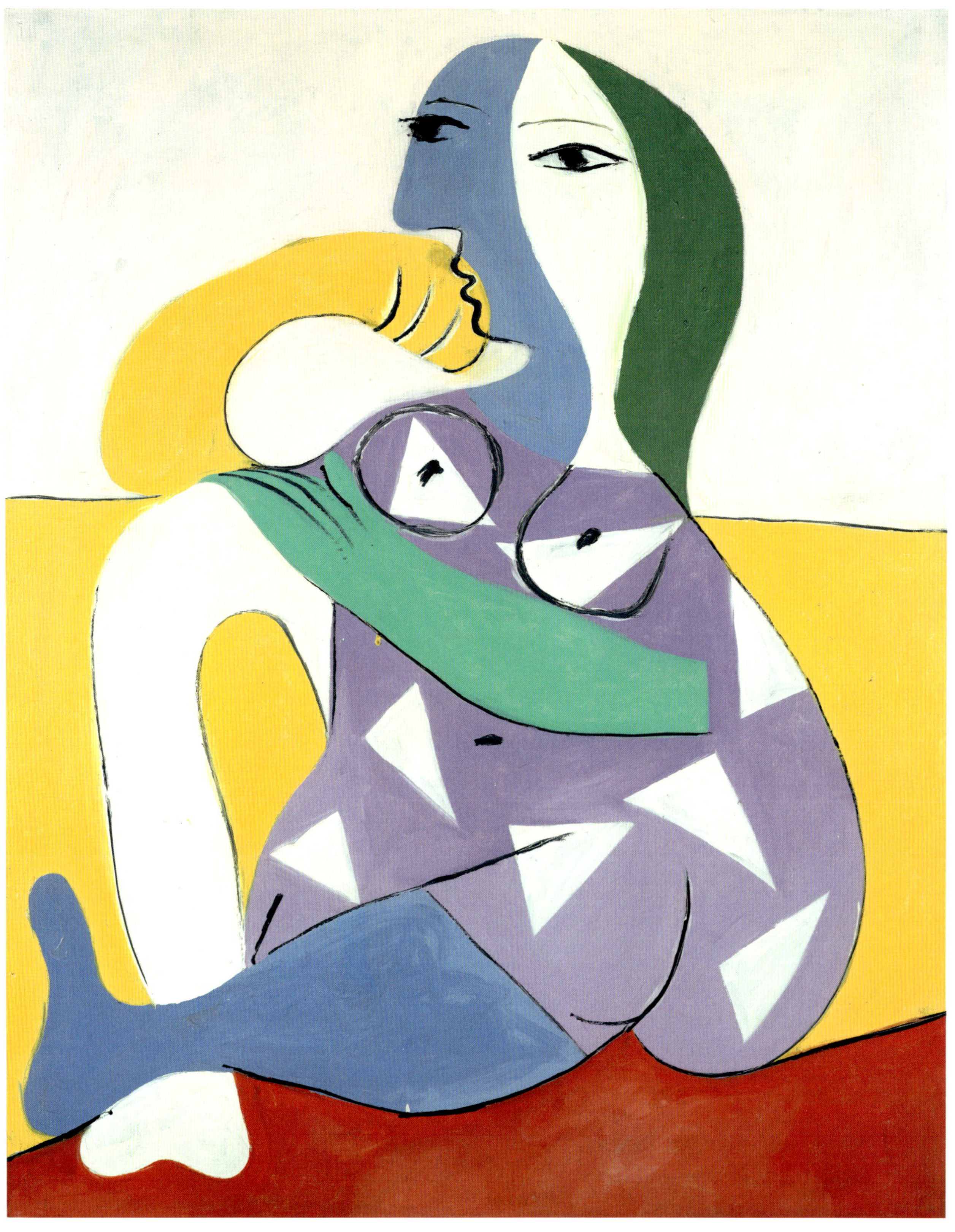

*Seated Woman with Elbow on Knee, Femme assise au coude appuyé sur le genou*

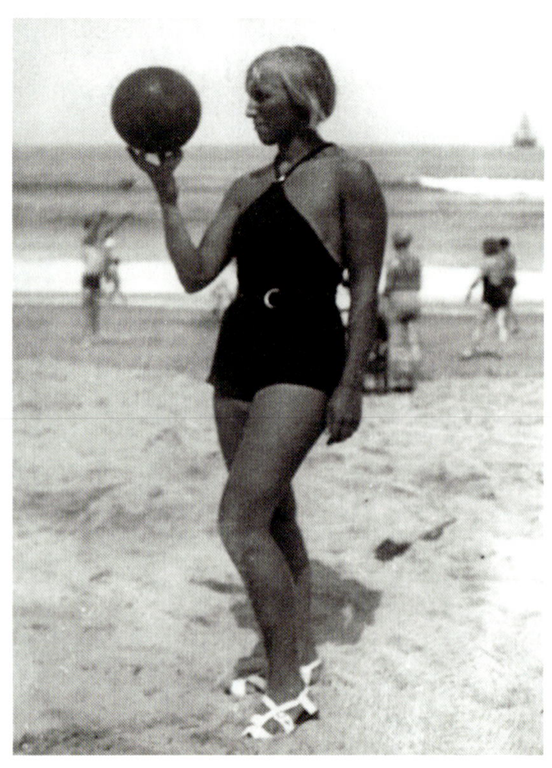

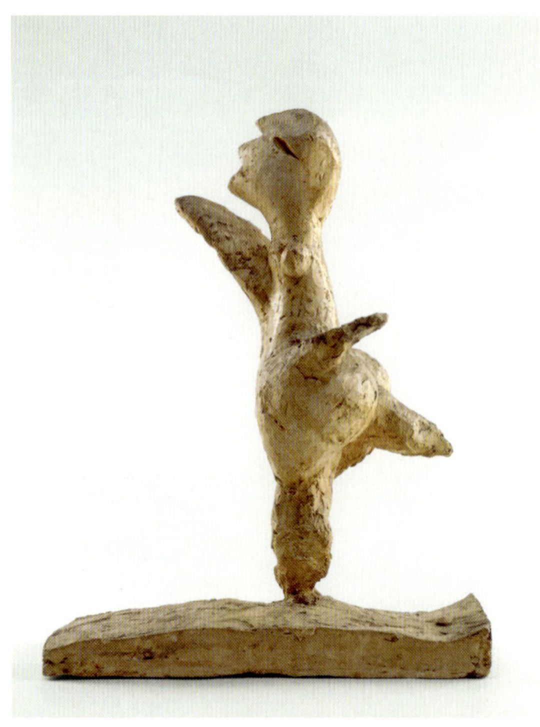

Marie-Thérèse Walter, Juan-les-Pins, 27 July 1932

*Bather, Baigneuse* 1931

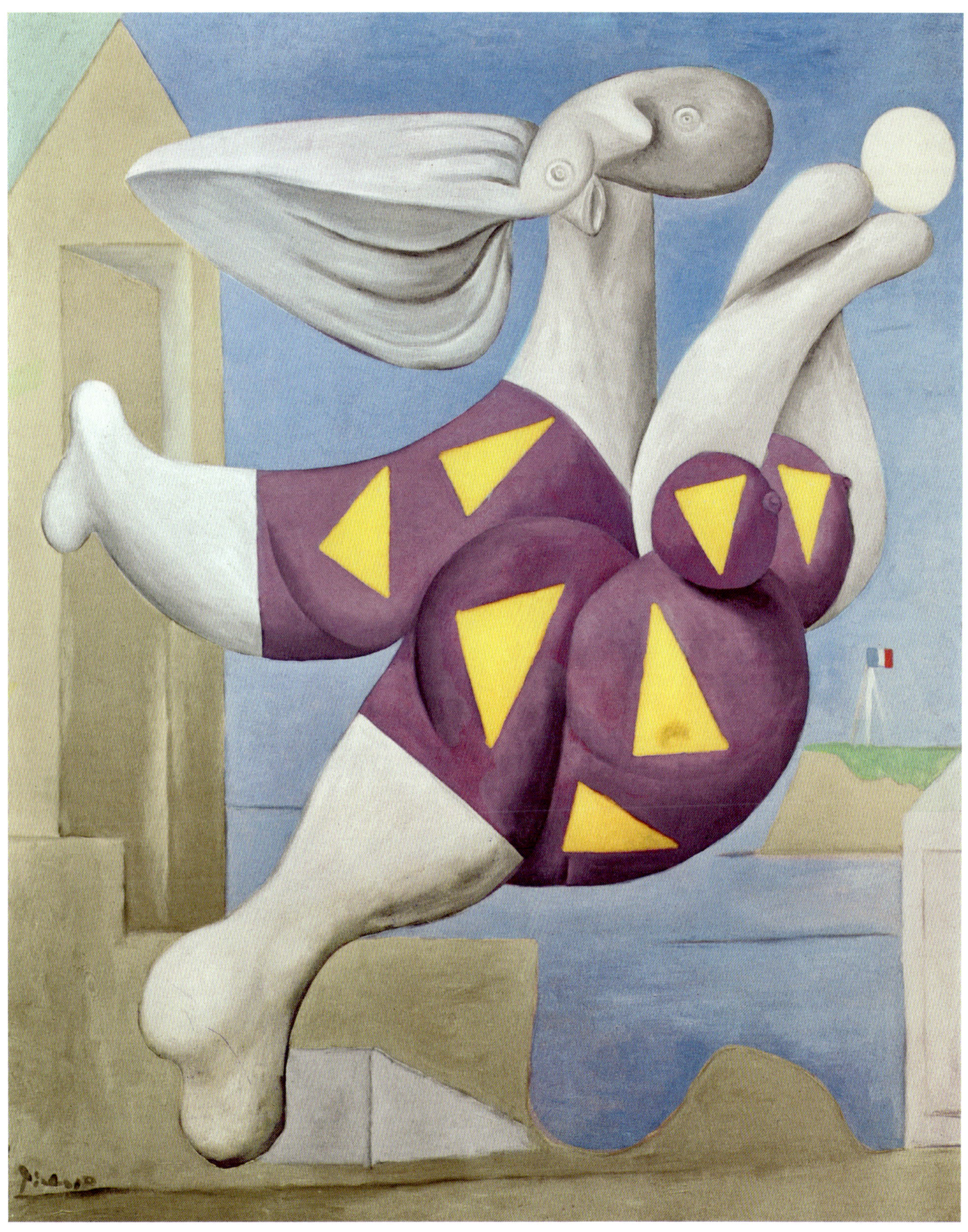

*Bather with Beach Ball, Baigneuse au bord de la mer*

# A Blank Canvas: Experiments in Black and White

Nancy Ireson

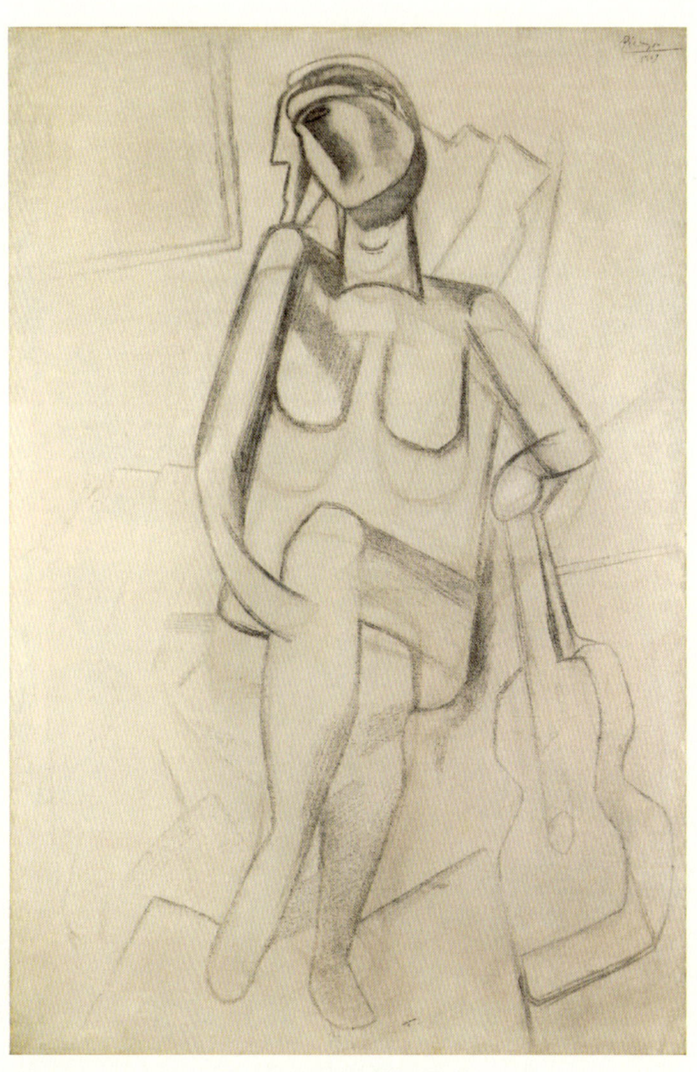

*Nude Woman with Guitar, Femme nue à la guitare* 1909

'All the interest of art lies in the beginning. After the beginning, it's already the end.'

Picasso, quoted in Tériade, 'En causant avec Picasso', *L'Intransigeant*, 15 June 1932, p.1

The defining images of Picasso's 1932 are brightly coloured but, throughout the year, he also worked in black and white. On different scales, using a range of materials, he addressed multiple themes. His choice of monochrome was hardly new: drawings had been a mainstay of his career since his earliest days as an artist.[1] But three kinds of black and white imagery from this period – drawings made in charcoal on canvas, experimental prints that he produced without the help of a professional printer, and pen and ink drawings – reveal his continuing thirst for reinvention. As his career reached new heights, the artist reconnected with his younger self, looking back in order to move forward.

The charcoal drawings are the largest of these works. Although Picasso had produced works like this in previous decades, they now seem to play a more active role in his creative process. This change of direction may have been prompted by his decision sometime in the early 1930s to release *Nude Woman with Guitar* 1909 (opposite) from his personal collection to the dealer Pierre Loeb, indicating that he now considered it suitable for exhibition. He had not displayed it in public previously.[2]

Although *Nude Woman with a Guitar* looks like a study for a painting, in composition the canvas relates more readily to experimental prints that the artist produced in the same year. As a young artist in Paris – in tentative drypoints that are not listed in the catalogue raisonné – Picasso made impressions

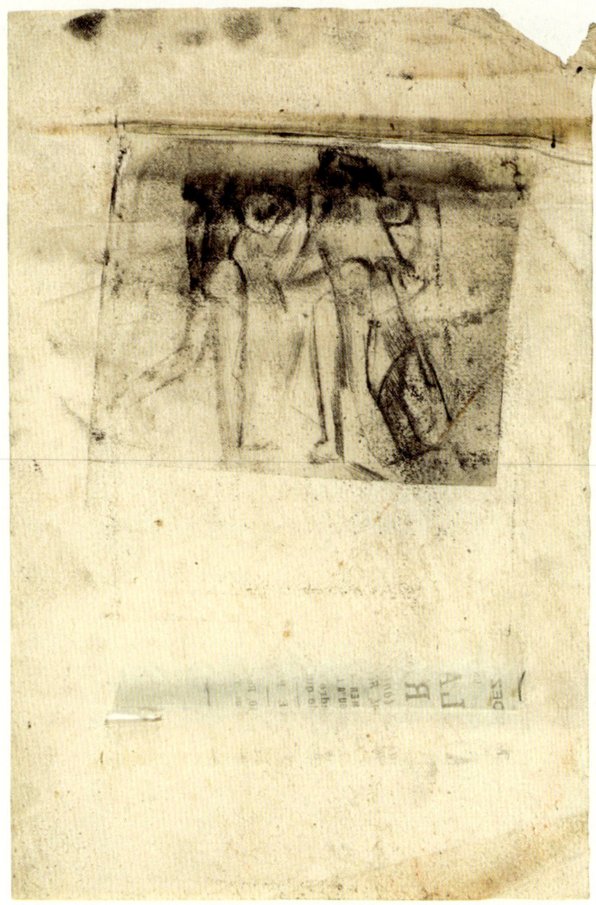

*Two Nude Figures: Woman with a Guitar and Boy with a Cup, Deux figures nues: femme à la guitare et garçon à la coupe* 1909

where, clearly, he struggled with the practicalities of using a press. Newspaper type bleeds onto the image; details are obscured in paper creases; the orientation of the printing plate is at odds with that of the sheet. These are the output of an artist at an early stage in his career; working for himself, not his public, testing a method to see what effects might result.[3] Now, at fifty, he would challenge his technical skill once again. In the last part of 1932 he brought a youthful energy to his independent printmaking, after a hiatus of more than twenty years.

As the year began, however, it was a 'woman with a mandolin' (though it might just as well have been a woman with a guitar, for the image is highly abstracted), that Picasso first tackled in charcoal on canvas. *Study for a Mandolin Player* of 2 February (p.162) came after the heavily worked *Woman in a Red Armchair* of 27 January and the *Seated Woman in a Red Armchair* of 30 January (pp.58, 59). Here, surrounded by a dark painted background, confident black charcoal lines demarcate a composition on the primed surface. Colour notations suggest work to come.[4] Yet what transpired, more than a week later, were new canvases, featuring anthropomorphic still lifes (pp.60, 61). Though the motif and medium had changed, clearly there was some sense of returning to the drawing process in order to move on to a new phase of work.

In *Sleeping Nude* of 13 March, where the connected curves of the figure stand out against the traces of erased lines, a similar sense of working through an idea is evident (p.99). This work (like some others of its kind) is not listed in the catalogue raisonné compiled by Christian Zervos; but, even if this is a deliberate omission because Picasso considered it incomplete, it no doubt served a purpose in allowing the artist to develop his ideas.[5] The composition evolved as part of an epic few days of creativity, in which he completed *Nude, Green Leaves and Bust* (8 March), *Nude in a Black Armchair* (9 March) and *The Mirror* (12 March) (pp.93, 95, 97). Following immediately after these three dazzling reclining nudes, *Sleeping Nude* forgoes the shaded undulation of their curves to settle on an arrangement of body parts aligned on a single plane: it is the visual equivalent of a palate cleanser. By reducing the theme to its essential components (and, tellingly, the background of the image is sparse), the next day Picasso could take the idea further still. The orientation of *Girl before a Mirror* is vertical rather than horizontal, as if the *Sleeping Nude* is raised to become a standing reflection (14 March, p.101). The round breasts of the actual figure appear in parallel, as they do in the drawing on canvas, but now a circular face and stomach complete the line up of spheres.

Increasingly, it seems, a sparse work serves as a creative springboard. As the artist explained to his former dealer Daniel-Henry Kahnweiler in 1933: 'Line drawing has its own light.'[6] In *Sleeping Nude* of 30 July (p.167), made three days after *Nude Woman in a Red Armchair* (p.137), the figure goes from seated to prostrate. Perhaps in a bid to push the idea further still, Picasso reversed additional aspects of the image: the woman's arms – pointed inwards to frame her face in the painting – now open to reveal her body. Her mons veneris, no longer rendered oblique by her thighs, becomes a rounded curve. The artist talked with Brassaï in 1943 about his tireless need to explore an idea: 'I can rarely keep myself from redoing a thing ... sometimes it gets to be a real obsession. After all, why work otherwise, if not to better express the same thing? You must always seek perfection'. But perfection was not a question of a level of finish. 'For me it means: from one canvas to the next, always go further and further.'[7]

If Picasso looked to the evolution of his works in order to move forward practically in 1932, similarly he looked to his past as an artist in order to reiterate his relevance as a contemporary practitioner. Though the two had not met since 1914, in March 1932 he tried unsuccessfully to start a new creative dialogue with his old collaborator Georges Braque.[8] His past was also – perhaps less agreeably – trying to forge new ties with him. In May he heard from Fernande Olivier – his partner from 1904 to 1911 – who, against his wishes, had recently published memories of their time together.[9] Despite this, Picasso had offered her financial help and writing to thank him, Olivier signed off: 'from the depths of my heart where you have always remained, and that the only years of happiness in my life were those I spent with you.'[10] For better or worse, undoubtedly, the early days in Paris remained a touchstone. In his conversations with Kahnweiler the following year, at the height of the financial crisis, his nostalgia for the era was palpable. 'What joy: soon it will all be over. I'll have no more money. Think of it, a second youth.'[11]

Certainly, by 1932, Picasso had come far in material terms. 'How had the painter, after living on the hills of Montmartre and Montparnasse, come to reside on rue La Boétie?' asked Brassaï, as he recalled his first visit to Picasso's Paris studio that December.[12] The photographer captured this tension in his photographs, using two paintings by Henri Rousseau to reiterate the point. In one image *The Representatives of the Foreign Powers Coming to Greet the Republic as a Sign of Peace* 1907 appears, propped on the studio floor (p.34). Picasso had acquired this painting in 1913 and he may have known it since as far back as the year it was made.[13] In another, a portrait that went unpublished when Brassaï's series of photographs first appeared in *Minotaure*, Picasso stands before Rousseau's *Portrait of a Woman* 1895, a canvas that he had owned since at least 1908 (p.34).[14] At the start of the twentieth century, before Rousseau's death in 1910, Picasso's taste for the older artist had been trailblazing. By

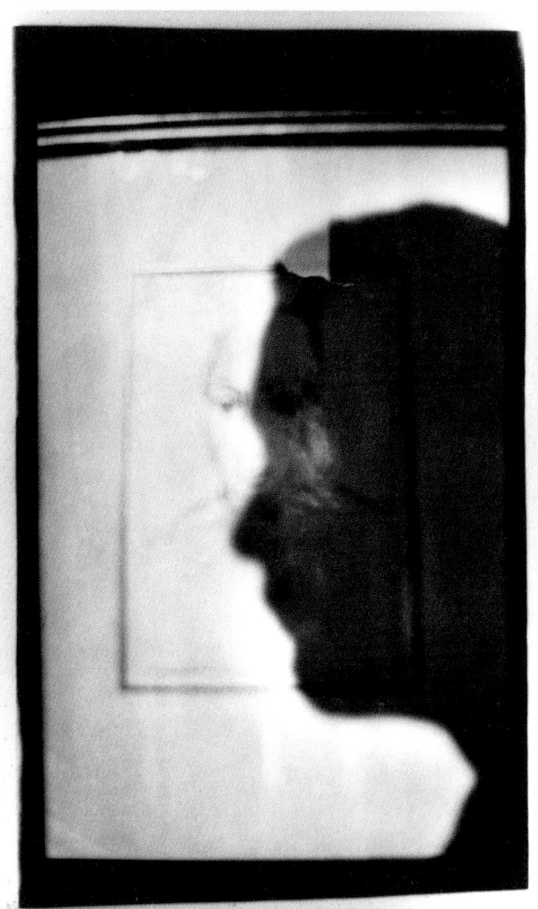

*Self-Portrait*, *Autoportrait*, Paris 1927

1932, prices were high, with Rousseau's critical reception stronger still. In 1925, collector Jacques Doucet (who also owned Picasso's *Demoiselles d'Avignon*) had persuaded the Louvre to accept a Rousseau – if not a Picasso – as part of his future bequest to the nation.[15] That Picasso was willing to pose museum-quality pictures on his floor, in the midst of studio debris, hints at a devil-may-care attitude to their transformed status. The photographs show Picasso unchanged in manner, ever the innovator, with Rousseau as much a talisman as the carved statuettes that similarly decorated the upstairs apartment (p.36).[16] He stares at the viewer provocatively.

Already, in his summer retrospective at Galeries Georges Petit, Picasso had made it clear that, regardless of age, as an artist he was unchanged. There it was his younger self (this time in a blue period self-portrait) that presided most immediately over images of his family but also, more widely, over all of his subsequent production in the comprehensive

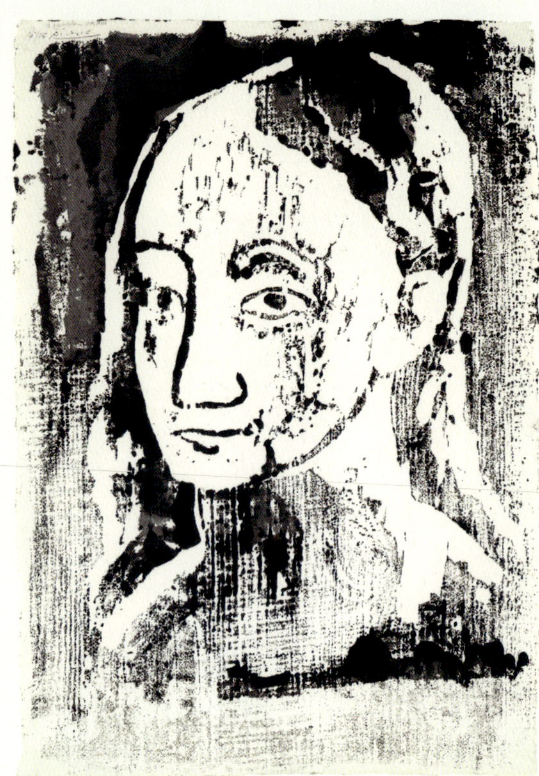

*Bust of Young Woman in Three-Quarter View, Buste de jeune femme en trois quarts* 1906, printed 1933

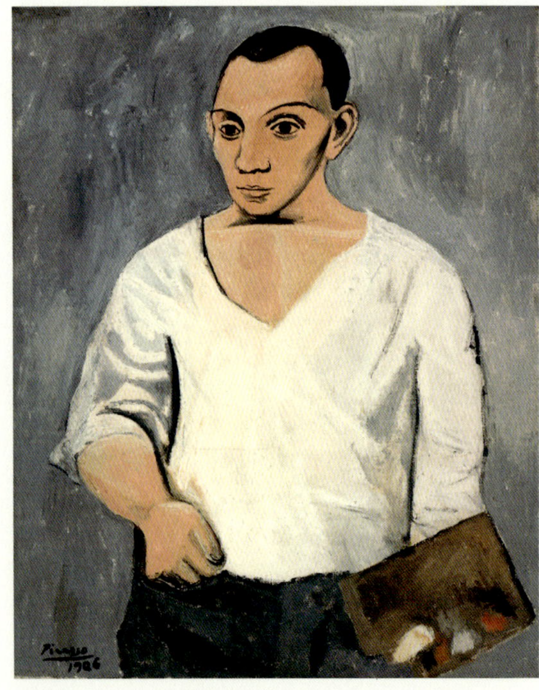

*Self-Portrait with Palette, Autoportrait à la palette* 1906

exhibition (p.128). Complimentary to this public assertion of youthful vitality, in the late 1920s (and by now in his mid-forties) Picasso had given Marie-Thérèse Walter three photographs privately that also convey the same message.[17] Two suggest a hint of vanity. One, retouched with pastel, makes the artist look younger. Another shows him years before the couple had met. But the most telling of the group aligns the older Picasso with his younger artistic self. In this *Self-Portrait* from 1927, the artist's middle-aged profile overshadows an earlier drawing, made around 1906 for the by-then legendary *Demoiselles d'Avignon*. As images meet and merge, the past and the present combine, suggesting that age is irrelevant to Picasso the creator.

In the juxtaposition of Picasso's own works, too, Brassaï's photographs linked the artist's career in the 1900s and 1930s. In a studio shot of a large group of prints and drawings from 1932 pinned to a board, in prominent position to the right there is an early state of his first known woodblock print (p.36).[18] Devised in 1906 (and despite its current title which indicates its subject is female), the appearance of this print is very much like his painted self-portrait of the same year. Judging from photographs, at the time of Brassaï's visit, Picasso had reworked a matrix that was by then twenty-six years old. The version from 1933 shows the composition in a further state of development, the back areas cut away more starkly, changing the appearance of the final impression (as is evident from a comparison of the image in Brassaï's photograph and the version reproduced here).

The other works on the board also hark back to the intaglio methods Picasso had tried in 1909. Particularly following the closure of the Zurich retrospective in November the artist was no doubt in the mood for fresh experimentation. In December he made different versions of *The Rescue of the Drowned Woman* (pp.228–9): appearing in the photograph above images of pipe players, the roughness of their printing is clear, with one creased heavily across its centre. Though Picasso had worked with professional printers in the 1920s and early 1930s – most notably in his illustrations for the art dealer Ambrose Vollard's edition of Honoré de Balzac's *The Unknown Masterpiece* in 1927, and for Albert Skira's edition of Ovid's *Metamorphosis* in 1931 – with a printing press installed in the sculpture studio in Boisegloup he could undertake, unaided, all the stages of the process.[19] However, as Brassaï's photographs suggest (and inscriptions on some of the prints also indicate), he was clearly able to make prints in Paris too (see pp.36–7). He did so inexpertly.[20] At times he seems to have forgotten to wipe the printing plate, with the acid residue causing the paper to bubble, forcing the surface of the heavy paper into sharp relief. Many of these images were not printed professionally until the 1960s,[21] although Picasso did allow his friend Tristan Tzara to use one (not seen in the Brassaï photographs) as the frontispiece to *Antitête*, published in 1933, a book that – appropriately – spanned a similarly wide time frame in its author's career.[22]

Perhaps emboldened by this 'stripping back', Picasso pushed the boundaries of appropriate media for making art further still in other 1932 prints, going so far as to use suet and nail polish.[23] In a series of prints on the theme of *The Diver*, he added found elements to his prints to make monotypes, including rose petals (that have since fallen off) on one more notable occasion (p.221).[24] These combinations of media are an extension of his bringing together of material in his *Composition with Butterfly* of 15 September (p.195), an assemblage that, in some ways, was a monochrome version of colourful works such as *Three Women Playing on the Seashore*, completed the same day (p.194). That André Breton would champion *Composition with Butterfly* in his seminal text 'Picasso in his Element', in which he also subscribed to the notion that Picasso's prints had a life of their own, is telling (p.184). 'It is simply that the engraving needle moving over the copper plate has suddenly caught itself dreaming.'[25] The 'stripping back', here, is taken to new extremes.

These connections to surrealism, coupled with the fact that the artist gave a few of his experimental prints to his eleven-year-old nephew Javier Vilató, shows another way in which black and white signified a return for the sake of renewal in Picasso's art.[26] Beyond any personal sense of looking back, given the intellectual preoccupations of his social circle, the idea of extreme regression – beyond conventional behaviours – also offered creative possibilities.

Child drawing had counted amongst the artist's interests since at least the mid 1920s, when he made a group of zinc etchings that each consist of a single line, including *Dancer*. By Picasso's own admission, this method was inspired by seeing children draw

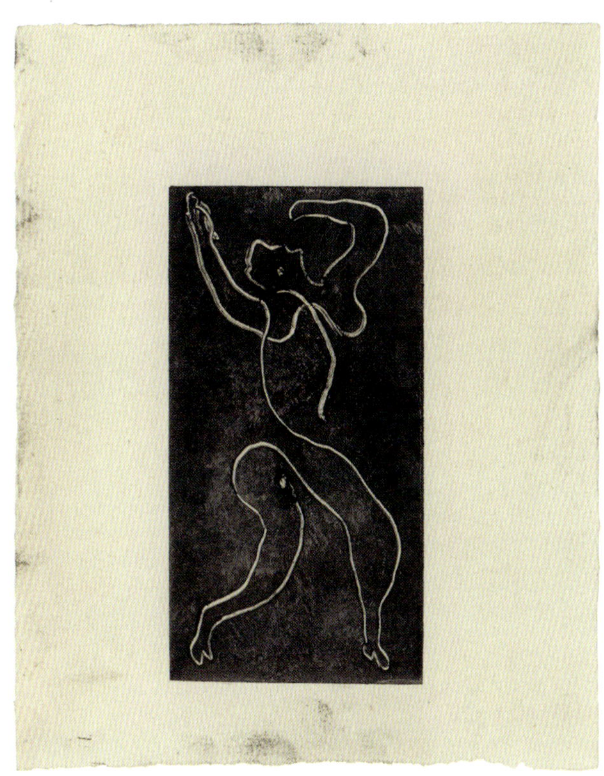

*Dancer*, *Danseuse* 1925

with sticks on the beach in Malaga, making continuous lines in the sand;[27] and it may in turn have informed the aesthetic of certain drawings on canvas (in particular *Woman with Flower Writing*, p.165, where the figure herself has a girlish appearance). Yet by this time childhood was no longer synonymous with innocence. The appearance of Sigmund Freud's *Three Essays* had transformed understanding of desire and sexual development in infancy and, in certain representations of his son Paulo as a very young boy, Picasso seems to have explored the idea of children as willfully transgressive.[28] In a further development, with the French publication of *Civilisation and its Discontents* and *Totem and Taboo* in 1930, the pre-social mentality of children and what Freud understood as the 'uncivilised' minds of tribal peoples came into comparison.[29] This was of significant interest to many of Picasso's peers.

One of them was Michel Leiris, who corresponded with the artist in 1932 from a far-flung expedition as part of a French ethnographic mission, also exchanging letters with Georges Bataille. While Leiris explained that his travels had been prompted in part by desire for 'breaking the circle' – a wish to escape the monotony of their unchanging social

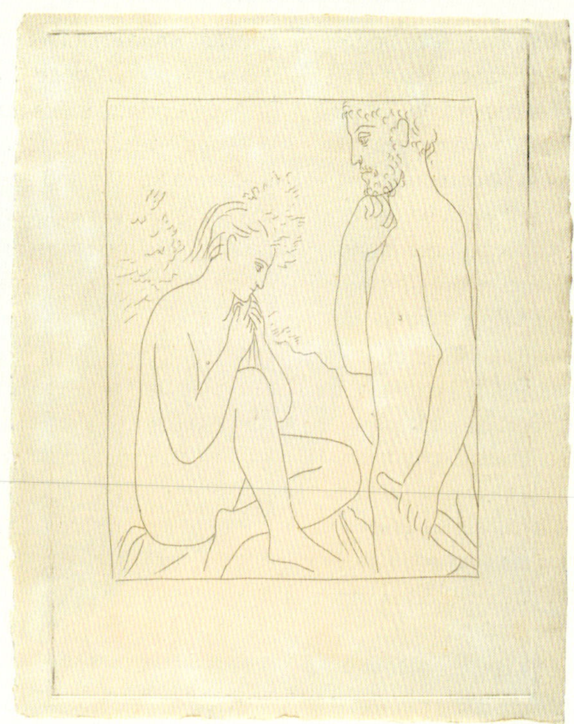

*Tereus and his Sister-in-law Philomela, Térée et sa belle-soeur Philomèle* 18 October 1930, illustration for *Ovid's Metamorphoses, Les Métamorphoses d'Ovide*

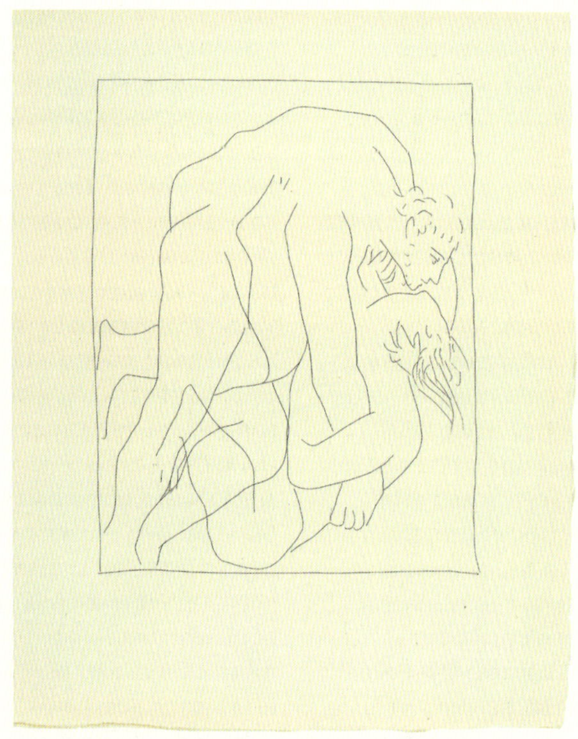

*Tereus Raping his Sister-in-law Philomela, Térée violant sa belle-soeur Philomèle* 18 October 1930, illustration for *Ovid's Metamorphoses, Les Métamorphoses d'Ovide*

world – Bataille conveyed not only dismay that people are unchanging but that, more significantly, the conventions of conversation prevent anything 'Other' from being discussed.[30] Transgression – a theme that had been key to Bataille's periodical *Documents*, which had ceased production in 1930 – would be central to writings in *Minotaure*, a new publication for which Picasso would design the cover of the first issue in 1933, as well as featuring heavily inside (see pp.178, 184–7).[31]

A conversation with Kahnweiler in November 1933 proves that such concerns were pertinent to Picasso across the late 1920s and early 1930s. The artist mentioned that he had been to see Jacques Lacan, where he had found himself in disagreement with the psychoanalyst, as the two discussed a notorious recent murder trial. The case in question was that of the Papin sisters, two working-class women who had murdered their employer's wife and daughter early in 1933. While Lacan believed that the women were mad, Picasso was unconvinced. The artist instead expressed admiration that the sisters had committed a crime that no one else – contrary to desire – would dare take on. 'To say that they're mad, it's to take away that wonderful thing, sin.' The judges in the case had declared that the women were sane. Picasso approved, claiming that theirs was 'a classical culture'. 'How antisocial is tragedy then? And what becomes of the great emotions? Hate? ... Modern psychiatrists are the enemies of tragedy and sanctity'.[32]

A wish for a return to a 'classical culture' (which might, by association, also connect with childhood or other supposedly 'pre-civilised' cultures) may explain the extremes of behaviour played out in some of Picasso's 1932 works on paper. Increasingly, towards the end of the year, his subject matter veered between idyllic and violent. The illustrations that Picasso had devised for Skira's edition of Ovid's *Metamorphoses* in 1931 (which, visually, bore a resemblance to surrealist 'automatic drawings')[33] already opened up the possibility that his flute players and Crucifixions might share common ground. In a period where Freud had employed classical myths to articulate his modern findings, Picasso's choice of subject invited psychological readings, which might account for how in the original version of *Tereus Raping his Sister-in-law Philomela* there is no physical evidence of violence. In subsequent versions, Tereus attacks, while Philomela rallies against the assault. Her thrown-back head – which surely informed Picasso's prints of *The Rape* and *The Rescue of the Drowned Woman* the following year (pp.218, 221–2) – is at once horrific and ecstatic. If Picasso's surrealist and classicising works are linked,[34] disturbingly, the motif covers the range of human emotion: another indication, perhaps, of his completeness as an artist.

A regressive return in Picasso's monochrome work – that might in turn spark something new – seems to play out most clearly in a series of ink drawings that he made on the theme of the Crucifixion in September and October of 1932 (pp.196–9, 201–3, 207). While the strange composition of Christ's body recalls the composite wooden crucifixes of Catalonia, which he would have known since his youth, one of the sheets makes a literal connection between his subject matter and infancy (p.205).[35] Focused on a detail of Christ's loincloth, it singles out a safety pin, which the artist labelled explicitly as a 'nappy pin'. This blasphemous reference indicates an ongoing exchange with dissident surrealism even as, in crude terms, it hints at the 'rebirth' of the resurrection.[36] Picasso – who had already made a painting on the theme of the Crucifixion in 1930 (p.180) – was no doubt mindful of how Bataille's 1928 book *The Story of the Eye* ends with an abusive parody of the Eucharist.

To take on Matthias Grünewald required a degree of artistic confidence that had only come to the artist in middle age. Brassaï had noticed this on a further visit to Picasso in 1932, when he saw and photographed the Crucifixion drawings, which at that stage were newly completed. The artist admitted to the photographer that his interpretation of the Isenheim altarpiece had become 'something completely different'. Brassaï noticed that that Picasso had gone to new lengths to unlock the secrets of the work; that he had reduced and reconstituted the image, and had left it transfigured. 'He was no longer bowing to an influence, as he had done earlier when he was infatuated with Lautrec, Cézanne, El Greco, or Ingrés. Picasso had himself become something of a Lautrec, a Cézanne, an El Greco, an Ingrés. Now it is the old masters inspiring him that become Picassos'.[37] For Brassaï, these black and white works indicated not only that Picasso was at one with himself as an artist, but also that he had taken his place in the history of art.

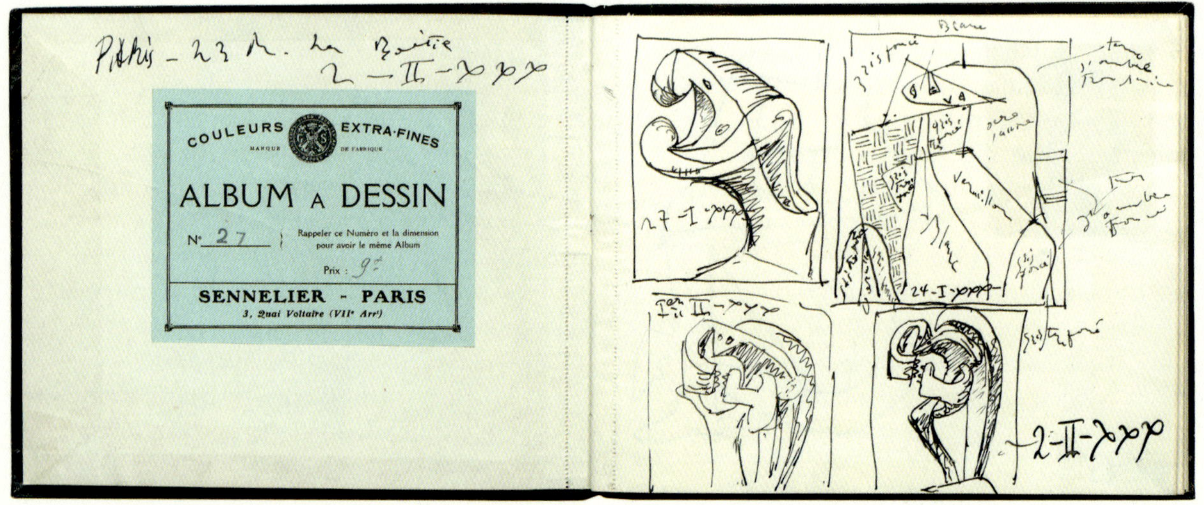
COULEURS EXTRA-FINES
MARQUE DE FABRIQUE
ALBUM A DESSIN
N° 27
Rappeler ce Numéro et la dimension pour avoir le même Album
Prix :
SENNELIER - PARIS
3, Quai Voltaire (VIIe Arr')

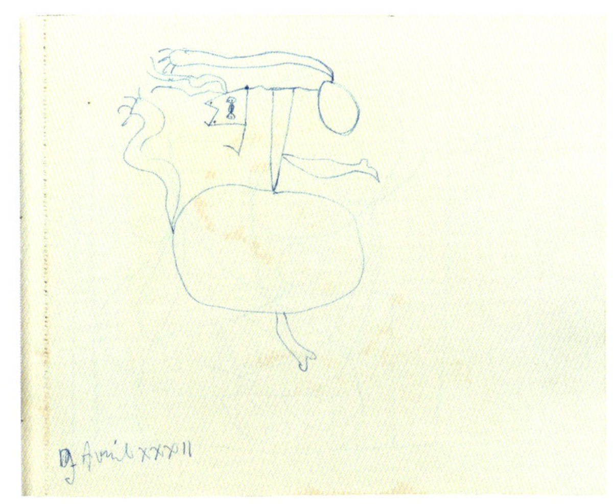


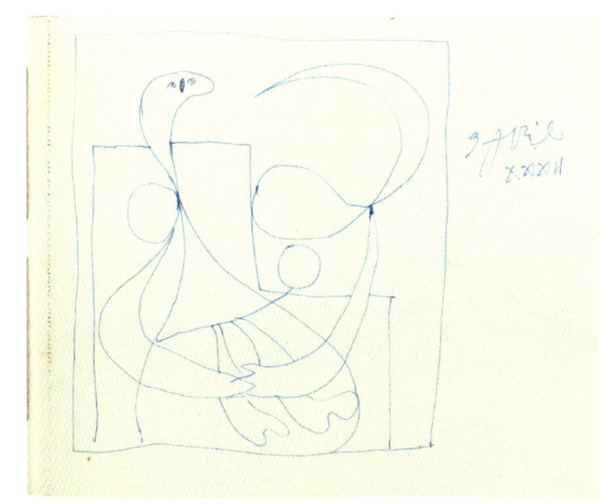


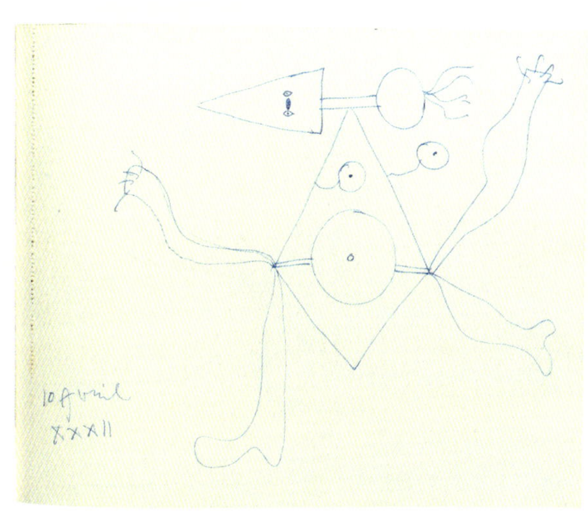


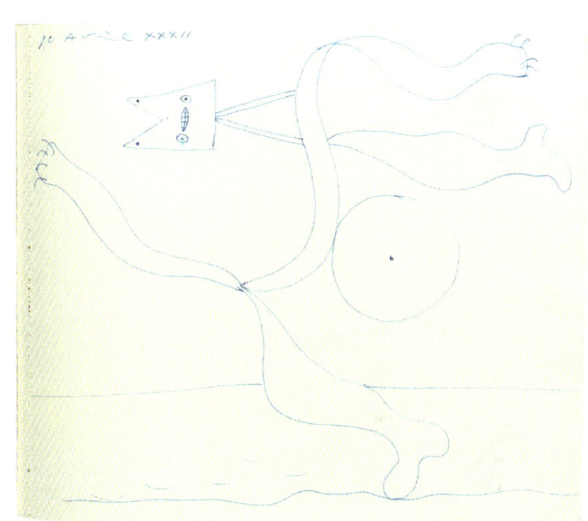


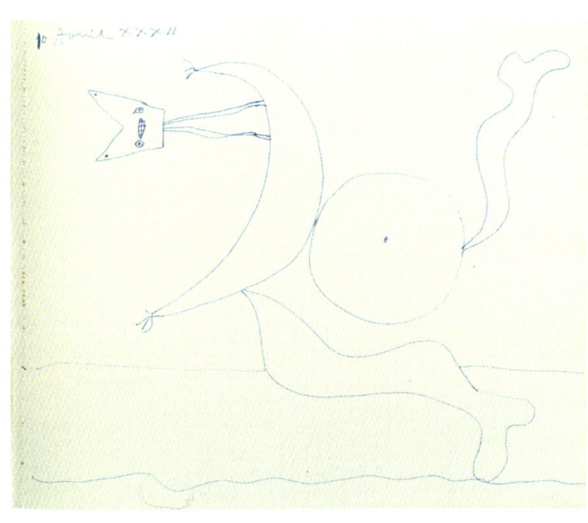


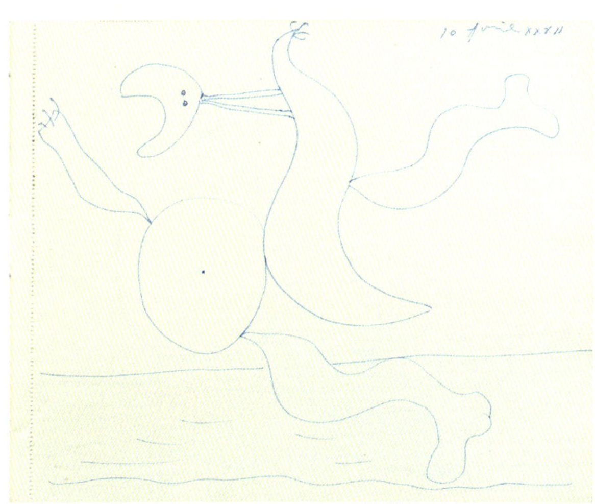


*Pages from Sketchbook no.17, Carnet no.17*

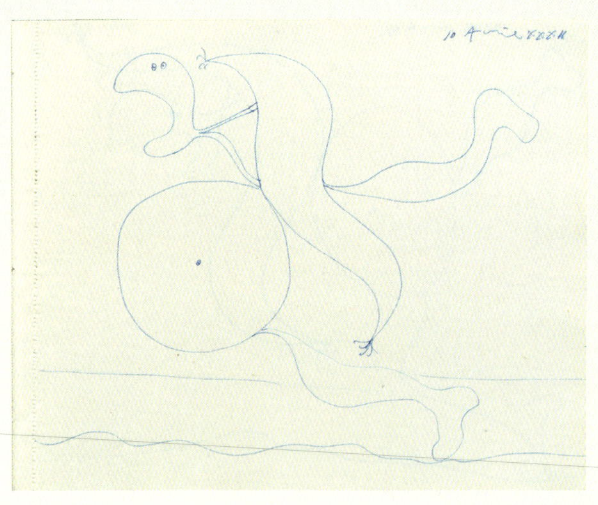

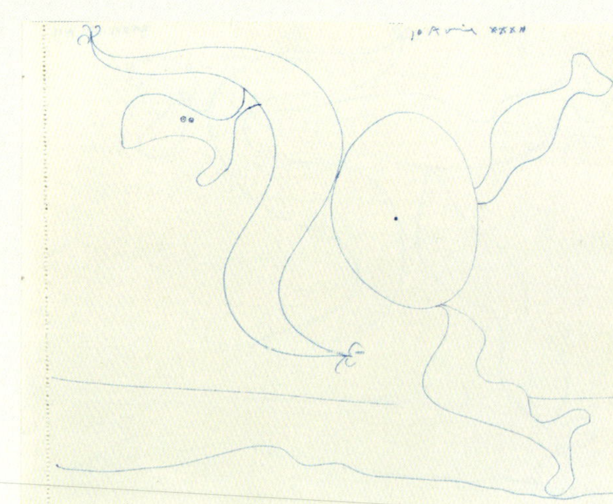

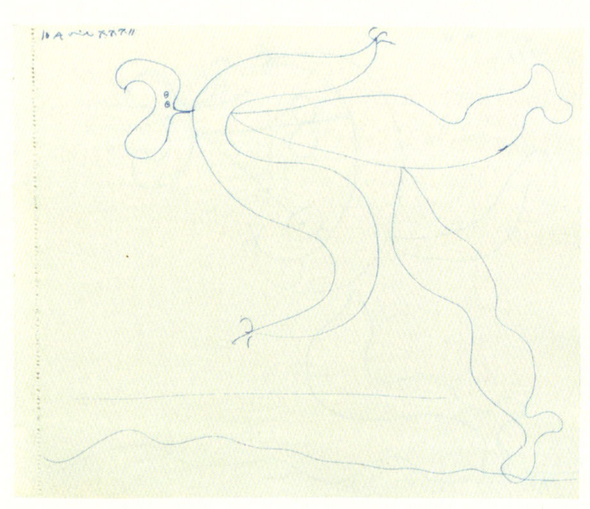

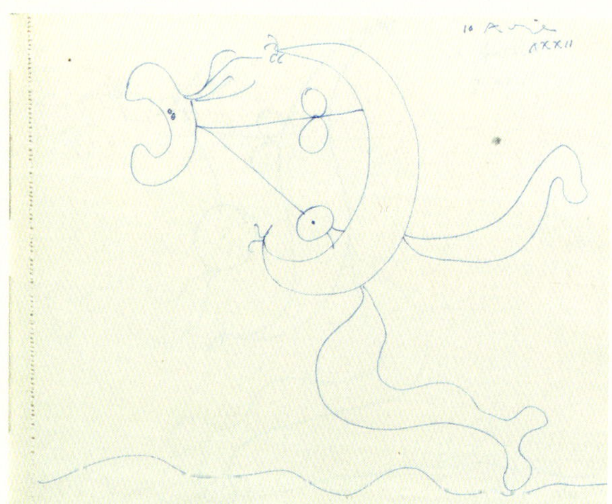

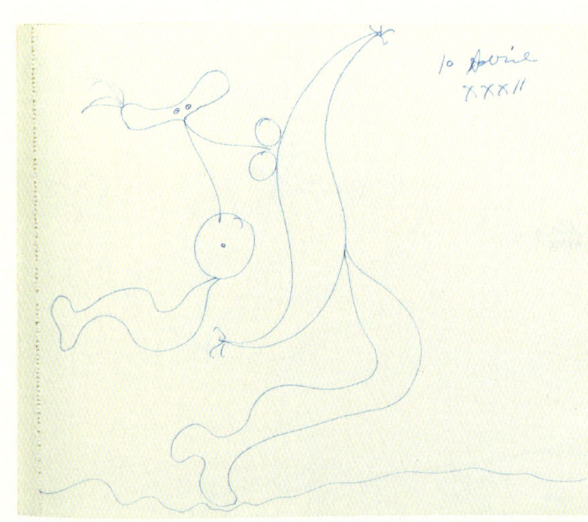

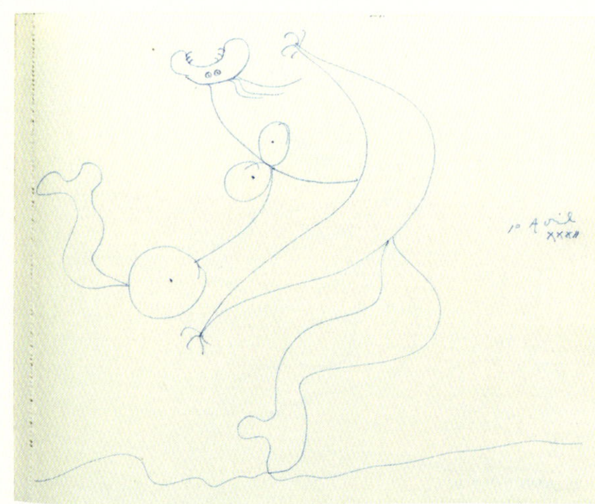

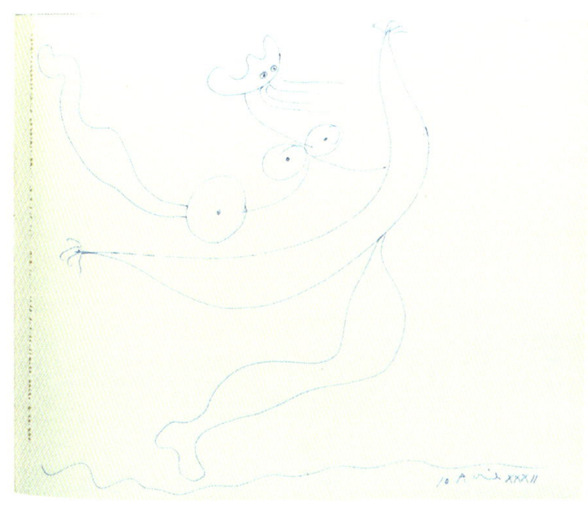

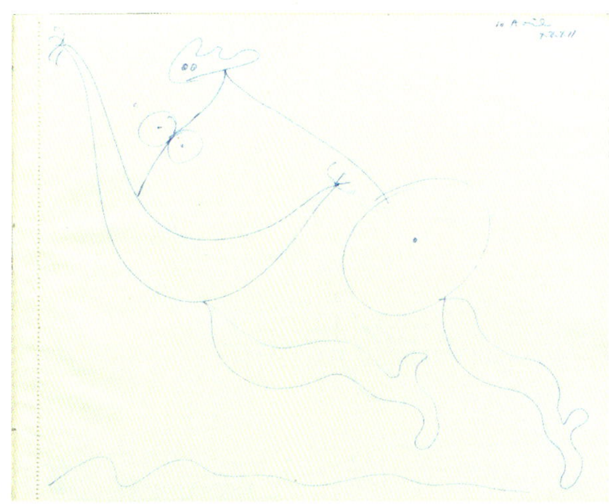

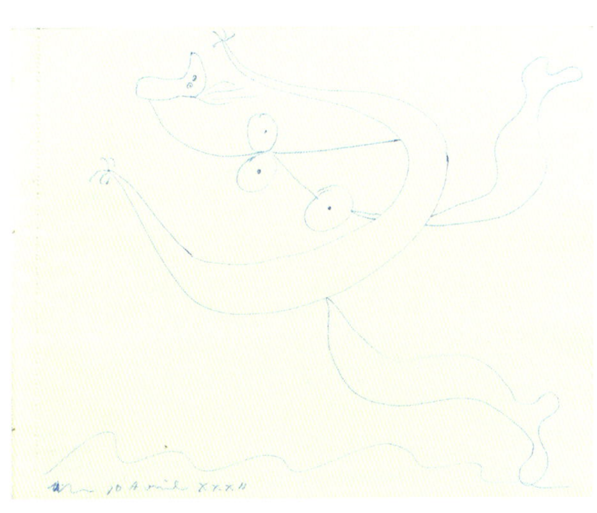

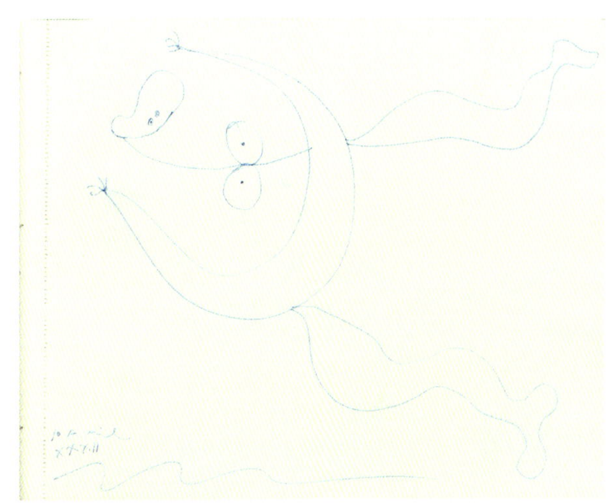

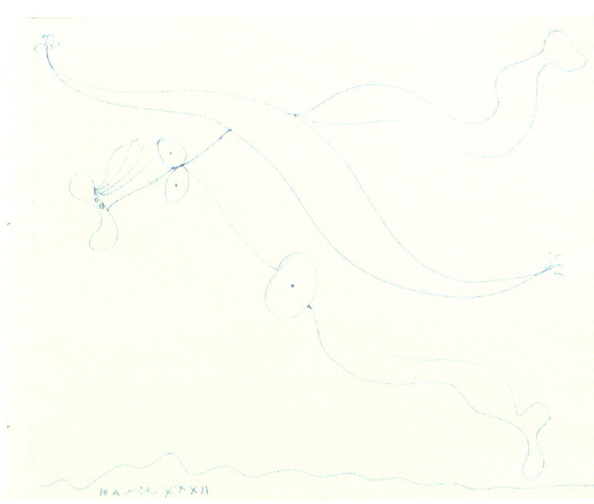

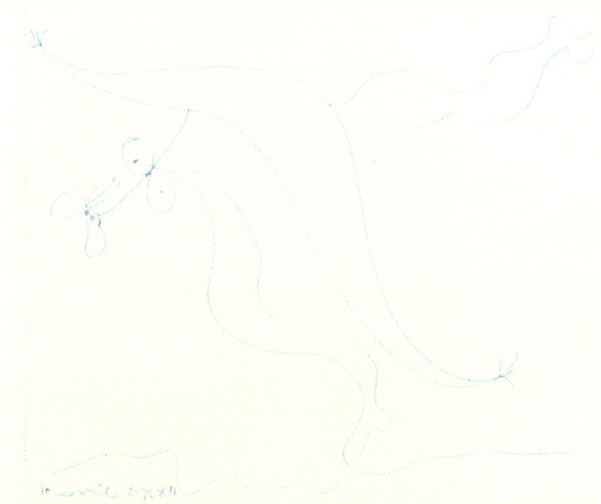

*Pages from Sketchbook no.17, Carnet no.17*

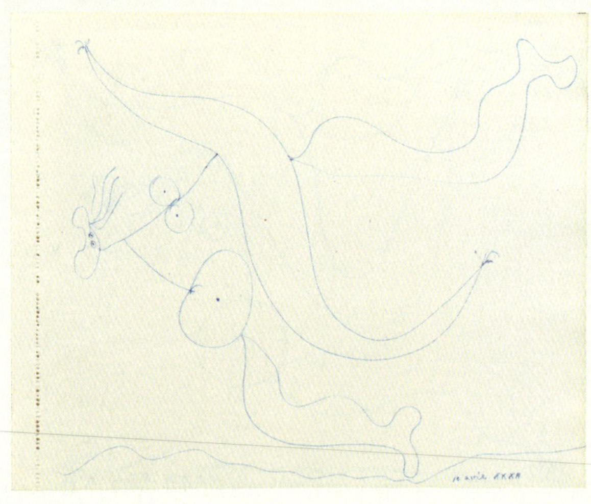

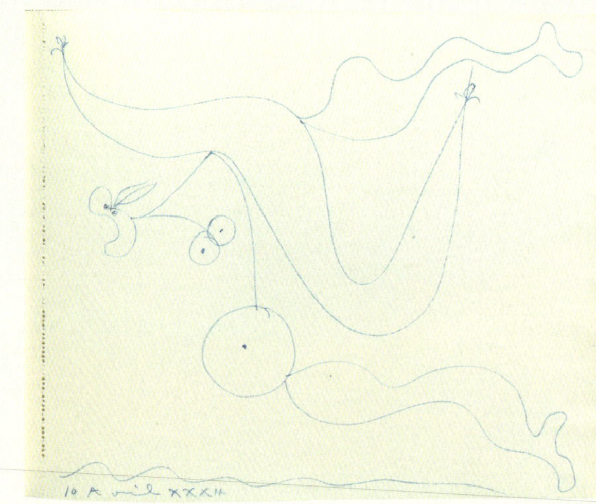

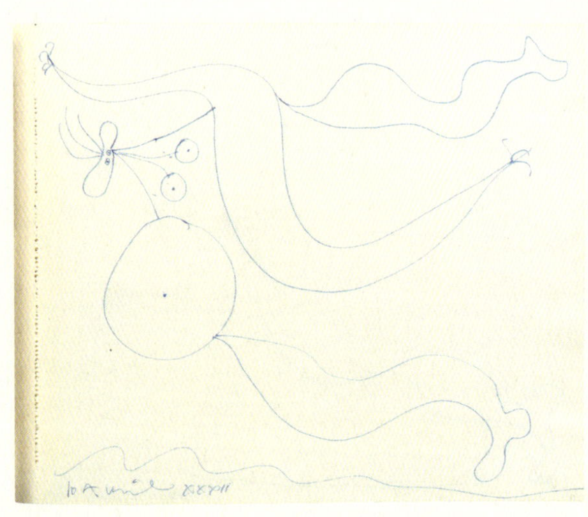

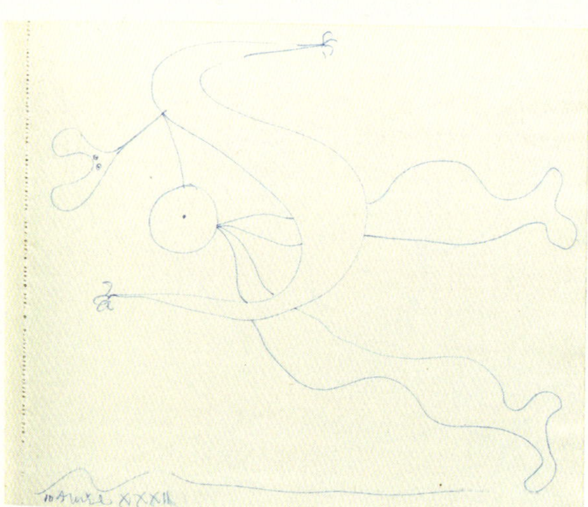

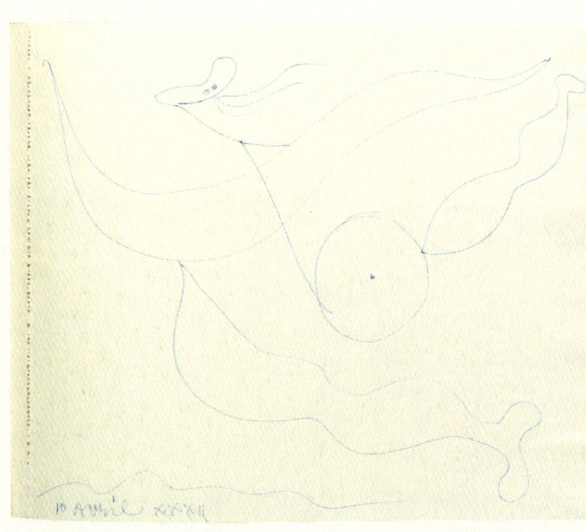

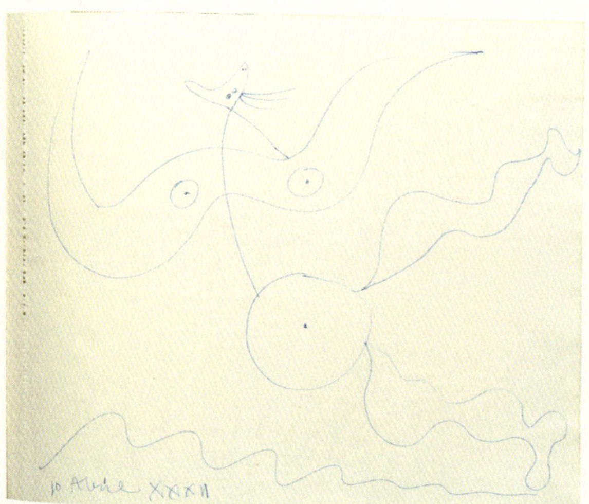

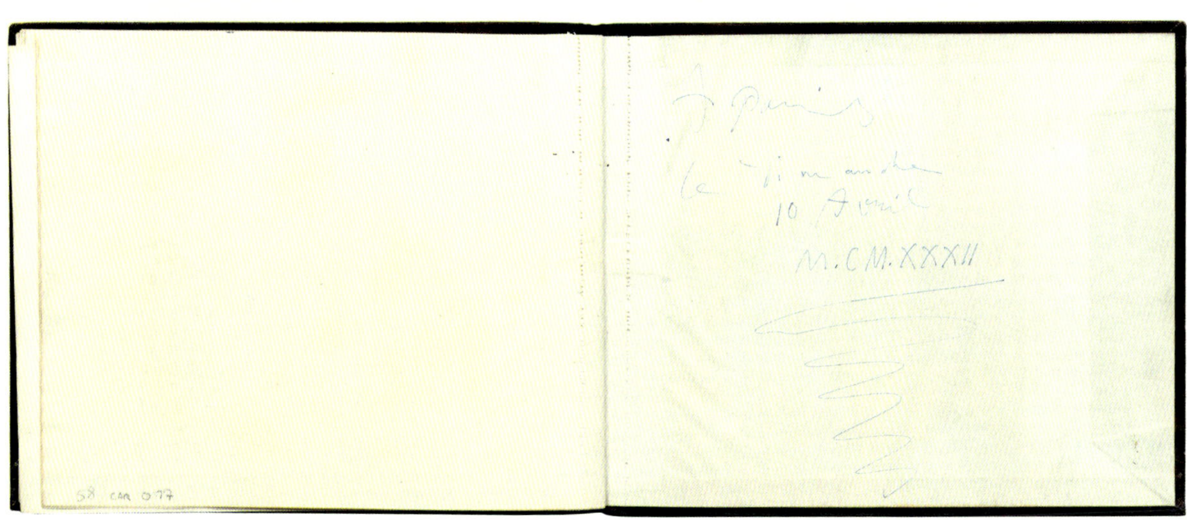

*Pages from Sketchbook no.17, Carnet no.17*

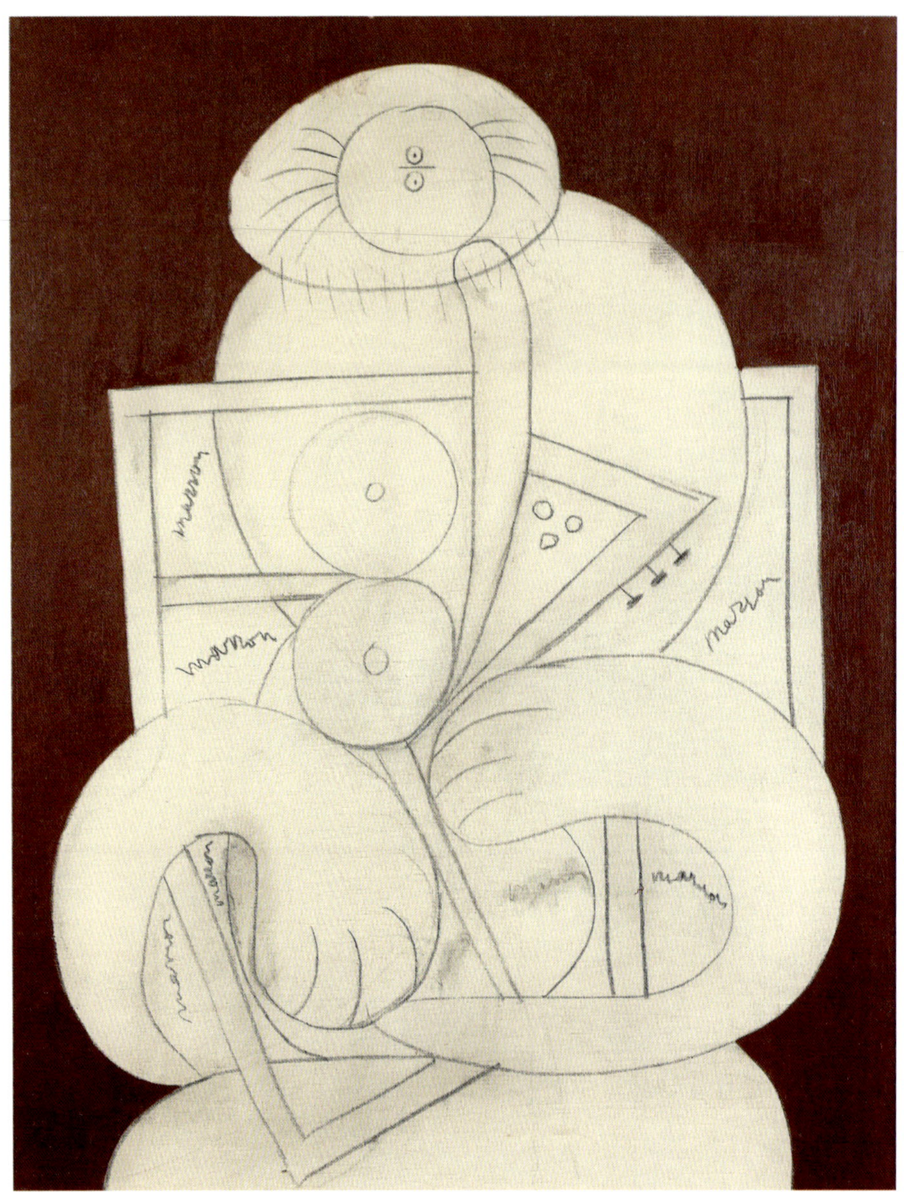


*Study for a Mandolin Player, Etude pour une joueuse de mandoline*

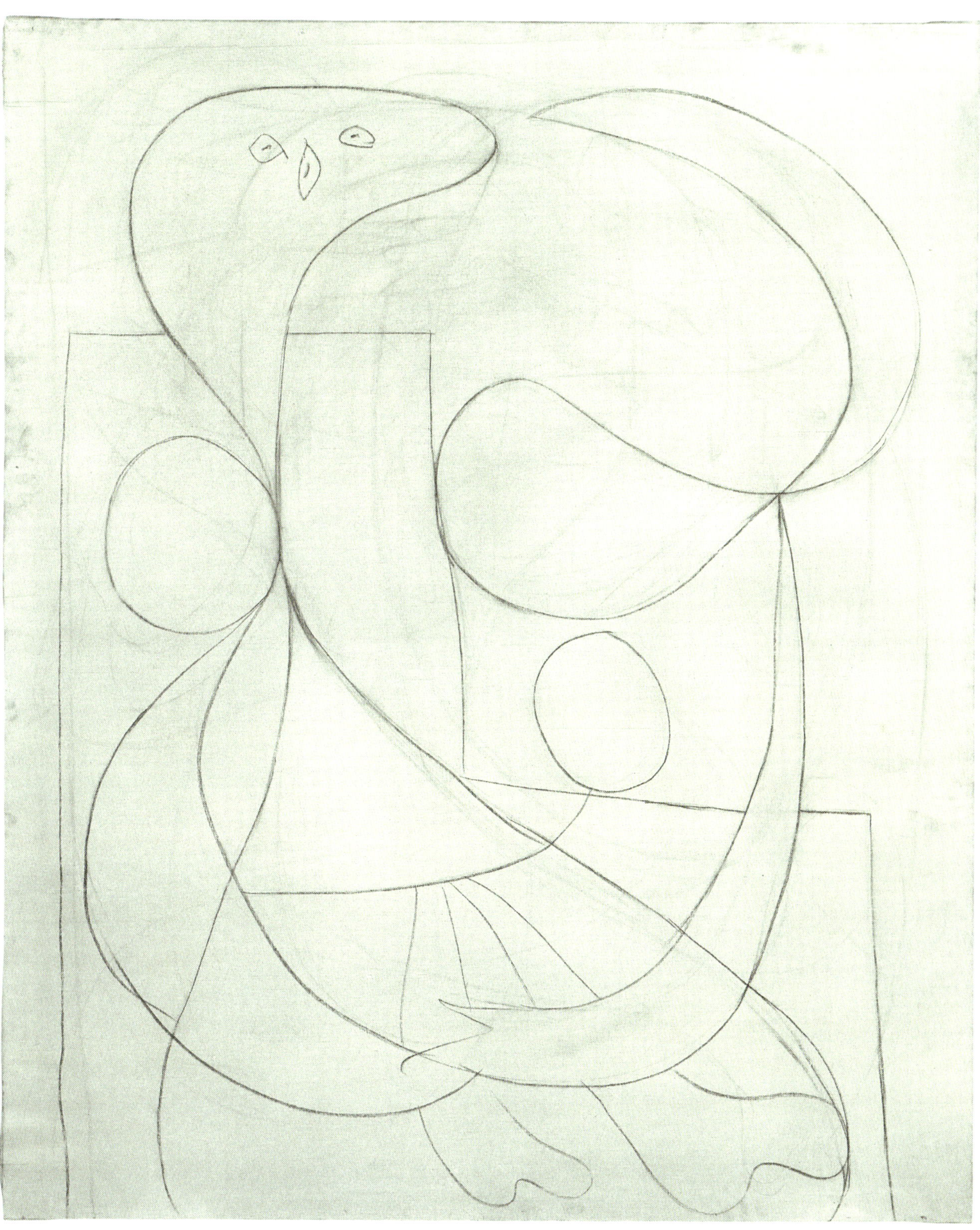

*Woman with a Flower, Femme à la fleur*

'When I'm painting a picture, I think of a white and I apply a white. But I can't continue working, thinking and applying white; colour like line follows the mobility of emotion.'

Picasso to Christian Zervos, in 'Conversation avec Picasso,' *Cahiers d'Art*, 1935, p.174

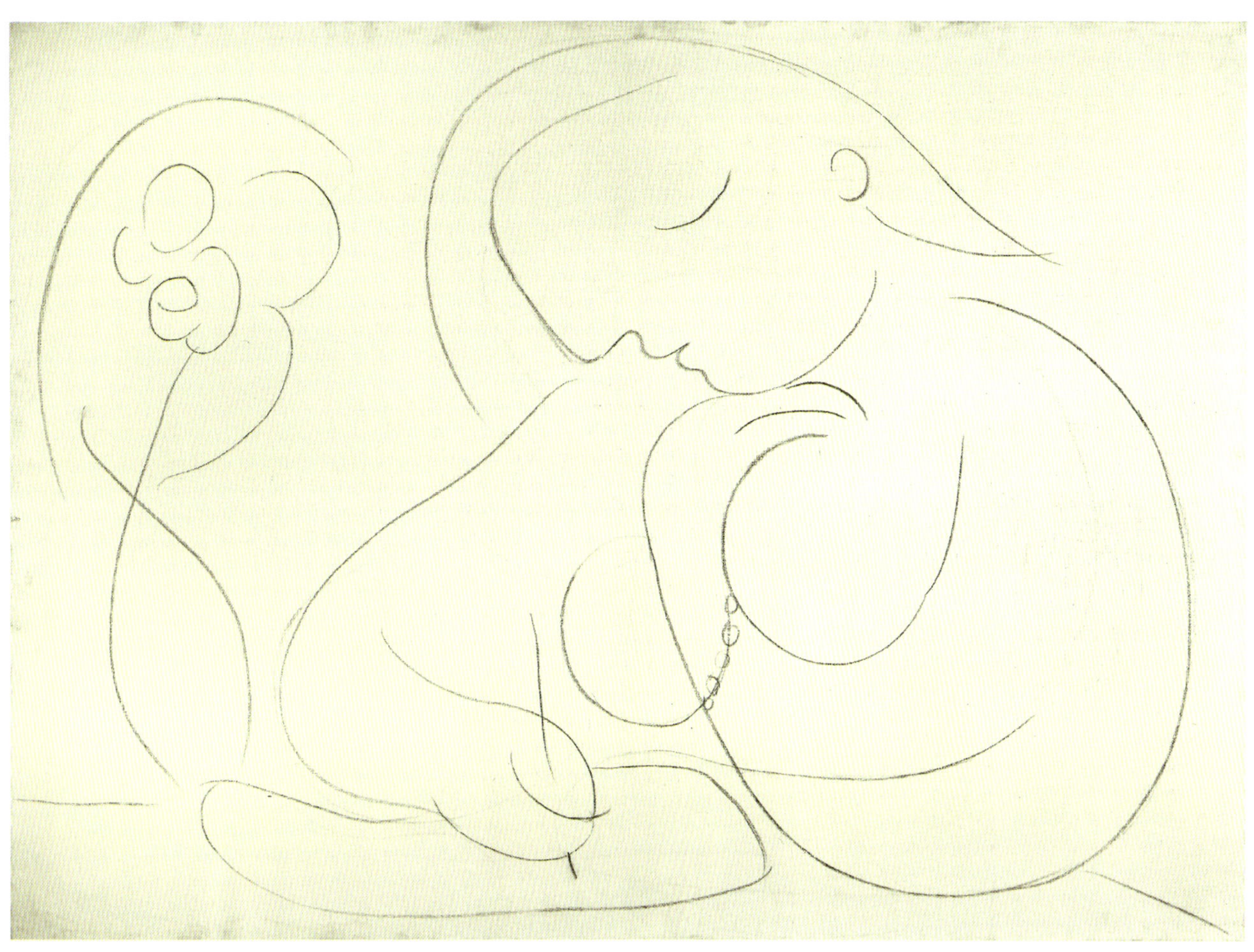

*Woman with Flower Writing, Femme à la fleur écrivant*

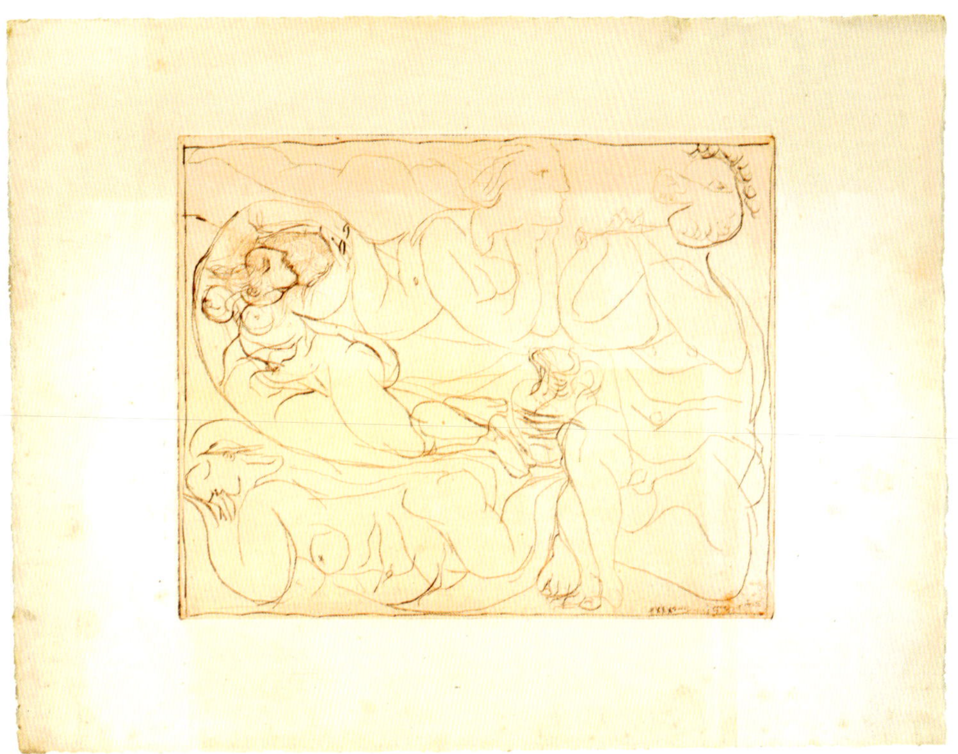

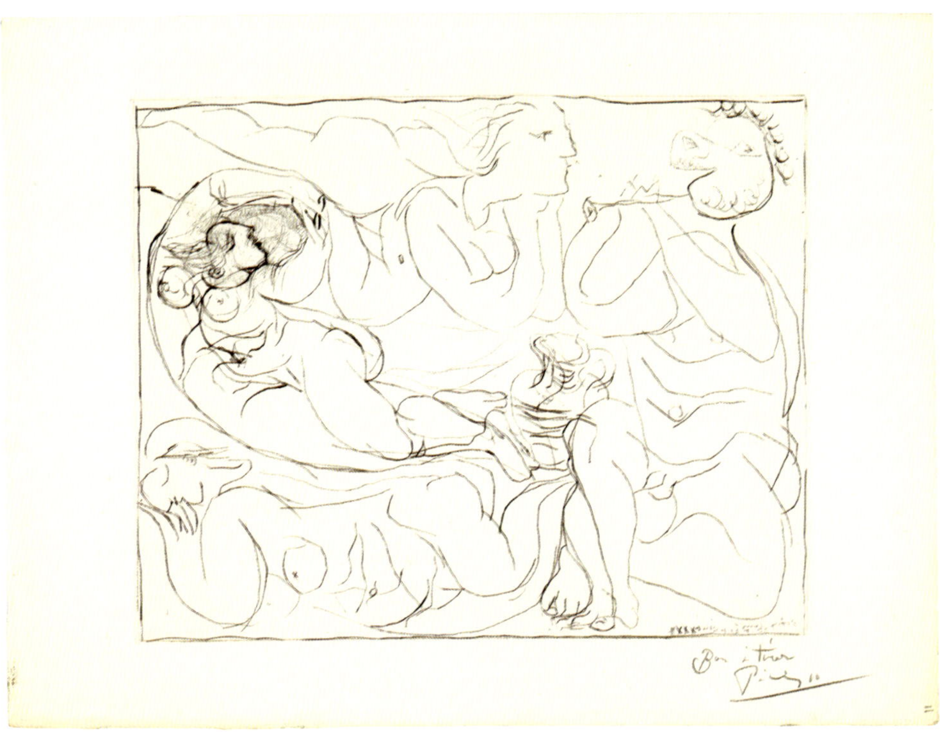

*Flute Player and Three Female Nudes, Flûtiste et trois femmes nues*

*Flute Player and Three Female Nudes, Flûtiste et trois femmes nues*

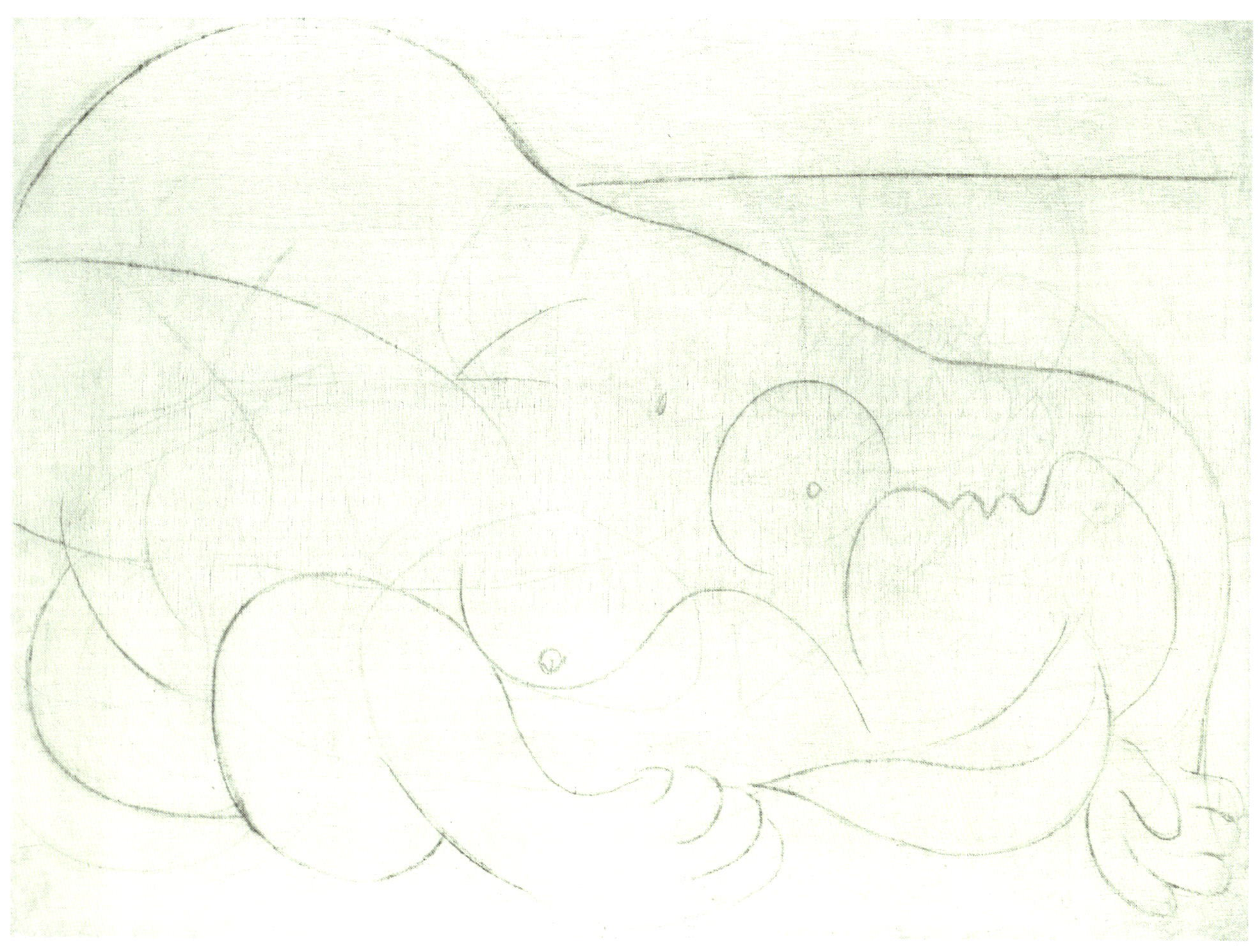

*Sleeping Nude, Nu endormi*

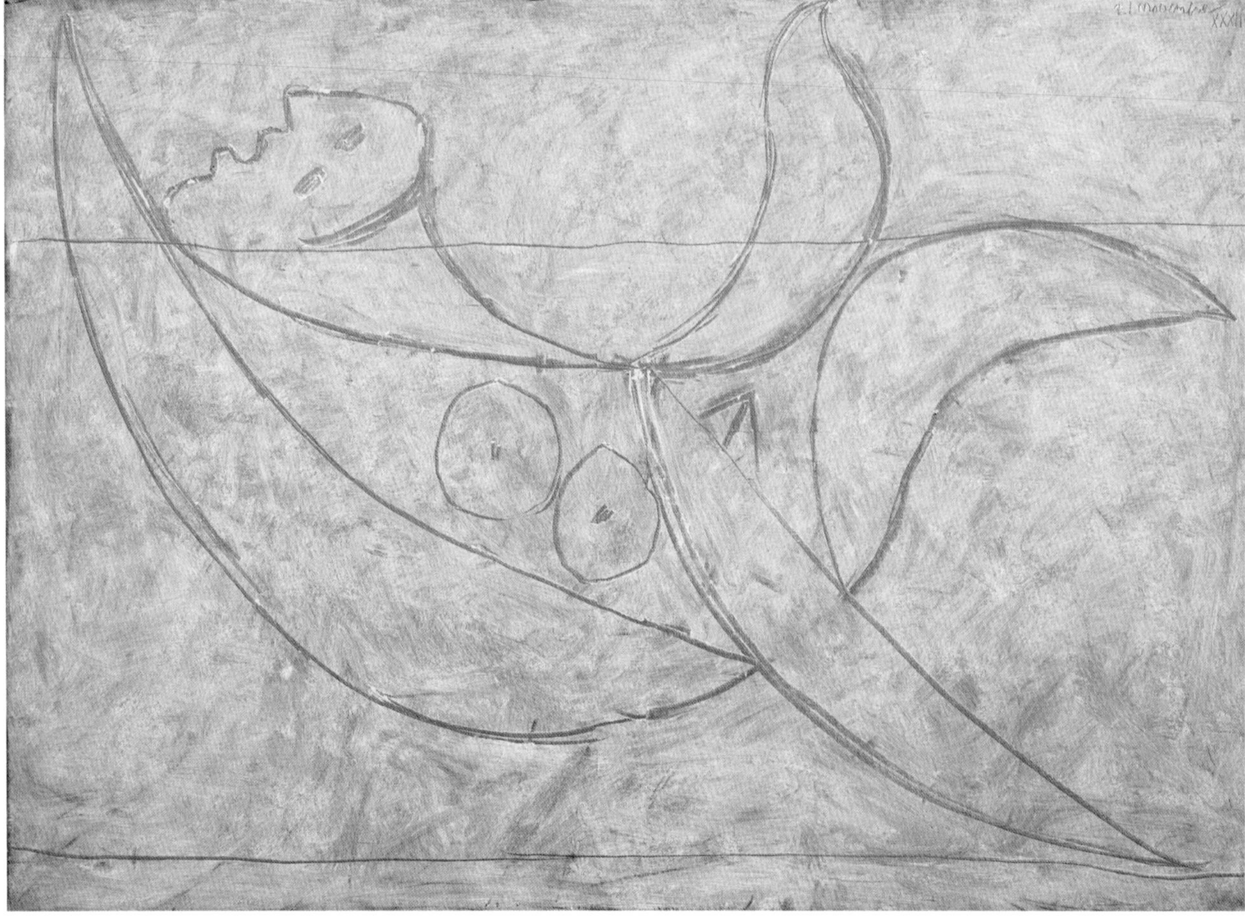

 *Swimmer, Nageuse*

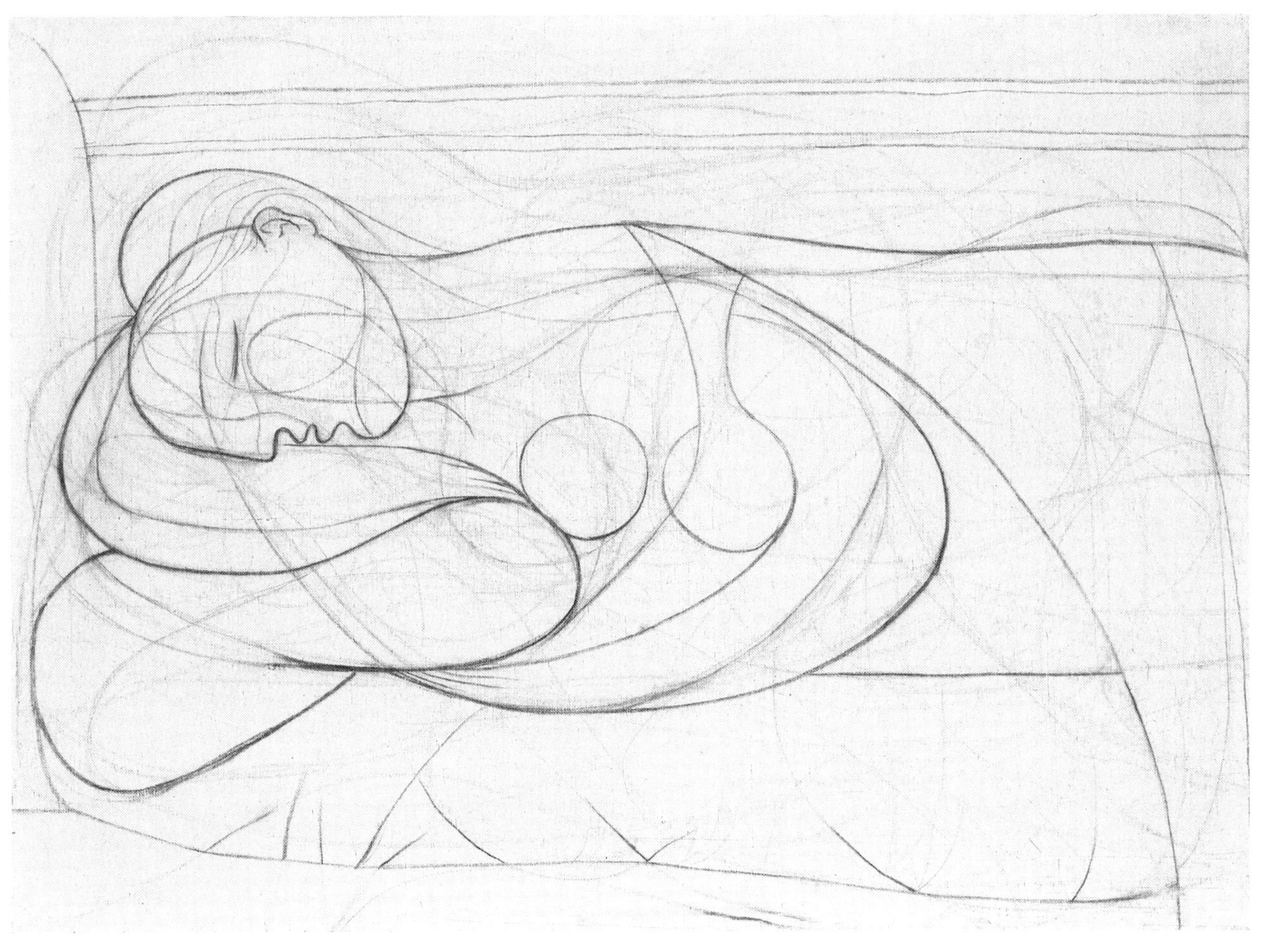

*Sleeping Woman, Femme nue couchée*

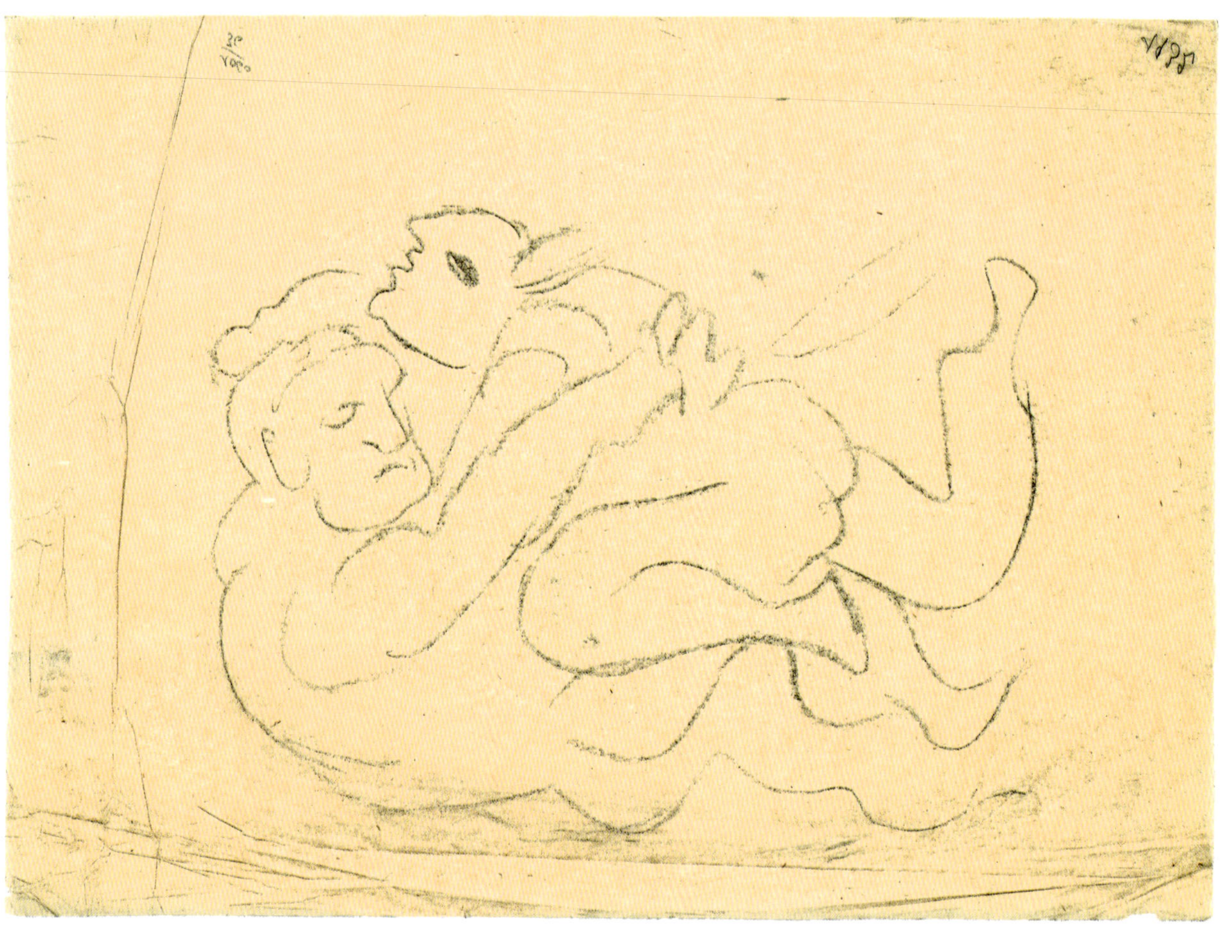

 *The Embrace, L'Etreinte*

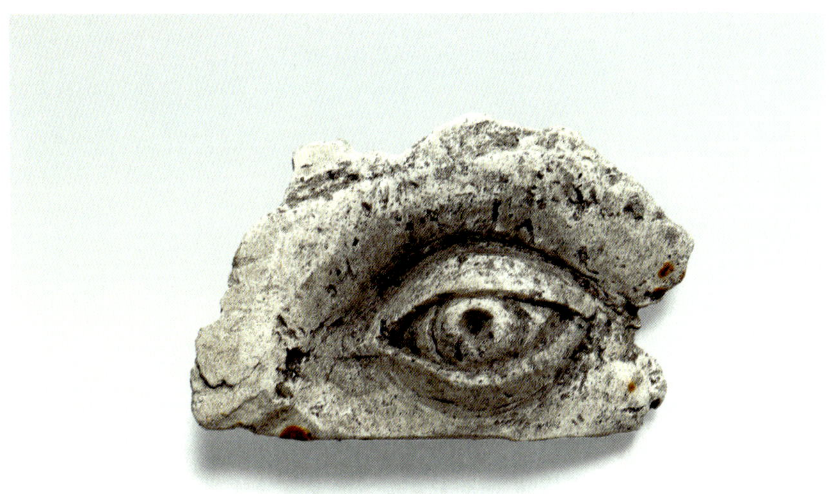

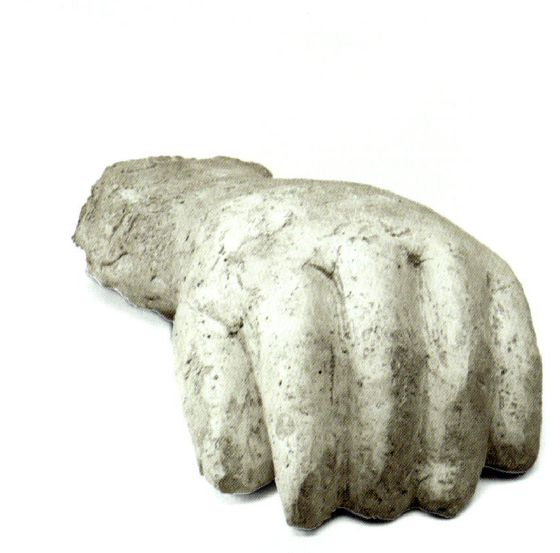

*Eye, Oeil*

*Hand, Main*

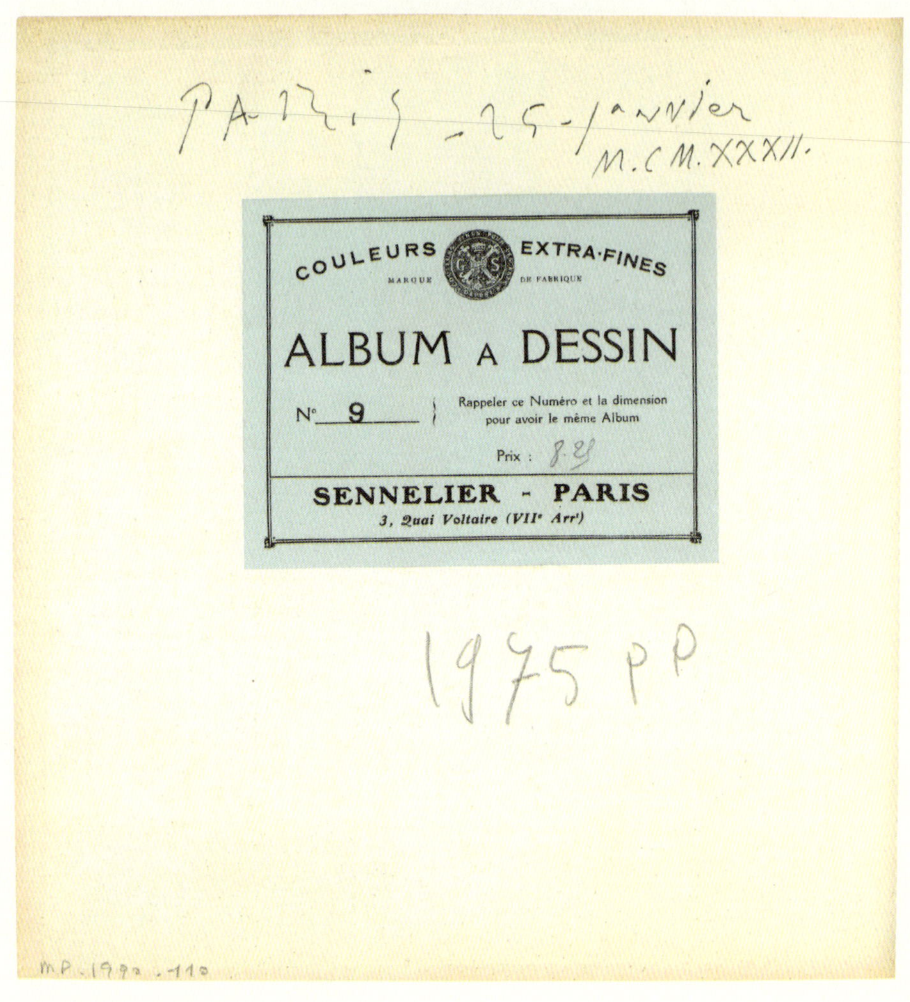
PARIS -29-janvier
M.CM.XXXII.
COULEURS EXTRA-FINES
MARQUE DE FABRIQUE
ALBUM A DESSIN
N° 9
Rappeler ce Numéro et la dimension
pour avoir le même Album
Prix :
SENNELIER - PARIS
3, Quai Voltaire (VIIe Arrt)
1975 PP

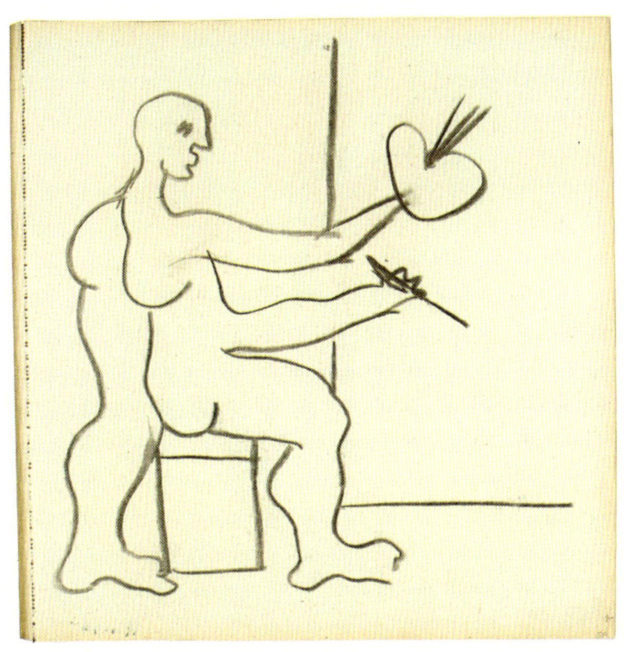

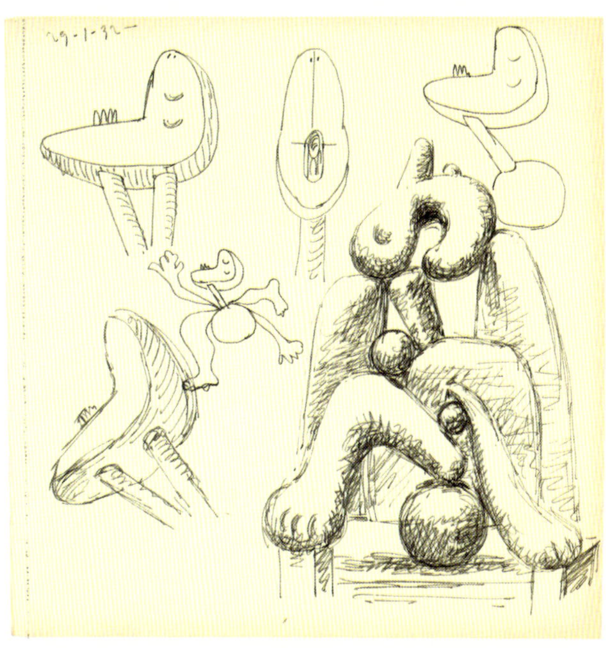


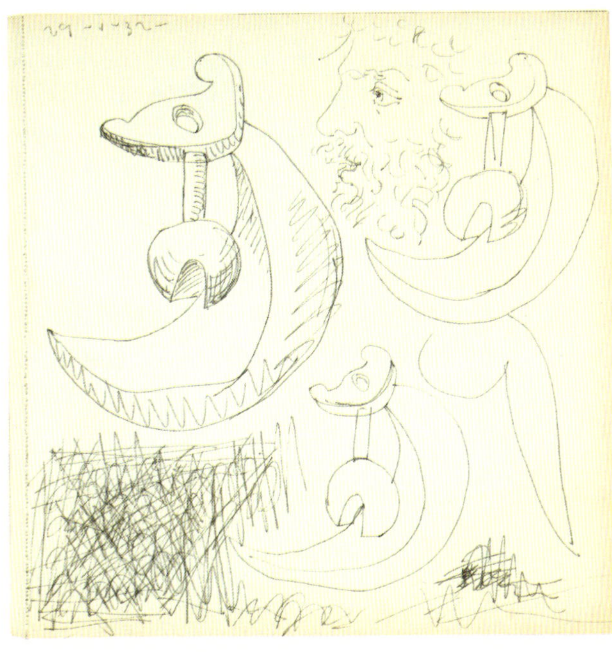

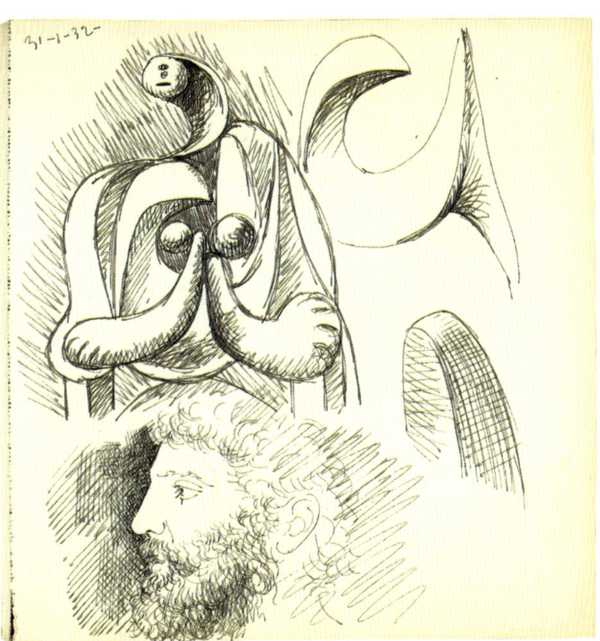


*Pages from Sketchbook no.40, Carnet no.40*

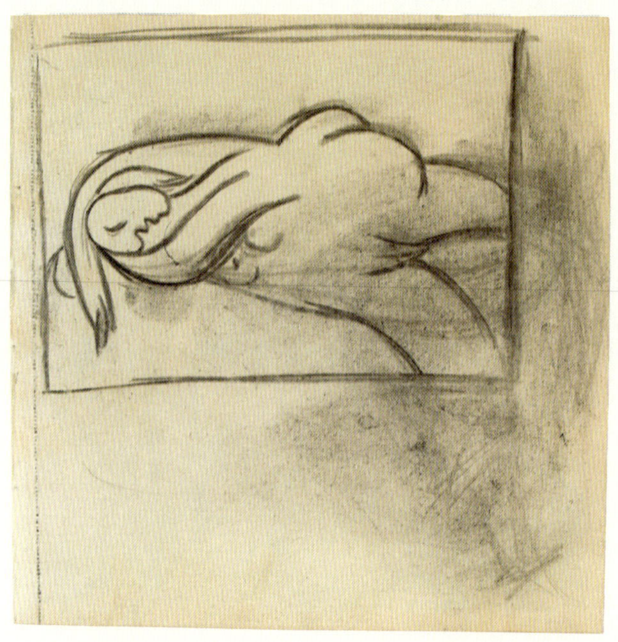

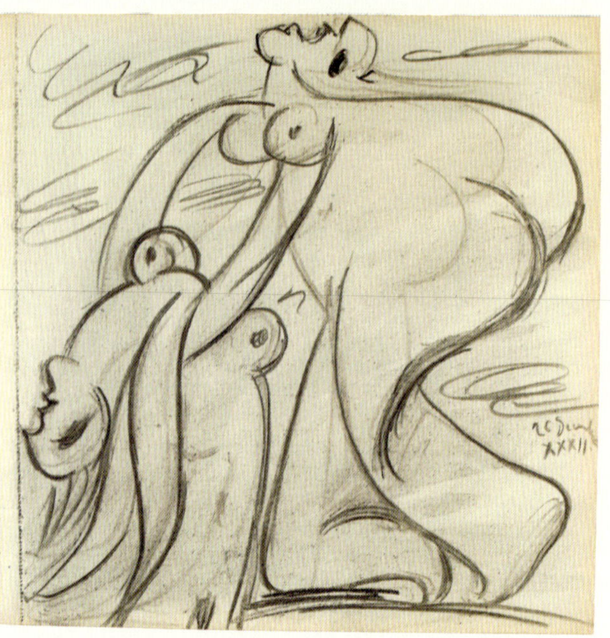

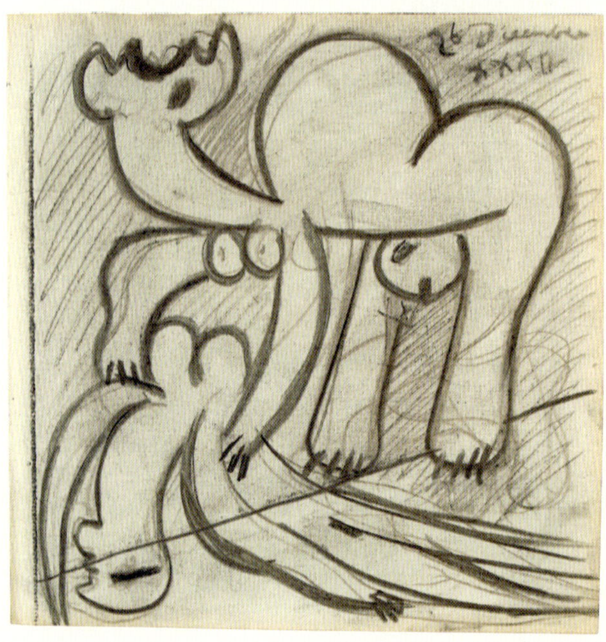

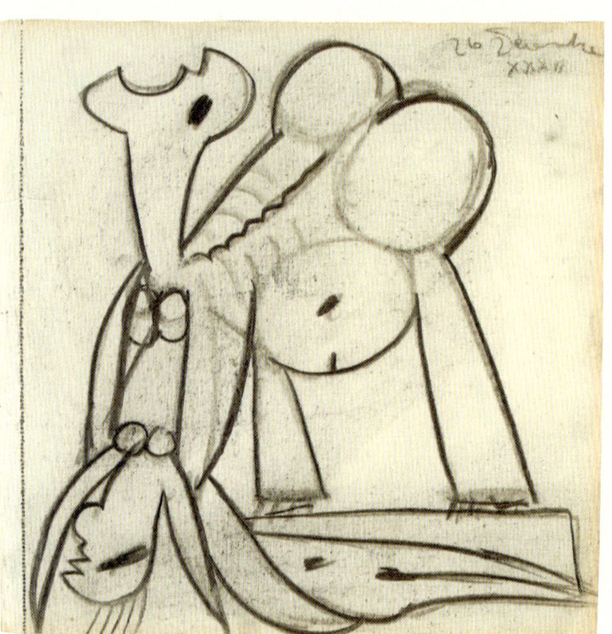

 *Pages from Sketchbook no.40, Carnet no.40*

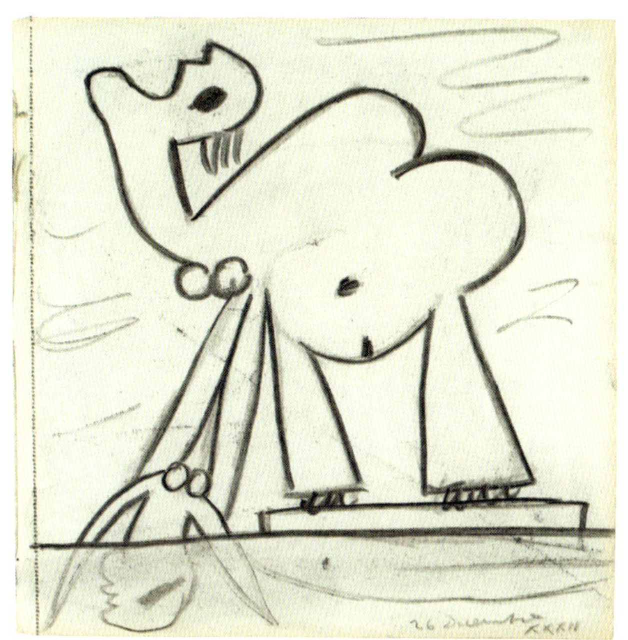

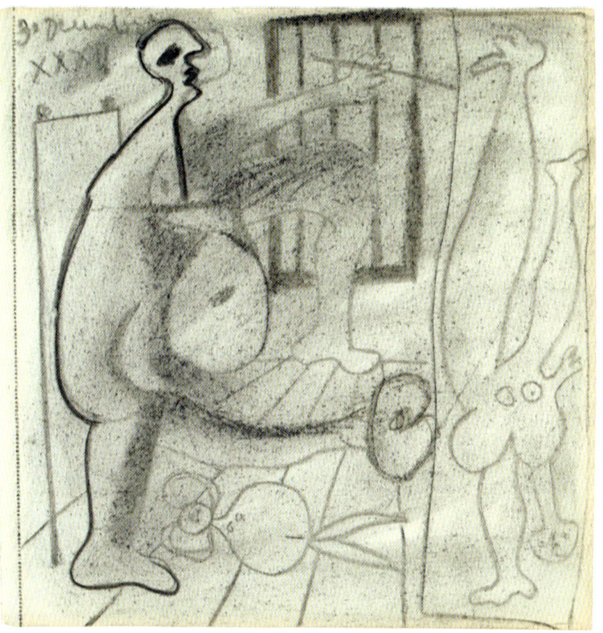

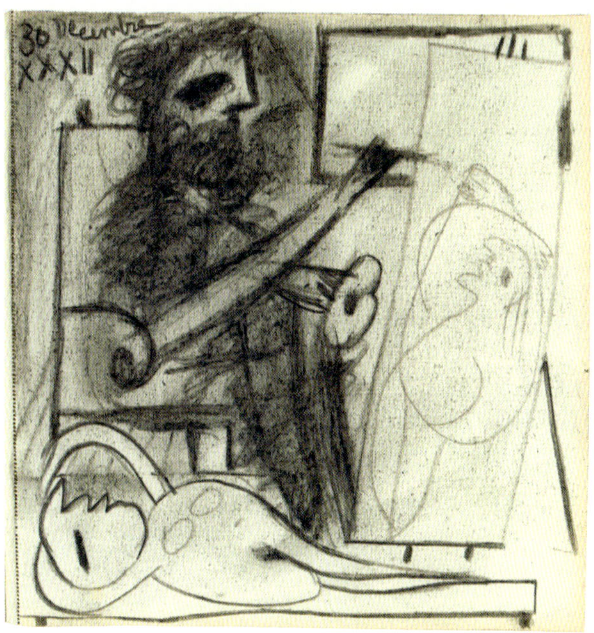


*The Painter and his Model, Le Peintre et son modèle* 30 December 1932. This was Picasso's final drawing of 1932

# Picasso in his Element? An Autumn of Surrealism

Neil Cox

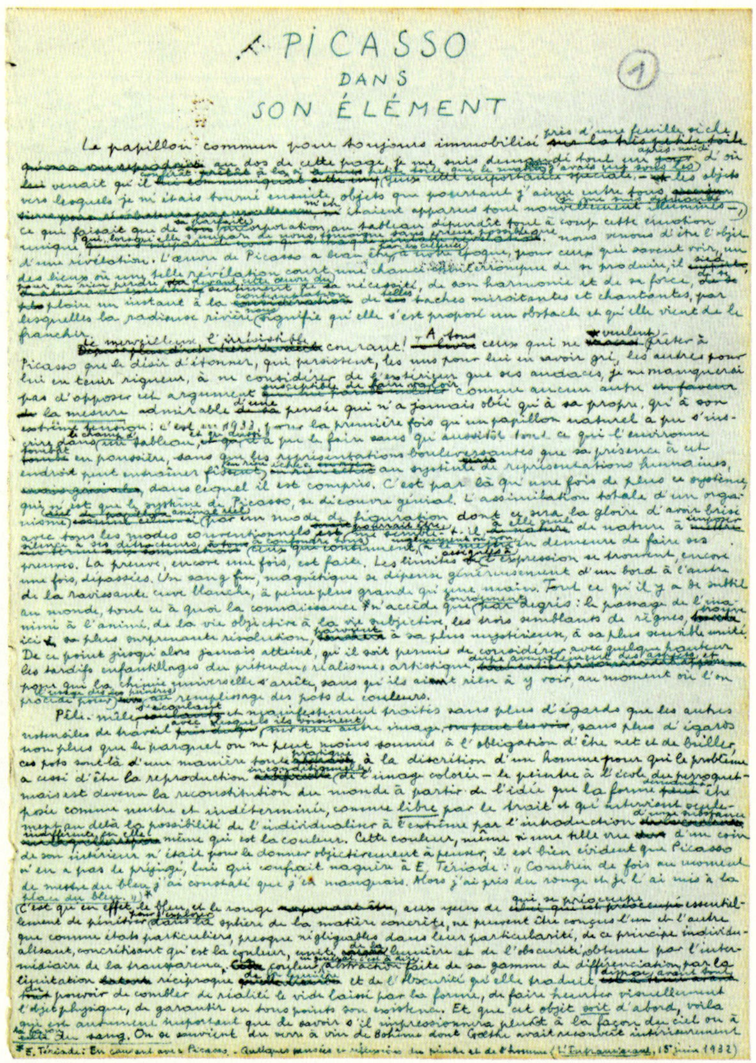

PICASSO
DANS
SON ÉLÉMENT

Page from the manuscript of André Breton's text 'Picasso in his Element' (1933)

'Do you know Matthias Grünewald's *Crucifixion,* the central panel of the Isenheim altarpiece? I like the picture and I tried to give an interpretation of it. But I'd hardly begun to draw it when it turned into something completely different.'

Picasso, quoted in Brassaï, *Conversations with Picasso*, p.36

In the autumn of 1932, Picasso invited the Hungarian-French photographer Brassaï to take a series of shots of his studios in both rue La Boétie and Boisgeloup. These highly atmospheric images were published for the first time in June 1933, together with a text by the leader of the surrealist movement, André Breton (pp.184–7). Evocatively entitled 'Picasso in his Element' the article appeared in the first issue of the luxury surrealist-leaning review *Minotaure*.[1] The full-colour cover featured a collage Picasso had made especially for the magazine the month before, depicting the legendary Minotaur brandishing a dagger (p.178). The title of the review seems to have come from surrealist artist André Masson and writer Georges Bataille. Masson's practice had developed in the early 1920s under the stimulus of Picasso's cubism, and Bataille was the erstwhile editor of the review *Documents*, which in spring 1930 had included a special issue 'homage' to Picasso. The figure of the Minotaur, that strange beast – half man, half bull – from Greek mythology, was both a metaphor for insurgent unconscious desire and, waiting in his labyrinth on the island of Crete for his sacrificial victims from Athens, also symbolised the violent eroticism of ancient cultures.[2] To a significant degree, the first issue of *Minotaure* was also a tribute to Picasso. It was illustrated with four of his Minotaur etchings and with a further three etchings of classicising studio scenes. Appearing under the title 'The Parable of the Sculptor' these three images acted as a prologue to Brassaï's dramatically lit photographs of the 1931 plaster sculptures (p.187).[3] These were followed by three pages illustrating pen and ink drawings from September

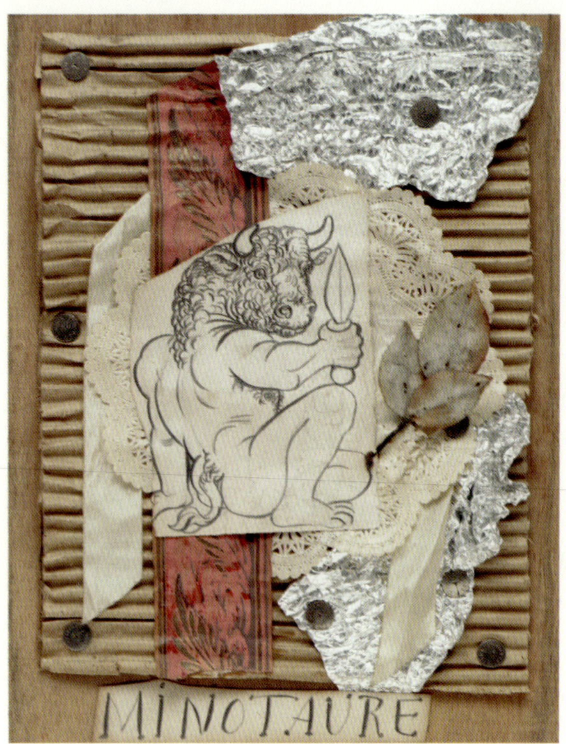


The front cover of *Minotaure*, vol.1, 1933, designed by Picasso

1932, all variations on the theme of the Crucifixion. A final five-page section, entitled 'An Anatomy', featured fantastical constructions, figure drawings made in February 1933. By any reckoning, this was an extraordinary display of the variety of Picasso's visual vocabulary, with a delicately drawn lyrical classicism cheek-by-jowl with monstrous violence on one side and voluptuous sculpture on the other.

In 1955 Picasso publicly insisted that *only* work of 1933, made during 'a brief period of darkness and despair' just before his final break with his Russian wife Olga Khokhlova, could legitimately be called surrealist. [4] The context for this statement was ill-tempered: Picasso was seeking to distance his art of the interwar period from surrealism, in order to protect the integrity of his image as self-sufficient 'genius' against unwanted interpretations by art historians. Yet Picasso's intervention does not explain what it meant to distinguish work of 1933 from what precedes or follows it, and nor in fact does it tell us what exactly Picasso *means* by 'surrealist'. Certainly, Picasso's 1955 position is broadly consistent with his refusal to become a fully committed member of the Parisian surrealist group throughout the 1920s and 1930s, despite the sustained campaign (led by André Breton in particular) to recruit the artist to the cause. Soon after the publication of the *Manifesto of Surrealism* in 1924, a purloined photograph of Picasso featured in a pantheon of key figures reproduced in *La Révolution surréaliste,* the inaugural journal of the movement. Over the next decade or so, sporadic illustrations and texts enabled Breton to claim the artist.[5] For example, the movement appropriated *The Three Dancers* 1925 (p.78), reproducing the work for the first time from a photograph taken explicitly for the purpose in Picasso's studio by Man Ray.[6] Yet, that Picasso allowed this to happen also points to his openness to surrealism, or at least to his acknowledging the opportunities it afforded.

At its root, the debate over the degree to which Picasso should be considered as (at any point) a surrealist artist goes deeper than the question over which year(s), if any, should count as surrealist. Rather, it points to a fundamental ambivalence in Picasso's practice, one that gets played out in striking ways during 1932, and in the pages of *Minotaure* not long after.[7] In the magazine *Documents*, founded in 1929 after a bitter split between those loyal to Breton and others close to Bataille, the writer and critic Michel Leiris had argued in 1930 that 'in most of Picasso's paintings, one remarks that the subject is almost always down to earth, in any case never borrowed from the hazy world of dreams, not susceptible to immediate conversion into symbol – that is to say in no way surrealist'.[8] Such strong claims reflect in part the 'dissident' position that *Documents* took in relation to Breton's surrealism. Leiris was close to the artist, but it now seems strange to think of Picasso's art in terms of an earthy pursuit of reality – of the particularity of things – since his work often deforms, abuses or refuses appearance. The surrealists 'were right,' Picasso said to Roland Penrose around the same time as his public renunciation: 'reality is more than the thing itself. I always look for its super-reality'.[9] What Picasso meant here can probably only be fleshed out in encounters with his work and debates over the nature of the 'reality' it produces. Breton's 1924 definition of surrealism focused on the 'true functioning of thought', free of any conscious controls. The truth at stake here is a psychological one, but it insists too that external reality is always itself a product of desires, obsessions, and fantasies. Hence, in its poetic statement of its vision, surrealism aimed to overcome the

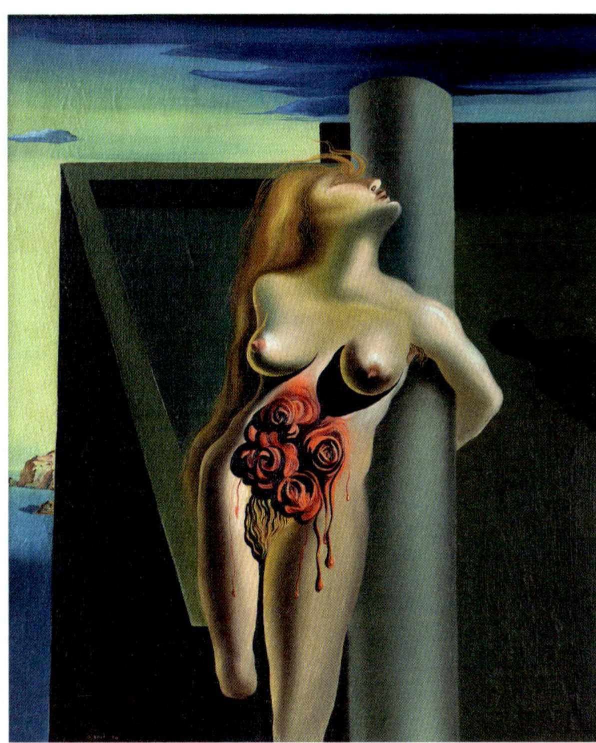

Salvador Dalí *The Bleeding Roses* 1930

distinction between dreaming and waking: this was to be the foundation of its revolution. It is this model of surrealism that captures the intensity of much of Picasso's work in the interwar period, and points too to the possibility of his own responsiveness to the inventions of other artists close to the movement, such as Salvador Dalí and Joan Miró.[10] To give but one example, the flowers in Dalí's *The Bleeding Roses* 1931 find their parallel in the bloodied lips and pose of *Sleeping Woman by a Mirror* 1932 (p.51).

One pattern of behaviour that might suggest the impact of surrealist preoccupations on Picasso is his increasing insistence during the 1920s and 1930s on recording ever more precise dates on paintings and drawings. Any connection to surrealism here depends on how we are to become readers of what the artist described as kind of visual diary – the basis, so he thought, for a future 'science of man'.[11] When the precise dating of works starts to highlight extraordinary leaps of style and content from day to day, it is easy to focus attention on the presumed vicissitudes of the artist's private life. This, of course, is how Picasso's most important biographer, John Richardson, sees it: he perceives Picasso's visceral depiction, completed on Christmas Day 1931, of the murder of Jean-Paul Marat (p.41) – a parody of Jacques-Louis David's *The Death of Marat* 1793 (p.40) – as a cathartic response to Olga Picasso's depressive illness. This emptying of rage is now thought to free the artist's psyche for a series of erotic manipulations of his secret mistress Marie-Thérèse Walter. 'If we obey the artist and interpret his work as a diary', Richardson continues, 'it would appear that Olga suffered another attack in mid-January', alluding to *Rest* (p.54).[12] Reading the visual diary here means inferring from a painting a woman's pathological episode on a particular day, for which there is no other historical evidence.

What is the alternative to this kind of biographical interpretation? One way is to rethink this unstable image of reality in Breton's terms: as an untrammelled flow of desires, fantasies and obsessions that *undo*, rather than confirm, the coherence, or logic of the desiring subject (as might, if we really take it seriously, the blurring of dreaming and waking). Although he draws our attention to significant calendar dates or events, the work Picasso makes on those dates constructs symmetries across his production that span months, years or even decades, resisting straightforward linear narrative. Perhaps such cycles, irruptions and repetitions of artistic vision formed the pattern by which Picasso perceived his life to be lived, and not, as we might normally conceive things (and as Richardson does), the other way round, where 'real' events determine art.[13] Although this proposition sounds strange in relation to our habitual ways of thinking, its radical reversal points to surrealism's rhetoric of a revolution founded in the transformation of life. Picasso's ultra-productivity is, in other words, a way of living visually, and living in that element is chaotic, repetitive, fragmented, impulsive and so on.

So that first issue of *Minotaure* exposes the surrealist form of life that is Picasso's work in the interwar period, and especially in the early 1930s. The work is 'reality' remade according to desire, a project to undo rather than reproduce the real; it is also the symptom of the cyclical or disruptive sense of artistic identity that must inevitably follow in its wake. Picasso's *Crucifixion* drawings, enterprises of a restless autumn, insert themselves in this unstable flow. I want now to look closely at them: their fitful process of production, and the almost schizophrenic oscillation to frivolity alongside them, arguably reveal something of Picasso's surrealist questioning of the self.

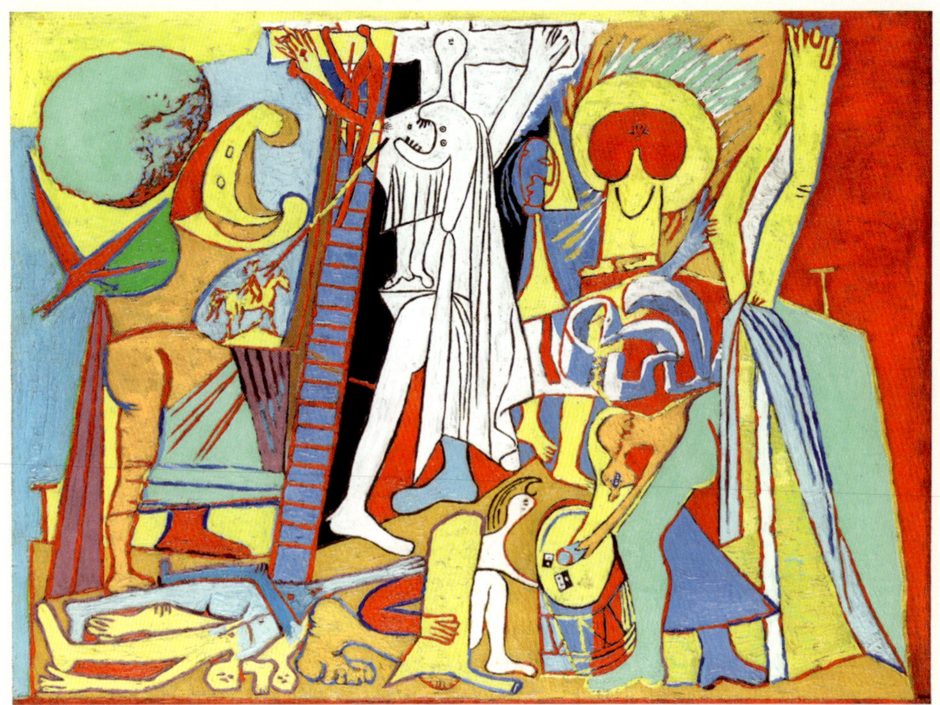

*The Cruxificion*, *La Crucifixion* 1930

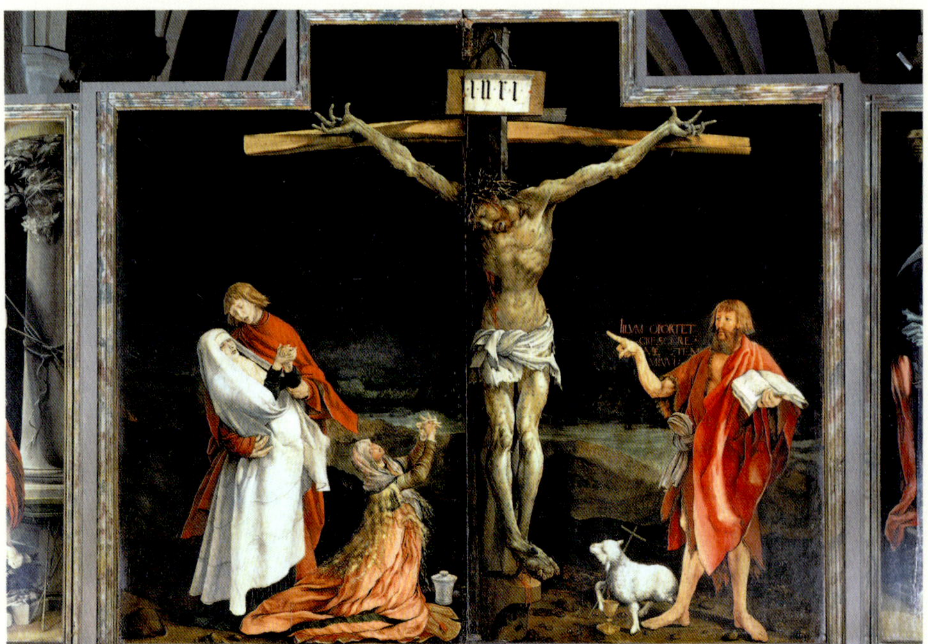

Matthias Grünewald, Isenheim altarpiece: *Crucifixion* c.1510–15

Picasso had made sporadic attempts to explore Crucifixion scenes in previous decades, including most significantly in the *Crucifixion* of 1930 (opposite), shown at both his 1932 retrospective exhibitions at Galeries Georges Petit and Kunsthaus Zürich; but also in studies of 1929, cubist Crucifixions of 1917, and occasional drawings dating back to his youth.[14] When the drawings of autumn 1932 were published in *Minotaure* in 1933, they bore the caption 'Drawings by Picasso after Grünewald's *Crucifixion*'.[15] The caption poses a historical and an interpretative challenge by inviting us to see all the drawings as responses to Matthias Grünewald's Isenheim altarpiece, then as now on display in Colmar, Alsace. Did Picasso visit Colmar before he made the drawings, and do the drawings show clear relationships to the Grünewald? The possibility that he stopped off at the Musée Unterlinden in Colmar around 13 September 1932, on his return from the Zurich showing of his retrospective, has been the subject of much speculation,[16] although recent research by Laurence Madeline makes such a visit look increasingly improbable.[17] It is possible that Christian Zervos, publisher of *Cahiers d'Art* and of Picasso's catalogue raisonné, who was preparing an issue of the journal dedicated to the Isenheim altarpiece, first brought the work to Picasso's attention.[18] But Picasso could hardly have been ignorant of the Grünewald painting before that: it had a particular charge in the interwar period as it had been appropriated as a masterpiece of German art during the First World War, then became part of French patrimony following the restoration of Alsace-Lorraine to France in the Versailles settlement. Picasso is not likely to have cared much for this nationalist tug-of-war, but it made the altarpiece the focus of much scholarship and photography, and also literary reading by authors such as Joris-Karl Huysmans, a writer admired in surrealist circles.[19] So, whether or not Picasso visited Colmar in September 1932, the question of the visual and conceptual relationships of his drawings to the Grünewald altarpiece remains open.

Curiously, grappling with the theme of the Crucifixion crossed over with a series of Dionysian beach-scene paintings (pp.191–4). In two seaside frolics of 15 September, the beach ball – which in previous versions had been the animating object making sense of the tumult – has disappeared. Now the apparent trampling of the woman recumbent on the beach looks violent rather than sporting, and the changing-cabins on the right start to look a little ominous, like the arches of a bullring (p.194). It is only a few steps from this position to *Women at the Seashore* of 22 November 1932, where the bodies of the figures begin to fragment in erratic pen strokes and wilful shapes.[20] All this is of course to suggest that the extreme affective distance of a Crucifixion from a game of beach ball might be narrowed, with visual analogies – the very stuff of fantasy – taking on new meaning. Indeed, in the *Minotaure* sequence 'An Anatomy' – which began on the page facing the end of the Crucifixion drawings – the vestiges of a beach scene, with schematic cabin, shore and sea, become the setting for three elemental object-bodies. Three bathers, three monsters, three figures in a Crucifixion: troubling metamorphoses, copulations and mutations are cultivated in the artistic self-analysis that follows the successes of the first half of 1932. What these different preoccupations also have in common is work that is mostly on an intimate rather than public scale, composed on loose sheets of paper, in sketchbooks, and in printmaking. In part, this retreat from the imposing nude paintings of the first half of the year may reflect a need to regroup after the two retrospectives, but it may also reflect the self-examination that went hand in hand with the questioning ethos of surrealism, as well as with the advent of Zervos's new catalogue raisonné project. A series of whimsical pastoral poesies showing a musician and a female companion that also flourish in the autumn of 1932 are symptoms of a retreat into Arcadia (pp.188–9, 200, 204, 205) – perhaps as the counterpoint in feeling to the Crucifixion drawings and their grotesque anatomies.

Picasso began to work on the Crucifixion drawings in Boisgeloup on 17 September 1932, and he produced three that day, in what order is uncertain. One is violent and uneven in its execution (p.196). As in Grünewald's altarpiece, the body of Christ looms unfathomably large over those of his witnesses and mourners. The gestures of these figures are partially preserved in cursory form: one is standing close to the cross, while another collapses to its knees. In Grünewald's painting it is the other way round, with Mary Magdelene kneeling close to the cross and the Virgin standing, but swooning back in the supporting arms of the disciple John. The intense gesture of the wringing hands and interlacing fingers of the kneeling figure echo not just Grünewald's Magdelene, but many another Magdalene.[21] In the end it is impossible to resolve the images in such rapidly drawn shapes: on the right, the figure that might be John the Baptist is enlarged and frantically rendered; his attendant lamb has more or less disappeared. The other two drawings of 17 September shroud the scene in deep black, responding no doubt to the darkness, the night that descended on land in the Gospels (p.197).[22] Picasso takes up the black as a compositional challenge, modelling the figures with all the resources of his late cubism (as for instance in *The Milliner's Workshop* 1926[23]) and also of printmaking processes, where whites and inky blacks are in dialectical relationships (as in the 1907 woodcut *Study for Standing Nude*[24]) or where cross-hatching acts, as it does in one drawing, as shading.

Picasso came back to the theme again two days later, producing three more drawings. One connects directly to the abstracted black drawings of 17 September (p.198), but the other two introduce a new mode, described by Elizabeth Cowling as 'chaplets of bones'.[25] In what may be the first of the two drawings, the black ink wash conceals the form of the cross, still faintly visible behind it (p.199, top). The removal of the supporting cross transmutes the array of bone-like objects into perverse life-forms (p.199, bottom). Picasso's association of an ossuary or charnel house with the Crucifixion is in a sense banal, given Golgotha iconography, but here the bones of monsters have been piled and jammed together in a grotesque parody of the scene. The fallen head of Christ is summoned up in the sickle, stirrup and bored out eyes at the top. The form of the Virgin/Magdalene on the left is part pitcher plant (her wailing mouth), part starfish (her wringing hands) and part vertebra (the mass of her clothed body). Bravura chiaroscuro is applied to uncanny effect, and the variant repetition of the configuration in the second drawing adds, perhaps, to the sense of disturbance.

On 4 October Picasso made two more variations, but – troubling to our sense of coherence and of the tragic sobriety of the Crucifixion – also made a relatively elaborate work in his pastoral series on the same day (p.200–1). The Crucifixions also have contrasting languages: one is probably most compellingly understood as a response to the compositional radicalism of Grünewald, attempting to capture the shape of the panel through an alternating high-contrast chiaroscuro. This is the only drawing that seems to step back enough to show the altarpiece as an object in space, and there is an extraordinary jump in the opposite direction in the other drawing made that day, which returns to the seemingly crude mark-making and scratching of the first drawing. In addition, it also thrusts the body of Christ forwards in space, as if we suddenly enter Grünewald's painting from a place above ground level. Some drawings thus seem to speak directly to the Isenheim altarpiece, while others, and especially those that end the sequence, could allude to myriad Crucifixion paintings.

More flute players intervene until 7 October, when Picasso makes four more variations on the Crucifixion (pp.202–3). One of these is a further exploration of the scene as boneyard, but here without the black night setting. Two others show a bone Christ, close up again, with the forms of bones, the construction of the body itself, metamorphosing from one drawing to another. It is perhaps these conceptions, so disturbing in their degree of resolution and clarity, that lead to a sardonic and irreverent diagrammatic exposition of Crucifixion technology, instructing executioners in proper use of tools: the application of a long woodscrew to the bone hand of Christ is detailed, and the method for fastening his loincloth with a safety pin is set out. The dénouement of this torturer's discipline is the last of Picasso's variations and the first drawing made in Paris (p.207). Dated 21 October 1932, it shows a bone Christ on a wide-shafted cross, titulus overhead, feet resting on a platform, and with his claw hands screwed rather than nailed in place. There is the ghostly suggestion of a Magdalene on the left, but this is an empty death.

John Golding once connected the Crucifixion drawings to *The Three Dancers* (p.78), suggesting that even in 1925 Picasso might have had Crucifixion iconography, including Grünewald, in mind when his painting transformed from revelry to Calvary.[26] Picasso could rhyme varieties of pictorial, compositional thinking to the point where one structure becomes another, and the latter's meaning is freighted with the former (three dancers, beach ball players, Crucifixions, anatomies). This capacity for the layering of meaning is in part what fascinated Breton in his *Minotaure* piece 'Picasso in his Element'. He begins this flagship essay with a memorable evocation of *Composition with Butterfly* of 15 September 1932 (p.195):

> *That ordinary butterfly, forever immobilized next to a dry leaf: for an entire afternoon I kept wondering how it could confer such particular importance on the little canvas I'd been looking at that morning in Picasso's studio, so that the objects I turned to afterward – objects I had nonetheless always loved above all the others – seemed freshly illuminated.*[27]

Here two stick figures pursue their quarry, its rapid flitting through the air signified by the wind rushing behind it. The enormous leaf that lies at the centre of this creamy liquid world, together with the insect (both of which are real), makes for a story of innocence masking violence: the poses of the two figures, and the creature permanently stuck in death, recall the expressive content of the Crucifixion drawings. For Breton, the achievement is in being able to recruit a living thing to art without the butterfly overwhelming the human imaginative work of representation, of art.

This rumination provides the opportunity to explore the question of Picasso's approach to the external world, which had been raised, as we have seen, by Michel Leiris. By 1933, the febrile atmosphere that had in part motivated Leiris's counterblast to those who saw Picasso as a surrealist had passed. Nevertheless, the question of how to address Picasso's apparently unrelenting grasping at the object world had not gone away. Meditating over several pages on the gesture of *Composition with Butterfly*, Breton recognises its exceptional character but also claims that it exposes the terms of Picasso's relationship to the external world, his exploration of 'the great enigma': 'Picasso is great in my eyes precisely because he has constantly remained on the defensive against these external things, including those he has drawn from himself, and he has never taken them to be anything but moments of *intercession* between himself and world.'[28] The idea of moments of intercession points to the notion of a flow of invention – or 'interminable gestation' – in which works are mere arrests or glimpses of a larger élan vital. 'In Picasso's life and person, this gestation appears in a series of optimal moments: we cannot forget that it began and must continue beyond them.'[29]

Breton's prose, however grandiloquent it may be, offers a radical perspective on the turning point in Picasso's work from 1932 to 1933. Each work is an optimal moment, crystallising a particular world, a strongly realised yet frighteningly unfamiliar life. Such imagined lives are sometimes pathologically vicious, as in the vision of the death of Marat from Christmas Day 1931, and sometimes comic, self-mocking, like the drawings that bring the year 1932 to a close.[30] For this year of extraordinary achievements ends a day early on 30 December 1932, with rough sketchbook drawings of an artist at his easel, painting a naked model (p.175). There is a self-conscious symmetry at work here: not only does it return to the theme with which the same sketchbook began on 29 January 1932, depicting the painter as an obsessive genius who is also absurd (p.173): driven by sexual desire for a particular model and striving to produce absolute art by painting and re-painting the female nude. Picasso's painters conjure up anamorphic bodies with their penile brushes – and sometimes a monstrous penis. That these assertions of virility are also burlesques. The humour is a defence against another striking undercurrent at work in the autumn of 1932: Crucifixion shows the male nude as object of torture. Given the possibility that Picasso could identify with this punished masculinity, the dismantled female creatures of 'An Anatomy' in *Minotaure* are perhaps the sadistic compensation for this masochistic fantasy of the male body in the Crucifixion drawings.

Such dizzying swings in mood, from a harrowing Crucifixion to a beach ball game, from pastoral scenes to sex in the studio, reflect the degree to which Picasso, whatever his later pronouncements, found in surrealism a poetic reimagining of the self. An endless chain of representations, the gestation of bodies over and over again, is not just a virtuoso artistic display: it makes visible multiple desiring existences, each belonging to another self. Those great erotic and violent paintings of early 1932 are not records of reality: they make desire real.

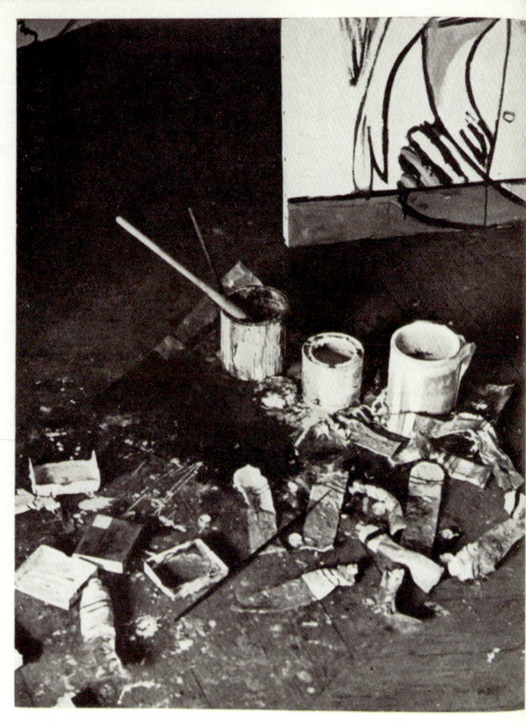

# PICASSO

## DANS SON ÉLÉMENT

par ANDRÉ BRETON

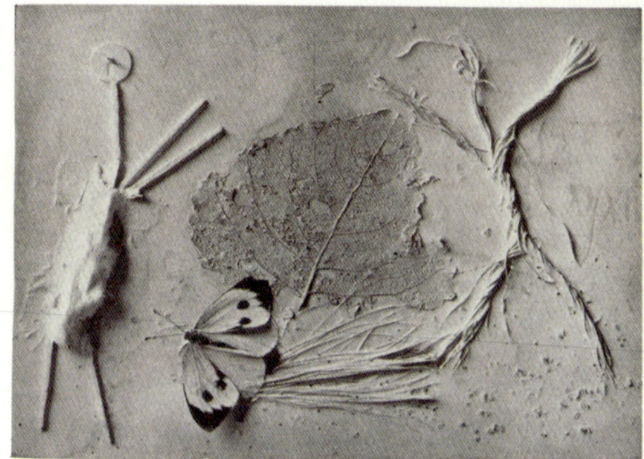

DANS LES ILLUSTRATIONS QUI ACCOMPAGNENT CETTE ÉTUDE, L'ON PEUT VOIR LA PALETTE DE PICASSO, LES DIVERS ASPECTS DE SON ATELIER A PARIS, SON ATELIER DE SCULPTEUR A BOISGELOUP ET SES SCULPTURES RÉCENTES.

(Photographies exécutées par Brassaï.)

Le papillon commun pour toujours immobilisé près d'une feuille sèche au dos de cette page, je me suis demandé tout un après-midi d'où venait qu'il conférât à la si petite toile que le matin même j'avais eue sous les yeux cette importance spéciale — les objets vers lesquels je m'étais tourné ensuite, objets que pourtant j'aime entre tous, m'en étaient apparus tout nouvellement illuminés — je me suis demandé ce qui faisait que de sa parfaite incorporation au tableau dépendît tout à coup cette émotion unique, qui, lorsqu'elle s'empare de nous, témoigne sans erreur possible que nous venons d'être l'objet d'une révélation. L'œuvre de Picasso a beau être par excellence, à notre époque, pour ceux qui savent voir, un des lieux où une telle révélation court une chance ininterrompue de se produire, il sied, pour ne rien perdre devant cette œuvre du sentiment de sa nécessité, de son harmonie et de sa force, de se plaire un instant à la contemplation de telles taches miroitantes et chantantes, par lesquelles la radieuse rivière nous signifie qu'elle s'est proposé un obstacle et qu'elle vient de le franchir.

Le merveilleux, l'irrésitible courant ! A tous ceux qui ne veulent prêter à Picasso que le désir d'étonner, qui persistent, les uns pour lui en savoir gré, les autres pour lui en tenir rigueur, à ne considérer de l'extérieur que ses audaces, je ne manquerai pas d'opposer cet argument susceptible de faire valoir comme aucun autre la *mesure* admirable d'une pensée qui n'a jamais obéi qu'à sa propre, qu'à son extrême tension : c'est en 1933 pour la première fois qu'un papillon naturel a pu s'inscrire dans le champ d'un tableau, et qu'aussi il a pu le faire sans qu'aussitôt tout ce qui l'environne tombât en poussière, sans que les représentations bouleversantes que sa présence à cet endroit peut entrainer fissent en rien échec au système de représentations humaines dans lequel il est compris. C'est par là qu'une fois de plus ce système, qui n'est que le système de Picasso, se découvre génial. L'assimilation totale d'un organisme animal réel par un mode de figuration dont ce sera la gloire d'avoir brisé avec tous les modes conventionnels pourrait être, me semble-t-il, à elle seule, de nature à imposer silence à ses détracteurs, à confondre tous ceux qui continuent, ingénument ou non, à le mettre en demeure de faire ses preuves. La preuve, encore une fois, est faite. Les limites assignées à l'expression se trouvent, encore une fois, dépassées. Un sang fin, magnétique, se dépense généreusement d'un bord à l'autre de la ravissante cuve blanche, à peine plus grande qu'une main. Tout ce qu'il y a de subtil au monde, tout ce que à quoi la connaissance n'accède que lourdement par degrés : le passage de l'inanimé à l'animé, de la vie objective à la vie subjective, les trois semblants de règnes, trouve ici sa plus surprenante résolution, parvient à sa plus mystérieuse, à sa plus sensible unité. De ce point jusqu'alors jamais atteint, qu'il soit permis de considérer avec quelque hauteur les tardifs enfantillages du prétendu « réalisme » artistique, dupe aveuglément des *aspects*, et pour qui la chimie universelle s'arrête, sans qu'il ait rien à y voir, au moment où l'on procède pour l'usage des peintres au remplissage des pots de couleurs.

Pêle-mêle s'écoulant et manifestement traités sans plus d'égards que les autres ustensiles de travail avec lesquels ils voisinent sur une autre image, sans plus d'égards non plus que le parquet on ne peut moins soumis à l'obligation d'être net et de briller, ces pots sont là d'une manière toute pratique à la discrétion d'un homme pour qui le problème a cessé d'être la reproduction inconditionnelle de l'image colorée — le peintre à l'école du perroquet — mais est devenu la reconstitution du monde à partir de l'idée que la forme demande à être posée comme neutre et indéterminée, comme *libre* par le trait et qu'intervient seulement au delà la possibilité de l'individualiser à l'extrême par l'introduction d'une substance indifférente en elle-même qui est la couleur. Cette couleur, même si une telle vue d'un coin de son intérieur n'était pour le donner objectivement à penser, il est bien évident que Picasso n'en a pas le préjugé, lui qui confiait naguère à E. Tériade : « Combien de fois au moment de mettre du bleu j'ai constaté que j'en manquais! Alors j'ai pris du rouge et je l'ai mis à la place du bleu * ». C'est qu'en effet le bleu et le rouge, aux yeux de qui se préoccupe essentiellement de

Au fond, le portrait de Yedwiga par le Douanier Rousseau (Collection Picasso).

* E. Tériade. — *En causant avec Picasso. Quelques pensées et réflexions du peintre et de l'homme.* (*L'Intransigeant*, 15 juin 1932).

10

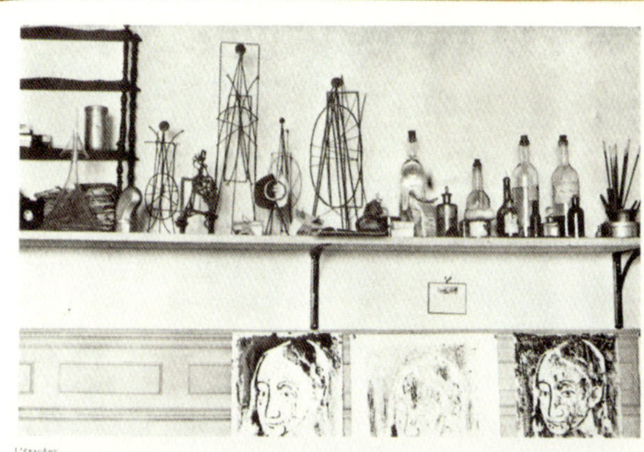

L'Étagère.

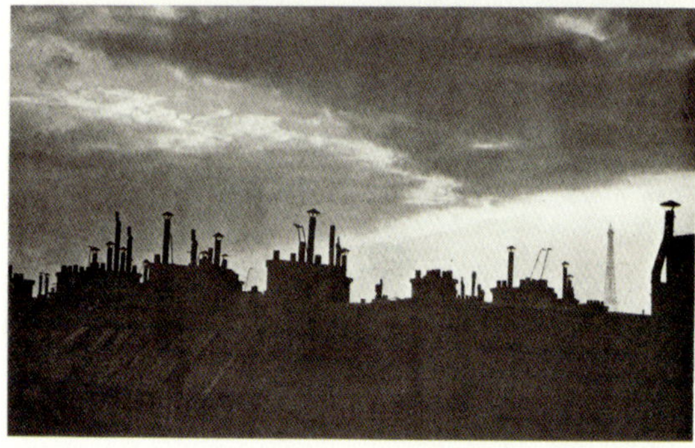

La fenêtre



pp.186–9: André Breton, 'Picasso dans son élément', with photographs by Brassaï, *Minotaure*, no.1, 15 June 1932, pp.4–27

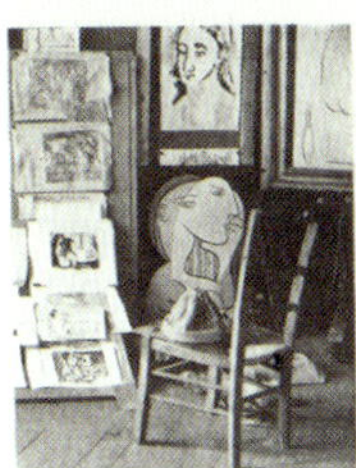

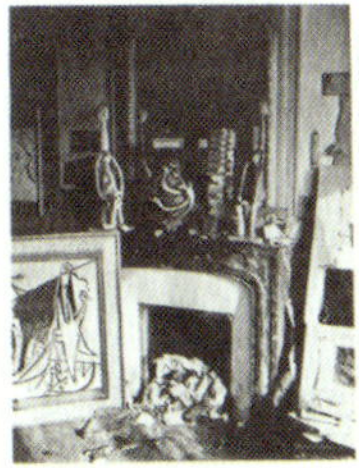

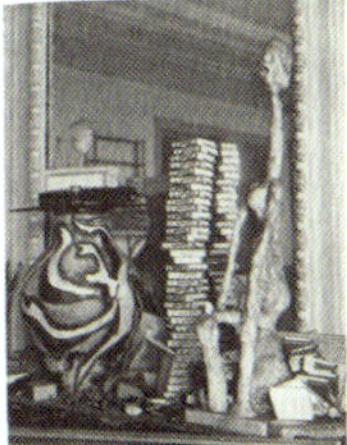

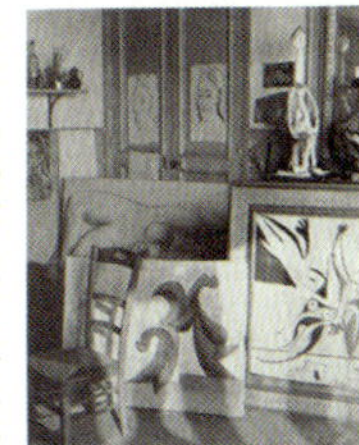

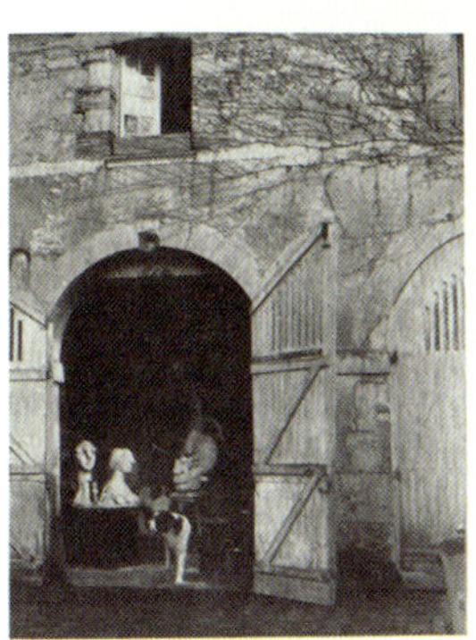

## L'ATELIER DE SCULPTURE

DANS L'INTÉRIEUR DE CET ATELIER PHOTOGRAPHIÉ DE JOUR ET DE NUIT, SE TROUVENT LES SCULPTURES EXÉCUTÉES AU COURS DE CES DERNIÈRES ANNÉES : LES STATUES MÉTALLIQUES, LES CONSTRUCTIONS EN FIL DE FER, LES SCULPTURES EN BRONZE DORÉ, LA SÉRIE DES TÊTES MONUMENTALES, LES PETITES STATUES DE PLATRE, L'OISEAU, LA GÉNISSE ET LE COQ.

(Photographies exécutées par Brassaï.)

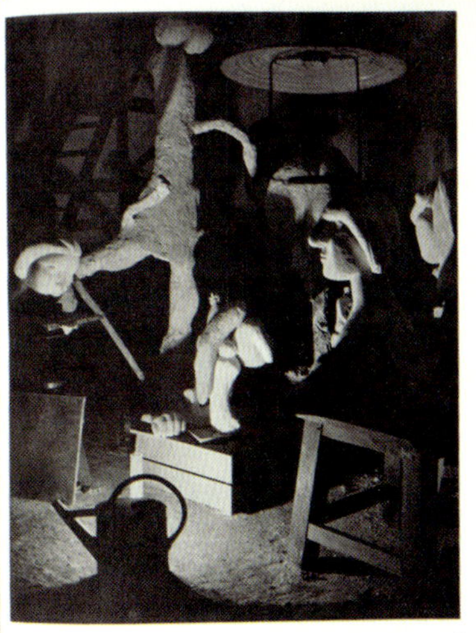

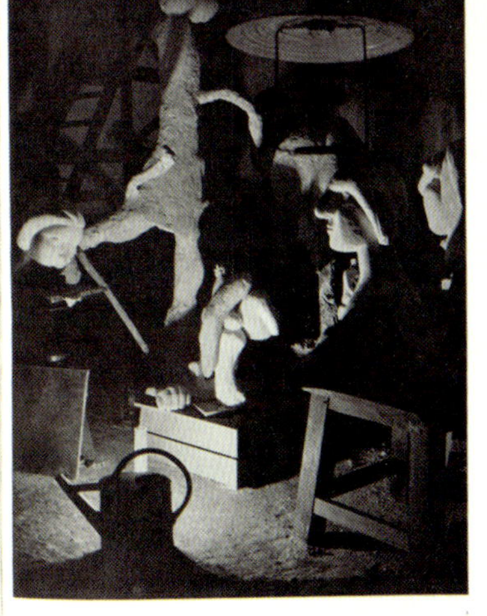

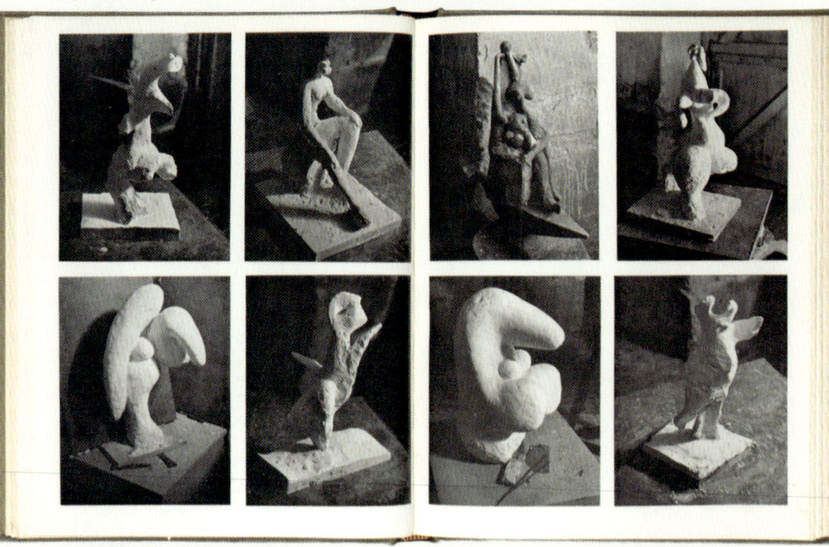

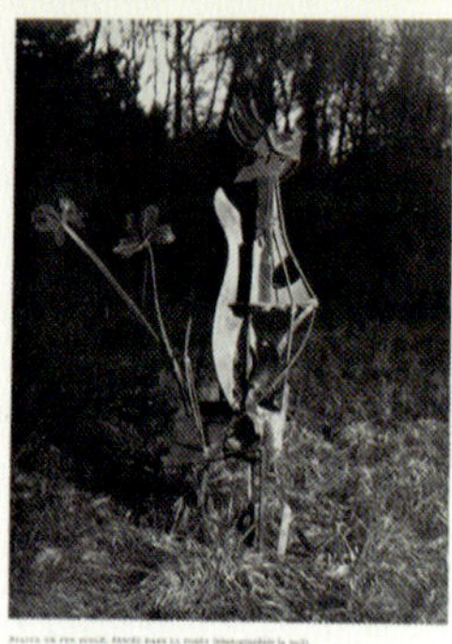

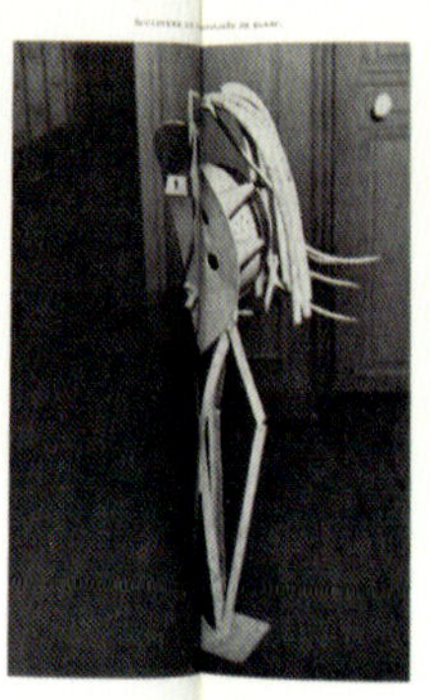

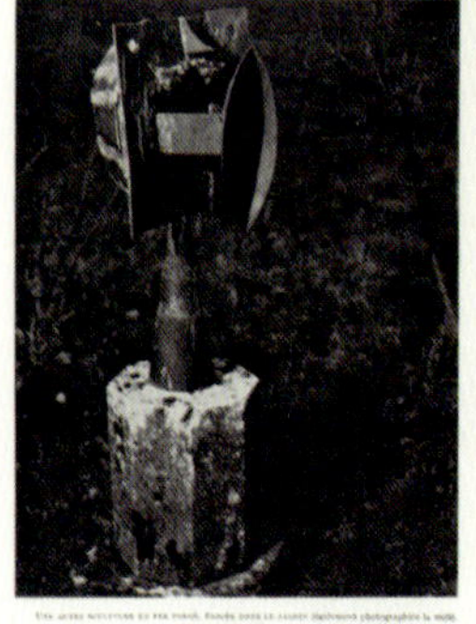

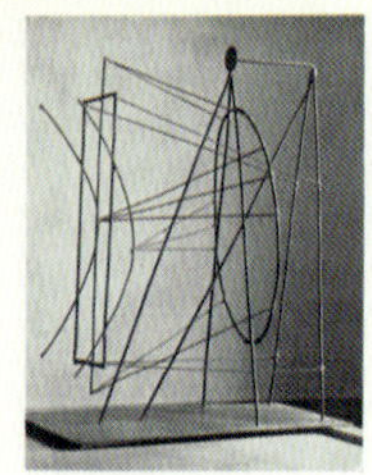

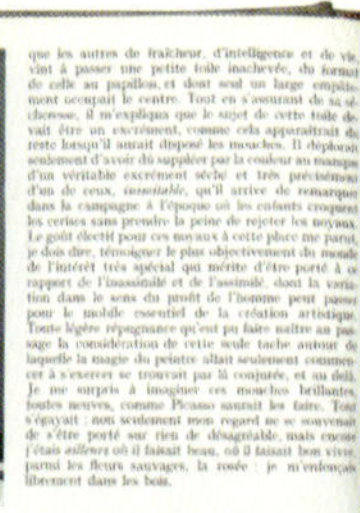

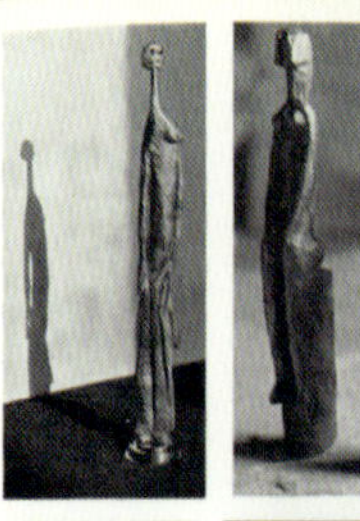

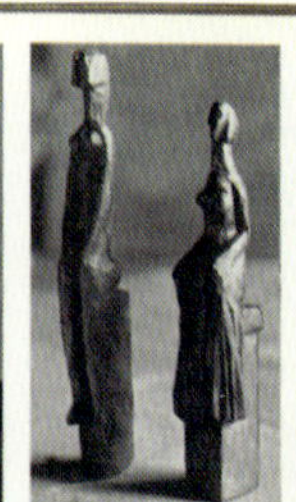

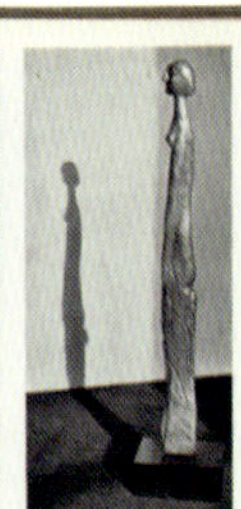

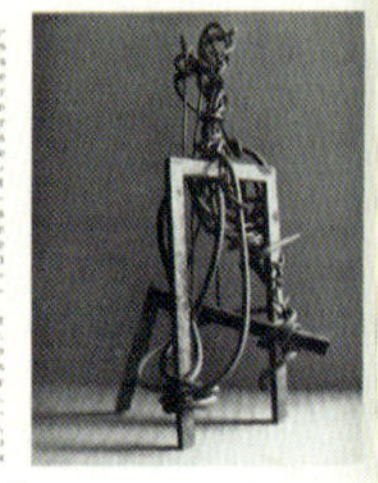

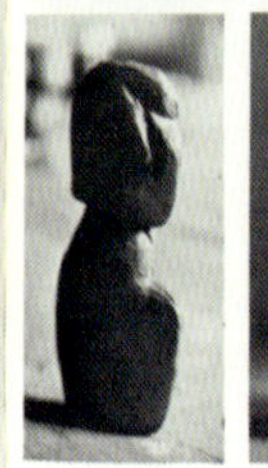

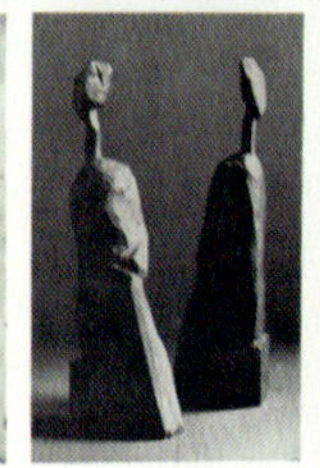

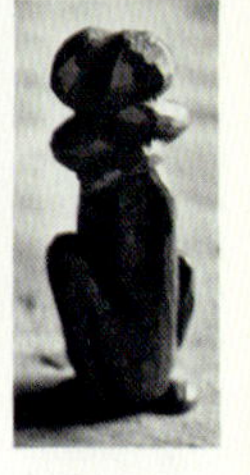

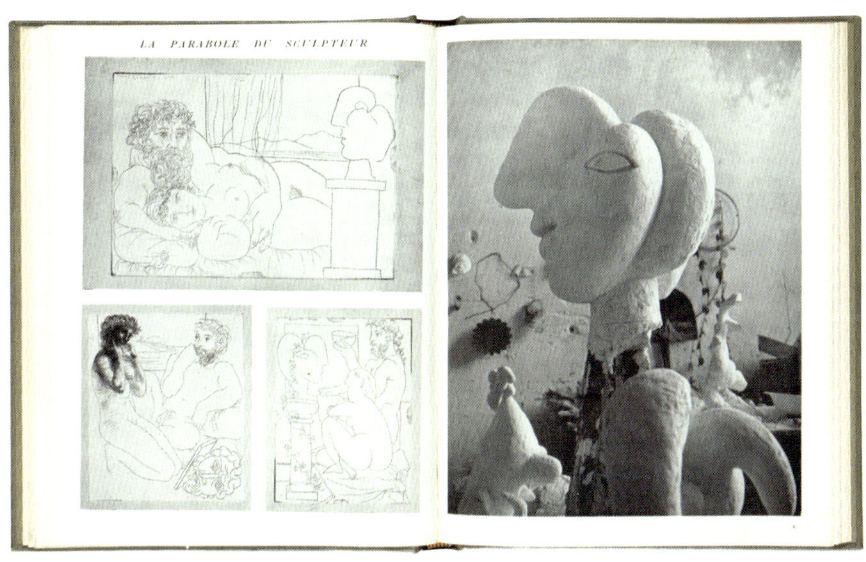
LA PARABOLE DU SCULPTEUR

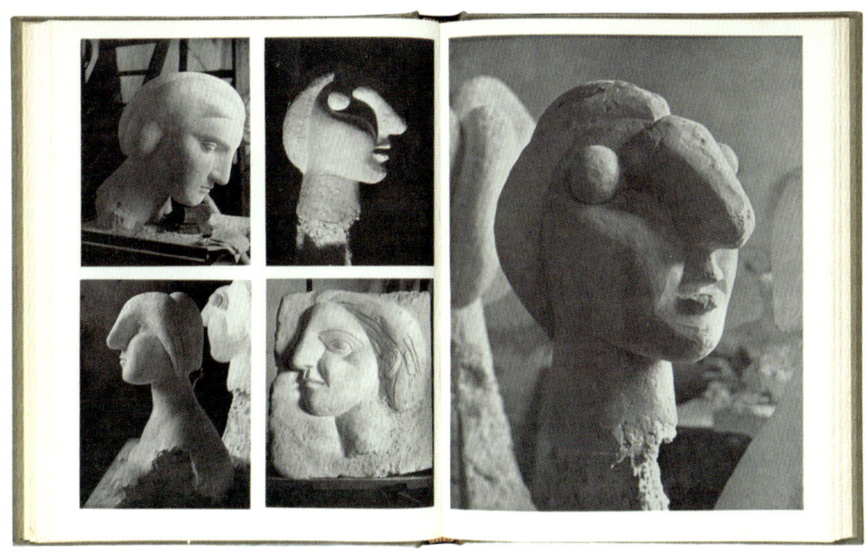

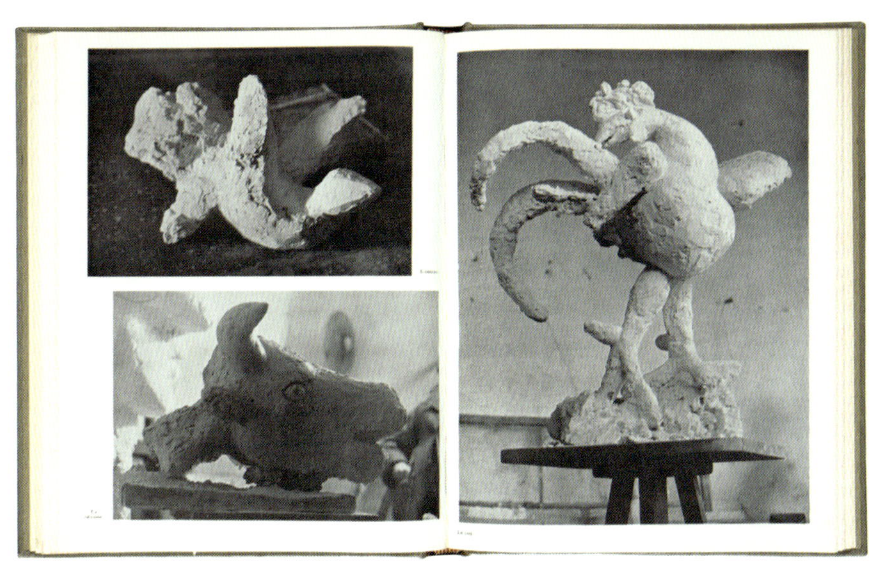

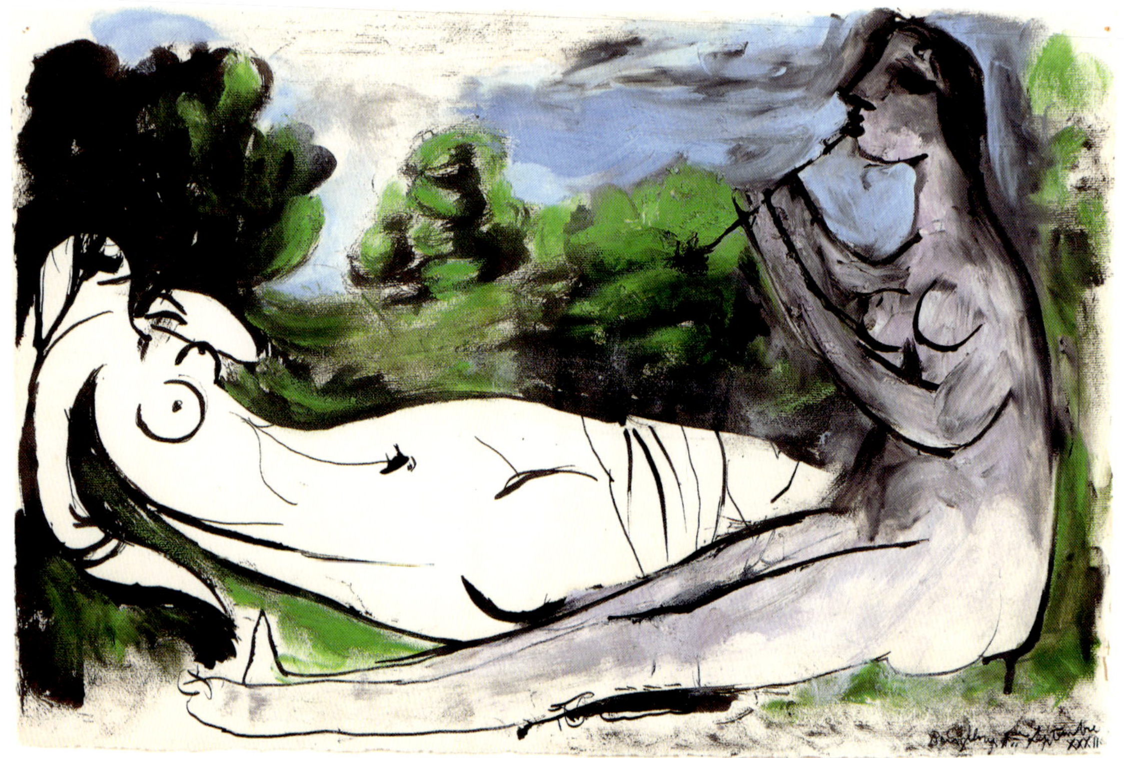

 *Flute Player and Reclining Nude, Joueuse de flûte et femme allongée*

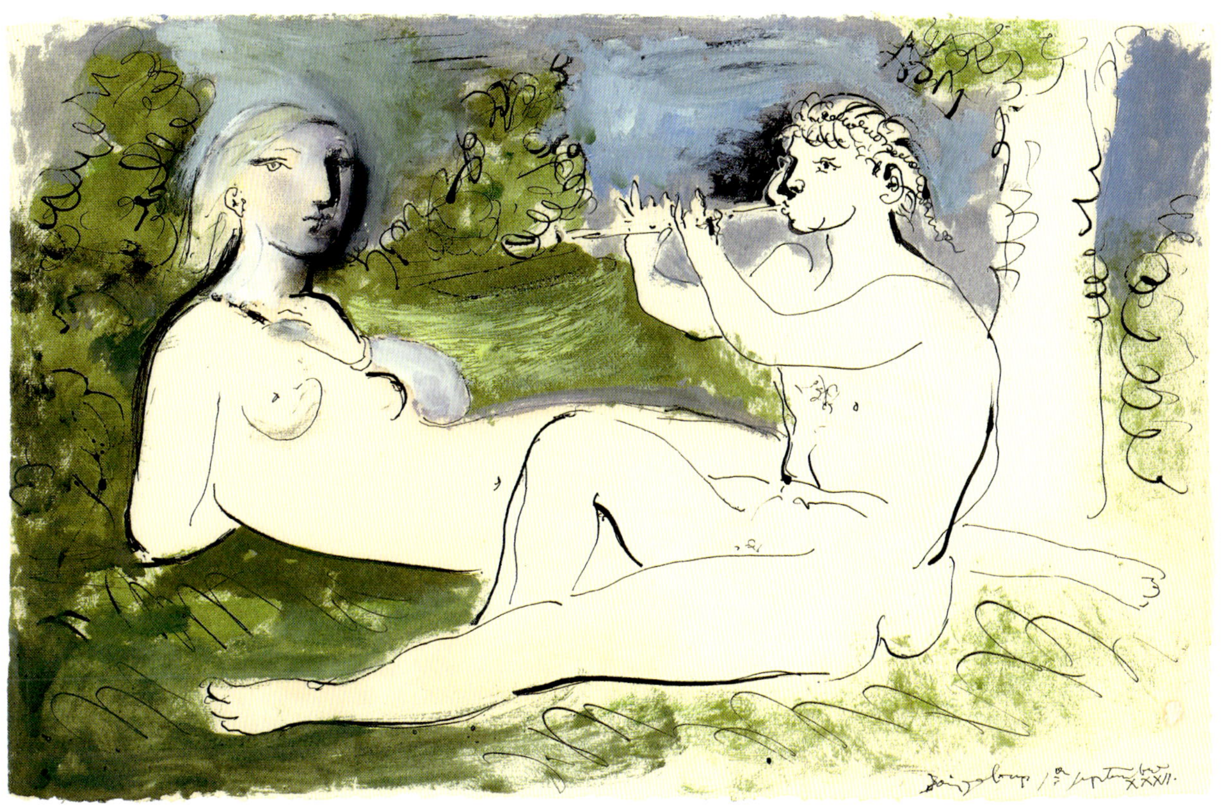

*Flute Player and Reclining Nude, Joueur de flûte et nu couché*

'I seek always to observe nature. I cling to resemblance, to a deeper resemblance, more real than the real, attaining the surreal. That is how I understood surrealism, but the word was used in a completely different way.'

Picasso, quoted in Brassaï, *Conversations with Picasso*, p.36

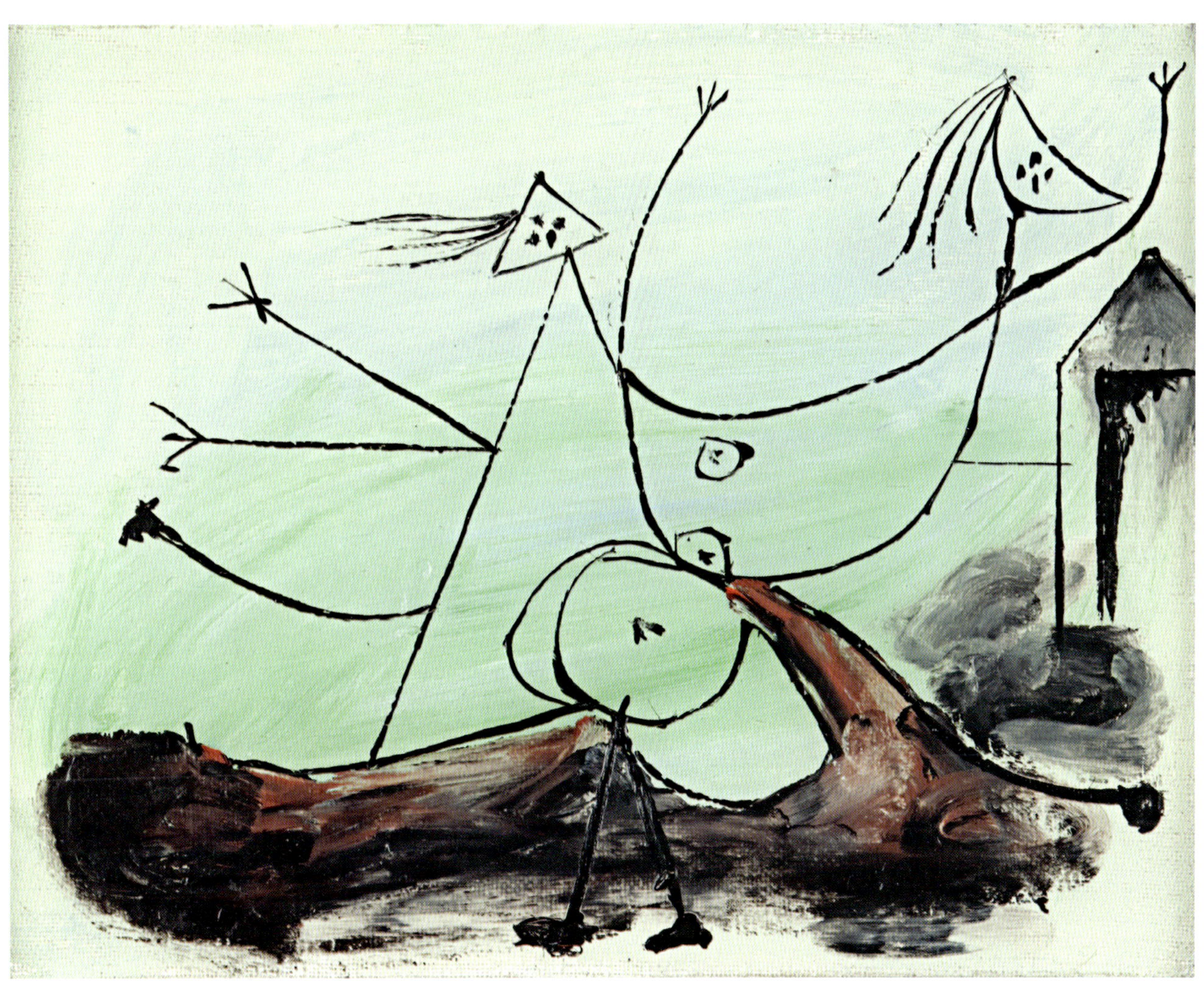

*Two Women on the Beach with Swimming Cabin, Deux femmes sur la plage, avec cabine de bain*

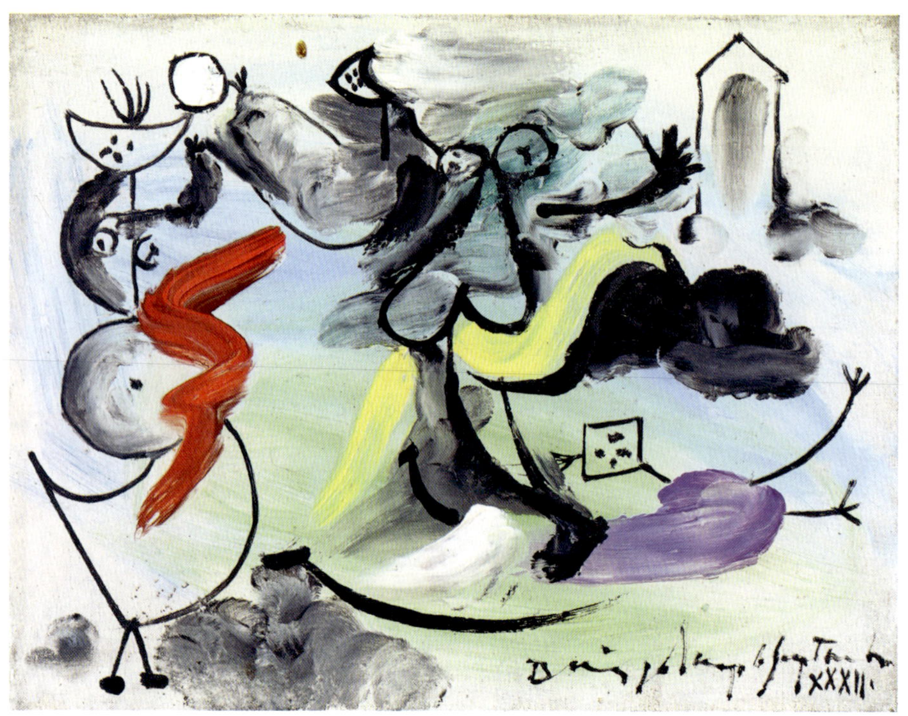

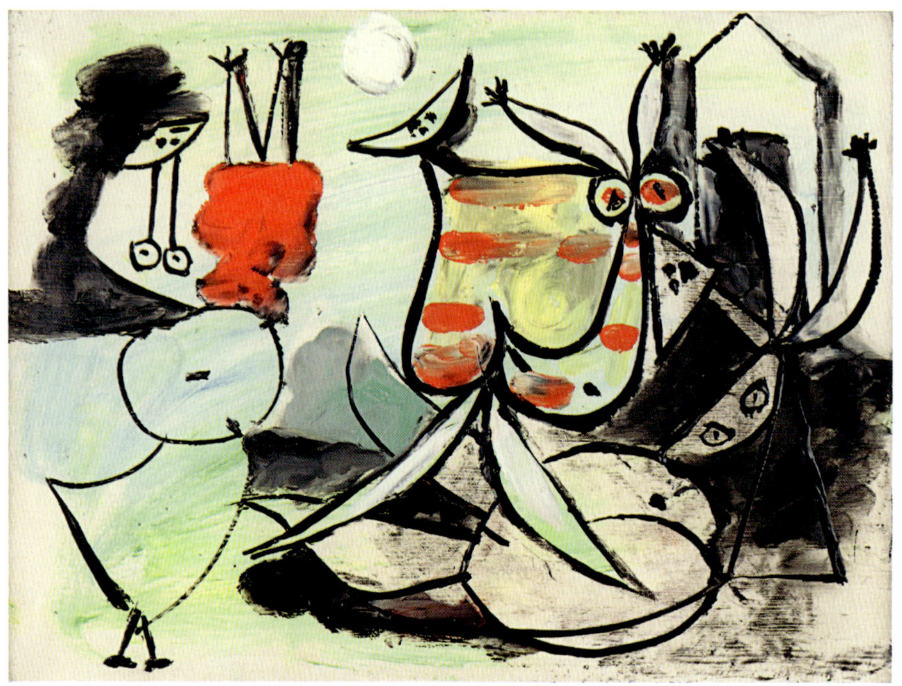

*Women Playing with a Ball on the Beach, Femmes jouant à la balle sur la plage*

*Swimmers with a Beach Ball, Bagneuses au ballon*

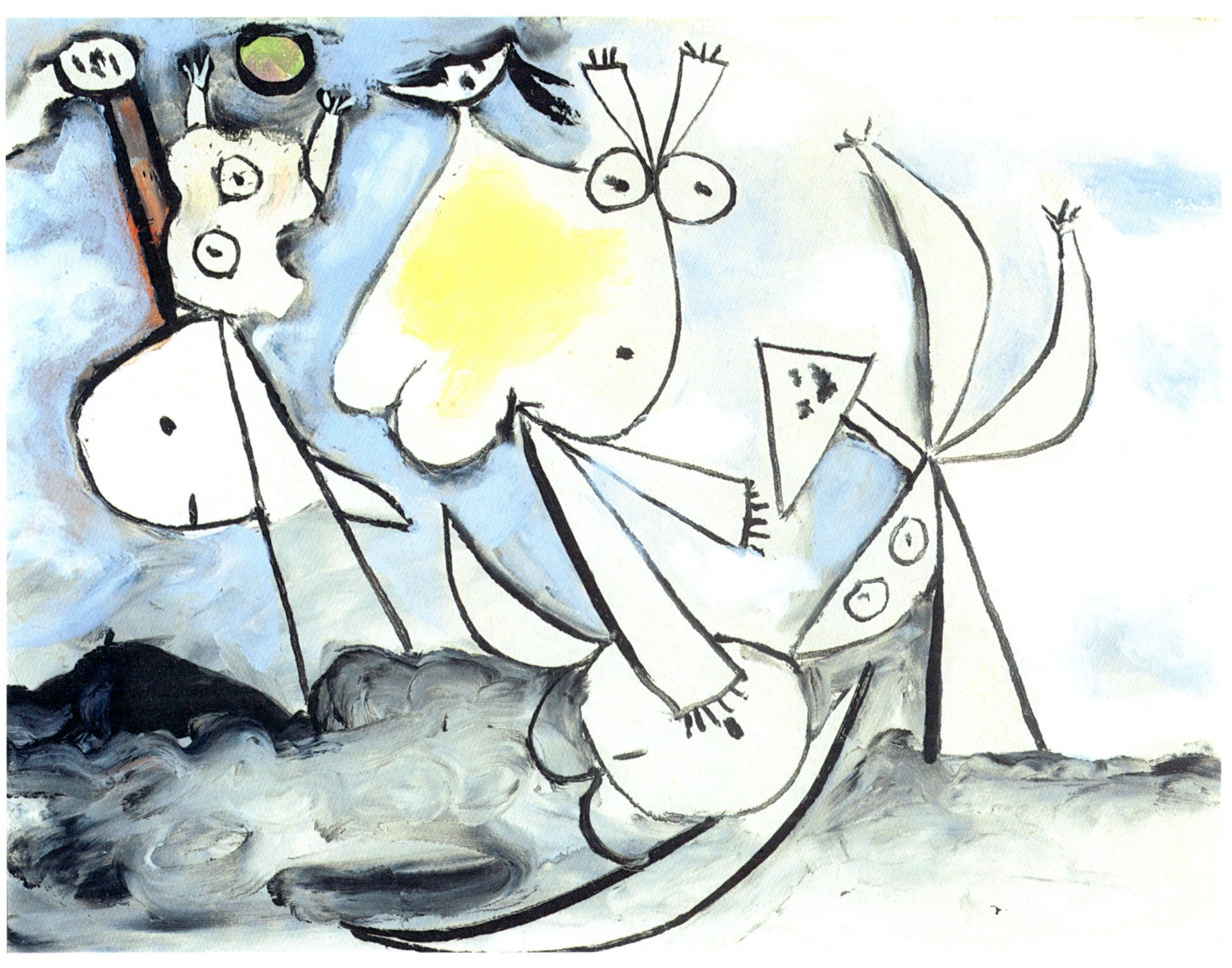

*Ball Players on the Beach, Joueuses de ballon sur la plage*

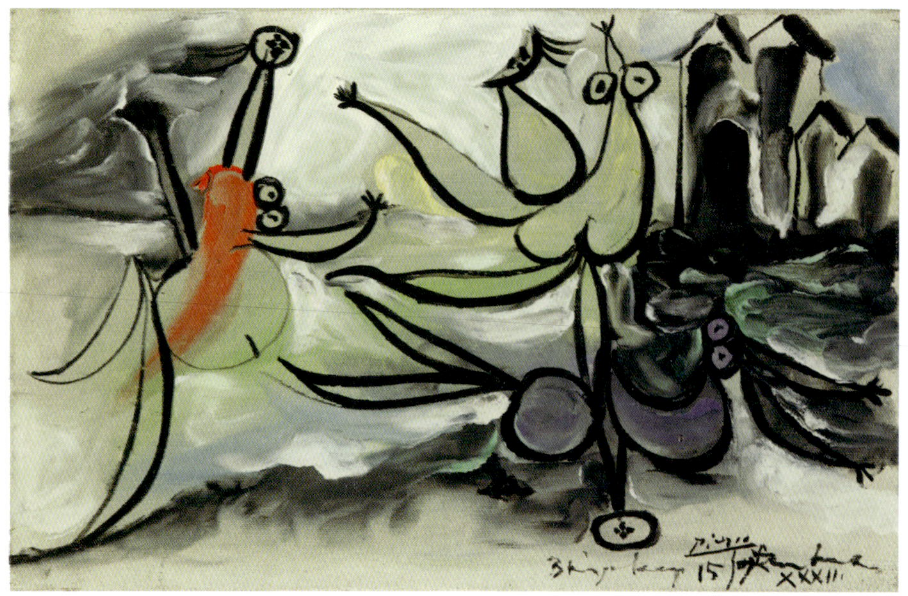

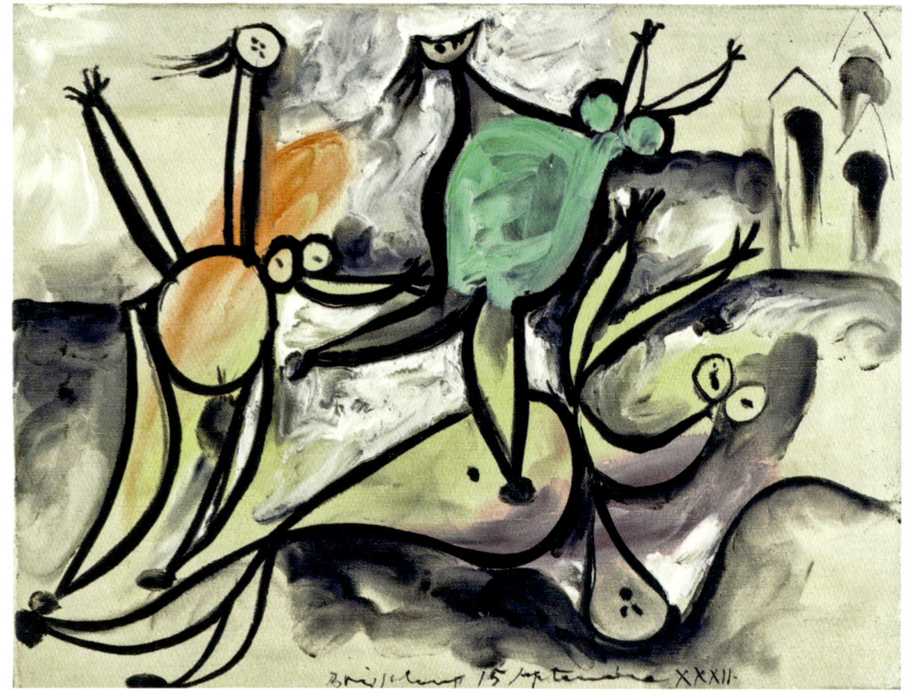

*The Three Bathers, Les Trois Baigneuses*

*Three Women Playing on the Seashore, Trois Femmes jouant au bord de la mer*

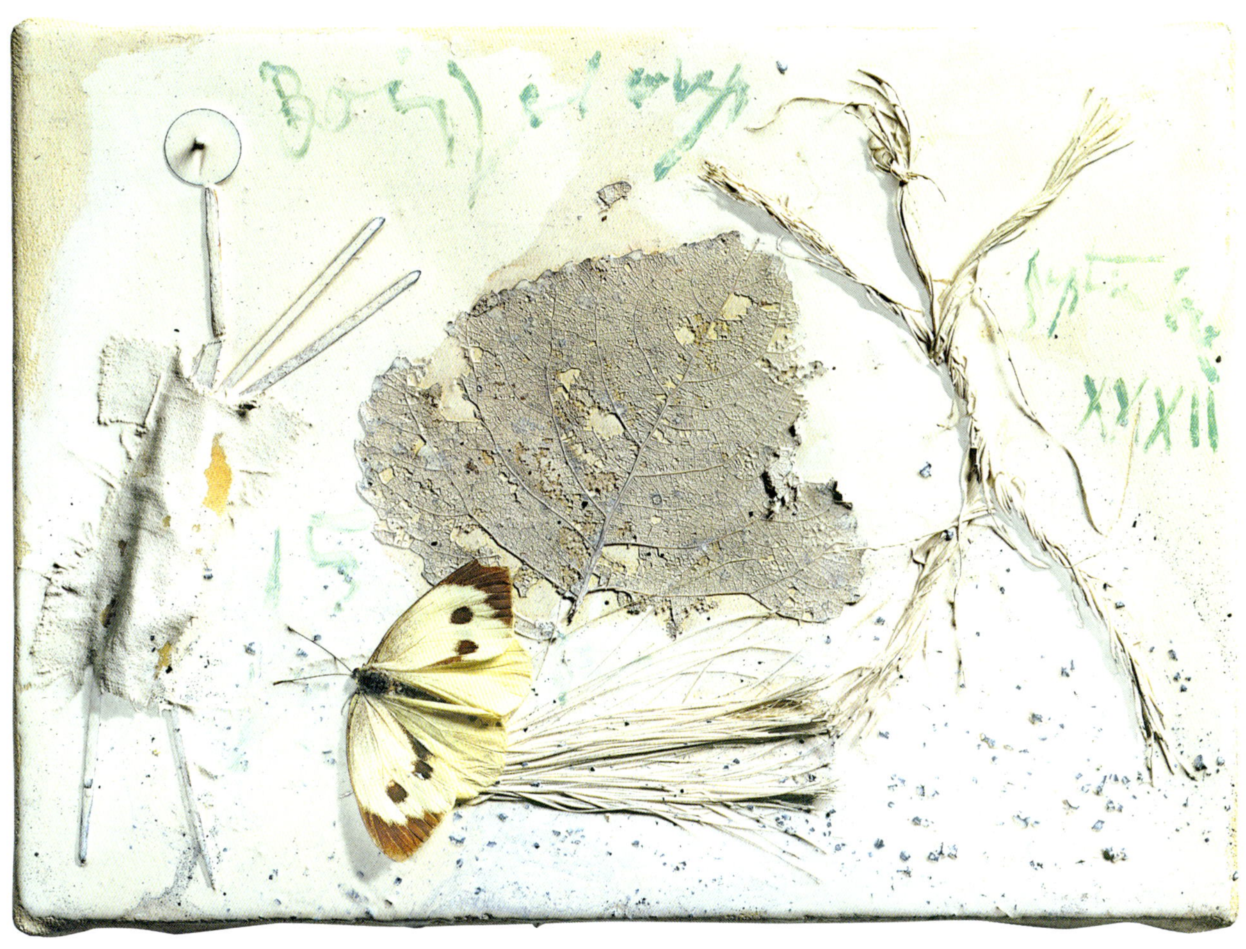

*Composition with Butterfly, Composition au papillon*

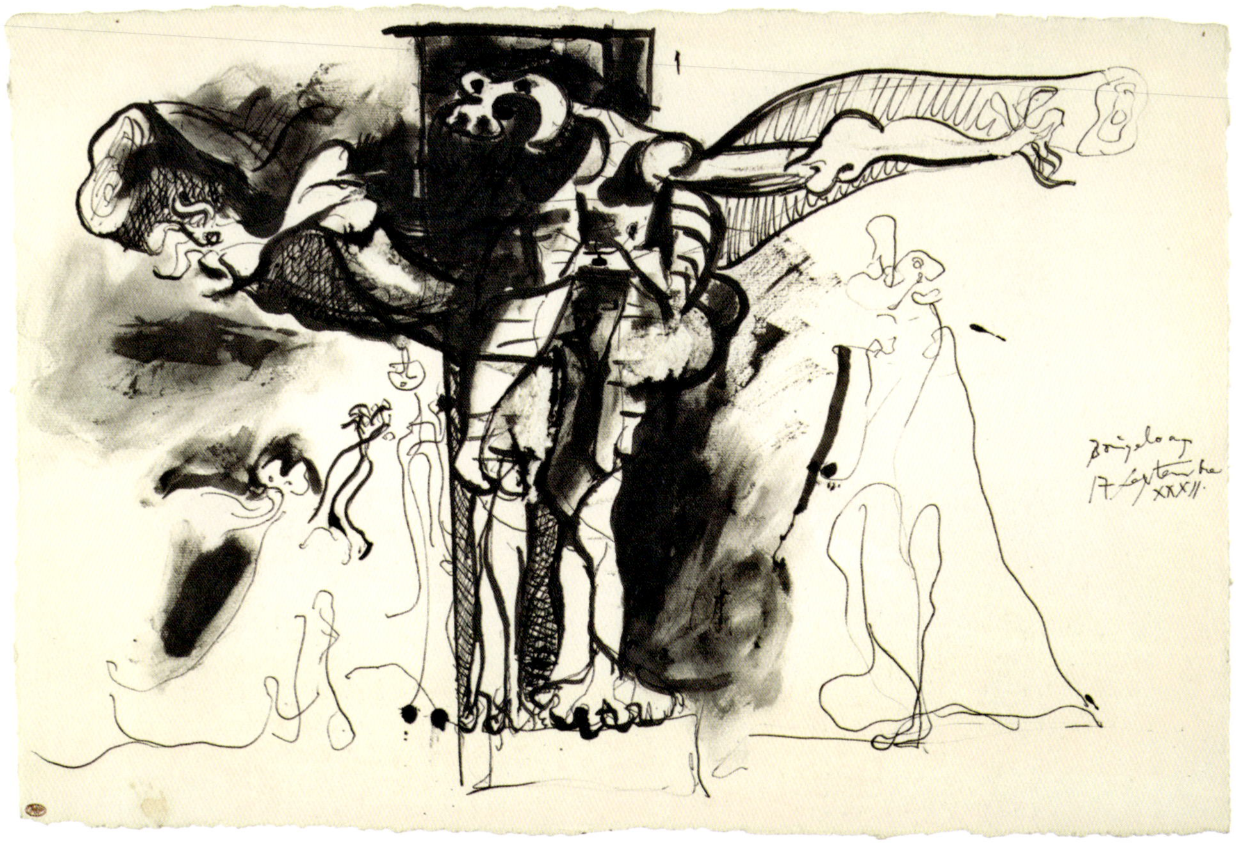


 *The Crucifixion*, *La Crucifixion*

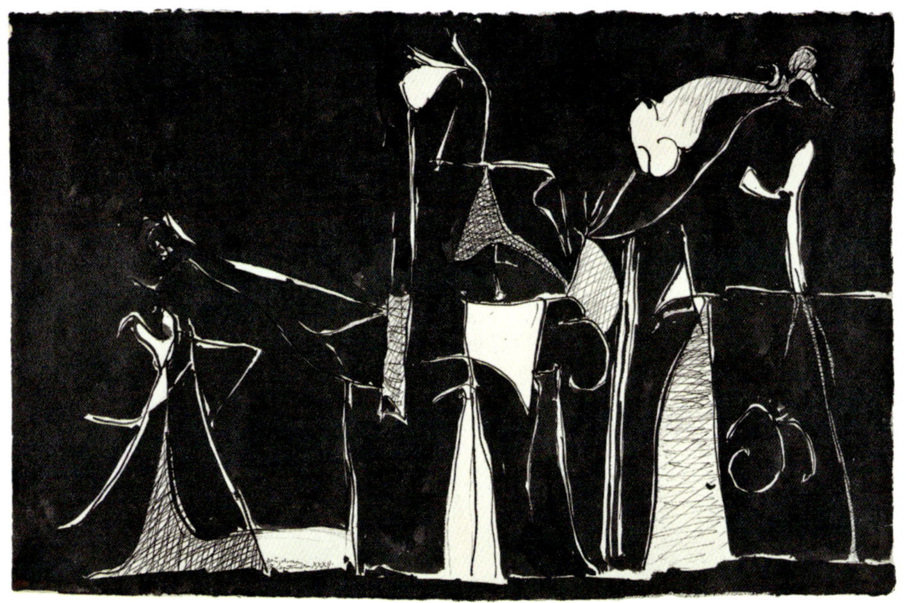

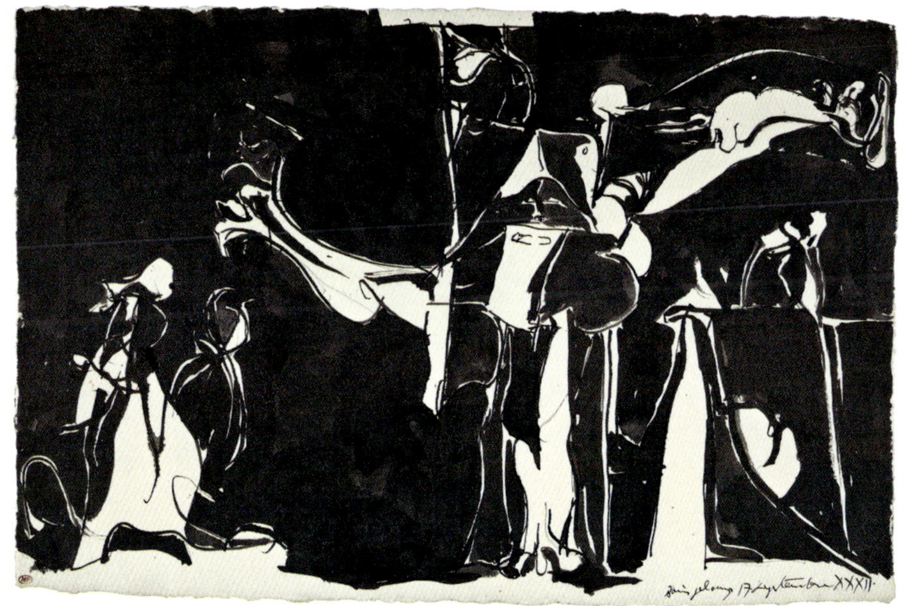

*The Crucifixion, La Crucifixion*

*The Crucifixion, La Crucifixion*

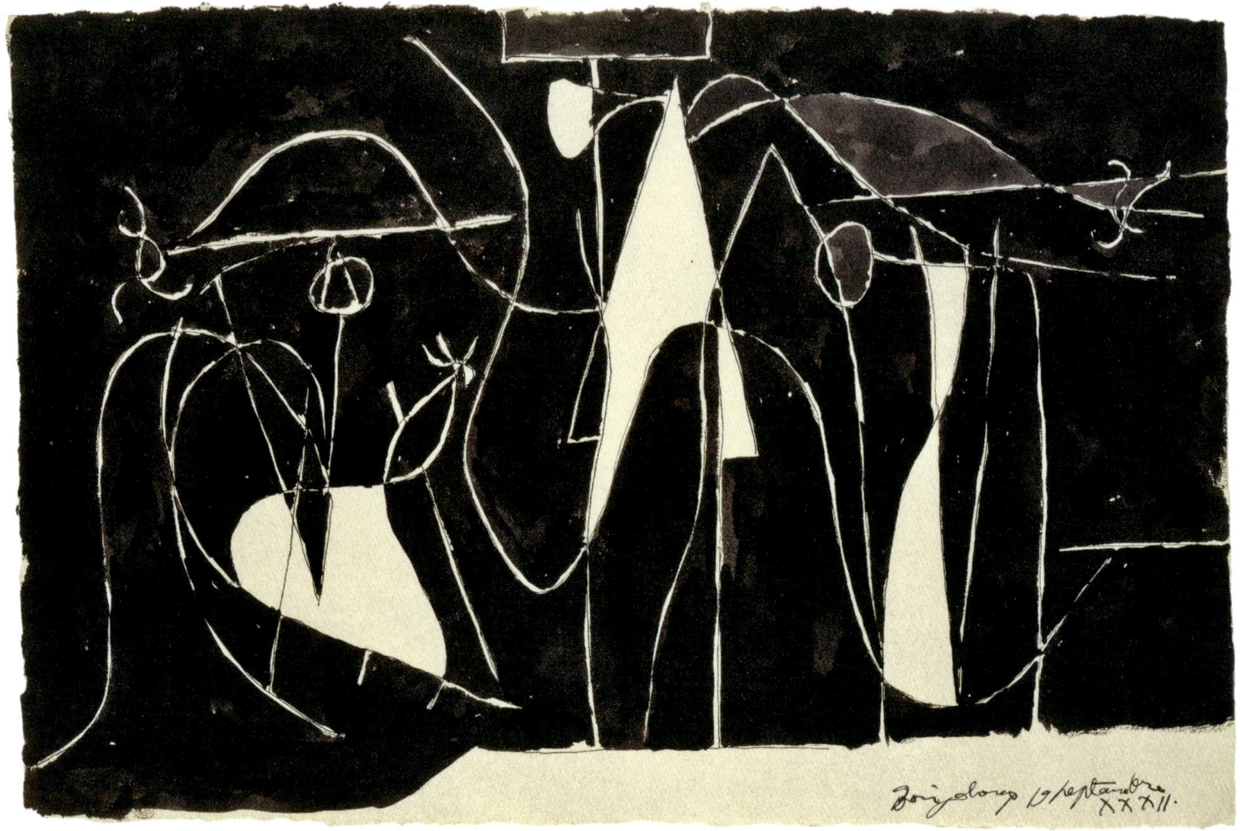

 *The Crucifixion, La Crucifixion*

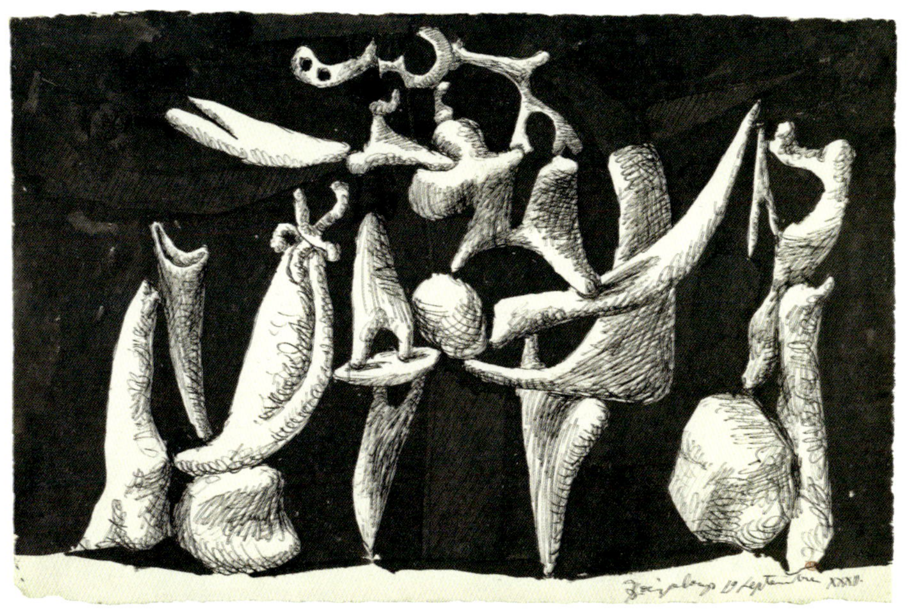

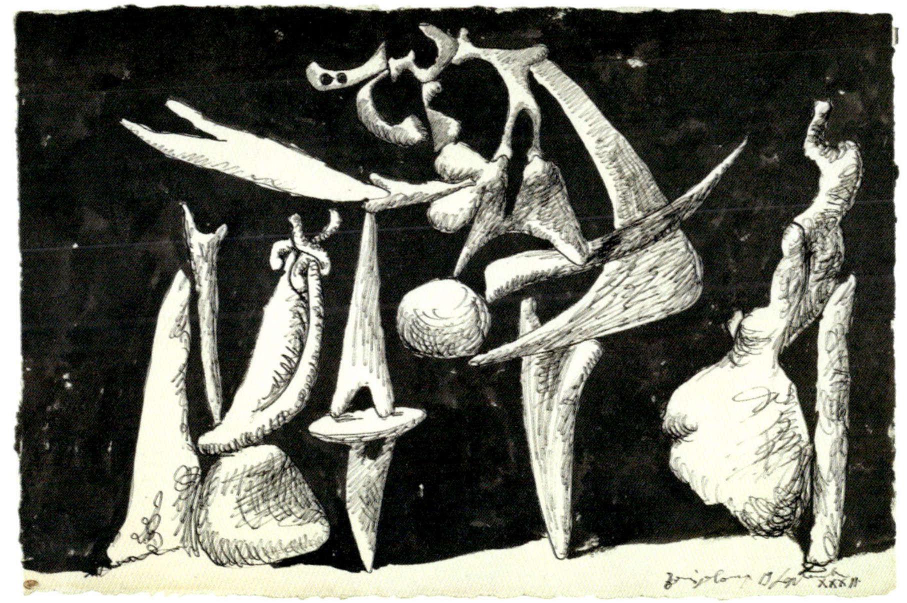

*The Crucifixion, La Crucifixion*

*The Crucifixion, La Crucifixion*

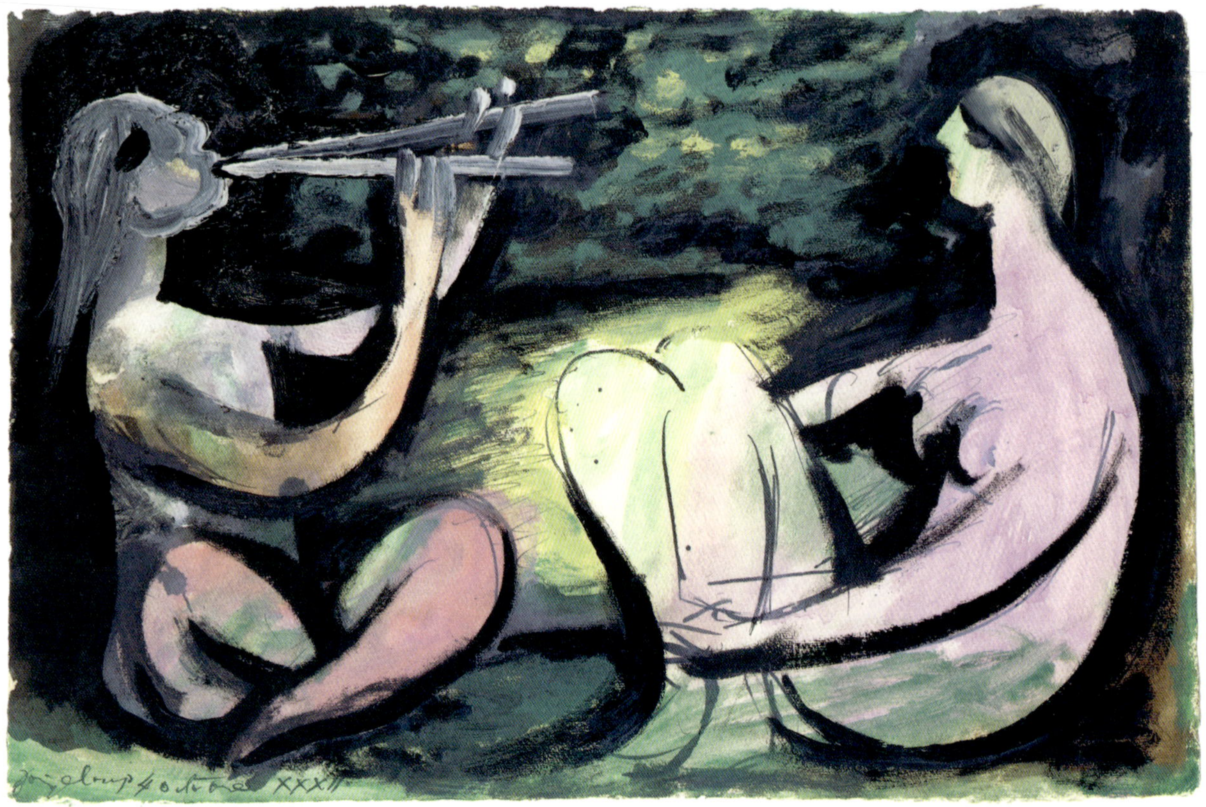

 *Flute Player and Seated Nude, Deux femmes nues dont l'une jouant de la diaule*

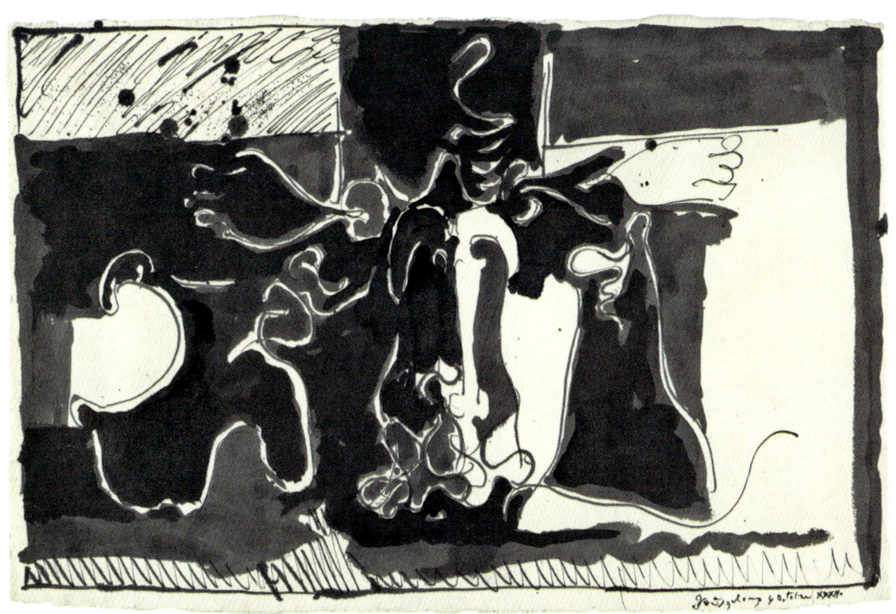

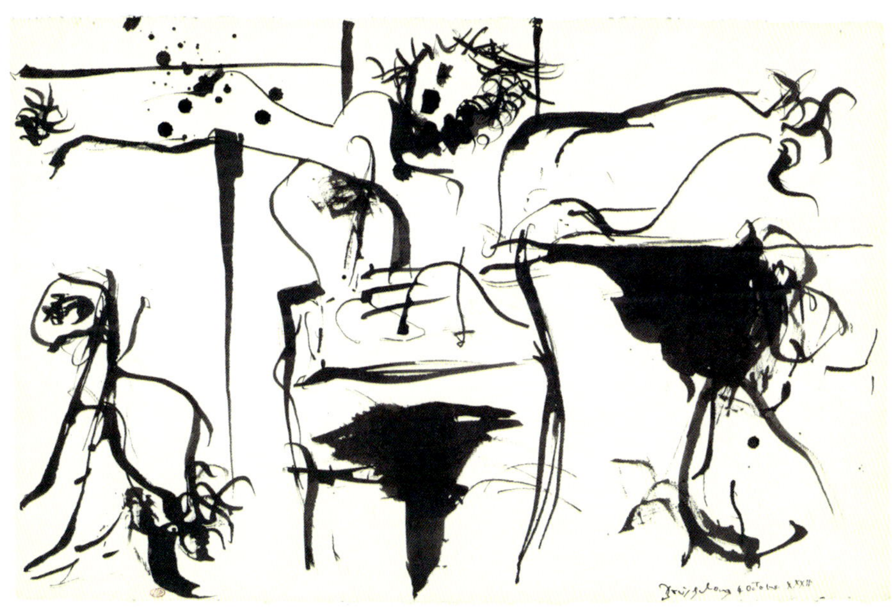

*The Crucifixion, La Crucifixion*

*The Crucifixion, La Crucifixion*

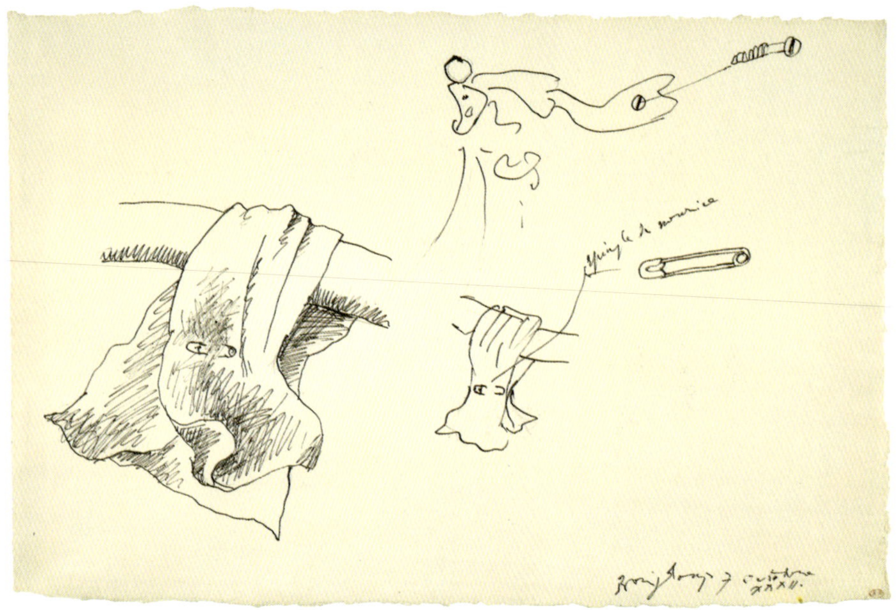

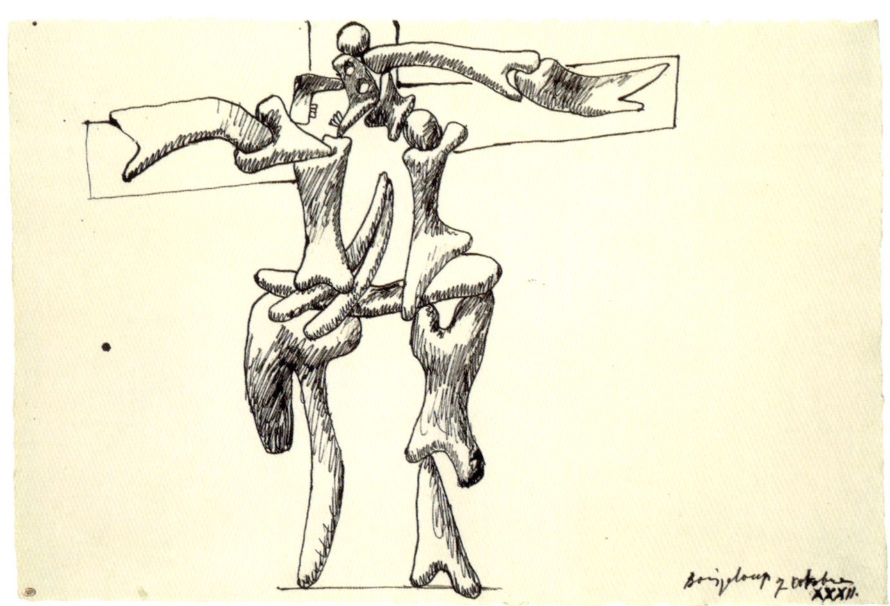

*The Crucifixion. Studies of Details, La Crucifixion. Etude de détails*



*The Crucifixion, La Crucifixion*

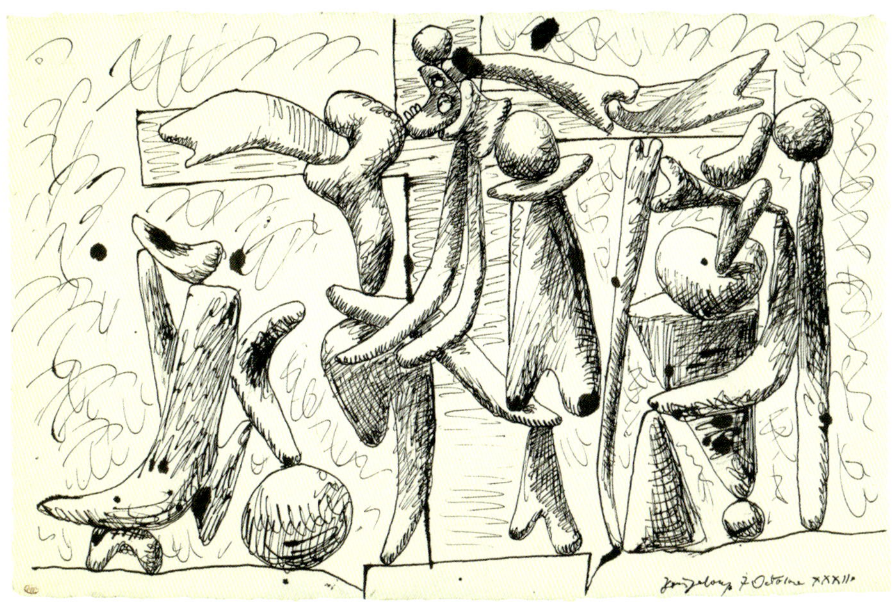


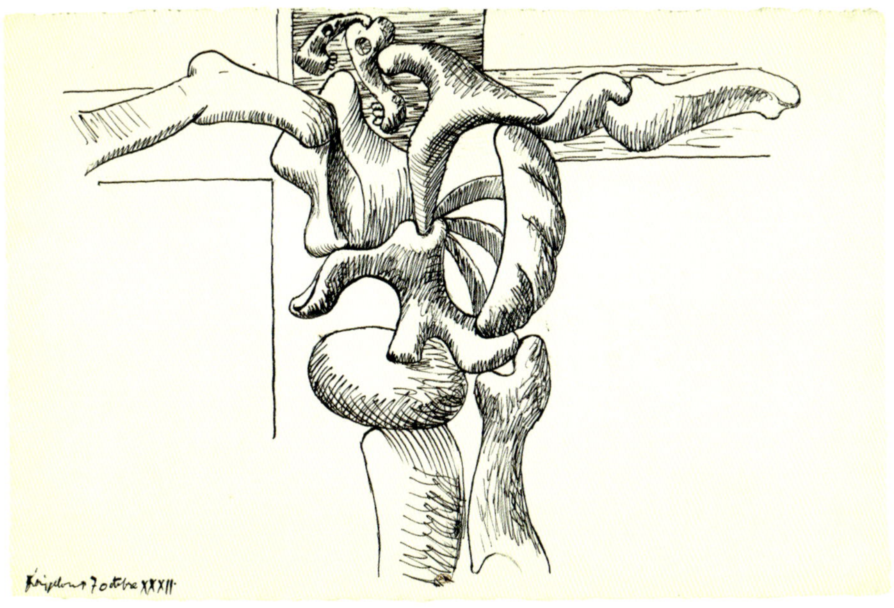


*The Crucifixion, La Crucifixion*

*The Crucifixion, La Crucifixion*

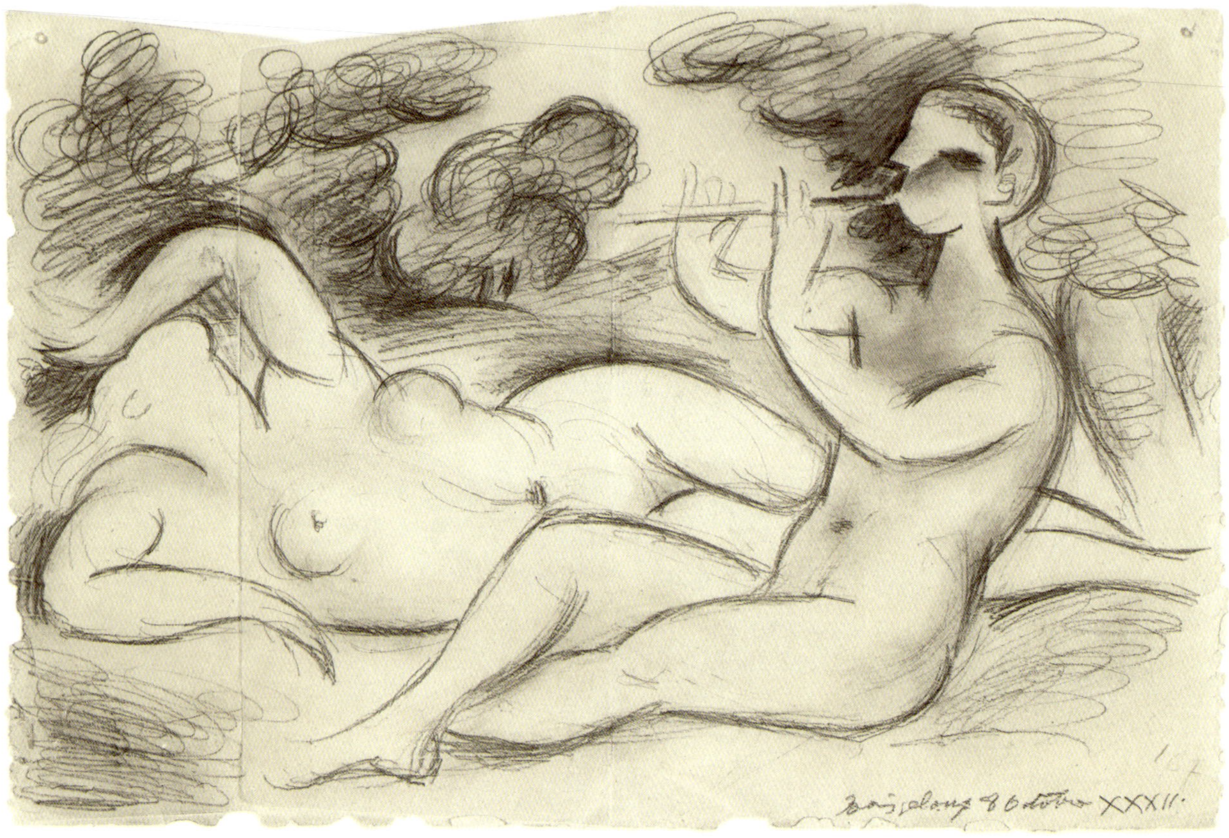

204 *Flute Player and Reclining Nude, Joueur de flûte et nu allongé*

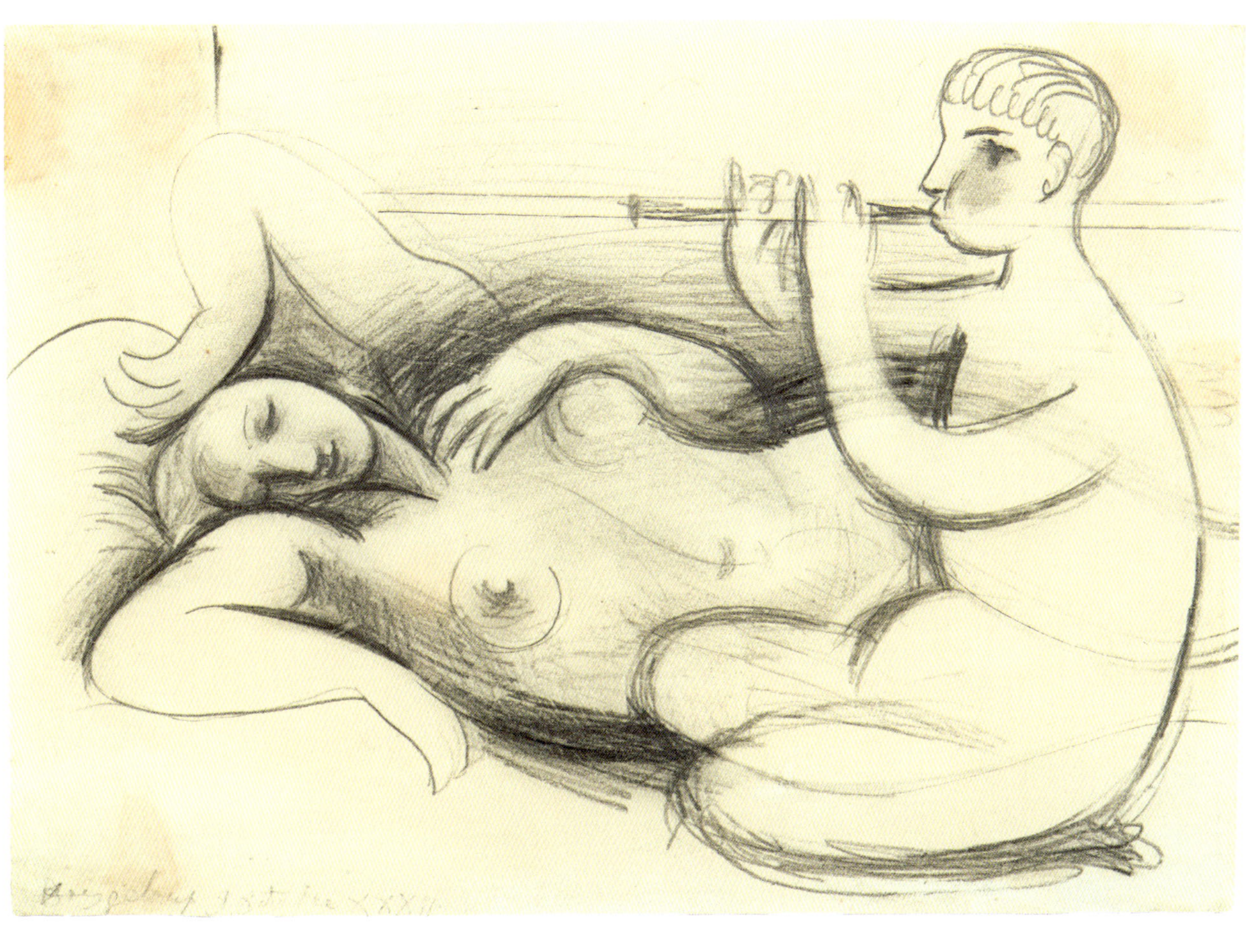

*Reclining Woman and Flute Player, Femme allongée, joueur de flûte*

'I can rarely keep myself from redoing a thing ... After all, why work otherwise, if not to better express the same thing? You must always seek perfection.'

Picasso, quoted in Brassaï, *Conversations with Picasso*, p.114

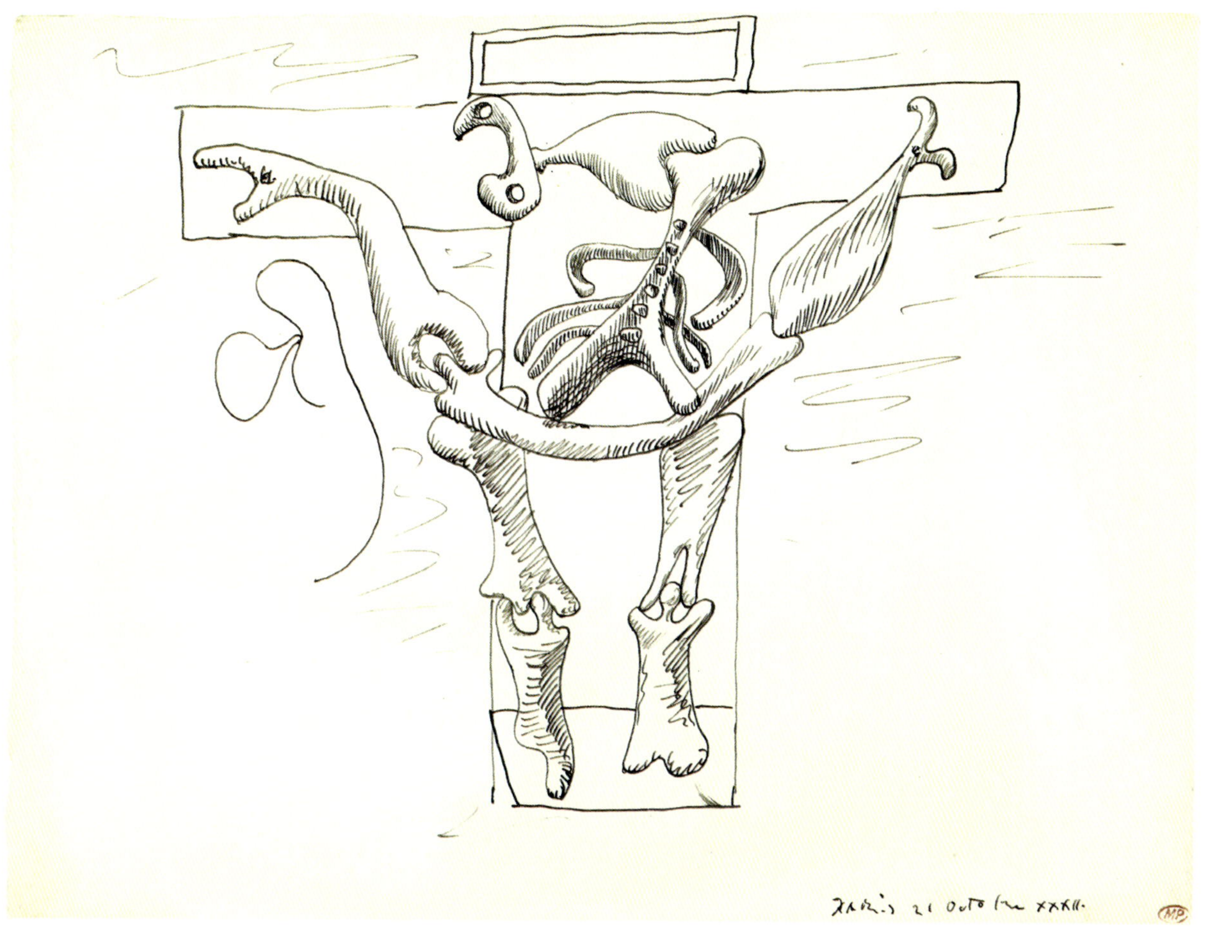


*The Crucifixion, La Crucifixion*

# Rescue: The End of a Year

Diana Widmaier Picasso

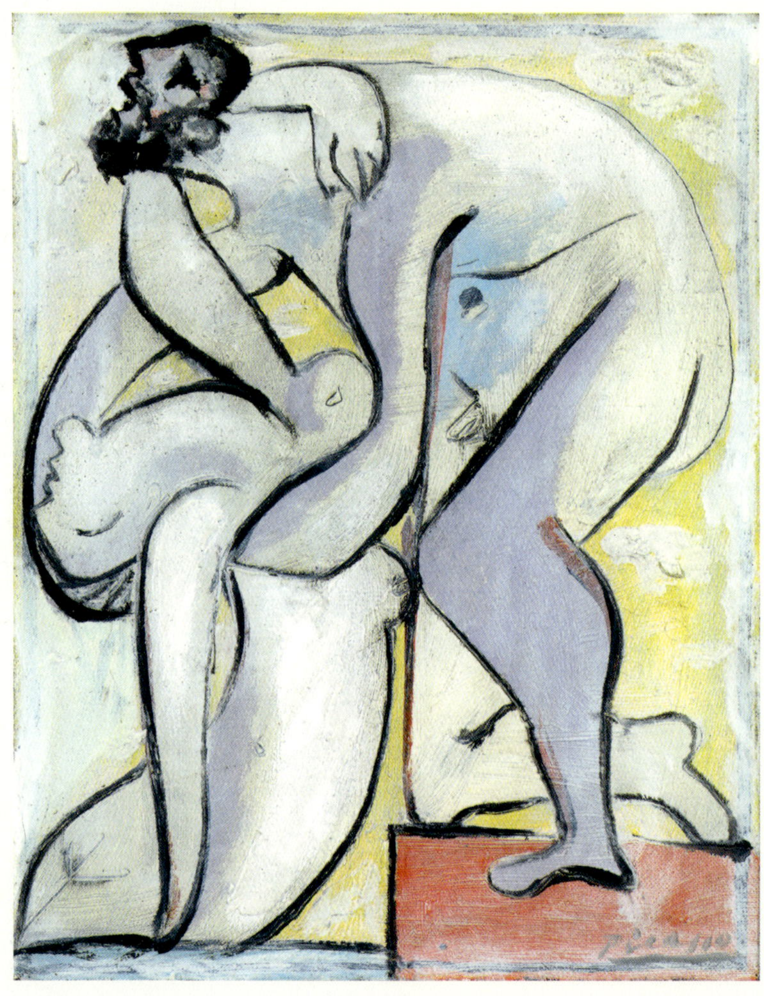

*The Rescue, Le Sauvetage* November 1932

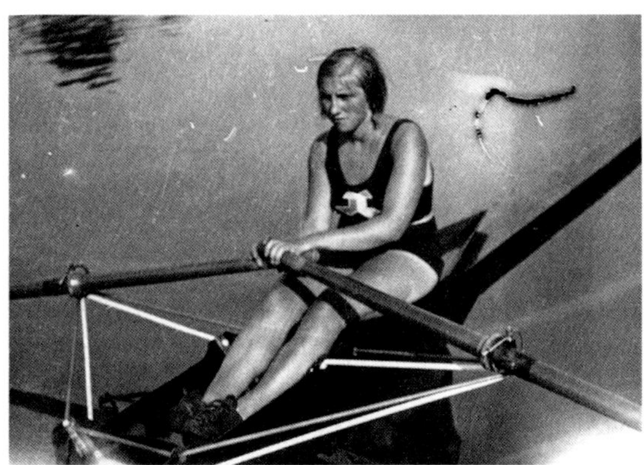

Marie-Thérèse Walter, Marne, Île de France, 1928

In June 1932, during a conversation with art critic and publisher Tériade, Picasso confided: 'the work that one does is a way of keeping a diary'.[1] The rhythm of Picasso's life can certainly be measured in his artistic creativity, but it was also affected by passionate love affairs and by certain events, tragic and otherwise, that occurred over the course of his career. At this time, though married to Olga Khokhlova,[2] Picasso was engaged in a five-year relationship with Marie-Thérèse Walter, the young woman he had met outside the Galeries Lafayette on 8 January 1927. Despite their twenty-eight year age difference, Picasso professed a boundless admiration for his young muse. In June 1930, when Walter was still living partly at her mother's house in the suburbs, and partly in Paris,[3] Picasso had purchased a chateau at Boisgeloup.[4] Picasso, Olga and their son often spent time together there, but equally the house played a key role in Picasso and Walter indulging in their passionate relationship, with the occasional clandestine getaway to the Normandy seaside.[5] This period gave rise to an unparalleled outpouring of creativity under the impulse of this *amour fou* (mad love),[6] with the resulting works presented publicly for the first time at the major retrospective that opened at Galeries Georges Petit in June 1932. It was then that the public discovered the existence of Marie-Thérèse Walter, whose identity remained unknown but whose physical attributes were evoked in a series of voluptous portraits.[7] Walter was a striking beauty and extremely athletic; in fact her body had a sculptural form that would inspire Picasso with a new formal vocabulary.

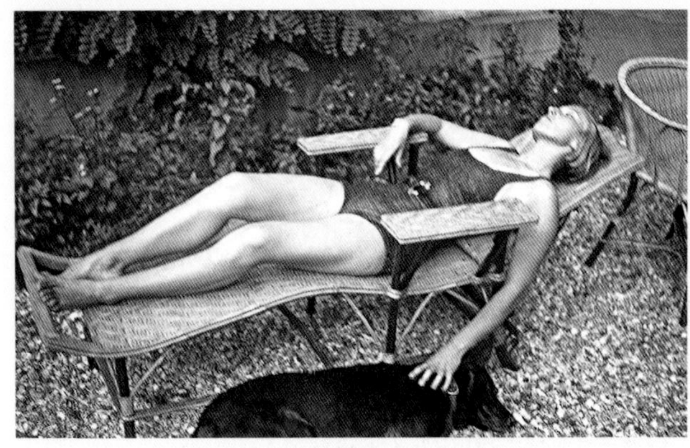

Marie-Thérèse Walter, Cité d'Alfort, Maisons-Alfort, c.1932

An accomplished and intrepid swimmer, in late 1932 Walter had the severe misfortune to fall victim to spirochetosis, a sometimes fatal disease that she contracted after swimming in the sewage-polluted waters of the river Marne, where she went rowing.[8] As a consequence, she spent time in hospital and then convalesced away for several months. In her absence Picasso became obsessed with the memory of their time together, depicting her constantly in his work and reliving the erotic nature of their relationship with scenes of naked female bathers and of drowning in which Walter is omnipresent as victim, witness and rescuer. Pierre Daix sees in this a parallel with Olga Picasso's return to Boisgeloup after a summer spent away from him,[9] while for John Golding the choice of subject is explained by the deterioration of their marriage.[10] However, the dramatic and harrowing atmosphere of these rescue scenes raises a number of questions. What is one to make of this latent disquiet in Picasso's work? What is the meaning of the many drawings, engravings and paintings on the repeated theme of drowning executed between November 1932 and January 1933? Are they votive offerings or symbols of a resurrection?

Over the summer of 1932 Olga and Paulo had gone on a long holiday to Juan-les-Pins while Picasso remained at Boisgeloup. He was visited there by Georges Braque, Julio González, Daniel-Henry Kahnweiler, Michel Leiris, Maurice Raynal and Christian Zervos, none of whom knew of the existence of Walter. Daix suggests that Picasso had also joined his mistress during this time, but it could not have been on the beaches of Étretat or Dieppe as he claims.[11] In fact, photographs[12] confirm that Walter spent the end of July and the month of August in the south of France in the company of her sister Jeanne,[13] moving between Juan-les-Pins, Monte Carlo, Île Saint-Honorat, Les Tourettes and Gorges du Loup (opposite). Picasso's separation from her inspired several paintings, including *Bather with Beach Ball*, painted on 30 August 1932 (a pictorial transposition of a photograph dated in ink on the reverse 'Juan-les-Pins, 27-7-32'), in which Walter resembles a playful, bouncy toy (p.147). The soft, round curves of her silhouette are completely transformed into a kind of inflatable ball, floating upwards, while her mouth takes on a sexually explicit oval form. In this work, we rediscover the dynamism of the series of *Bathers* executed during the summer of 1928 in Dinard, where Picasso spent a holiday with his family, with Walter lodging nearby. Every day he would go to meet her clandestinely and take her to the beach hut he had rented. During this time, Picasso painted a collection of twenty-six bathers running on the beach, opening beach huts and playing ball. His approach is carefully documented in a sketchbook filled with bather after bather, each transformation giving birth to a different canvas.[14] In *Bather (Project for a Monument)* 1928,[15] the background is simplified in the extreme and Walter's body is distorted and metamorphosed into a curious anthropomorphic structure: a button-shaped head, boomerang torso, conical breasts and sticks for limbs – like bones assembled on a beach. By allowing Picasso to study the relationship between the dimensions of the body and the movement of the figure, the *Bathers* series became a boundless landscape providing him with ample opportunity to experiment with new forms. The unsettling strangeness emanating from these 'sexually monstrous monumental creatures'[16] recalls the highly erotically charged beach scenes beloved of the surrealists – but above all it represents the very peak of Picasso's imagination.

A large number of drawings, engravings and paintings executed between September 1932 and January 1933 – such as *Ball Players on the Beach*, painted on 6 September 1932 (p.193), and *The Three Bathers*, painted nine days later, on 15 September (p.194) – combine these experimental representations of beach games with the anecdotal theme of rescue. From November 1932, Walter's illness – which had caused high fever and significant weight loss – continued to haunt Picasso. Like a recurring nightmare, the theme of rescue began to repeat itself in his work. Josep Palau i Fabre sees this as a product

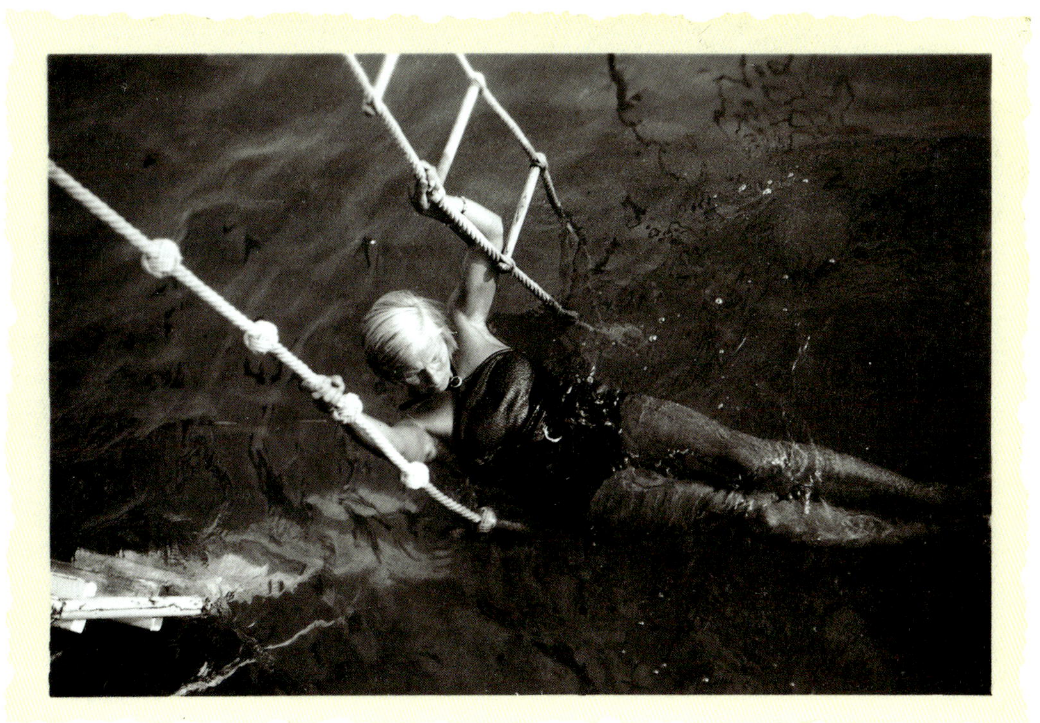

Marie-Thérèse Walter, Monte-Carlo, August 1932

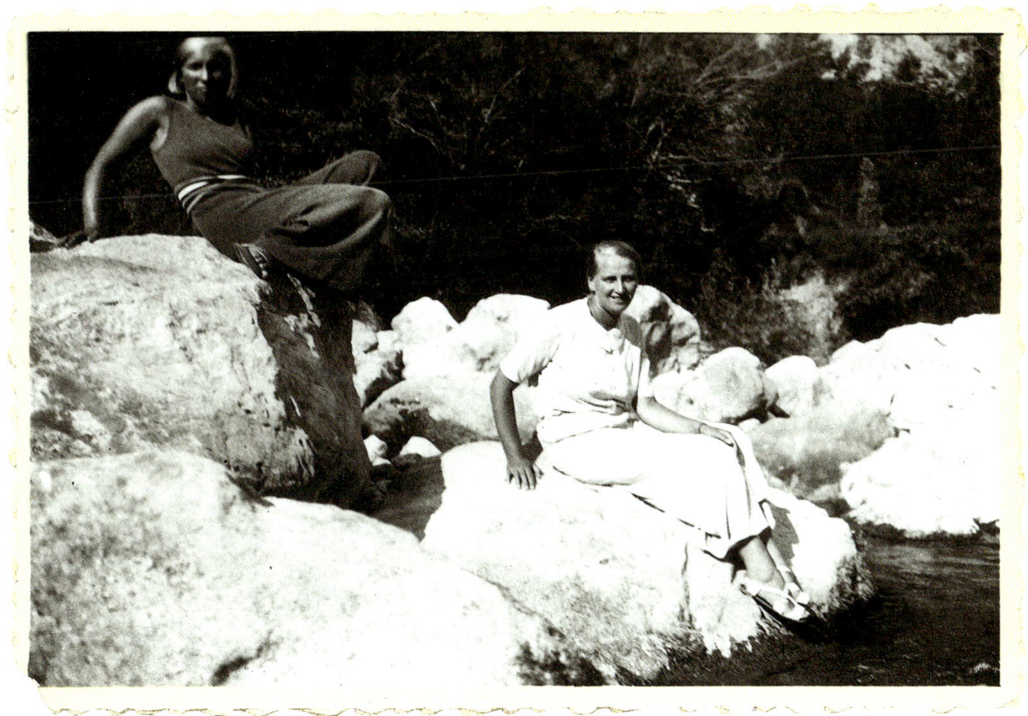

Marie-Thérèse Walter with her sister Jeanne, Gorges du Loup, 22 August 1932

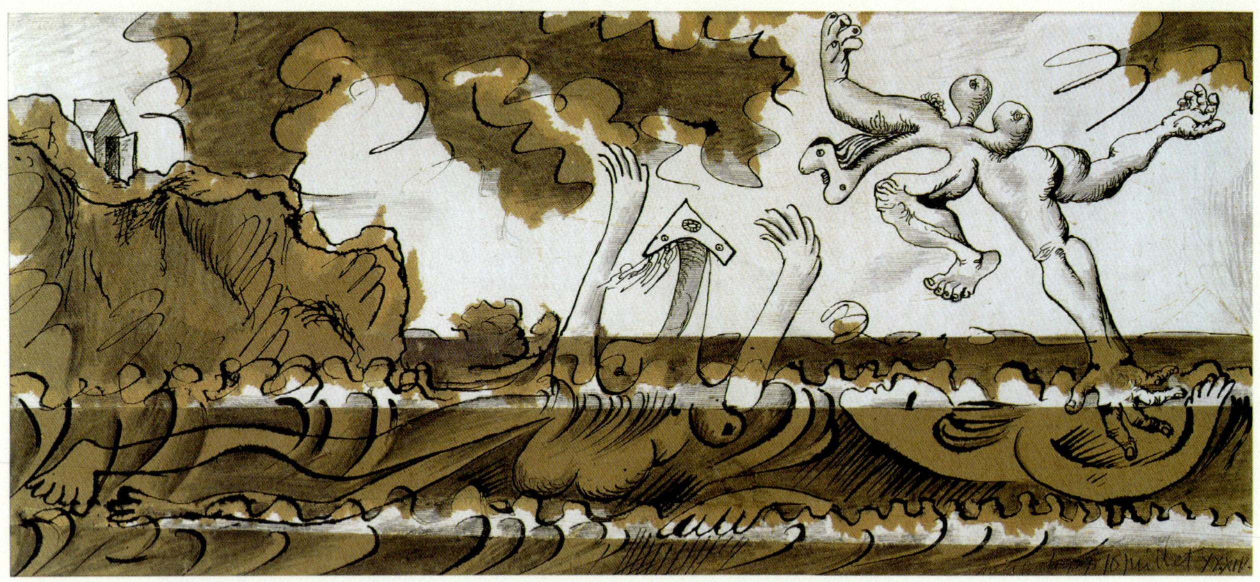

*Bathers, Baigneuses* Boisgeloup, 10 July 1934

of the artist's imagination: on many occasions Picasso will have seen Walter diving with great agility and may even have seen her save someone from drowning; this theory is perhaps illustrated in the painting *Woman Running towards a Swimmer*, painted at Boisgeloup on 4 September.[17] Brigitte Baer suggests, quite correctly, that the subject of rescue is a visual transposition of the virus.[18] Probably in November 1932, Picasso painted a bearded man – a reference to the sculptor, the painter's alter ego in his etchings portfolio *Les Métamorphoses d'Ovide* (Ovid's *Metamorphoses*)[19] – saving a young woman from drowning (p.208). The canvas is somewhat evocative of the composition of the sculpted group *Menelaus Supporting the Body of Patroclus* 240–30 BCE,[20] or the posture of the two protagonists in Antonio Canova's *Psyche Revived by Cupid's Kiss* 1789–93 or Ary Scheffer's *Orpheus Mourning the Death of Eurydice* 1814.[21] Picasso adopts the same arrangement of the figures in a canvas also titled *The Rescue*, dated 20 November 1932, but here adds a third person (p.217). The three women depicted all have the same features as Walter, who here plays every role: the central figure, inanimate, her head and arms thrown back as she is lifted from the water, appears to be a reflection of the figure receiving her.[22] The 'Greek profile'[23] of the latter figure recalls the monumental busts executed at Boisgeloup a few months earlier,[24] just as it anticipates the face of one of the principal figures in *Guernica* (p.27). The rhythm and grace of the painting as a whole contrast with the flat tints and background work. In the white flowers in the background, Reinhold Hohl sees an allusion to the myth of Narcissus who, in Ovid's *Metamorphoses*, falls in love with his own reflection and who, when he dies, is transformed into the flower that now bears his name.[25] One could also associate these flowers with pictorial representations of Shakespeare's Ophelia,[26] the subject of a poem by Rimbaud that underlines the symbiosis with nature.[27] The erotic tension of the painting is accentuated by the nudity and intertwinement of the bathers – like nymphs emerging from the water, their limbs transformed into tentacles and fins[28] – also found intermixed with ball games in *The Rescue* of December 1932 (p.231).[29] Here Picasso combines two scenes – one of pleasure, to which he later returns in monochrome tones in *Bathers with Beach Ball* and *Women Playing with a Ball on the Beach* on 4 December 1932 (pp.224, 225); the other of terror, in which we find the customary alliance of the colours yellow, red and violet, characteristic of his depictions of Marie-Thérèse Walter.[30] Against a highly simplified background, the figures are transformed into surrealist creatures resembling birds, with wings instead of arms and legs, and evocative of the small group of bathers modelled by the artist at Boisgeloup in 1931.[31] Picasso takes this biomorphic transformation to its extreme on 11 January 1933 (p.233). The bodies of rescuer and rescued merge and twist like a bud about to burst. That same year, Picasso also executed a number of drawings in which the Minotaur, the artist's sexual alter ego, draws his victim to him, her profile and her abandoned body evoking that of Walter, in a movement that recalls the earlier rescue compositions.[32] Certain rape scenes, such as *The Rape*, painted on 10 August 1933,[33] bear witness to the iconographic proximity of the two subjects – rescue and Minotaur – while also suggesting that Picasso's desire is responsible for the young woman's death. A few years later, Picasso would merge the two themes with *Minotaur in a Boat Saving a Woman* 1937.[34]

In the years that followed, the theme of victimhood or rescue returned episodically to haunt the artist's work and then took a dramatic turn. In the summer of 1934, death stalked Picasso's art. At Boisgeloup he drew numerous scenes of bulls being put to death,[35] and an earlier theme of the death of Marat reappeared as *The Murder* 7 July 1934, with Marie-Thérèse Walter in the role of the victim. While in *Woman with Dagger* from November 1931 the focus was Olga's jealous fury (p.41), the subject now revolved around Marie-Thérèse, her body prostrate and unconscious in the bath. In fact it is difficult to know whether the imposing hand of the figure at the top right in the *Bathers* drawing of 10 July 1934 is benevolent or, on the contrary, is pushing the young woman down into the depths. Here the stylistic treatment of the figures differs from earlier representations of *The Rescue*, with surrealist distortion of the faces and limbs. Picasso returned to this subject in a series of drawings of spring 1936 (including *Composition*, 4 May, right),[36] and the motif resonates once again the following year, in May 1937, to express the suffering of a mother carrying her dead child in *Guernica*.

The iconography of Walter as a drowning woman plunging backwards is also somewhat reminiscent of Crucifixion scenes in which a fainting Mary is supported by John the Baptist, and of depictions of the Lamentation of Christ, in which the Virgin cradles her dead son's body upon her knees.[37] This may also be seen in relation to Picasso's interest in September 1932 in the early sixteenth-century Isenheim Altarpiece by Matthias Grünewald, whose central panel becomes the inspiration for graphic and pictorial variations.[38] This was followed by a series of drawings executed between 17 September and 21 October 1932 (pp.196–9, 201–3, 207) which foreshadow the troubling paintings on the theme of rescue – a common theme in religious painting of biblical subjects such as Moses being saved from the waters[39] and Christ saving the apostle Peter from drowning.[40]

Though Picasso was not a believer and his work is, as William Rubin points out, 'areligious',[41] the artist seems to abide by a personal form of spirituality. *The Rescue* series, like a 'tool of domestic piety',[42] allows him to project and exorcise his internal conflicts. In it he initiates an existential reflection on life and death, joy and gravity, beauty and horror, possession and loss. The artist makes the link between a real event (Marie-Thérèse's illness), a religious subject (the Crucifixion, Pietà and Resurrection) and the universal themes of suffering and death. The subject of drowning is made secret and through this Picasso transforms Marie-Thérèse Walter into martyr and saint.

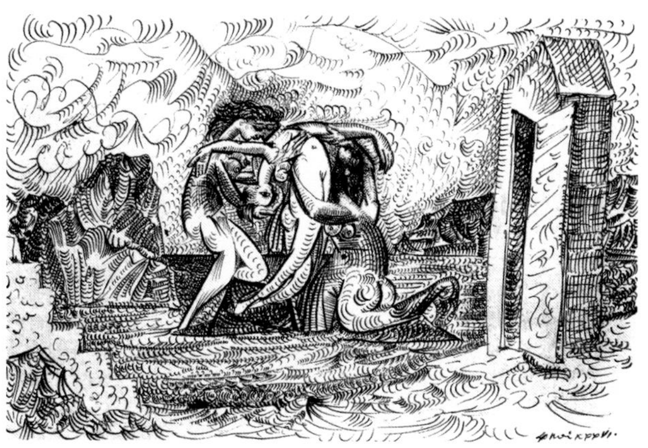

*Composition*, *Composition* Juan-les-Pins, 4 May 1936

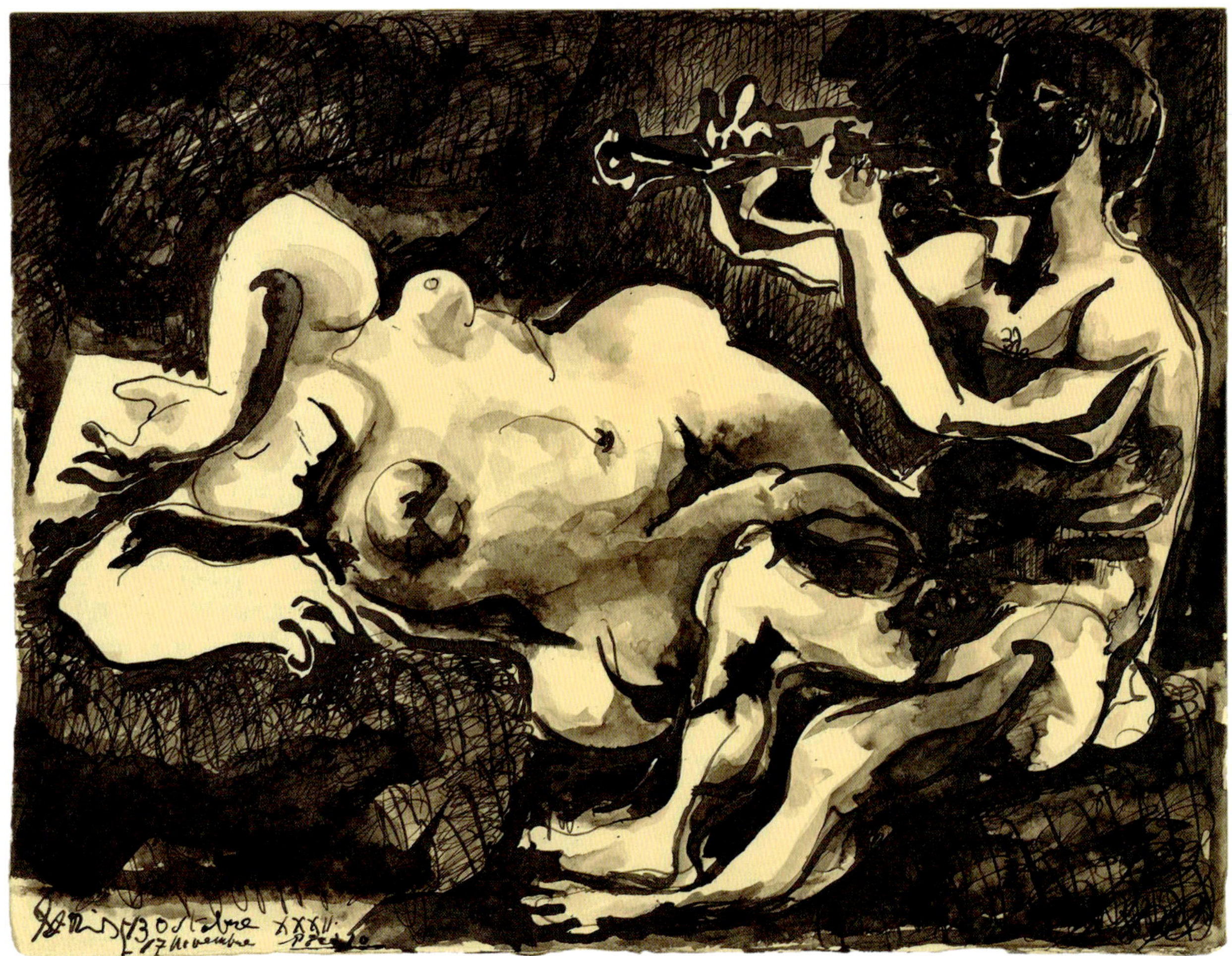

 *The Clarinet Player*, *Le Joueur de clarinette*

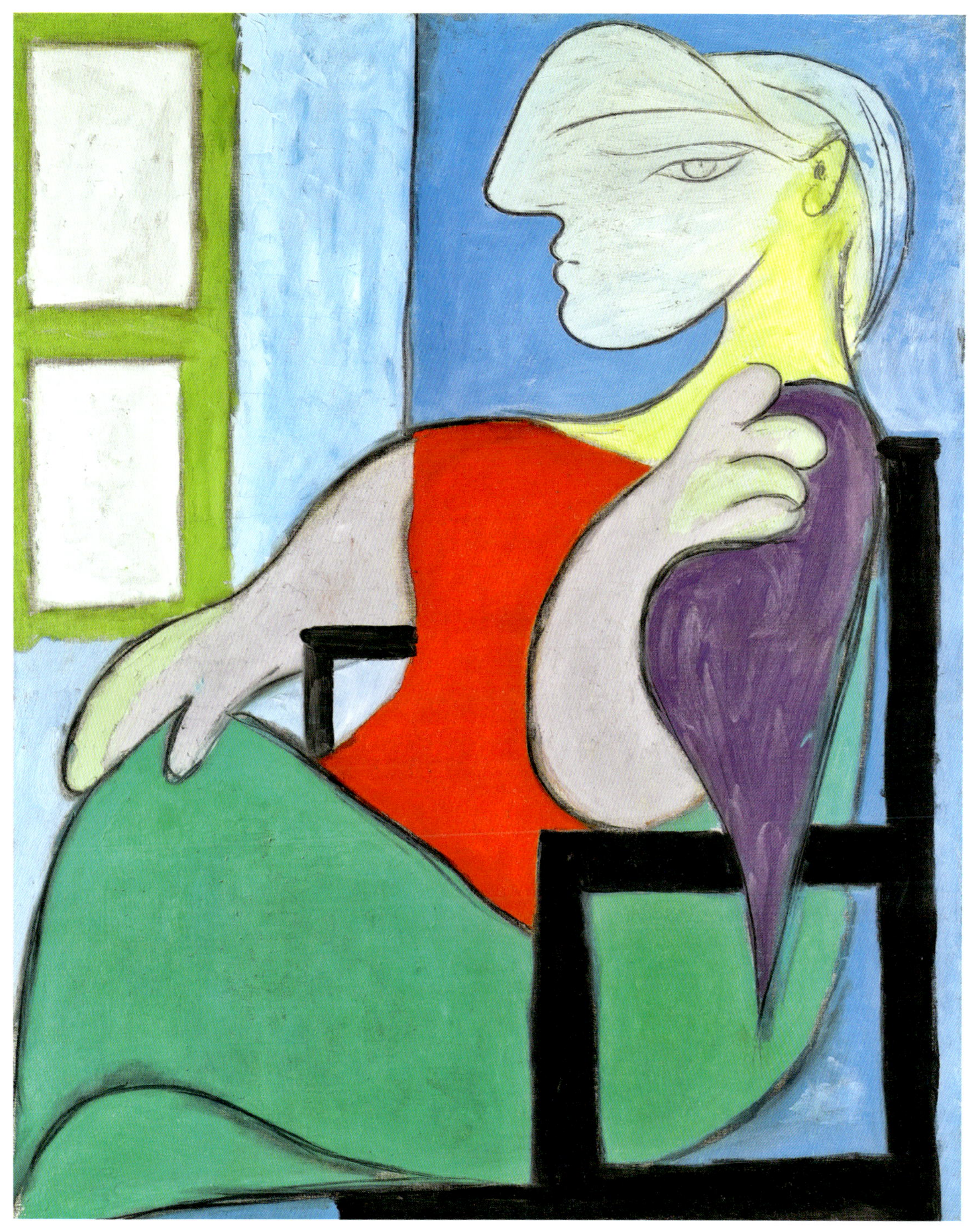

*Seated Woman by a Window, Femme assise près d'une fenêtre*

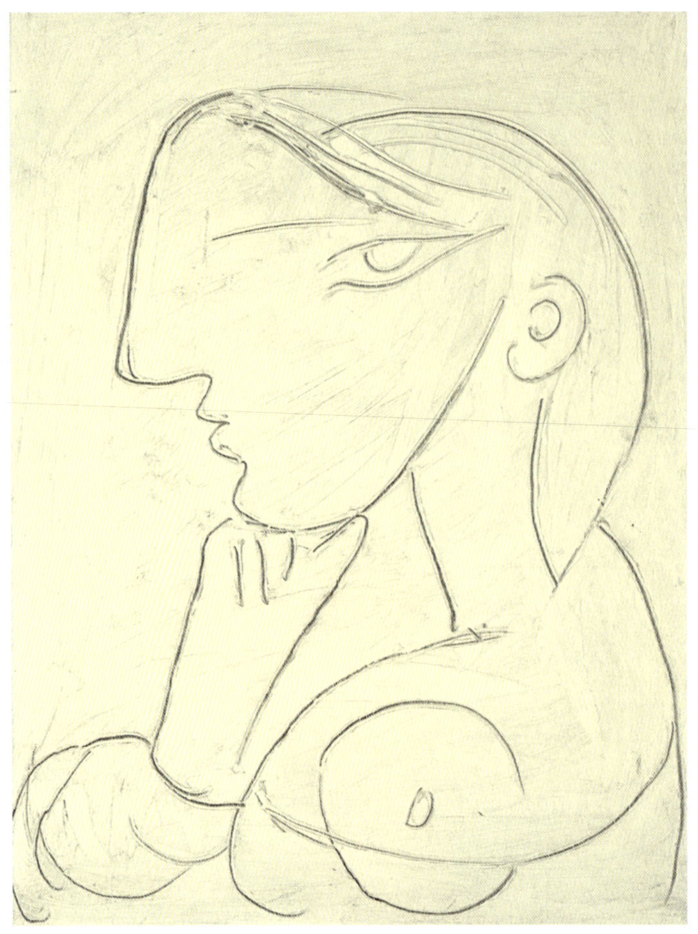

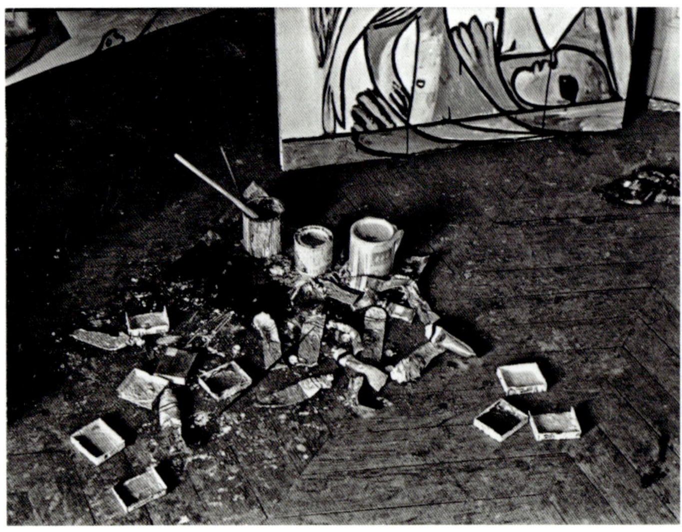

*Marie-Thérèse in a Pensive Mood, Marie-Thérèse pensive*

Pots and tubes of paint on the floor of the upstairs studio at 23 rue La Boétie, in front of *The Rescue*. Photograph by Brassaï

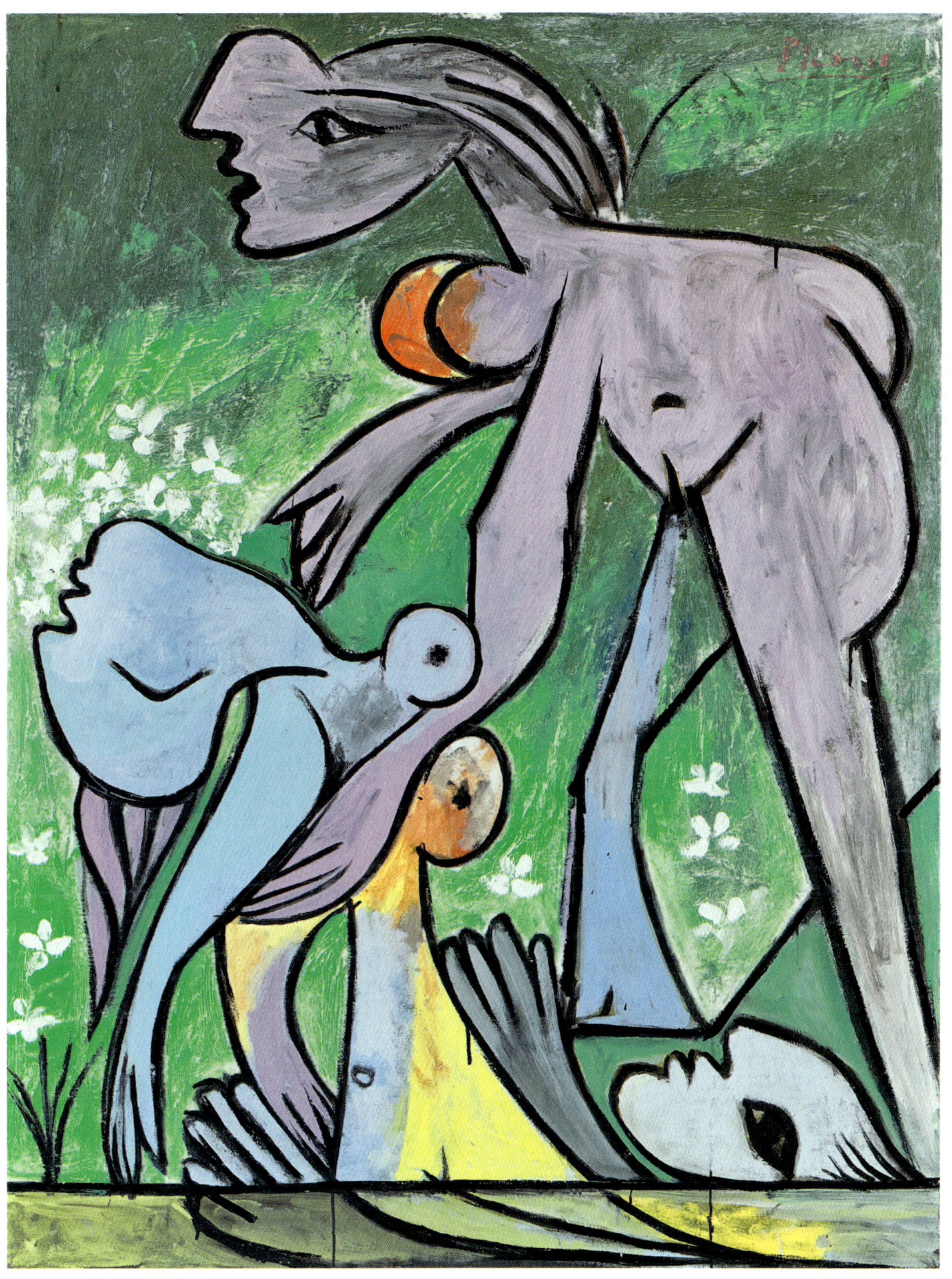

*The Rescue, Le Sauvetage*

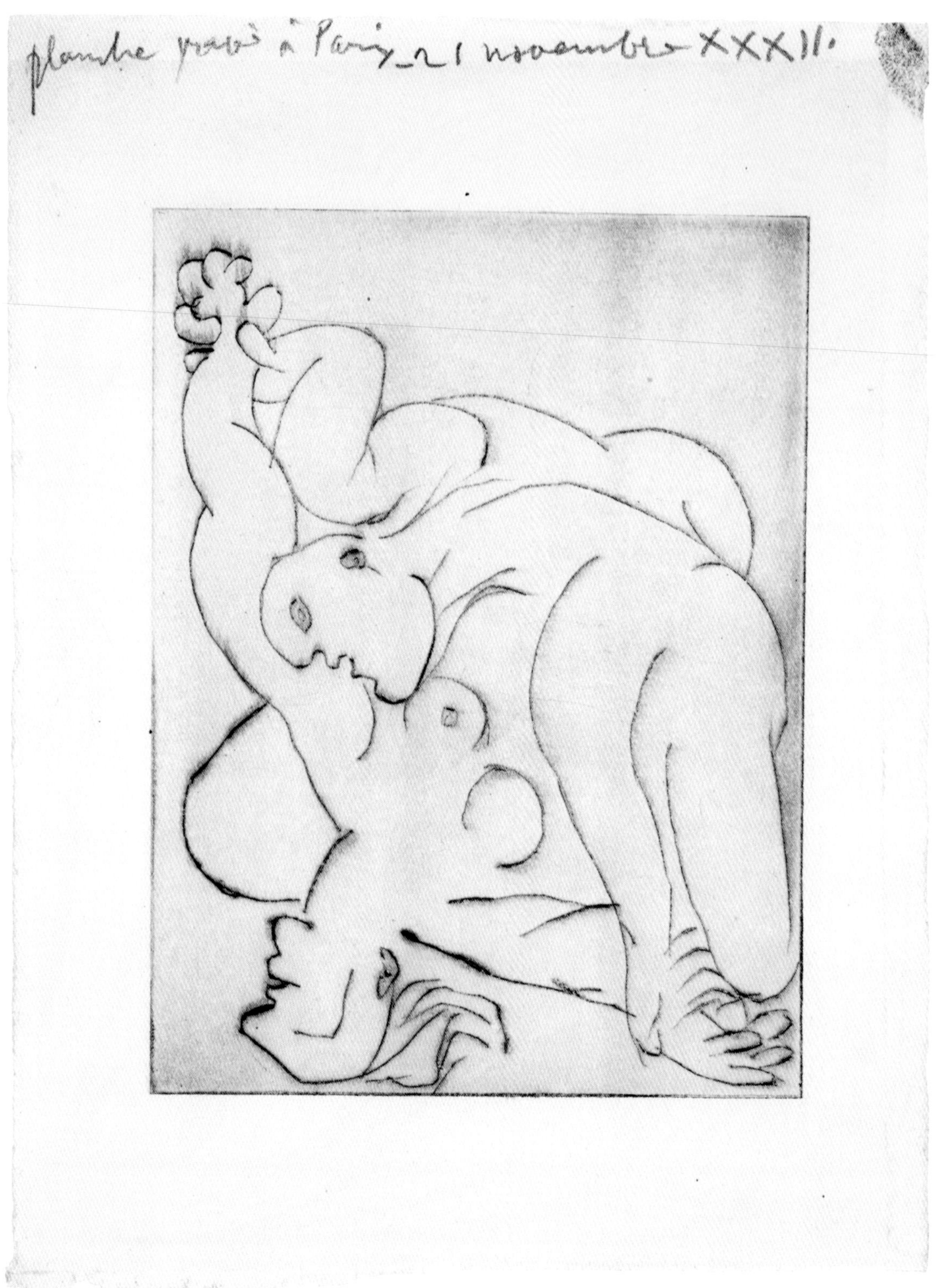




*The Rape, Le Viol*

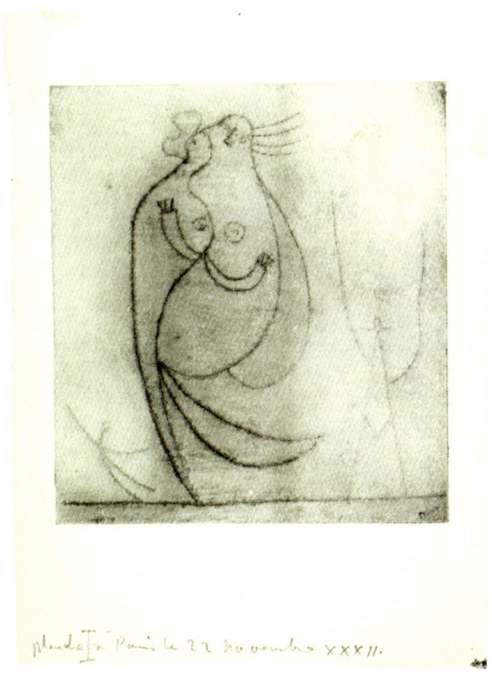

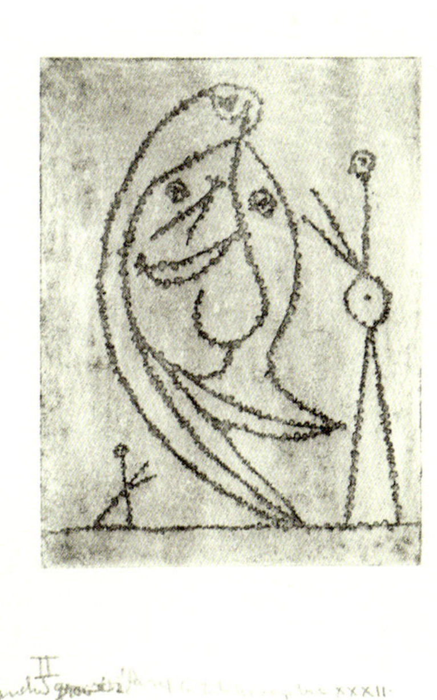

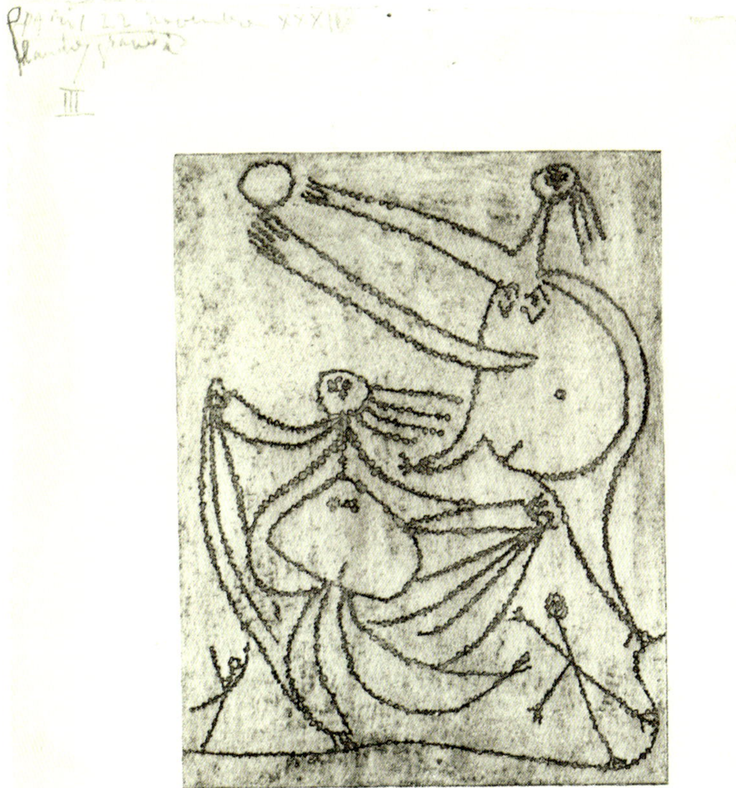

*Bathers on the Beach I, Baigneuses sur la plage I*

*Bathers on the Beach II, Baigneuses sur la plage II*

*Bathers on the Beach III, Baigneuses sur la plage III*

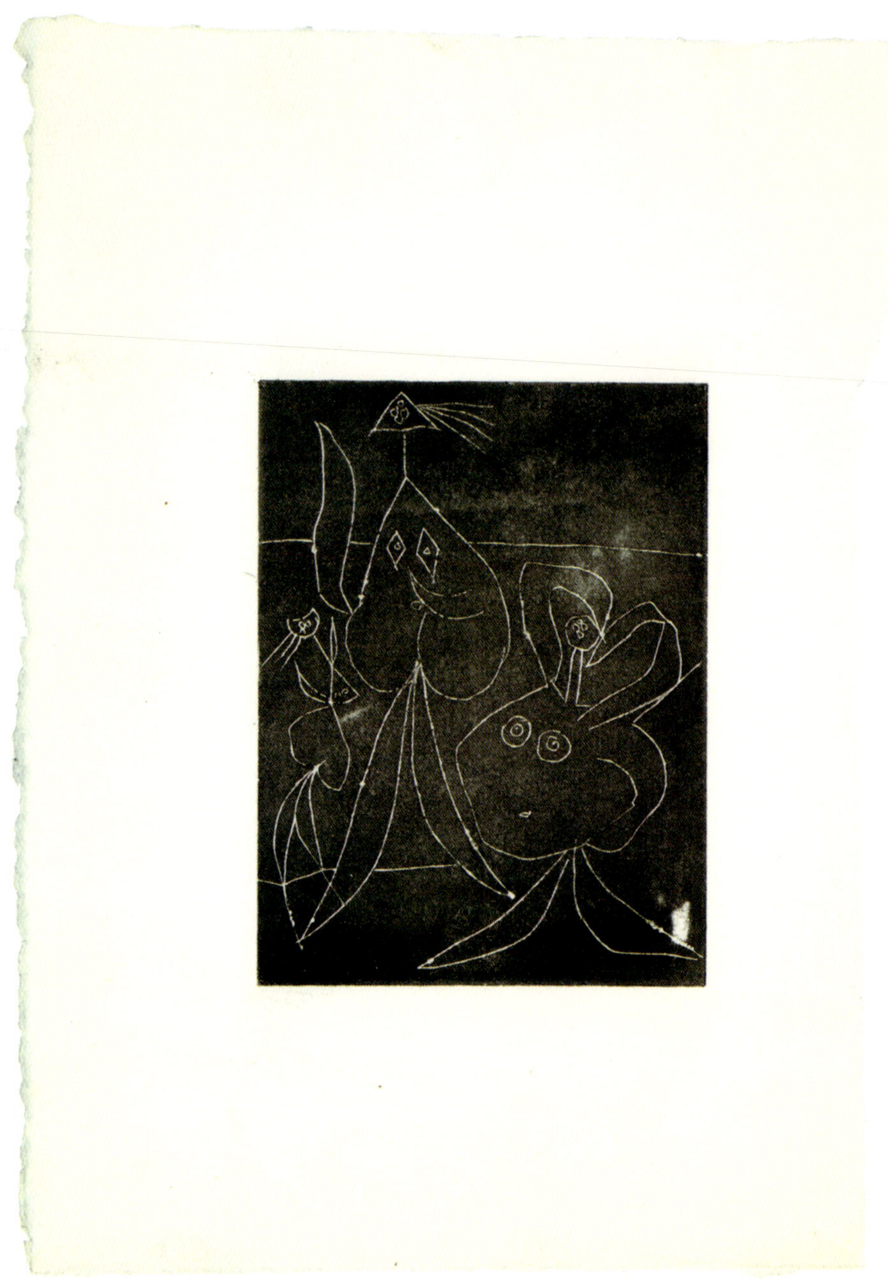



*On the Beach. Three Bathers, Sur la plage. Trois baigneuses*

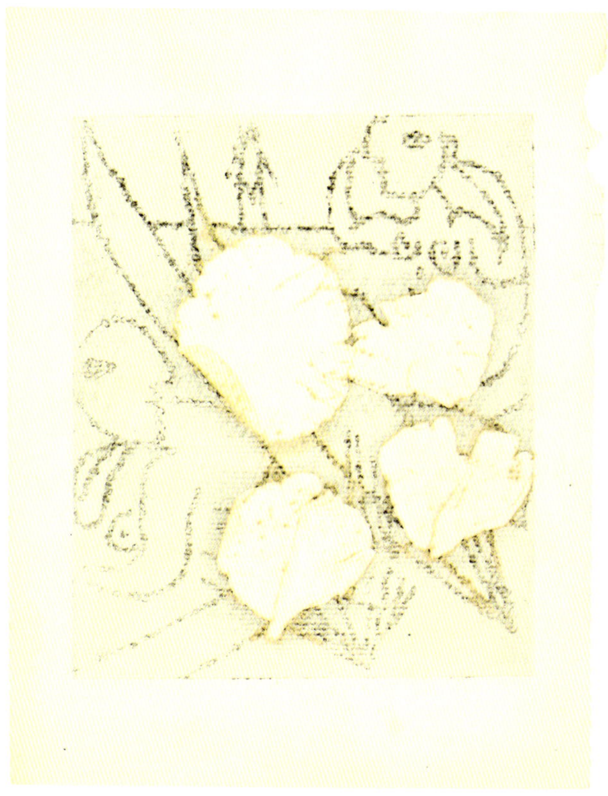

The Diver, La Plongeuse

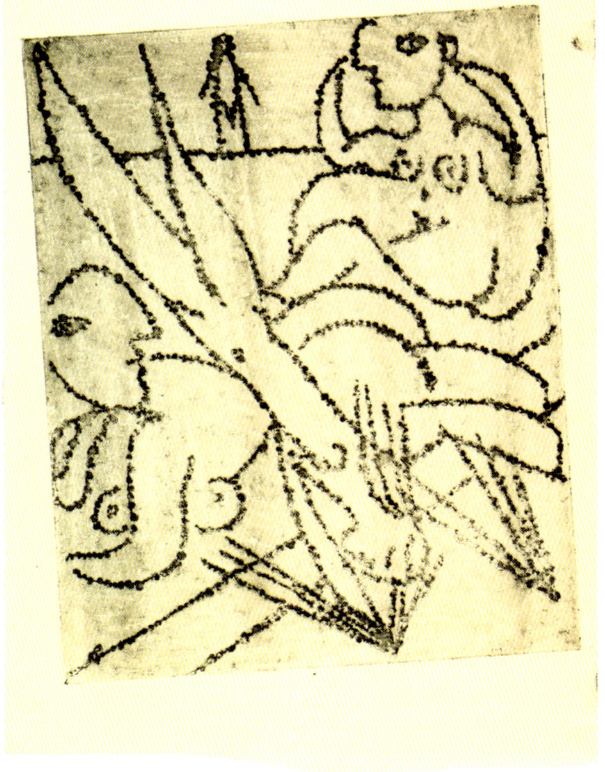

The Diver, La Plongeuse

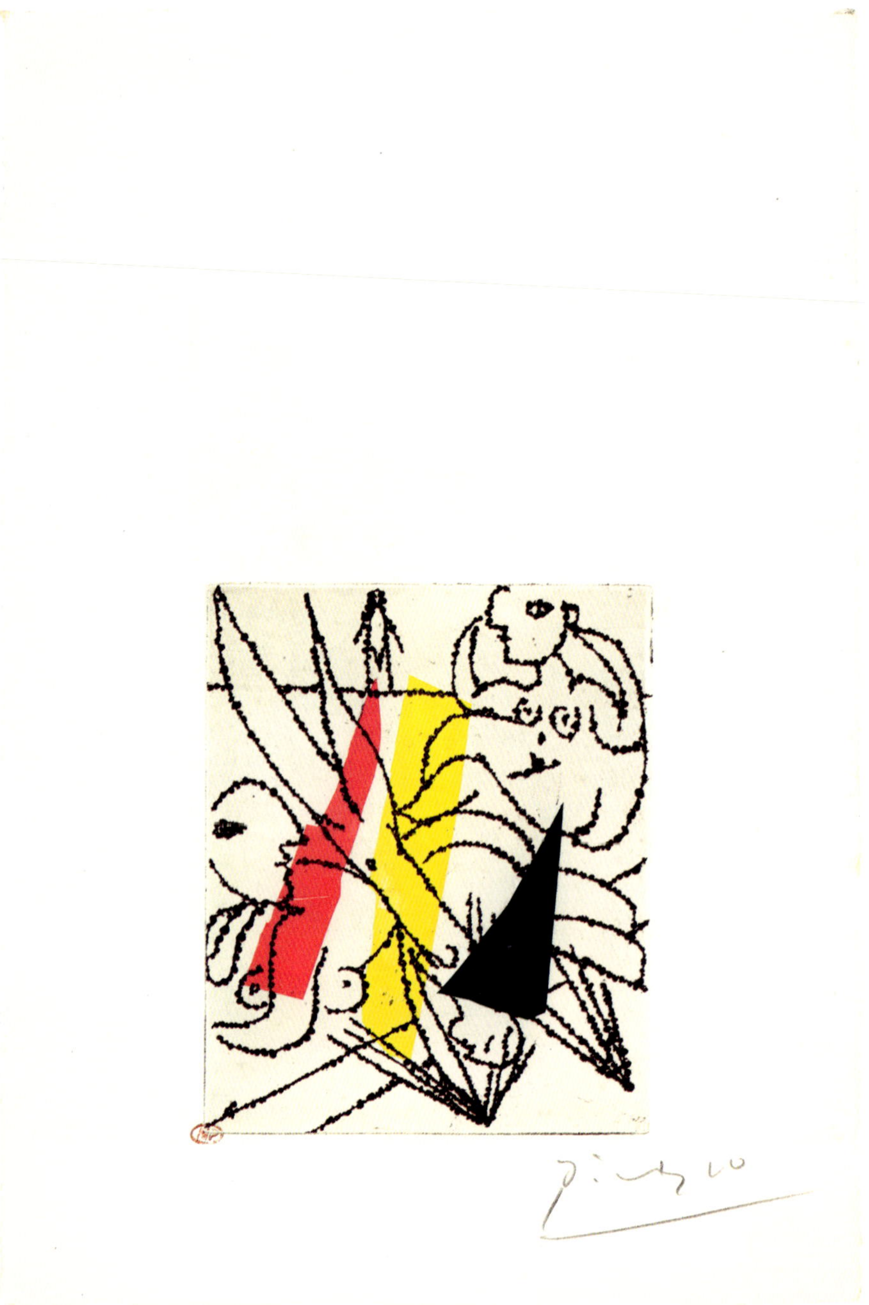



*The Diver, La Plongeuse*

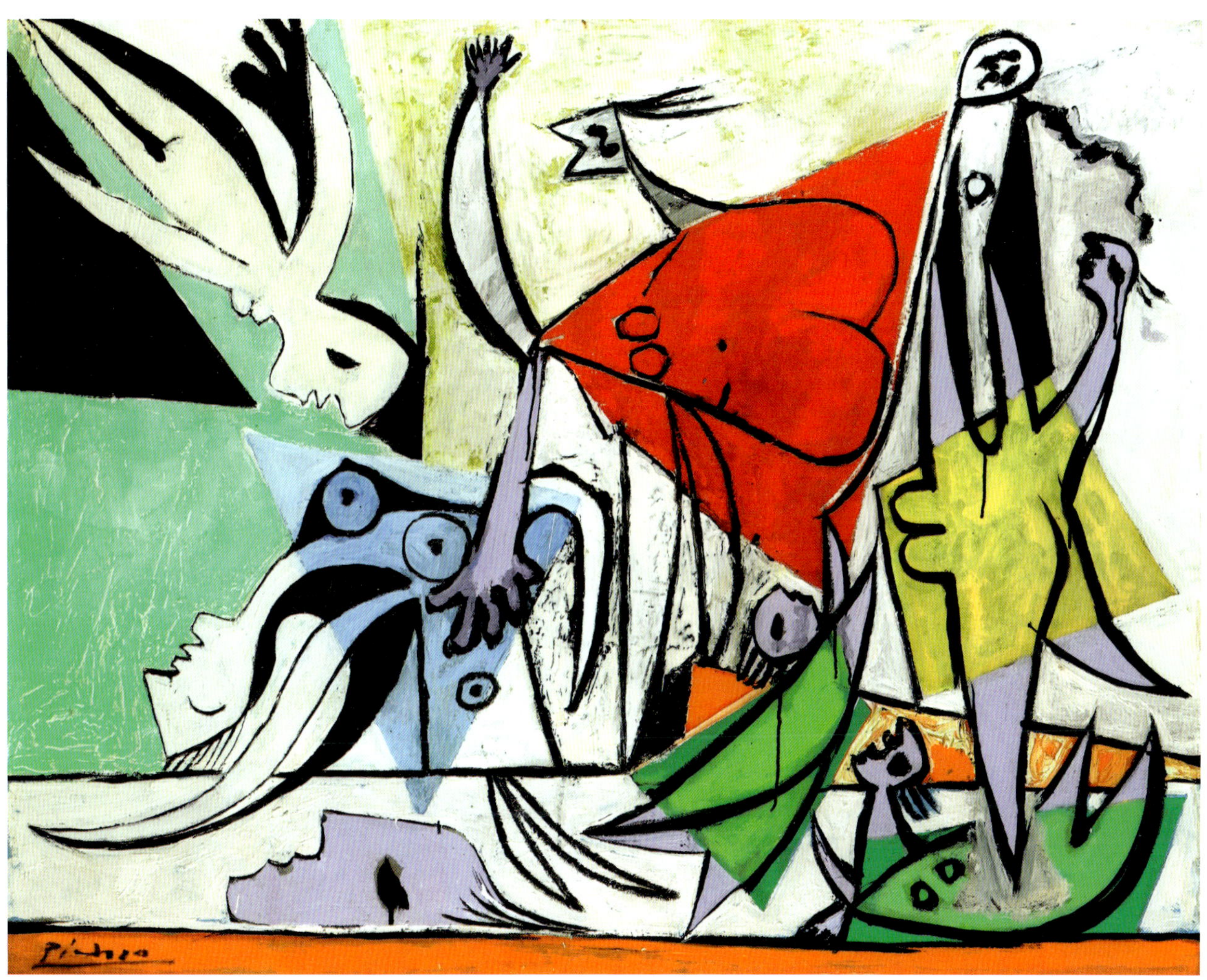

*The Rescue, Le Sauvetage*

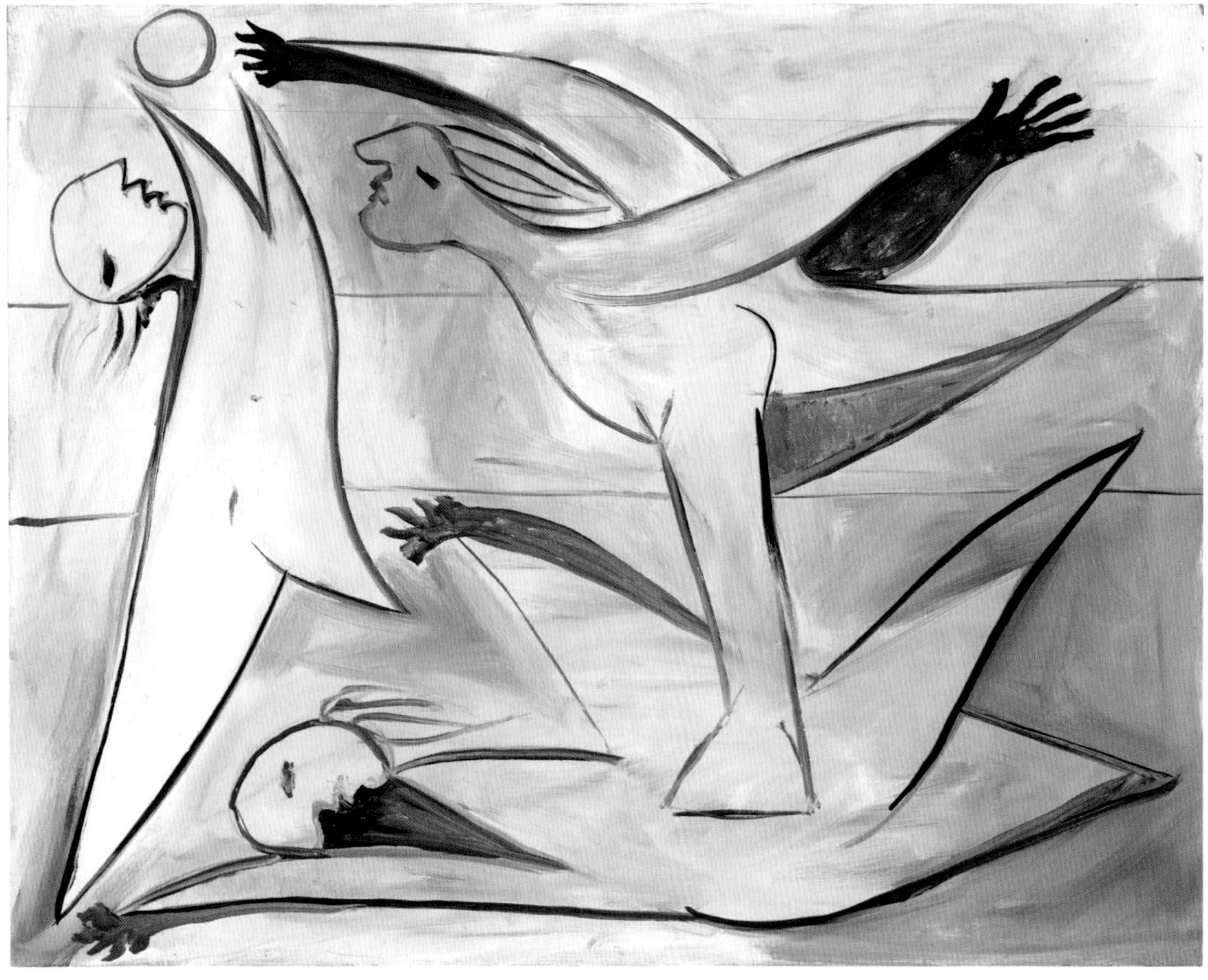

 *Bathers with Beach Ball, Baigneuses au ballon*

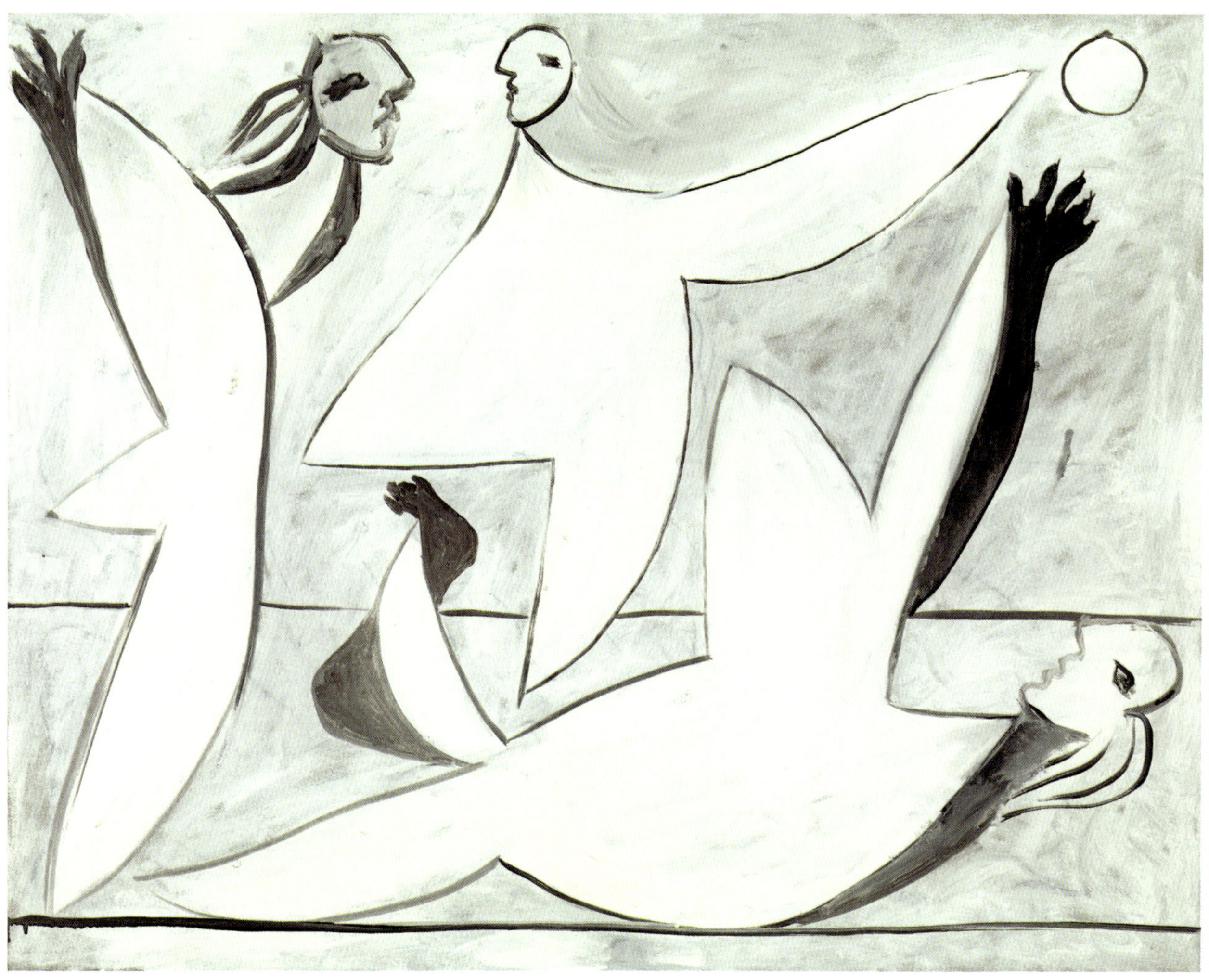

*Women Playing with a Ball on the Beach, Femmes jouant à la balle sur la plage*

'I shall not make art with the preconceived idea of serving the interests of the political, religious or military art of any country.'

Picasso, quoted in Felipe Cossío del Pomar, *Con los buscadores del camino* (1932)

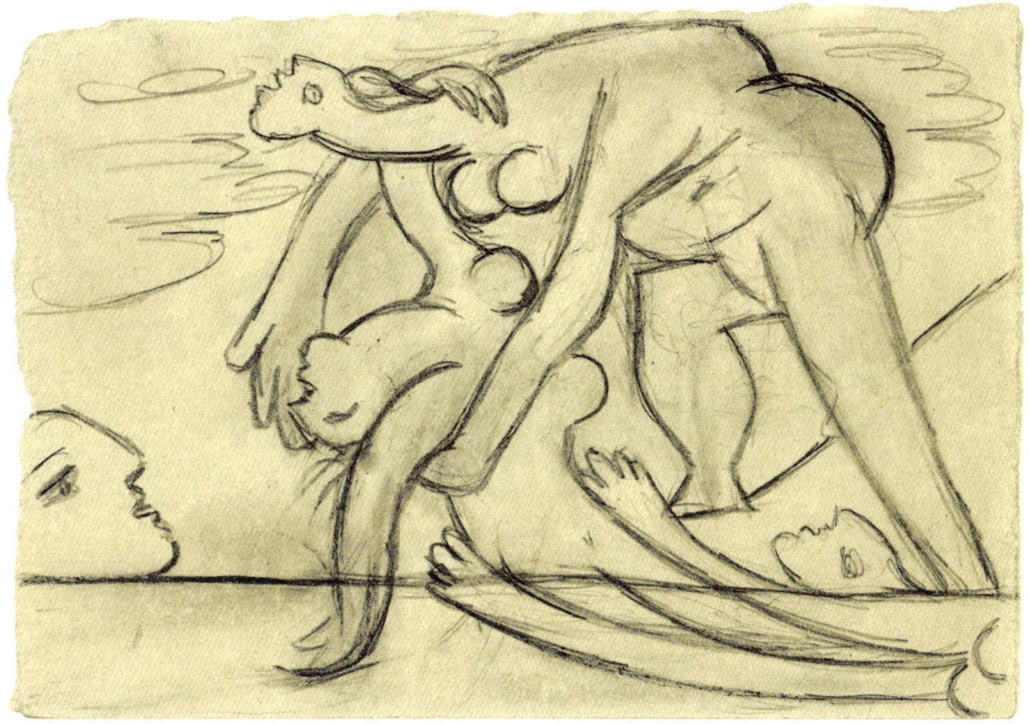

*The Rescue, Le Sauvetage*

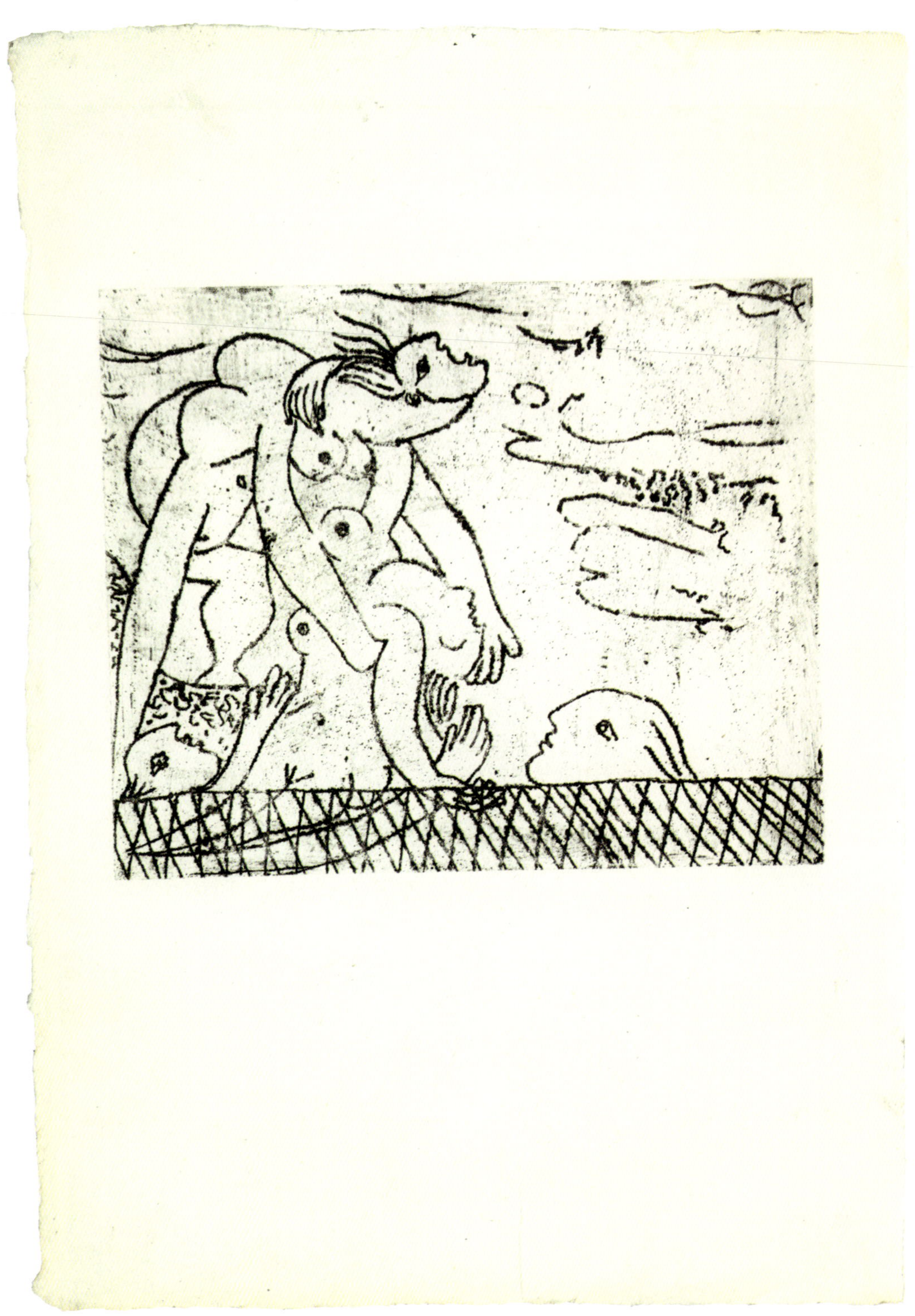

*The Rescue of the Drowned Woman I, Le Sauvetage de la noyée I*

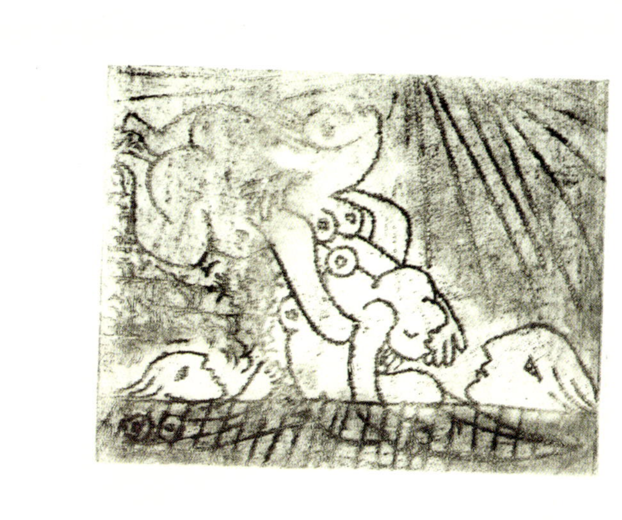

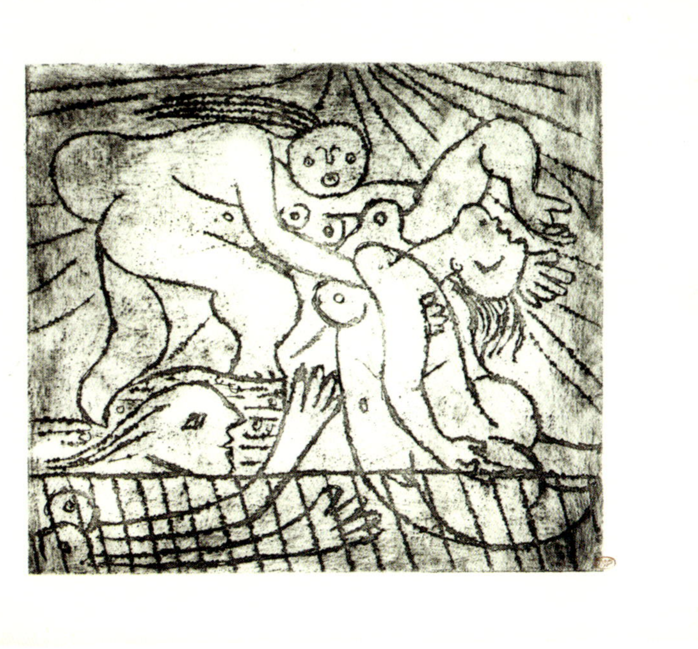

*The Rescue of the Drowned Woman II, Le Sauvetage de la noyée II*

*The Rescue of the Drowned Woman III, Le Sauvetage de la noyée III*

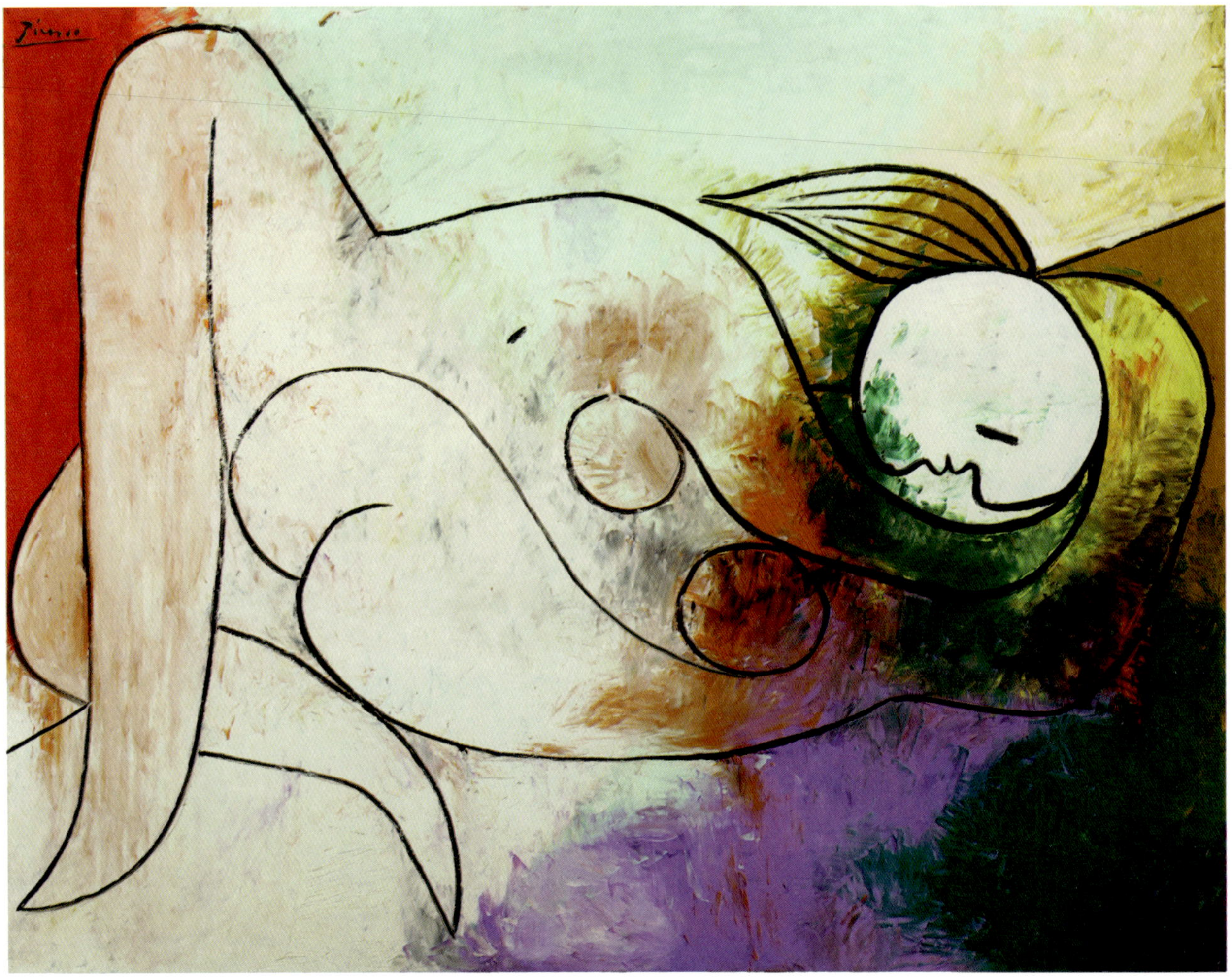

 *Sleeping Nude with Blonde Hair, Femme couchée à la mèche blonde*

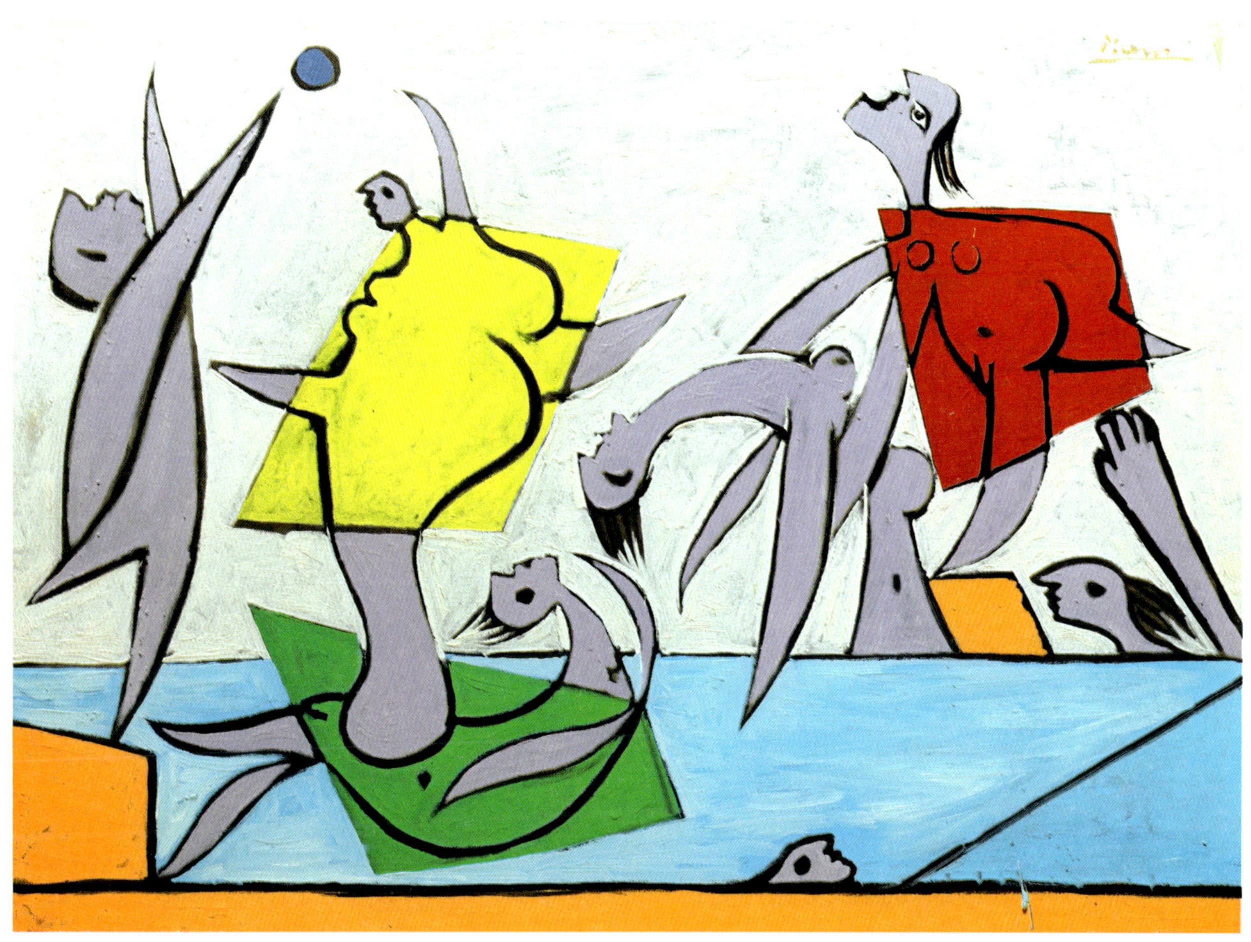

*The Rescue, Le Sauvetage*

'Everything we love is about to die, and that is why everything we love must be summed up, with all the high emotion of farewell, in something so beautiful we shall never forget it.'

Michel Leiris, 'Death Notice', *Cahiers d'Art*, no.4-5, 1937, p.128

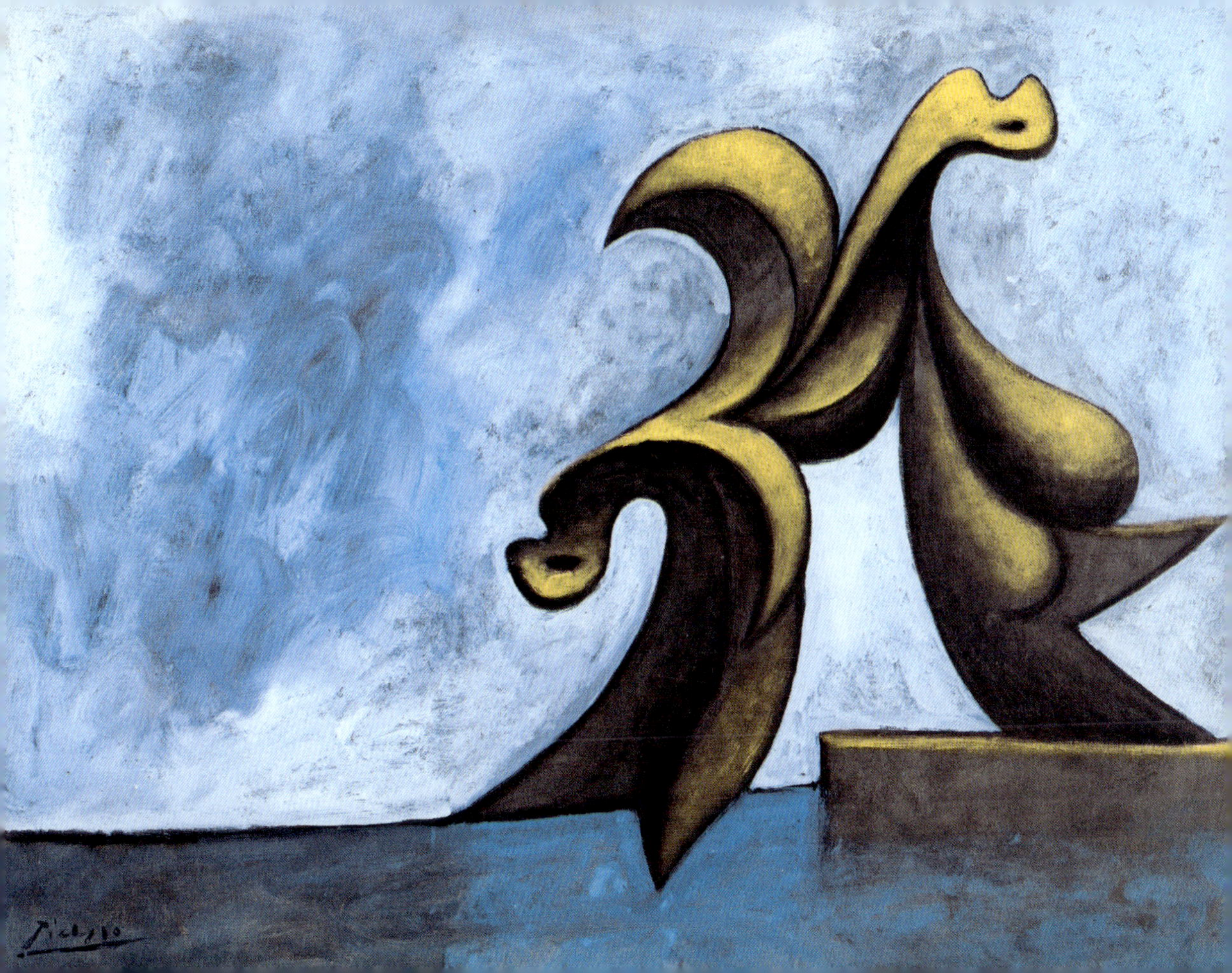

# 366 Days

## Laurence Madeline

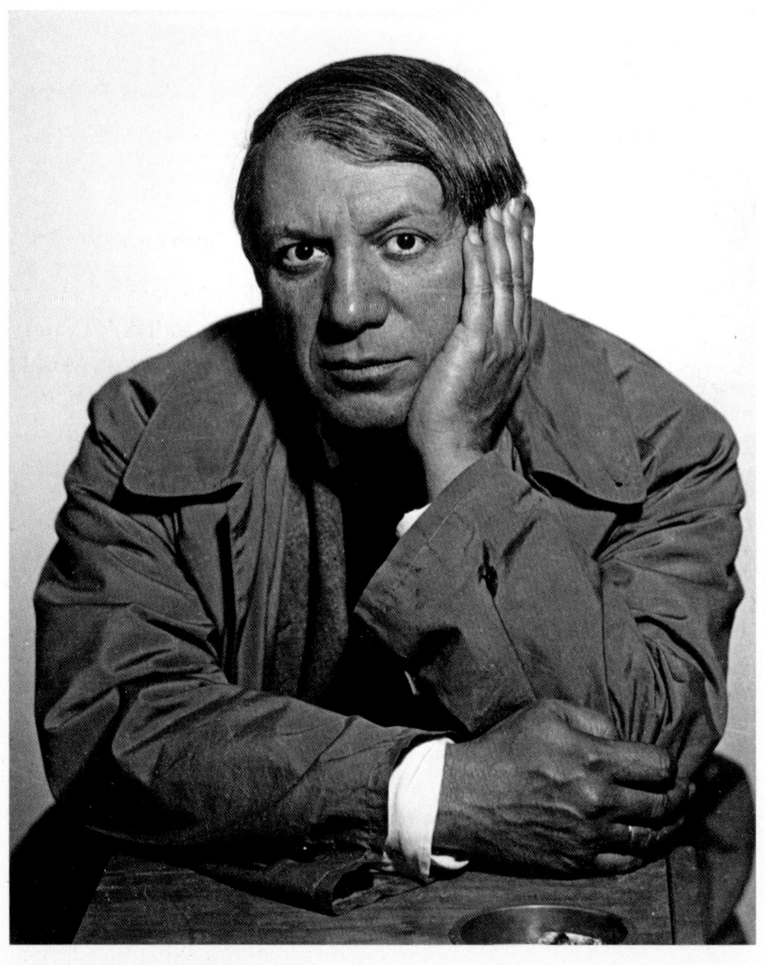

Portrait of Picasso by Man Ray, 1932

This chronology is based principally on research in the archives of the Musée national Picasso–Paris, to which the documents and correspondence amassed by Picasso during his lifetime were donated by his heirs in 1978. Unless otherwise stated, the records cited come from this source: see further *Picasso 1932*, exh. cat., Musée national Picasso–Paris, 2017. Due to the secretive nature of his relationship with Marie-Thérèse Walter at this stage in their lives, their letters feature very little in these archives.

The number of artworks that Picasso made during the year are too many to mention every one of them here.

## January

**2** After spending Christmas Eve in Paris surrounded by friends and not having worked for five days, Picasso completes *Figures by the Sea I* (p.45) and *The Reading* (p.46).

**6** *The Yellow Belt* (p.47)

Picasso attends the premier of Darius Milhaud's opera *Maximilien* at the Paris Opera, according to a report in the newspaper *L'Intransigeant* the following day.

**9** *Reading* (p.48)

**10** *Young Woman with Mandolin* (p.49)

**14** *Sleeping Woman by a Mirror* (p.51)

**18** *Still Life at the Window* (p.53)

**22** *Rest* (p.54)

**23** *Sleep* (p.55)

**24** *The Dream* (p.57)

**25** Picasso dates the first page of his sketchbook, *Carnet* no.40: 'Paris 25 janvier M.CM.XXXII' (pp.172–5). Four days later, on 29 January, he starts to draw in it; he returns to it on 31 January, before abandoning it until 26 December.

**26** Count Giuseppe Volpi of Misurata (1877–1947), President of the Venice Biennale, sends an official invitation to Picasso to exhibit at the next Venice Biennale.[1]

Alfred H. Barr, Jr, founding director of The Museum of Modern Art, writes to Picasso informing him of the decision of the exhibition committee, chaired by Anson Conger Goodyear (1877–1964), to postpone the retrospective Barr had hoped to show in New York in the autumn of 1932. Although conversations had begun back in spring 1930 it has meanwhile become increasingly clear that Picasso would prefer to have a Paris exhibition. The artist is particularly keen to include current works from 1932 in a retrospective show.

**27** *Woman in a Red Armchair* (p.58)

The sculptor Julio González (1876–1942), who has previously assisted the artist in the realisation of his sculptures, cancels a meeting scheduled for the next day at Picasso's studio in Paris.

**30** Olga Picasso spends the weekend in Boisgeloup drawing up an inventory of household linen.[2] In Paris Picasso paints *Seated Woman in a Red Armchair* (p.59).

## February

**2** *Study for a Mandolin Player* (p.162)

**3** The writer Michel Leiris, who is a member of the Paris ethnographic mission led by Marcel Griaule travelling to Dakar and Djibouti from May 1931 to February 1933, writes a long letter to the Picasso family. He thanks them for the postcard he has received with a view of the village of Boisgeloup on which Picasso has drawn African animals.[3]

4 Eleventh birthday of Picasso and Olga's son Paul, or Paulo as he is known in the family.

6 The surrealists circulate a leaflet entitled 'The Aragon Affair', defending the poet Louis Aragon. He has been charged with 'inciting soldiers to disobey and provocation to murder for the purpose of anarchist propaganda' through his poem 'Front rouge' (The Red Front), published in December 1931. Picasso is one of the signatories in the leaflet: it is one of his first engagements with French intellectuals and a rare moment in which he gets openly involved in politics.

7 The Uruguayan painter Joaquín Torres-García (1874–1949), who had known Picasso in Barcelona, writes to suggest he will visit Picasso at his Paris studio on 9 February at noon.

11 *Fruit Bowl and Guitar* (p.60)

13 *Still Life with Fruit Bowl and Mandolin* (p.61)

17 Torres-García, who has met Picasso at some point since his letter of 7 February, writes to tell him of the book he wants to write about Picasso after studying his work. In his autobiography *Histoire de ma vie*, Torres-García says that Picasso in the end refused him permission to publish, so he threw the text into the fire.[4] The cover of the destroyed work, designed by the painter, is now preserved by the Torres-García Foundation in Montevideo.

22 Olga and Pablo Picasso attend a concert at the Conservatoire, organised by the chamber music society 'La Sérénade'.[5] The programme includes the musical piece 'Before the Cinema' composed by Francis Poulenc after a poem by Guillaume Apollinaire, and dedicated to Olga.

The art critic, adviser and sometime lover of Benito Mussolini, Margherita Sarfatti (1880–1961), writes to Picasso to notify him of her imminent arrival in Paris. She is responsible for organising his participation in the Venice Biennale.

26 At the sale of *Modern Paintings, Watercolours, Pastels, Drawings ... Collection of an Amateur* at the Hôtel Drouot auction house, a painting by Picasso, *La Coiffure* 1906 sells for 56,000 francs.[6] The newspapers comment widely on this record price, which is taken as a positive sign for an art market hit by the Great Depression. The painting is bought by Picasso's dealer, Paul Rosenberg (1881–1959).

29 Picasso attends a boxing gala at the Palais des Sports.[7]

## March

2 *Still Life with Tulips* (p.89)

3 *Still Life, Bust, Cup and Palette* (p.91)

Olga is in Boisgeloup to continue work on the inventory of household linen.[8]

8 *Nude, Green Leaves and Bust* (p.93)

9 *Nude in a Black Armchair* (p.95)

*Le Figaro* mentions Olga Picasso has attended one of the first performances of the ballet production of Jules Supervielle's play *The Sleeping Beauty in the Wood* (*La Belle au bois dormant*) at the Théâtre de l'Avenue. Mr and Mrs Edouard Bourdet, Max Jacob, Anne-Jules de Noailles, the Comtesse de Polignac, Mrs Paul Valéry are also in the audience. The precise date of this attendance is unspecified.

12 *The Mirror* (p.97)

13 *Sleeping Nude* (p.99)

14 *Girl before a Mirror* (p.101)

Christian Zervos (1889–1970), who is preparing the first volume of the catalogue raisonné of works from 1895 to 1906, writes to Picasso:

My dear Picasso

Will you be kind enough to leave the proofs of your book with your wife. I will have them collected tomorrow around 2:30 to 3 p.m.

15 *L'Intransigeant* mentions that Picasso, Pierre Bost, Georges Braque, Constantin Brancusi, Le Corbusier, Kees van Dongen, Othon Friesz, Demetrios Galanis, Pablo Gargallo, André Gide, Henri Laurens, Henri Lévy, André Lhote, Jacques Lipchitz, Ossip Zadkine, and Mesdames Halicka, Marthe Laurens, Marguerite Matisse, Valentine Prax were among those who

attended a showing of the film *Voyage aux Cyclades* (Voyage to Cyclades), by Roger Vitrac, Jacques-Bernard Brunius and Eli Lotar. The precise date of the presentation is not mentioned. Christian Zervos devotes a text to the film in *Cahiers d'Art*, no.1–2, p.84.

A butcher's bill from Epicerie centrale in Gisors shows that Olga Picasso is in Boisgeloup.

**16** Olga Picasso completes the inventory of the household linen in Boisgeloup.[9] While it is not possible to determine Picasso's whereabouts with certainty, a mid-week stay during Paulo's school term would seem unusual.

**17** Daniel-Henry Kahnweiler (1884–1979) visits Picasso in his Paris studio together with an unidentified person. He is one of the first to see the large nudes made earlier in the month.

**18** Back in Paris, Olga ships food parcels to her family in Moscow and St Petersburg.[10]

**19** Kahnweiler starts a letter to Leiris in Africa:

Yes, as you say, painting is only being kept alive by Picasso, but how marvellously. Two days ago, at his place, we saw two paintings he had just done. Two nudes that are perhaps the greatest, most moving things he has produced. 'It seems as though a satyr who had just killed a woman could have painted this picture,' I said to him about one of the two. It's not cubist, not naturalistic, it's without any painterly artifice, it's very alive, very erotic, but with the eroticism of a giant. Picasso has done nothing comparable for many years. 'I would love to paint like a blind man,' he'd said a few days before, 'who pictures an arse by the way it feels.' That's it exactly. We came away from there stunned.[11]

Paulo is on school holidays and the Picasso family stay in Boisgeloup for a few days.

**22** Kahnweiler finishes his letter to Leiris begun on 19 March and writes:

On the other hand, visit to Braque a complete disappointment ... his work is like Picasso in 1926, but diluted, lacking power.'[12]

**25** As the long Easter weekend begins, Picasso starts a series of reclining women on the beach. The first work he makes that same day is a small oil and charcoal drawing on tracing paper, together with the largest in the series, an oil and charcoal on canvas (p.102).

**26** Picasso continues the series of reclining women, producing three paintings (p.103).

The magazine *Les Nouvelles Littéraires* announces that the Jeu de Paume, the Paris museum housing work by foreign artists, has reopened with new rooms:

Let us look for some Spaniards, and first Picasso, as they didn't see fit to put him in the Luxembourg [the Musée du Luxembourg, housing contemporary art]. We must resign ourselves – the most astonishing visual artist of our time, this protean-painter, does not feature on the official museum walls of Paris.

**28** After a break on Easter Sunday, Picasso completes the last work in his series of reclining women on the beach (p.105).

**29–30**

Picasso paints several views of the village of Boisgeloup in the rain (pp.106–7).

## April

**2** *Reclining Nude* (p.109)

The daily newspaper *Comoedia* announces that the painter and curator Carl Montag (1880–1956) is organising an exhibition of Picasso, Braque and Léger at the Kunsthaus in Zurich. The newspaper says:

With regard to Picasso, you may see, in Zurich, a sufficient number of canvases to give the fullest possible idea of his work as a whole and the evolution of his talent.

**4** *Reclining Nude* (p.111)

**6** The Picasso family is back in Paris, though from now on stays in Boisgeloup become more frequent, generally during the weekends.

Picasso, having received a message from González, replies that he wants to talk to him and invites him to spend 7 April 'at the house'.

**9** Picasso takes up a sketchbook, first begun in January 1930 (*Carnet* no.17, p.156–61), and executes two drawings, one of which (p.157 top) is related to *Woman with a Flower* (p.112).

**10** *Woman with a Flower* (p.112)

Picasso makes twenty-two more drawings in *Carnet* no.17, finishing the sketchbook.

**11** Picasso has a meeting with Etienne Bignou (1891–1950) and the German critic Carl Einstein (1885–1940) to prepare his retrospective exhibition planned for June at Galeries Georges Petit, 8 rue de Sèze. Bignou, together with Gaston and Josse Bernheim-Jeune and the Alex Reid & Lefevre Gallery in London, formed part of a consortium that had bought Galeries Georges Petit in 1920 to stage major sales exhibitions. At this point, Picasso stops making works to be included in the retrospective: he starts to act as the curator of the show rather than as the artist.

**12** Bignou sends Picasso the minutes of the meeting, including the list of the works to be exhibited, the names of the owners, and who to contact to obtain loans. As the owner of about twenty works, Picasso is the single most important lender and is fully involved in the preparation of the exhibition. Einstein also plays an important role, contacting German and Swiss-German collectors. They also rely on the help of others, including: collector Gottfried Friedrich Reber (1880–1959); the Pierre Colle gallery; Georges Keller (1899–1981), director of Galeries Georges Petit; the New York gallery of Valentine Dudensig (1892–1967); and Max Pellequer, Picasso's personal banker and a collector of his work. Rosenberg figures solely as a lender, despite having been Picasso's principal dealer since 1918. At this stage 150 paintings are selected, almost a hundred fewer than will appear in the final exhibition.

**20** Picasso must certainly participate in the further meeting with Bignou and Einstein suggested in the letter of 12 April.

**23** Picasso receives an invitation for him and Olga to have lunch with Alphonse Kann (1878–1948) to discuss potential loans to the retrospective. Bignou's initial list includes four paintings belonging to Kann, of which three will eventually be shown.

**25** The tourist office in Gisors, the small town where the chateau of Boisgeloup is located, invites Picasso to exhibit with local painters.

**27** The American critic, collector and painter Albert Eugene Gallatin (1881–1952) asks to visit Picasso with his camera. His portrait photograph of Picasso at 23 rue La Boétie is doubtless the result.[13]

**28** Paulo Picasso attends his First Communion, an occasion for a large gathering of family and friends. Picasso's mother, Doña Maria, and his brother-in-law Juan Batista Vilató come from Barcelona and spend a few days between Paris and Boisgeloup. Picasso's old friend, the writer and collector Gertrude Stein (1874–1946), and the pianist Misia Sert (1872–1950) attend the ceremony.

The Venice Biennale is inaugurated by King Victor Emmanuel III. France is represented by Joseph Bernard, André Derain, Léon-Ernest Drivier, François Pompon and Henry de Waroquier. Picasso is not included.

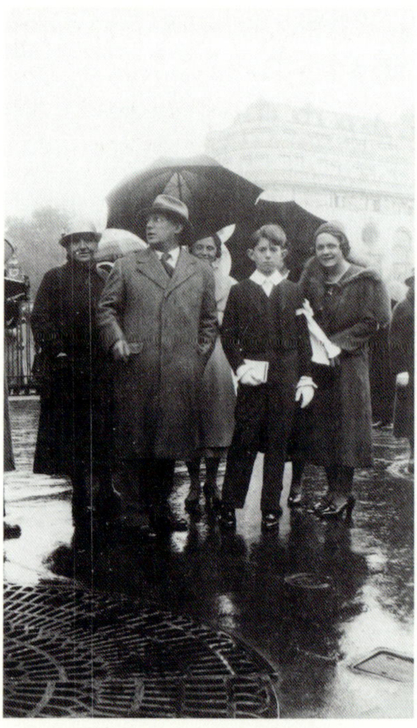

Gertrude Stein, Pablo, Olga and Paulo Picasso and Misia Sert, on the day of Paulo's First Communion, Paris, 28 April 1932

**29–30**

The Picasso family spends the weekend in Boisgeloup.

**30** On the occasion of the opening of the exhibition *The Heroic Era of Cubism* at Galerie Bonjean, the magazine *Les Nouvelles Littéraires* publishes an article by Max Jacob (1876–1944) which states:

None of those who should feature in the cubist parade knew Picasso in 1906. Picasso alone is the creator of this art.[14]

## May

**4** Opening of the Alberto Giacometti exhibition at Galerie Pierre Colle. On 6 May Giacometti writes to his parents:

The first to arrive was Picasso, who came at half past midday! He looked round and said 'very nice' like a child ... but then he never commits, in fact he's known for that.[15]

**5** Fernande Olivier (1881–1966), with whom Picasso had been in a relationship from 1904 to 1912, writes to him:

Dear Pablo

To say thank you seems inadequate, especially when, knowing you as I do, I'm aware how little notice you would take of this.

All the same, I need to tell you how very grateful and touched I am by your generous gesture, which has made my life, which I doubt you could possibly imagine now, so much easier.

Emotionally even more so – I feel liberated – and physically too as I can breathe more easily.

So, I call out to you nevertheless, to declare my thanks, knowing you will reject them, that they will of course mean so little, though they come to you from the depths of my heart where you have always remained, and that the only years of happiness in my life were those I spent with you.

In the daily newspaper *Le Temps* the critic Guillaume Janneau gives an account of the International Congress of Contemporary Art which has just been held in Venice, and repeats a remark by Filippo Tommaso Marinetti (1876–1944), the founder of the futurist movement: 'How is it that no work by Picasso is on display in the Luxembourg or in the French pavilion at the Venice Biennale?' The response of Louis Hautecoeur (1884–1973), curator of the Luxembourg Museum and head of the French pavilion of the Biennale, is also given:

Picasso is not French but Spanish, and we have no reason to alter the facts in support of such arguments. French society and its members, who above all, are taxpayers, might well be astonished if we were to go to the considerable expense of promoting abroad the reputation and influence of an artist who, indeed, is not a member of the French community and, furthermore, represents a way of thinking that may be considered to have concluded some ten years ago. So let us have an end to this contention that has already gone down in history by dint of constant repetition.

**5–8**

Picasso, Olga and Paulo spend the Ascension holidays in Boisgeloup. The weather is changeable, with sun and showers: Picasso paints views of the village with rainbows.

**11** Dr Erwin Quedenfeldt, chemist and photographer (1869–1948), 'Inventor of the Erwin process. Transfer printing without machinery or press', writes to Picasso asking to present his invention.

**14–16**

Picasso is in Boisgeloup, most likely together with Olga and Paulo, who enjoys an extra day off school for the Feast of Pentecost.

**16** *Woman Sleeping* (p.114)

A letter[16] from the Czech collector Vincenc Kramář (1877–1960) to Christian Zervos, publisher of the *Cahiers d'Art*, indicates that Zervos has prepared a summary of the Picasso special issue, and has contacted various contributors. In another letter, Joan Junyer (1904–94) asks for details about the proposed exhibition of two paintings belonging to his uncle Sebastià Junyer (1878–1966) that have been solicited for the retrospective, showing that preparation is in full swing.

**17** *Rest* (p.115)

**20** The painter Wolfgang Paalen (1905–59) asks if he may visit Picasso's studio.

**21** Although the Venice Biennale has already opened and Picasso is not represented, the painter Gino Severini (1883–1966) sends a card:

My dear Picasso,

In Venice the young people are waiting for your exhibition with very keen interest, and this year the officials appear disposed to fulfil to the very best of their abilities their duties of hospitality; in short, we can expect a serious success. Gino Severini.

**26** Picasso, who must have met Quedenfeldt at some point following his letter of 11 May, creates his first erwinograph.[17]

**30** The poet Georges Hugnet (1906–74), informs Picasso that he has finished his text, commissioned by Zervos for the Picasso special issue of *Cahiers d'Art*, and says that he will be going to see the forthcoming exhibition.

## June

**10–15**

According to Carl Einstein,[18] and the journalist Guy Hickock, who interviews Picasso at Galeries Georges Petit on 15 June,[19] the artist says he has spent the past six days installing his retrospective.

**14** The critic Efstratios Tériade (1889–1983) interviews Picasso in the exhibition space while he is hanging the works. The painter and critic Jacques-Émile Blanche (1861–1942) also visits the gallery.[20]

**15** Gertrude Stein sends a telegram to Picasso: 'HOW WONDERFUL MY FRIENDSHIP ALWAYS – GERTRUDE'.

Tériade's interview appears in the daily *L'Intransigeant*.

At 11 p.m., Francisco de Melgar, correspondent for the Spanish newspaper *Ahora*, interviews Picasso in the gallery. Picasso says:

Why should I deny myself the joy of seeing once again everything that I produced over a third of a century? So here I am, reinvigorated and full of life, taking care of an exhibition of my works for the first time, like a lad of twenty. It feels as if I'm witnessing a retrospective vision of myself ten years after my death.[21]

**16** In the course of the day, the first copies of volume one of the catalogue raisonné of Picasso's works are being delivered to a handful of privileged recipients. Olga receives the first, 'hors-commerce', copy and Christian Zervos the second. The Picasso special issue of *Cahiers d'Art* and the exhibition catalogue are on sale in the gallery. Picasso dedicates the catalogue to Chester Dale, member of the exhibitions committee at The Museum of Modern Art, New York.

The Spanish newspapers *Ahora* and *Luz*[22] and the Parisian daily newspaper *Paris-Soir* announce the private view of the *Picasso* exhibition. The dress code is evening dress. The opening is one of the highlights of the social season. The bill for champagne cocktails is estimated at 40,000 francs and around two thousand curious bystanders squeeze into rue de Sèze outside the gallery:

So many people! A true Parisian soiree, by which I mean cosmopolitan, with every language being spoken. Ministers, bankers, famous artists, beautiful women – yesterday evening a glittering crowd attended the private view of Picasso's greatest exhibition to date.[23]

Among the guests are: two ministers; writers Blaise Cendrars, Jean Cocteau, Max Jacob; artists Georges Braque, Charles Despiau, Raoul Dufy, Moses Kisling, Fernand Léger, Jean Lurçat and Zadkine; composers Darius Milhaud and Francis Poulenc; dealers Georges Bernheim, Paul Guillaume, Ambroise Vollard and Georges Wildenstein; collectors Maja Hoffmann, G.F. Reber and Wilhelm Uhde.

Everyone is aware of Picasso's absence:

Just one was missing. People called for the artist. But in vain.[24]

**17** Olga Picasso turns forty-one.

*Picasso* opens to the public. The first reviews are published: by September more than eighty will have appeared in French, Spanish, German and American newspapers.

A large Edouard Manet retrospective opens at the Musée de l'Orangerie. Picasso,

who no doubt visits at some point, writes on the back of an envelope:
When I see Manet's *Déjeuner sur l'herbe* I think about the pain to come.

**18** Picasso is in Boisgeloup, where he resumes painting after a hiatus of more than twenty days (*Woman Sleeping on a Red Cushion*, p.130; *Reclining Nude with a Necklace*, p.131). He receives a telegram from Webster Todd (1899–1989) who wants to commission a mural for the Rockefeller Center in New York. The same request has been sent to Henri Matisse. Matisse refuses; Picasso never replies.

**19** *Reclining Nude* (p.133)

Wilhelm Wartmann (1882–1970), director of the Kunsthaus Zürich, which plans to show the Picasso exhibition, writes to the show's organiser Carl Montag that the Zurich version will have to be 'more beautiful and more serious ... That would be its only justification.'[25]

**20** In a telegram addressed to the painter Mario Tozzi (1895–1979), who together with the critic Eugenio d'Ors (1881–1954) had been in charge of organising Picasso's participation in the Venice Biennale, Antonio Maraini (1886–1963), secretary general of the Biennale, puts an end to such plans.[26]

**21** Max Jacob writes to his friends François de Gouy d'Arcy (1883–1941) and Russell Greeley (1878–1956):
The Picasso exhibition is exquisite torture.[27]

**24** In the Madrid daily newspaper *El Sol*, Juan de la Encina (1883–1963)[28] calls for the exhibition shown at Galeries Georges Petit to be taken up by the National Museum of Modern Art in Madrid.[29]

Léonce Rosenberg, who, on 17 June, warmly congratulated Picasso on his exhibition,[30] writes to Francis Picabia:
Clearly his exhibition is a means of publicity for the enormous 'fiddle' that his art has become. As I was saying yesterday to our friend Léger, P.'s misfortune is that his painting has become a pretext for speculation.[31]

**25** The Spanish art historian María-Luisa Caturla (1888–1984) informs Picasso of her imminent arrival in Paris to invite him to exhibit in Madrid. She is representing the Society of Iberian Artists, the Society of Friends of Art, the National Museum of Modern Art, the Society of Courses and Conferences, with the support of the Ministry of Public Education.

Picasso buys thirty-seven canvases at Castelucho Diana, 16 rue de la Grande Chaumière in the Montparnasse district of Paris. Originally from Barcelona, Antonio Castelucho Diana (1879–1939) is the artist's main supplier.

**26** Back in Boisgeloup with Olga and Paulo, Picasso paints three nudes (pp.134–5). The smallest of them, painted on the lid of a cardboard box, is made to be sent to Michel Leiris, who is still in Africa (*Reclining Nude*, p.134).[32] His wife Louise looks after it for the meantime, sending Leiris a photograph instead.

Picasso must have received his friend Sebastià Junyer (1878–1966), who, on his return home, writes on 3 July:
Imagine what an impression the grandiose manifestation of your art at Galeries Georges Petit made on me, then during that memorable afternoon at your chateau, and then at your place in Paris ... May God repay your love. For the wonderful kindness of your good wife and the amiability of your lovely son.

**27** Picasso is probably in Paris. He receives a letter from Gertrude Stein:
Everyone is writing to me about the beauty and the success of the exhibition ... I'm still working and amusing myself.
with all my friendship to the three of you Gtde

Kahnweiler writes to the Swiss collector Hermann Rupf (1880–1962):
Picasso's last works in particular are among the most grandiose he has ever produced. Rarely in painting has one ever seen such spontaneous monumentality, such an absence of preconception and such liberty.[33]

**29** The Munich merchant Justin K. Thannhauser (1892–1976), who is staying in Cabourg on the Normandy coast, sends a telegram to the Picassos to suggest a visit to Boisgeloup the following weekend.

**30** Invoices for various purchases attest that the Picassos are in Paris.

## July

**1** The City of Barcelona and the Government of Catalonia purchase the Plandiura collection. This includes twenty-two works by Picasso (subsequently transferred to the Museo Picasso).

**5** In Paris, Picasso buys thirty-six canvases from his supplier Castelucho Diana and pays the invoice for 1,600 francs by cheque.

**9** The prize-giving ceremony at the Hattemer school that Paulo attends marks the beginning of the summer holidays, with the family settling in Boisgeloup.

**10** The Thannhausers spend Sunday in Boisgeloup. The residence is cosy and plans for a swimming pool, drawn up in Bern in 1932 and sent to Picasso, show that either the artist or his wife are thinking to improve comfort further.

**13** Marie-Thérèse Walter turns twenty-three.

Max Jacob writes to his friend Joseph Pérard:

The Picasso exhibition makes you suffer, that's all I can say about it. One might respond that a period may suffer from an art it does not yet understand. Picasso is what he wishes to be: a vigilante executioner.[34]

**15** Serge Férat (pseudonym of Count Sergei Nikolaevich Yastrebzov, 1881–1958) thanks Picasso for the money he gave him which has helped at a difficult time.

**19** The date on a medical prescription indicates that Picasso is in Paris for the day.

**20** In the Madrid daily *La Noche*, the painter and critic Miquel Utrillo (1862–1934) publishes a polemical article entitled 'A Desertion. A Bad Spaniard: The Painter Pablo Ruiz Picasso'.[35] He is vehemently against the proposed Picasso exhibition in Spain.

**21–23**
Picasso, who has installed a printing press in Boisgeloup, produces the first of his engravings (p.166). During the month of July, he also produces four erwinographs.

**22** Paul Rosenberg lets Picasso know when he is next away on holiday, saying that he hopes to see him before he goes.

**23** Adolf Jöhr (1878–1953), president of the Zurich art association, Zürcher Kunstgesellschaft, writes to Picasso:

At our request, Mr Charles Montag has been kind enough to covey to you an invitation to an exhibition planned by the Kunsthaus – the Zurich Fine Art Museum – which will include, along with two collections of forty to fifty canvases by Georges Braque and Charles Léger [sic], a series of 150 to 200 of your works assembled to provide the most complete representation possible of your artistic endeavours and production. We would be so grateful if you would agree to our proposal and collaborate personally by loaning a large number of the works belonging to you.

As, generally, we are keen that our exhibition should as a whole satisfy your intentions and wishes, may we ask you kindly to agree to meet with us in the coming days so that we know your thoughts on the exhibition itself and what framework we might give it, so that we can then make any modifications that may be required. Mr Wartmann, the Kunsthaus director, will be leaving Zurich next Tuesday. He will be in touch with you once he is at the Georges Petit gallery, and will be working there for a week.

**25** Rosenberg regrets not having been able to see Picasso after all, as he is now leaving for Gstaad.

**27** *Nude Woman in a Red Armchair* (p.137)

Following Jöhr's letter, Picasso sends a telegram to Wartmann in Paris. He offers him an appointment at his studio in rue La Boétie on 29 July.[36]

The artist and choreographer Oskar Schlemmer (1888–1943) writes, from Breslau, to Willi Baumeister:

Picasso, the Kreuger of painting (!), a 'bon mot' that is not without merit. He's immensely successful. A vast quantity of paintings, that he has hung himself ... It is indeed still astonishing. Wonderful use of colour.[37]

Timoteo Pérez Rubio, deputy director of the Museum of Contemporary Art in Madrid (whose new director is the art critic Juan de la Encina), has just arrived in Paris. He says at a press conference:
I have come to Paris to find the elements for a Picasso exhibition for Madrid ... Spain is still quite unfamiliar with the work of Pablo Picasso. Far less familiar than France. And yet Picasso is Spanish ... This exhibition will take place in our museum in November.[38]

Marie-Thérèse Walter is photographed on the beach of Juan-les-Pins (p.146).[39]

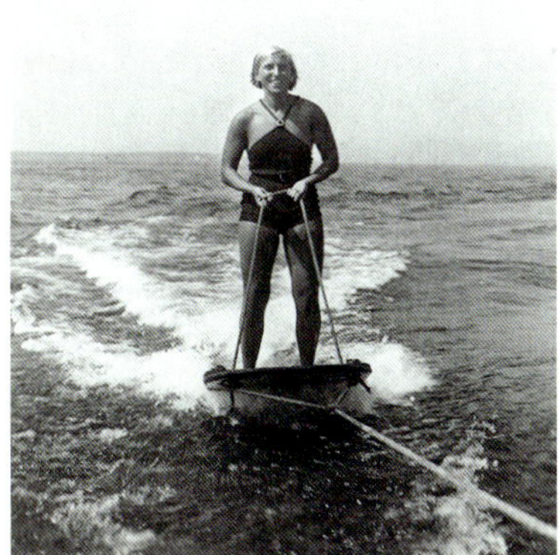

Marie-Thérèse Walter, Juan-les-Pins, 28 July 1932

**29** Picasso meets Wartmann and Montag in Paris. Plans for a joint exhibition of Braque, Léger and Picasso at the Kunsthaus in Zurich transform into monographic Picasso exhibition. Wartmann promises a large number of loans and favourable conditions for the retrospective, in particular the purchase by the Kunsthaus of one of his paintings.

**30** Picasso executes several drawings as well as a charcoal on canvas (p.167).

Close of the exhibition at Galeries Georges Petit.

## August

**1** Margaret Scolari Barr, the wife of Alfred H. Barr, Jr, goes round Galeries Georges Petit in the company of the artist:
Picasso was kind and walked up and down the largest room in the gallery. He is content and reassured by his success.
She also records seeing Vollard there.[40] She annotates a series of installation photographs, now held in The Museum of Modern Art Archives, New York. Many of these photographs are identical to those in the Georges Reber Archive, suggesting that they were supplied by either the gallery or the artist.

**3** The composer Igor Markevitch (1912–83) writes to Picasso at rue La Boétie, from La Tour de Peilz in Switzerland:
Massine has written to tell me that you have given favourable consideration to the possibility of designing the set for our *Rebus*; he asked me to write to let you know my thoughts on this: I hardly need to say that I would be very happy indeed to see such a wonderful project come to fruition?
Markevitch had presented *Rebus* in its concert form on 15 December 1931 in the Salle Gaveau. The ballet version he is now working on has been commissioned by Léonide Massine in memory of Serge Diaghilev.

**7** Matisse writes to his son Pierre that Georges Keller, director of Galeries Georges Petit, had invited the Philadelphia-based collector and philanthropist Albert Barnes (1872–1951) to Boisgeloup and that Barnes (one of Matisse's greatest supporters) had refused:

He [Barnes] told me ... that Picasso could not see colour and that he had made a travesty of Matisse. Keller sent Barnes an invitation to dinner at Picasso's chateau and he refused it. It seems that Picasso is devastated that B. is not interested in his work. Bignou wanted him to buy a large blue painting, with a male and a female nude one in front of the other; the woman appears pregnant and the painting is called *La Vie*. B. told me that he already has around 10 Picassos and that is quite enough. He said that P. was an artist if compared with Derain and Friesz, etc.[41]

15 Valentine Hugo, André Breton and Paul Eluard, on holiday together in Castellane, send a postcard to Pablo and Olga Picasso:

Dear Olga. Where are you both? We think of you all the time. We talk about you constantly. We love you more and more. Where are you? Olga, I send my love.
My affection to you both
Valentine

Our very dear Friends, we never tire of thinking about the wonderful rue de Sèze exhibition, which we visited so often and which should never have ended.
Thinking of you most affectionately,
André Breton
and Paul Eluard

The transmission receipt for a telegram sent from Dieppe to Boisgeloup suggests that Olga has gone for a short stay on the Normandy coast.[42]

18 *Sleep* (p.143)

19 The journalist Joseph Diner-Dénes (1857–1937) publishes the final article in his series on 'Bourgeois Decadence' in the socialist daily *Le Populaire*. Devoted to Picasso, it compares the artist's production and marketing style with that of the industrialised Ford motor company.

20–21
A bill from the Régina Hôtel in Dieppe shows that the Picasso family spend the weekend on the Normandy coast.

22 Marie-Thérèse and her sister Jeanne are pictured in photograph taken in the Gorges du Loup in southern France (p.211). The pair also appear in two photographs taken in Monte Carlo the same summer.[43]

24 *Seated Woman with Elbow on Knee* (p.145)

26 Newspapers report on the publication of the fifth volume of the Grand Larousse encyclopedia of the twentieth century, with an entry devoted to Picasso.[44] The entry says that his art 'with its difficult to interpret, jumbled lines and an appearance bearing no relation to reality, can only be decorative (still lifes, portraits).'

27 Wartmann notifies Picasso by telegram that his fifty-eight paintings have arrived safely in Zurich for installation in the exhibition.

Junyer writes to Picasso, saying he had been shocked by Utrillo's article of 20 July denouncing the proposed exhibition in Madrid and asks Picasso not to abandon plans to show there. On the same day, the daily *Heraldo de Madrid* announces that the project has been cancelled.[45]

30 *Bather with Beach Ball* (p.147)

The American photographer Thérèse Bonney (1894–1978) writes to Boisgeloup, asking to take pictures of the house. She had taken photographs of the exhibition at Galeries Georges Petit (p.128)[46] but it is unknown whether she did ever work at Boisgeloup.

31 Gertrude Stein asks Picasso for news: 'Where are you and what are you doing'.

## September

1 Paul Fierens publishes an article on the influence of Picasso on modern decoration in *Art et Décoration*.

4 Picasso begins the cycle of *Bathers on the Beach* with nine small canvases, including *Two Women on the Beach with Swimming Cabin* (p.191).

6 The series continues with five more paintings (pp.192–4).

7 At 10 a.m., the Picasso family leaves Paris in their chauffeur-driven Hispano-Suiza car.[47] They stop in Strasbourg and visit the cathedral before staying overnight at the Hôtel des Trois Rois in Basel.

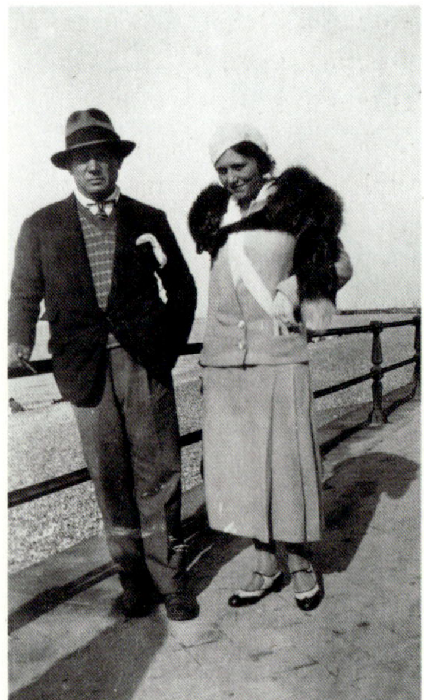

Pablo and Olga Picasso in Normandy, 1932

8 The family arrive in Zurich where they stay in the Hôtel Baur au Lac. They visit the city and the Kunsthaus where the painter Sigismund Righini (1870–1937), who is head of the exhibitions committee, is hanging the Picasso show. The artist does not intervene.

9 Accompanied by Jöhr and Wartmann, Picasso meets members of the Art Society.

10 The Picasso family, accompanied by the photographer Gotthard Schuh (1897–1969), Lucy Turel-Welti and her brother, the painter Hans Welti (1894–1935), who have been sent by the magazine *Zürcher Illustriert*, take a boat trip on the lake. They visit Welti's workshop in Wollishoffen, the new neighbourhood of Neubühl, a real estate complex built between 1930 and 1932, where they are welcomed by the president of the co-ownership project, the architect Robert Winkler and his wife Renée Winkler. They attend a reception held in their honour at the Belvoir Park restaurant with the art historian Doris Wild (1900–90). Welti and Wild tell the story of Picasso in detail[48] and recount Picasso's words:

On no account shall I attend the private view of my exhibition. It would be too strange.[49]

11 On the morning of the opening of his exhibition, Picasso leaves Zurich for St Moritz with Olga and Paulo. They stay at the Badrutt's Palace Hotel.

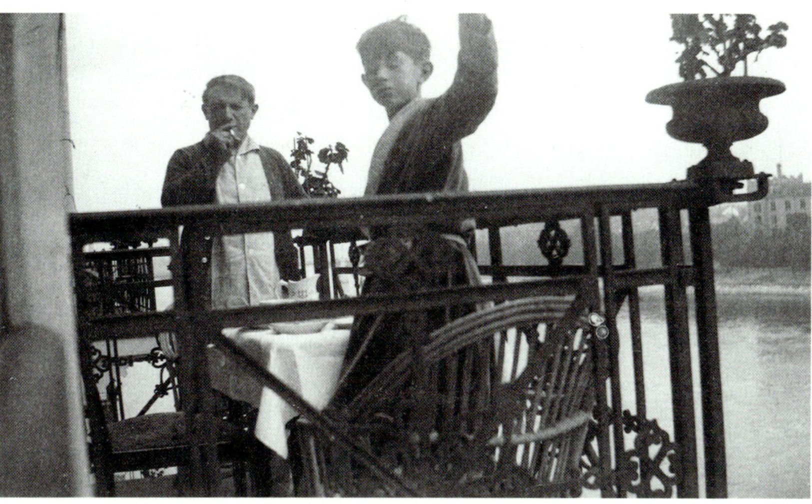

Pablo and Paulo Picasso at the Hôtel des Trois Rois, Basel, 8 September 1932

12 The family is in Interlaken, staying at the Beau Rivage & Grand Hotel.

13 The family leave Switzerland for Paris, then Boisgeloup.

15 *Composition with Butterfly* (p.195)

In Boisgeloup, Picasso takes up his work where he had left it and realises four beach scenes (p.192).

17 Picasso begins the series of Crucifixions 'after Grünewald' with three drawings (pp.196–7).

19 The series continues with three new compositions (pp.198–9).

21 In a long letter, Zervos explains to Picasso why the artist did not find his catalogue raisonné on sale in Zurich. Picasso, who supports Zervos's company financially, asks to see the accounts.

30 Francis Jourdain (1876–1958), president of the French Association of Revolutionary Writers and Artists, writes to Picasso to ask him to protest against the forced dissolution of the Association for the Protection of German Writers in Berlin. Founded on 4 January 1932, the Association of Revolutionary Writers and Artists is closely aligned to the Communist Party. The request is indicative of the hardening of political positions between the communists on the one hand and the fascists on the other.

In his book *Con los buscadores del camino*[50] published in September 1932, Felipe Cossío del Pomar (1888–1981), quotes Picasso:

As far as I'm concerned, I intend to continue in an aesthetic direction, or if you prefer, purely cerebral. I shall continue to make art without concerning myself about its influences, or whether it 'humanises' our life, as you put it. If it contains truth, my work will be useful without my explicit desire, if not, well, too bad ... I shall not make art with the preconceived idea of serving the interests of the political, religious or military art of any country.[51]

**October**

**3** In a postcard addressed to Olga and Picasso, Massine says he is looking forward to working with Picasso on *Rebus* (see 3 August). This project does not come to fruition.

**4–9** Picasso alternates Crucifixions and flute players (pp.200–7).

**7** Paul Klee (1879–1940) visits the retrospective in Zurich and writes to his wife: The Picasso exhibition has won me over me once again and the latest very colourful paintings were a true surprise. He has even incorporated some Matisse. Most of the time the formats are larger than one might think. Many of the amusing bather pieces gain a great deal from their tended painting. All in all: the painter of today.[52]

**10** In a telegram to Wartmann, Picasso authorises the extension of the Zurich show until 13 November.[53]

End of the summer holidays. The Picasso family leaves Boisgeloup.

**11** The Zurich social-democratic daily *Volksrecht* contains an article by 'H.O.': 'Should the City Contribute to Financing the "Picasso" Exhibition?' The writer says not, because Picasso's art is 'typical of bourgeois decadence'.

**16** Closing of the Automobile Fair at the Grand Palais. It opened on 10 October; Picasso visits on an unknown date.[54]

**21** Last drawing in the series of Crucifixions (p.207).

**25** Picasso turns fifty-one.

**30** *Seated Woman by a Window* (p.215)

Picasso spends the weekend at Boisgeloup.

**November**

**3** Galka E. Scheyer (1889–1945), representing the Oakland Gallery, writes to Picasso as she wants to buy one of his paintings shown in the Zurich exhibition. Picasso's reply is not known but on 9 December the Percier gallery sells her *Head of a Woman* 1927 for 7,500 francs.[55]

**10** The American sculptor Alexander Calder (1898–1976) invites Picasso to see the *Circus Calder* in Paris.

**12** Wartmann writes to Picasso: Your exhibition at the Kunsthaus closes tomorrow, Sunday evening. It has been a huge artistic success and the public's interest has continued to grow throughout. What has been disastrous, however, is that the financial crisis has made buyers apprehensive and has even forced Zurich's Municipal Council to reduce their planned subsidies heavily; as a result, we ourselves have only very limited means available to make acquisitions for the Zurich Museum. The canvas on which we have settled first is 'Le Guéridon' [*The Pedestal Table*], no.91 in the Zurich exhibition, and no.100 in the Georges Petit exhibition. Due to the very considerable cost of transport, insurance and installation, and the reduced subsidy from the city of Zurich, the figure of 150,000 francs that we believed we could offer you has now been halved, i.e. 75,000 francs.[56]

**13** Closing of the Picasso exhibition at the Kunsthaus Zürich. The show has attracted 34,027 visitors, including 14,078 paying entries at 1.50 francs each; 5,644 copies of the list of works have been sold at 50 centimes each and 716 catalogues have sold at 5 francs each.

Carl Gustav Jung (1875–1961) publishes an article on Picasso in the German-language Swiss daily newspaper *Neue Zürcher Zeitung*. He writes: On the basis of my experience, I can confirm to the reader that, insofar as it is expressed in his art, Picasso's problematic is in every respect analogous to that of my patients.

**15** *Marie-Thérèse in a Pensive Mood* (p.216)

**16** Following Wartmann's letter of 12 November, Picasso replies by telegram: 'ACCEPT PRICE PAINTING NINETY-ONE CATALOGUE PICASSO'.[57]

**17** Picasso completes *The Clarinet Player*, which had been started on 13 October then set aside (p.214).

**20** *The Rescue* (p.217)

**22 November – 18 December**

Picasso intensifies his practice of engraving restarted on 15 November (pp.219–221).

**28** Michel Leiris writes from Gondar in Ethiopia:

I've received the photo of the painting via Zette. It increases my desire to return and I thank you with all my heart.

Picasso will be at the Gare de Lyon to welcome Leiris on his return on 20 January 1933.

**29** Picasso makes etchings of *The Diver* (pp.221–2).

**30** Mr Raymond, the examining magistrate, dismisses Picasso's complaint of breach of trust against Mrs Zak, a gallery owner in Paris, and Michel Calvet, a broker, filed on 9 May 1930. Calvet had stolen several hundred drawings from Picasso's mother in Barcelona.

**December**

**1** The *Gazette des Beaux-Arts*, the oldest French art review, publishes a study by Eustache de Lorey entitled 'Picasso and the Muslim East'.[58]

**2** In *Cahiers d'Art* (no.8–10), Zervos defends Picasso against Jung's text. The article is illustrated with a new portrait of the artist photographed by Man Ray (p.234).

**4** *Bathers with Beach Ball*; *Women Playing with a Ball on the Beach* (pp.224, 225)

**6** Picasso telegraphs Wartmann: 'SEND ME CHEQUE PARIS PICASSO'.

**12** Jim Ede (1895–1990), Assistant Curator at the Tate Gallery in London, asks Picasso to receive his friend, the British painter Ben Nicholson (1894–1982).

**14** The Russian ballerina Lydia Keynes (née Vassilievna Lopokova, 1891–1981) writes to Picasso asking if he would be willing to sell her *Woman with a Flower*, number 221 in the Zurich exhibition catalogue, for £150 (p.112).

Before the end of the year, on a Thursday or a Sunday, Brassaï is sent by Tériade to produce a photographic reportage on Picasso's studios in rue La Boétie and in Boisgeloup. The photographs will accompany Breton's text 'Picasso in his Element' to be published in the first issue of *Minotaure* in June 1933 (pp.184–7).

**26** Picasso starts to use again the sketchbook abandoned on 29 January.

**21** *Sleeping Nude with Blonde Hair* (p.230)

**24** The Picasso family spend Christmas at the Lascauxs' home with the Desbois, Max Jacob, Armand Salacrou, Gertrude Stein and Alice B. Toklas.[59]

The Picassos also organise a Christmas party. A guest list drawn up by Olga shows that there are twenty-eight guests, including seven children: among these are Eugenia Errázuriz, Kahnweiler and his wife, Elie Lascaux and his wife, André Level and his wife, Zette Leiris and her sister, Darius Milhaud and his wife, and Albert Skira and his wife. Picasso makes a Christmas tree from old objects and toys; it seems that the party and dinner with friends, and the making of a Christmas tree, is something of a ritual. The 1932 tree is visible in photographs taken by Cecil Beaton in the family apartment at rue La Boétie in the spring of 1933 (pp.32–3); Brassaï had photographed the tree made in 1930; and the one created in 1931 appears in a photograph taken by Gallatin takes in April 1932 (see 27 April).

**26** The German critic Max Raphaël, who is preparing his book *Proudhon, Marx, Picasso: Three Studies on the Sociology of Art*,[60] asks to meet Picasso.

**30** Picasso draws two sketches of *The Painter and his Model* in Sketchbook no.40 (p.175, right).

## Notes

### The Painter of Today
Achim Borchardt-Hume

This text is indebted to the work of numerous Picasso scholars, not least my fellow contributors to this publication, and every effort has been made to reference published sources. I would especially like to acknowledge the research undertaken by Laurence Madeline in the run-up to this exhibition and her close study of primary source material in various archives to correct some of the historic assumptions about Picasso's life and work in 1932. I am particularly grateful to Laura Bruni, Assistant Curator, for her assistance with and meticulous attention to some of the detailed research informing this introduction.

1 In the auction catalogue and the related press-cuttings the work is referred as *La Femme se faisant coiffer*. Later, it came out that the buyer of the work was Picasso's dealer Paul Rosenberg. *La Coiffure* 1905 is now in the collection of the Baltimore Museum of Art, Baltimore (Z.I, 309).

2 Alex Ross, *The Rest Is Noise: Listening to the Twentieth Century*, London 2012, p.339.

3 John Richardson, *A Life of Picasso*, vol.3: *The Triumphant Years 1917–32*, New York 2007, p.465.

4 See also Marisa García Vergara, 'The Deaths of Marat', in T.J. Clark, Rosario Peiró, Anne M. Wagner, *Pity and Terror: Picasso's Path to Guernica*, exh. cat., Museo Nacional Centro de Arte Reina Sofía, Madrid 2017, pp.89–100.

5 See André Breton, 'Picasso dans son élément', *Minotaure*, no.1, June 1933, pp.4–27; Brassaï and Daniel-Henry Kahnweiler, *Les Sculptures de Picasso*, Paris 1949 and *Picasso 1930–1935*, Paris 1936.

6 See 'Annus Mirabilis II: The Paintings (1931–1932)' in Richardson 2007, chap.38, pp.457–72.

7 The Bateau-Lavoir, or 'Floating Laundry', as it was nicknamed, was a former piano factory in the Montmartre district of the 18th arrondisement of Paris where Picasso had a studio when he first arrived in Paris. The dilapidated building became the residence and meeting place for a group of influential early twentieth-century artists, writers and poets, theatre people and art dealers.

8 See Michael C. FitzGerald, *Making Modernism: Picasso and the Creation of the Market for Twentieth-Century Art*, New York 1995. See also Anne Sinclair, *My Grandfather's Gallery: A Family Memoir of Art and War*, London 2014.

9 These expenditures are recorded by a number of original documents which are now part of the Archives of the Musée national Picasso-Paris. See for example, the invoice for Picasso's Hispano-Suiza car, sent to rue La Boétie, Paris, 7 July 1932 (Series A, box 17); a bill from Meyer & Mortimer Tailors (London) sent to rue La Boétie, Paris, 13 August 1932 (Series A, Box 14). I should like to thank Laurence Madelaine for bringing this material to my attention.

10 'Je suis un grand maître maintenant, il faute avoir une automobile.' H[arold] S[tanley] Ede, 'Picasso', *Cahiers d'Art*, vol.7, no.3–5, 1932, p.133. The Tate Gallery officially adopted its name only in 1932, hence Ede is still listed as Assistant Curator at the National Gallery in the article.

11 Brassaï (born Gyula Halász), *Conversations with Picasso*, trans. Jane Marie Todd, Chicago and London 1999, p.6.

12 Ibid., p.7.

13 'l'époque des duchesses': Max Jacob cited in Richardson 2007, p.46.

14 Brassaï 1999, p.4.

15 Ibid.

16 Ibid., p.5.

17 The separation was not fully formalised until the end of the decade. A divorce was not possible under Spanish law after Franco had seized power in 1936, while under French law Picasso would have had to split half his assets, including half his stock of works, a prize too high for an artist the most stellar collection of whose work was his own.

18 Although they were reproduced in 1933, 1936 and 1949, none of the sculptures was shown in the Galeries Georges Petit or Zurich retrospectives. The works Picasso had made at his Boisgeloup studio were shown to the public for the first time at the Spanish Pavilion in Paris in 1937. Picasso's total achievement as sculptor was revealed only at his eighty-fifth birthday, as late as 1967, when for the first time he allowed a full-scale retrospective of all his sculptures. The majority of these sculptures remained in Picasso's possession until his death. For an in-depth study of the sculptures, see Ann Temkin and Anne Umland (eds.), *Picasso Sculptures*, exh. cat., The Museum of Modern Art, New York 2015.

19 Brassaï 1999, p.16.

20 Thomas Chaineux, 'Olga Picasso entre France et Russie', in Emilia Philippot et al. (eds.), *Olga Picasso*, exh. cat., Musée national Picasso–Paris 2017, p.109. Chaineux suggests that Olga may have been aware of the presence of another woman in Picasso's life as early as July 1928.

21 Roland Penrose, *Picasso: His Life and Work*, London 1958, p.243.

22 Françoise Gilot and Carlton Lake, *Life with Picasso*, London 1990, p.222.

23 See also Michael C. FitzGerald, 'Post 1932: From the Paris and Zurich Retrospectives to "Guernica"', in Tobia Bezzola (ed.), *Picasso: His First Museum Exhibition 1932*, exh. cat., Kunsthaus Zürich, Zurich 2010, pp.132–55. When asked by André Breton and his fellow surrealists to sign a petition in support of Louis Aragon, Picasso refused to do so until having consulted with a lawyer, for fear of deportation.

24 Ibid., pp.40–1.

25 Picasso quoted in Brassaï 1999, p.36.

26 See *Picasso and Marie-Thérèse: L'Amour Fou*, exh. cat., Gagosian Gallery, New York 2011.

27 'Croyez-vous que cela m'intéresse que ce tableau représente deux personnage? Ces deux personnages ont existé, ils n'existent plus. Leur vision m'a donné une émotion initiale, petit à petit leur presence réelle s'est estompée, ils sont devenus pour moi une fiction, puis ils ont disparu, ou plutôt, ont été transformés en problems de toute sorte. Ce ne sont plus pour moi deux personnages, mais des forms et des couleurs, entendons-nous, des forms et des couleurs qui résument cependant l'idée des deux personnages et conservent la vibration de leur vie.' Picasso in Christian Zervos, 'Conversation avec Picasso,' *Cahiers d'Art*, vol.10, no.7–10, 1935, special issue, *Picasso 1930–1935*, p.176. Translation by Myfanwy Evans and published in Alfred H. Barr, Jr, *Picasso: Forty Years of his Art*, exh. cat., The Museum of Modern Art, New York 1939, p.17.

28 'L'Oeuvre qu'on fait est une façon de tenir son journal.' Quoted in Tériade (Efstratios Eleftheriades), 'En causant avec Picasso', *L'Intransigeant*, 15 June 1932, p.1.

29 See Michael C. FitzGerald, 'A Question of Identity' in *Picasso's Marie-Thérèse*, exh. cat., Acquavella Galleries, New York 2008, pp.8–29.

30 Barr 1939, p.155.

31 Marie-Thérèse Walter, interview with Pierre Cabanne on the radio broadcast *Présence des arts*, 13 April 1974.

32 See Richardson 2007, pp.467–8 and Anne Umland, *Picasso: Girl before a Mirror*, New York 2012, pp.30–1.

33 See, for example, Yve-Alain Bois, *Matisse and Picasso*, exh. cat., Kimbell Art Museum, Forth Worth 1999; Yve-Alain Bois, *Matisse and Picasso*, Paris 2001; Elizabeth Cowling et al., *Matisse/ Picasso*, exh. cat., Tate Modern, London 2002. See also T.J. Clark's text in this catalogue.

34 Henri Matisse, *The Dance I* 1932–3, The Barnes Foundation, Merion Station, PA.

35 The trip is recounted in Richardson 2007, pp.470–1.

36 See Elizabeth Cowling, *The 'Reclining Woman on the Beach' Series*, exh. cat., Museo Picasso Málaga, Malaga 2007, especially pp.36–40. Joan Miró, *Person Throwing a Stone at a Bird* 1926, The Museum of Modern Art, New York; Max Ernst, *Men Shall Know Nothing of This* 1923, Tate.

37 Letter from Daniel-Henry Kahnweiler to Michel Leiris, 19 March 1932, published in *Daniel-Henry Kahnweiler, marchand, éditeur, écrivain*, exh. cat., Centre Georges Pompidou, Musée national d'art moderne Paris 1984, p.147: '[Deux nus qui sont] peut-être ce qu'il a produit de plus grand, de plus émouvant'. Translated in T.J. Clark, *Picasso and Truth: From Cubism to Guernica*, Princeton and Oxford 2013, p.6.

38 'Non, je refuse d'avoir des trous de cul dans ma galerie.' The episode is recounted in Roland Penrose, *Scrap Book 1900–1981*, London 1981, p.68.

39 *Picasso 1930–1935*, Paris 1936, p.61. The issue is undated but was published late January or February 1936. It was in this reproduction that the painting first caught the eye of Roland Penrose. The story of Penrose's acquisition of the work and subsequent lifelong friendship with Picasso is recounted in Elizabeth Cowling, *Visiting Picasso: The Notebooks and Letters of Roland Penrose*, London 2006, pp.29–30.

40 'Picasso Speaks, *The Arts* (New York), vol.7, no.5, May 1923, pp.315–29. Reprinted in Barr 1939, p.9 and in Alfred H. Barr, Jr, *Picasso: Fifty Years of his Art*, New York 1946, pp.270–1; Bibliography, item no.1, p.286.

41 See Simonetta Fraquelli, 'Picasso's Retrospective at the Galeries Georges Petit, Paris 1932: A Response to Matisse', in Bezzola 2010, pp. 76–93.

42 As Jeffrey Weiss has discussed elsewhere, the continued attention given to his past work while he was focusing on the production of new work, and the mounting awareness of all these works forming one oeuvre whose whole was bigger than its parts had a profound impact on Picasso from the publication of the first volume of the catalogue raisonné in summer 1932 onwards. Jeffrey Weiss, 'Picasso *Raisonné*' in Patricia G. Berman and Gertje R. Utley (eds.), *A Fine Regard: Essays in Honor of Kirk Varnedoe*, Aldershot 2008, pp.119–33.

43 From the transcript of the board meeting of 8 June 1931, it emerges that Maraini – then General Secretary of the Venice Biennale – was against the idea of including Picasso in the XVIII Biennale as he thought his work was no longer representing of a modern trend and it had become obsolete: '[I] had been thinking to organise an exhibition on Picasso ... But then I stopped, partly because of the cost of the insurance, partly because, thinking about it, I do not know if Picasso either still represents a young and lively style and trend, or he is not rather an obsolete.' (Translation by Laura Bruni.) Busta 62, Archivio Storico delle Arti Contemporanee, Fondazione La Biennale di Venezia; published in Jean-François Rodriguez, *Picasso alla Biennale di Venezia (1905–1948): Soffici, Paresce, De Pisis e Tozzi intermediari di cultura tra la Francia e l'Italia*, Padova 1993, pp.70–1.

44 Letter from Alfred H. Barr, Jr to Jacques Mauny, 20 June 1931. Alfred H. Barr, Jr. Papers, The Museum of Modern Art Archives, New York, XI.J, folder 2; published in FitzGerald 1995, p.213: 'After several conversations Picasso refused on the grounds that he wished to carry through to its culmination his present "period" before holding a retrospective exhibition.' For a further account of the events, see also FitzGerald 1995, pp.204–14.

45 Barr succeeded on mounting the first Picasso retrospective show at the Museum of Modern Art only seven years later: *Picasso: Forty Years of his Art*, 15 November 1939 – 7 January 1940. This was followed by *Picasso: 75th Anniversary Exhibition*, 22 May – 8 September 1957. Both exhibitions were curated in collaboration with the Art Institute of Chicago where each travelled after the first venue. Between the two exhibitions, Barr wrote a further book on Picasso's works, *Picasso: Fifty Years of his Art*, New York 1946. While lobbying Picasso to show in New York in 1932, Barr had already developed the model of distinct periods which soon would become the norm for almost all monographic exhibitions and much of the literature on the artist.

46 Ruth Green Harris, 'Great Picasso Show in Paris a One-Man Medley', *New York Times*, 24 July 1932.

47 Penrose 1958, p.243.

48 See Annette King, Joyce H. Townsend and Bronwyn Ormsby, 'Nude Woman in a Red Armchair 1932 by Pablo Picasso', Tate Papers, no.28, Autumn 2017, http://www.tate.org.uk/research/ publications/tate-papers/28/picasso-nude-woman-red-armchair, accessed 12 December 2017.

49 See Bezzola 2010; esp. Christian Geelhaar, 'Picasso: The First Zurich Exhibition', pp.26–45.

50 See Carl Gustav Jung, 'Picasso', *Neue Zürcher Zeitung*, 13 November 1932, p.107, written in response to the Zurich retrospective. Later translated in *The Collected Works of C.G. Jung*, vol.15: *Spirit in Man, Art, and Literature*, London and New York 1966, pp.136-41 and reproduced in Marilyn McCully (ed.), *A Picasso Anthology*, London 1981, pp.182–6. Jung's article was partly translated and strongly criticised by Christian Zervos in 'Picasso étudié par le Dr. Jung', *Cahiers d'Art*, vol. 7, no.8–10, 1932, pp.352–4.

51 See Reinhold Hohl, 'C.G. Jung on Picasso (and Joyce)', *Source: Notes in the History of Art*, vol.3, no.1, Fall 1983, pp.10–18, www.jstor.org/stable/23202362, accessed 6 September 2016.

52 *Grand Larousse XXe siècle*, edited by Paul Augé, vol.5, Paris 1932, p.566.

53 See also Carmen Giménez (ed.), *Picasso Black and White*, exh. cat., Solomon R. Guggenheim Museum, New York 2012.

54 Michael Cary, 'Tentacle Erotica', *Art in America*, 1 September 2011, pp.104–11.

55 I thank my colleague, Jenny Batchelor, Convenor, Interpretation, Tate for first bringing Renoir's film to my full attention.

56 This was Picasso's first work to be acquired by a museum. See Geelhaar 2010, pp.41–3.

57 In 1956 the photographer David Douglas Duncan went to visit Picasso and in front of one painting, portraying a woman and dated 30 April 1936, he declared to Picasso that it was the saddest of the paintings he had ever seen. Picasso replied it was because 'It was the worst time of my life' ('C'était la pire époque de ma vie'). See David Douglas Duncan, *Picasso's Picassos*, New York and Evanston 1961, p.111. The episode is then reported in Pierre Cabanne, *Pablo Picasso: His Life and Times*, trans. Harold J. Salemson, New York 1977, pp.282–4 and Charles Stucky, 'Olga dans les années 1930: "la pire époque de ma vie" Pablo Picasso' in Philippot 2017, p.249.

58 Felipe Cossío del Pomar, *Con los buscadores del camino*, Madrid 1932; cited and translated in Michael C. FitzGerald 2010, pp.135 and 154, n.2.

59 For a detailed study of this figure, see Anne M. Wagner, '*Mater dolorosa*: The Women of *Guernica*' in T.J. Clark, Rosario Peiró, Anne M. Wagner, *Pity and Terror: Picasso's Path to Guernica*, exh. cat., Museo Nacional Centro de Arte Reina Sofía, Madrid 2017, pp.107–24.

60 'Au fond, il n'y a que l'amour. Quel qu'il soit.' Picasso in Tériade 1932, p.1.

61 'En un rectangle noir et blanc telle que nous apparait l'antique tragédie, Picasso nous envoie notre lettre de deuil: tout ce que nous aimons va mourir, et c'est pourquoi il était à ce point nécessaire que tout ce que nous aimons se résumât, comme l'effusion des grands adieux, en quelque chose d'inoubliable-ment beau.' Michel Leiris, 'Faire-part', *Cahiers d'Art*, vol.12, no.4–5, 1937, p.128. Translation by T.J. Clark and AM. Wagner in wall text for the exhibition *Pity and Terror: Picasso's Path to Guernica*, Museo Nacional Centro de Arte Reina Sofía, Madrid 2017.

62 'Alles in Allem: der Maler von Heute': postcard from Paul Klee to Lily Klee, 7 October 1932, Zentrum Paul Klee, Bern. Published in Felix Klee (ed.), *Paul Klee: Briefe an die Familie 1893–1940*, vol.2: *1907–1940*, Cologne 1979, p.1189.

### 'I am a woman': The Spring Nudes
T.J. Clark

Some elements of the present essay are reworked from: T.J. Clark, *Picasso and Truth: From Cubism to Guernica*, Princeton and Oxford 2013; from the lecture 'Picasso's Two Great Nudes from 1932' given at the Wexner Center for the Arts at The Ohio State University, Columbus, Ohio, on 7 October 2014; and from the lecture 'A Room of One's Own: Reflections on Picasso's *Nude, Green Leaves and Bust* 1932' given at the New York Institute for the Humanities at NYU, New York, on 14 November 2013.

1 For an English translation of 'Toiles récentes de Picasso', see *Pity and Terror: Picasso's Path to Guernica*, exh. cat., Museo Reina Sofía, Madrid 2017, pp. 71–3.

2 See *Daniel-Henry Kahnweiler, marchand, éditeur, écrivain*, Centre Georges Pompidou, Musée national d'art moderne, Paris 1984, p.147.

3 Romuald Dor de La Souchère, *Picasso à Antibes*, Paris 1960, cited in Marie-Laure Bernadac and Androula Michael (eds.), *Picasso propos sur l'art*, Paris 1998, p.135. Dor de La Souchère was the first Keeper of the Picasso Museum in Antibes.

4 Christian Zervos, 'Conversation avec Picasso', *Cahiers d'Art* (1935). Cited in Bernadac and Michael 1998, p.33.

5 Daniel-Henry Kahnweiler, 'Entretiens avec Picasso au sujet des *Femmes d'Alger*', *Aujourd'hui*, Sept. 1955. Cited in Bernadac and Michael 1998, p.72.

6 Kahnweiler and Picasso had Mallarmé's poem 'L'après-midi d'un faune' as a shared point of reference: in it a faun-satyr does something unspecified, but possibly lethal, to a nymph he desires. Picasso had painted a backdrop for Nijinski's ballet drawn from Mallarmé's poem in 1922. Matisse did etchings for 'L'après-midi' as part of his *Poésies de Stéphane Mallarmé*, published in October 1932.

7 'Quand je peins une femme dans un fauteuil, le fauteuil, c'est la vieillesse et la mort, non? Tant pis pour elle. Ou bien, c'est pour la protéger.' André Malraux, *La Tête d'obsidienne*, Paris 1974, p.128.

8 See Clark 2013, pp.72–109 and passim.

9 For instance, *Figure and Profile* (*Figure et profile)* 1927–8, private collection (Z.VII, 144): *Figure and Profile (Figure et profile)* 1928, Musée Picasso, Paris (Z.VII 129); and *Bust of a Woman with Self-Portrait (Buste de femme et autoportrait)* 1929, private collection, (Z.VII 248). Reproduced in Clark 2013, pp.12, 202.

10 Daniel-Henry Kahnweiler, 'Gespräche mit Picasso', *Jahresring 59/60*, 1959. Cited in Bernadac and Michael 1998, p.92.

11 See Yve-Alain Bois, *Matisse and Picasso*, exh. cat., Kimbell Art Museum, Fort Worth 1998 and Elizabeth Cowling et al., *Matisse Picasso*, exh. cat., Tate Modern, London, 2002, especially pp.123–75.

12 Alfred H. Barr, Jr, *Matisse: His Art and his Public*, New York 1951, p.214.

13 William Blake, 'Infant Sorrow', in *Songs of Innocence and of Experience*, published 1794.

14 See Bois 1998, pp.41, 46, and p. 245, n.101, for discussion of the exhibition history of Matisse's 1914–18 paintings in the later 1920s.

15 *Poissons rouges et palette* 1914, oil on canvas. The Museum of Modern Art, New York. Gift and bequest of Florene M. Schoenborn and Samuel A. Marx.

16 The idea that the coexistence of such images can be explained by some of them being 'of' Marie-Thérèse Walter, and others, like *Rest*, being 'of' Picasso's wife, Olga Khokhlova (the Picasso marriage had apparently been foundering since 1923) seems wrong-headed to me. Picasso could hardly have made it clearer, formally, that *The Dream* is a transform of *Rest*, not a portrait of *Rest*'s opponent. Both paintings are 'dreams', dreamt by the 'I' that is someone else. *Woman with a Flower* is tied even closer than *Rest* into a set of variations on the 'same' distinctive (but completely malleable) body and face. And even if we could trace particular pictures to this or that sitter, how that might affect (let alone determine) our reaction to any one picture remains obscure. As Picasso said to Malraux: 'If I do a nude, you should think it's a nude. Not a picture of Madame Machin.' (Malraux 1974, p.110.)

17 See Clark 2013, pp.172–81, 204–33.

18 Pablo Picasso, *The Four Little Girls*, trans. Roland Penrose, London 1970, p.17.

19 'Au fond il n'y a que l'amour. Quel qu'il soit.' See Tériade, 'En causant avec Picasso', *L'Intransigeant*, 15 June 1932, p.1. Cited in Bernadac and Michael 1998, p.27.

20 Françoise Gilot and Carlton Lake, *Vivre avec Picasso*, Paris 1965, p.235; Françoise Gilot and Carlton Lake, *Life with Picasso*, New York 1964, p.252.

21 Gilot and Lake 1965, p. 203. Gilot borrows the phrase from Zervos, 'Conversation avec Picasso', *Cahiers d'Art* (1935), cited in Bernadac and Michael 1998, p.33.

22 Gilot and Lake 1964, p.266.

23 Gilot and Lake 1965, p.278. (Not in the English edition. I have reversed the order of Picasso's sentences.)

24 'Je suis une femme'. Geneviève Laporte, *'Si tard le soir, le soleil brille', Pablo Picasso*, Paris 1973, p.127. Cited in Bernadac and Michael 1998, p.131.

25 Laporte 1973, p.127.

26 'Je pense que tout, c'est inconnu, c'est ennemi!' Malraux 1974, p.18.

### An Art without Past or Future: The Summer Retrospective
Alma Mikulinsky

1 Margaret Scolari Barr, 'Our Campaigns: Alfred H. Barr Jr and the Museum of Modern Art: A Biographical Chronicle of the Years 1930–1944', *New Criterion*, special issue, 1987, p.29.

2 Roger Lesbats described the beauty of the Petit gallery in 'Le Cas étrange de Picasso', *Le Populaire*, 12 July 1932. The wallpaper design is described in Pierre Cabanne, *Pablo Picasso: His Life and Times*, trans. Harold J. Salemson, New York 1977, p.270. Simonetta Fraquelli claims that the owners of Petit gallery 'install[ed] a modern light system but preserv[ed] the building's nineteenth-century character': Simonetta Fraquelli, 'Picasso's Retrospective at the Galeries Georges Petit, Paris 1932: A Response to Matisse', in Tobia Bezzola (ed.), *Picasso: His First Museum Exhibition 1932*, exh. cat., Kunsthaus Zürich, Zurich 2010, p.78. For modern gallery decor, see installation photographs of Picasso's exhibition at Paul Rosenberg's, reproduced in Michael C. FitzGerald, *Making Modernism: Picasso and the Creation of the Market for Twentieth Century Art*, New York 1995, pp.185–6.

3 See also Yves-Alain Bois, *Matisse and Picasso*, Fort Worth 2001, pp.72–4 and Fraquelli 2010, pp.77–93.

4 See Jean-François Rodriguez, *Picasso alla Biennale di Venezia (1905–1948)*, Padua 1993, p.67 and FitzGerald 1995, pp.204–15.

5 See G. and J. Bernheim-Jeane and E. Bignou, *Exposition Picasso, Paris*, exh. cat., Galeries Georges Petit, Paris 1932: references to specific paintings in this text appear as GP followed by the corresponding number in the exhibition catalogue. See also Dorothy Kosinski, 'G.F. Reber: Collector of Cubism', *Burlington Magazine*, vol.133, no.1061, Aug. 1991, pp.519–31.

6 *Cahiers d'Art*, vol.7, no.3–5, 1932.

7 Christian Zervos, *Pablo Picasso: Oeuvres 1895–1906*, Paris 1932; Jeffrey Weiss, 'Picasso Raisonné' in Patricia G. Berman and Gertje R. Utley (eds.), *A Fine Regard: Essays in Honor of Kirk Varnedoe*, Aldershot 2008, pp.119–23.

8 Christopher Green, *Picasso: Architecture and Vertigo*, New Haven and London 2006, p.4; Weiss 2008.

9 André Malraux, *The Psychology of Art*, New York 1949, p.53. At that point only two volumes of the Zervos catalogue had been released: Christian Zervos, *Pablo Picasso: Oeuvres 1895–1906*, Paris 1932 and *Pablo Picasso: Oeuvres de 1906–1912*, Paris 1942.

10 Bezzola 2010, pp.16–17; Fraquelli 2010, pp.77–93.

11 Barr summarised his idea for the retrospective in an undated document naming and dating thirteen stylistic periods to be exhibited chronologically. See Alfred H. Barr, Jr., Papers, Box 12.XII.1, The Museum of Modern Art Archives, New York. For an analysis in light of Barr's relationship to Picasso's dealers see FitzGerald 1995, pp.208–9.

12 'Someone asked me how I was going to hang my exhibition. "Badly," I replied, because an exhibition is like a picture: whether it is well or badly "arranged", it comes to the same thing. What counts is the sense of continuity in [the artist's] ideas. And when it exists, everything ends up falling into place' (*Quelqu'un me demandait comment j'allais arranger cette exposition. Je lui ai répondu 'Mal'. Car une exposition, comme un tableau, bien ou mal "arrangée", cela revient au même. Ce qui compte c'est l'esprit de suite dans les idées. Et quand cet esprit existe, comme dans les plus mauvais* ménages, tout *finit par s'arranger.*). Quoted in Efstratios Tériade, 'En causant avec Picasso', *L'Intransigeant*, 15 June 1932, p.1. For a thorough analysis of Picasso's curation see Alma Mikulinsky, 'How to Curate Badly: Forked Temporality in Pablo Picasso's Retrospective at the Galeries Georges Petit, 1932,' *Journal of Curatorial Studies*, vol.6, no.1, 2017, pp.2–28.

13 'Picasso Speaks: Statement to Marius de Zayas', *The Arts*, New York, May 1923, pp.315–26.

14 Jacques-Emile Blanche, 'Retrospective Picasso,' *L'Art Vivant*, no.162, July 1932, pp.333–4. Quoted in Pierre Daix, *Picasso: Life and Art*, New York 1993, pp.223–4.

15 Thirteen installation photographs of Picasso's 1932 retrospective are found in Alfred H. Barr, Jr Papers, 12a.8, The Museum of Modern Art Archives, New York. Eighteen additional prints from the estate of the Picasso collector Dr Gottlieb Friedrich Reber have recently emerged, three of which are copies of Barr's prints. See Bezzola 2010, pp.95–100. Two additional images also provide information regarding the hang: Rogi's image of the private view that is reproduced here and an article published in June 1932 in the Swiss daily *Zürcher Illustrierte* (p.21, above).

16 Scolari Barr 1987, p.29.

17 The two versions of *The Three Musicians* (*Les Trois Musiciens*) are in the collections of the Museum of Modern Art, New York, and the Philadelphia Museum of Art; *The Three Dancers*, Tate (p.78); *The Painter and his Model*, Teheran Museum of Contemporary Art; *The Painter and the Model*, The Museum of Modern Art, New York.

18 *Picasso*, exh. cat., Galeries Georges Petit, Paris 1932, with annotations by Margaret Scolari Barr: Alfred H. Barr, Jr Papers, 12a.5, The Museum of Modern Art Archives, New York.

19 Siegfried Bing, owner of the gallery Maison de L'Art Nouveau, was the first gallerist to integrate live plants, when staging his display of the latest furniture designs at the 1900 Universal Exhibition as a real house. Nancy Troy, *Modernism and the Decorative Arts in France: Art Nouveau to Le Corbusier*, New Haven, CT 1991, p.35.

20 Roland Penrose, *Picasso: His Life and Work* (1958), New York 1962, p.242.

21 André Breton, 'Picasso in his Element' in *Break of Day*, trans. Mark Polizzotti and Mary Ann Caws, Lincoln, NE 1999, pp.116–17.

22 Penrose 1962, p.242.

23 Germain Bazin, 'Un Bilan: L'Exposition Picasso', *L'Amour de l'Art*, vol.13, no.7, July–Aug. 1932, p.247.

24 Waldemar George, 'Aut Caesar Aut Nihil (Reflections on the Picasso Exhibition at the Georges Petit Galleries)', *Formes: An International Review of Plastic Art*, no.25, 1932, pp.268–71.

25 Jacque Guenne, 'Retrospective Picasso,' *L'Art Vivant*, July 1932, p.333.

26 George Lesbat, 'Le Cas étrange de Picasso', *Le Populaire*, 12 July 1932, n.p.

**A Blank Canvas**
Nancy Ireson

1 For an overview of Picasso's use of black and white, see Carmen Giménez (ed.), *Black and White*, exh. cat., Solomon R. Guggenheim Museum, New York 2012.

2 The exact date that the work was passed from Picasso to Loeb is unknown. In 1937 it was one of the pieces that represented the artist in the influential exhibition *Les Maîtres de l'art indépendant* (no. 20), organised by the City of Paris, which celebrated the best of French contemporary art. It is now in the Metropolitan Museum of Art, New York. Promised gift from the Leonard A. Lauder Cubist Collection.

3 Conversation with Mark Pascale, The Janet and Craig Duchossois Curator of Prints and Drawings, The Art Institute of Chicago, 12 September 2017. These prints were not issued formally until 1911–12.

4 Diana Widmaier Picasso has suggested to Laurence Madeline that this work was a preparatory study for a tapestry, see *Picasso 1932*, exh. cat., Musée national Picasso–Paris 2017, p.40.

5 The 'non finito' as part of a Picasso's working process is discussed in Diana Widmaier Picasso, 'Picasso Finished / Unfinished', in *Unfinished: Thoughts Left Visible*, exh. cat., The Metropolitan Museum of Art, New York 2016, pp.188–93.

6 'le dessin au trait a sa proper lumière'. Picasso, 2 October 1933, cited by Kahnweiler, in Daniel-Henry Kahnweiler, *Huit entretiens avec Picasso* (1988) Paris 2014, n.p.

7 Picasso, quoted by Brassaï, in Brassaï, *Conversations with Picasso*, Chicago 1999, p.114.

8 John Richardson, *A Life of Picasso*, vol.3: *The Triumphant Years 1917–32*, New York 2007, pp.182–3; 470–1.

9 Fernand Olivier, 1930. 'Neuf ans chez Picasso: Picasso et ses amis'. Originally serialised in the evening newspaper *Le Soir* (Summer 1930) under the title 'Quand Picasso était pompier'. Reprinted in *Mercure de France*, 1 May 1931, pp.549–6; 'La Naissance du cubisme', *Mercure de France*, 15 June 1931, pp.558–8; 'L'Atelier du boulevard de Clichy', *Mercure de France*, pp.352–68.

10 'du plus profound de mon coeur qui ne t'a jamais oublié, que les seules années de bonheur de ma vie je les ai passées près de toi'. Letter from Fernande Olivier to Picasso, 5 May 1932, reproduced in *Picasso 1932* 2017, p.80.

11 Picasso to Kahnweiler, 2 December 1933, cited in Daniel-Henry Kahnweiler, *Six Entretiens avec Picasso* (1988), Paris 2014, n.p.

12 Brassaï 1999, p.5.

13 Henri Rousseau – whom Picasso knew as a staunch Republican – claimed in his lifetime that the work's display coincided with the second Hague international peace conference of June–September 1907. This was untrue – it was exhibited before the conference took place – but Picasso could have known the work from the twenty-third Salon des Indépendants of March–April 1907. Henri Certigny, *Le Douanier Rousseau et son temps: Biographie et Catalogue Raisonné*, vol.1, Tokyo 1984, p.500.

14 Picasso had purchased the painting, allegedly touted as a canvas to reuse, from small-time picture dealer Eugène Soulier. The painter Max Weber recalled seeing it in the artist's studio in November 1908. Max Weber, 'Rousseau as I Knew him', *Art News*, 15 February 1942, pp.17 and 35.

15 On Doucet's Rousseau entering the Louvre see André Salmon, 'L'Entrée au Louvre du Douanier Rousseau', *L'Art Vivant*, Paris, November 1925, pp.29–30.

16 On Picasso's conception of art as a form of magic, which impacts on her reading of Picasso's 1932 work in the same volume, see Lydia Gasman, 'Mystery, Magic and Love in Picasso, 1925–38', Pt.2, 'Picasso and the Surrealist Poets', unpublished Ph.D thesis, Columbia University, New York 1981.

17 Diana Widmaier Picasso, 'The Marie-Thérèse Years: A Frenzied Dialogue for the Sleeping Nude', in John Richardson and Diana Widmaier Picasso (eds.), *L'Amour fou: Picasso and Marie-Thérèse*, exh. cat., Gagosian, New York 2011, p.76.

18 Brigitte Baer, *Picasso the Engraver: Selections from the Musée Picasso*, Paris, exh. cat, The Metropolitan Museum of Art, New York 1997, pp.18–19. Baer dates the impression from 1933 but its presence in the Brassaï photograph suggests that it was pulled in December 1932.

19 Coline Zellal, 'La Presse et la crayon: Boisgeloup ou la fabrication du mythe', in *Picasso: Boisgeloup*, Paris 2017, p.105. He would only find technical help the following year, from Montmartre printmaker Roger Lacourière.

20 Patrick Elliott, *Picasso on Paper*, exh. cat., Dean Gallery, Scottish National Gallery of Modern Art, Edinburgh, 2007, p.14.

21 The various states of *The Rescue of the Drowned Woman* were printed in 1960 by Frélaut and in a 1961 edition by the Galerie Louise Leiris (released in 1981). Post-edition prints were also made in 1979: G.272–4.

22 Tzara had begun work on the book in 1916 and continued sporadically until 1932.

23 Baer 1997, p.72.

24 Earlier in the year, he had also begun to try his hand at Erwinography, a novel technique that also allows the introduction of diverse objects. See Brigitte Baer, *Picasso the Printmaker: Graphics from the Marina Picasso Collection*, exh.cat., Dallas Museum of Art 1983, p.64. A letter in the archives of the Musée national Picasso-Paris – from Erwin Quedenfeldt to Picasso on 13 May – answers Baer's question as to how the artist knew of the technique. See *Picasso 1932* 2017, p.87.

25 Breton, 'Picasso dans son élément', *Minotaure*, no.1, 15 June 1933, pp.4–27.

26 Picasso gave his nephew prints he had pulled of G.272–4. It seems unlikely that Picasso assumed his recipient was completely innocent.

27 Baer 1997, p.33.

28 Christopher Green, *Picasso: Architecture and Vertigo*, New Haven and London 2006, pp.193–220.

29 On Picasso, Freud and child art, see ibid.

30 Letter from Leiris to Bataille, 1 May 1932; letter from Bataille to Leiris, September or October 1932. *Georges Bataille and Michel Leiris: Correspondence*, ed. Louis Yvert, trans. Liz Heron, Oxford 2008, pp.92–6.

31 On *Documents*, see Dawn Ades and Simon Baker (eds.), *Undercover Surrealism: Georges Bataille and Documents*, exh. cat), Hayward Gallery, London 2006.

32 'Que deviant la tragédie, alors? Et les grands sentiments? La haine? ... dire que les soeurs Papin sont folles, c'est enlever cette chose admirable, le péché'. Picasso, 30 November 1933, cited in Kahnweiler, *Six Entretiens avec Picasso* 2014, pp.7–8.

33 Lisa Florman, *Myth and Metamorphosis: Picasso's Classical Prints of the 1930s*, Cambridge, MA and London 2000, p.15.

34 Elizabeth Cowling, *Picasso: Style and Meaning*, New York 2002, p.543. Ruth Kaufmann also links the motif seen in images

including *The Rape* to the Saint-Sever manuscripts: 'Picasso's Crucifixion of 1930', *Burlington Magazine*, vol.III, no.798, September 1969, pp.553–61.

35 Juxtapositions in a 2016 exhibition of Picasso's work have suggested that these images might look to history since, from the early 1900s, Picasso would have known about the carved and jointed wooden crucifixes that were typical of Catalonia: Romanesque-Picasso, Museu Nacional d'Art de Catalunya, Barcelona,

36 On Bataille, Picasso, and the significance of the 1930 *Crucifixion* see C.F.B. Miller, 'Bataille with Picasso: Crucifixion, 1930, and Apocalypse', *Papers of Surrealism*, vol.7, Manchester 2007, pp.1–24. Noticeably, in his brightly coloured 1930 painting on the theme, Picasso depicted the central motif only in black and white.

37 Brassaï 1999, pp.33–4.

### Picasso in his Element? An Autumn of Surrealism
Neil Cox

1 'Picasso dans son élément', *Minotaure,* no.1, 15 June 1933, pp.4–27.

2 Masson stated in 1942 that he and Bataille had invented the title *Minotaure*. See Dawn Ades, *Dada and Surrealism Reviewed*, exh. cat., Hayward Gallery, London 1978, p.279. For the *Documents* homage, see C.F.B. Miller, 'Picasso', in Dawn Ades and Simon Baker (eds.), *Undercover Surrealism: Georges Bataille and Documents*, exh. cat., Hayward Gallery, London 2006, pp.214–21.

3 These studio scenes later featured in the so-called *Vollard Suite,* a print portfolio of some one hundred etchings executed between 1931 and 1937. The portfolio was commissioned by Picasso's friend and early dealer, Ambroise Vollard. Vollard's death in a car accident in 1939, and then the onset of war, delayed publication for a decade or so. For detailed analysis see Lisa Florman, *Myth and Metamorphosis: Picasso's Classical Prints of the 1930s*, Cambridge, MA, chap.3.

4 Picasso to Daniel Henry-Kahnweiler in the catalogue of his 1955 retrospective exhibition at the Musée des arts decoratifs, Paris. Cited in John Richardson, *A Life of Picasso*, vol.III: *The Triumphant Years 1917–1932*, London 1991, p.350. For Richardson's support of this view, see p.488.

5 Elizabeth Cowling, '"Proudly we claim him as one of us": Breton, Picasso and the Surrealist Movement', *Art History*, vol.8, no.1, March 1985, pp.82–104.

6 *La Révolution Surréaliste*, 15 July 1925. For two recent contrasting readings of this work, see C.F.B. Miller, 'Rotten Sun', *Art History*, vol.34, no.2, April 2011, pp.388–411; and T.J. Clark, 'Window', in *Picasso and Truth: From Cubism to Guernica*, Princeton 2013, pp.111–46.

7 For a range of views see, among others, Michael C. FitzGerald, 'Post 1932: From the Paris and Zurich Retrospectives to Guernica' in Tobia Bezzola (ed.), *Picasso: His First Museum Exhibition 1932*, exh. cat., Kunsthaus Zürich, Zurich 2010, p.140; John Golding, 'Picasso and Surrealism' in *Visions of the Modern*, London 1994; Elizabeth Cowling, *Picasso: Style and Meaning*, London 2002, chap.8; Anne Baldassari, *The Surrealist Picasso*, Paris 2005. All recognise the complexity of the problem.

8 Michel Leiris, 'Toiles récentes de Picasso', *Documents*, no.2, 1930, translated in Bezzola 2010, p.142.

9 Cited in Richardson 1991, p.350. The phrasing here suggests that Picasso remained in part wedded to Guillaume Apollinaire's conception of 'sur-realism', a term he coined in 1917. For more on English surrealist Penrose's relationship to Picasso, see Elizabeth Cowling, *Visiting Picasso: The Notebooks and Letters of Roland Penrose*, London 2008.

10 For discussions of these connections, see William Jeffett et al., *Picasso/Dalí: Dalí/Picasso*, exh. cat., Museu Picasso, Barcelona 2015; Eugenio Carmona et al., *Picasso, Miro, Dalí: Angry Young Men. The Birth of Modernity*, exh. cat., Palazzo Strozzi, Florence 2011.

11 The phrase comes from a reported conversation with Brassaï on 6 December 1943 (see Brassaï, *Conversations avec Picasso*, Paris 1964, p.123), but the notion of Picasso's work as diary-like is floated by Michel Leiris: see Leiris 1930.

12 Richardson 1991, p.466.

13 See Neil Cox, 'Picasso's Mirrors: The Mobility of Thoughts' in *Picasso: Eleven Paintings from International Collections*, exh..cat., Vancouver Art Gallery, Vancouver, BC, 2005, pp.3–13, and the excellent brief discussion in Christopher Green, *Picasso: Architecture and Vertigo*, London 2005, pp.3–17.

14 In Zurich the 1930 *Crucifixion* was no.196 in the catalogue. See Bezzola 2010, p.242.

15 'Crucifixions: Dessins de Picasso d'après la *Crucifixion* de Grünewald', *Minotaure*, no.1, 1933, n.p.

16 The visit is disputed. See the sceptical Christian Heck, 'Entre le mythe et le modèle formel: Les Crucifixions de Grünewald et l'art du XXe siècle', *Corps Crucificié*, exh. cat., Musée Picasso, Paris 1992, p.104, and the confident Richardson 1991, p.486.

17 I am very grateful to Laurence Madeline for sharing her research with me.

18 See also Diane Apostolos-Cappadona, 'The Essence of Agony: Grünewald's Influence on Picasso', *Artibus et Historiae*, vol.13, no.26, 1992, pp.31–47.

19 Ann Stieglitz, 'The Reproduction of Agony: Toward a Reception-history of Grünewald's Isenheim Altar after the First World War', *Oxford Art Journal*, vol.12, no.2, 1989, pp.87–103. Huysmans's reading of the work is in *Trois Primitifs*, Paris 1905. Zervos would publish a special issue on the painting in *Cahiers d'Art* in 1936, when the prophetic dimension of the surrealist revision of Grünewald was already coming to pass in Spain and when the grotesque bodies in the Isenheim painting could be used to speak the truth to Nazi culture.

20 Private collection, Z.VIII, 57.

21 See for example the right-hand figure in Rogier van der Weyden's *Descent from the Cross* 1435 in the Prado, Madrid, and thus well known to Picasso.

22 The point is made by Richardson 1991, p.487.

23 *L'Atelier de la modiste*, Musée National d'Art Moderne, Centre Georges Pompidou.

24 Bernhard Geiser and Brigitte Baer, *Picasso: Peintre-Graveur*, vol.1, Bern 1990, no.217, p.357.

25 Cowling 2002, pp.522–3.

26 Golding 1994, pp.217–18.

27 André Breton, 'Picasso in his Element', in *Break of Day*, trans. Mark Polizzoti and Mary Ann Caws, London 1999, p.111.

28 Ibid., p.116.

29 Ibid.

30 On *Woman with Dagger*, see Neil Cox, 'Marat/Sade/Picasso', *Art History*, vol.17, no.3, Sept. 1994, pp.383–417.

## Rescue: The End of a Year

Diana Widmaier Picasso

1 'L'Oeuvre qu'on fait est une façon de tenir son journal.' Quoted in Efstratios Tériade, 'En causant avec Picasso', *L'Intransigeant*, 15 June 1932, p.1. Cited in Pierre Daix, *Picasso*, Paris 2007, pp.308–9.

2 In 1917, Picasso joined Diaghilev in Rome to work on the sets for *Parade*. It was there that he met Olga Khokhlova (1891–1955), a twenty-six year old dancer with the *Ballets Russes*. On 12 July 1918 they married and on 4 February 1921 their son Paulo was born. Their break-up was made official in June 1935 but their legal separation was not granted by the courts until 15 February 1940.

3 Anne Baldassari has suggested that in the summer of 1930, Picasso moved Marie-Thérèse Walter into 44 rue La Boétie, opposite the apartment where he was living with Olga and Paulo: see 'Chronologie', in *Musée Picasso Paris*, Paris 2014, p.312. However, there is no firm evidence that Marie-Thérèse moved to rue La Boétie in 1930 as, up to 1935, Picasso continued to send letters to her at her mother's house at 6 cité d'Alfort in Maisons-Alfort, where she lived with her sister Jeanne (Archives Maya Widmaier-Picasso).

4 On Boisgeloup, see pp.64–73 above.

5 It is probable that Olga knew from 1928 of the existence of Marie-Thérèse Walter; a postcard from Marie-Thérèse dated 28 July was found in her cabin-trunk, as if she had intercepted the mail intended for her husband. In addition, Picasso's 1929 diary contains the address '11, rue de Liège' in the entry for 27 October, the address where Marie-Thérèse was installed. See Thomas Chaineux, 'Olga Picasso entre France et Russie', in Emilia Philippot et al. (eds.), *Olga Picasso*, exh. cat., Musée national Picasso–Paris 2017, p.109.

6 The term refers here to the novel *L'Amour fou* (Mad love) by the poet and leader of surrealism André Breton, written between 1934 and 1936 and published in 1937.

7 Although none of the works bore the title 'portrait' or even a name, this exhibition will have given Olga Picasso some insight into the woman who had taken her place in her husband's heart and work. Although Marie-Thérèse Walter's name does not appear in the nominal index of Alfred H. Barr, Jr's exhibition catalogue for the 1946 Museum of Modern Art exhibition *Picasso: Fifty Years of his Art*, Michael C. FitzGerald points out ('A Question of Identity' in *Picasso's Marie-Thérèse*, exh. cat., Acquavella Galleries, New York 2008, p.9, n.1) that Roland Penrose does mention Walter in his book *Picasso: His Life and Work*, New York 1958, p.243 – the first biographer to do so.

8 The term 'spirochetosis' is often used to mean leptospirosis, a bacterial disease indirectly transmitted by infected water. The date of this event – 1932 – which seems most likely, however, is nuanced, given the interview of Marie-Thérèse Walter by Pierre Cabanne shortly before her death. This emotional interview, which is not always consistent, was broadcast on the radio programme 'Présence des arts', France Culture, 13 April 1974 (Fonds d'archives Pierre Cabanne, INHA-Collection Archives de la critique d'art, Rennes).

9 Pierre Daix, *Picasso: Life and Art*, New York 1993, p.234. Quoted in Marilyn McCully, 'Boisgeloup, L'Olympe de Picasso', in *Picasso érotique*, exh. cat., Galerie nationale du Jeu de Paume, Paris 2001, p.149.

10 John Golding, 'Introduction', in *Picasso: Sculptor/Painter*, exh. cat., Tate Gallery, London 1994, p.29. Quoted in McCully 2001, p.149.

11 Daix 2007, pp.339–40.

12 These photographs are held in the Archives of Maya Widmaier Ruiz Picasso, who was born on 5 September 1935 to Walter and Picasso.

13 Marie-Thérèse was the youngest of four children; the others were Maurice (b.1903), Geneviève (b.1904) and Jeanne (b.1906). Both her sisters studied medicine and became ophthalmologists.

14 Sketchbook 1044, Dinard, 1928, private collection.

15 *Baigneuse, projet pour un monument* 1928, oil paint on canvas Philadelphia Museum of Art, Philadelphia (Z.VII, 209).

16 Lazlo Glozer, *Picasso und der Surrealismus*, Cologne 1974, p.76.

17 *Femme courant vers un nageur*, oil paint on canvas, private collection (not in Z.). Josep Palau i Fabre, *Picasso 1927–1939: From the Minotaur to Guernica*, Barcelona 2011, p.123.

18 Brigitte Baer in Bernhard Geiser et al., *Picasso Peintre-Graveur*, vol. II: *Catalogue raisonné de l'œuvre gravé et des monotypes 1932–1934*, Bern 1992, p.36.

19 *Les Métamorphoses d'Ovide* (Ovid's Metamorphoses) is a collection of thirty-two etchings executed at Boisgeloup between 13 September and 25 October 1930. They were published by Albert Skira on 25 October 1931.

20 Roman copy from the Flavian period after a Greek original dated 240–230 BCE, Loggia dei Lanzi, Piazza della Signoria, Florence.

21 Antonio Canova, *Psyche Revived by Cupid's Kiss* 1789–93, Louvre, Paris; Ary Scheffer, *Orpheus Mourning the Death of Eurydice* 1814, Musée des Beaux-Arts, Blois.

22 According to John Richardson, it is likely that Picasso wanted to depict Marie-Thérèse Walter being saved from drowning by her two sisters, Jeanne and Geneviève. See his, *A Life of Picasso*, vol.3: *The Triumphant Years 1917–1932*, New York 2007, p.487.

23 Françoise Gilot and Carlton Lake, *Life with Picasso*, London 1964, p.224.

24 *Head of a Woman (Marie-Thérèse)*, plaster (S.128); *Bust of a Woman (Marie-Thérèse)*, plaster (S.131); *Head of a Woman (Marie-Thérèse)*, plaster and wood (S.132); *Head of a Woman*, plaster and wood (S.133), all made at Boisgeloup, 1931.

25 Reinhold Hohl in Reinhold Hohl, Markus Brudelin, Gottfried Boehm et al., *Fondation Beyeler*, Munich 1997, p.90.

26 William Shakespeare's *Hamlet*, published in 1603, recounts the impossible love between Hamlet and Ophelia, whose fateful death by drowning inspired many artists including, in the nineteenth century, painters such as Eugène Delacroix (*The Death of Ophelia* 1838, Neue Pinakothek, Munich) John Everett Millais (*Ophelia* 1851–2, Tate), and Alexandre Cabanel (*Ophelia* 1883, private collection).

27 'On the calm, black water where the stars are sleeping / White Ophelia floats like a great lily' (*Sur l'onde calme et noire où dorment les étoiles / La blanche Ophélia flotte comme un grand lys*). Arthur Rimbaud wrote the poem 'Ophelia' in May 1870. He enclosed the manuscript with a letter dated 24 May 1870 to Théodore de Banville.

28 According to John Richardson, Picasso may have taken inspiration from the work of the director and biologist Jean Painlevé and in particular from his film *La Pieuvre* (*The Octopus*) (1928) shown at the Studio Diamant in December 1928, which fascinated the surrealists (see the film still reproduced on p.110, above). See John Richardson, *Picasso and the Camera*, exh. cat., Gagosian Gallery, New York 2014, p.171.

29 See also the two etchings *The Rescue of the Drowned Woman I* of 17 December 1932 and *The Rescue of the Drowned Woman II* of 18 December 1932 (pp.228, 229).

30 In this work, Yve-Alain Bois perceives an anticipated response to Matisse's *Dance* 1931–3, taking as its starting point Matisse's illustrations for Stéphane Mallarmé's *Poésies*, published in October 1932. Yve-Alain Bois, *Matisse and Picasso*, Paris 1999, p.90.

31 *Young Girl with Ball* (*Fillette au ballon*); *Bather* (*Baigneuse*); *Bather with Raised Arms* (*Baigneuse aux bras levés*); *Bather* (*Baigneuse*); all plaster, Boisgeloup, 1931 (S.112–15).

32 Both works are entitled *Minotaur and Nude Woman (Minotaure et nu)*, both charcoal on paper, Paris, 12 December 1933 (Z.VIII, 145, 146).

33 *The Rape* (*Le Viol)*, 10 August 1933.

34 *Minotaur in a Boat Saving a Woman* (*Minotaure dans une barque sauvant une femme*), March 1937, ink and gouache on board (Z.IX, 097).

35 *Woman with Candle, Fight between Bull and Horse* (*Femme à la bougie, combat entre le taureau et le cheval*), graphite and ink on canvas mounted and glued to plywood, Boisgeloup, 24 July 1934.

36 *The Rescue* (*Le Sauvetage*), pastel and charcoal on canvas, Juan-les-Pins, 29 April 1936; *Study for The Rescue series* (*Etude pour la série du Sauvetage*), graphite on paper, Juan-les-Pins, 4 May 1936; *Study for The Rescue series* (*Étude pour la série du Sauvetage)*, ink on paper, Juan-les-Pins, 4 May 1936 (Z.VIII, 284). The same month, Picasso executed *Minotaur and Mare before a Cave, in front of a Girl with a Veil (Minotaure et jument morte devant une grotte face à une jeune fille au voile)*, gouache and ink on paper, Juan-les-Pins, 6 May 1936, the composition and postures of which recall those of *The Rescue*, among others.

37 Picasso's rescue scenes make particular reference to the theme of the Pietà. For example, the print *The Rescue of the Drowned Woman II* (*Le Sauvetage de la noyée II*) of 17 December 1932 (see p.227) may be compared with the uncompleted marble sculpture by Michelangelo known variously as *The Deposition*, the *Bandini Pietà* or *The Lamentation of the Dead Christ* c.1547–55, which depicts Nicodemus carrying the body of Jesus, assisted by the Virgin Mary and Mary Magdalene (Museo dell'Opera del Duomo, Florence).

38 The motifs of Christ Crucified and Christ the Benefactor appear very early in the artist's career, on the pages of the 'little journals' he kept at the age of twelve, before reappearing at each stage of his work and in particular in 1930, such as the oil painting *The Crucifixion* of 7 February 1930 (p.180).

39 The Old Testament story of Moses being saved from the waters (Exodus 2: 1–10) inspired painters such as Tintoretto (*Moses Saved from the Waters* c.1555), Paolo Veronese (*Moses Saved from the Waters of the Nile* c.1580) and Nicolas Poussin (*Moses Rescued from the Water* 1638).

40 In the Gospel of St Matthew (14: 22–33), the apostle Peter is saved by Jesus while walking on the waters of the Sea of Galilee. In the fourteenth century, Giotto illustrated this subject with the monumental *Navicella* c.1305–13, a mosaic now almost entirely lost.

41 William Rubin, *Dada and Surrealist Art* (1968), Paris 1976, p.292.

42 Anne Baldassari, presentation text for *The Crucifixion* 1930, at the exhibition *La Madonna nell'arte contemporanea: Omaggio ai XXV anni di pontificato di S.S. Giovanni Paolo II*, Basilica di Santa Maria and Martyres – Pantheon, Rome, 14 Oct. 2003 – 30 Nov. 2004.

## 366 Days

Laurence Madeline

1 Historical Archives of Contemporary Arts, Venice Biennale Foundation.

2 Archives Fundación Almine y Bernard Ruiz-Picasso para el Arte (FABA Archives).

3 Bibliothèque Littéraire Jacques Doucet, chancellerie des universités de Paris, Paris.

4 Joaquín Torres-García, *Histoire de ma vie,* Neuchâtel 1998, pp.252–3.

5 Two admission tickets are conserved in the archives of the Musée national Picasso-Paris.

6 Baltimore Museum of Art, Maryland. The Cone Collection, formed by Dr Claribel Cone and Miss Etta Cone of Baltimore, Maryland.

7 See the admission tickets conserved in the archives of the Musée national Picasso-Paris.

8 FABA Archives.

9 Ibid.

10 Ibid.

11 Bibliothèque Littéraire Jacques Doucet.

12 Ibid.

13 Albert Eugene Gallatin, *Picasso in his Studio, rue La Boétie,* Paris 1932. Bibliothèque Kandinsky, Paris, Fonds Gallatin.

14 Max Jacob, 'Naissance du cubisme et autres', *Les Nouvelles littéraires*, 30 April 1932, p.7.

15 Agnès de La Beaumelle, 'Sous le signe de l'informe: Picasso et Giacometti dans les années 1927–1930', *Picasso–Giacometti*, exh. cat., Musée national Picasso–Paris 2016, p.42, n.19.

16 Archives of the Bibliothèque Kandinsky, Centre national d'art et de culture Georges Pompidou, Paris.

17 *Head of a Bearded Man*. See Brigitte Baer, *Picasso peintre-graveur: Catalogue raisonné de l'oeuvre gravé et des monotypes, 1899–1972*, vol.II: 1932–1934, Bern 1988, no.572.

18 Letter to Maja Hoffmann, March 1933. I am grateful to Liliane Meffre for this information.

19 Guy Hickok, *Brooklyn Daily Eagle*, 7 July 1932, Part 7, p.71.

20 Jacques-Émile Blanche, 'Exposition Picasso', *L'Art Vivant*, 8 July 1932.

21 Francisco Melgar, 'Hoy se inaugura en parís la gran exposición de Picasso', *Ahora*, 16 June 1932, p.8.

22 Corpus Barga, 'Esta noche en Paris...', *Luz*, 16 June 1932, p.7.

23 S.M., 'Le Tout-Paris hier soir a verni l'oeuvre de Picasso', *Paris Soir*, 18 June 1932.

24 Ibid.

25 Christian Geelhaar, *Picasso. Wegbereiter und Förderer seines Aufstiegs 1899–1939*, Zurich 1993, p.184.

26 Historical Archives of Contemporary Arts, Venice Biennale Foundation.

27 Max Jacob, *Les Propos et les jours: Lettres 1904–1944*, edited by Annie Marcoux and Didier Gompel-Netter, Paris 1989, p.361.

28 Pseudonym of Gùtierez Abascal.

29 Juan de la Encina, 'Un acontecimiento. Pablo Picasso', *El Sol*, 24 June 1932, p.1.

30 Letter to Picasso, archives of the Musée national Picasso–Paris.

31 'Francis Picabia. Lettres à Léonce Rosenberg', *Les Cahiers du MNAM*, Hors-Série/Archives, Paris, p.87.

32 Musée National d'Art Moderne, Paris. Gift of Louise and Michel Leiris, 1984.

33 Letter from Daniel-Henry Kahnweiler to Hermann Rupf, Archives of the Hermann and Margritt Rupf Foundation, Kunstmuseum, Bern.

34 Cited by Hélène Seckel in *Max Jacob et Picasso*, exh. cat., Musée des beaux-arts, Quimper and Musée Picasso, Paris 1994, p.225.

35 Miguel Utrillo, 'Una desercion. Un mal español. El pintor Pablo Ruiz Picasso', *La Noche*, 20 July 1932, p.3.

36 Swiss Art Archive, SIK-ISEA, Zurich.

37 *Oskar Schlemmer: Lettres et journaux*, translated from German into French by Claude Rabant, Dijon 2014, p.205. 'Kreuger' refers to the Swedish industrialist Ivar Kreuger, the 'king of matches', whose empire was ruined in the aftermath of the Wall Street Crash. His suicide in Paris on 12 March 1932 was widely reported in the media.

38 *Comoedia*, 27 July 1932, p.1.

39 Archives Maya Widmaier Ruiz Picasso.

40 Margaret Scolari Barr, 'Our Campaigns: 1930–1944', *New Criterion*, Features, 1 August 1987.

41 Cited by John Russell in *Matisse: Père et fils*, Paris 1999, pp.67–8.

42 Archives FABA.

43 Archives Maya Widmaier Ruiz Picasso.

44 *Grand Larousse du xxe siècle*, vol.5 (1932), p.566.

45 Criado y romero, '¿Ha fracasado el proyecto de la Exposición Picasso en Madrid?', *Heraldo de Madrid*, 27 August 1932, p.4.

46 Olga had kept one of the photographs; FABA Archives.

47 Telegram from Picasso to Carl Montag, Swiss Art Archive, SIK-ISEA, Zurich.

48 Hans Welti, 'Picasso in Zurich', *Sie und Er*, 24 September 1932.

49 Doris Wild, 'Begegnung mit Picasso', *Neue Zürcher Zeitung*, 2 October 1932.

50 Felípe Cossio del Pomar (1888–1981), *Con los buscadores del Camino*, Madrid 1932.

51 Cited in Michael C. FitzGerald, 'Post 1932: From the Paris and Zurich Retrospectives to "Guernica"', in Tobia Bezzola (ed.), *Picasso: His First Museum Exhibition 1932*, exh. cat., Kunsthaus Zürich, Zurich 2010, pp.133–53, p.135.

52 *Klee rencontre Picasso*, exh. cat., Zentrum Plau Klee, Bern 2010, pp.22–3.

53 Archives of the Art Society, Kunsthaus Zürich, Zurich.

54 Entrance tickets conserved in the archives of the Musée national Picasso–Paris.

55 The painting had been shown at Galeries Georges Petit as no.171 and at the Kunsthaus Zürich as no.173. Gelka Scheyer bequeathed it to Pasadena Art Museum in 1953.

56 The painting *Le Guéridon* is listed in the Zurich exhibition catalogue as belonging to Picasso and available for sale.

57 Archives of the Art Society, Kunsthaus Zürich.

58 See pp.299–314. The essay had previously appeared in an untraced English journal (see René-Jean, 'Pablo Picasso grand artiste et caméléon', *Comoedia*, 23 June 1932, p.3.

59 Xavier Vilato, *Elie Lascaux: Un enfant du Paradis*, Paris 2009.

60 Max Raphaël, *Proudhon, Marx, Picasso: Trois études sur la sociologie de l'art*, Paris 1933.

## List of Works

This list details the works by Pablo Picasso (1881–1973) exhibited in The Eyal Ofer Galleries at Tate Modern. It also includes additional works by the artist that are reproduced as plates within this publication. The page number for the illustration is given in brackets, together with an indication if the work is not exhibited.

The list appears in reverse chronological order by year, with works then arranged alphabetically by title within each year.

Archival material displayed in the exhibition is not listed.

For details of supplementary figure illustrations, see p.262.

Abbreviations

G/B
Bernard Geiser and Brigitte Baer, *Picasso: Peintre-graveur. Catalogue raisonné de l'oeuvre grave et des monotypes*, vols.I–VII and adddendum, Bern and Kornfeld 1986–1996

S.
Werner Spies, *Picasso: The Sculptures,* catalogue raisonné compiled in collaboration with Christine Piot, revised editon Berlin 2000

Z.
Christian Zervos, *Pablo Picasso: Catalogue raisonné des oeuvres*, vols.I–XXXIII, Paris 1932–78

### 1933

*Flaming Heart*
Graphite and ink on paper (with writing by Marie-Thérèse Walter) 12.7 × 9.5
Coeur enflammé
Private collection
[p.42]

*The Rescue* 11 January
Le Sauvetage
Oil paint on canvas 73 × 92
Fondation Jean et Suzanne Planque, en dépôt au Musée Granet (Aix-en-Provence)
[p.233] Not in Z.

### 1932

*Ball Players on the Beach*
6 September
Joueuses de ballon sur la plage
Oil paint on canvas 27 × 35
Private collection
[p.193] Not in Z.

*Bather with Beach Ball*
30 August
Baigneuse jouant avec un ballon
Oil paint on canvas 146.2 × 114.6
The Museum of Modern Art, New York. Partial gift of an anonymous donor and promised gift of Jo Carole and Ronald S. Lauder
[p.147; not exhibited] Z.VIII, 147

*Bather with Parasol*
1932
Baigneuse au parasol
Graphite on paper 23.5 × 28.3
Musée national Picasso–Paris. Dation Pablo Picasso, 1979. MP1068
[p.108; not exhibited] Z.VIII, 186

*Bathers on the Beach I*
22 November
Baigneuses sur la plage I
Etching on paper 17.3 × 12.5
Musée national Picasso–Paris. Dation Pablo Picasso, 1979. MP2205
[p.219; not exhibited] G/B 265

*Bathers on the Beach II*
22 November
Baigneuses sur la plage II
Etching on paper 17.4 × 12.6
Musée national Picasso–Paris. Dation Pablo Picasso, 1979. MP2206
[p.219; not exhibited] G/B 266.a

*Bathers on the Beach III*
22 November
Baigneuses sur la plage III
Etching on paper 19.6 × 17.5
Musée national – Picasso, Paris. Dation Pablo Picasso, 1979. MP2209
[p.219; not exhibited]
G/B 267.A.a

*Bathers with Beach Ball*
4 December
Baigneuses au ballon
Oil paint on canvas 81 × 100
Musée national Picasso–Paris. Dation Pablo Picasso, 1979
MP143
[p.224] Not in Z.

*Boisgeloup in the Rain*
30 March
Boisgeloup sous la pluie
Oil paint on fabric 47.5 × 83
Musée national Picasso–Paris. Dation Pablo Picasso, 1979. MP141
[p.107] Z.VII, 339

*Boisgeloup in the Rain*
30 March
Boisgeloup sous la pluie
Oil paint on canvas 19 × 24
Fundación Almine y Bernard Ruiz-Picasso para el Arte
[Not illustrated]. Not in Z.

*Boisgeloup in the Rain, with a Rainbow* 6 May
Vue de Boisgeloup sous la pluie, et arc-en-ciel
Oil paint on canvas 27 × 46
Fundación Almine y Bernard Ruiz-Picasso para el Arte
[Not illustrated]. Not in Z.

*The Clarinet Player*
13 October and 17 November
Le Joueur de clarinette
Ink and wash on paper 28.5 × 33
Nahmad Collection, Monaco
[p.214]

*Cock* 1932, cast 1952
Coq
Bronze 65.5 × 58.2 × 39.5
Tate. Purchased 1953
[p.140] S.134

*Composition with Butterfly*
15 September
Composition au papillon
Cloth, wood, plants, string, bug, butterfly and oil paint on canvas 16 × 21.5 × 2.5
Musée national Picasso–Paris. Achat 1982. MP1982-169
[p.195] S.116

*The Crucifixion* 17 September
La Crucifixion
Ink on paper 34.5 × 51.5
Musée national Picasso–Paris. Dation Pablo Picasso, 1979. MP1073
[p.196] Z.VIII, 49

*The Crucifixion* 17 September
La Crucifixion
Ink on paper 34.5 × 51.5
Musée national Picasso–Paris. Dation Pablo Picasso, 1979. MP1072
[p.197 bottom] Z.VIII, 51

*The Crucifixion* 17 September
La Crucifixion
Ink on paper 34.5 × 51.5
Musée national Picasso–Paris. Dation Pablo Picasso, 1979. MP1071
[p.197 top] Z.VIII, 52

*The Crucifixion* 19 September
La Crucifixion
Ink on paper 34.5 × 51.5
Musee national Picasso–Paris. Dation Pablo Picasso, 1979. MP1074
[p.199 top] Not in Z.

*The Crucifixion* 19 September
La Crucifixion
Ink on paper 34.5 × 51.5
Musée national Picasso–Paris. Dation Pablo Picasso, 1979. MP1075
[p.199 bottom] Z.VIII, 55

*The Crucifixion* 19 September
La Crucifixion
Ink on paper 34.5 × 51.5
Musée national Picasso–Paris. Dation Pablo Picasso, 1979. MP1076
[p.198 bottom] Not in Z.

*The Crucifixion* 4 October
La Crucifixion
Ink on paper 34 × 51
Musée national Picasso–Paris. Dation Pablo Picasso, 1979. MP1078
[p.201, top] Z.VIII, 56

*The Crucifixion* 4 October
La Crucifixion
Ink on paper 34 × 51
Musée national Picasso–Paris. Dation Pablo Picasso, 1979. MP1079
[p.201, bottom] Z.VIII, 50

*The Crucifixion* 7 October
La Crucifixion
Ink on paper 34.5 × 51
Musée national Picasso–Paris.
Dation Pablo Picasso, 1979.
MP1080
[p.203, bottom] Not in Z.

*The Crucifixion* 7 October
La Crucifixion
Ink on paper 34.5 × 51
Musée national Picasso–Paris.
Dation Pablo Picasso, 1979.
MP1081
[p.202, bottom] Z.VIII, 53

*The Crucifixion* 7 October
La Crucifixion
Ink on paper 34.5 × 51.5
Musée national Picasso–Paris.
Dation Pablo Picasso, 1979.
MP1082
[p.202, top] Not in Z.

*The Crucifixion* 21 October
La Crucifixion
Ink on paper 25.5 × 33
Musée national Picasso–Paris.
Dation Pablo Picasso, 1979.
MP1085
[p.207] Z.VIII, 54

*The Crucifixion: Studies of Details* 7 October
La Crucifixion. Etude de détails
Ink on paper 34.5 × 51.5
Musée national Picasso–Paris.
Dation Pablo Picasso, 1979.
MP1083
[p.202, top] Not in Z.

*The Diver* 29 November
La Plongeuse
Etching on paper 19.4 × 14.8
Musée national Picasso–Paris.
Dation Pablo Picasso, 1979.
MP2249
[p.221, left]

*The Diver* 29 November
La Plongeuse
Etching on paper 17 × 12.8
Musée nationai Picasso–Paris.
Dation Pablo Picasso, 1979.
MP2247
[p.221, right] G/B 277 A.a

*The Diver* 29 November
La Plongeuse
Etching on paper 32.9 × 21.8
Musée national Picasso–Paris.
Dation Pablo Picasso, 1979.
MP2250
[p.222] G/B 277 B.a

*The Dream* 24 January
Le Rêve
Oil paint on canvas 12.9 × 96.8
Private collection
[p.57] Z.VII, 364

*The Dreamer* July
Nu couché aux fleurs
Oil paint on canvas 101.3 × 93.3
The Metropolitan Museum of Art, New York. The Mr and Mrs Klaus G. Perls Collection, 1997
[p.138; not exhibited] Z.VII, 407

*The Embrace* 1932
L'Etreinte
Charcoal on silk paper 28 × 38
Fundación Almine y Bernard Ruiz-Picasso para el Arte
[p.170] Not in Z.

*Figures by the Sea I* 2 January
Figures au bord de la mer I
Oil paint and chalk on canvas 130 × 97
Museo Nacional Centro de Arte Reina Sofía, Madrid
[p.45] Not in Z.

*Flute Player and Reclining Nude* 1 September
Joueuse de flûte et femme allongée
Oil paint and ink on paper 34.5 × 50.5
Private collection
[p.188] Z.VIII, 34

*Flute Player and Reclining Nude* 1 September
joueur de flûte et nu couché
Ink, gouache and oil paint on paper 34.5 × 50.5
Private collection
[p.189] Z.VIII, 39

*Flute Player and Reclining Nude* 8 October
Joueur de flûte et nu allongé
Graphite on paper 25.5 × 37.2
Musée national Picasso–Paris.
Dation Pablo Picasso, 1979.
MP1084
[p.204] Z.VIII, 38

*Flute Player and Seated Nude* 4 October
Deux femmes nues dont l'une jouant de la diaule
Oil paint and ink on paper 34.5 × 50.5
Musée national Picasso–Paris.
Dation Pablo Picasso, 1979.
MP1077
[p.200] Z.VIII, 43

*Flute Player and Three Female Nudes* 21 July
Flûtiste et trois femmes nues
Drypoint on paper 45.6 × 57.9
Musée national – Picasso, Paris.
Dation Pablo Picasso, 1979.
MP2481
[p.166, top] G/B 258 A

*Flute Player and Three Female Nudes* 21 July
Flûtiste et trois femmes nues
Drypoint on paper 38.4 × 50.4
Musée national – Picasso, Paris.
Achat 1982. MP1982-70
[p.166, bottom; not exhibited] G/B 258 B.a

*Fruit Bowl and Guitar* 11 February
Compotier et guitare
Oil paint on canvas 97 × 130
Nahmad Collection, Monaco
[p.60] Z.VII, 354

*Girl before a Mirror* 14 March
Jeune Fille devant un miroir
Oil paint on canvas 162.3 × 130.2
The Museum of Modern Art, New York. Gift of Mrs Simon Guggenheim, 1937
[p.101] Z.VII, 379

*Hand* 1932
Main
Plaster 37 × 19.5 × 11
Musée national Picasso–Paris.
Dation Pablo Picasso, 1979.
MP323
[p.171] S. 222

*Head of a Woman* 1932
Tête de femme
Plaster 65 × 43 × 25
Musée national Picasso–Paris.
Dation Pablo Picasso, 1979.
MP295
[p.90] S.120.I

*Marie-Thérèse in a Pensive Mood* 15 November
Marie-Thérèse pensive
Oil paint on wood 63.8 × 47.2
Private collection
[p.216] Not in Z.

*The Mirror* 12 March
Le Miroir
Oil paint on canvas 130 × 96.8
Private collection
[p.97] Z.VII, 378

*Nude in a Black Armchair* 9 March
Nu au fauteuil noir
Oil paint on canvas 162 × 123
Private collection, USA
[p.95] Z.VII, 377

*Nude, Green Leaves and Bust* 8 March
Femme nue, feuilles et buste
Oil paint on canvas 162 × 130
Private collection
[p.93] Not in Z.

*Nude before a Mirror* 26 June
Nu devant la glace
Oil paint on canvas 27 × 35
Bettina and Donald L. Bryant, Jr.
[p.134] Z.VII, 388

*Nude in front of a Mirror* 26 June
Femme entendue les bras sous la nuque sur un lit rouge
Oil paint on canvas 27 × 35
Private collection
[p.135] Not in Z.

*Nude with Necklace* July–October
Nu au collier
Oil paint on canvas 92 × 73
European private collection, courtesy Libby Howie
[p.142; not exhibited] Z.VIII, 69

*Nude Woman in a Red Armchair* 27 July
Femme nue dans un fauteuil rouge
Oil paint on canvas 129.9 × 97.2
Tate. Purchased 1953
[p.137] Z.VII, 395

*On the Beach. Three Bathers* 23 November
Sur le plage. Trois baigneuses
Etching on paper 25.6 × 7.9
Musée national Picasso–Paris.
Dation Pablo Picasso, 1979.
MP2217
[p.220; not exhibited] G/B 268 A.b

*The Rape* 21 November
Le Viol
Etching on paper 17.6 × 12.7
Musée national Picasso–Paris.
Dation Pablo Picasso, 1979.
MP2204
[p.218] G/B 264 A.a

*Reading* 9 January
La Lecture
Oil paint on wood 65.5 × 51
Private collection
[p.48] Z.VII, 363

*Reading* 2 January
La Lecture
Oil paint on canvas 130 × 97.5
Musée national Picasso–Paris.
Dation Pablo Picasso, 1979.
MP137
[p.46] Z.VII, 358

*Reclining Nude* 2 April
Femme nue couchée
Oil paint on canvas 129.5 × 162
Private collection
[p.109] Z.VIII, 331

*Reclining Nude* 4 April
Nu couché
Oil paint on canvas 130 × 161.7
Musée national Picasso–Paris.
Dation Pablo Picasso, 1979.
MP142
[p.111] Z.VII, 332

*Reclining Nude* 19 June
Femme couchée
Oil paint on canvas 38 × 46
Centre Pompidou, Paris. Musée national d'art moderne / Centre de création industrielle.
Donation Louise at Michel Leiris, 1984
[p.133] Not in Z.

*Reclining Nude* 19 June
Nu couché
Oil paint on paper 26.5 × 31.5
Musée national Picasso-Paris.
Dation Pablo Picasso, 1979.
MP1070
[Not illustrated] Z.VII, 386

*Reclining Nude* 26 June
Femme couchée
Oil paint on lid of cardboard box 10.5 × 19.3 × 3.5
Centre Pompidou, Paris. Musée national d'art moderne / Centre de création industrielle.
Donation Louise et Michel Leiris, 1984
[p.134] Not in Z.

*Reclining Nude with a Necklace* 18 June
Femme nue couchée au collier
Oil paint on canvas 41 × 41
Private collection
[p.131; not exhibited] Z.VII, 383

*Reclining Nude Sunbathing on the Beach* 25 March
Femme étendue au soleil sur la plage
Oil and charcoal on tracing paper 24.4 × 35.2
Musée national Picasso–Paris.
Dation Pablo Picasso, 1979.
MP1069
[p.102, top] Z.VII, 356

*Reclining Woman* 6 August
Femme couchée
Oil paint on canvas 23.8 × 34.9
McNay Art Museum. Jeanne and Irving Mathews Collection
[p.139; not exhibited] Not in Z.

*Reclining Woman on the Beach* 25 March
Femme étendue sur la plage
Oil and charcoal on canvas 130 × 162
Private collection
[p.102, bottom] Z.VII, 355

*Reclining Woman on the Beach* 26 March
Femme nue couchée au soleil sur la plage
Oil paint on canvas 24 × 33
Fundación Almine y Bernard Ruiz-Picasso para el Arte
[p.103, top] Not in Z.

*Reclining Woman on the Beach* 26 March
Femme étendue sur la plage
Oil paint on canvas 22 × 27
Private collection
[p.103, middle] Not in Z.

*Reclining Woman on the Beach* 26 March
Femme étendue sur la plage
Oil paint on canvas 22 × 27
Private collection
[p.103, bottom; not exhibited] Not in Z.

*Reclining Woman and Flute Player* 9 October
Femme allongée, joueur de flûte
Graphite on paper 24.5 × 32.5
Private collection
[p.205]

*The Rescue* 20 November
Le Sauvetage
Oil paint on canvas 35 × 27
Grace, Sean, Lauren, and David Carpenter
[p.208] Z.VIII, 68

*The Rescue* 20 November
Le Sauvetage
Oil paint on canvas 130.5 × 97.5
Fondation Beyeler, Riehen/ Basel, Sammlung Beyeler
[p.217] Z.VIII, 66

*The Rescue* November
Le Sauvetage
Oil paint in canvas 35 × 27
Private collection
[p.223; not exhibited] Z.VIII, 63

*The Rescue* December
Le Sauvetage
Graphite on paper 11.5 × 16
Musée national Picasso–Paris.
Dation Pablo Picasso, 1979.
MP1086 (r)
[p.227; not exhibited] Z.VIII, 65

*The Rescue* 22 December
Le Sauvetage
Oil paint on canvas 97.2 × 130
Private collection
[p.231] Z.VIII, 64

*The Rescue of the Drowned Woman I* 17 December
Le Sauvetage de la noyée I
Etching on paper 34.2 × 24
Musée national Picasso–Paris.
dation Pablo Picasso, 1979.
MP2226
[p.228] G/B 272 A.a

*The Rescue of the Drowned Woman II* 18 December
Le Sauvetage de la noyée II
Etching on paper 25.7 × 34.2
Musée national Picasso – Paris.
Dation Pablo Picasso, 1979.
MP2232
[p.229] G/B 273 A.a

*The Rescue of the Drowned Woman III* 18 December
Le Sauvetage de la noyée III
Etching on paper 25.8 × 35.1
Musée national Picasso–Paris.
Dation Pablo Picasso, 1979.
MP2238
[p.229] G/B 274 A.a

*Rest* 22 January
Le Repos
Oil paint on canvas 162 × 130
Private collection
[p.54] Z.VII, 361

*Rest* 17 May
Le Repos
Oil paint on canvas 27.3 × 46.3
Collection of Mr Giancarlo Giammetti, London
[p.115] Not in Z.VII

*Sculpture of a Head* 1932
Sculpture d'une tête
Charcoal on prepared fabric 92 × 73 × 2.5
Fondation Beyeler, Riehen/ Basel, Sammlung Beyeler
[p.73] Not in Z.

*Seated Woman with Elbow on Knee* 1932
*Femme assise au coude appuyé sur le genou*
Oil paint on canvas 146 × 114
Private collection
[p.145; not exhibited] Not in Z.

*Seated Woman in a Red Armchair* 30 January
Femme assise dans un fauteuil rouge
Oil paint on canvas 130 × 97.5
Musée national Picasso–Paris.
Dation Pablo Picasso, 1979.
MP139
[p.59] Not in Z.

*Seated Woman by a Window* 30 October
Femme assise près d'une fenêtre
Oil paint on canvas 146 × 113.9
Earth Light Foundation, Vaduz
[p.215] Not in Z.

*Sleep* 23 January
Le Sommeil
Oil paint on canvas 130 × 97
Private collection
[p.55] Z.VII, 362

*Sleep* 18 August
La Sieste
Oil paint on canvas 97 × 130
Fundación Almine y Bernard Ruiz-Picasso para el Arte.
En dépôt temporaire au Museo Picasso Málaga
[p.143] Not in Z.

*Sleeping Nude* 13 March
La Dormeuse (Femme nue couchée)
Charcoal and oil paint on canvas 130 × 162
Private collection
[p.99; not exhibited] Not in Z.

*Sleeping Nude* 30 July
Nu endormi
Charcoal on gessoed canvas 97 × 130
Private collection, courtesy Gagosian Gallery
[p.167] Not in Z.

*Sleeping Nude with Blonde Hair*
21 December
Femme couchée à la mêche blonde
Oil paint on canvas 130 × 162
Nahmad Collection, Monaco
[p.230] Not in Z.

*Sleeping Woman* 1932
Femme nue couchée
Charcoal on canvas 97.2 × 130.2
Private collection
[p.169] Not in Z.

*Sleeping Woman by a Mirror*
14 January
La Dormeuse au miroir
Oil paint on panel 130 × 97
Nahmad Collection, Monaco
[p.51] Z.VII 360

*Still Life: Bust, Cup and Palette*
3 March
Nature morte: buste, coupe et palette
Oil paint on canvas 130.5 × 97.5
Musée national Picasso–Paris.
Dation Pablo Picasso, 1979.
MP140
[p.91] Not in Z.

*Still Life with Fruit Bowl and Mandolin* 13 February
Compotier et mandoline
Oil paint on canvas 97 × 130
Private collection
[p.61; not exhibited] Z.VII, 375

*Still Life with Tulips* 2 March
Nature morte aux tulipes
Oil paint on canvas 130 × 97
Private collection
[p.89] Z.VII, 376

*Still Life at the Window*
18 January
Nature morte à la fenêtre
Oil paint on canvas 130 × 162
Private collection
[p.53] Z.VII, 374

*Study for a Mandolin Player*
2 February
Etude pour une joueuse de mandoline
Charcoal and oil paint on canvas 130 × 97
Private collection
[p.162] Not in Z.

*Swimmer* 21 November
Nageuse
Oil paint on canvas 97 × 130
Private collection
[p.168; not exhibited]. Not in Z.

*Swimmer* 1932
Nageuse
Oil paint on canvas 22 × 27
Fundación Almine y Bernard Ruiz-Picasso para el Arte
[p.141] Not in Z.

*Swimmers with a Beach Ball*
6 September
Baigneuses au ballon
Oil paint on canvas 27 × 35
Private collection
[p.192, bottom] Not in Z.

*The Three Bathers*
15 September
Les Trois Baigneuses
Oil paint on canvas 27 × 41
Nahmad Collection, Monaco
[p.194, top] Not in Z.

*Three Women Playing on the Seashore*
15 September
Trois femmes jouant au bord de la mer
Oil paint on canvas 27 × 35
Fundación Almine y Bernard Ruiz-Picasso para el Arte
[p.194, bottom] Not in Z.

*Two Women on the Beach with Swimming Cabin* 4 September
Deux femmes sur la plage, avec cabine de bain
Oil paint on canvas 22 × 27
Private collection
[p.191] Not in Z.

*View of Boisgeloup* 29 March
Vue de Boisgeloup
Oil paint on canvas 27 × 41
Fundación Almine y Bernard Ruiz-Picasso para el Arte
[p.106] Z.VII, 340

*Village in the Rain. Rainbow*
6 May
Village sous la pluie. Arc-en-ciel
Oil paint on canvas 27 × 46
Private collection
[Not illustrated] Not in Z.

*Woman on the Beach* 28 March
Nu sur la plage
Oil paint on canvas 33 × 40
The Penrose Collection
[p.105] Z.VII, 353

*Woman with a Flower* 10 April
Femme à la fleur
Oil paint on canvas 162 × 130
Private collection
[p.112; not exhibited] Z.VII, 381

*Woman with a Flower* April
Femme à la fleur
Charcoal on canvas 162 × 130
Fundación Almine y Bernard Ruiz-Picasso para el Arte
[p.163] Not in Z.

*Woman with Flower Writing*
April
Femme à la fleur écrivant
Charcoal on canvas 97 × 130
Private collection
[p.165] Not in Z.

*Woman in a Red Armchair*
27 January
Femme au fauteuil rouge
Oil paint on canvas 130.2 × 97
Musée national Picasso–Paris.
Dation Pablo Picasso, 1979.
MP138
[p.58] Z.VII, 330

*Woman Sleeping* 16 May
Femme endormie
Oil paint on canvas 46 × 46
Private collection
[p.114] Not in Z.

*Woman Sleeping on a Red Cushion*
18 June
Dormeuse au coussin rouge
Oil paint on canvas 33 × 55
Private collection
[p.130] Not in Z.

*Woman in a Yellow Armchair*
April
Femme dans un fauteuil jaune
Oil paint on canvas 116 × 89
Private collection
[p.113] Z.VII, 380

*Women Playing with a Ball on the Beach* 6 September
Femmes jouant au ballon sur la plage
Oil paint on canvas 19 × 24
Private collection
[p.192, top] Not in Z.

*Women Playing with a Ball on the Beach* 4 December
Femmes jouant à la balle sur la plage
Oil paint on canvas 81 × 100
Private collection
[p.225] Not in Z.

*The Yellow Belt* 6 January
La Ceinture jaune
Oil paint on canvas 130 × 97
Nahmad Collection, Monaco
[p.47] Z.VII, 357

*Young Woman with Mandolin*
10 January
Jeune Fille à la mandoline
Oil paint on board
83.8 × 66.9 × 63.5
The University of Michigan Museum of Art, Ann Arbor, Michigan. Gift of The Carey Walker Foundation
[p.49] Z.VII, 359

**1931–2**

*Eye*
Oeil
Plaster 7 × 11 × 3
Private collection
[p.171] S.122

*Head of a Woman*
Tête de femme
Bronze 128.5 × 54.5 × 62.5
Musée national Picasso–Paris .
Dation Pablo Picasso, 1979.
MP302
[Not illustrated] S.133.II

**1931**

*Bather*
Baigneuse
Plaster 40.5 × 13.2 × 31.5
Musée national Picasso–Paris.
Dation Pablo Picasso, 1979.
MP303
[p.146] S.113.I

*Bust of a Woman*
Buste de femme
Cement 78 × 44.5 × 50
Musée national Picasso–Paris.
Dation Pablo Picasso, 1979.
MP299
[p.75] S.131.III: cement cast after S.131, Ia

*Bust of a Woman*
Buste de femme
Plaster 62.5 × 28 × 41.5
Musée national Picasso–Paris.
Dation Pablo Picasso, 1979.
MP293
[p.74 right] S.111.I

*Head of a Woman*
Tête de femme
Plaster 71.5 × 41 × 33
Musée national Picasso–Paris.
Dation Pablo Picasso, 1979.
MP291
[p.74, left] S.110.I

*Head of a Woman*
Tête de femme de profil
Bronze. Unique cast
68.5 × 60 × 9
Musée national Picasso–Paris.
Dation Pablo Picasso, 1979.
MP297
[p.88] S.130.II.

*The Sculptor* 7 December
Le Sculpteur
Oil paint on plywood 128.5 × 96
Musée national Picasso–Paris.
Dation Pablo Picasso, 1979.
MP135
[p.39] Z.VII, 346

*Seated Woman*
Femme assise
Plaster 35 × 23.2 × 30.5
Musée national Picasso–Paris.
Dation Pablo Picasso, 1979.
MP288
[p.38] S.105.I

*Woman with Dagger*
19–25 December
La Femme au stylet
Oil paint on canvas 46.5 × 61.5
Musée national Picasso–Paris.
Dation Pablo Picasso, 1979.
MP136
[p.41]. Not in Z.

*Woman in a Red Armchair*
25 December
Femme au fauteuil rouge
Oil paint on canvas 162 × 98
Fundación Almine y Bernard
Ruiz-Picasso para el Arte
[p.43] Not in Z.

**1929–30**
*Woman in the Garden*
1929–30
La Femme au jardin
Welded iron painted white
206 × 117 × 85
Musée national Picasso–Paris.
Dation Pablo Picasso, 1979.
MP267
[p.124] S.72.I

**1925**
*The Three Dancers*
Les Trois Danseuses
Oil paint on canvas
215.3 × 142.2
Tate. Purchased with a special
Grant-in-Aid and the Florence
Fox Bequest with assistance
from the Friends of the Tate
Gallery and the Contemporary
Art Society 1965
[p.78] Z.V, 426

**1924**
*Paulo as a Harlequin*
Paulo en arlequin
Oil paint on canvas 130 × 97.5
Musée national Picasso–Paris.
Dation Pablo Picasso, 1979.
MP83
[p.129] Z.V, 178

**1923**
*Portrait of Olga*
Portrait d'Olga
Oil paint on canvas 33 × 24
Museo Picasso Málaga.
Depósito del Ministerio de
Cultura
[Not illustrated] Z.IV, 438

**1921**
*Portrait of Paul*
Portrait de Paul
Oil paint on canvas 33.5 × 27
Fundación Almine y Bernard
Ruiz-Picasso para el Arte
[Not Illustrated] Z.IV, 434

*Child with a Toy*
L'Enfant au jouet
Charcoal, pastel and gouache
on paper 103.5 × 73.5
Fundación Almine y Bernard
Ruiz-Picasso para el Arte
[Not illustrated] Z.V, 52

**1918**
*Portrait of Olga in an Armchair*
Spring 1918
Portrait d'Olga dans un fauteuil
Oil paint on canvas 130 × 88.8
Musée national Picasso–Paris.
Dation Pablo Picasso, 1979.
MP55
[p.129] Z.III, 83

**1909–10**
*Seated Nude*
Femme nue assise
Oil paint on canvas 92.1 × 73
Tate. Purchased 1949
[Not illustrated] Z.2a, 201

**c.1905**
*Girl in a Chemise*
Jeune Femme en chemise
Oil paint on canvas 72.7 × 60
Tate. Bequeathed by C. Frank
Stoop 1933
[Not illustrated] Z.I, 307

**1901**
*Self-Portrait*
Late 1901
Autoportrait
Oil paint on canvas 81 × 60
Musée national Picasso–Paris.
Dation Pablo Picasso, 1979. MP4
[Not illustrated] Z.I, 91

**Sketchbooks used during 1932**
*Sketchbook no.40*
25 January 1932 – 1 May 1934
*Carnet no.40*
Ink and graphite on 38 sheets of
paper 29 × 27
Musée national Picasso–Paris.
Dation en 1990. MP1990-110
[pp.98, 172–5]

*Sketchbook no.17*
22 February 1930 – 20 April
1932
*Carnet no.17*
Ink on paper 20.5 × 24.5
Fundación Almine y Bernard
Ruiz-Picasso para el Arte
[pp.156–61]

## List of Figure Illustrations

This list includes artworks that appear as supplementary figure illustrations. It does not include documentary photographs or reproductions in publications. Works are listed chronologically by artist.

## Credits

### Copyright

All artworks by Pablo Picasso © Succession Picasso/DACS, London 2018

© The Cecil Beaton Studio Archive at Sotheby's 12, 30 top and bottom left, 32–3, 76

© Estate Brassaï – RMN-Grand Palais 15 right, 18, 34–7, 65, 66 bottom, 69 bottom right, 70, 72, 132, 140 right, 184–7, 216 bottom, inside front and back flap

© Estate of Albert Eugene Gallatin 52

© Archives Jean Painlevé, Paris 110

© Estate of Rogi André 118 top

© Salvador Dalí, Fundació Gala-Salvador Dalí, DACS 2018 179

© Man Ray Trust/ADAGP, Paris and DACS, London 2018 234

Henri Matisse © Succession H. Matisse / DACS 2018 82–4

© Estate of Margaret Scolari Barr 116–17, 118 bottom, 121 bottom, 126 bottom left, 127, 128

### Photographic credits

For archival images, the photographer is named in the accompanying caption whenever possible; if there is no attribution, their identity is unknown.

Maurice Aeschimann Photographe SA 135, 165, 193

AF archive / Alamy Stock Photo 25

© Archives Jean Painlevé, Paris 110

© Archives Maya Widmaier-Ruiz-Picasso 19, 42, 56, 146 top, 209–11, 243

© Archives Olga Ruiz-Picasso, Fundación Almine y Bernard Ruiz-Picasso para el Arte Photographer unknown, all rights reserved 23 bottom, 30 bottom right, 238, 244, 245

© 2017. The Art Institute of Chicago / Art Resource, NY/ Scala, Florence 150

Colección de Arte ABANCA 179

Courtesy Axel Vervoordt Gallery 168

Photo: © Basel-Riehen, Fondation Beyeler 73, 181 top, 217

© The Cecil Beaton Studio Archive at Sotheby's 12, 30 top and bottom left, 32, 76

© Bridgeman Images 147

© Cahiers d'Art, Paris 21 right, 104

Photo © Centre Pompidou, MNAM-CCI, Dist. RMN-Grand Palais / Droits réservés 133, 134 bottom / Philippe Migeat 83, 234

Photo © Crane Kalman, London / Bridgeman Images 112

© 2018 Christie's Images Limited 93, 115

Photo © Christie's Images / Bridgeman Images 48, 61, 89, 97, 131, back cover image

Colmar, Musee d'Unterlinden. © 2017. Photo Scala, Florence 180 bottom

European Private Collection courtesy of Libby Howie 142

© FABA Photo: Eric Baudouin 141, 143; / Marc Domage 43, 103 top, 106, 163; / Hugard & Vanoverschelde Photography 156–61, 170, 194 bottom

Fondation Jean et Suzanne Planque, on deposit at the Musée Granet, Aix-en-Provence (inv. FJSP-998-129) © photo Luc Chessex 233

Courtesy Gagosian Gallery 54

Courtesy Gallery Helly Nahmad, London 47, 51, 60, 194 top, 214, 230

© Photographie Claude Germain 102, 103 centre, 189, 192 top, 227

© Photo: Patrick Goetelen / Courtesy Krugier Contemporain 53

Photo Béatrice Hatala 130, 145, 191, 192 bottom, 216 top

© Photo: Béatrice Hatala, Courtesy Gagosian 167

Jane Corking Collection, Toronto 118 top

© 2017 Kunsthaus Zürich 116–17, 118 bottom, 121 bottom, 126 top and bottom left, 127, 128

© Photo: Rob McKeever 109

Collection of the McNay Art Museum, Jeanne and Irving Mathews Collection 139

Photo © The Metropolitan Museum of Art, Dist. RMN-Grand Palais / image of the MMA 138

Musées Royaux des Beaux-Arts, Brussels © 2017. Photo Scala, Florence 40

Colección Museo Nacional Centro de Arte Reina Sofía / Photographic Archives Museo 27 bottom, 45

The Museum of Modern Art Archives, New York. / Copyright: Unknown. Cat. no.: MA1245.6. 50 / Cat. no.: ARCH.1070.16. © 2017. Digital image, The Museum of Modern Art, New York / Scala, Florence 100

© 2017. Digital image, The Museum of Modern Art, New York / Scala, Florence 84, 101, 119, 121 top, 124 bottom, 126 bottom right, 152 top

National Galleries of Scotland. Long loan in 1994 105

© Photo: Ellen Page Wilson, Courtesy Pace Gallery 55, 99

© 2017. Photo The Philadelphia Museum of Art / Art Resource / Scala, Florence 152 bottom

Tom Powel Imaging, New York, courtesy Mitchell-Innes & Nash 134 top

Private collection front cover image, 57, 113, 205, 213

Photo © RMN-Grand Palais (Musée national Picasso–Paris) / image RMN-GP 15, 17, 18, 23 top, 33, 34–7, 52, 65–72, 85, 132, 140 right, 151, 154, 200, 216 bottom, inside front and back flaps; / Jean-Gilles Berizzi 91; / Adrien Didierjean 75, 129 right; / Béatrice Hatala 38–9, 74, 90, 146 bottom, 195, 198, 202 bottom; / Thierry Le Mage 98, 102 top, 108, 153, 154 bottom, 172–6; / René-Gabriel Ojéda 111; / Mathieu Rabeau 41, 46, 58–9, 88, 107, 124 top, 129 left, 125, 166, 171 bottom, 180 top, 196–7, 199, 201, 202 top, 203, 204, 207, 218–22, 224–6, 228–9; / Franck Raux 154 top

Estate of David Rockefeller 82

The Paul Rosenberg Archives, New York 16

Courtesy of Richard Gray Gallery. Private collection, USA 95

Image courtesy of Sotheby's 215

Photograph courtesy of Sotheby's, Inc. © 2017 114, 223, 231

© Tate, 2018 78, 86, 136–7, 140 left; / Samuel Cole 178, 184–7; / Joe Humphrys 208

© 2002 Topham / AP 26 top

University of Michigan Museum of Art, Gift of The Carey Walker Foundation, 1994/1.69 49

Serge Veignant, Paris 103 bottom

Photo: Zarko Vijatovic 162, 171 top, 188

Wide World / ullstein bild / Getty Images 24

World History Archive / Alamy Stock Photo 14

© Nancy Whyte Fine Arts, New York 169

© Zentralbibliothek Zürich 21 left

Photo: Jens Ziehe. © 2017. Photo Scala, Florence/bpk, Bildagentur fuer Kunst, Kultur und Geschichte, Berlin 212

*The publishers have made every effort to trace all the relevant copyright holders and apologise for omissions that may have been made.*

## Index

Page numbers in *italic* type refer to illustrations

**Supporting Tate**

Tate relies on a large number of supporters – individuals, foundations, companies and public sector sources – to enable it to deliver its programme of activities, both on and off its gallery sites. This support is essential in order for Tate to acquire works of art for the Collection, run education, outreach and exhibition programmes, care for the Collection in storage and enable art to be displayed, both digitally and physically, inside and outside Tate. Please contact us at:

Development Office
Tate
Millbank
London SW1P 4RG
Tel: +44 (0)20 7887 4900
Fax: +44 (0)20 7887 8098

Tate Americas Foundation
520 West 27 Street Unit 404
New York, NY 10001
USA
Tel: 001 212 643 2818
Fax: 001 212 643 1001

Donations, no matter the size, are gratefully received, either to support particular areas of interest, or to contribute to general activity costs.

**Legacies**
A legacy to Tate may take the form of a residual share of an estate, a specific cash sum or item of property such as a work of art. Legacies to Tate are free of inheritance tax, and help to secure a strong future for the Collection and galleries. For further information please contact the Development Office.

**Offers in lieu of tax**
Inheritance Tax can be satisfied by transferring to the Government a work of art of outstanding importance. In this case the amount of tax is reduced, and it can be made a condition of the offer that the work of art is allocated to Tate. Please contact us for details.

**Tate Members**
Tate Members enjoy unlimited free admission throughout the year to all exhibitions at Tate, as well as a number of other benefits such as exclusive use of our Members' Rooms and a free annual subscription to *Tate Etc*. Whilst enjoying the exclusive privileges of membership, members also help secure Tate's position at the very heart of British and modern art. Members support actively contributes to new purchases of important art, ensuring that Tate's collection continues to be relevant and comprehensive, as well as funding projects in London, Liverpool and St Ives that increase access and understanding for everyone.

**Tate Patrons**
Tate Patrons share a passion for art and are committed to supporting Tate on an annual basis. The Patrons help enable the acquisition of works across Tate's broad collecting remit, support the staging of major exhibitions in the galleries, and also give their support to vital conservation, learning and research projects. The scheme provides a forum for Patrons to share their interest in art and meet curators, artists and one another in an enjoyable environment through a regular programme of events. These events take place both at Tate and beyond and encompass curator-led exhibition tours, visits to artists' studios and private collections, art trips both in the UK and abroad, and access to art fairs. The scheme welcomes supporters from outside the UK, giving the programme a truly international scope. For more information, please contact the Patrons Office on +44(0)20 7887 8740 or at patrons.office@tate.org.uk.

**Corporate Membership**
Corporate Membership at Tate Modern, Tate Britain and Tate Liverpool offers companies opportunities for corporate entertaining and the chance for a wide variety of employee benefits. These include special private views, special access to paying exhibitions, out-of-hours visits and tours, invitations to VIP events and talks at members' offices.

**Corporate Investment**
Tate has developed a range of imaginative partnerships with the corporate sector, ranging from international interpretation and exhibition programmes to local outreach and staff development programmes. We are particularly known for high-profile business to business marketing initiatives and employee benefit packages. Please contact the Corporate Partnerships team for further details.

**Charity Details**
The Tate Gallery is an exempt charity; the Museums & Galleries Act 1992 added the Tate Gallery to the list of exempt charities defined in the 1960 Charities Act. Tate Members is a registered charity (number 313021). Tate Foundation is a registered charity (number 1085314).

**Tate Americas Foundation**
Tate Americas Foundation is an independent charity based in New York that supports the work of Tate in the United Kingdom. It receives full tax exempt status from the IRS under section 501(c)(3) allowing United States taxpayers to receive tax deductions on gifts towards annual membership programmes, exhibitions, scholarship and capital projects. For more information please contact the Tate Americas Foundation office.



**Tate Modern Donors to the Founding Capital Campaign**
29th May 1961 Charitable Trust
Alan Cristea Gallery
AMP
The Annenberg Foundation
Arts Council England
The Asprey Family Charitable Foundation
Lord and Lady Attenborough
The Baring Foundation
Ron Beller and Jennifer Moses
Alex and Angela Bernstein
David and Janice Blackburn
Mr and Mrs Anthony Bloom
BNP Paribas
Mr and Mrs Pontus Bonnier
Lauren and Mark Booth
Mr and Mrs John Botts
Frances and John Bowes
Ivor Braka
Mr and Mrs James Brice
The British Land Company plc
Donald L Bryant Jr Family
Melva Bucksbaum
Cazenove & Co
CGU plc
Clifford Chance
The Clore Duffield Foundation
Edwin C Cohen
The John S Cohen Foundation
Ronald and Sharon Cohen
Sadie Coles
Carole and Neville Conrad
Giles and Sonia Coode-Adams
Douglas Cramer
Thomas Dane
Michel and Hélène David-Weill
Julia W Dayton
Gilbert de Botton
Pauline Denyer-Smith and Paul Smith
Sir Harry and Lady Djanogly
The Drapers' Company
Energis Communications
English Heritage
English Partnerships
The Eranda Foundation
Esmée Fairbairn Charitable Trust
Donald and Doris Fisher
Richard B and Jeanne Donovan Fisher
The Fishmongers' Company
Freshfields Bruckhaus Deringer
Friends of the Tate Gallery
Bob and Kate Gavron
Giancarlo Giammetti
Alan Gibbs
Mr and Mrs Edward Gilhuly
GKR
GLG Partners
Helyn and Ralph Goldenberg
Goldman Sachs
The Horace W Goldsmith Foundation
The Worshipful Company of Goldsmiths
Lydia and Manfred Gorvy
Noam and Geraldine Gottesman
Pehr and Christina Gyllenhammar
Mimi and Peter Haas
The Worshipful Company of Haberdashers
Hanover Acceptances Limited
The Headley Trust
Mr and Mrs André Hoffmann
Anthony and Evelyn Jacobs
Jay Jopling
Mr and Mrs Karpidas
Howard and Lynda Karshan
Peter and Maria Kellner
Madeleine Kleinwort
Brian and Lesley Knox
Pamela and C Richard Kramlich
Mr and Mrs Henry R Kravis
Irene and Hyman Kreitman
The Kresge Foundation
Catherine and Pierre Lagrange
The Lauder Foundation – Leonard and Evelyn Lauder Fund
Lazard Brothers & Co., Limited
Leathersellers' Company Charitable Fund
Edward and Agnès Lee
Lehman Brothers
Lex Service Plc
Ruth and Stuart Lipton
Anders and Ulla Ljungh
The Frank Lloyd Family Trusts
London & Cambridge Properties Limited
London Electricity plc, EDF Group
Mr and Mrs George Loudon
Mayer, Brown, Rowe & Maw
Viviane and James Mayor
Ronald and Rita McAulay
The Mercers' Company
The Meyer Foundation
The Millennium Commission
Anthony and Deirdre Montagu
The Monument Trust
Mori Building, Ltd
Mr and Mrs M D Moross
Guy and Marion Naggar
Peter and Eileen Norton, The Peter Norton Family Foundation
Maja Oeri and Hans Bodenmann
Sir Peter and Lady Osborne
William A Palmer
Mr Frederik Paulsen
Pearson plc
The Pet Shop Boys
The Nyda and Oliver Prenn Foundation
Prudential plc
Railtrack plc
The Rayne Foundation
Reuters

Sir John and Lady Ritblat
Rolls-Royce plc
Barrie and Emmanuel Roman
Lord and Lady Rothschild
The Dr Mortimer and Theresa Sackler Foundation
J Sainsbury plc
Ruth and Stephan Schmidheiny
Schroders
Mr and Mrs Charles Schwab
David and Sophie Shalit
Belle Shenkman Estate
William Sieghart
Peter Simon
Mr and Mrs Sven Skarendahl
London Borough of Southwark
The Foundation for Sports and the Arts
Mr and Mrs Nicholas Stanley
The Starr Foundation
The Jack Steinberg Charitable Trust
Charlotte Stevenson
Hugh and Catherine Stevenson
John Studzinski
David and Linda Supino
The Government of Switzerland
Carter and Mary Thacher
Insinger Townsley
UBS
UBS Warburg
David and Emma Verey
Dinah Verey
The Vintners' Company
Clodagh and Leslie Waddington
Robert and Felicity Waley-Cohen
Wasserstein, Perella & Co., Inc.
Gordon D Watson
The Weston Family
Mr and Mrs Stephen Wilberding
Michael S Wilson
Poju and Anita Zabludowicz
*and those who wish to remain anonymous*

**Donors to The Tate Modern Project**
Artist Rooms Foundation
Abigail and Joseph Baratta
Blavatnik Family Foundation
Lauren and Mark Booth
The Deborah Loeb Brice Foundation
The Lord Browne of Madingley, FRS, FREng
John and Michael Chandris, and Christina Chandris
James Chanos
Paul Cooke
The Roger De Haan Charitable Trust
Ago Demirdjian and Tiqui Atencio Demirdjian
Department for Digital, Culture, Media and Sport
George Economou
Stefan Edlis and Gael Neeson
English Partnerships
Mrs Donald B. Fisher
Jeanne Donovan Fisher
Mala Gaonkar
The Ghandehari Foundation
Thomas Gibson in memory of Anthea Gibson
Lydia and Manfred Gorvy
The Granville-Grossman Bequest
The Hayden Family Foundation
Peter and Maria Kellner
Madeleine Kleinwort
Catherine Lagrange
Pierre Lagrange
London Development Agency
LUMA Foundation
Allison and Howard W. Lutnick
Donald B. Marron
Scott and Suling Mead
Sami and Hala Mnaymneh
Anthony and Deirdre Montagu
Mori Building Co Ltd
Elisabeth Murdoch
Eyal Ofer Family Foundation
Maureen Paley
Simon and Midge Palley
Stephen and Yana Peel
Daniel and Elizabeth Peltz
Catherine Petitgas
Franck Petitgas
The Roman Family
The Dr Mortimer and Theresa Sackler Foundation
The Sackler Trust
Lily Safra
Stephan Schmidheiny Family / Daros Collection
Helen and Charles Schwab
London Borough of Southwark
John J Studzinski, CBE
Tate Americas Foundation
Tate Members
Julie-Anne Uggla
Lance Uggla
Viktor Vekselberg
Nina and Graham Williams
Manuela and Iwan Wirth
The Wolfson Foundation
*and those who wish to remain anonymous*

**Tate Modern Benefactors and Major Donors**
We would like to acknowledge and thank the following benefactors who have supported Tate Modern prior to September 2017.
Mr Roman Abramovich
Alireza Abrishamchi
Abrishamchi Family Collection
Tomma Abts
Mohammad and Mahera Abu Ghazaleh
Acquavella Galleries, Inc.
Aigboje and Ofovwe Aig-Imoukhuede
Raad Zeid Al-Hussein
Dilyara Allakhverdova and Elchin Safarov
Olga de Amaral
The Fagus Anstruther Memorial Trust in memory of the late Hartley Ramsden and Margot Eates
Art Fund
Art Mentor Foundation Lucerne
Arts and Humanities Research Council
Arts Council England
The Artworkers Retirement Society
Celia and Edward Atkin, CBE
Axel Vervoordt Gallery
Roger Ballen
Lionel Barber
The Estate of Peter and Caroline Barker-Mill
Beckett Fonden
David Alfredo Benatar
Big Lottery Fund
Anton and Lisa Bilton
Bloomberg Philanthropies
Anne Donovan Bodnar
Oliver Bolitho
The Charlotte Bonham-Carter Charitable Trust
Mr John Botts
Estate of Louise Bourgeois
Frank Bowling, Rachel Scott, Benjamin and Sacha Bowling, Marcia and Iona Scott
Alan Bowness
Pierre Brahm
The Estate of Dr Marcella Louis Brenner
The Deborah Loeb Brice Foundation
Rory and Elizabeth Brooks Foundation
Beatrice Bulgari | In Between Art Film
Susan and John Burns
Piers Butler
Jamal Butt
Carl Freedman Gallery / Counter Editions, London
Mr and Mrs Nicolas Cattelain
The Estate of Marigold Ann Chamberlin
Priti Chandaria
Trustees of the Chantrey Bequest
The Chaplaincy to the Arts and Recreation in North East England, Durham
Judy Chicago in honour of Frances Morris
The Clore Duffield Foundation
The Clothworkers' Foundation
R and S Cohen Foundation
Sadie Coles
Contemporary Art Society
The Ernest Cook Trust
Douglas S. Cramer
The Cranford Collection
Alan Cristea
Danish Ministry for Culture and The Embassy of Denmark, London
Darat al Funun - The Khalid Shoman Foundation
Dimitris Daskalopoulos
David Kordansky Gallery
Kate-Jane Davie
Tiqui Atencio Demirdjian and Ago Demirdjian
Department for Business, Innovation and Skills
Department for Digital, Culture, Media and Sport
The Estate of F.N. Dickins
Mr Paul Dickins
Braco Dimitrijevic
Anthony and Anne d'Offay
Joe and Marie Donnelly
Peter Dubens
The Easton Foundation
Lonti Ebers
Maryam and Edward Eisler
John Ellerman Foundation
Carla Emil and Richard Silverstein
Tracey Emin
Mr Mehmet Riza Erdem and Mrs Elif Erdem
European Union
The Estate of Maurice Farquharson
The Estate of Mary Fedden and Julian Trevelyan
Mr Paul Findlay
The Finnis Scott Foundation
Wendy Fisher
Dr. Kira and Neil Flanzraich, in honor of Anthony D'Offay and ARTIST ROOMS
Ford Foundation
Eric and Louise Franck
Freelands Foundation
The Estate of Lucian Freud
Froehlich Foundation, Stuttgart
Gagosian
Gaia Art Foundation, UK
Galeria Luisa Strina, São Paulo
Frank Gallipoli
Georg Geyer
Adrian Ghenie
Glenstone Foundation
The Estate of Kaveh Golestan, with assistance from Dr. Nina Ansari
Sir Nicholas and Lady Goodison
Antony Gormley
Lydia and Manfred Gorvy
The Granville-Grossman Bequest
Cornelia Grassi
Great Britain Sasakawa Foundation
Guaranty Trust Bank Plc
Calouste Gulbenkian Foundation
The Hakuta Family
Paul Hamlyn Foundation
Thomas Hartland-Mackie
Hauser & Wirth
Sanford Heller in Honour of Sir Nicholas Serota
Barbara Hepworth Estate
Heritage Lottery Fund
The Hintze Family Charitable Trust
Damien Hirst
David Hockney
Trustees of Lord Howard of Henderskelfe's Will Trust
Michael and Ali Hue-Williams
The Estate of Malcolm Hughes
Yvonne Alexandra Ike
The J Isaacs Charitable Trust
Yasuharu Ishikawa
Italian Cultural Institute
Amrita Jhaveri
Kikuji Kawada
Kiran Nadar Museum of Art
The Estate of Fay Elspeth Langford
The Leathersellers' Company Charitable Fund
Agnès and Edward Lee
Legacy Trust UK
The David M Leuschen Charitable Foundation in honor of Abigail and Joseph Baratta
The Leverhulme Trust
Dominique Lévy
Linyao Kiki Liu
Peter Louis and Chandru Ramchandani
Henry Luce Foundation
LUMA Foundation
Mace Foundation
The Manton Foundation
The Estate of Sir Edwin Manton
Marian Goodman Gallery
Marlborough Fine Art
Salman Matinfar
David Mayor
Lord McAlpine of West Green
Fergus McCaffrey
Susan McDonald
The Estate of Kenneth McGowan
The Andrew W. Mellon Foundation
The Paul Mellon Centre for Studies in British Art
Patrizia Memmo Ruspoli
Kamel Mennour
Gustav Metzger
Tobias Meyer and Mark Fletcher
Boris and Vita Mikhailov
Sir Geoffroy Millais
Mondriaan Fund, Amsterdam
Montana
Henry Moore Foundation
Les Morgan
Elisabeth Murdoch
National Heritage Memorial Fund
The National Trust
Novatek
Elisa Nuyten and David Dime
James O'Connell
Ordovás
Outset Contemporary Art Fund
Pace Gallery
Maureen Paley
The Pasmore Estate
Catherine Petitgas
Stanley Picker Trust
The Pivovarov Family
The Porter Foundation
David W. Posnett, OBE
Gilberto Pozzi
Massimo Prelz Oltramonti
Emilio Prini
Qatar Museums Authority
Maya and Ramzy Rasamny
The Robert Rauschenberg Foundation
The Redfern Gallery
Roman Family Collection
The Estate of Eugene and Penelope Rosenberg
Edward Ruscha
Keith and Katherine Sachs
SAHA – Supporting Contemporary Art from Turkey
The Estate of Simon Sainsbury
Salon 94
Nadia and Rajeeb Samdani
Fondazione Sandretto Re Rebaudengo
Julião Sarmento
John Schaeffer
Lisa Schiff
Gregor Schneider
Jake and Hélène Marie Shafran
Monir Shahroudy Farmanfarmaian
Stuart Shave
Jack Shear
Taryn Simon
Andy Simpkin
Lorna Simpson
The Estate of Sylvia Sleigh
Bob and Roberta Smith
Chris Steele-Perkins
Richard Stephens in memory of his father Brian Thomas Stephens
Emile Stipp
The Estate of Michael Stoddart
Norman and Norah Stone
Mercedes and Ian Stoutzker
Swiss Art Council – Pro Helvatia
Tamares Real Estate Holdings Inc. in collaboration with the Zabludowicz Collection
Aldo Tambellini
Dayana Tamendarova
Honus Tandijono
Tate 1897 Circle
Tate Africa Acquisitions Committee
Tate Americas Foundation
Tate Asia-Pacific Acquisitions Committee
Tate International Council
Tate Latin American Acquisitions Committee
Tate Members

Tate Middle East and North Africa Acquisitions Committee
Tate North American Acquisitions Committee
Tate Outreach Appeal
Tate Patrons
Tate Photography Acquisitions Committee
Tate Russia and Eastern Europe Acquisitions Committee
Tate South Asia Acquisitions Committee
Terra Foundation for American Art
The Estate of Mr Nicholas Themans
Thomas Gibson Fine Art
Wolfgang Tillmans
Tomasso Brothers Fine Art Ltd
Phillip Trevelyan
The Hon Robert H Tuttle and Mrs Maria Hummer-Tuttle
Luc Tuymans
Two Palms Press
V-A-C Foundation
Reginald Van Lee
Mercedes Vilardell
Marie-Louise von Motesiczky Charitable Trust
The Estate of Kenneth Ernest Webster
David and Maria Wilkinson
Jane and Michael Wilson
WME | IMG
The Lord Leonard and Lady Estelle Wolfson Foundation
Bill Woodrow
Erwin Wurm
The Estate of Mrs Monica Wynter
Mr. Xue Bing, the Co-Founder of New Century Art Foundation
Yuz Foundation
The Estate of Mr Anthony Zambra
*and those who wish to remain anonymous*

**Platinum Patrons**
Ghazwa Mayassi Abu-Suud
Maria Adonyeva
Mr Shane Akeroyd
Basil Alkazzi
Celia and Edward Atkin, CBE
Alex Beard
Beecroft Charitable Trust
Jacques Boissonnas
Natalia Bondarenko
Rory and Elizabeth Brooks
The Lord Browne of Madingley, FRS, FREng
Karen Cawthorn Argenio
Caroline Cole
Mr Stephane Custot
Pascale Decaux
Sophie Diedrichs-Cox
Mira Dimitrova and Luigi Mazzoleni
Valentina Drouin
Mr David Fitzsimons
The Flow Foundation
Edwin Fox Foundation
Stephen Friedman
Mrs Lisa Garrison
Hugh Gibson
Alexis and Anne-Marie Habib
David Herro
Misha and Theresa Horne
Mr and Mrs Yan Huo
Mr Phillip Hylander
Ms Natascha Jakobs
Mrs Gabrielle Jungels-Winkler
Maria and Peter Kellner
Judith Licht
Mr and Mrs Eskandar Maleki
Lali Marganiya
Scott and Suling Mead
Pierre Tollis and Alexandra Mollof
Mr Donald Moore
Mary Moore
Ife Obdeijn
Idan and Batia Ofer
Anthony and Jacqueline Orsatelli
Hussam Otaibi
Simon and Midge Palley (Chair)
Jan-Christoph Peters
Mr and Mrs Paul Phillips
Mr Gilberto and Mrs Daniela Pozzi
Frances Reynolds
Ralph Segreti
Jake and Hélène Marie Shafran
Andrée Shore
Maria and Malek Sukkar
Annie Vartivarian
Michael and Jane Wilson
Lady Wolfson of Marylebone
Chizuko Yoshida
Poju Zabludowicz and Anita Zabludowicz, OBE
Meng Zhou
*and those who wish to remain anonymous*

**Gold Patrons**
Yasmine Abou Adal
Eric Abraham
Fahad Alrashid
Shoshana Bloch
Elena Bowes
Louise and Charlie Bracken
Nicolò Cardi
Angela Choon
Melanie Clore
Beth and Michele Colocci
Harry G David
Ms Miel de Botton
Mr Frank Destribats
Mrs Maryam Eisler
Michael Herzog
Tiina Lee
Fiona Mactaggart
Paul and Alison Myners
Mr Francis Outred
Mathew Prichard
Garance Primat
Valerie Rademacher
Debra Reuben
Mr and Mrs Richard Rose
Almine Ruiz-Picasso
Carol Sellars
Mr and Mrs Stanley S Tollman
Nicholas Wingfield Digby
Manuela and Iwan Wirth
Barbara Yerolemou
*and those who wish to remain anonymous*

**Silver Patrons**
Sharis Alexandrian
Ryan Allen and Caleb Kramer
Gregor Alpers
Mrs Malgosia Alterman
The Anson Charitable Trust
Toby and Kate Anstruther
Mr and Mrs Zeev Aram
Mrs Charlotte Artus
Aspect Charitable Trust
Mrs Liz Astaire
Peter Barham
Mrs Jane Barker
Oliver Barker
Mr Edward Barlow
Victoria Barnsley, OBE
Jim Bartos
Dr Amelie Beier
Mr Harold Berg
Ms Anne Berthoud
Madeleine Bessborough
Janice Blackburn
David Blood and Beth Bisso
Bruno Boesch
Mrs Sofia Bogolyubov
Laurel Bonnyman
Mr Brian Boylan
Viscountess Bridgeman
Mr Dan Brooke
Ben and Louisa Brown
Beverley Buckingham
Michael Burrell
Mrs Marlene Burston
Piers Butler
Mrs Aisha Cahn
Sarah Caplin
Timothy and Elizabeth Capon
Mr Francis Carnwath and Ms Caroline Wiseman
Sir Roger Carr
Countess Castle Stewart
Roger Cazalet
Lord and Lady Charles Cecil
Dr Peter Chocian
Cynthia Clarry
Frank Cohen
Mrs Jane Collins
Dr Judith Collins
Terrence Collis
Mr and Mrs Oliver Colman
Mayte Comin
Carole and Neville Conrad
Giles and Sonia Coode-Adams
Cynthia Corbett
Mark and Cathy Corbett
Pilar Corrias
Tommaso Corvi-Mora
Mr and Mrs Bertrand Coste
Kathleen Crook and James Penturn
James Curtis
Daniella Luxembourg Art
Fiona Davies
Sir Howard Davies
Sir Roger and Lady De Haan
Elisabeth De Kergorlay
Giles de la Mare
Mr Damon and The Hon Mrs de Laszlo
Alexander de Mont
Anne Chantal Defay Sheridan
Jackie Donnelly Russell
Michael Donovan
Joan Edlis
Lord and Lady Egremont
John Erle-Drax
Dr Nigel Evans
Stuart and Margaret Evans
Eykyn Maclean LLC
Leonie Fallstrom
Mrs Heather Farrar
David Fawkes
Mrs Margy Fenwick
Mr Bryan Ferry, CBE
Laurie Fitch
Lt Commander Paul Fletcher
Katherine Francey Stables
Mr and Mrs Laurent Ganem
Mala Gaonkar
Geoffrey and Julian Charitable Trust
Mr Mark Glatman
Ms Emily Goldner and Mr Michael Humphries
Emma Goltz
Aphrodite Gonou
Kate Gordon
Dimitri Goulandris
Penelope Govett
Svitlana Granovska
Judith and Richard Greer
Martyn Gregory
Richard and Odile Grogan
John Howard Gruzelier
Mrs Helene Guerin-Llamas
Ms Nathalie Guiot
Jill Hackel Zarzycki
Louise Hallett
Diane Hamilton
Arthur Hanna
Mark Harris
Michael and Morven Heller
Christian Hernandez and Michelle Crowe Hernandez
Muriel Hoffner
James Holland-Hibbert
Lady Hollick, OBE
Holtermann Fine Art
Jeff Horne
John Huntingford
Helen Janecek
Sarah Jennings
Mr Haydn John
Mr Michael Johnson
Mike Jones
Jay Jopling
Mrs Brenda Josephs
Tracey Josephs
Mr Joseph Kaempfer
Andrew Kalman
Ghislaine Kane
Dr Martin Kenig
Mr David Ker
Mr and Mrs Simon Keswick
Sadru Kheraj
Mrs Mae Khouri
David Killick
Mr and Mrs James Kirkman
Brian and Lesley Knox
David P Korn
Kowitz Trust
Mr and Mrs Herbert Kretzmer
Linda Lakhdhir
Simon Lee
Mr Gerald Levin
Leonard Lewis
Sophia and Mark Lewisohn
Yuandao Liu
Mr Gilbert Lloyd
George Loudon
Mrs Elizabeth Louis
Mark and Liza Loveday
Jeff Lowe
Alison Loyd
Mrs Ailsa Macalister
Kate MacGarry
Sir John Mactaggart
Marsh Christian Trust
Stephen and Sharon Mather
Daniele Mattogno
Ms Fiona Mellish
Mrs R W P Mellish
Professor Rob Melville
Dr Helen Metcalf
Dr Basil Ross Middleton
Victoria Miro
Jan Mol
Lulette Monbiot
Mrs Bona Montagu
Mrs William Morrison
Ms Terrina Narbett
Louise Nathanson
Ms Deborah Norton
Julian Opie
Pilar Ordovás
Sayumi Otake
Desmond Page
Maureen Paley
Dominic Palfreyman
Michael Palin
Mrs Kathrine Palmer
Mathieu Paris
Mrs Véronique Parke
Anna Pennink
Frans Pettinga
Trevor Pickett
Frederique Pierre-Pierre
Mariela Pissioti
Mr Alexander Platon
Penelope Powell
Susan Prevezer, QC
Mr and Mrs Ryan Prince
Ivetta Rabinovich
Patricia Ranken
Mrs Phyllis Rapp
The Reuben Foundation
Lady Ritblat
David Rocklin
Frankie Rossi
Mr David V Rouch
Mr James Roundell
Mr Charles Roxburgh
Hakon Runer and Ulrike Schwarz-Runer
Naomi Russell
Mr Alex Sainsbury and Ms Elinor Jansz
Mr Richard Saltoun
Cherrill and Ian Scheer
Sylvia Scheuer
Mrs Cara Schulze
Melissa Sesana
Ellen Shapiro
The Hon Richard Sharp
Neville Shulman, CBE
Ms Julia Simmonds
Simon C Dickinson Ltd
Louise Spence
Mr Nicos Steratzias
Marie-Claude Stobart
Mrs Patricia Swannell
Mr James Swartz
The Sylvie Fleming Collection
The Lady Juliet Tadgell
Isadora Tharin
Elaine Thomas
Marita Thurnauer
Mr Henry Tinsley
Ian Tollett
Victoria Tollman O'Hana
Karen Townshend
Andrew Tseng
Melissa Ulfane
Mrs Jolana Vainio and Dr Petri Vainio
Nazy Vassegh
Mrs Cecilia Versteegh
Gisela von Sanden
Andreas Vourecas-Petalas
Audrey Wallrock
Stephen and Linda Waterhouse
Offer Waterman
Miss Cheyenne Westphal
Professor Sarah Whatmore
Mr David Wood
Mr Douglas Woolf
Alice Zhou
Sharon Zhu
*and those who wish to remain anonymous*

**Young Patrons**
10 Hanover
Katrina Aleksa
Miss Noor Al-Rahim
HRH Princess Alia Al-Senussi
Miss Sharifa Alsudairi
Miss Katharine Arnold
Lucy Attwood
Miss Olivia Aubry

Daniel Axmer
Charles and Tetyana Banner
Katrina Beechey
Penny Johanna Beer
Francesca Bellini Joseph
Dr Maya Beyhan
Poppy Boadle
Roberto Boghossian
Georgina Borthwick
Chantal Bradford
Kit Brennan
Ms Blair Brooks
Verena Butt d'Espous
Jamie Byrom
Mr Tommaso Calabro
Alexandre Carel
Federico Martin Castro Debernardi
Alexandra and Kabir Chhatwani
Yoojin Choi
Arthur Chow
Aidan Christofferson
Bianca Chu
Zuzanna Ciolek
Harriet Clapham
Julia Clemente
Thamara Corm
Tara Wilson Craig
Eleonore Cukierman
Henry Danowski
Mr Joshua Davis
Countess Charlotte de la Rochefoucauld
Giacomo De Notariis
Agnes de Royere
Raphaele Deghaye
Indira Dyussebayeva
Alexandra Economou
Eleanor A Edelman
Danae Filioti
Jane and Richard Found
Aude Fourcade
Sylvain Fresia
Laurie Frey
Mr Andreas Gegner
Lana Ghandour
David Goldstein
Molly Grad
Alex Haidas
Zoe Haldane
Shiori Hamada
Sara Harrison
Max Edouard Friedrich Hetzler
Louise Holten
Andrew Honan
Simona Houldsworth
Kamel Jaber
Karim Jalbout
Aled Jones
Sophie Kainradl
Miss Meruyert Kaliyeva
Mrs Vasilisa Kameneva
Miss Tamila Kerimova
Zena Aliya Khan
Marika Kielland
Ms Chloe Kinsman
Maria Korolevskaya
Zoe Kuipers
Nicholas M Lamotte
Nadja Laub
John Lellouche
Alexander Lewis
Claire Livingstone
Guy Loffler
Lucy Loveday
Thomas Luypaert
Yusuf Macun
Frederic Maillard
Ms Sonia Mak
Dr Christina Makris
Mr Jean-David Malat
Kamiar Maleki
Daria Manganelli
Zoe Marden
Ignacio Marinho
Magnus Mathisen
Charles-Henri McDermott
Fiona McGovern
Mary McNicholas
Chelsea Menzies
Miss Nina Moaddel
Mr Fernando Moncho Lobo
John-Christian Moquette
Jacopo Moretti
Vanita Nathwani
Natasha Norman
Ikenna Obiekwe
Aurore Ogden (Co-Chair, Young Patrons Ambassador Group)
Reine and Boris Okuliar
Berkay Oncel
Periklis Panagopoulos
Christine Chungwon Park
Alexander V Petalas (Co-Chair, Young Patrons Ambassador Group)
Robert Phillips
Mr Mark Piolet
Megan Piper
Courtney Plummer
Nadim Rabaia
Mr Eugenio Re Rebaudengo
Sydney Rogers
Ms Nadja Romain
Tarka Russell
Nour Saleh
Umair Sami
Paola Saracino Fendi
Rachel Schaefer
Rebekka Schaefer
Franz Schwarz
Mr Richard Scott
Count Indoo Sella Di Monteluce
Nasiha Shaikh
Robert Sheffield
Eric Shen
Henrietta Shields
MinJoo Shin
Ms Marie-Anya Shriro
Amar Singh
Jag Singh
Evgenia Slyusarenko
Tammy Smulders
Dominic Stolerman
Miss Claire Sussmilch
Nayrouz Tatanaki
Vassan Thavaraja
Soren S K Tholstrup
Omer Tiroche
Milan Tomic
Simon Tovey
Mr Giancarlo Trinca
Mr Philippos Tsangrides
Ms Navann Ty
Mr Lawrence Van Hagen
Steffan Vaughan Griffiths
Alexandra Warder
Ewa Wilczynski
Elizabeth Wilks
Kim Williams
Kate Wong
Alexandra Wood
Edward Woodcock
Tyler Woolcott
Vanessa Wurm
Jian Xu
Shelly Yang
Miss Burcu Yuksel
Evgeny Zborovsky
Marcelo Osvaldo Zimmler
*and those who wish to remain anonymous*

**International Council Members**
Mr Segun Agbaje
Staffan Ahrenberg, Editions Cahiers d'Art
Mr Geoff Ainsworth, AM
Dilyara Allakhverdova
Mrs Maria Baibakova and Mr Adrien Faure
Anne H Bass
Nicolas Berggruen
Mr Pontus Bonnier
Paloma Botín O'Shea
Frances Bowes
Ivor Braka
The Deborah Loeb Brice Foundation
The Broad Art Foundation
Andrew Cameron, AM
Nicolas and Celia Cattelain
Mrs Christina Chandris
Richard Chang (Vice Chair)
Pierre Chen, Yageo Foundation, Taiwan
Mr Kemal Has Cingillioglu
Mr and Mrs Attilio Codognato
Sir Ronald Cohen and Lady Sharon Harel-Cohen
Mr Douglas S Cramer and Mr Hubert S Bush III
Mr Dimitris Daskalopoulos
Mr and Mrs Michel David-Weill
Ms Miel de Botton
Tiqui Atencio Demirdjian and Ago Demirdjian
Joseph and Marie Donnelly
Mrs Olga Dreesmann
Barney A Ebsworth and Rebecca L Ebsworth
Füsun and Faruk Eczacibaşi
Stefan Edlis and Gael Neeson
Mr and Mrs Edward Eisler
Carla Emil and Rich Silverstein
Fares and Tania Fares
Mrs Doris Fisher
Mrs Wendy Fisher
Dr Kira Flanzraich
Dr Corinne M Flick
Amanda and Glenn Fuhrman
Mrs Belma Gaudio and The Butters Foundation
Candida and Zak Gertler
Mrs Yassmin Ghandehari
Mr Giancarlo Giammetti
Alan Gibbs
Lydia and Manfred Gorvy
Mr Laurence Graff
Ms Esther Grether
Konstantin Grigorishin
Mr Xavier Guerrand-Hermès
Mimi and Peter Haas Fund
Margrit and Paul Hahnloser
Andy and Christine Hall
Mrs Susan Hayden
Marlene Hess and James D. Zirin
André and Rosalie Hoffmann
Ms Maja Hoffmann
Vicky Hughes
Dakis and Lietta Joannou
Sir Elton John and Mr David Furnish
HRH Princess Firyal of Jordan
Pamela J Joyner
Mr Chang-Il Kim
Jack Kirkland
C Richard and Pamela Kramlich
Mrs Grazyna Kulczyk
Andreas and Ulrike Kurtz
Catherine Lagrange
Mr Pierre Lagrange
Bernard Lambilliotte
The Lauder Foundation - Leonard and Judy Lauder Fund
Agnès and Edward Lee
Mme RaHee Hong Lee
Jacqueline and Marc Leland
Panos and Sandra Marinopoulos
Mr and Mrs Donald B Marron
Mr Ronald and The Hon Mrs McAulay
Mark McCain and Caro MacDonald
Mr Leonid Mikhelson
Naomi Milgrom, AO
Mr Donald Moore
Simon and Catriona Mordant
Mrs Yoshiko Mori
Mr Guy and The Hon Mrs Naggar
Fayeeza Naqvi
Mrs Judith Neilson, AM
Dr Mark Nelson
Mr and Mrs Takeo Obayashi
Mr and Mrs Eyal Ofer
Andrea and José Olympio Pereira
Hideyuki Osawa
Irene Panagopoulos
Young-Ju Park
Yana and Stephen Peel
Daniel and Elizabeth Peltz
Catherine Petitgas (Chair)
Sydney Picasso
Jean Pigozzi
Lekha Poddar
Miss Dee Poon
Ms Miuccia Prada and Mr Patrizio Bertelli
Laura Rapp and Jay Smith
Maya and Ramzy Rasamny
Patrizia Sandretto Re Rebaudengo and Agostino Re Rebaudengo
Robert Rennie and Carey Fouks
Sir John Richardson
Michael Ringier
Lady Ritblat
Ms Hanneli M Rupert
Ms Güler Sabanci
Dame Theresa Sackler, DBE
Mrs Lily Safra
Muriel and Freddy Salem
Rajeeb and Nadia Samdani
Alejandro Santo Domingo
Dasha Shenkman, OBE
Dr Gene Sherman, AM
Poonam Bhagat Shroff
Uli and Rita Sigg
Norah and Norman Stone
Julia Stoschek
John J Studzinski, CBE
Maria and Malek Sukkar
Mr Christen Sveaas
Mr Robert Tomei
The Hon Robert H Tuttle and Mrs Maria Hummer-Tuttle
Mrs Ninetta Vafeia
Paulo A W Vieira
Mercedes Vilardell
Robert and Felicity Waley-Cohen
The Hon Hilary M Weston
Angela Westwater and David Meitus
Diana Widmaier Picasso
Christen and Derek Wilson
Mrs Sylvie Winckler
The Hon Dame Janet Wolfson de Botton, DBE
Poju Zabludowicz and Anita Zabludowicz, OBE
Michael Zilkha
*and those who wish to remain anonymous*

**Africa Acquisitions Committee**
Kathy Ackerman Robins
Anshu Bahanda
Adnan Bashir
Priti Chandaria Shah
Mrs Kavita Chellaram
Salim Currimjee
Harry G David
Mr and Mrs Michel David-Weill
Robert and Renee Drake
Mrs Wendy Fisher
Diane B. Frankel
Aita Ighodaro Menet
Andrea Kerzner
Samallie Kiyingi
Alexander Klimt
Matthias and Gervanne Leridon
Caro Macdonald
Dale Mathias
Professor Oba Nsugbe, QC
Ms Ndidi Okpaluba
Mr Hussam Otaibi
Pascale Revert Wheeler
Emile Stipp
Mr Varnavas A Varnava
Mercedes Vilardell (Chair)
Alexa Waley-Cohen
Peter Warwick
Ms Isabel Wilcox
Marwan G Zakhem
*and those who wish to remain anonymous*

**Asia-Pacific Acquisitions Committee**
Sara A Alireza
Matthias Arndt
Bonnie and R Derek Bandeen
Mrs Bambi Blumberg
Andrew Cameron, AM
Mr and Mrs John Carrafiell
Richard Chang
Jasmine Chen
Adrian Cheng
Lawrence Chu
Mr Yan d'Auriol
Katie de Tilly
Ms Kerry Gardner
Mrs Yassmin Ghandehari
Mr Reade and Mrs Elizabeth Griffith
Philippa Hornby
Mr Yongsoo Huh
Shareen Khattar Harrison
Mr Chang-Il Kim
Mr Jung Wan Kim
Ms Yung Hee Kim
Ms Ellie Lai
Alan Lau (Co-Chair)
Woong-Yeul Lee
Jasmine Li
Mr William Lim
Ms Dina Liu
Alan and Yenn Lo
Ms Kai-Yin Lo
Anne Louis-Dreyfus
Lu Xun
Elisabetta Marzetti Mallinson
Elaine Forsgate Marden
Marleen Molenaar
Mr John Porter
The Red Mansion Foundation
Dr Gene Sherman, AM (Co-Chair)
Leo Shih
Ed Tang
Chikako Tatsuuma
Dr Andreas Teoh

Dr Neil Wenman
Yang Bin
Fernando Zobel de Ayala
*and those who wish to remain anonymous*

**Latin American Acquisitions Committee**
Monica and Robert Aguirre
José Antonio Alcantara
Luis Benshimol
Celia Birbragher
Estrellita and Daniel Brodsky
Miguel Angel Capriles Cannizzaro
HSH the Prince Pierre d'Arenberg
Tiqui Atencio Demirdjian (Chair)
Renata Dias de Moraes
Marta Regina Fernandez Holman
Barbara Hemmerle-Gollust
Carola Hinojosa
Julian Iragorri
Anne Marie and Geoffrey Isaac
Nicole Junkermann
Aimee Labarrere de Servitje
José Luis Lorenzo
Francisca Mancini
Felipe and Denise Nahas Mattar
Susan McDonald
Veronica Nutting
Victoria and Isaac Oberfeld
Silvia Paz Illobre
Esther Perez Seinjet
Catherine Petitgas
Claudio Federico Porcel
Mr Thibault Poutrel
Frances Reynolds
Erica Roberts
Alin Ryan Lobo
Catalina Saieh Guzman
Lilly Scarpetta
Camila Sol de Pool
Juan Carlos Verme
Juan Yarur Torres
Teresita Soriano Zucker
*and those who wish to remain anonymous*

**Middle East and North Africa Acquisitions Committee**
Ahmad and Sirine Abu Ghazaleh
HRH Princess Alia Al-Senussi
Abdelmonem Bin Eisa Alserkal
Mr Abdullah Al-Turki
Mehves Ariburnu
Marwan T Assaf
Niloufar Bakhtiar Bakhtiari
Perihan Bassatne
Ms Isabelle de la Bruyère
Füsun Eczacibaşi
Maryam Eisler (Co-Chair)
Shirley Elghanian
Delfina Entrecanales, CBE
Noor Fares
Hossein and Dalia Fateh
Negin Fattahi-Dasmal
Raghida Ghandour Al Rahim
Mareva Grabowski
Aysegül Karadeniz
Mr Elie Khouri
Maha and Kasim Kutay
David Maupin
Tansa Mermerci Ekşioğlu
Basma Haout Monla
Falak Naqvi
Dina Nasser-Khadivi
Shulamit Nazarian
Ebru Özdemir
Mr Moshe Peterburg
Ramzy and Maya Rasamny (Co-Chair)
Thomas Rom
Mrs Madhu Ruia
Shihab Shobokshi
Maria and Malek Sukkar
Faisal Tamer
Berna Tuglular
Yesim Turanli
Sebnem Unlu
Madhi Yahya
Mr Zahid and Ms Binladin
Roxane Zand
*and those who wish to remain anonymous*

**North American Acquisitions Committee**
Carol and David Appel
Jacqueline Appel and Alexander Malmaeus
Abigail Baratta
Dorothy Berwin and Dominique Lévy
Dillon Cohen
Michael Corman and Kevin Fink
Theo Danjuma
Anne Dias
James E Diner
Wendy Fisher
Jill Garcia
Victoria Gelfand-Magalhaes
Amy Gold
Nina and Dan Gross
Pamela J Joyner
Monica Kalpakian
Elisabeth and Panos Karpidas
Christian Keesee
Naznin and Mahmood Khimji
Marjorie and Michael Levine
James Lindon
Rebecca Marks
Lillian and Billy Mauer
Nancy McCain
Jeff Menashe
Stavros Merjos
Gregory R Miller
Rachelli Mishori and Leon Koffler
Sami Mnaymneh
Shabin and Nadir Mohamed
Jenny Mullen
Elisa Nuyten and David Dime
Amy and John Phelan
Laura Rapp and Jay Smith
Carolin Scharpff-Striebich
Komal Shah
Eleanor and Francis Shen
Dasha Shenkman, OBE
Kimberly Richter Shirley and Jon Shirley
Beth Swofford
Juan Carlos Verme
Christen and Derek Wilson
Leyli Zohrenejad
*and those who wish to remain anonymous*

**Photography Acquisitions Committee**
Ryan Allen
Artworkers Retirement Society
Nicholas Barker
Cynthia Lewis Beck
Carolin Becker
Pierre Brahm
Mrs William Shaw Broeksmit
Elizabeth (Co-Chair) and Rory Brooks
Marcel and Gabrielle Cassard
Nicolas (Co-Chair) and Celia Cattelain
Beth and Michele Colocci
Mr and Mrs Michel David-Weill
Mr Hyung-Teh Do
Nikki Fennell
David Fitzsimons
Lisa Garrison
Ms Emily Goldner and Mr Michael Humphries
Ann Hekmat
Alexandra Hess
Bernard Huppert
Jack Kirkland
David Knaus
Mr Scott Mead
Sebastien Montabonel
Mr Donald Moore
Tarek Nahas
Kristin Rey
David Solo
Saadi Soudavar
Nicholas Stanley
Maria and Malek Sukkar
Francois Trausch, in memory of Caroline Trausch
Michael and Jane Wilson
*and those who wish to remain anonymous*

**Russia and Eastern Europe Acquisitions Committee**
Dmitry Aksenov
Dilyara Allakhverdova
Maria Baibakova
David Birnbaum
Maria Rus Bojan
Maria Bukhtoyarova
Francise Hsin-Wen Chang
Dr Kira Flanzraich (Chair)
Lyuba Galkina
Dr Joana Grevers
Konstantin Grigorishin
Cees Hendrikse
Mr Vilius Kavaliauskas and Rita Navalinskaite
Carl Kostyál
Mrs Grażyna Kulczyk
Peter Kulloi
Eduard Maták
Teresa Mavica
Luba Michailova
Maarja Oviir-Neivelt
Neil K Rector
Valeria Rodnyansky
Robert Runták
Ovidiu Şandor
Zsolt Somlói
Elena Sudakova
The Tretyakov Family Collection
Miroslav Trnka
Jo Vickery
Veronika Zonabend
Mr Janis Zuzans
*and those who wish to remain anonymous*

**South Asia Acquisitions Committee**
Shohidul Ahad-Choudhury
Mrs Sheetal Ansal
Maya Barolo-Rizvi
Krishna Bhupal
Dr Arani and Mrs Shumita Bose
Akshay Chudasama
Jai Danani
Zahida Habib
Shalini Hinduja
Aparajita Jain
Simran Kotak and Vir Kotak
Ms Aarti Lohia
Yamini Mehta
Mr Yogesh Mehta
Mohammad N. Miraly
Shalini Misra
Mr Rahul Munjal and Mrs Pooja Munjal
Mrs Chandrika Pathak
Puja and Uday Patnaik
Lekha Poddar (Co-Chair)
Nadia Samdani
Rajeeb Samdani (Co-Chair)
Mrs Tarana Sawhney
Osman Khalid Waheed
Manuela and Iwan Wirth
Ambreen Zaman
*and those who wish to remain anonymous*

**The 1897 Circle**
Marilyn Bild
David and Deborah Botten
Geoff Bradbury
Charles Brett
Sylvia Carter
Eloise and Francis Charlton
Mr and Mrs Cronk
Alex Davids
Jonathan Davis
Professor Martyn Davis
Sean Dissington
Ronnie Duncan
Joan Edlis
V Fabian
Lt Cdr Paul Fletcher
Mr and Mrs R.N. and M.C. Fry
Tom Glynn and Margaret Anne Glynn
Richard S Hamilton
LA Hynes
John Janssen
Dr Martin Kenig
Isa Levy
Jean Medlycott
Susan Novell and Graham Smith
Martin Owen
Simon Reynolds
Dr Claudia Rosanowski
Ann M Smith
Deborah Stern
Jennifer Toynbee-Holmes
Estate of Paule Vézelay
D Von Bethmann-Hollweg
Audrey Wallrock
Professor Brian Whitton
Kay and Dyson Wilkes
Simon Casimir Wilson
Andrew Woodd
Mr and Mrs Zilberberg
*and those who wish to remain anonymous*

**Tate Modern Corporate Supporters**
Amorim
Bank of America Merrill Lynch
BMW
Deutsche Bank AG
EY
HTC VIVE
Hyundai Card
Hyundai Motor
IHS Markit
Kvadrat
Qantas
Red Hat Inc
Solarcentury
Sotheby's
Tiffany & Co.
Uniqlo
*and those who wish to remain anonymous*

**Tate Modern Corporate Members**
Allen & Overy LLP
Ashmore Group
Bank of America Merrill Lynch
BCS Consulting
Bloomberg
Christie's
The Cultivist
Deutsche Bank AG London
Dow Jones
Finsbury
Floreat Group
Holdingham Group
HSBC
Hyundai Card
Imperial College Healthcare Charity
JATO Dynamics
Linklaters
The Moody's Foundation
Morgan Stanley
Oliver Wyman
Otis Elevator Company
QBE
Saatchi & Saatchi
Siegel + Gale
Slaughter and May
Tishman Speyer
Vitality
Zenith
*and those who wish to remain anonymous*